THE LONG ARM OF C(
THE FRUSTRATED CONNECTION BETWEEN
BEOWULF AND *GRETTIS SAGA*

Scholars in Old Norse and Old English studies have for years sought to find connections between *Beowulf* and *Grettis saga*, despite great differences in the composition, time period, and country of origin of the two works. Based on some striking surface similarities, the assumption of kinship, or genetically related analogues, has inspired scholars to make more and more daring conjectures regarding the actual relationship between the two works.

Magnús Fjalldal has written a lively challenge to those notions, carefully demonstrating how even tangential resemblances that at one point would have been considered questionable, have become progressively assimilated into mainstream Old English and Old Norse scholarship. The author's refutations are closely tied to the primary texts, and he makes constructive and plausible suggestions as to how the apparent parallels could have arisen in two texts so separated by time, culture, and geography.

Passionately and engagingly written, occasionally forceful, *The Long Arm of Coincidence* successfully reopens a classic argument in Old Norse and Old English studies, and will be sure to provoke strong reactions on both sides of this question.

MAGNÚS FJALLDAL is an associate professor of English literature at the University of Iceland in Reykjavík.

MAGNÚS FJALLDAL

The Long Arm of Coincidence: The Frustrated Connection between *Beowulf* and *Grettis saga*

UNIVERSITY OF TORONTO PRESS
Toronto Buffalo London

© University of Toronto Press Incorporated 1998
Toronto Buffalo London
Printed in Canada

ISBN 0-8020-4301-1 (cloth)
ISBN 0-8020-8128-2 (paper)

Printed on acid-free paper

Canadian Cataloguing in Publication Data

Fjalldal, Magnús
    The long arm of coincidence : the frustrated connection between
    Beowulf and Grettis saga

    Includes bibliographical references and index.
    ISBN 0-8020-4301-1 (bound)   ISBN 0-8020-8128-2 (pbk.)

    1. Beowulf.   2. Grettis saga.   I. Title.

    PR1585.F52 1998   829.3   C98-930145-1

University of Toronto Press acknowledges the financial assistance to its publishing
program of the Canada Council for the Arts and the Ontario Arts Council.

Contents

Introduction

For over a century most scholars in the fields of Anglo-Saxon and Old Norse have been convinced that *Grettis saga* and *Beowulf* are related, although the two works are on the whole very different, separated by several centuries in time and composed in different countries in different languages. This belief in a mutual relationship of some kind has rested on the perception that certain passages in both texts are so similar that the resemblance between them ruled out any possibility of accidental likeness. And there are indeed striking similarities, at least at first glance: Grettir and Beowulf both cleanse haunted houses by fighting supernatural opponents; they both wreck buildings in the process of doing so; and a monster loses an arm before succumbing in the struggle.[1]

The assumption of kinship between *Beowulf* and *Grettis saga* has understandably inspired scholars to make further and more daring comparisons between the saga and the poem. Each text has already been used extensively to interpret or clarify its counterpart, and many critics believe that the question of a genetic relationship between the analogues in *Beowulf* and *Grettis saga* has been resolved once and for all. As early as 1881, C.S. Smith declared that 'in the unbiased mind, no real doubt can arise of the parallelism between these two legends,'[2] and ninety years later Larry D. Benson concluded that the resemblances were 'so many, so obvious, and so detailed' that he could not be bothered to 'belabor them.'[3] Unfortunately, the issue in question is not quite this crystal-clear, and the supposed resemblances between the two works raise a number of problems that do indeed deserve a bit of belabouring.

The various problems that I perceive in the analogy-making process itself will be dealt with in subsequent chapters, but before going into detail, I would like to offer a few reasons for being sceptical about the so-called parallel texts that scholars have accepted as evidence of a genetic relationship in this case. In the first place, the human mind is 'a pattern-producing machine [that] sees shapes in random constellations,'[4] as T.A. Shippey – commenting on the end-less stream of allegorical readings of *Beowulf* – observed some years ago, and texts that appear to resemble each other can turn out to be very false friends. Take, for example, the following Japanese analogue to *Beowulf* that was offered by F. York Powell in 1901:

There was in the tenth century, in Japan, a great nobleman, Yorimitsu of the famous Minamoto family, who had four champions famous for wisdom, courage, strength, and skill; one of these, Kintoki, is the Japanese Orson or Perceval, brought up by the Lady of the Mountain away from mankind, with bears for his playfellows. Another is the Watanabe-no-Tsuna, the Japanese Béowulf.

He was sent upon an errand on a wild and stormy night by his lord, Yorimitsu, and as he came back, by a certain deserted, haunted temple, a demon (at first trying to deceive him by falsely appearing as a forlorn maiden) suddenly seized him up and attempted to carry him off. With his master's renowned blade *Hinge-kiri*, which he was wearing that night, Watanabe freed himself, cutting off at a sweep the demon's arm that had grappled him by the helmet. This arm with its huge claws he bore off as a trophy, and, locking it up in a stone chest, congratulated himself on his exploit, which would, he believed, free the temple from the evil beings that made its neighbourhood dreadful and dangerous. Next day, however, the old lady who had fostered him, an aged kinswoman to whom he owed reverence, was ushered before him and he was prayed to show his trophy to her. He could not refuse so slight a favour; but as soon as the chest was opened the old lady turned to a horrid demon, caught up the grisly arm and dashed off through the roof, half wrecking the room as she left, before Watanabe was able to do anything to hinder her or recapture his enemy's arm. In the end, however, the demons are disposed of.[5]

In some respects, this story presents a closer analogy to *Beowulf* than *Grettis saga*, but any resemblance here is certainly nothing but a coincidence. In other words, because this analogue cannot be genetically related to *Beowulf*, it is merely an amusing literary curiosity, and if, by the same token, the analogues in *Grettis saga* that we shall soon be examining cannot be shown to be genetically related to *Beowulf*, they too can only be regarded as literary curiosities.

Secondly, there is the matter of loose ends. Beowulf and Grettir have never been altogether comfortable as bedfellows, partly because of the uncertainty over what material concerning the two was genuinely analogous, and partly because the proposed genetically related analogues differ sharply on a number of points. As we shall later see, the criteria that scholars have tried to use as their basis for accepting or rejecting any proposed genetically related analogue have always been quite subjective, and a century of scholarship aimed at smoothing away problems and deepening the reader's understanding of the relationship between the two texts has in reality done just the opposite. It has produced enough reasonable evidence to question many of the basic arguments that have been used to link *Beowulf* to *Grettis saga*.

A third reason for being sceptical is the context of some of the proposed genetically related analogues in *Grettis saga*. Take, for instance, the Sandhaugar episode (chapters 63–7), which is normally seen as the best parallel to Beowulf's fight with Grendel and his dam. The literary fate of these two supposedly genetically related episodes is amazingly different. In *Beowulf* the story of this epic struggle occupies centre stage in the entire first half of the poem and is the vehicle that elevates Beowulf to his heroic stature. In *Grettis saga* the Sandhaugar episode is no more than a small and insignificant digression and perhaps, as Wolf von Unwerth has argued,[6] an episode which is mainly made up of items borrowed from other Icelandic sagas or even earlier episodes in *Grettis saga* itself.

Finally, there is the matter of how to explain a kinship between *Beowulf* and *Grettis saga*. This is the most difficult problem that 'the faithful' have had to tackle, and it is here that the weakness of the whole argument becomes most apparent. Four different hypotheses have been proposed, and none of them is very convincing.

These are some of the doubts that brought this study about, and I now leave it to my readers – and their unbiased minds, of course – to assess the evidence for themselves.

MAGNÚS FJALLDAL

PART I
THE PROPOSED GENETICALLY
RELATED ANALOGUES

1

Determining Analogous and Genetically Related Material

This chapter presents a survey of the five episodes in *Grettis saga* that have been proposed as genetically related analogues[1] to *Beowulf*, as well as a look at the methods and the arguments of the scholars who originally suggested them. Criticisms concerning the validity of individual analogues – when such criticisms are to be found – are limited to those that were offered in the scholarly debate that took place at the time. In short, my aim in the following pages is primarily to sum up the academic work that established these five episodes as analogues to *Beowulf*, and in doing so, insisted that they were related to the poem.

1: The Sandhaugar Episode[2]

Grettir learns that a farm called Sandhaugar is haunted. The owner of the farm had disappeared one night while his wife attended a Christmas service, and the following year one of the farm workers vanished at Christmas as well. On the next Christmas eve Grettir comes to the farm to rid it of the hauntings. First, however, he carries the lady of the farm, Steinvǫr, and her daughter across an icy river, Eyjardalsá, so they can attend the Christmas service. Grettir then waits fully clothed and with a light burning for the troll to attack in the night. A troll woman carrying a trencher and a knife appears in the hall. They wrestle inside the farmhouse, and great damage is done to the building. The troll-woman drags Grettir out of the hall and all the way to the brink of a gorge. Grettir then succeeds in freeing one arm, reaches for his short-sword, and cuts off the troll-woman's arm. She falls into the gorge and disappears. The narrator then explains that according to local legend she did not fall into the gulf but was at sunrise turned into a stone image which can still be seen at the edge of the cliff.

Grettir is curious to discover the fate of the two missing men. He goes to the gorge with a single companion, lets down a rope, which his helpmate is to guard, and dives into the chasm and underneath a waterfall which is there. Behind the waterfall he finds a cave which he enters. Inside the cave he discovers a huge giant sitting by a fire. The giant attacks him with a weapon with a wooden handle (a *heptisax*). Grettir cuts the weapon off its handle and kills the giant as he tries to reach for a sword that is hanging on the wall of the cave. Grettir's companion sees blood stains on the river, concludes that Grettir is dead, and deserts the rope. Grettir searches the cave and finds the bones of the two men who had disappeared as well as treasure. No mention is made of the troll-woman. Grettir then climbs up the rope unaided and leaves the bones of the men at a local church with a rune staff on which he has carved two stanzas that relate his adventure in the cave.

Since Guðbrandur Vigfússon first compared this episode with events in *Beowulf* in his edition of *Sturlunga Saga ... and Other Works* more than a century ago and claimed that it proved a genetic relationship between the saga and the epic, it has become one of the best known and most frequently cited analogues to the Old English poem. There is a good reason for its primary status: in the first place it relates the only self-contained story within *Grettis saga* that invites a full-fledged comparison with a section of *Beowulf*, and secondly, all other attempts to see further analogies in the saga either depend on the Sandhaugar episode or relate to it in one way or another.

Although Vigfússon claimed a general resemblance between *Beowulf* and *Grettis saga* by arguing that 'Gretti's fight with Glam, and afterwards with the troll-wife and the monster below the water-fall, [was] the Icelandic version of the Gothic hero's struggle with Grendel and his witch-mother,'[3] he did not attach much importance to specific similarities between the two stories, except for one: 'Where everything else is transformed,' he wrote, 'one word remains as a memorial of [the story's] origin, viz. in the English epic *hæft-méce* and in the Icelandic Saga *hefti-sax*, both occurring in the same place of the legend, and both *hapax legomena* in their respective literatures.'[4] How Vigfússon came to see *hæftmece* and *heptisax*,[5] terms for different weapons that only share the same prefix, as 'one word,' he never explained, nor has it ever been clear precisely how their respective uniqueness should link the two texts. In light of this, it is somewhat strange that Vigfússon should put so much emphasis on the importance of this pair, unless he mistakenly thought that *heptisax* was a special term for Grettir's weapon, and that both heroes thus had swords described by words that sounded somewhat similar and that were not to be found anywhere else. *Corpus Poeticum Boreale*, published five years after *Sturlunga saga* and edited jointly by Vigfússon and York Powell, sums up the Sandhaugar episode in a way that might hint at this: 'Having dived below the force [waterfall], [Grettir] gets into a cave, where he finds a giant, whom he slays with a thrust of the famous short sword (hefti-sax, Beowolf's hefti-mæci).'[6] But whether the analogy between *Beowulf* and *Grettis saga* might have come about through Vigfússon's faulty memory is immaterial; the keystone of his argument – the *heptisax-hæftmece* parallel – was universally accepted and gradually became a myth in its own right.

Vigfússon's comparison implied that the general outline of the two stories was roughly similar; however, the analogy that actually proved them to be related, as far as he was concerned, really hinged on the *heptisax-hæftmece* pair, because in *Grettis saga* everything else had been transformed. This argument was short-lived. As other medieval scholars took notice of Vigfússon's discovery, everything in the two texts that could possibly be seen as similar was eventually accepted as evidence of their relationship, and the possibility of an accidental likeness between the poem and the saga was categorically rejected.[7] The following list contains the points of resemblance that critics proceeded to find in the Sandhaugar episode after Vigfússon had first presented his discovery:

- The hero learns there is a haunted place and comes from afar to seek adventure.
- He is strong and a good swimmer and performs a feat of strength that involves swimming prior to the battle (Beowulf's contest with Breca; Grettir's carrying Steinvǫr, the lady of the haunted farm, and her daughter across a swollen river).
- He fights a battle with a pair of cannibalistic monsters – one male, the other female – in two successive fights.
- The first battle takes place in a human dwelling at night. The hero wrestles with a monstrous creature and great damage is done to the building in the process.
- Like Beowulf in the battle with Grendel's dam, Grettir is tightly clutched by the troll-woman. Here, 'striking similarity in the phraseology' has also been claimed.[8]
- The monster loses an arm in the battle but escapes.
- The hero battles with a second monster that lives in a cave under water (under a waterfall). The hero has to dive to the bottom before reaching the cave.
- A fire burns in the cave, and a sword hangs on the wall.
- The hero's helper(s) see(s) blood on the water and depart(s) thinking that he is dead.
- The second monster is killed, but both in *Grettis saga* and in *Beowulf* there is a weapon – the *hæftmece* or *heptisax* – that fails.

- There is treasure in the monster's cave.
- After the second battle, an object with runes carved on it (the ancient sword in *Beowulf*, the rune staff in *Grettis saga*) is presented.
- The hero is rewarded by the host of the haunted place.

Which of these points different scholars have chosen to emphasize has of course varied, and the same item has not always been considered analogous for the same reason. Klaeber[9] and Halldórsson,[10] for example, see the icy river that Grettir crosses as a challenge to test his strength, whereas Malone[11] thinks its unseasonable rising recalls the mystery and terror of the marshes in *Beowulf*. But the different reasons that scholars may have had are not important in this context; what matters is that all these items have been brought forward as evidence, not just to show that the two texts are similar, but that they are genetically related.

Differences between the Sandhaugar episode and *Beowulf* were also noted in the course of the discussion that Vigfússon's discovery generated. As early as 1880, James Garnett observed that in spite of striking general resemblances, the differences were 'so numerous and so material' that accidental likeness could not be ruled out.[12] His criticism, however, did not go beyond this single comment and appears to have had no impact. The same may be said of the objections of the few other scholars who were either sceptical or refused to see the Sandhaugar episode as analogous to *Beowulf*, in the sense of proving that the saga and the poem were related.[13] Klaeber, Chambers, and other influential critics found the differences to be neither numerous nor material; and the ones they did find they waved away with the magic wand of textual corruption. Chambers, for instance, addresses the issue as to why Grettir first fights against a female monster and then a male one (in *Beowulf* the order is reversed) as follows:

In this the *Grettis saga* probably represents a corrupt tradition: for, that the female should remain at home whilst the male searches for his prey, is a rule which holds good for devils as well as for men. The change was presumably made in order to avoid the difficulty – which the Beowulf poet seems also to have realized – that after the male has been slain, the rout of the female is felt to be a deed of less note – something of an anticlimax.[14]

The only other difference that Chambers appears to notice is that the sword on the wall in the monster's cave has somehow changed hands. In *Beowulf* the hero uses it to attack the monster, whereas the giant reaches for it in his attack on the hero in the saga. Klaeber blames these and other changes in *Grettis saga* on what he calls 'an obscuration of the original folk-tale elements,' which explains why the female monster 'is not stated explicitly to be the giant's mother' in the saga and also why their 'natural roles' have been reversed.[15] This form of literary decay is, furthermore, responsible for making the motivation for the hero's visit to the cave in *Grettis saga* 'mere curiosity,' omitting all mention of the wounded she-demon in the second adventure, and 'completely blurring the motive of the wonderful sword which is hanging in the cave.' Among early commentators on the Sandhaugar episode as a genetically related analogue to *Beowulf*, only Stedman was concerned about the thorny problem of differences in landscape and setting:

However different the mere of the Grendels be from the force of the trolls, however they themselves differ in nature from the Grendel-kin, it seems to me that this is to be ascribed to the racial differences of thought, of imagination, of fear of the supernatural between the peoples by whom the stories were fostered and among whom they grew up.[16]

A simpler answer would later be found by moving Grendel and his dam into a waterfall and giving them a family tree that traced their ancestry to Scandinavian waterfall trolls, as we shall see in a subsequent chapter.

2: Glámr[17]

The reader first meets Glámr as a big and surly Swede who is employed by the farmer of Þórhallsstaðir to look after his sheep. He is warned that the place is haunted but pays no heed to the warning. At Christmas Glámr is killed in a fight with some kind of a monstrous creature. He is buried but does not lie still in his grave and begins to haunt the farm and its neighbourhood. Eventually, Grettir goes to the farm to meet the horrid living dead that Glámr has now become. Grettir waits for his arrival in the night under the cover of a cloak but fully dressed and with a light burning in the hall. Glámr enters the hall, grabs at the cloak, and a tug of war ensues until Grettir and the fiend tear it apart. Glámr and Grettir then wrestle and break up everything in their way during the struggle. Glámr manages to pull Grettir out of the house, but Grettir throws himself at him, and Glámr falls in the process. Grettir decapitates Glámr with his sword and places the head at the thigh of the fiend, but before that comes to pass, Glámr has spoken a curse: Grettir's deeds will turn against him, he will become a lonely outlaw, the eyes of Glámr will always follow him, and he will be afraid of the dark. As a result, Grettir will crave company, which in turn will lead to his death.

Those who accept the Glámr episode as a genetically related analogue have always considered him and/or his role in *Grettis saga* to be comparable to that of Grendel in *Beowulf*. This is by no means surprising, as even a cursory look at the poem and the saga is enough to show that Grendel and Glámr have special positions among the supernatural opponents of Beowulf and Grettir. To begin with, they both have names; in fact, Grendel is the only monster in *Beowulf* to be given one (cf. the nameless troll-woman and the giant at Sandhaugar). Like Grendel, Glámr has a considerable background – more detailed than any of Grettir's other opponents in the saga. They may both possess magic powers,[18] there is something sinister about their eyes, and they haunt human dwellings. Vigfússon and York Powell considered the story of Glámr to be even more important than the Sandhaugar episode, because they believed that the cursing of the Icelandic hero by the monster supplied vital clues to explain the fate of Beowulf, such as his childlessness and his unhappy end:

Here the haunting, the broken hall, the wrestling, the farmer's attitude, his gifts are all identical in poem and tale; the riven coverlet is paralleled by the torn limb of the fiend; only the curse is a fresh feature, and this may be a trait of the original legend which our poem has not preserved. It is almost needed as a thread to bind the whole life of Beowolf together.[19]

But although the Glámr episode had, in addition to all these features, the advantage over the Sandhaugar episode of being a central event in *Grettis saga*, there were still two knotty problems. Grettir's fight with Glámr could only be partly analogous to Beowulf's adventure, inasmuch as it was only a single fight against one Grendel-like adversary, and since Grettir's wrestling with the troll-woman at Sandhaugar was also supposed to be a parallel to the fight with Grendel, how could there be two analogues in the saga, considerably different from each other, recounting the same event as in the poem? Vigfússon and York Powell suggested that the Sandhaugar episode included 'a certain repetition of the Grendel story,'[20] but further than that they did not get. Much later, Nora K. Chadwick tried to solve this dilemma by making Glámr and the giant in the cave at Sandhaugar into the same monster, which she equated with Grendel. According to this argument the troll-woman at Sandhaugar is analogous to his mother, and as Grendel is finally disposed of after his mother's death, so is the Glámr-giant monster.[21] This solution, however, is not obtained without a sacrifice or two. Whatever differences there are between a ghost, a troll, and a giant are obviously immaterial in Nora Chadwick's argument, and so is the fact that in *Grettis saga* a distinction is normally made between the Glámr and Sandhaugar episodes. Chadwick's ideas concerning Glámr will be discussed in more detail in chapter 2, but we must now return to a time when critics still considered him to be a motherless ghost.

In the case of Glámr, as opposed to the Sandhaugar episode, a genuine tug of war between believers and non-believers was soon under way. The Glámr story was dismissed as a genetically related analogue by Gering on the grounds that there was no equation between a torn cover and an arm, that indoor wrestling matches with consequent damage to the building and the gifts that Grettir receives were commonplaces in the sagas, and, last but not least, that Glámr and the water monsters in *Beowulf* were very different creatures.[22] A number of scholars, including R.C. Boer, Sophus Bugge, W.W. Lawrence, Guðni Jónsson, and Joan Turville-Petre, have since concurred, although they do not necessarily agree with Gering's reasoning.[23] R.W. Chambers seems to have hesitated. He included the Glámr section as a genetically related *Beowulf* analogue in the first edition of his study of the poem (1921), presumably because of its 'great, if possibly accidental likeness to the Grendel story,' and then completely dismissed it in an article published a few years later with the comment that although many details were the same, there was but one struggle, the foe was disposed of, and there was no hint of any sequel.[24]

But various critics came to Vigfússon's defence by insisting that the Glámr section was truly analogous, and some even produced fresh evidence to bolster the original argument. C.S. Smith, although he did not like the idea that a rent cloak could substitute for Grendel's arm, addressed the problem of the two different saga versions by maintaining that Grettir's fight in the Sandhaugar episode was but a poor copy of the Glámr section – in other words the saga author was just repeating himself – and thus Glámr should be given priority status as a *Beowulf* analogue.[25] Douglas Stedman recognized additional similarities between Grendel and Glámr, such as: their mutual loathing of the sound of music,[26] the size and the ugliness of the monsters' heads, the horror in the eyes of both of them as they glare into the hall, and the fact that the hero in each case fights with his bare hands (as opposed to the troll-woman in the Sandhaugar episode, who is armed with a long knife and disposed of with Grettir's short-sword).[27] Fernand Mossé emphasized the gigantic size of the monsters and the fact that the hero lies down as he waits for them.[28] Vigfússon's supporters, however, remained divided on the question as to whether Glámr *per se* was related to Grendel or whether the two were merely attached to the same legend.[29]

And so the feud over the status of the Glámr story as an analogue that proves something or nothing about *Grettis saga* being related to *Beowulf* has continued. Klaeber, who in his edition of *Beowulf* tried the diplomatic approach by suggesting that the episode was 'of less significance' than Sandhaugar but 'worthy of mention as a parallel to the Grendel fight,'[30] has been noticeably short of followers.

3: Kárr the Old[31]

Grettir, while outlawed from Iceland, stays as a guest of a farmer who lives on an island in Norway. He sees a mysterious fire and is told that the farmer's father, Kárr the Old, a revenant who occupies a gravemound and has driven all his son's competitors for land away, lives there with his treasure. Grettir, accompanied by a single companion, breaks into the gravemound, lowers himself into it by using a rope, and puts the ghost to permanent rest. The noise from their struggle makes his companion, who has been left to guard the rope,[32] think that Grettir is dead, and he deserts his post. Grettir, however, gets out of the gravemound unaided and brings the treasure back to his host. Later, Grettir saves the farm from an attack by a group of berserks and is rewarded with a splendid short-sword (*sax*) from the grave-mound treasure.

Klaeber, in his edition of *Beowulf*, recognized that parts of this story resemble the Sandhaugar and Glámr episodes:[33] the fight with Kárr shares certain traits of both the wrestling match with Glámr and the encounter with the trollwoman at Sandhaugar, and, in the case of the latter adventure, a watchman who leaves a rope and presumes the hero to be dead as well. Klaeber did not consider the story of Grettir's encounter with Kárr the Old to be an analogue to *Beowulf*, in the sense of being genetically related to the poem, however, and neither did anyone else until A.R. Taylor argued for its admission into the canon in a short but seminal article published in 1952.[34] Taylor departed radically in his approach from the conventional method which had been used in respect to Sandhaugar and Glámr; i.e., the consideration of each episode as a whole and the use of the similarity of its narrative ingredients and sequence of events to make a case for it as a *Beowulf* analogue. Instead, he simply took it for granted that the authors of *Grettis saga* and *Beowulf* had both known and used the same legend and proceeded to assume that the saga author had been so interested in this old legend that he had decided to implant and re-implant bits and pieces of it into various parts of his work. Taylor readily admitted that the connection between the Kárr episode and the attack on the monsters' lair in *Beowulf* was slight and consisted mainly of the desertion of the hero by his companion and the removal of a sword from a chamber, but given his basic premise that did not really matter because the nature of the quest for analogous materials had changed. Taylor's argument clearly implied that the burden of proof for claiming new genetically related analogues was considerably lighter now that the relationship between *Grettis saga* and *Beowulf* could be dealt with as an established fact. This novel approach threw the critical discussion of the subject into an entirely different dimension and set an example which several later scholars have found immensely appealing.

R.W. McConchie, who thirty years later set out on the same mission as Taylor, is not, however, one of his disciples. McConchie seems to have been unaware of Taylor's article, and his approach is conventional in the sense that he tries to claim the whole episode as a genetically related analogue to the Grendel fight without relying on Taylor's *a priori* assumption of kinship between *Beowulf* and *Grettis saga*:

There are several obvious points of similarity between Beowulf's struggle with Grendel's mother and Grettir's fight with Kárr. Both take place as a result of a series of violent hauntings. The heroes are both possessed of extraordinary powers and skill. Despite this their companions do not believe that they can succeed. The place of combat is reached by solitary descent, leaving companions, or a companion behind. These desert the hero, believing him to be dead. There is a hand-to-hand combat between the hero and the monster in which the hero comes close to defeat. In both instances there is a decapitation – in *Beowulf* it is Grendel, not Grendel's mother, who is beheaded. There is a splendid sword found in the place of combat, and the hero recovers some kind of treasure. Fire, or light, appears in each version.[35]

Nevertheless, McConchie also admits that there are 'many points of significant difference between the two versions.'

4: The Slaying of the Bear[36]

Grettir stays as a guest with a farmer named Þorkell in Hálogaland in Norway. A kinsman of Þorkell's, Bjǫrn, is also staying there. Bjǫrn is a vain, quarrelsome man who often drives Þorkell's guests away with his taunts. Predictably, he and Grettir do not get along well together. In the winter, a ferocious bear begins to ravage the area, including the farm of Grettir's host, preying on men and cattle at night. People blame this calamity on Bjǫrn and his companions because of their habit of loud merrymaking every night. The bear lives in a cave in a cliff that overlooks the sea and can only be reached by a single narrow track. Bjǫrn boasts that he will kill the beast but does not succeed in his attempt and is derided for his failure. At Christmas a group of men, including both Bjǫrn and Grettir, try to attack the bear but are forced to turn back. As he is making his way home Grettir, egged on by Bjǫrn, returns to the lair of the animal. He cuts off its paw, and then wrestles with the bear. Grettir and the bear both tumble down the cliff, but Grettir lands on top of the animal and kills it. He brings the bear's paw back as a trophy, and his feud with Bjǫrn becomes even more embittered than it had been.

It was A.R. Taylor, in the same article that made a case for Kárr the Old, who first proposed that this section of the saga should be considered as a genetically related analogue to *Beowulf*. Previously, Klaeber had noted Beowulfian touches in the way the saga describes the bear's den as being 'in a cliff by the sea where there was a cave under an overhanging rock, with a narrow path leading to the entrance,'[37] but Klaeber took the issue no further. Lawrence, who briefly considered the episode in his book on *Beowulf* in 1928, rejected it as a genetically related analogue: 'A fight with a brown bear recalls a bit the contests with Grendel,' he writes, but then discards the bear (and Glámr) as 'obvious reminiscences of the Bear's Son tale.'[38]

Taylor, on the other hand, pointed to the night attacks of the bear, to the cutting off of the paw and its use as evidence, to Grettir's remarkable short-sword, to his wrestling match with the animal, and last but not least, to the character and actions of Bjǫrn, which Taylor believed to mirror those of Unferð, the enigmatic courtier who insults Beowulf before he embarks on his mission against Grendel. To Taylor it seemed clear that 'the same basic legend' was present in Grettir's encounter with the bear as in the other parallels to *Beowulf*.[39] As he had done before in the case of Kárr the Old, Taylor carefully limited his comparison to certain details rather than insisting that the episode as a whole bore a close resemblance to Beowulf's fight with Grendel.

A. Margaret Arent, who was the next scholar to make a case for Grettir's fight with the bear as a *Beowulf* analogue, took a very different approach: 'No one, to my knowledge,' she declared, 'has taken into account the fact that both Grendel and dragon motifs appear in a recombined form in the Halogaland bear episode.' Arent's case for this discovery relies mainly on the following points:

- 'The bear in *Grettis saga* is roused by noise and gaiety like Grendel in his attack on Heorot.'
- 'Grendel holds such sway over Heorot and the misty moors that men may not venture forth (*Beowulf*, lines 161–3); the bear comes forth to stalk man and beast, particularly plaguing Thorkel's farm; the dragon lays waste the whole region with fire (*Beowulf*, lines 2333–5). (Similarly, Kár spirits away all the farmers on the island, Glám ravages cattle and men, the troll woman at Sandhaugar causes two men to vanish.)'
- 'The bear, like Grendel, the dragon and all the other ghosts and trolls, haunts at night.'
- 'Hand-to-hand grappling takes place when the bear and Grettir topple down over the precipice and when Beowulf struggles with the mere-wife in the cave (*Beowulf*, lines 1539–46). (Similarly, Kár falls over on his back, as does Glám with Grettir.)'
- 'Boastfully, like Beowulf in the fights against Grendel and the dragon –

although Beowulf in his eagerness disclaims all boasting (lines 2527–8), illustrative of the poet's innovation in handling his theme – Grettir wants to demonstrate his prowess and courage single-handed against the bear.'

- 'That the bear wards off all spear thrusts with his teeth and is hard to get at recalls an invulnerability to weapons and the bite of iron continually referred to in respect to Grendel, Grendel's dam and the dragon.'
- 'Grettir also follows well-known tradition by striking the bear to the heart ... The dragon, too, succumbs only when pierced in his most vulnerable spot.'
- 'Grendel, the Sandhaugar ogress, and the bear are all mutilated in a similar manner.'
- The bear's cave lair near the sea, with a narrow path, difficult of access, and with rocky cliffs plunging into the sea (*Grettis saga*, chapter 21, 74), recalls the dragon's lair (*Beowulf*, lines 2241–3).[40]

There has been no critical reaction to the different methods that Taylor, McConchie and Arent employ to obtain their results, and on the whole their findings have been met with approval. Subsequent commentators on *Grettis saga*, for instance Óskar Halldórsson,[41] Richard Harris[42] and Peter Jorgensen,[43] have all accepted Grettir's encounter with the bear along with the story of Kárr the Old as valid genetically related analogues to Beowulf's struggles with Grendel and his dam.

5: The Death of Grettir in Drangey[44]

Grettir takes refuge in Drangey, a fortress-like island in the North of Iceland, accompanied by his brother Illugi and a slave named Glaumr. The island is owned by a group of farmers who use it for their sheep over the summer. Grettir refuses to leave the island or give up the sheep and thereby incurs the wrath of the farmers. The job of ridding them of Grettir eventually falls to one Þorbjǫrn ǫngull. Þorbjǫrn first tries to plead with Grettir but meets with no success. He then sends an assassin to kill him, but the attempt on Grettir's life fails. Þorbjǫrn now seeks advice from his old nurse, Þuríðr, who is a known sorceress, and together they make a trip to the island. Þorbjǫrn pretends to offer peace in return for Grettir's departure, but Grettir declines the offer. Þuríðr then curses him, and Grettir retaliates by breaking her thighbone with a stone that he throws at her. Some time later the old witch carves runes on a piece of wood, sprinkles it with blood and magic, and sets it adrift. The log finds its way to Drangey where Grettir twice refuses to use it as firewood, but on a third occasion the slave brings it to their hut, and Grettir injures his leg as he attempts to split the log with his axe. Grettir's injury seems to heal at first but then takes a turn for the worse, and it becomes clear that the wound is fatal. Þuríðr now advises Þorbjǫrn to gather troops and set sail for Drangey. He does so and reaches the island successfully despite seemingly impossible weather conditions. The slave Glaumr, whose job it is to pull up the ladder which is the only means of reaching the hut occupied by Grettir, Illugi, and himself and who is also to stand guard that day, does neither, as he is overcome by sleep. Þorbjǫrn reaches the hut, kills Grettir on his deathbed and has Illugi executed. After Grettir's death Þorbjǫrn tries to remove his short-sword from his grip, but cannot wrench it loose and has to cut Grettir's hand off to release it. Þorbjǫrn then smites the short-sword against Grettir's head and nicks the weapon in the process. Finally, he decapitates Grettir and takes his head and sword with him as a trophies. Grettir's death is eventually avenged by his half-brother, Þorsteinn drómundr, who follows Þorbjǫrn ǫngull to Constantinople and kills him there.

In 1973, Richard Harris claimed that the story of Grettir's death contained a fifth genetically related analogue to *Beowulf*, as it resembled the poem – particularly the episode depicting the fight at Grendel's mere – in at least eleven of its details. Harris summed up his findings, insofar as they relate to this episode and *Beowulf*, in the following chart:

Grettir's Death	Beowulf
1/ Grettir occupies Drangey.	Grendel haunts Heorot.
2/ Grettir has a hut on Drangey; nearness to the sea.	Grendel has a waterfall cave, possibly near the sea.
3/ Þorbjörn arrives at Drangey toward the end of the day.	Beowulf takes most of day to reach bottom of mere.
4/ Þorbjörn climbs a ladder to reach Grettir's hut.	Beowulf plunges into mere.
5/ Glaumr sleeps, betrays Grettir.	Danes desert mere at sight of blood.
6/ Grettir previously disabled.	Beowulf wounds Grendel mortally in Heorot – dead in cave.
7/ Grettir loses his hand posthumously.	Beowulf tears off Grendel's arm.
8/ Grettir is beheaded in his hut by Þorbjörn.	Grendel is beheaded in cave by Beowulf.
9/ The beheading is done with Grettir's own sword, Kársnautr.	Sword found in cave.
10/ Sword is damaged by the blow.	Blade melts in blood of Grendel and mother.
11/ Head and sword are kept as trophies.	Head and sword hilt are kept as trophies.[45]

On the basis of this comparison of elements relating to the deaths of Grettir and Grendel and with complete faith in the four previously established analogues in *Grettis saga*, Harris concludes that 'the saga's author knew more of the material, in some form or other, upon which Grendel's story is based, than could be assumed without an awareness that Grettir's death does indeed offer another parallel to the narrative in *Beowulf*.'[46] Within the Drangey episode of *Grettis saga*, in which – up to now – the reader's sympathy has generally been considered to be on the side of the hunted outlaw, we have, in other words, a hidden story, cunningly embedded, in which the hero changes sides with the monster. It is not clear, however, from Harris's remarks, whether he is referring to a fuller story about Grendel as 'a victim' than the one that we have in *Beowulf*, or to a full-fledged story about Grendel (in his struggle against Beowulf?) told from the monster's point of view.

Aside from the eleven details that Harris offers as evidence, his argument involves a double role reversal: Grettir is made to take Grendel's place as a monster, and Þorbjǫrn ǫngull dressed up to be the hero who kills it. To explain the first of these two, Harris points to Arent's argument that the names Grettir and Grendel are related etymologically, that Grettir is spoken of as a troll and has troll-like qualities, that an attempt is made to kill Grettir with his own sword in chapter 55 of the saga, as if he was a giant ogre who could not be killed with any other weapon, and that Grettir's head and sword are kept as trophies; to N.K. Chadwick's idea that in *Grettis saga* Grendel has been transformed into a hero, and that a story originally told from the monster's point of view has left traces on him; and finally to James Carney's thesis that the curse of Cain carried by Grendel as his descendant was transferred to Grettir by an author who otherwise removed Cain from his material.[47] Harris believes that Þorbjǫrn's surly nature and the brutalities he commits as a young man give him, like Grettir, a hero's background as far as his youth is concerned. 'But what sort of hero does Þorbjörn actually become?' asks Harris. 'His exploit is accomplished with the help of a foster mother's magic. His only thanks for the act of cleansing is banishment. His glory as the slayer of Grettir, when he boasts of it in Constantinople, is short-lived. Grettir, on the other hand, is recognized as a hero and cleanser of the land for doing away with various harmful creatures.'[48]

The only criticism of Harris's ideas and of his treatment of the source materials has, so far, come from Anatoly Liberman, who in 1986 surveyed critically the various theories that seek to relate *Grettis saga* and *Beowulf*.[49] Liberman rejects the notion that a close identity of the hero's and the monster's nature has ever been proven to exist in Old English poetry or in the Icelandic sagas:

It is easy to admit that a monster will yield only to its equal in strength, ferocity, and, if necessary, magic powers. That in a mortal fight both opponents acquire awesome proportions can also be granted. Finally, there is nothing surprising in the constant dehumanization of Grettir (what else could be expected?) ... From the point of view of the audience, role reversal is unthinkable: a word of compassion for Grendel the exile does not diminish the distance between him and Beowulf the *aglæca*, and in the saga our sympathy is always with Grettir, whether he preys on the local farmers' sheep or not. It is only this sympathy that matters, unless we are prepared to substitute a motif index for the reader's/listener's reaction.[50]

Other critics have been more receptive. Peter Jorgensen[51] and Stephen Mitchell[52] have both noted Harris's discovery of a new analogue with approval, and Óskar Halldórsson lists his essay among those sources that he believes to be the most important in the study of the saga's relationship to *Beowulf*.[53]

These five analogues that have now been presented are all supposed to reflect material in *Grettis saga* that corresponds to Beowulf's fight with Grendel and his dam, or parts of that story, but as we have seen, the types of arguments that have been used in support of these five candidates are quite different. Most importantly, they vary in their approach to the text of the saga and the poem, and on the question as to what constitutes sufficient evidence to claim a genetically related analogue. In the first place, there are arguments that rely on specific points in the two texts in comparing the nature and deeds of heroes and monsters, the role of various objects and settings that surround them, and the sequence of events. For the most part, these concern the Sandhaugar and Glámr episodes. We have also seen arguments that take lesser or greater liberties with both texts, which obviously must be done if Grettir's fight with a gravemound ghost and a bear, and Þorbjǫrn ǫngull's struggle against Grettir as a monster are to be considered genetically related *Beowulf* analogues. It should also be noted that the last three genetically related analogues that critics claim to have found in *Grettis saga* hinge very heavily on the presumed existence of the first, or the first two. But let us now proceed to take a closer look at the heroes and monsters to see how well they actually compare.

2

The Making of Heroes and Monsters

The purpose of this and of the next three chapters is to examine the basic ingredients of the five genetically related analogues that critics claim to have found
in *Grettis saga* against the relevant sections of *Beowulf*. Although a great deal
of literature has accumulated around these five texts, comparisons have never
been very detailed or thorough, even in the case of the most widely accepted
analogues, namely, the Sandhaugar and Glámr episodes. Critical discussion has
in most cases revolved around a few fragments of a given analogue, usually to
reach the quick conclusion that they presented ample evidence to relate the two
works. Differences have, for the most part, been ignored. In this respect, later
scholars have too often followed the example of Guðbrandur Vigfússon and
F. York Powell, who only touched upon a few examples from the Sandhaugar
and Glámr episodes and then pronounced their conviction that in the first text
events described in *Beowulf* were repeated 'with little alteration' and that correspondence of incident was 'so perfect' in the second.[1]

Beowulf and Grettir as Heroes

The lives of Beowulf and Grettir are to a large extent dictated by the fact that as
king and outlaw they inhabit opposite ends of the social spectrum. Before
Guðbrandur Vigfússon lumped them together as monster killers no one had
seen anything to compare in Beowulf and Grettir,[2] but soon after Vigfússon had
published his findings critics began to peel away their differences to find a core
of attributes that the two heroes might have in common. Four points seemed
obvious: Beowulf and Grettir are sluggish youths; they possess great physical
strength; they swim long distances; and, most importantly, they volunteer to
overcome evil supernatural beings. But is this sufficient evidence to argue that
as a character Grettir is partly fashioned with Beowulf in mind, or that the two

share a common ancestor in their heroic exploits? Some critics have not found these apparent similarities enough to outweigh the differences. Guðni Jónsson, for instance, regards Grettir, in his land-cleansing efforts, merely as a new player in an old role,[3] but other critics have insisted that the two heroes are basically cut from the same cloth.[4] Textual comparison is always a treacherous business, and in this case it is more treacherous than usual because of the different techniques that the authors of the poem and the saga employ to present their main characters. *Grettis saga* is cast as the story of Grettir's life in the sense that it relates, in considerable detail, his origin, his career, and his death as an outlaw. *Beowulf*, on the other hand, is not a biographical poem, whether or not a king by that name ever existed. Only certain critical moments in Beowulf's life are ever described. Other information about him as a character is sketchy and incidental.

This lack of concrete information in the Old English poem has often forced critics who wish to claim a special affinity between the two heroes into a position of having to fall back on rather superficial comparisons and speculative arguments as evidence. We have, for example, already come across the observation that both Beowulf and Grettir come from afar to do their deeds and prefer to fight alone.[5] It has also been pointed out that each is a lonely man, who only has one friend in the final struggle, and who ends his life unhappily.[6] These factors do indeed apply to Beowulf and Grettir, albeit in different ways; but they are equally applicable to any number of heroes from Gilgamesh to Tin Tin. Guðbrandur Vigfússon and F. York Powell believed that, like Grettir, Beowulf had been cursed (by Grendel), and suggested that the curse had been 'a trait of the original legend which our poem has not preserved.'[7] They saw the curse as a missing link which explained Beowulf's childlessness and his sad fate as a ruler. But in the poem Grendel is silent on this and other matters, except for one mighty howl, and efforts of this kind have not produced any firm ground for comparing the two heroes beyond the four points mentioned at the beginning of this chapter.

The first of these concerns the question as to whether a background as an inglorious or a sluggish youth can be claimed as a common trait for both Beowulf and Grettir. The idea was first proposed by Friedrich Panzer, who believed that both Beowulf and Grettir were derived independently from the folktale figure of the Bear's Son, a creature who is often unmanageable or lazy in his youth.[8] The issue, however, is a great deal more complex than Panzer makes it appear. *Grettis saga* devotes a whole chapter (14) to Grettir's youth. We learn that he is not a precocious youngster, and the saga emphasizes this fact by specifically mentioning that Grettir is ten when he begins to show signs of any real growth. When his father asks him to pull his weight on the farm, Grettir promptly explains that he is not suited for such labour. Making the boy do domestic chores only results in a series of memorable, but nasty, pranks. Grettir obviously finds farm work demeaning and has presumably at the age of ten already decided on a career that involves more heroic exploits. In this sense, Grettir's youth may be disappointing or sluggish from a diligent farmer's point of view, but it is not necessarily inglorious for a hero to be. The question as to whether Grettir spent his youth as an ash-lad by the fire is addressed by the narrator of the saga and answered in the negative.[9]

We know that Beowulf is, on his mother's side, related to the royal family of the Geatas, but otherwise the story of his youth and upbringing is very unclear in the poem. The hero's undistinguished boyhood is alluded to only once (lines 2183b–9), where it is stated that he was long despised by the Geatas, who found him slack and lacking in courage and rewarded him accordingly until a change came about. But there are also passages in *Beowulf* that seem to contradict this statement. At the age of seven the boy is at the court of his grandfather, King Hreðel, enjoying treasures and feasts and being treated like one of Hreðel's own sons (lines 2428–31). Furthermore, when Beowulf, presumably still a very young man, arrives at the court of King Hroðgar to fight against Grendel, he does so with impressive credentials. According to the poem he has already performed many illustrious deeds (lines 408b–9a) and is an accomplished destroyer of sea monsters and giants (lines 418–24a and 549–76).[10]

Some scholars, especially those who believe that the poem seeks to depict a model prince, have found it impossible to reconcile these different pieces of information concerning Beowulf's youth and have therefore dismissed the reference to his inglorious early years as incompatible.[11] Others have sought to create a picture of Beowulf's youth that could accommodate his accomplishments as well as a period when something is seriously amiss.[12] There is, in other words, no clear-cut evidence to establish Beowulf as a youngster without promise of becoming a hero, and even if such a case could be made the comparison with Grettir as a boy would still be highly questionable because Grettir rebels against mundane tasks that he considers unworthy of a hero's attention.

Ever since Guðbrandur Vigfússon claimed that *Grettis saga* and *Beowulf* derived from the same legend, the great physical strength of the two monster killers has been considered one of the most obvious traits that they have in common. Ironically, this factor separates them no less than it unites them. The author of *Grettis saga* measures the strength of his hero on various occasions: he bails water like eight seamen (chapter 17); carries an ox single-handedly (chapter 50); and successfully wrestles against two men, each twice as strong as an ordinary person (chapter 72). These and other feats of strength that Grettir performs allow the saga author to conclude that he was indeed the strongest man in Iceland in his time (chapter 93). But strong though Grettir is, his physical prowess is always kept close to the borders of the humanly possible; what he might have become had Glámr's curse not stunted his growth by half we can only guess.

Beowulf, on the other hand, has no constraints of 'realistic' presentation imposed upon his strength. He is the strongest man alive (lines 789–90), with the strength of thirty men in his hand-grip (lines 379b–81a). These references would not necessarily indicate a strength of mythological proportions were they not coupled with descriptions of Beowulf's feats of swimming, which include five days in the sea in full armour (line 545a)[13] and a five hundred mile swim home after Hygelac's disastrous raid on Frisia (lines 2359b–72). Scholars have quibbled over various details in these descriptions, but there is no question that the author of *Beowulf* endows his hero with superhuman qualities of strength and endurance.[14] By comparison, Grettir's achievements in fresh or salt water are understandably paltry, as they are kept within the range of what a strong swimmer can actually do.[15]

The superhuman qualities of Beowulf make it very unlikely that the author of *Grettis saga* merely borrowed the physical attributes of his hero from the poem, but could the two hearken back to a legendary forefather – a strong swimmer who killed monsters? Larry D. Benson has argued along these lines in a well-known article entitled 'The Originality of Beowulf,' in which he maintains that whereas wrestling is a common accomplishment among Germanic heroes, great feats of swimming are more unusual. The idea of combining the two leads him to conclude that 'the fact that both Grettir and Beowulf demonstrate skill at swimming and wrestling raises the possibility that both works are based on some longer work that included the Grendel episode and had other similarities to the central fable in Beowulf.'[16] Benson's observation – i.e., that Germanic heroes who are both strong and can swim are few and far between – is incorrect insofar as it ignores the evidence of the later mythic-heroic *fornaldarsǫgur*, some of which are known to have influenced *Grettis saga*. *Örvar-Odds saga, Hálfdanar saga Brönufóstra, Egils saga einhenda*, and *Þorsteins saga Víkings-sonar* all include swimming heroes, so in this respect Grettir and Beowulf are not as exceptional as Benson would like to think. If, in the original story, it mattered that the hero had to swim to reach a second monster, his journey is not easily reconstructed by comparing the poem and the saga. Beowulf, in full armour, sinks to the bottom of the mere where he is immediately attacked by Grendel's dam and her ilk, whereas Grettir dives beneath a waterfall and uneventfully scales the rock behind it to reach the giant's cave. The real swimming feats of both heroes are reserved for other occasions.

The mythical strength of Beowulf and the human limitations of Grettir do not point to a common ancestor; on the contrary, they indicate different concepts of what comprises heroic prowess. The attitudes of the poem and the saga towards supernatural beings also reveal a wholly different definition of what forces the hero must combat. In *Beowulf*, not only Grendel, his mother, and the dragon, but all mystical creatures, are evil. They are all enemies of man and God alike, and Beowulf fights them and overpowers them by virtue of superior strength (and divine assistance) until his final battle with the dragon. In *Grettis saga*, supernatural beings more or less mirror the world of people in the story: some are hostile, like Kárr, Glámr, and the Sandhaugar trolls, and Grettir destroys them in much the same way as he does his human enemies; others are friendly towards him, like the half-troll Þórir and the mysterious Hallmundr.[17] Furthermore, the saga author always assumes that supernatural creatures are stronger than Grettir. This is abundantly clear in his wrestling bouts with Kárr, Glámr, Hallmundr, and the troll-woman. Grettir's victories against hostile supernatural creatures are won with the aid of good luck or cunning or both; either they trip over something in the course of the struggle and fall flat on their backs, like Kárr and Glámr, or they fail to avoid a wrestling trick, like the troll-woman at Sandhaugar.

Grendel and His Mother

In their comparisons of Beowulf and Grettir, Guðbrandur Vigfússon and F. York Powell paid little attention to differences in the heroes' supernatural opponents, although the nature of such creatures obviously mattered to the saga author and, even more so, to the *Beowulf* poet. Vigfússon and Powell regarded Grendel and his dam, Glámr, the troll-wife, and the giant at Sandhaugar primarily as hostile otherworldly creatures – 'fiends' and 'monsters' – not the same thing, perhaps, but easily interchangeable in the two different versions of the legend.[18] This trend has continued, and it is still common practice among critics to lump the supernatural adversaries of Beowulf and Grettir together on the facile assumption that they are all more or less the same, functionally speaking.[19] A structural approach is in itself neither better nor worse than any other, but the problem begins when the same critics start extracting sundry details in the description of the monsters, such as the cannibalism of the Grendels and the Sandhaugar trolls or the evil eyes of Grendel and Glámr, and then proceed to serve them up as evidence to support the idea that the poem and the saga are related.

The shortcuts that have been taken by various comparatists have not stemmed from a lack of critical efforts to determine the origin and nature of Grendel and his mother. The earliest views, however, which favoured rather abstract interpretations of them, did little to support Vigfússon's theory. The

Grendels were most commonly thought to originate in nature myths and Beowulf's victory against them was seen in the context of the prevailing of spring against the forces of winter. Alternatively, they were taken to be symptoms of diseases like malaria or hallucinations by the Danes, brought on by too much drink and lack of proper ventilation. But gradually Grendel and his mother took on more concrete shapes, and scholars began to trace their ancestry to the male–female rulers of the underworld of Persian and Greek mythology.[20] These developments opened the possibility of finding a more immediate forefather of the Grendels, preferably with descendants in *Grettis saga* as well.

In 1912, W.W. Lawrence published an article that offered new and persuasive evidence to link *Beowulf* and *Grettis saga*.[21] Lawrence was convinced that from the bewildering and seemingly contradictory description of the Grendels' abode in different parts of the poem it was possible to glimpse a reference to a waterfall in two places.[22] The waterfall linked the description of the landscape in *Beowulf* to Sandhaugar and led Lawrence to conclude that the original story, a *Märchen* of the Bear's Son type, had been set in Scandinavia and involved waterfall trolls as the hero's adversaries. From such stock the author of *Beowulf* had eventually fashioned Grendel and his mother.[23] Lawrence found further support for his ideas on the habitat of trolls in Icelandic materials such as the *Story of Grímur Helguson* and *Orms þáttr*, and in the presence of water sprites in Norwegian folklore. 'A waterfall among high rocks, in which a supernatural being is believed to dwell, is a common and characteristic feature of Scandinavian mountain scenery,' Lawrence declared.[24] It now seemed as though Vigfússon's hunch about a Scandinavian homeland from which the legend had derived had been correct after all.

Although there are glaring weaknesses in his argument, Lawrence's ideas concerning the origin of Grendel and his mother have had a lasting influence on *Beowulf* studies.[25] To begin with his thesis hinges on the notion that there is indeed a waterfall with a cave behind it to be found in the poem; an assumption that has come under stinging criticism from Kemp Malone, as we shall see in chapter 5. Furthermore, there is nothing in the poem's complex and ambiguous description of Grendel and his dam – other than their enormous size – to support the idea that waterfall trolls were the raw material from which the *Beowulf* poet formed his monsters. But the weakest link in Lawrence's theory is probably the fact that Scandinavian trolls do not as a rule live in waterfalls. They are roaming creatures who traditionally choose to live in mountains or hills.[26]

Grendel and his mother are no ordinary trolls; that much is certain from the poem. They may be huge, misshapen, diabolical, and beastly cannibals, but they are much more 'aristocratic' and have more human attributes than monsters in Scandinavian lore usually do. In *Beowulf* one of the first things we discover about the Grendels is their, criminally speaking, respectable background as descendants of Cain and inheritors of his curse. Like the Danes, they also keep their own court, in the sense that they occupy an underwater hall (*niðsele*) guarded by a band of water-monsters. Furthermore, we learn that for a number of years Grendel literally ruled over the Danes (*rixode*), until Beowulf put an end to his reign. The touch of magic that makes the Grendels immune to normal weapons also sets them apart from ordinary monsters in the poem, and as a tangible sign of family pride, mother and son possess an heirloom, a sword whose hilt records the history of their race. Other human touches are added as Grendel is on several occasions referred to as a man (*rinc, wer, healðegn*), and his misery as an outlaw equated with ordinary human feelings of loss and rejection (*wonsæli, dreamum bedæled*). His mother is similarly presented as a woman (*ides*), and in avenging her son she fulfils her duty as any self-respecting Germanic mother would.

Another factor that separates the Grendels from ordinary trolls in Scandinavian literature is the mystery in which the author of *Beowulf* shrouds them. His audience is never allowed to satisfy their curiosity by having a good look at them, or to discover a simple answer as to what kind of creatures they are. We have to imagine them to be unlike any known monsters, and their strangeness is emphasized by the frequent variation among terms that highlight their threefold nature: human, bestial, and diabolical. In the description of Grendel's mother the *Beowulf* poet goes still further by teasing his audience with contradictory statements about her. She is supposed to be weaker than a male warrior (lines 1282b–7) but, as Beowulf discovers, she is a far more dangerous opponent than Grendel.[27] With the proposed Sandhaugar analogue in mind, however, it is even more important that the poem refers to her with a masculine pronoun on four different occasions (lines 1260a, 1392b, 1394b and 1497b). Is this done to suggest that her sex is unimportant, as Lawrence and Goldsmith have argued,[28] or do we have to think of her separately as a mother and a monster, as Wrenn seems to think?[29] Whatever the answer is, these androgynous qualities make her more analogous to certain modern pop stars than to the troll-woman at Sandhaugar.

Grendel's name is of no help in determining family traits; it only adds to the mystery. Lawrence's theory that the word *grendel* may have been a generic term for a water monster in Old English[30] is pure guesswork, and there is no evidence to suggest that the poem's Anglo-Saxon audience had any more clues as to what the name actually means than modern scholars, who have proposed no less than five different etymologies to account for it:

1 / Old English *grindan* = 'to grind' (Old Norse *grand* = 'evil').
2 / Old English *grindel* = 'bar,' 'bolt.'

3 / Old Norse *grindill*   = a poetic term for 'storm.'
4 / Latin *grandis*   = 'full-grown,' 'great,' 'large.'
5 / Old English *grund*   = bottom, cf. Old Norse *grandi* = sand, bottom ground
                             of a body of water.[31]

Not everything about Grendel is as enigmatic as his name and nature, however. The facts that can be gleaned from different parts of the poem about his physical attributes and behavior as a man-eating monster are briefly as follows:

- Grendel is an (in)famous rover[32] of the fens and the moors that lie outside the borders of human habitation (lines 103–4).
- He is huge. Four men struggle to carry his head back to Heorot after Beowulf's final victory (lines 1637b–9).
- His fingers have nails that seem like steel-tipped spurs (lines 985–7b).
- An ugly, flame-like light emanates from his eyes (lines 726b–7).
- Unlike his mother, he does not care to fight with weapons (lines 433–4), and they do not wound him (lines 794–805b), except for his mother's magic sword (lines 1588b–90), if that is indeed the sword with which Beowulf decapitates him.
- Poisoned or corrosive blood runs through his veins (lines 1615b–17).
- Grendel is a ferocious cannibal who behaves much like an ordinary predator. For twelve years (line 147) he persecutes the Danes with frequent attacks at night (lines 1577b–9) to feast on them.
- Grendel's feeding habits have both predatory and human characteristics. He snatches as many as thirty Danes at a time, eats fifteen on the spot in one go, and carries another fifteen away with him for a later meal (lines 1581b–4a). He tears his victims apart, drinks the blood from their veins, and eats their bodies in huge mouthfuls, leaving nothing behind (740–5a).
- Grendel has a huge pouch or glove made of dragon skins (lines 2085b–8) in which he presumably carries victims that he intends to eat later.
- Grendel has no career as a 'living corpse,' (cf. Glámr and Kárr) either before or after Beowulf cuts his head off.

Glámr

Glámr is an uncommon name in Old Norse. Although the origin and meaning of the name are somewhat uncertain, it does not appear to be related etymologically to that of Grendel in any way. Glámr comes from Germanic **glé*, 'to shine with a dim or a faint light' (cf. Modern English 'gloom'), and later derivations of the word are usually associated with light or whiteness of some kind.[33]

Scholars are agreed that as a name, or a nickname, Glámr originally denotes someone who stares or looks foolish, but this association has attracted far less attention than the occurrence of his name as a poetic term for a giant and for the moon in Snorri's *Edda*. This latter connection has led some critics to believe that it might be indicative of his nature in the saga. Thus R.C. Boer associated Glámr with a moon myth and saw him (or rather his ghost) as the personification of the moonlight in winter.[34] Others, particularly Wolf von Unwerth, have stressed the giant-like size and nature of Glámr as a ghost.[35] But Glámr also occurs as an ordinary name in *Sturlunga* (*Íslendinga saga*), so it is by no means certain that the author of *Grettis saga* intended his audience to interpret it in a particular way, except to associate it with *glámsýni* (illusions), as he himself suggests.

It is not clear either what kind of creature Glámr is supposed to have been before he became one of the living dead. Boer and von Unwerth regard him as a demon or a magician who only feigns a human form and has evil intentions, whether he is living or dead.[36] No one, however, had seen any connection between the pre-ghostly Glámr and Grendel until James Carney found a way to unite them. In *Beowulf* (line 107) we are told of Grendel's descent from the exiled Cain, who becomes the progenitor of monsters and giants in medieval lore, and Grendel thus owes his monstrous form to inherited guilt. Carney maintains that this account in the poem has been transformed in the story of Glámr into his 'personal guilt,' because of his failure as a 'normal human being' to observe Christian rites, for which he is punished by becoming 'not a mere ghost, but a physical monster':

just as Hrothgar's palace was changed into an Icelandic farmhouse, so too the tale was brought up to date in medieval Iceland by discarding the idea of Cain's guilt for an analogical idea – failure to practice religious observance – that had some relevance in contemporary Iceland ... Grettir slew the monster Glam who became a monster because he, in his own person, had refused to attend Mass and had eaten meat on a fast-day.[37]

This is pretty far-fetched stuff, and Carney has to make a few shortcuts through the facts of the matter on his way to his conclusion. In the first place, Glámr hardly qualifies either as a 'normal human being' or as a 'monster,' the term under which Carney conveniently lumps Glámr and Grendel together. Secondly, he has no convincing means of explaining why the idea of monsters springing from Cain should have been replaced by a more relevant notion in medieval Iceland. There is indeed a hint of divine retribution in the tale of how Glámr meets his end, but there is no suggestion in *Grettis saga* that his existence as a ghost is a form of punishment or due to anything other than his own evil nature.[38] As opposed to Grendel, Glámr seems to enjoy his supernatural state; the punishment is reserved for Þórhallr's farm and the rest of the community.

Although Glámr as a ghost haunts farms and kills people, he is in most respects entirely different from Grendel. Glámr has no taste for human flesh, he can speak, he is as vulnerable to weapons as anyone else in the saga, and no mother or a female partner avenges his second and permanent death at the hands of Grettir. Icelandic ghosts are as a rule 'more material than the ghosts of English tradition,'[39] as E. V. Gordon so aptly put it, and Glámr is no exception, so a physical presence after death does not *per se* make him a monster on par with Grendel, as some critics like to think. Glámr's ghostly exploits: riding housetops, making a whole region desolate, driving people mad, breaking the bones of and killing animals and people, are all well known ghost story motifs from Icelandic texts, many of which the author of *Grettis saga* has been shown to have been familiar with.[40] It is also possible, as Hermann Pálsson has suggested,[41] that the account of Glámr's nature and powers is sprinkled with ideas that can be traced to medieval commentaries on the subject of ghosts and demons. But the main traits that Glámr and Grendel share – haunting places and killing people – are far too common among ghosts and monsters to establish any particular link between the two. Of the contact points between Glámr and Grendel that have been suggested, only three are specific enough to indicate that they might hearken back to a common origin or be directly related in some other manner: their great size, their evil eyes, and the matter of cursing or being cursed.

Grettis saga makes it quite clear that Glámr's size varies. As he enters the farmhouse where Grettir awaits him (chapter 35), he towers up to the ceiling, but a moment later the two wrestle in a manner that would be impossible if Glámr was the giant that he had just appeared to be. Hermann Pálsson has explained this with a reference to the illusionary powers that *Antoníus saga* ascribes to demons,[42] and the note which the saga author inserts into his text to relate the word *glámsýni* to the story of Glámr supports Pálsson's reading. Grettir's vision of Glámr as a giant is only a fleeting illusion, whereas Grendel's gigantic size is an integral part of his ancestry from Cain.

It is only as Glámr is about to meet his death that his evil eyes and his stare begin to play a part in the story, whereas the ugly flame-like light from Grendel's eyes presumably scared the Danes all along. The idea that evil persons who possess magic powers can do harm by looking at someone at the moment of their death was, however, already well established in Icelandic literature before *Grettis saga* was composed[43] and has nothing whatsoever to do with Grendel.

Finally, there is the matter of the curse. James Carney includes Grettir in the second part of his Cain hypothesis and presents the following argument:

Part of the curse of Cain was that he was to be a *'vagus et profugus in terra.'* When the monster Glam is dying he curses Grettir and part of his curse is: 'Thou shalt be outlawed and doomed ever to dwell alone, away from men.' This suggests that Cain figured in the author's source material; when Cain was eliminated the terms in which he was cursed were retained; but he is made, in the person of Glam, to utter the curse of which, in the source material, he was the recipient.[44]

Carney's theory is based on his conviction that the author of *Grettis saga* had direct access to a manuscript of *Beowulf*, something which is very unlikely, as we shall see in chapter 6. But the most amazing part of Carney's speculation is that, having just explained how the author of *Grettis saga* felt compelled to substitute Grendel's ancestral guilt for Glámr's personal guilt in order to emphasize the importance of observing Christian customs in Iceland, the same author decided to cast the ghost of that stubborn heathen Glámr in the role of God almighty to banish and curse Grettir, as Cain was banished and cursed.

Whether Glámr's role in the 'old legend' is the same as Grendel's we have yet to examine, but nothing about the origin, nature, or behaviour of Glámr seems to point to any special affinity with Grendel. The differences between them far outweigh any superficial traits that they might seem to share, and statements to the effect that 'after his death [Glámr] distinctly resembles Grendel'[45] are not based on much more than wishful thinking.

The Troll-Woman and the Giant of the Sandhaugar Episode

Some scholars think that the Old Norse terms *trǫll* ('trolls') and *jǫtnar* ('giants') may have indicated a degree of difference between the two at a very early stage, i.e., that giants were considered to be remote, prehistoric figures in comparison to trolls. In late sagas (especially *fornaldarsǫgur*) and in folktales, trolls and giants have merged and for the most part share the same characteristics.[46] In this literature, trolls and giants are huge, supernatural beings who live in the mountains far to the north and are as a rule hostile towards people. This is, of course, not without exceptions, as we see in *Grettis saga* itself.

Unlike the battle against Glámr, whose curse follows Grettir to the end of his days, the Sandhaugar episode is self-contained and independent; much like a chapter in a picaresque novel. Late in the saga (chapter 64), the reader is informed that at a farm called Sandhaugar in Bárðardalur people are spooked by the presence of trolls. For two years in a row a man has been kidnapped from the farm at Christmas, a season that also inspired Glámr to do evil deeds; however, unlike Glámr, whose persecutions extended throughout the dark months of winter, these creatures only strike once a year. During the first attack, when the farmer was snatched away, there were other people present in the hall of the farmhouse, which clearly shows that these evil beings are only interested in taking a single person. The farmer disappeared without a trace, and no one saw anything, although a great deal of noise was heard by his bed. Then, in one sentence, the saga author makes a year go by and has nothing to say about anyone's reaction to the man's disappearance. It is only after the second attack, when traces of blood are found by the front door of the hall, that people conclude that some evil beings must be responsible for the kidnapping of the two men. Unlike with Grendel and his mother or Glámr, nothing is known about these trolls; they are (and remain) nameless, and no one knows where they come from. This is how matters stand when Grettir – who after his tangle with Glámr is the last person the reader expects to turn up in a haunted place – appears on the scene.

The above-mentioned account looks like a summary of a story, but in fact it is not; there is no more information in the saga concerning the famous hauntings at Sandhaugar prior to Grettir's fight with the trolls. What little we have is a disappointingly short and incomplete story, especially if we keep in mind that Vigfússon believed his 'old legend' to have been percolating in people's imaginations for hundreds of years. And it is not just that the saga version is short. As it stands, this first part of the Sandhaugar episode, i.e., the counterpart to the national disaster that Grendel brought on the Danes, leaves some awkward questions unanswered. There is no explanation as to why these evil beings only strike at Christmas,[47] why they kidnap people but only take one person at a time, or what they actually do with their victims. The fact that when the troll-woman attacks Grettir she is armed with a long knife and carries a *trog*,[48] and the discovery of the bones of the two missing men in the giant's cave, would seem to indicate that the Sandhaugar trolls are cannibals like Grendel. But if that is indeed the case, it does not say much for their monstrous appetite that they strike only once a year and take one person at a time. Grettir's discovery of the bones in the cave also shows that their eating habits must be a good deal more sophisticated than those of Grendel's. If, on the other hand, we are not meant to think of the Sandhaugar trolls as cannibals, there is no explanation as to why they kidnap people. These uncertainties, which affect the very nucleus of the story, do not give the impression of a legend polished by centuries of oral transmission. The hints which the author drops are inconsistent, as if he has not fully formulated the story that he wants to tell. The blood by the front door would, for example, seem to suggest that someone was attacked and perhaps eaten on the spot, and the troll-woman's long knife and *trog* could create the same impression. But the bones in the cave point in the opposite direction, i.e., towards people being abducted live and in one piece and killed there.

Grettir's involvement does not add a great deal of knowledge about the Sandhaugar trolls, as the reader is never given any information beyond what little Grettir actually sees. They remain without a background, there is no attempt to develop them as characters, and there is nothing about them to suggest that they enter the story with the identifying marks of a long tradition. The troll-woman is big and is armed with a long knife (*skálm*), as troll-women in Icelandic lore commonly are.[49] The *trog* she carries is, however, a more interesting and unusual prop. In his introduction to *Beowulf*, Klaeber states his belief that the *trog* and Grendel's *glof* ('glove,' 'pouch'?) point to a connection between the two stories, as both articles serve the identical purpose of holding food,[50] but this comparison is somewhat misleading. Grendel obviously uses his glove to store and carry his victims, whereas the troll-woman's *trog* might be used as a cutting tray or a container in which to store food, but as a substitute for Grendel's 'rucksack' it will not do. The giant's entry into the story adds very little to what we know (or rather what we do not know); he is huge, black, and ugly, as giants in folklore are expected to be,[51] and like the troll-woman, but unlike Grendel, he uses weapons.

Critics who wish to equate the Sandhaugar pair with Grendel and his mother have usually chosen to ignore the fact that *Grettis saga* suggests no relationship of any kind between the giant and the troll-woman, although in recent years some scholars have seen a ray of hope in one of the kennings that Grettir uses to refer to the giant in a stanza (no. 61) that he composes about the battle against him in the cave. The epithet in question is *mellu vinr*, which literally means 'the troll-woman's friend.' The two main editors of *Grettis saga*, R.C. Boer and Guðni Jónsson, take this kenning to mean 'a giant' and read nothing else into it. It is therefore somewhat surprising to encounter the giant as the 'she-troll's ugly husband' in the translation of this stanza in *Beowulf and Its Analogues*.[52] Unfortunately, the translator does not explain how and when this match has come about. Another attempt to establish a relationship has been undertaken by Peter Jorgensen, who maintains that *mellu vinr* might be taken to mean 'a lover,' but the kennings for lovers that he points to as a basis for his reading are too far removed from *mellu vinr* to prove his point.[53]

The only thing that the Sandhaugar trolls really have in common with Grendel and his dam is the fact that they are male and female, and even that evidence comes with certain caveats. It must be kept in mind that, unlike in *Beowulf*, their sex is of no importance, and that in the saga they appear in the wrong order. Critics who have the imagination to see Grendel and his mother 'in all their monstrosity and superhuman powers' in the giant and the troll-woman of Sandhaugar[54] are only testifying to the might of Glámr's eyes.

Kárr the Old

Nothing but the art of finding the lowest common denominator through a play on words can make Kárr the Old resemble Grendel or his mother. Kárr is a ghost (one of the living dead) who lives in a gravemound on Háramarsey. According to the saga he has managed to increase the wealth and power of his son, Þorfinnr, by scaring other farmers off the island and making Þorfinnr the sole owner of all property there. Only those who enjoy Þorfinnr's favour are unmolested by Kárr's hauntings.[55] R.W. McConchie, who, as we have already seen, maintains that the story of Kárr the Old is a genetically related and neglected *Beowulf* analogue, readily admits that Kárr is quite unlike Grendel, and that the whole episode is relatively unimportant in the context of the saga. Instead he chooses to emphasize the similarity of events and how the two heroes react to them. McConchie suggests that the first of 'several points of similarity between Beowulf's struggle with Grendel's mother and Grettir's fight with Kárr' is the fact that both 'take place as a result of a series of violent hauntings.'[56] It is, of course, a matter of literary sensibility whether we see fit to equate a national disaster, like Grendel's reign of terror, and Kárr's spooking a few farmers away (he does not kill anyone) under the neat semantic umbrella of 'a series violent hauntings.' However, it is simply not true that Grettir tangles with Kárr as a result of his hauntings, as McConchie maintains. *Grettis saga* makes it quite clear that the hero's motive has nothing to do with cleansing the island of an evil being; Kárr has achieved his goal anyway, and there is nothing to be gained by his destruction except treasure. Like all others who break into gravemounds in the sagas, Grettir does so for precisely this reason.[57]

The Bear

A.R. Taylor and A. Margaret Arent, the first scholars to maintain that the bear episode was analogous and genetically related to *Beowulf*, saw nothing in the description of the brown bear that Grettir fights except a brown bear. Their readers were thus spared a detailed comparison of the nature and characteristics of the beast and Grendel. But is there no way of equating the two? Recently, Arthur A. Wachsler has attempted to do so and presents his case as follows:

According to Norse Lore, a man was said to possess a soul called a '*fylgja*' which could leave the body and reappear in the form of an animal. Indeed, the *fylgja* often shared the personality of its human partner. 'The animal *fylgja* often had some corresponding aspect to that of the character of its owner – bulls and bears attended great chiefs, foxes people of crafty nature.' Along with the bull, then, the bear, according to Norse tradition, was the spirit form of a great leader.

The supernatural and manlike qualities of the bear are attested also in the Norse belief in lycanthropy. Men who had the gift of shape-shifting frequently changed into animals, often appearing as bears as well as wolves ...

Besides the Scandinavians, other northern races held the bear in special esteem. The Lapps, Finns, Ostiaks and Voguls regarded the bear as the most holy of wild animals and held feasts in its honor. They considered the animal to be more intelligent and stronger than a man. One northern race, the Votiaks, believed that the bear could understand human speech. In addition, these people believed that the bear, if provoked enough, could return from the dead to punish its enemies. The awe in which the Votiaks held the bear was based no doubt on its ghostly nature, on its ability to return from the dead ...

The evidence in ancient northern lore suggests that the bear, along with more obvious examples, was considered to be a revenant, one of the *draugar* or animated dead. For that reason, the bear can be considered no less formidable and worthy an opponent than Glamr, the female troll at Sandhaugr and Kar the Old to all of whom the animal is related.[58]

Wachsler's method puts the cart squarely before the horse. Even if we accept all his findings at face value, it is still not easy to see how they lead to the desired conclusion. If there is a connection to be made between Scandinavian beliefs in *fylgjur*, or shape-shifting – which, as it happens, only affect living persons – and the Votiaks' belief that the bear could return from the dead, it certainly does not turn the brown bear in *Grettis saga* into a *draugr* on par with Glámr and Kárr, as Wachsler would like us to think. None of this has anything to do with the bear in *Grettis saga*, unless we are meant to think of the animal as someone's *fylgja*, a chief who has taken on the shape of a bear, or the ghost of the beast rather than an ordinary brown bear of flesh and blood.

Various other points that concern the bear episode, in addition to Grettir's fight against the beast and the descriptions of its lair, have been thought to show contact with *Beowulf*. There is, first of all, Taylor's contention that the character and actions of Bjǫrn, the obnoxious relative of Þorkell, mirror those of Unferð. Taylor based his comparison on their 'discourtesy towards guests and strangers,' which he found so strongly emphasized in the saga writer's portrait of Bjǫrn that he believed it to have been a 'characteristic of the prototype of the two men.'[59] However this comparison is not as simple as it looks. It is quite true that Unferð challenges Beowulf's credentials in the poem (lines 499–528), but it is by no means certain that he does so out of discourtesy or hostility. As

Hroðgar's ryle ('spokesman'?), it may well be that he is merely carrying out his duties.[60] Later in the poem, Unferð appears as Beowulf's friend and lends him Hrunting – the famous *hæftmece* – to use against Grendel's mother. Although Bjǫrn and Unferð may both be jealous men, there are too many other factors that separate them in the poem and the saga to suggest that they go back to a common ancestor. In the first place, Bjǫrn has no official position at Þorkell's farm, and he has no skeletons in his closet like Unferð (who is guilty of fratricide). Secondly, Unferð makes no attempt to tangle with Grendel, whereas Bjǫrn tries to kill the bear. Finally, it must be kept in mind that Bjǫrn is eventually killed by Grettir. As Geoffrey Hughes has rightly observed, there is no character in Germanic literature with whom Unferð can be readily compared, and Bjǫrn is no better than previous candidates.[61]

Wachsler, however, thinks that he can detect echoes from 'the original stories' in the way in which Bjǫrn and his companions arouse the 'primal monster':

> It is not unreasonable to suppose that Bjorn and his company drank to excess and celebrated by playing instruments, singing loudly and generally behaving as drunk men do. They 'lifted their voices' (*reysta*) causing a din (*háreysti*). And there is nothing to suggest the Danes in Heorot were any less boisterous than their Icelandic [*sic*] counterparts. They expressed their joy by celebrating loudly (drēam). During their noisy celebration, both groups, apparently, provoked their neighbors who in great anger retaliated by attacking their inconsiderate tormentors. In keeping with his Christian background, the *Beowulf* poet places Grendel in league with the kin of Cain. In contrast, the author of the saga, with his monstrous bear, remains squarely in the pagan world, and he is probably closer to the original stories. In each case, however, it is loud noises or the sounds of celebration which arouse a primal monster and cause it to attack those who have disturbed its peace.[62]

This may look convincing, but most of the analogous material that Wachsler claims to find in *Grettis saga* either is not there or is made to appear in a greatly emended form. In the saga Bjǫrn and his cronies are said to have loitered outside and to have made loud noises (74), but there is no mention of singing or drinking or other forms of celebration; nor are such activities normally practised outdoors in Scandinavia during the winter. It is a also a mere play on words to argue that both Grendel and the bear are 'roused' by noises, which cause them to attack, or to compare them as 'primal monsters.' Grendel is attracted – and presumably tormented – by the happy noises of celebration that he hears coming from Heorot every day; the brown bear is awoken from its hibernation and behaves as a hungry bear might be expected to do: it attacks sheep – anyone's sheep. Þorkell suffers more damage than other farmers simply because he is the wealthiest of the lot, as *Grettis saga* duly explains. To find in the brown bear episode of the saga essentially the same story line as in *Beowulf* can obviously be done, but only if we are prepared to emend both texts in the manner that Procrustes employed to make his visitors fit his infamous bed.

Grettir as a Monster

The hypothesis that Grettir has an alter ego as a monster was first suggested by Nora Chadwick in 1959, and has since become increasingly fashionable among *Beowulf* scholars. Chadwick's transformation of Grettir seems to have come about as a result of her failure to fit him into a theory that would make *Beowulf* and *Grettis saga* (along with several other texts in Old Norse) ritualistic repetitions of an ancient story, which supposedly involved 'a hereditary feud between a heroic member of a ruling Scandinavian dynasty and a closely knit group of supernatural foes [a *draugr*, an evil supernatural woman and a dragon], located to the east of the Baltic.'[63] Chadwick finds two of these foes in *Grettis saga*, but no trace of landscapes east of the Baltic or a dragon. As luck would have it, *Bjarnar saga Hítdælakappa* contains these missing elements, and that leads Chadwick to the following extraordinary conclusion:

It is strongly to be suspected that Grettir's adventures against monsters nowhere else associated with Iceland, but consistently located east of the Baltic in 'Bjarmaland,' have been derived by the author from traditions proper to Björn Hítdælakappi's Russian sojourn with King Cnut.[64]

What Chadwick omits to explain is why, if these traditions are indeed associated with Bjǫrn, they are not included in his saga? And where does this leave poor Grettir? Given a family tree with half-trolls and warlocks on its distant branches and with no immediate prospects of qualifying as 'a heroic member of a ruling Scandinavian dynasty,' his fate at Chadwick's hands is rather predictable. As she meditates on Grettir's name – which she believes to be unusual and sinister – his metamorphosis from a hero to a monster is a matter of smooth speculation:

Is it possible that the name itself carries with it a troll connotation? What is its origin? Can it be a Norse form derived from *grandi-*, and is the corresponding Anglo-Saxon form *Grend-il*? Is it possible that in origin Grendel and Grettir are identical, and that in the Norse story the monster has been transformed into the hero – that a story, originally told from the monster's point of view, has left traces on this strange and capricious, pitiful yet very sinister, outlaw?[65]

Nora Chadwick's ideas have been firmly opposed by Anatoly Liberman, who, as we have already seen, also rejects the notion that there could have been an Old English text in which Grendel's story was related from the monster's point of view. But is it possible that the names Grettir and Grendel are related through *grandi-*[66] or *grenja* ('to bellow'), as Margaret Arent has proposed?[67] Grettir's name is normally traced to *grantian* (i.e., related to words meaning 'to snarl' or 'to growl'), but it has also been argued that the name might not be of Norse origin and hence that it is uncertain what it means.[68] Liberman, who has discussed the possible etymologies of the names Grettir and Grendel in detail, sees no possibility of tracing their origin to the same root. His argument may be summarized as follows:

1 / Although the etymology of Grendel is debatable, the root *grend* is probably the umlauted form of **grand*.

2 / Another Germanic root, *gran-*, is related to the root *grant-*, as in **grantjan*, from which we have the verbs *grenja* and *gretta*, and eventually Grettir as a name.

3 / The relevant question is thus whether the roots **grand-* and **grant-* can be related, which they cannot be unless we can find a way of explaining the last consonant in each word: i.e., the *d* in **grand-* and the *t* in **grant-*. This was indeed attempted during the last century by Sophus Bugge, but his hypothesis was demolished by historical linguists a long time ago. In short, the bottom line is that **grand-* and **grant-* have to be taken to be two separate and unrelated etyma and, given that conclusion, there is no possibility of tracing the names of Grettir and Grendel to the same root.[69]

Arent and Chadwick have also used chthonic connotations, which they claim to be present in the names of Grettir and Grendel, as evidence to link them. It goes without saying, however, that in the final analysis the argument stands or falls on etymological evidence, and any speculation about common connotations, chthonic or otherwise, which critics may feel that they share, is simply irrelevant.[70] It may well be that Nora Chadwick's ideas represent 'the most daring questioning to date,' as Richard Harris has stated,[71] but there is not a shred of reasonable evidence to support her hypothesis concerning Grettir's monstrous origin.

As we saw in chapter 1, the fifth analogue that Harris claimed to have found in *Grettis saga* represents an attempt to develop Chadwick's ideas much further than she herself was prepared to do. Harris looks for textual evidence and finds that 'the death of Grettir resembles in at least eleven details the first part of *Beowulf*, particularly the fight at Grendel's Mere.'[72] Harris's evidence inevitably consists of sundry events and details that are extracted from the two texts. Apart from this, his approach to the two texts does not appear to follow any particular method, except to connect them at any cost.[73] Sometimes the order of these elements, as they originally appear in *Grettis saga* and *Beowulf*, seems to matter – and is kept; in other instances it must be re-shuffled to make a comparison.[74] But this is not the only liberty that Harris takes in the presentation of his evidence. There is also a tendency to 'emend' some of it in the process. Take points 2 and 3, for example:

Grettir has a hut on Drangey; nearness to the sea.	Grendel has a waterfall cave, possibly near the sea.
Þorbjörn arrives at Drangey toward the end of the day.	Beowulf takes most of day to reach bottom of mere.

Grendel has no waterfall cave like the giant at Sandhaugar; he has an underwater hall, and according to the poem it takes Beowulf *hwil dæges* (line 1495) – 'a good part of the day,' not most of it – to reach the bottom of the mere.

In the course of Harris's discussion these seemingly unrelated items are stitched together with literary exegesis of the kind that Isidore of Seville practised to perfection in the seventh century. Take point 4, for example:

Þorbjörn climbs a ladder to reach Grettir's hut.	Beowulf plunges into mere.

For the reader who is slow to see a connection between Þorbjǫrn's climbing a ladder to reach Grettir's hut, and Beowulf's plunging into the mere, Harris offers the following explication:

> Þorbjörn climbs a ladder to reach Grettir's hut. Panzer's description of the Bear's Son Tale includes the motif of the hero climbing to a world, the Demon Kingdom, above or below the earth to confront the monster. Presumably an ascent would be involved where the opening in the earth, by which access is gained to the other world, is on a mountain or the top of a hill. The monster is reached only by descent elsewhere in *Beowulf* and *Grettis saga*. The necessity of climbing in the opposite direction doesn't seem to me to rule out the possibility of this being an element parallel to the climbing in the other episodes. The ladder would simply be a modification of the rope used by Grettir in the Háramarsey and Sandhaugar adventures.[75]

In *Grettis saga,* it is perfectly true that Grettir plays many and sometimes contradictory roles,[76] and in conclusion, I want to emphasize that I do not reject

Nora K. Chadwick's role reversal theory because I find it shocking that Grettir could be cast as a monster; I reject it because there is no reasonable evidence to support that particular role reversal for Grettir, and Harris's attempt to develop the original theory further changes nothing in that respect. In essence, Harris's fifth analogue shows Grettir to be a sheep-eating outlaw whose death, scene by scene, does not mirror that of Grendel, unless we are prepared to suspend common sense altogether in reviewing the evidence. However, Harris's argument is neither better nor worse than others that we have examined in this chapter from the hands of critics who would like to equate Beowulf and Grettir as heroes or their various adversaries as monsters. Undoubtedly, these arguments are inspired by academic climates that place a great value on critical imagination in literary analysis, but some issues – like the questions we have examined in this chapter – simply cannot be resolved on the basis of what critics would like to imagine. Having considered the ingredients that make up the heroes and the monsters in *Beowulf* and *Grettis saga*, I do not think there is convincing evidence to suggest a relationship between the two. As 'heroes' Grettir and Beowulf have little in common, and as 'monsters' their supernatural adversaries have even less.

3

The Hero's Fight against the Monsters

The five episodes in *Grettis saga* which have been claimed to be analogous and genetically related to *Beowulf* all contain battle scenes, and in all five the battle between the hero and his adversary is the climax of that episode. If there was indeed an old legend about a hero who overcame two monsters – a story that served as a common source for the authors of both *Beowulf* and *Grettis saga* – there is no reason why the form of the struggle, or parts of it, might not have survived intact, even if the original protagonists were no longer the same. An argument along these lines has been proposed by Guðni Jónsson, who in his edition of *Grettis saga* describes Grettir in his fight with the Sandhaugar trolls as a new player in an old role.[1] There is common agreement among critics who see a connection between *Beowulf* and *Grettis saga* that the 'old role' in both works included two fights against different monsters, and with that pattern in mind we can begin to look at the first fight in the poem and the saga.

Beowulf's Fight against Grendel

During the nineteenth century *Beowulf* scholars, German for the most part, tended to view the hero's battles with Grendel and his dam allegorically and therefore paid little attention to the actual details of the two battle scenes. But ever since Guðbrandur Vigfússon claimed that there was a genetic relationship between Beowulf's struggle with Grendel and the Sandhaugar and Glámr episodes, critics have analysed these combat scenes on the assumption that both authors were attempting to describe the battle in realistic terms. In the case of Beowulf's encounter with Grendel, there are some questions that remain unanswered, but the main outline of what takes place is fairly clear:

1 / Beowulf waits for Grendel to attack Heorot.
2 / When Grendel enters the hall in the night, Beowulf is awake and awaits him. He watches Grendel devour one of his retainers but does nothing to stop him.
3 / Grendel then reaches for Beowulf, who is lying down, with his hand. Beowulf seizes it – with one hand, apparently – and holds it firmly in his grip. Grendel struggles to get out of Beowulf's hand-grip, and in the course of their struggle Heorot is damaged.
4 / Beowulf's retainers hack at Grendel with their swords but to no avail.
5 / Beowulf tears Grendel's arm off, and the monster flees, leaving a trail of blood.
6 / Grendel's arm is kept as a trophy, and he is presumed to be mortally wounded.

There is some very strange stuff in this description. Take, for instance, the question as to why the hero, while waiting for Grendel, lies calmly on his bed while one of his men (Hondscioh) is eaten by the monster. The motif of waiting does indeed occur in the Sandhaugar and Glámr episodes of *Grettis saga*, and it also occurs in *Þorsteins þáttr uxafóts* and in *Þórodds þáttr Snorrasonar*, but the part of the scene that has the hero watch the monster eat one of his followers as a preamble to battle has no counterpart in Icelandic literature. Fr. Klaeber believes that the attack on Hondscioh was inserted into the original story by the author of *Beowulf*, but the only evidence that such an interpolation actually took place is Klaeber's faith in the above-mentioned episodes from *Grettis saga* as proof that there was indeed a literary ancestor.[2] But even if we accept that *Grettis saga* preserves the original story by making the hero fight the monster unaided, there are still some very important differences between the first fight in *Beowulf* and any of the genetically related analogues that critics claim to have found in *Grettis saga*. For the most part, these differences concern the actual form that the fight takes, the manner in which victory is achieved, and the aftermath of the battle.

Let us first consider the manner of fighting. In *Beowulf* the hero 'wrestles' with Grendel, and in *Grettis saga* the hero also 'wrestles' with a troll-woman and with Glámr, but these fights in the saga and the poem have little in common, although the same word is often used to apply to both in English.[3] In *Beowulf* it is not certain whether the fight begins with the hero sitting up, leaning on his own arm and then proceeding to fight the monster's hand, or whether he grasps Grendel's hand straightaway,[4] but what happens during the rest of the struggle is something like this: As soon as Beowulf has locked the monster's hand in the grip of his own hand, Grendel seeks to pull himself free with the well-known result that his entire arm is torn off. In other words, it is the hero's (one) hand that fights the monster's hand, and the poem offers no suggestion that Beowulf uses his free hand or his feet in the ensuing struggle with Grendel.[5]

This unusual method of fighting is the essential feature of the whole battle scene at Heorot, and it dictates what the hero must do in order to succeed, namely, tear the monster's arm off. It leaves Beowulf and Hroðgar's court in possession of Grendel's arm as a trophy, which in turn leads to his mother's visit to collect it and to Beowulf's subsequent battle with her at the mere. Thus everything in this account hangs together, and everything comes down to the fate of Grendel's hand or arm as an instrument of fighting and an instrument of his own fate and the fate of Hroðgar's court, as has been amply demonstrated by a number of studies.[6] Critics who view this battle scene simply as one in which 'a monster loses an arm' and readily equate it with Grettir's fight at Sandhaugar are obviously prepared to ignore the logic behind this chain of events. As we shall soon see, the fact that Grettir cuts the troll-woman's arm off is only a means of disposing of her; it has no integral relationship with their battle or later developments in the saga.

Grettir's Fight with the Troll-Woman at Sandhaugar[7]

As we saw in chapter 1, various critics have sought to account for some of the most obvious differences between this episode and Beowulf's fight with Grendel. Efforts of this kind have explained why Grettir fights with the female before the male, noted the saga author's omission to relate the two trolls and lamented his failure to motivate Grettir's visit to the giant's cave by anything other than mere curiosity. The two different versions that the saga offers of the troll-woman's fate,[8] both without much similarity to that of Grendel, seem also to have been discussed and settled to the satisfaction of most scholars.[9] Our concern at the moment, however, is not with these so-called textual corruptions of the poem and the saga, but rather with Grettir's fight with the troll-woman. What happens between them may be summarized as follows:

1 / She enters the farm house carrying a long knife and a *trog* and goes straight to Grettir's bed to attack him. He jumps up to meet the attack.
2 / The troll-woman pulls him out of the farm house, and having done great damage to it, they find themselves outside wearing the frame for the front door around their shoulders.
3 / Grettir feels exhausted but realizes that if he cannot do better than this, she will succeed in tossing him into the ravine.
4 / The troll-woman has so far held Grettir tightly to herself, making it impossible for him to use either of his hands, as he can only clasp his arms around her waist.

5 / As they reach the edge of the chasm, Grettir gives the ogress a swing, frees his right hand, grabs his short-sword, and cuts off her right arm. Whichever version of the saga we choose to follow, this leads to her death and disappearance from the story.

Aside from the manner of fighting as compared to the Grendel fight, three other differences may be noted. In the first place, the troll-woman's arm plays no special role, either in the fight itself, or as a trophy, or in Grettir's later encounter with the giant. Secondly, she is portrayed as being stronger than the hero. We see this from the fact that she is on the offensive until the final moment of the fight, and that she, rather than Grendel, decides how the battle is fought. As Martin Puhvel has observed, the troll-woman, like Grendel, is struggling to get out of the building, but for an entirely different reason: she is not trying to escape; she wants to throw Grettir into the ravine;[10] and it is luck rather than strength which brings Grettir victory. From a different point view, we need only examine what prospects of victory the authors of the poem and the saga assign to their respective heroes to confirm this. In Beowulf's fight against Grendel there is no element of suspense; the poet drops hints to his audience from the first moment of the battle, and then at regular intervals while it lasts, to indicate that his hero will prove victorious.[11] By contrast, the author of *Grettis saga* invites the reader to expect that Grettir may lose: the troll-woman is stronger than Grettir, stronger than any being that Grettir has ever fought, and he can see that he is about to be defeated, etc.[12]

The third point of difference concerns the hero's use or non-use of weapons – the fact that Beowulf fights Grendel barehanded, whereas Grettir uses his sword against the troll-woman. The usual way to account for this is to point out that Grendel is gifted with magic powers that make swords useless against him, whereas the troll-woman has no such powers or protection. Another possibility has been suggested by Larry Benson in his article 'The Originality of *Beowulf.*' Benson argues that in the first fight of the common original, the hero has to grapple with a monster who tries to drag him from a hall. Consequently, the hero must be a proficient at wrestling. Beowulf, according to Benson, evidently does 'not have previous experience as a wrestler, since he makes quite a point of facing Grendel without his usual weapons (a point that Grettir, who has already demonstrated his skill at wrestling, need not make).'[13]

This theory may well work for Beowulf as a hero but for Grettir it will not do. The fight against the troll-woman demonstrates to Grettir (and to the reader) that, for all his prowess at wrestling, there are beings out there who are stronger than he and who must be defeated with the aid of a good weapon. The supposed common original hardly made much of that point in respect to the hero. Furthermore, Benson's argument ignores a very simple pattern of poetic justice which

the author of the saga follows in Grettir's dealings with Glámr and the
Sandhaugar trolls:

- Glámr likes to break the backs of men and beasts. He meets his own death
lying on his back with Grettir on top.
- The troll-woman arrives armed with meat-processing instruments and presumably intends to go to work on Grettir. He carves her arm off.
- The giant reaches for a sword to use against Grettir, who promptly kills him
with a sword.[14]

Here the comparison with *Beowulf* does not contribute much to our understanding of *Grettis saga*.

Grettir's Fight with Glámr

Grettir's fight with Glámr may be divided into the following stages in the saga:

1 / Glámr enters the farm house, his head towering up to the rafters, and notices
that something is lying on a bench covered by a cloak. He pulls at the cloak
so hard that Grettir, who is hiding underneath it, is pulled up from the bench.
Between them, they rip the cloak apart.
2 / Grettir leaps under Glámr's arms, grasps him around the waist, and clasps
him as hard as he can, but Glámr grips Grettir's arms so tightly that he is
forced to break away.
3 / Glámr now seeks to drag Grettir out of the hall, but it is clear to Grettir that it
will be worse to deal with the fiend once they are outside, so he resists all he
can. As they struggle, they break everything in their way.
4 / Glámr pulls Grettir to the vestibule of the hall, and Grettir realizes that
he cannot resist any longer. He puts his feet against a half-sunken boulder
and throws all his weight against Glámr, who is pulling in the same direction. Glámr falls out of the door and lands on his back with Grettir on
top.
5 / Glámr meserizes Grettir with his eyes and utters his curse. Grettir comes to,
cuts Glámr's head off, and places it against his buttocks.[15]

Some critics have been reluctant to accept this account as a *bona fide* genetically related analogue to *Beowulf*. R.W. Chambers, for example, eventually
rejected it on the grounds that *Grettis saga* offered no sequel to Grettir's fight
with Glámr.[16] In his edition of the saga, Guðni Jónsson makes no attempt to
relate this fight to Beowulf's tangle with Grendel, but unlike Chambers he does
not do so for structural reasons. Jónsson seems to think that there is a kernel of

truth to the Glámr episode; that it somehow relates to an event that actually took place in Grettir's life.[17] Others have objected because they have failed to find much in Grettir's fight with Glámr that compares with the Grendel fight in *Beowulf*. As we have just seen, Grettir fights alone, the only tug of war is over a cloak (the actual wrestling part is entirely different from Beowulf's fight with Grendel), Grettir is weaker than Glámr, and uses a trick to beat him.[18]

These two fights in the poem and the saga may also be compared according to their relevance *per se* to each work, and in terms of how victorious each hero actually is. The Glámr fight in *Grettis saga* is indisputably the climax of the story and a turning point in Grettir's life, but it is hardly an event of national importance. Furthermore, it is a Pyrrhic victory. Grettir defeats the demon but loses to the forces of darkness, which will haunt him for the rest of his life as a consequence of Glámr's curse. In *Beowulf*, the hero's victory over Grendel is a career move and no climax, although it affects the fate of an entire nation; and it is an absolute victory, although it leads to the hero's discovery of another evil being that also must be defeated.

Some *Beowulf* scholars have been much less fastidious than Chambers with regard to the absence of a sequel in the Glámr episode. They accept that the 'old legend' probably contained an account of two fights against monsters, and that each story – or even fragments of each of them – might have survived independently. Armed with this conviction, these critics have looked at the Glámr fight and found what they wanted to find. A century ago John Earle concluded that the circumstances of Grettir's encounter with Glámr were 'full of parallels' with the Grendel fight,[19] and some later commentators have found themselves in agreement with him.[20] In the literature on the subject, the number of parallels that I have been able to find is rather smaller than Earle's pronouncement would lead one to think – five to be exact – and there is much to be imagined and explained before they fit the circumstances of Beowulf's battle with Grendel:

1 / We are asked to accept that the tug of war over the cloak is a distant echo of the tearing off of Grendel's arm.
2 / The destruction of the farmhouse during the battle is to be read as equivalent to the damage of Heorot.
3 / Grettir's moment of weakness when he is sitting on top of Glámr is a parallel to Beowulf's brief 'lapse' in the battle with Grendel's mother.
4 / The ugly, flame-like light that shines from Grendel's eyes (lines 726b–7) is the same as the evil stare of the ghost.
5 / Glámr's curse relates to Grendel's descent from Cain and to the curse of Cain.

The matter of the curse was discussed in chapter 2 in connection with Glámr's nature, but the other four items merit further attention. As early as the 1920s, Heinz Dehmer showed that the tug of war over the cloak in *Grettis saga* matches a similar scene in *Hávarðar saga Ísfirðings* and is quite common in later Icelandic folktales.[21] Dehmer believes that in the Glámr episode Grettir hides underneath the cloak as a means of protection against the evil powers of the demon, whereas the tug of war part is a traditional first test of strength (Old Norse *skinnleikr*, which literally means 'a game involving a hide') in a fight between two parties. If Dehmer is right, it is very hard to imagine that these two uses of the cloak in the saga have much to do with Grendel's arm. In his study, Dehmer also looked for examples of damage to houses as a result of fights in the Icelandic sagas and found the motif to be fairly commonplace. It occurs in sagas that describe a ghost fight, a fight against a bear, and ordinary fights between men of flesh and blood.[22] There is, in other words, no reason to think that this aspect of the fight relates *Beowulf* to *Grettis saga* any more than to other Icelandic stories in which the same motif occurs.

Grettir's inability to draw his sword and kill Glámr has been linked to *Beowulf* from two very different angles. Peter Jorgensen maintains that there is a connection between *Beowulf* and *Grettis saga* through what he calls 'the useless sword motif,' which supposedly originated in a legend where the sword is the gift of a king whose court is plagued by an ogre. Hrunting, the sword that fails Beowulf against Grendel's mother, goes back to this 'original version,' according to Jorgensen, and 'another remnant of the useless weapon, realized as the sword which can't be drawn, may occur in Grettir's battle with Glámr.'[23] The validity of Jorgensen's 'useless sword' theory is beyond the scope of this discussion, but as it relates to *Grettis saga*, suffice it to say that Grettir's shortsword is drawn and turns out to be a very useful weapon indeed against Glámr. Furthermore, the saga attributes the hero's faintness to a combination of his exhaustion after the struggle and the effect on him of Glámr's evil stare,[24] so in his speculation Jorgensen is simply asking us to brush the text aside.

Commenting on the same moment of suspense in the hero's fight with Glámr, Martin Puhvel wonders aloud whether 'Grettir's fateful faintness from the gaze of Glám's baleful eyes may recall Beowulf's startling weakness in his grapple with Grendel's Mother.' 'Is this coincidence,' Puhvel asks, 'or an instance of a confused, muddled connection?'[25] The parallel that Puhvel proposes is a new one, but the methodology on which it rests is not. It has indeed been argued before that 'the old legend' exploded into tiny fragments which scattered all over Icelandic literature, and the various ideas that this thesis has spawned stand or fall on the basis of the approach itself. What we are really dealing with in respect to Puhvel's 'muddled connection' is a theory concerning the transmission of literary motifs from one country to another, and that aspect of the question of affinity between the poem and the saga is not our concern at the moment but will be in a later chapter.[26]

Finally, there is the issue of the frightening eyes of Glámr and Grendel. Margaret Goldsmith, who accepts the Glámr episode as 'the closest analogue we have to the scene of the wrestling in Heorot,' explains the relationship between the two in this way:

it is a fair inference that the adversary's gleaming eyes were a traditional feature of the story, which each author has fitted to the surroundings, the eyes of the *draugr* reflecting the moonlight, the eyes of the giant glinting red in the glow of the fire so that they seem to emit flame. We have no means of knowing at what stage in the transmission of the story the detail of the frightening eyes appeared; it is quite conceivable that it had become a commonplace of horrifying tales.[27]

Of course the eyes of Grendel and Glámr are frightening, but that is hardly surprising since everything else about these creatures is frightening as well. The important issue is how and why their eyes are frightening and whether the answers to these questions suggest a common ancestor. Goldsmith's idea that the common denominator in both stories is the reflection of light – moonlight in the case of Glámr, a fire burning in the hall in the case of Grendel – has no support in either text. *Grettis saga* does not tell us that Grettir became frightened because he could see the moon reflected in Glámr's eyes; on the contrary, it suggests that he was struck with fear because the moonlight enabled him to perceive the evil stare of the ghost. (Here Goldsmith seems to forget the role that Glámr's eyes are made to play, in the sense that they are his ultimate weapon in the fight against Grettir.) As for the theory that 'the glow of the fire' made Grendel's eyes 'seem to emit flame,' we first have to imagine that there is in fact a fire burning in Heorot on the night of his attack, because the text of the poem does not mention it. I do not see much point in rationalizing the ugly light which shines from Grendel's eyes in this fashion, unless one wants to rationalize everything else about him as a monster. The flame-like light is more likely to be a reminder of his hellish origin,[28] and at the same time a useful prop, because it lights up the field of battle in Hroðgar's presumably darkened palace.

The basic question thus remains unanswered: how and why would the eyes of the monster have been frightening in the original story? In the descriptions of Glámr and Grendel I cannot see anything that gives us much of a clue in reconstructing this aspect in the monstrous make-up of their supposed common ancestor.

Other First Fight Analogues in *Grettis saga*

Two other fight descriptions in *Grettis saga* have been claimed to be partly related to Beowulf's battle with Grendel. These involve Grettir as a hero in the scene where he kills the brown bear and as a monster in the Drangey episode, when he is killed by Þorbjǫrn ǫngull. In Grettir's fight with the brown bear the following items have been offered as evidence of its relationship to Beowulf's contest with Grendel:

- The bear wards off spear thrusts and is hard to get at, and these two features compare with Grendel's invulnerability to weapons.
- Grettir's wrestling match with the animal is reminiscent of Beowulf's battle with Grendel.
- The cutting off of the paw and use of it as evidence or a trophy parallels what is done with Grendel's arm in Heorot.
- The hero is deserted by his companions both in the bear episode and at the mere.[29]

In the Drangey analogue, two items from Richard Harris's list are said to correspond to battle descriptions in *Beowulf:*

6 / Grettir previously disabled.	Beowulf wounds Grendel mortally in Heorot – dead in cave.
7 / Grettir loses his hand posthumously.	Beowulf tears off Grendel's arm.

It complicates any discussion of these points that they have been submitted by four critics who view the issue of what constitutes analogous and genetically related material in *Grettis saga* from somewhat different premises. Thus Arnold Taylor and Richard Harris, who also allow for role reversals, think it permissible to search for matching if unconnected details, A. Margaret Arent sees Grendel and the dragon appearing in the brown bear in a recombined form, and Arthur Wachsler stresses similarity in what he calls 'essential plot and major themes.' But it is not by what tricks of literary imagination these observations have come about that really matters; what these scholars have in common is that they have all set out to seek further evidence for a relationship which they already believe to have been established beyond any shadow of a doubt.

In the comparison concerning the brown bear there is little new. Two of the points of comparison are variations of similar items from the Sandhaugar and Glámr fights, and the other two (the bear's invulnerability and the desertion of Grettir by his companions) are simply not in accordance with the text of the saga. In Harris's case the point has already been made that his findings cannot be isolated from the method that he uses to obtain them, and for the purpose of this discussion his comparisons are much too general. Grettir's leg wound is thus equated with Grendel's loss of his arm, and in the next item Grettir's cut-off hand becomes a variation of his previous wound.

Beowulf's Fight with Grendel's Mother

I have already discussed the various links which the second monster fight has with the first one in the poem, and it is worth emphasizing that in the two fights in *Grettis saga* that have been considered as possible genetically related analogues, no elements of continuity are present. This is not, of course, to say that the second fight in *Beowulf* proceeds predictably in all respects in comparison to the first. It comes as a surprise, for instance, that Beowulf should arm himself at the mere, although he knows that Grendel has proved invulnerable to (ordinary?) weapons, and, contrary to all expectation, Grendel's mother turns out to be a far more dangerous opponent than her son. Finally, it is to be noted that whereas the first battle is rather simple and unexciting in its format, the second contains a number of different stages in which the fortunes of the combatants are reversed:

1 / Beowulf dives into the mere. Grendel's mother grabs him, tries to stab him with her (steel-tipped?) fingers and drags him to the bottom.
2 / The monster carries Beowulf, who cannot wield his weapons, into her underwater hall. Sea monsters attack him in the process.
3 / Inside the hall Beowulf is suddenly free. (The poem does not tell us how this comes about, but it is as though Grendel's mother carries him to her water-free den and then releases her grip on him.) Beowulf can now draw Hrunting, and he strikes at her head. The famous sword will not penetrate, and Beowulf throws it away.
4 / Beowulf then seizes Grendel's mother by the hair and pulls her to the floor.
5 / She clutches at him, and Beowulf falls.
6 / The ogre sets upon Beowulf and tries to stab him with a knife.[30] Beowulf's coat of mail and God protect him.
7 / Beowulf somehow gets up again.[31] He sees a sword belonging to Grendel's mother, grabs it and swings at her neck with it, and (we assume) cuts her head off.
8 / Beowulf notices Grendel's dead body and cuts his head off as well.[32] The blade of the giant sword begins to melt.
9 / The mere becomes stained with blood. The Danes leave, but Beowulf's

retainers keep to their station, although they do not expect to see their lord again.

10 / Beowulf sees many treasures in the cave but returns to the surface with only Grendel's head and the hilt of the giant sword.[33]

In a recent article, Ward Parks has compared the behaviour of Grendel and his mother in their respective battles and finds it strangely different. He sees Grendel's reaction in his fight with Beowulf as characteristic 'of a predator suddenly meeting up against more than he has reckoned on,' as opposed to the second fight, which 'proceeds much as a battle of champions ... a single combat on fairly equal terms,' marked by the internal symmetry of the action.[34] Critics who have tried to reconcile the second fight with Grettir's battle against the giant at Sandhaugar would probably be reluctant to subscribe to Parks's analysis of it. Both R.W. Chambers and Fr. Klaeber were unhappy about the inglorious manner in which Beowulf enters the underwater hall, and both sought to explain it away. Chambers put it down to inconsistencies in the poem:

We may note the further inconsistency that Beowulf is seized by Grendel's mother in the water and carried powerless to her den: when he reaches the den, the words used seem to imply that he perceives Grendel's mother and attacks her, as if he had entered free.[35]

But Chambers does not specify what vocabulary he has in mind, and there is nothing in lines 1512b–20 that readily supports his idea. He is merely looking at the poem through the spectacles of the Sandhaugar analogue, and Klaeber's proposed solution is an even better example of where too much faith in a genetically related analogue can lead us:

In the *Grettissaga* the hero straightaway enters the cave to fight the monster; in the *Samsonssaga* the hero is seized by the troll-woman in the water and dragged by her to the bottom. This dual conception, possibly, is responsible for the lack of clearness in *Beowulf.*[36]

Klaeber does not care to elaborate on this cryptic explanation, which may be interpreted in two different ways: (a) the old legend had a hero who was both seized by the monster and also entered his or her cave freely. Later Icelandic authors had the good fortune to inherit this schizophrenic account in separate parts, which surface in the two different sagas, whereas the poor *Beowulf* poet was stuck with a contradictory description of the hero's entry into battle and could only respond to the tyranny of the original story by obfuscating this part of it as best he could. Or (b) *Grettis saga* inherited its version of events from one 'old legend' (descended from the original story) and *Samssons saga* from another, in which case there was a confused ur-story that influenced *Beowulf,* or the author knew two conflicting versions of the 'old legend' and tried to combine them for some reason.

Critics who lament inconsistencies or lack of clearness in this part of *Beowulf* are hardly going to find much consolation in this theory of Klaeber's.

Grettir's Fight with Kárr the Old

R.W. McConchie, who believes that Kárr the Old has been grossly neglected in the discussion of analogous and genetically related material in *Grettis saga,* maintains that the following aspects of Grettir's fight with the gravemound ghost in Norway are comparable with Beowulf's struggle against Grendel's mother:

1 / Despite the extraordinary powers and skill of the hero, his companions do not believe that he can succeed.
2 / The place of combat is reached by a solitary descent, leaving a companion or companions behind.
3 / There is a hand to hand combat between the hero and the monster in which the hero comes close to defeat.
4 / In both instances there is a decapitation.
5 / The hero is deserted by his companions, who believe that he is dead.
6 / There is a splendid sword found in the place of combat, and the hero recovers some kind of treasure.[37]

This list of items is obviously not an actual comparison of two events. It is simply an abstract which may be said to fit a very broad summary of two different stories. As soon as we go beyond generalities, misrepresentations, and plays on words, the so-called analogous and genetically related material evaporates into thin air. There is, for instance, not a word of doubt uttered by Beowulf's followers before he sets out to fight Grendel's mother; Grettir's lowering himself into a gravemound and Beowulf's jumping into the mere become their 'solitary descent'; Grettir is, as it happens, never 'close to defeat' in his battle with Kárr; it is not Grendel's mother who is decapitated after the battle; Beowulf is not deserted by his retainers, and the giant sword does not become his special weapon, in contrast with the splendid short-sword that Grettir recovers. Add to this list the fact that Grettir enters the gravemound to look for treasure and that no land-cleansing comparable to the killing of the monsters in *Beowulf* takes place, and what is there left to compare?

Neither McConchie nor Taylor before him seem to have realized that the Kárr episode in *Grettis saga* follows a very traditional pattern of describing an entry into a gravemound:

- A ghost in a burial place is also found in *Andra saga, Harðar saga*, and *Hrómundar saga*.
- Descent by means of a rope into a cave or a gravemound of a ghost or a dragon takes place in *Játmundar saga, Andra saga, Gull-Þóris saga, Harðar saga*, and *Hrómundar saga*.
- Odour or preternatural stench is described in *Andra saga, Gests þáttur, Harðar saga, Hrómundar saga*, and *Orkneyinga saga*.
- The fight with the dragon or the ghost is delayed in *Gull-Þóris saga, Gests þáttur, Harðar saga*, and *Hrómundar saga*.
- A light is there in *Gull-Þóris saga* and *Harðar saga*.
- A sword is discovered in *Andra saga, Gull-Þóris saga, Harðar saga*, and *Hrómundar saga*.
- The hero is abandoned in *Játmundar saga* and *Harðar saga*.[38]

This episode is not simply traditional; it also resembles the second half of Grettir's Sandhaugar adventure in containing a descent, a rope, and a watchman who is frightened off. It has been argued that the story of Kárr the Old is merely a copy of the Sandhaugar episode in which the din from the gravemound substitutes for the blood on the water of a proper Beowulfian tale,[39] but given the traditional nature of gravemound entries, it is more likely that the relationship between the two is precisely the reverse.

Grettir's Fight with the Giant at Sandhaugar

Even before Kárr the Old, the brown bear, and the Drangey analogues were entered into the debate over the relationship between *Beowulf* and *Grettis saga*, there was always some confusion as to what to compare to what. Those critics who accepted the Glámr fight as genetically related and comparable to Beowulf's struggle against Grendel faced a bit of a dilemma in dealing with Grettir's two fights at Sandhaugar. Most chose to regard the Glámr and the troll-woman fights as variants of the first fight in *Beowulf*, but some wanted to include both the troll-woman and the giant in the comparison with Beowulf's fight with Grendel's dam.[40] A third solution has been proposed by Nora K. Chadwick, who equates Grendel and Glámr, and also Grendel's mother and the troll-woman, who is Glámr's mother in Chadwick's theory. Accordingly, Grettir's killing of the giant in the cave is 'the quietus of the *draugr* Glámr, and, as in *Beowulf*, the final episode.'[41]

Before we look at the actual contest between Grettir and the giant, it will be interesting to compare the nature of the hero's mission at Sandhaugar to that of Beowulf in Heorot. The poem tells us very clearly that Beowulf makes his journey from Geatland to Denmark for the express purpose of cleansing Hroðgar's land of a single monster.[42] A second monster is discovered, and dealt with, only because of circumstances that arise in the wake of the killing of the first. It has been argued that *Grettis saga* matches the poem on this point, i.e., that Grettir knows nothing of a second monster when he sets out to explore the cave behind the waterfall.[43] This is not so. In his introduction to the Sandhaugar episode the saga author informs his readers that the region was known to be haunted by trolls, and this information is given before anyone is reported to have disappeared from the farm.[44] Since it is public knowledge that there is more than one troll about, we must assume that Grettir knows this as well and is not surprised by the discovery of a second troll, although his reason for wanting to explore the cave is not to look for one. Grettir's unwillingness to dive into the waterfall with a rope tied around him, and the fact that he carries his sword with him, also suggest that he expects to have to fight with someone in the course of his exploration.

The actual battle between Grettir and the giant is an extremely simple and straightforward affair:

1 / A rope is let down into the ravine for Grettir to make his way back, and Steinn, the priest, is instructed to look after it.
2 / Grettir dives underneath the waterfall and scales the cliff behind it until he reaches a cave.
3 / Grettir enters the cave and sees a giant sitting on a chair by a fire. The giant grabs his *heptisax*[45] and strikes a blow at Grettir.
4 / Grettir meets the blow with his short-sword and cuts the handle of the giant's weapon apart.
5 / The giant reaches for a sword that is hanging on the wall in the cave, but before he can reach it, Grettir cuts his chest and belly open with a blow and continues striking at the giant until he is dead.
6 / The priest sees blood on the water and runs off. Grettir climbs up the rope unaided with the bones of the missing men and treasure from the cave.
7 / Grettir leaves the bones and a rune staff, on which two verses that describe his adventure are carved, on the porch of the local church.

Those who have compared this battle description to Beowulf's adventure at the mere have been forced to note two obvious differences.[46] In the first place, there is Grettir's motivation: he is convinced that the missing men have been taken into the ravine, but the priest Steinn has his doubts. The only reason Grettir undertakes his mission is to prove the priest wrong. That this is one of the many 'latter [*sic*] alterations in the tale,' as W.W. Lawrence argues in making his comparison,[47] is pure speculation. Secondly, there is the complete lack of proper introduction of the giant as Grettir's adversary, and, perhaps not surprisingly, the embarrassingly short and simple account of the actual battle: the giant goes to attack the hero; the hero is faster and kills him; end of story. In addition, the saga relates this unexciting battle scene in a strangely casual manner; in fact, it reads much like a short newspaper article. There is little drama in the account, and the reader is never in doubt about the outcome of the fight. In short, it goes without saying that it takes no small amount of imagination to equate this part of the Sandhaugar episode with Grendel's mother and her fight with Beowulf at the mere.

The manner in which the giant meets his death is also of some interest. Like Grendel's dam, he is killed with a sword. But to argue, as one analogue enthusiast has done, that the two are stabbed to death 'in more or less the same way' is stretching the truth a bit too far.[48] Then there is the matter of the giant's weapon, the *heptisax*. It would undeniably strengthen the analogy with Hrunting, Beowulf's *hæftmece*, if it were Grettir and not the giant who wielded the weapon. In an effort to get past this obstacle, Peter A. Jorgensen has proposed an emendation of the stanza in which the giant's weapon is named by combining readings from the three extant vellum manuscripts of *Grettis saga*. His emendation would change the traditional reading of the lines in question from 'I cut the shaft of his *heptisax*' to 'I caused the *heptisax* to chop the hard edges from the shaft.'[49] This editorial 'improvement' of the saga text has not, however, met with everyone's approval. Anatoly Liberman, in particular, has been critical of Jorgensen's methods:

He views the extant variants of the verses as attempts to change the meaning of a text that was no longer understood. It is likely, says he, 'that scribes intentionally made changes in the verses, for the word heptisax had obviously become archaic by the saga-writing period, making it almost impossible for a familiar, beloved Icelandic hero to brandish a mysterious weapon no one had even seen or heard of' (1973.58–59). The emendation is Jorgensen's, but the idea behind it belongs to York Powell (1900.413, Note 2); Powell also thought that 'the Beowulf sword incident ... was probably difficult to reconcile with what was known of Grettir and his weapons.' Neither the emendation nor the idea of an incongruous weapon is supported by weighty arguments. Emending three texts in order to obtain a satisfactory version is hardly a tenable procedure, and, as far as a difficult word is concerned, Icelanders would certainly have forgiven the saga-man a touch of antiquarian spirit.[50]

Let us now proceed from the question of weapons to look at Grettir's return from battle. Critics who view the Sandhaugar episode as a genetically related analogue to *Beowulf* have uniformly endorsed the idea that the blood on the water and the cowardly priest correspond to the bloodstained mere and the Danes who choose to leave in the poem. There is no question that blood and gore on the water, misinterpreted to signal the death of the hero, is a motif that *Grettis saga* shares with *Beowulf*, but does this have to indicate a special rela- tionship between the two works? J. Michael Stitt points out that this motif has its roots in Indo-European dragonslayer tales (a passage of the *Ramayana* and the Vedic account of Indra's battle with Vrtra),[51] and there no reason to assume that its only occurrence in Northern Europe was limited to a common ancestor of *Beowulf* and *Grettis saga*.[52]

The matter of desertion is a great deal more complicated, as R.W. Chambers readily admits:

it is true that the departure of the Danes homeward because they believe that Beowulf has met his death in the water below, bears only the remotest resemblance to the deliber- ate treachery which the companions in the folktale [i.e., the Bear's Son Tale] mete out to the hero. But when we compare the *Grettir*-story, we see there that a real breach of trust is involved, for there the priest Stein leaves the hero in the lurch, and abandons the rope by which he should have drawn Grettir up. This can hardly be an innovation on the part of the composer of the *Grettis saga*, for he is quite well disposed towards Stein, and has no motive for wantonly attributing treachery to him. The innovation presumably lies in the *Beowulf*-story, where Hrothgar and his court are depicted in such a friendly spirit that no disreputable act can be attributed to them, and consequently Hrothgar's departure home must not be allowed in any way to imperil or inconvenience the hero. A compari- son of the *Beowulf*-story with the *Grettir*-story leads then to the conclusion that in the oldest version those who remained above when the hero plunged below *were* guilty of some measure of disloyalty in ceasing to watch for him. In other words we see that the further we track the *Beowulf*-story back, the more it comes to resemble the folk-tale.[53]

Chambers is right. There is no treachery involved in the Danes' leaving the mere, but nor is there in Steinn's leaving the rope in *Grettis saga*. He does not purposely 'betray' Grettir by any stretch of the imagination; he merely makes a mistake by wrongly assuming that the hero is dead. Grettir, who is not the sort of person to leave treachery against him unpunished, later reminds the priest that he was slack in his rope-watching duties. Steinn admits to his shortcom- ings, and with that the matter is over. In other words, the folktale desertion motif that Chambers would like to see in *Grettis saga* is not really there. Conse- quently, the idea that the *Beowulf* poet had to deviate from an original story, which prescribed desertion at this point in the chain of events because of deference to Hroðgar and his court, is quite simply ridiculous. In his desire to find a folktale origin for the poem, Chambers commits the intentional fallacy of presuming to know both the original story and why the *Beowulf* author decided to change it. Hroðgar and his court have known nothing but cowardice and humiliation for twelve years; would one more instance have made much difference?

Finally, we can compare how success in the second battle benefits the two heroes and how they perceive it. To Beowulf, the victory over Grendel's mother is, strangely enough, not the zenith of his career; the contest with Grendel is. In preparing to meet the dragon, he wishes that he might fight it as he fought Grendel in the old days (line 2521). As Larry D. Benson has put it, he 'seems aware that his entire life has been a falling off from that one moment of triumph.'[54] Still, the aftermath of the second fight brings Beowulf all the recognition and treasure that a hero can desire. By contrast, the Sandhaugar fights do not do much for Grettir, except to grant him a temporary refuge. The killing of either the troll-woman or the giant brings Grettir no glory that he has not already achieved.

At the beginning of this chapter we set out to examine whether the form of the two monster battles, or even parts of their form, might have survived intact in *Grettis saga*. In the course of this examination we have seen that there are indeed certain specifics that some of the proposed genetically related analogues share with *Beowulf*. Both texts include, for instance, male and female adversaries, an arm that is lost, a head that is cut off, blood on the water, companions who leave, etc., as we have already seen in the individual analogues. But the form that each of the two battles takes in *Beowulf* is not to be found in *Grettis saga*, if by form we mean some kind of a pattern in a chain of events, or even the details that make up a single link in such a chain.

Within the context of the saga, Grettir's battles against Kárr the Old, the brown bear, Glámr, and others hang together as a series of tests – a form of initiation perhaps, as Mary Danielly has argued.[55] They create the impression of some unfulfilled greatness in Grettir which vanishes after his battle with Glámr. Whether or not we choose to ascribe his bad luck to the effects of the curse, everything still turns to his misfortune. Even his stay at Sandhaugar is ultimately a sad story, in the sense that it gives Grettir a son who is seen to have the strength and valour of his father, but who dies in his youth. Beowulf also has an unusual career as a hero because of the strange absence of triumphs in his life after his defeat of Grendel and his mother, but the curse that Guðbrandur Vigfússon believed Grendel to have put on him simply is not there in *Beowulf*, and thus the poem and the saga must be reckoned to follow their separate ways in terms of what fortunes the killing of monsters brings the hero.

4

A Sword by Any Other Name

When Guðbrandur Vigfússon proclaimed the Sandhaugar and Glámr episodes of *Grettis saga* to be analogous and genetically related to *Beowulf*, he offered the *heptisax-hæftmece* parallel as his best evidence. Vigfússon gave three reasons for the special importance of this pair: as far as he was concerned, the two were one and the same word, they occurred at the same place in the legend, and they were unique in their respective literatures.[1] Although the first two points are obvious exaggerations, the idea of equating the two words has gone unchallenged for more than a century, and such is the faith of the converted that it now seems acceptable to translate *hæftmece* as 'the sword with a long wooden hilt,' a gloss which clearly echoes the words that the author of *Grettis saga* uses to define the *heptisax* of the giant at Sandhaugar.[2] This translation effort is merely a single example; a great deal of scholarly work aimed at bringing *Grettis saga* into line with *Beowulf* also rests on the basis of Vigfússon's equation. But how secure is the kinship between *hæftmece* and *heptisax*, and do these two words actually provide a definite link between the poem and the saga?

Beowulf, as the poem tells us, borrows the famous sword Hrunting from Unferð, and Hrunting, in line 1457a (as Beowulf arms himself before his dive into the mere), is referred to as a *hæftmece*. The *heptisax*, on the other hand, belongs to and is used by the giant in the saga, so our starting point in this story of swords must be the mess which the author of *Grettis saga* makes of the old legend by failing to place either the giant's *heptisax* or the sword on the wall in the hands of the hero. Peter A. Jorgensen, as we saw in the previous chapter, has tried to correct the misplacement of the first weapon, and H.R. Ellis Davidson has made a similar attempt for the second:

It is not clear either from the verses or the prose account with what weapon he [i.e., Grettir] actually slew the giant, but the prose account refers to a sword hanging up in the cave which the giant tries to reach, and the introduction of this into the story is quite pointless unless it was used in some way.[3]

Davidson does not actually say that the giant is killed with his own sword, but she implies it. It is true that *Grettis saga* does not say with which sword the giant is killed, but the introduction of the giant sword is far from being pointless, even if he is not actually killed with it. In the cave scene, the saga shows Grettir holding his short-sword, which he has just used to cut apart the handle of the *heptisax* in a moment of great suspense, while the giant goes for another weapon which is within easy reach behind him. Davidson would like us to imagine that in this situation Grettir puts his own sword down, gets past the giant and behind him to collect the other sword, then traces his steps back to his original position so that he can face the giant – who has politely waited while all this took place – and cut his guts open. This kind of sophistry is hardly to the point, since we are dealing with a literary text and not a real estate contract. The sword on the wall does play its part in this story, but not the one that Davidson thinks that it should play.

The only weapon that the giant actually uses against Grettir has no name but is described with a word (*heptisax*) that would seem to identify it as a particular and recognizable type of weapon. But what does the term *heptisax* mean, and where does the word come from? Although the compound is only recorded in *Grettis saga*, there is nothing very strange or mysterious about it. In Old Norse the handle of a full-length sword was usually called a *meðalkafli* (i.e., 'the middle piece'), whereas the corresponding part of a short-sword (Old Norse *sax*) or a long knife (Old Norse *skálm*) was called either *hepti* or *mundriði*. Hjalmar Falk, who lists this vocabulary in his *Altnordische Waffenkunde*, gives an example of a sentence from a Norse text where both components of Vigfússon's mystery word are actually present: '*fell saxit or hepti*'; i.e., 'the blade of the short-sword was detached from its handle.'[4] It follows from this that neither of the two nouns that make up the compound is rare or obscure, nor is the meaning of the word which they combine to form. *Heptisax* must mean a short-sword with a plain handle, as opposed to the sword-type handle (*meðalkafli*) that Grettir's own *sax*, the *Kársnautr*, has.

Perhaps because it is so transparent, the meaning of the word *heptisax* has never interested the analogue makers very much; however, its single occurrence in Old Norse has always had its romantic appeal. On the basis of this limited circulation, and nothing else, it has been generally assumed from early on that the word *heptisax* must be of foreign stock, although the critical camp has always been sharply divided over where to seek its origin. Scholars who believe *Grettis saga* to have been directly or indirectly influenced by *Beowulf* have looked to Old English as a source, whereas those who favour the idea of a common source – preferably Scandinavian – for the saga and the poem, have promptly rejected any such ideas. R.C. Boer, who produced the first scholarly edition of *Grettis saga*, was inclined to think that *heptisax* was a literary borrowing from a now lost Anglo-Saxon poem because he found it hard to believe that an oral tradition could preserve a single unique term for centuries.[5] Other *Beowulf* scholars, such as Hermann Schneider[6] and Carl W. von Sydow,[7] were also convinced that the word had to hearken back to a literary source. By contrast, Joan Turville-Petre, who sees a common source for the poem and the saga, thinks that the *heptisax-hæftmece* is originally a technical term, specifically associated with cave-warfare, which each author interprets in his own way.[8]

In *Beowulf* the word *hæftmece* occurs as a sword term for Hrunting with no greater fanfare than other synonyms for swords in the poem. In *Grettis saga*, on the other hand, the author pauses to add a brief comment on the weapon of the giant:

when Grettir came to him, the giant leaped up and seized a pike, and hewed at the newcomer: for with the pike he could both cut and stab. It had a handle of wood: men at that time called a weapon made in such a way a *heptisax*.[9]

Much has been made of this brief comment. John Earle called attention to it in a translation of *Beowulf* that he made only a few years after Guðbrandur Vigfússon had advanced his theory on the relationship between the poem and *Grettis saga* : 'The author of the Saga ... treats the word [*heptisax*] as curious and strange, by the explanation which he offers of it. There must be some common source ...'[10] This statement has been repeated and elaborated on by various scholars since Earle's time.[11] It has even been hypothesized that the author of *Grettis saga* had problems understanding the stanza (no. 61) in which the hero describes his battle with the giant. According to this theory, the stanza was his only source, and he wanted to include it but felt compelled to explicate the meaning of *heptisax* – which he did not quite understand – in the prose account of Grettir's adventure.[12]

In this effort to provide the giant's *heptisax* with an ancient and mysterious origin, the first assumption that everyone seems to take for granted is that the slightest digression, in the form of an explanation or a comment that the author of *Grettis saga* makes, is a sign that something extraordinary is happening in the text. For the saga as a whole this is hardly the case, since its author is not averse to tagging explanatory notes and even longer digressions on to his narrative on sundry occasions, as may be seen from the following examples:

Then the king ordered his berserks to advance. They were called wolfskins and could not be injured by any iron weapons. (5)

Þorgeirr was in charge of the farm of the brothers at Reykjarfjǫrðr. He regularly went fishing, for then the fjords were full of fish. (26)

The ship which the merchants had built was very broad, and people called it the Wooden Sack, and from this epithet the inlet takes its name. (32–3)

Þorsteinn had had a church built on his farm. He had a bridge made which led away from the farm. It was built with great ingenuity. On the bridge, underneath the support beams, there were rings and chiming bells, so that if anyone walked across it, the rings shook so much that the din could be heard all the way to Skarfsstaðir, a couple of miles away. Þorsteinn, who was a very skilled blacksmith, put a great effort into this bridge. Grettir took great turns at hammering the iron, when he could be bothered to do it.[13] (173)

If the *heptisax* comment was a rare occurrence in an otherwise sparsely worded saga, there might be some merit to this argument, but *Grettis saga* is not that kind of text.

It is also very difficult to imagine that the two stanzas in which Grettir sums up his battle with the giant and mentions the *heptisax* go back to high antiquity, as Jorgensen has maintained. Since the nineteenth century, scholars have agreed that most, if not all, of the forty-seven stanzas which the saga attributes to Grettir were composed later than the eleventh century,[14] and Jorgensen does not *per se* dispute that conclusion. His argument, however, is perfectly circular, because the attempt to prove that these two verses are older than other stanzas in the saga rests on an *a priori* assumption that they contain genetically related parallels with the Grendel fight in *Beowulf*.[15]

Jorgensen further maintains that the saga author's description of the giant's *heptisax* is inconsistent both with the meaning of the word itself and with the reference to it as *fleinn*, in other words, as yet another sign of a misunderstood relic from the old legend:

It seems highly improbable that the word *heptisax* should occur only once in all of the extensive battle descriptions in Old Icelandic prose and, by chance, at precisely the same point in a narrative where the corresponding English text employs the cognate term. There is no reason, no special motivation for its occurrence at this point or, indeed, for its occurring at all. Furthermore, the Icelandic prose passage in which the word appears makes little sense. The reader is told that the giant came at Grettir with a *fleinn* and chopped at Grettir with it. But the Icelandic term *fleinn* is normally used to denote an arrow or javelin. Having once informed the reader that the giant attacked Grettir with a *fleinn* or javelin, the writer hastily adds that one could both thrust and chop with this instrument and that it was called a *heptisax*, which etymologically should be some sort of sword. The use of the weapon would bear this out, but we are also told that the handle was made of wood, which would further indicate a spear or javelin. Much more usual expressions in Old Icelandic for the weapon evidently intended in the prose text are *hǫggspjót, kesja, brynþvari,* and *atgeirr.*

The preservation of the word *heptisax* is more likely due to its presence as a necessary formal entity in a poetic line.[16]

The issue of a dichotomy between *fleinn* and *heptisax* has also been discussed by Joan Turville-Petre, who concludes that the author of *Grettis saga* is describing 'an impossible composite weapon.'[17]

The basic assumptions behind both these theories are that the word *fleinn* cannot mean the same as *heptisax* and that neither term fits the spear-sword type weapon in question.[18] Haakon Shetelig and Hjalmar Falk address both issues in their *Scandinavian Archaeology,* and fail to notice the drama that Jorgensen and Turville-Petre would like to see in the text:

A special type of *fleinn* is mentioned in *Grettis saga* (chap. 66) under the name *heptisax.* This weapon consisted of a sword-like blade fixed at the end of a wooden shaft, and differed from the other types of *fleinn* in not being a throwing spear, but was used as a *hǫggspjót,* for hewing and thrusting. It must have been similar to the *kesjufleinn,* or, more probably, identical with it; this was evidently a *kesja* ... with a longer blade than usual. It was doubtless by reason of the long narrow blade that the *heptisax* was classed by *Grettis saga* as a *fleinn.* The same sort of weapon was known in other Germanic lands, too: OE [Old English] *stæfsweord,* glossing 'dolo' and OHG [Old High German] *stapaswert,* 'framea,' must also have consisted of a sword-like blade on a wooden shaft.[19]

If Shetelig and Falk are correct in their analysis, we may safely assume that the author of *Grettis saga* was neither trying to gloss over his ignorance of that 'ancient' term *heptisax,* nor allowing his imagination to fashion an impossible weapon.

Like *heptisax,* the term *hæftmece* only occurs once; and Guðbrandur Vigfússon, and many others after him, firmly believed that this uniqueness somehow related the two and made them special. But just how special is *hæftmece* within the context of *Beowulf* as a whole? It is often conveniently forgotten that several terms and kennings for swords – other than Hrunting – also appear only in the poem and nowhere else in the Old English corpus,[20] although the old legends that gave us *beado-mece, eald-sweord, guð-sweord, hilde-mece, maðþum-*

sweord, sceaden-mæl, and *hilde-leoma* have obviously yet to be discovered. It is only the presumed relationship with the Norse term that has elevated *hæft-mece* to the special position that it enjoys among these peers.[21]

As a weapon, the *hæftmece* was very different from the *heptisax*; that much at least is undisputed. In Old English the *mece* was a long two-edged sword with a long handle. What precisely the *hæft* was meant to indicate is uncertain. The usual meaning of the word is 'fetter' or 'captive,' which would make it likely that the compound either denoted a sword whose blade was attached in some special way, or that it was fastened to its scabbard, or had a hilt with some kind of fastening, perhaps like the *fetelhilt*, the sword that Beowulf finds in the cave.

It further complicates the *hæftmece* issue that the sword in question, Hrunting, is not always called a *mece*: on one occasion the *Beowulf* poet also refers to it as a *hildebill* (line 1520b). According to Caroline Brady, both *bill* and *mece* are terms that denote long, slender two-edged swords with either sharply pointed or rounded tips, but although archaeologists are not in agreement as to what precisely the difference between the two is supposed to have been, the two words appear to refer to two distinct sword types in the poem. Brady points out that the *Beowulf* poet is, on the whole, 'remarkably consistent in maintaining a distinction between the two types,'[22] with this one notable exception. Even if we accept that calling Hrunting a *bill* is an isolated error on the part of the poet or a later copyist, however, it remains to be explained why the author of *Beowulf* uses the word *hæftmece* so extremely sparingly. As we have already seen, a variety of other terms are applied to Hrunting, and if *hæftmece* was a key word in the old legend on which he was basing his story, one would expect this term to play a more important role.

As a legacy of Guðbrandur Vigfússon's faith in the secrets that the *heptisax-hæftmece* parallel might unlock, Hrunting, the actual name of the sword, has received much less attention than the illustrious pair. But if Hrunting is the sword with which the hero kills the monster in some version of the old legend, then what is it doing in the hands of the coward and fratricide Unferð? The poem makes no attempt to explain this, and yet it is obvious that the sword must have qualities that make it special. Beowulf, who has brought his own excellent sword to Heorot and been given another by Hroðgar,[23] rejects both in favour of Hrunting as he prepares to fight with Grendel's mother, and we may thus assume that Beowulf perceives that Hrunting is superior to these other swords.

Names of swords sometimes give an indication of their appearance or special qualities, but unfortunately the etymology of Hrunting remains uncertain. The word has been connected with **hrut*, 'to resound' (cf. Old Norse *hrjóta*, 'to fall' or 'to snore') and with **hrunt* (cf. Modern English 'runt' and Hrotti, the name

of Fáfnir's sword).[24] Kemp Malone, who has been one of the proponents of the
latter etymology, believes that Hrunting originally got its name from an owner
nicknamed Hrunta; a name which, like Hrotti, indicated the owner's great size
and grimness. Malone also notes that Hrunting is probably related to Old
English *hrung*, 'rung' or 'pole,' which ultimately derived from a Germanic base
denoting a thick, stout segment of a tree or a branch.[25] Norman E. Eliason also
takes Hrunting to be a nickname, although unlike Malone he thinks it stemmed
from the shortness of the weapon rather than the characteristics of its original
owner.[26] Haakon Shetelig and Hjalmar Falk, on the other hand, interpret Hrunt-
as an extended form of the Old English base *hrung*; i.e., as a 'long piece of
wood' or a 'rung.'[27] If the name Hrunting does indeed indicate that the sword
had a wooden handle, it would seem to give us something to compare with the
giant's *heptisax* in *Grettis saga*, although it does not explain what was special
about the wooden handle in the original story. But even if we accept that Hrotti
and Hrunting are cognates, it does not lend much strength to this argument that
saga author knows the sword name Hrotti and uses it in two early stanzas, nos. 4
and 17, without the slightest hint that the word has any special significance
either for Grettir's weapons or for Grettir himself.

Another method which has been tried in order to find out more about Hrunting is to assume that the author of *Beowulf* meant his audience to take the few
references that are made to the sword literally. The clues that this gives us are:

hringmæl, (adj.)   = 'ring-marked'[28] (line 1521b)
wundenmæl, (n.)   = 'a sword with curved markings'[29] or a 'twisted pattern'[30]
                  (line 1531a)
ecg wæs iren   = the edge – or the entire sword – was made of iron (line
                  1459a)
atertanum fah   = decorated with 'poison twigs'[31] or 'gleaming with tiny ser-
                  pents'[32] or 'of gleaming or fiery hilt or pommel.'[33] (line
                  1459b)

The sundry details that may be deduced from this vocabulary do not form any
coherent picture and obviously leave a good deal of room for speculation. Not
surprisingly, two contradictory lines of interpretation have emerged. Thus, H.R.
Ellis Davidson thinks that the poet is describing a sword with a pattern-welded
blade, whereas W.P. Lehmann believes Hrunting to be a weapon which had an
iron edge covering a wooden shaft.[34] It does not matter which of these readings
we favour, for neither one sheds any light on the connection between the sword
and the *heptisax* of the saga. The best link between Hrunting and the *heptisax*
remains the same: they are both weapons that fail, albeit for very different rea-

sons. To reconstruct a legend that could function as a common ancestor, it must furthermore be assumed that one of these weapons is in the wrong hands, and somehow both heroes must be found with a victorious sword with a special haft or hilt, a task which various *Beowulf* critics have been more than willing to perform.

One further possibility is to wrest the *hæftmece* from its association with the useless Hrunting and turn it into a reference to the sword with the wonderful hilt that actually kills Grendel's dam. This is precisely what R.W. Chambers does in his *Introduction to the Study of the Poem*:

Presumably, in the original story, as it existed before our *Beowulf* was composed, an important part was played by the sword with a wonderful hilt which the hero met in the cave. In *Beowulf* ten lines are devoted to describing the presentation of the hilt to Hrothgar, twelve lines to describing the hilt itself. The sword is characterized by its hilt ...

When we turn to the prose of the *Grettis saga*, we find that much is made of the 'hafted cutlass' (*hepti-sax*) which Grettir encounters in the hands of the giant in the cave. Further, that this was an important part of the story, as the compiler of the *Saga* knew it, is also indicated by the important part the *hepti-sax* is made to play in the verses, late as these doubtless are. Just as Beowulf brings back to Hrothgar the rune-inscribed hilt which is all that is left of the sword, so Grettir leaves with Stein a stave of wood upon which is inscribed in runes an account of the separation of the haft of the 'hafted cutlass' from its blade ...

In the original story – say of the sixth century – the sword was probably described in a number of words compounded with the element *haft* or *hilt*: one of these *haft*-compounds survives in the *Grettis saga*, whilst in *Beowulf* it also survives, but has got into a different context.[35]

Several other scholars have also favoured this avenue of approach towards establishing the old legend.[36] Of course, we must assume that both authors made a bit of a mess of the story in the process of retelling it, the *Beowulf* poet by putting a key word 'into a different context' – to use Chambers's polite phrase – and the composer of *Grettis saga* by failing to have the giant at Sandhaugar killed with his own *heptisax*. As Martin Puhvel has observed, it makes no sense that the role of the essential weapon – Chambers's *hæftmece* of the original legend – could be so greatly altered in both the poem and the saga,[37] even if we turn a blind eye to his method of emending both stories to reconstruct the original.

It is not easy to determine what kind of a weapon the cave sword is meant to be before its blade melts. The poem informs us that it was wrought by giants (line 1562b) and huge, but mostly refers to it with very ordinary synonyms for swords: *bil(l)* (line 1557b), *ealdsweord* (line 1558a), *fetelhilt* (line 1563a), *hringmæl* (line 1564b), *ecg* (line 1575b), *wigbil* (line 1607a), *brogden-mæl* (line 1616a), *hildebil* (line 1666b), and *wreopenhilt* (line 1698a). From this list of references, *hringmæl* and *brogden-mæl* would seem to indicate that the cave sword was damascened, and *fetelhilt* might refer to a hilt furnished with a ring or a chain.[38] As these sword references have no apparent connection with Grettir's second adventure at Sandhaugar, critics have preferred to look for one by comparing the story that is carved on the hilt of the cave sword to the rune-staff that Grettir leaves behind for the incredulous Steinn. However, it is far from clear what Hroðgar actually sees as he muses over the hilt in lines 1687–98. The poem tells us that it has something to do with the beginning of an ancient strife (*on þæm wæs or writen / fyrngewinnes*), and then seems to proceed to allude to the Genesis story about the deluge that destroyed the race of giants (*syðþan flod ofsloh / ... giganta cyn*). Given the genealogy of the Grendels, it seems feasible to take *syðþan* as an explanatory conjunction ('when'), and thereby link the ancient strife and the ultimate destruction, but *syðþan* may be an adverb ('afterwards'), in which case we have no means of knowing what the ancient strife was all about. A runic inscription on the hilt also tells Hroðgar for whom the sword was originally made.

But how does the hilt of the wondrous sword relate its story? In their editions of the poem, Fr. Klaeber and C.L. Wrenn assume that it did so through engraved designs,[39] but scholars who are more analogue-minded have favoured runes. The most ambitious attempt to link this scene in *Beowulf* to *Grettis saga* is to be found in H.R. Ellis Davidson's study, *The Sword in Anglo-Saxon England*:

Heptisax is the name given to the weapon of the giant whom Grettir meets under water, and Grettir, using his famous short sword, cuts the giant's weapon from its shaft. Later on Grettir leaves in the church a bag of bones he has brought up from the giant's cave and with it a piece of wood carved in runes, a *rúnakefli*, on which two verses are said to have been 'excellently carved.' Could this possibly be the wooden shaft of the Heptisax? The saga does not tell us what became of the giant's weapon after Grettir destroyed it, but the coincidence of the strange term, the separation of the giant's weapon from its hilt (as in *Beowulf*), and the reading of runes on it after the battle is over (again as in *Beowulf*) is certainly striking, all the more so because there is so much difference in the two accounts.[40]

Davidson furthermore rejects the idea that the reference which the poem makes to rushing waters and the destruction of giants has anything to do with Genesis, and finds it 'not impossible' that Beowulf recorded his struggle against the Grendels on the hilt before presenting it to Hroðgar. Another possibility that

Davidson suggests is 'that the hilt bore some prophetic inscription in runes, emphasizing the fact which we know from the poem, that it was the only weapon which could kill Grendel's mother and cut off Grendel's head.'[41] Vera I. Evison, who reviewed Davidson's book, flatly rejects this speculation. She points out that most armour in *Beowulf* appears to be of the sixth century, and that it is 'quite impossible that a sword of this period should have an inscription in runes long enough to tell a story,' as inscriptions from this age are extremely short, giving little more than a name.[42]

Departing from the more usual rune staff comparison, A.R. Taylor focuses his analogy on Grettir's own weapon, the *Kársnautr*:

Professor Chambers has tried to show that *Grettis saga* is clearer in its account of the weapons used. But it would seem more probable that the real purpose behind the *hepti-sax-hæftmece* has been obscured by both authors; possibly in the original story it was the sword which the hero found in the cave and used to slay his opponent. It is, however, certain that the weapons used to slay the monsters in both *Grettis saga* and *Beowulf* have one thing in common: they are both remarkable for their hilt. This common characteristic is almost certainly a reminiscence of the original legend. In *Beowulf* the sword blade melts away in Grendel's blood, and the hero can bring only the hilt to Hroðgar. The hilt is noteworthy, and the poet makes this clear by spending twenty-two lines on it. Grettir's short-sword is unique in Old Norse literature. It is the only *sax* with a regular sword hilt. Normally, the name given to the handle or grip of a *sax* is *hepti* or *mundriði*, but the handle of Grettir's *sax* is twice called a *meðalkafli*, a name usually reserved for the grip of a sword. It may perhaps be argued that the thirteenth-century Icelandic author of the *Grettis saga* made a slip when he gives this name to the hilt of Grettir's short-sword, but the uniqueness of the nomenclature argues rather that tradition had preserved this remarkable feature of the weapon.[43]

I have commented before on the both-authors-got-it-wrong approach, and suffice it to add that if this kind of methodology becomes acceptable in medieval studies, we shall see an astronomical growth of analogue-making efforts at the expense of common sense. In Taylor's case, however, not even this questionable approach can carry the argument. That Grettir's *sax* is unique in Old Norse in having a sword hilt is entirely correct, but I wonder if the author of *Grettis saga* realized how unique he was being in endowing the *sax* with a handle of this kind. What Taylor omits to mention is that there is nothing special about the hilt, except the saga author's placement of it on Grettir's *sax*. The hilt is casually mentioned twice in the saga, first when Grettir ties the weapon to his hand before going to meet the bear (76), and again when an unsuccessful attempt is made to wrest the *sax* is from the hero's grip after his death (261). In both instances it is as if the author assumes that he is referring to an ordinary type of a handle for a short-sword, and, as we saw, even Taylor has to admit that this might have come about through sheer ignorance. The unique *meðalkafli* of Grettir's *sax* plays no role in the saga over and above being a handle for his short-sword, and with that in mind, the comparison of a word that occurs twice in the saga to the twenty-two lines of musings over the hilt of the ancient cave sword in *Beowulf* becomes rather far-fetched.

It should be clear from the various critical efforts that I have just cited that it is no easy task to make Guðbrandur Vigfússon's theory of equating *heptisax* with *hæftmece* pan out. On the matter of weapons, *Grettis saga* and *Beowulf* – as we have them – simply cannot be made to fall into line. If a relationship between the actual weapons cannot be established in the texts without emending them both, we are bound to come back to the starting point of our enquiry, namely, the assumption of a special relationship between the two words.

Vigfússon never cared to elaborate on what precisely constituted their kinship,[44] so later critics have had to discover this for themselves, and they have done so in a variety of manners. Ideally, the kind of proof of a relationship that one would want would be etymological, one that would account for the two words as cognates descending from a Germanic etymon that could be reconstructed, but there is no such proof to be had. This, however, has not prevented some analogue-minded critics from describing *heptisax* and *hæftmece* as cognate terms.[45] It is true, of course, that *hæft* and *hepti* are cognate prefixes, but taken as a whole the two words are not otherwise related. Another linguistic avenue which has been tried is to find a 'semantic resemblance' between the two: *hæftmece* glossed as the 'hilted sword,' and *heptisax* as the 'hafted short-sword.'[46] This may appear to be a promising approach, but it is extremely misleading. As we have already seen, the prefix *hepti-* in the saga almost certainly means a 'plain handle,' and, as it happens, we have nothing with which to compare this reading because we do not know what precisely the first part of *hæftmece* is supposed to mean. Under the umbrella of 'semantic resemblance' we can presumably also include statements that link the two words as 'counterparts' or take them to be 'of the same kind.'[47]

Other attempts, i.e., ones that are neither linguistic nor based on the texts, to account for a relationship between the pair are – and only can be – pure speculation. Most commonly, critics have turned their imagination towards ancient rituals and magic. Vera I. Evison has suggested that the meaning of the two words 'may be connected with something altogether unsuspected and be a lost memory of the ritual of exorcism.'[48] Anatoly Liberman believes that in the original story there was magic contained in the haft of the weapon, and that the terms *hæftmece* and *heptisax* originally 'belonged to a stock of ritual words.'[49] The latest and most ambitious hypothesis in this vein comes from Carlo A. Mastrelli, who argues that the elements *hæft-* and *hepti-* originally implied divine or demonic power. According to Mastrelli, the two words go back to a version of the Indo-Iranian myth about Indra's victory over the demon Valla and the snake Vrtra, in which a marvelous sword with its power contained in the handle was of central importance. In *Beowulf* the characteristics of this sword are divided among three weapons: the *hæftmece* Hrunting, the dagger with which Grendel's mother attacks Beowulf, and the magical giant sword. *Grettis saga* is also found to have corresponding weapons. With the transition from paganism to Christianity, the myth itself and the meaning of the key word gradually faded so that by the time that the poem and the saga were recorded, the magical associations of *hæftmece* and *heptisax* had been forgotten, and they had come to denote no more than a weapon with a handle.[50]

However, not all critics – not even scholars who are convinced that *Beowulf* and *Grettis saga* must be somehow related – have been equally impressed by the importance that Guðbrandur Vigfússon attached to his discovery of the unique pair. Henrik Schück, for example, voiced his criticism as early as 1909. Schück rightly observes that in Anglo-Saxon literature there is not a great deal of secular poetry that has survived and consequently finds it questionable to read too much into the single occurrence of *hæftmece* in *Beowulf*. According to Schück there is a similar danger in the saga, because although the compound is unique, both components of *heptisax* are common words. He also wonders about the incomplete correspondence between Vigfússon's pair; after all we should expect to find a **heptimækir* in *Grettis saga* or a **hæftseax* in *Beowulf*.[51] More recently, A. Margaret Arent has maintained that the occurrence of the two forms 'should not carry too much weight in establishing a dependency or common source for the motifs in *Beowulf* and *Grettis saga*.'[52]

It goes without saying that these objections have not been greeted with much enthusiasm, nor have they inspired other scholars to re-examine the elusive relationship that Vigfússon postulated. In the eyes of the faithful, the magic of the verbal talismans *hæftmece* and *heptisax* is both proven and sacrosanct. Perhaps the most fallacious idea in all the literature on this pair is the general assumption that it is their uniqueness in Old English and Old Icelandic that makes them so special. We are tacitly asked to believe that they could only be associated with one particular 'old legend' and could not have come about in any other manner. But it is only through the hindsight of good dictionaries in both languages that we know the two words to be unique, and critics – awestruck, as it would seem, by the presence of two words recorded only once –

often tend to forget that the authors of *Beowulf* and *Grettis saga* hardly shared this information with us. Given this scenario, the unbeliever feels like the child in Hans Christian Andersen's story 'The Emperor's New Clothes,' who saw that His Highness was naked even though the rest of the court kept admiring his fine new suit.

5

Hell and High Water

In this chapter we round up the examination of the proposed genetically related analogues by inspecting the dwellings in which the monsters of saga and poem live, and the landscape through which Beowulf and Grettir must travel to reach them. The logic behind this comparison is much the same as in chapter 3, namely, that similarities in respect to settings, or perhaps some details relating to their description, might have survived in the two stories that supposedly developed from the same original legend. Landscape and other settings are indeed one of the main areas of comparison where Guðbrandur Vigfússon's followers felt there was work to be done, and armed with the kind of methodology that I have just described, they have generated more books and articles on this one subject than on any other concerning the relationship between *Beowulf* and *Grettis saga*. In the early decades of this century Carl W. von Sydow tried to stem this tide by arguing that details of the landscape of an original legend were quickly stripped away in the process of transmission within an oral tradition.[1] But the triumvirate of Klaeber, Lawrence, and Chambers thought differently. To them it seemed entirely logical that even though this part of the poem described a battle between a hero of superhuman qualities against a pair of supernatural enemies the landscape of the monsters' abode should meet all rational criteria – and in the ensuing critical battle, their ideas won the day.

If we retrace the journey that Beowulf makes to the abode of the monsters, the first parallel to *Grettis saga* that has been proposed is the road he must take: the narrow footpath (*'enge anpaðas, uncuð gelad,'* line 1410). In his edition of *Beowulf*, Klaeber notes that Grettir must also follow a narrow path to reach the bear's cave lair, but stops short of suggesting that it might be an analogous feature.[2] Later critics, particularly A. Margaret Arent and Peter A. Jorgensen, have been less hesitant, and both have maintained that the narrow path was part of the original legend.[3] There are, however, a number of reasons that make this very unlikely. The most obvious one is the absence of a narrow footpath to take Grettir to his fights with otherworldly creatures, such as the giant at Sandhaugar or Glámr. Secondly, the narrow footpath in *Beowulf* is part and parcel of a description which seems to be aimed at giving an impression of the hero's entry into a hellish realm, as opposed to the *einstigi* in *Grettis saga*, which merely serves as a precariously narrow battle ground for the bear fight.

The next feature of landscape which has been claimed to have a counterpart in *Grettis saga* is the famous mountain stream (*fyrgenstream*, line 1359b) that goes down under the darkness of the hills and forms a flood under the earth, to which King Hroðgar alludes in his description of what is in store for Beowulf on the perilous journey that he must undertake to reach the abode of Grendel's mother. This allusion is somewhat mysterious, because the lines that actually describe Beowulf's trip to the mere (1399–1417a) make no mention of a mountain river. As early as 1881, C.S. Smith suggested that there was a parallel between the mountain stream of the poem and the waterfall of the Sandhaugar episode,[4] but it was not until later – after W.W. Lawrence had fully developed Smith's idea – that the 'waterfall theory' gained critical momentum in *Beowulf* studies. It must be borne in mind, however, that the waterfall is only a part of a larger landscaping effort which Lawrence had in mind. His general aim was to clear up and rationalize the surrealistic and conflicting images of natural scenery that *Beowulf* seems to offer, and he did this by assuming that *Grettis saga* preserves features of landscape that are closer to the hypothetical original legend than the English poem. Lawrence then proceeds to superimpose the Icelandic inland scenery of the waterfall in *Grettis saga* onto the salty surroundings of the mere, and here, as might be expected, he runs into the difficulty of reconciling the vocabulary of the poem with the landscape that he wants to see. His solution to this obstacle, however, is both sweet and simple: 'Anglo-Saxon poetry was not particular about the propriety of its synonyms ... Hence poetic elaborations were often used with considerable looseness.'[5] In other words, the *fyrgenstream* in *Beowulf* was not really a mountain stream, as the elements that make up the compound would seem to suggest, but a waterfall:

It will be observed, in the first place, that the general location of Grettir's contest under water is much like what we may believe to be the original scenery of Beowulf's second adventure. There are in the Scandinavian tale the same high cliffs, from which one looks down to the waters below, and the same waterfall breaking down over the rocks, and plunging into a turbulent whirlpool. These general and essential features of inland mountain scenery are the same. Certain details naturally vary; there is less suggestion of a river in the Anglo-Saxon, although a waterfall such as is there described could hardly exist without something like a river as tributary to it ... The place where the demon has dragged Beowulf is a cave behind the waterfall – *under firgen-stréam*, 2128, – where, as the poet tells us, she had previously taken the luckless Æschere. Beowulf dives to the bottom, just as Grettir did, in order to avoid the whirlpool and thus get up underneath the waterfall.[6]

Both R.W. Chambers and Fr. Klaeber warmly embraced this theory and did their share to promote it, Chambers by incorporating it into his highly influential study on *Beowulf*, and Klaeber by glossing the crucial word *fyrgenstream* as 'waterfall' in his edition of the poem.[7] Chambers's account of how Lawrence's theory brought the light of reason to his and W.P. Ker's understanding of the mere episode in *Beowulf* illustrates well what Margaret E. Goldsmith has called 'an ingrained preference for naturalism in literature':

To many of us this [i.e., the waterfall setting] now seems clear – but only with the *Grettis saga* before us, and even then only after reading Lawrence's excellent demonstration: I remember W.P. Ker saying, 'Strange, that none of us ever noticed that before.' The waterfall-setting in *Beowulf* is almost obliterated, visible only when searched for, like the original writing of some palimpsests. It is one of those things which, however obvious after they are pointed out, are not noticed till they *are* pointed out ...

In any case it is certain that in *Beowulf* there is no suggestion that the cave is just behind the waterfall. Beowulf plunges to the bottom, and in course of time finds himself in a cave free from the water. Nothing is said of his rising after his dive – the cave appears to be at the bottom of the mere: it is sheer un-reason. Of course such un-reason *does* occur elsewhere in *Beowulf*. But when we confront the *Beowulf* account with the Sandhaugar episode, the episode reveals itself as eminently reasonable. The hero, in order to get *under* the waterfall, *has* to dive to the bottom. 'Can it be done?' I remember asking W.P. Ker. 'Yes,' said Ker, 'I have done it.' (All depends, of course, upon the volume of the waterfall.)[8]

Although Lawrence's theory has convinced many *Beowulf* scholars, in addition to Klaeber and Chambers,[9] there have always been those who found it simply too good to be true. One of the first critics to voice his objections was W.S. Mackie, who bluntly rejected the idea of a waterfall in the poem as an interpolation from *Grettis saga*:

Lawrence translates *fyrgenstréam* by 'waterfall,' and suggests that *under næssa genipu* may refer to 'the fine spray thrown out by the fall in its descent, and blown about the windy nesses.' There is a waterfall in the *Grettissaga*; is there one in *Beowulf* also?

Fyrgenstréam, 'mountain stream'; *fyrgen* is translated 'mountain' because that is the meaning of the cognate Gothic *fairguni*, which translates Greek ὄρος. In Old English *fyrgen* never occurs as a simplex, but only as the first element in three compounds found only in poetry. Only one of these, *fyrgenstréam* itself, occurs outside of *Beowulf*; and then it seems always to mean 'the sea,' or, at most, 'the flowing sea,' 'the sea waves.' See, for example, *Andreas* 390, *Anchor Riddle* 2, *Cotton Gnomic Verses* 47. So it would seem that the original meaning of the archaic *fyrgen* had weakened to vanishing point, and that the word survived in poetic compounds principally for the sake of providing an *f* alliteration. *Fyrgenholt* in *Beowulf* 1393 probably means nothing more than 'forest,' and the *fyrgenbéamas* that lean over the grey rock (*Beowulf* 1414) are merely trees. Similarly *fyrgenstréam* is simply equivalent to *stréam*, 'stream,' 'running water,' or merely 'water.' 'The running water descends, a stream below the level of the earth' is most probably meant to describe a stream running into the mere through a gorge, but it is possible that what the poet has in mind is a whirlpool in the mere, or even the turbid mere itself. At any rate, notwithstanding *niþer gewíteð*, the translation of *fyrgenstréam* by 'waterfall' is very doubtful indeed.[10]

In addition to his criticism of Lawrence's interpretation of *fyrgenstream*, Mackie also called attention to the fact that the poem describes Beowulf's return from the abode of the monsters as a dive up through the water without any hint that he must dive under a waterfall.

Lawrence replied to Mackie's objections and tried to defend his translation, but he could neither refute Mackie's argument nor offer anything new. As before, Lawrence simply insisted that Anglo-Saxon poetry 'possessed a large choice of epithets for its own limited range of subjects, but few for those outside its range. Consequently, in the obligatory repetition, variation, and alliteration, terms not strictly applicable were often used.'[11]

A few years before Mackie's article appeared, Lawrence's waterfall theory had come under attack from Kemp Malone who, in a review of the second edition of Chambers's study of *Beowulf*, flatly rejected Lawrence's ideas and criticized Chambers for promoting them. Like Mackie, Malone did not believe that it would have occurred to anyone to interpret *fyrgenstream* as a waterfall, were it not for the supposedly analogous and genetically related Sandhaugar episode. In his review Malone argued that the first element of *fyrgenstream* should be read as an intensifier ('mountainous,' 'vast'), and that the word as a whole could only mean 'the great stream of the Ocean (the sea pure and simple).'[12] Years later, Malone came back to this subject in an article entitled 'Grendel and his Abode,' in which he thoroughly examined the variety of simplex nouns and compounds that appear in *Beowulf* for bodies of water, and concluded, as he had done previously, that *fyrgenstream* could only mean a 'stream that is a mountain (of intensity)' and that the word most likely referred to the ancient notion that a stream of gigantic size – the world river Oceanus – encircled the world.[13] These objections from Mackie and Malone to Lawrence's waterfall argument have, insofar as I know, never been refuted, and yet they seem to have had very little impact on analogue-minded scholars, who have simply ignored them.[14]

From the point of view of *Grettis saga* there is also a serious weakness in Lawrence's line of reasoning. If the Sandhaugar episode is supposed to clear up ambiguities and contradictions in the physical settings of the mere scene in *Beowulf*, then we must assume that the saga is crystal-clear in its description of the relevant details. Lawrence indeed made this claim in his original article on the subject of landscape in the poem, 'The Haunted Mere in *Beowulf*,' and later repeated it in his *Beowulf and Epic Tradition*.[15] This opinion has since come to be generally accepted, apparently both by Lawrence's followers and his critics.[16] But just how accurate is this assessment of the waterfall scenery in the saga?

The waterfall described in the saga does not reflect any actual scenery in Bárðardalur, where Grettir's fight with the giant is said to have taken place. Lawrence assumed that this was further proof that *Grettis saga* had faithfully preserved the scenery of the ancient legend,[17] but of course that need not be the case. The saga author might just as easily have fashioned an imaginary landscape for Grettir's battle, and the ambiguities in his account of the waterfall and the cave would seem to suggest that this is indeed what he did. One such ambiguity – the question of the location of the cave in respect to the waterfall – was well known before Lawrence published his 'Haunted Mere in *Beowulf*.' When Grettir goes with the priest to explore the gorge, the passage in question can be read to mean that they see either a cave behind the waterfall or simply the precipitous sides of the ravine, and whatever they see is said to be ten fathoms away from something which the text does not clearly identify.[18] It says all that needs to be said about the supposed crystal clarity of this landscape that, for instance, Friedrich Panzer, R.C. Boer, and W.W. Lawrence all see in it a cave, specifically, the cave in which Grettir later has his fight with the giant, behind the waterfall, but cannot agree as to what the ten fathoms are meant to refer,[19] whereas R.W. Chambers does not believe that there is any cave, and even if there was one, he maintains, it would surely have to be yet another cave, different from the one in which the giant lives.[20]

Turning from the landscape of the Sandhaugar episode to the details of what takes place in the cave, the reader who wishes to seek consolation in the clarity of *Grettis saga* after the muddy waters of *Beowulf* is also likely to be disappointed. As we have already seen, the Sandhaugar episode as a whole is riddled with question marks and inconsistencies, and its final chapter is no exception. The prose account of chapter 66 of the saga informs us that Grettir dives under the waterfall and scales the cliff until he reaches a ledge from which he enters the cave. He walks into the cave, which is huge, and well inside the cave fights his battle with the giant. But this course of events is squarely contradicted by the two stanzas, nos. 60 and 61, which Grettir composes to inform the priest of his adventure. Stanza 60 describes Grettir's difficulty in battling against the strong current of a river which runs through the cave, and in stanza 61 the giant is said to have left his cave and come outside to meet him.[21] This is confusing, to say the least. Is the cave dry or does a river run through it; and if a river runs through it, is it supposed to be the same river as the one that forms the water-fall? In the prose account the reader is definitely intended to visualize Grettir in a dry place – after all there is a fire burning in the cave – but at the same time we are also told that the entrails of the giant fell into the river. Are we meant to imagine a virtual avalanche of blood and gore, which flows from the cave and into the river below, or is the saga author being inconsistent at this moment in the narrative by reaching for a a stage prop in the form of a stream, because a river is a handy means of carrying the gory message that signals the outcome of the battle to the timid priest? How we choose to resolve these textual difficulties is actually immaterial for the purpose of this discussion; it is their presence in the text that matters. The description of Grettir's journey to the giant's cave and what takes place once he is there is not a realistic narrative by any stretch of the imagination.

In presenting his waterfall argument Lawrence insisted that the scenery sur-rounding the mere was characterized by inconsistent features. According to his view, the poem's description of the haunted mere revealed no less than three different conceptions of its nature and location: (a) in a moor or fen, (b) in high and rocky land, and (c) in or near the sea.[22] These could not be reconciled to produce a single consistent picture of natural scenery, in his opinion, because they represented traces of older versions of the story, which had had different stage settings, and which had left their traces on his work when the *Beowulf* poet drew on them for his poem.[23] Furthermore, Lawrence argued that at the core of the poem, in particular in its description of the landscape of the mere, lay a Scandinavian original set in the mountainous country of the Scandinavian peninsula, which was preserved in *Grettis saga*.[24] In other words, the original conception of the scene in *Beowulf* was an inland body of water set in rocky heights, and any traces of the sea or fens were merely secondary stages intro-duced later in the evolution of the original story.[25]

There is no small amount of arrogance implicit in this analysis. If this is the process through which *Beowulf* came about, we are forced to assume that the author was a bungling realist, a poet who presumably tried to harmonize and digest a number of conflicting versions of his story and who failed miserably in attempting to do so. A less heavy-handed approach might be to accept the contradictions in the scenery of the mere and to allow for the possibility that the author of *Beowulf* set out to create a certain kind of mood rather than realistic scenery. This line of interpretation was in fact suggested by James R. Hulbert as early as 1929,[26] and has influenced some of the later criticisms of Lawrence's reading of the poem.[27] But the waterfall theory was soon criticized for more than being a heavy-handed interpretation. Serious doubts were raised with regard to two of the basic ingredients of Lawrence's theory: first, his claim that references to the sea in the description of the mere were late and unimportant additions to the original legend, and secondly his assumption that the general landscape of the poem could not be visualized as one consistent image.

With respect to Lawrence's dismissal of terms related to the sea in the mere scene, Mackie found numerous examples of words of that kind that Lawrence had overlooked, as well as flaws in the conclusions drawn from the vocabulary that he had examined. Mackie showed beyond any shadow of a doubt that, in the vocabulary of the poem, the mere becomes the sea as soon as the Geatas and the Danes have reached it, and he concluded that the mere must be considered to be a large landlocked arm of the sea, 'even though the resemblance of the scenery in *Beowulf* to that in the *Grettissaga* becomes thereby more distant than before.'[28] Malone, who later examined the entire vocabulary of words denoting bodies of water in *Beowulf*, came to the same conclusion. In the course of his discussion, Malone also had some harsh words for Klaeber, whom he accused of being completely inconsistent in his glossing of sea vocabulary in his edition of the poem in order to accommodate Lawrence's theory.[29]

In his article Malone also examines Lawrence's notion of the three inconsistent descriptions in *Beowulf* of the mere and its surroundings and completely rejects it. Malone's conclusion is that 'the poet gives us not a confused and distorted description of natural scenery but a consistent and carefully-wrought picture of a hell on earth.'[30] Malone shows that Grendel is on numerous occasions referred to by words and phrases that would appear to identify him as a member of a tribe of devils. Grendel is 'a devil in thought and deed,' although he is 'no fallen angel but a monster of human stock and the poet gives him an abode to fit, a hell on earth.'[31] But the strongest evidence for such a reading is undoubtedly, as Malone emphasized, the close resemblance between St. Paul's vision of hell in Blickling Homily XVI, and the passage in *Beowulf* that describes the landscape of the mere.[32] A relationship between the two texts was recognized long before Malone published his article, but there has never been any agreement among scholars as to whether the poem borrowed its description of hell from the homily or the homily from the poem, or whether they both drew from the same source, and this debate still continues.[33] It might be added that Malone's interpretation of the mere scene has not escaped criticism either, as some scholars do not think that the image of hell that he finds in it is hellish enough.[34] What matters for the purpose of this discussion, however, is that a key element in Lawrence's theory, namely, his notion of three conflicting pictures of landscape in the descriptions of the mere in *Beowulf*, has thus been shown to be wrong, and with that the idea of superimposing the landscape of *Grettis saga* upon the poem no longer has any foundation. The shift that has occurred in respect to the issue of landscape in the poem has recently been summed up by Charles D. Wright, who suggests that Lawrence was on the wrong track all along:

Although Lawrence and other earlier scholars believed that the famous analogue in the Icelandic *Grettissaga* preserved 'the original conception of the dwelling of the demons' in *Beowulf*, most recent scholarship concurs that the *Beowulf*-poet has adapted conventional features of hell for his description.[35]

Much of the context of Lawrence's thesis was, as we have seen, demolished decades ago, but strangely enough, some *Beowulf* scholars still cling to certain aspects of the saga's description of landscape as analogues to the poem. In a fairly recent edition of *Beowulf*, for example, we are told that the 'scenery [of Grendel's mere] generally follows the pattern of the waterfall and cave in chapter 66 of *Grettis saga*,'[36] and these two features of landscape still commonly crop up in comparisons between the poem and the saga.

Let us now turn to the caves of Grendel's dam and the giant at Sandhaugar. The first difference between the two that meets the eye is the matter of their respective locations. However we choose to interpret the landscape of the mere in *Beowulf*, at least it is clear that it is set in a howling wilderness, a place which both men and animals avoid at all costs. The giant at Sandhaugar, by contrast, has his cave in the midst of a human settlement, and Grettir's actual journey to the cave is as short as it is uneventful. If we follow the prose of the saga, there is no doubt that the cave is located behind and under a waterfall. In his edition of *Beowulf*, Klaeber, taking his cue from and partly quoting Lawrence, also places Grendel's mother in a corresponding location:

Grendel's dam, aroused by a stranger's appearance in the water, goes to the bottom of the lake (to which Bēowulf had plunged, like Grettir, 'in order to avoid the whirlpool and thus get up underneath the waterfall'), and drags him to her cave.[37]

But there is absolutely nothing in the text to indicate a cave under or behind a waterfall; Grendel's dam in all likelihood inhabits a cave at the bottom of or under the sea. This is what everything points to in the description of Beowulf's entry into the world of the monsters:

- Beowulf dives in, and a long time passes until he has descended far enough to see the floor of the sea, the *grundwong* (line 1496a).
- Unlike the giant at Sandhaugar, Grendel's mother goes to meet her visitor, and after she has grabbed Beowulf, they come to the sea bottom, *to botme* (line 1506b).
- Grendel's dam then carries Beowulf into her cave, and since nothing in the lines of this passage of the poem suggests that they move upwards after having reached the bottom, it seems easiest to suppose that Grendel's mother takes Beowulf into a submarine cave.

In his article entitled 'Grendel and his Abode,' Kemp Malone calls attention to an interesting speech that Beowulf makes just before he sets out on his mission to seek the haunt of Grendel's mother (lines 1392–4), in which he accurately predicts where he intends to look for her:

> Ic hit þe gehate,   no he on helm losaþ,
> ne on foldan fæþm,   ne on fyrgenholt,
> ne on gyfenes grund,   ga þær he wille!

'I promise you, she will never escape into a safe place, not (if she flees) to the bosom of the earth nor to the grove of gigantic trees nor to the bottom of the sea, go where she will.'

In the search that followed, Beowulf first reached the *fyrgenbeamas* 'giant trees' (1414), the *wynleasne wudu* 'joyless wood' (1416) that overshadowed the *mere*. He then dived into the *mere*. Hours later he got far enough down to see the *grundwong* 'bottom' (1496). There, as he said in his report to King Hygelac (made after his return to Geatland), he found the *grundhyrde* 'keeper of the deep' (2136), Grendel's mother. She carried him off to her *hof* in the bosom of the earth, where he killed her after a hard fight. In my opinion the three places of refuge that Beowulf mentioned in lines 1393–1394 foreshadow the three places that he later reached in the course of his search.[38]

It is common enough to see analogue-minded critics equate Beowulf and Grettir as two heroes who battle a 'monster who dwells under water,'[39] but such comparisons conveniently stretch the meaning of 'under water' to unite very different circumstances under the same umbrella.

If the 'old legend' contained a description of the monster's abode, that description cannot be said to have been evenly divided among the supposed literary offspring. Chapter 66 of *Grettis saga* informs the reader that the giant's cave was big, and makes no further attempt to describe his dwelling place. By contrast, the *Beowulf* poet shows considerable interest in the home of the Grendels. As might be expected in a habitation where the occupants are supernatural beings, the place has magic properties. The sea floor forms the roof of the cave and keeps it dry, we are told, even if the cave is 'open,' in the sense that it must have a doorway or some kind of an entrance. Sheer un-reason, as Chambers would say, but for a hero who has held his breath for the better part of the day, this incredible feature must be a welcome relief.

There is another aspect concerning the home of the Grendels that firmly separates it from the cave at Sandhaugar. As James L. Rosier notes in an article entitled 'The Uses of Association: Hands and Feasts in *Beowulf*,' the vocabulary that the poem uses to describe the cave of the monsters often has curiously royal overtones:

Grendel's abode at the bottom of the mere and the description of Beowulf when he descends to that abode are not dissimilar to Hrothgar's hall and the depiction of Grendel at Heorot. For example, the mere-dwelling is called *niðsele*, 'hostile hall,' and *hrofsele*, 'roofed hall.' Just as Grendel is ironically referred to as a 'hall-thane,' so Beowulf is here called a *gist* (1522) and the *selegyst* (1545).[40]

The band of water monsters that guard the hall of the Grendels and attack Beowulf in his effort to reach them also give the impression of a court with its band of retainers. In comparison to all this pomp, the Sandhaugar cave has nothing to offer except its great size, and it is entirely fitting that for all we know about the underwater abode of the Grendels, the poem never mentions whether it is large or small.

It has long been an established fact among analogue enthusiasts that the fires that burn inside the caves of the monsters provide yet another proof of the relationship between *Beowulf* and *Grettis saga*. The following statement exemplifies the casual equation between saga and poem that some critics are ready to make concerning this supposedly analogous point: 'The fire, in each work, is the focus of domestic life, showing that these underwater creatures use the same means of heating and cooking as human beings.'[41] This may sound convincing, but actually there is not so much as a grain of truth in the whole sentence. In the first place, contrary to popular belief, there is no fire in the monster's cave in *Beowulf*; there is only some kind of light, *fyrleoht* (line 1516b), translated by Klaeber as 'fire-light.' In the text another phrase, *blacne leoman* (1517a), 'a shining light,' follows as a variation on *fyrleoht*. As *fyrleoht* is a nonce word, it is difficult to be certain what exactly the compound is supposed to mean, but since in both phrases a particular type of light is being described, it seems most logical to take *fyr-* as a qualifying prefix meaning 'fiery.'[42] It further complicates this discussion that in the poem another light is described just as Beowulf has succeeded in cutting off the head of Grendel's mother:

> Lixte se leoma,   leoht inne stod,
> efne swa of hefene   hadre scineð
> rodores candel, (lines 1570a–2a)

i.e., 'the gleam shone, a light streamed within, even as the candle of the sky shines brightly from heaven.' Is this the same light as the *fyrleoht* in line 1516b, or is this yet another light? Klaeber takes them to be the same, and so does Mackie,[43] but not all critics have concurred with his view. Both Chambers and Lawrence wanted to keep the fire-in-the-cave analogy between the poem and the saga and insisted that the second light should be seen as a 'miraculous radiance sent to help the hero.'[44] However, the issue that matters in this context is the question of a fire or no fire in this passage of the poem, and on this point I agree with Mackie's 'one-and-the same light' interpretation:

the supernatural abode of the demons in *Beowulf* is illuminated not by the large, almost homely fire beside which sits the giant in the *Grettissaga*, but by a lurid supernatural light, bright as the sun in the skies.[45]

As we have seen so often before in our discussion, *Grettis saga* simply does not compare with *Beowulf* on this point unless Procrustean methods are applied to stretch the text of the poem.

After having killed the giant, Grettir kindles a light to examine the interior of the cave. As might be expected, this action has been compared to the 'second light' in Beowulf's battle with Grendel's mother. What is perhaps most striking about this comparison is the lack of sensitivity that parallel-hunting critics have shown for the nature of the texts that are being compared. In *Beowulf*, the essence of the second light that flashes in line 1570 is its strange and unexplained appearance and its mysterious nature. In the poem it comes about at a moment which is in between the main events of Beowulf's adventure in the cave: Grendel's mother has been killed, Grendel has yet to be decapitated, and the blade of the ancient sword has yet to melt. This light comes about despite the hero and not because he wills it. Lawrence's explanation of this light as a 'miraculous radiance sent to help the hero' is somewhat strange, because the great light appears after the battle with Grendel's mother, not before or during the struggle, and therefore appears too late to be of any help to the hero. It is, as so much else that happens in this supernatural region, totally inexplicable. By contrast, the description of Grettir's striking a light in the cave is motivated entirely by realism. The purpose of his journey is to search for the two people who had been abducted by the trolls, and after his brief encounter with the giant, this is precisely what he does, and what the reader expects him to do. The cave is big, more light than just the giant's fire is needed to explore it, and so Grettir strikes a light. As Martin Puhvel has remarked, 'lights illuminating dark or dim places need not necessarily have any connection,' and in this instance *Beowulf* and *Grettis saga* have none.[46]

In this chapter we have examined analogous and genetically related features that critics claim to have discovered in respect to landscape descriptions and other elements of settings in the two works. In respect to all such features – be they narrow footpaths, waterfalls, caves, or fires – there can only be one conclusion. What these so-called genetically related analogues have in common is that none of them can stand up to much scrutiny, and as a rule they are established by seriously distorting the text of the poem or the saga or both. Presumably, analogues are sought in *Beowulf* and *Grettis saga* so that a passage in one work may illuminate or clarify a corresponding section in the other. In this first section of the book, I have looked at all genetically related analogues that I know to have been proposed between the two works, and I have not found a single instance where this has actually been successfully achieved. The deeper one probes in examining these supposed genetically related analogues, and the harder that *Beowulf* and *Grettis saga* are pushed together, the more they tend go their separate ways, so that in the final analysis, no mental acrobatics can bridge the gap between them as different and unrelated texts. However, this is obviously not what analogue-minded critics have thought in the past, and ironically this last point brings us to the next section of this enquiry, which will deal with the question as to how critics have sought to explain the relationship between *Beowulf* and *Grettis saga*, and the different theories that have been proposed to account for their alleged kinship.

PART II
TO CEMENT A RELATIONSHIP

6

The English Hypothesis

It goes without saying that postulating a genetically related analogue to a literary work demands that some form of contact be established between the work in question and the source of the prospective analogue. In presenting his original discovery, Guðbrandur Vigfússon did not shirk from the duty of informing his readers how certain episodes in *Beowulf* and *Grettis saga* had come to be related:

[The Beowulf legend] gives the clue to Grettis Saga, which is otherwise obscure. The old legend shot forth from its ancient Scandinavian home into two branches, one to England, where it was turned into an epic, and one to Iceland, where it was domesticated and embodied in a popular Saga, tacked to the name of an outlaw and hero.[1]

Vigfússon never elaborated much on this brief pronouncement, although, he did remark in a later publication that he took his newly discovered analogues in *Grettis saga* 'to be an echo, not of the present diluted epic [i.e., *Beowulf*], but of the lays from which the epic was later made up.'[2]

Vigfússon's theory was, however, soon challenged by one of the leading medievalists of the Victorian era, Sophus Bugge. Bugge preferred to think that the analogues in *Grettis saga* originated from a saga composed in the North of England, which in turn had been based on an ancient song that was either identical to *Beowulf* as we now have it or closely related to it.[3] In an article entitled 'Beowulf-Grettir,' Liberman calls this type of approach 'the English hypothesis,' and defines it in general terms as a 'solution, according to which the episode in the *Grettla* [i.e., the Sandhaugar episode] owes its origin to a similar episode in *Beowulf*.'[4] The term 'English Hypothesis' actually denotes a number of different but related theories that can fall under Liberman's definition, and in this chapter I take the liberty of using both Liberman's name for this type of approach and his definition of it.

It weakened Bugge's claim for an English origin for *Grettis saga* that he seemed inadvertently to contradict himself in the article in which his hypothesis was first proposed. Critics who came to Vigfússon's defence therefore had an easy first round in defending his ideas,[5] although several early critics voiced their support of Bugge's thesis.[6] In the following debate R.C. Boer eventually emerged as the main advocate and defender of the English Hypothesis. Boer made his case first in an article on *Grettis saga* published in 1898, and then in his edition of the saga two years later. Boer argued for the English Hypothesis in its simplest form, namely, that the saga was directly or indirectly influenced by the poem. He rejected Vigfússon's idea that the Glámr episode was analogous and genetically related to *Beowulf*, and maintained that the saga author was merely copying that episode in Grettir's fight with the troll-woman at Sandhaugar. Grettir's fight with the giant in the cave Boer believed to be an interpolation from *Beowulf*; according to his view the interpolator had taken an indigenous story about a hero who fights against a troll-woman (cf. the local account of how the fight ends, in which she is petrified at daybreak) and combined it with an English version of the Beowulf legend. The *heptisax-hæftmece* analogy was, in Boer's opinion, too close to suggest any solution other than a direct influence from *Beowulf* on the saga.[7]

It shows how much room for different views there actually was among followers of the English Hypothesis that many scholars had ideas that were quite different from those of R.C. Boer as to how much and what kind of a relationship there was between the poem and the saga. Thus Axel Olrik foreshadowed the arguments of several later *Beowulf* scholars (for example, Peter A. Jorgensen, Richard L. Harris, and George Clark) by suggesting that the Beowulf legend had left its mark not only on *Grettis saga*, but also on other Icelandic *þættir* and *fornaldarsǫgur*.[8] Andreas Heusler, on the other hand, believed the Sandhaugar episode of *Grettis saga* to be an eleventh century reworking of the *Beowulf* poem,[9] and Carl W. von Sydow and Hermann Schneider thought that the Grendel part of the Beowulf legend had been brought to Iceland in the twelfth century by someone who had travelled to England, picked up the story, and retold it once he was back home.[10]

In the decades that followed Boer's edition of *Grettis saga*, more and more scholars began to detect *Beowulf* analogues which they believed to be of Irish origin, and they too were bound to favour the English Hypothesis and reject Vigfússon's old Scandinavian legend as a means of contact between *Beowulf* and *Grettis saga*. Richard L. Harris, who surveys the claims for Irish ancestry for Beowulf's fight against Grendel and his mother in an article entitled 'The Deaths of Grettir and Grendel: A New Parallel,' sums them up as follows:

The Irish school is ... made up of two groups, the former having been interested chiefly in oral sources, especially The Hand and Child Tale. In this tale, a hero waits in a room from which, over a period of time, children have previously disappeared one by one. As he waits, an arm comes down the chimney, its hand reaching out into the room. The hero seizes the arm and pulls it off the intruding monster. He then chases and kills it and returns the children.

The latter group is concerned also with possible literary and ecclesiastical sources, in such works as the early eighth century *Táin Bó Fráich*, the *Vita Columbae* of Adomnán, upon which the former story is itself partially dependent, and the *Sex Aetates Mundi*, from which the brood of Cain as it is described in *Beowulf* is supposed to come.[11]

No potential common source has been found for the Irish materials. Consequently, proponents of the Irish version of the English Hypothesis, who have proven to be highly analogue-minded critics, can only assume that *Beowulf* directly (or indirectly) influenced *Grettis saga* if their own discoveries of Irish analogues are supposed to hold. Among critics who belong to the Irish school, only Martin Puhvel has been able to imagine a hypothetical compromise with Guðbrandur Vigfússon:

It should ... [in] this discussion of the thorny problem of the origin of the Grendel story, be admitted that the possibility of some form of basic influence by Scandinavian folk-tale, so much theorized about, cannot be totally dismissed, even if there seems, to me, no need for any such assumption – the pieces of the jigsaw puzzle seem to fall reasonably well into place without it. Yet it is not inconceivable that, as so many a scholar thinks, some extinct Scandinavian tale may lurk in the background. It may have fused in England with somewhat similar Celtic folktale elements and possibly elements of Anglo-Saxon folklore ... to provide the basic plot of the Grendel story; and, just conceivably, this story may then, to the further bedevilment of the *Beowulf* student, have travelled to Iceland to fuse there with an offshoot of its partial ancestor from Scandinavia, thus rearing its bewildering head in *Grettis saga*. All this complication seems to me altogether unlikely – yet, who truly knows?[12]

The debate between proponents of the English Hypothesis and those who favoured a common origin of some sort – either as Guðbrandur Vigfússon had originally proposed or by viewing *Beowulf* and *Grettis saga* as different versions of the same folktale (the Bear's Son Tale), as Friedrich Panzer maintained[13] – soon turned into a quarrel over what oral transmission could or could not preserve. Oral transmission was, of course, the vehicle on which all theories of common origin had to rest, and this is what Carl W. von Sydow, who emerged as a leading critic of such ideas, chose to focus his attention on.

Von Sydow had earlier believed that both *Beowulf* and *Grettis saga* went back to a common but now lost Irish source which had contained the original version of the poem; however, he later modified his position and formulated his own version of the English Hypothesis.[14]

In his criticism of theories that postulated a common origin, von Sydow's basic line of argument was that the process of oral transmission was incompatible with the nature of various key analogues that it was supposed to have delivered to different countries and thereby into different languages. To demonstrate his case, von Sydow singled out three analogous points of contact between the saga and the poem: the *hæftmece-heptisax* parallel, the runes on the handle of the giant sword and Grettir's rune staff, and Lawrence's thesis of confused and clear landscape descriptions in the two branches of the old legend. In respect to the analogy between *hæftmece* and *heptisax*, von Sydow found it highly improbable that the latter word – an unimportant term for a weapon – could have been passed on for six hundred years or so within an oral tradition, only to surface once in an insignificant episode of *Grettis saga*. As a result, he felt that the analogy between the two words could only point to direct or indirect literary borrowing.[15] Concerning the issue of runic messages in both works, von Sydow maintained that in *Beowulf* the runes on the handle of the giant sword played absolutely no role in the series of events that are described in the poem. To him it was a clear example of a motif that the author of *Grettis saga* had reworked into a rune staff carrying a message to Steinn the priest in order to make it meaningful.[16] Finally, von Sydow turned to Lawrence's waterfall theory and rejected it on general grounds. An oral tradition, he argued, could not contain at one and the same time two conflicting descriptions of a landscape, one clear and the other one confused, as Lawrence had postulated. Given enough time, one of the two would always be obliterated by the other within the tradition.[17]

The Irish-English Hypothesis is still being kept alive, by scholars such as Martin Puhvel, for example, but it has always been a version of the English Hypothesis that only a minority of scholars, most of them Irish, have embraced. There are great many 'ifs' in this approach, and one has to agree with Anatoly Liberman when he says in his criticism of it that 'the Irish-English hypothesis should be rejected not because the Old English and Icelandic texts use nearly the same word in the same situation, but because none of its theses can be proved.'[18]

Whatever version of the English Hypothesis its proponents chose to embrace, a means of ferrying the Beowulf story across the ocean to Iceland had to be found. It goes without saying that scholars had to resort to pure guesswork when it came to this part of the effort to bridge the gap between the poem and the saga, but vacuums of knowledge in medieval studies have never failed to attract attention, and there has been no lack of solutions proposed in this area either. Kemp Malone suggested that the legend could have reached Iceland through bilingual Viking settlers in England, and that 'through those who spoke both languages English tales like the Grendel story could spread all over the Scandinavian world.'[19] Douglas Stedman and Alois Brandl favoured the idea that the Beowulf legend had been brought to Iceland by Anglo-Saxon missionaries who had indeed worked there in the early decades of the eleventh century,[20] and, as I have already mentioned, Carl W. von Sydow and Hermann Schneider believed that an Icelander travelling in England had brought the legend home with him.[21] By far the most ambitious piece of speculation however, came from Eiríkur Magnússon who went so far as to discover the person responsible for the introduction of the Beowulf legend into Icelandic culture. According to his biographer, Magnússon suggested 'that the tales from *Beowulf* had been brought to Iceland from the British Isles with a settler named Auðunn Skökull, whose kin lived in the same district and was related by marriage to that of Grettir.'[22]

It is not an understatement to say that the English Hypothesis has been under constant attack since Sophus Bugge first suggested it, and nowadays it seems to have very few spokesmen among *Beowulf* scholars. Critics who subscribed to a common origin for *Beowulf* and *Grettis saga* quickly discovered several weak spots in the process that the English Hypothesis implicitly postulated and wasted no time in hammering away at them. One of the first targets was the fact that Old English and Old Norse are obviously different languages. As early as 1909, in his *Studier i Beowulfsagan*, Henrik Schück categorically stated that Old English would have been incomprehensible in thirteenth-century Iceland, so that even if the *Beowulf* poem had somehow found its way to the country, it could still not have been a source for *Grettis saga*.[23] R.W. Chambers, in an article entitled 'Beowulf's Fight with Grendel and its Scandinavian Parallels,' took up this argument and added several others to show that Old English was not likely to have been much understood in medieval Iceland:

My reasons for thinking that a thirteenth century Scandinavian could not have drawn from a MS of *Beowulf* are (1) the absurd blunders made when Icelanders drew from the Old English genealogies; (2) the difficulties which Thorkelin, despite his acquaintance with Icelandic and many years of study, found in understanding *Beowulf;* (3) the fact that, already in the early twelfth century, a writer like Henry of Huntingdon, who can understand Anglo-Saxon prose, finds the poetry difficult and its terms strange (*extranea*). For these and other reasons, the idea of an Icelander about the year 1300 reading a MS of *Beowulf* seems to me fantastic.[24]

And Chambers concluded this train of thought in his book on *Beowulf* by dryly remarking that if the Sandhaugar episode was derived from the poem, 'we have an interesting literary curiosity, but nothing further.'[25]

Another glaring weakness in the English Hypothesis is its failure to explain exactly how *Beowulf* could have inspired the supposed analogues in *Grettis saga*, in particular the Sandhaugar episode. W.W. Lawrence attacked this flaw in an article entitled 'The Haunted Mere in *Beowulf*' published in 1912: 'It is clear that the Anglo-Saxon *Beowulf*, in anything like the form in which we have it at present, could not have given a hint for the description of Grettir's adventure at the waterfall.'[26] In *Beowulf and Epic Tradition*, Lawrence comes back to this point and is even more critical of the English Hypothesis than before: 'One thing is obvious: that the straightforward account in the saga cannot have been derived, even indirectly, from the epic. The saga is clear where the epic is confused.'[27] In his book on *Beowulf* Chambers continued Lawrence's line of attack and singled out landscape descriptions in the poem and the saga as evidence against the possibility of an English origin for the latter:

Now it is in the highest degree improbable that, after the landscape had been blurred as it is in *Beowulf*, it could have been brought out again with the distinctness it has in the *Grettis saga*. To preserve the features so clearly the *Grettir*-story can hardly be derived from *Beowulf*: it must have come down independently.[28]

More recently, the issue of landscapes and settings has been raised by Joan Turville-Petre, who also rules out direct influence of the poem on the author of the saga: 'Even if he could have read the poem, the saga writer could not possibly have constructed his account from this source,'[29] and also by J. Michael Stitt, who concurs with the critics of the English Hypothesis that *Beowulf* cannot be the only source for the Sandhaugar episode of the saga.[30]

In his criticism of the possibility that *Beowulf* might have directly or indirectly influenced the author of *Grettis saga*, Chambers also used literary arguments. In 'Beowulf's Fight with Grendel, and its Scandinavian Parallels,' he wonders aloud why the saga author chose not to make use of the finer points of the Grendel section of the poem:

Now, when we turn to the *Sandhaugar* episode, we find that the heroic epic setting has absolutely disappeared. There is nothing even corresponding to it, *except for the things in which the Danes take over functions from folk tale*: the only sufferings or doings of the Danes which have their counterpart in the *Sandhaugar* episode are things like their victimization before Beowulf appears, and their departure leaving Beowulf in the water. But, apart from this, the whole Danish setting is wanting; even the motive of the vengeance for Æschere, which would have appealed to an Icelandic audience of the thirteenth century. In the *Sandhaugar* episode there is no second raid of the monster-brood, although this would have supplied what is so obvious a fault in that episode, a reason why Grettir, whose fear of the dark is haunting him, should nevertheless have felt bound to go out of his way to seek the monster in the cavern. If the compiler of the *Grettis saga* knew the story in the *Beowulf* form, why should he have reverted to the looser construction of the folk tale? For the Danish setting, which places the combat in a royal hall, makes a fine tale, eminently suited to Grettir's early adventures at the court of a king. Why abandon the courtly setting? And, above all, why abandon the vengeance motive? Is it likely that an Icelandic saga-man, borrowing his tale from *Beowulf*, would have omitted a detail so entirely congenial to him?[31]

In the final analysis the English Hypothesis must be rejected. It is clear that it fails to account properly for how *Beowulf* is supposed to relate to the saga, and proponents of this thesis have never managed to defend it successfully against the criticisms of Chambers, Lawrence, and other scholars. Furthermore, I agree with Richard L. Harris when he calls the idea of the saga's dependence on *Beowulf* 'naive.' 'Too many stories,' he adds, 'once told have been long forgotten, and the conflagrations damaging the Cotton and Arnamagnaean collections should be sufficient lessons in the uncertainties of preservation of the written word.'[32]

7

Panzer's 'Bear's Son' Thesis

In 1910 there appeared in Munich a remarkably ambitious and impressive work under the innocuous title of *Studien zur germanischen Sagengeschichte I. Beowulf.* The author, Friedrich Panzer, had collected and collated more than two hundred versions of a particular folktale, known as 'The Bear's Son Tale,'[1] from a variety of different languages and cultures. From these Panzer reconstructed in the first part of his book what he believed to be the original elements of the different versions of the tale. In the second part, he turned his attention to *Beowulf* and proceeded to argue that both the Grendel section of *Beowulf* and the Sandhaugar episode of *Grettis saga* were to be regarded as mutually independent versions of the Bear's Son Tale and related only insofar that they were two branches on the same stem.[2] Panzer was not the first critic to note similarities between *Beowulf* and the Bear's Son Tale, this had been done by Ludwig Laistner some twenty years earlier.[3] What was original about his theory was the revolutionary way that it proposed of linking *Beowulf* and *Grettis saga*, a way that was incompatible both with Guðbrandur Vigfússon's ideas of an old Scandinavian legend shooting its branches to England and Iceland and with the different versions of the English Hypothesis.

The folktale that Panzer believed to be the missing link between *Beowulf* and *Grettis saga* exists in several different versions, but the main outline of the story is something like this: The hero sometimes has an animal, usually a bear, as his ancestor, or he is raised by bears. He is often immensely strong and performs incredible feats of strength, but is otherwise an unpromising youth. He leaves home, or his master, and gathers around him two or three strong companions that he meets along the road. The companions often turn out to possess some special powers as well. Together, the hero and his companions come upon a deserted dwelling place, sometimes a castle, in the woods. The hero and his companions cook food, but an evil supernatural being steals it. The hero's companions fight the demon unsuccessfully, but the hero himself prevails against the monster, wounds it, and ties it to a tree, often by its beard. The wounded demon flees to his subterranean lair, tearing off a part of himself in the process of escaping and leaving a trail of blood behind him. The hero follows the trail and usually lowers himself by a rope into the underworld. There he beheads his supernatural enemy or enemies, a male and in some cases a related female as well, sometimes with a magic sword that he discovers in the demon's lair. After that he frees a princess or princesses (usually three) who have been held captive by the demon and has them and much treasure pulled up to the world above. His companions, who have been watching over or holding the rope, covet the princesses and the treasure and betray the hero by leaving him in the underworld, sometimes by cutting the rope, as soon as the princesses and the treasure have been pulled up. The hero eventually makes his way up, sometimes aided by a surviving demon or a magic bird, hunts down and punishes the treacherous companions and marries one of the princesses.[4]

In examining the Grendel section of *Beowulf*, Panzer noted a number of points where he thought that the poem followed the pattern of the folktale:

- Hroðgar's splendid hall matches the house in the woods.[5]
- Grendel compares with the 'Earthman' demon (*Erdmann*) in the folktale.[6]
- Like the demon in the folktale, Grendel appears at night, provoked by the merry noises of Hroðgar's court.[7]
- Beowulf's youth, unusual strength, early heroic deeds (such as the swimming match with Breca), and lack of promise as a boy all match the characteristics of the hero in the Bear's Son Tale.[8]
- The poem's description of Beowulf lying awake to wait for the monster while his companions sleep, the fight itself, the demon's immunity to weapons, the wounding of the demon and his escape as his arm is torn off, and finally, the display of Grendel's severed limb as a trophy, were all, according to Panzer, motifs which were to be found in the different versions of the folktale as well.[9]
- In the folktale the demon also leaves a bloody track, which the hero follows, and he sometimes has a mother, although revenge of the kind that we find in *Beowulf* does not occur in any versions of the folktale.[10]
- Unferð is cast in the mould of the Bear Son's cowardly retainers.[11]
- The demon's treasure-filled underwater lair in *Beowulf*, the fire burning in the cave, the hero's battle against Grendel's mother, his discovery of a magic sword, the killing of the demon with her own weapon, and Beowulf's attack on the already dead Grendel and the Danes who leave the mere were all items that matched the folktale in Panzer's view. He had to admit, however, that in *Beowulf* no princesses are rescued by the hero.[12]

Panzer then turned to the account of Beowulf's fight against the dragon and, as he had done previously with the Grendel section, found it to contain essential folktale elements, although he did not find them to stem from the Bear's Son Tale.[13]

In his analysis of *Grettis saga*, Panzer determined that the folktale had left the same unmistakable marks on it that he had discovered in *Beowulf*:

- As in the folktale, the demon appears three times at Sandhaugar and is attacked by the hero on her third visit.[14]
- The troll-woman, her knife, and her trencher all have their counterparts in the different versions of the Bear's Son Tale, and so does her disappearance following the loss of her arm.[15]
- Steinn, the priest, corresponds to the companions of the folktale in his failure to guard the rope properly. His name is also close to that of the *Steinmensch* in a Faroese version of the folktale.[16]
- In some versions of the Bear's Son Tale the hero must pass through water to reach the abode of the monsters. The cave, the fire, the sword on the wall, and the discovery of treasure are all familiar features, although the author of the saga is not keeping to the pattern of the folktale when he has Grettir kill the giant with his own weapon instead of with the sword for which the giant reaches during his encounter with the hero. The bones that Grettir carries from the cave do not fit the folktale pattern either; however, Panzer believed that they played a role in shaming the priest for his cowardice.[17]
- Although, unlike the Bear Son's unfaithful companions, Steinn is not directly punished, he is reprimanded by Grettir.[18]
- There are, of course, no princesses in the Sandhaugar episode, but Steinvǫr, the lady of the farm, is certainly a lady in distress. The affair that she has with Grettir, and the son that they have together, easily casts her into the role of one of the princesses of the Bear's Son Tale in Panzer's view.[19]
- Panzer also believed that as a hero Grettir conformed with the model of the strong but unruly and unpromising boy of the folktale who, like Grettir, performs various feats of strength, although he has no taste for ordinary work.[20]
- Grettir's adventure in the gravemound of Kárr the Old, Panzer considered to be a variant of the Bear's Son Tale. It included standard elements such as entry into the underworld, an unfaithful companion watching over a rope, and the presence of a treasure, and, in addition, Panzer felt that Þorfinnr's calm reaction to Grettir's breaking into his father's burial place made no sense unless versions of the folktale in which a boy goes out in search of treasure for his master were taken into account. In other words, Panzer believed the Kárr episode to be a substitute for an earlier passage of the Bear's Son

type in the saga, of which Þorfinnr's emotional tranquility over Grettir's breaking into his father's burial mound was a relic.[21]

- Grettir's fight with the bear, his swimming trips to fetch fire while in Norway and in Drangey, and many of the various feats of strength that the saga ascribes to him, as well as the story of the maiden who sees Grettir naked on the beach, were all features for which Panzer found corresponding episodes in some version of the folktale.[22]

In comparing *Beowulf* and *Grettis saga* in terms of how well each work had preserved the original folktale, Panzer found the Old English poem, generally speaking, closer to it than the saga. He noted that in the Sandhaugar episode the troll-woman should not be out of her lair, that the motivation given by the saga for Grettir's journey into the gorge is poor, that a lame sword motif is present in the episode which occurs once he is inside the giant's cave, and that the wounded troll-woman is completely absent from the cave. On the other hand, however, he believed that *Grettis saga* had preserved features from the original tale such as the threefold appearance of the unknown demon, her arrival at midnight armed with a sword and a trencher, the cutting off of the demon's arm, the descent to the underworld by means of a rope, and the discovery of the giant alive once the hero is inside his cave.[23] It may also be noted that in spite of his initial categorical insistence that *Beowulf* and *Grettis saga* were independent versions of the same folktale,[24] Panzer appears to have revised his ideas on this subject towards the end of his book, where he allows for the possibility of some form of contact either with an early Scandinavian version of the *Beowulf* story or with a poem close to the version of *Beowulf* we now have.[25] Perhaps he made this unexpected concession in order to defend himself against foreseeable criticism, because in his discussion of *Beowulf* and *Grettis saga* hardly a word had been said about the literary parallel upon which so much of the debate in previous scholarship had focused – namely the famous *hæftmece-heptisax* pair – and this allowed Panzer to get past that obstacle.

In the decades that followed the publication of his book, many *Beowulf* scholars accepted Panzer's ideas, either partially or fully. It is for instance obvious from Chambers's work on *Beowulf* that, although it did not quite convince him, Panzer's theory gave him much case for thought. Chambers was prepared to accept that bits and pieces of the Bear's Son story had influenced the common ancestor of *Beowulf* and *Grettis saga*, and he was even willing to admit that a version of the tale might have left its mark on the Sandhaugar episode.[26] But he was, at the same time, critical of Panzer's method,[27] and he did not agree with him that the Bear's Son story formed the core of both works or that no further connection between them need be postulated. After having con-

sidered the elements of the folktale, Chambers argued his case against Panzer
as follows:

Now it may be objected, with truth, that this is not like the *Beowulf*-story, or even particularly like the *Grettir*-story. But the question is not merely whether it resembles these
stories as we possess them, but whether it resembles the story which must have been the
common origin of both. And we have only to try to reconstruct from *Beowulf* and from
the *Grettis saga* a tale which can have been the common original of both, to see that it
must be something extraordinarily like the folk-tale outlined above.

For example, it is true that the departure of the Danes homeward because they believe
that Beowulf has met his death in the water below, bears only the remotest resemblance
to the deliberate treachery which the companions in the folk-tale mete out to the hero.
But when we compare the *Grettir*-story, we see there that a real breach of trust is
involved, for there the priest Stein leaves the hero in the lurch, and abandons the rope by
which he should have drawn Grettir up. This can hardly be an innovation on the part of
the composer of the *Grettis saga*, for he is quite well disposed towards Stein, and has no
motive for wantonly attributing treachery to him. The innovation presumably lies in the
Beowulf-story, where Hrothgar and his court are depicted in such a friendly spirit that no
disreputable act can be attributed to them, and consequently Hrothgar's departure home
must not be allowed in any way to imperil or inconvenience the hero. A comparison of
the *Beowulf*-story with the *Grettir*-story leads then to the conclusion that in the oldest
version those who remained above when the hero plunged below *were* guilty of some
measure of disloyalty in ceasing to watch for him. In other words we see that the further
we track the *Beowulf*-story back, the more it comes to resemble the folk-tale.[28]

Chambers expanded on this view later in his book and added that the chosen
retainers whom Beowulf has taken with him on his journey to combat Grendel
'could not be represented as unfaithful, because the poet was reserving the episode of the faithless retainers for the death of Beowulf.'[29] He also pointed to the
hæftmece-heptisax parallel and the strange conclusion drawn by the watcher(s)
in *Beowulf* and *Grettis saga* from the blood-stained water as elements that were
altogether absent from Panzer's folktale.[30] Chambers's final verdict on Panzer's
theory was that he had indeed shown that the Grendel episode of *Beowulf* was
an epic glorification of a folktale motif, but the absence of the three princesses
in the poem made it impossible to regard it as one of the different versions of
Panzer's Bear Son's Tale. 'At most,' Chambers concluded, 'it is a version of a
portion of them. The omission of the princesses in *Beowulf* and the *Grettis saga*
is fundamental. With the princesses much else falls away. There is no longer
any motive for the betrayal of trust by the watchers. The disguise of the hero
and his vengeance are now no longer necessary to the tale.'[31]

Chambers was not the only critic to give Panzer's work a mixed review. Carl W. von Sydow failed to see much of a comparison between Steinn's leaving the rope in *Grettis saga* and the treason of the Bear's Son's companions in the folktale.[32] Von Sydow was, like Chambers, inclined to think that the saga had borrowed both Steinn and the rope that he is supposed to watch over from the folktale; however, the two parted company over Chambers's supposition that the Bear's Son Tale might have influenced the common ancestor to *Beowulf* and *Grettis saga*, a theory that von Sydow rejected completely.[33] Fernand Mossé, in the introduction to his French translation of *Grettis saga*, included a brief chapter devoted to explicating Panzer's analysis of the saga which Mossé, for the most part, accepted. Mossé thought that Panzer had gone too far, though, in trying to discover stolen princesses in the Sandhaugar episode; it did not have any, and Steinvǫr would not do as a substitute.[34]

Nevertheless, many critics have been prepared to accept Panzer's theory with all of its ramifications. In America, W.W. Lawrence hailed it as 'a landmark in the investigation of *Beowulf*,'[35] and, on the other side of the Atlantic, Walter J. Sedgefield, in his 1935 edition of *Beowulf*, also praised Panzer's contribution: 'The great merit of Panzer's exhaustive study is that it throws new light upon the development of those Scandinavian sagas which deal with strong men fighting with monsters, and enables us to view the Beowulf story in something like a proper perspective.'[36] In recent years Panzer's line of investigation has been defended and continued by scholars such as E.E. Wardale,[37] Gwyn Jones,[38] Joaquín M. Pizarro,[39] Richard L. Harris,[40] and Peter A. Jorgensen.[41]

In their efforts to keep Panzer's ideas alive, these and other sympathetic scholars have, however, had to fight a constant battle against the tide of criticism to which Panzer's book has been exposed ever since its publication. First of all, his basic method has certain disturbing implications. Panzer collected relatively modern versions of the Bear's Son Tale, and in using them to construct an ancient original version and for comparison with *Beowulf* and *Grettis saga*, he obviously had to assume that the basic story had remained unchanged in its structure for more than a thousand years. Although folklorists like Vladimir Propp, Antti Aarne, and Stith Thompson insist on the relative stability of the folktale as a form of narrative,[42] their views hardly justify Panzer's assumption.[43] Secondly, Panzer's method of reducing different versions of the story to schematized summaries has come under intense criticism. Decades ago, Carl W. von Sydow pointed out that two very different stories can be made to produce the same composite pattern, and argued that a pattern which is obtained in this manner proves nothing about a relationship between the stories in question. He also drew attention to how different the narrative elements of the Bear's Son Tale are from the Grendel episode, although structurally they might be made to appear similar:

- In the different versions of the Bear's Son Tale, the demon most commonly only inhabits the house in the woods during the day.
- The demon is almost always a little dwarf with a long beard.
- The hero always uses a rope to get to the demon's under-ground lair.
- In most versions of the folktale there is no water that the hero has to pass through in his quest of the demon, and hence no swimming either.
- A princess or all three princesses are present in 190 of the 200 variants of the story.
- The hero's discovery of the princesses is always what motivates his helpers to betray him.

Von Sydow also pointed to several essential elements of the Grendel episode that are completely missing in the Bear's Son Tale:

- The king is harassed by the demon in his palace until the hero comes to his aid.
- The warriors who are supposed to keep watch have fallen asleep when the demon attacks.
- The hero tears off the demon's arm.
- Revenge is exacted by the demon's mother.
- No rope is used to reach the demon's abode.
- The magic sword is only discovered by the hero when it looks as though he will succumb to the demon in the fight against her.
- One of the demons is beheaded in order to bring its head back as a trophy.
- The demon's sword melts.
- The demon's blood on the water leads the hero's companions to think that it is the hero who is dead.[44]

In this comparison von Sydow came to the same conclusion as Klaeber, namely that similarities between the Bear's Son Tale and the Grendel episode were 'remote and generally vague.'[45] R.C. Boer went even further by accusing Panzer of assembling unrelated bits and pieces, particularly in *Grettis saga*, to make the Sandhaugar episode fit into the narrative pattern of the folktale.[46]

Furthermore, von Sydow and Chambers were critical of Panzer for his lack of geographical discrimination or attention to landscape in his comparisons of the Bear's Son Tale with *Beowulf* and *Grettis saga*.[47] It was also pointed out that Old English literature on the whole showed no signs of being influenced by this folktale.[48] The same may be said about early Scandinavian literature. J. Michael Stitt, who surveys the Scandinavian versions of the folktale in his book *Beowulf and the Bear's Son*, notes that only two motifs from it – those of treacherous abandonment and the abduction of women – are present in two late medieval Icelandic sagas, and that there is no firm evidence of the actual presence of the Bear's Son Tale in Scandinavia until the beginning of the eighteenth century.[49] Stitt also notes that in Scandinavian versions of the folktale, the hero is never associated with water.[50]

In conclusion, it must be said that, all in all, the criticism against Panzer's 'Bear's Son' theory outweighs his evidence concerning the supposed relationship between *Beowulf* and *Grettis saga* as two versions of the Bear's Son Tale. The basic shortcomings of Panzer's thesis, particularly the alleged connection between the folktale and the Sandhaugar episode, have, in the decades that have passed since his book appeared, not been repaired by anything that his followers have had to offer. The great weakness in Panzer's theory is that several of the motifs that he found in the three stories and used as special evidence to connect them – for example, the unpromising youth, great feats of strength, and the abandonment of the hero by his companions – are commonly found in medieval texts that have nothing whatsoever to do with the Bear's Son Tale.[51] As Theodore M. Andersson has recently pointed out, the folktale context that Panzer insisted on using as a basis for his comparison is simply 'too universal.'[52] In his investigation of the two hundred variants of the tale, Panzer never succeeded in finding a single version that corresponded motif by motif to the saga episode, and only a discovery of that kind would have been the sort of proof that might have clinched his argument. The few real similarities that are to be detected between the Grendel episode of *Beowulf*, the Sandhaugar episode of *Grettis saga*, and the different versions of the Bear's Son Tale can only be a coincidence that has probably come about because all three share a basic theme in the sense that they describe a hero's destruction of an evil being.

8

The Common Origin Theory

Among the different theories that compete to offer an explanation as to how *Grettis saga* and *Beowulf* might be related, there is no question that the original one suggested by Guðbrandur Vigfússon more than a century ago has always been the most popular among medievalists. As with the English Hypothesis, the Common Origin Theory is here used as an umbrella term, because there are, as we shall see in this chapter, considerable differences in how Vigfússon's followers imagine contact between the poem and the saga to have come about. However, the core of agreement that all variants of this theory share is that they postulate a common ancestor for the two works: Vigfússon's 'old legend.' In its most conservative form, the Common Origin Theory has it that the author of *Grettis saga* knew poems or stories related to the Old English epic.[1] Most Common Origin Theory critics, however, are not this modest. They usually work on the assumption that both the saga author and the composer of *Beowulf* had access to and used the same form of the 'old legend' and, armed with this conviction, they have mercilessly used *Grettis saga* to emend *Beowulf* or vice versa.

What commonly characterizes critics who have embraced this theory is a desire to find rational solutions to problems in both the saga and the poem. It is to this group that we owe the myth about the so-called realism of the Sandhaugar episode. Their line of approach demands *a priori* that the saga preserve a clearer version of the 'old legend' than *Beowulf*. This attitude is particularly explicit in W.W. Lawrence's *Beowulf and Epic Tradition*: 'One thing is obvious: that the straightforward account in the saga cannot have been derived, even indirectly, from the epic. The saga is clear where the epic is confused; it preserves the original form of the story so much better that it may even be used to explain obscure incidents and description in the Anglo-Saxon.'[2]

Along with W.W. Lawrence, R.W. Chambers gradually emerged as the chief promoter and defender of the Common Origin Theory. Chambers rejected the English Hypothesis on the grounds that Old English had been unintelligible in medieval Iceland and that the Sandhaugar episode could not have been constructed from *Beowulf*. He also rested his case on the strong cultural ties between England and Scandinavia:

> Other stories which were current in England in the eighth century were also current in Scandinavia in the thirteenth. Yet this does not mean that the tales of Hroar and Rolf, or of Athils and Ali, were borrowed from English epic accounts of Hrothgar and Hrothulf, or Eadgils and Onela. They were part of the common inheritance – as much so as the strong verbs or the alliterative line. Why then, contrary to all analogy, should we assume a literary borrowing in the case of the *Beowulf-Grettir* story?[3]

As for the logic behind the Common Origin Theory, Chambers believed that Lawrence's landscape theory had proven once and for all the validity of Vigfússon's original hypothesis.[4] However, Chambers must have found the Sandhaugar episode a meagre tale, because gradually he began to look for other Icelandic materials that could qualify as *Beowulf* analogues and make it possible for him to put together an outline of what he believed to be the original story. Eventually, his reconstruction of the 'old legend' rested not only on *Beowulf* and *Grettis saga*, but also on two other late sagas, *Samsons saga fagra*[5] and *Gull-Þóris saga*, and on an Icelandic folktale, *Gullbrá og Skeggi*. What Chambers distilled from these raw materials to 'reconstruct' his 'old legend' we shall see later in this chapter.

On most aspects of the Common Origin Theory, Lawrence and Chambers were in perfect agreement, but as we saw in the previous chapter, they – and Common Origin Theory critics in general – disagreed on the question as to how much the Bear's Son Tale was supposed to have influenced the 'old legend.' The location of the homeland of the 'old legend' was another issue on which Common Origin Theory critics have traditionally differed. Some, like Lawrence and Chambers, preferred a solution based on Vigfússon's idea:

> A widespread *märchen*, in a form determined by the mountainous country of the Scandinavian peninsula, was attached, in Scandinavian territory, to the hero Beowulf, and placed in a historical setting. In one incident of this story, the hero fought with a supernatural being in a cave under a waterfall. Brought to England, still in the form of lays, it was ultimately worked over, with other material, into the present epic ... The tale continued to live on in Scandinavia, both in its independent *märchen*-form, and as united with *Beowulf*. In a version pretty close to that taken to England and made the basis of the Anglo-Saxon epic, it was added to the exploits of Grettir Asmundarson, a historical per-

sonage of the eleventh century. The *Grettissaga*, which preserves much of original form of the story, thus enables us to see more clearly what was the original setting of the second adventure in *Beowulf*.[6]

Henrik Schück, on the other hand, imagined an even more complicated scenario:

1 / In its earliest form the 'old legend' is Danish but has no attachments to historical figures or events.

2 / In the next stage the legend incorporates historical material in Denmark. That version of the story is brought to England, but the unhistorical form of the story also lives on in Denmark.

3 / In Denmark the unhistorical version of the legend also eventually becomes a historical epic and is again brought to England, where in the meantime the legend has degenerated to an unhistorical folktale which, in that form, spreads to Scandinavia where it ultimately links up with stories about Grettir.[7]

Daring as Schück's proposed meandering of the 'old legend' may seem, he is still not nearly as imaginative as an earlier critic, John Earle, who gives the transmission of the 'old legend' a fixed date in his *Anglo-Saxon Literature*:

The identity [of events in the Sandhaugar episode and in *Beowulf*] is so manifest that we only have to ask which people (if either) was the borrower, the English or the Danes. And here comes in the consideration that the geography of the 'Beowulf' is Scandinavian. There is no consciousness of Britain or England throughout the poem. If this raises a presumption that the Saxon poet got his story from a Dane, we naturally ask, When is this likely to have happened? and the answer must be that the earliest probable time begins after the Peace of Wedmore in 878.[8]

Other critics have been more careful about committing themselves to a specific set of circumstances. Thus Klaeber, in his edition of the poem, merely states that 'a genetic relation of some kind must clearly be admitted between the *Beowulf* and certain Scandinavian stories, in particular the one attached to Grettir the Strong.'[9] H. Munro and Nora Chadwick are uncommitted about the location of the 'old legend' over and above placing it somewhere in the North,[10] and Eugen Mogk also belongs to this moderate camp, in the sense that he does not believe that it is possible to decide whether the story ultimately had a Danish or an English origin.[11]

There is also disagreement among whose who subscribe to the Common Origin Theory over the Glámr episode in *Grettis saga*. As we saw in chapter 1, some critics accept it as a bona fide genetically related analogue to *Beowulf* while others have rejected it. Scholars who accept Glámr usually maintain that his fight with Grettir corresponds to Beowulf's struggle against Grendel in Hroðgar's hall. It then follows that the first fight in the Sandhaugar episode loses its primary status since it is only an echo of a previous chapter of the saga. C.S. Smith, who argues along these lines, presents his case as follows:

> Comparing now the descriptions in Gretti [i.e., *Grettis saga*] of his two encounters in the hall, first with Glám and second with the evil-spirit, we shall find them to be identical. The same incidents are repeated in the same order. It is a trait well known to Icelandic students that the same incident is made at times to do double duty in the same saga. Hence in our mind there rests little doubt as to the identity between Glám and the hall-haunter of the second tale, for the difference in the catastrophe does not, to our view, entitle the latter to other distinction than that of being regarded as another form of the same legend. But how much more graphic, more masterly in all its parts, is the story of the wrestling with Glám. Unquestionably that is the original, and the other the copy.[12]

But on the status of Glámr, Smith is probably only speaking for a minority of Common Origin Theory critics. Most of them seem to have accepted Chambers's argument that the double fight of the Grendel story only compares to the double fight at Sandhaugar.[13]

Common Origin Theory critics have also disagreed on the question as to how to view the female monsters in the poem and the saga. On this issue Chambers maintained – with a curiously anti-feminist slant – that *Beowulf* preserved the original story while *Grettis saga* had altered the roles of the male and the female monsters:

> in the *Grettis saga* it is the female monster who raids the habitation of men, the male who stays at home in his den. In this the *Grettis saga* probably represents a corrupt tradition: for, that the female should remain at home whilst the male searches for his prey, is a rule that holds good for devils as well as for men. The change was probably made in order to avoid the difficulty – which the *Beowulf* poet seems also to have realized – that after the male has been slain, the rout of the female is felt to be a deed of less note – something of an anti-climax.[14]

In *The Art of Beowulf*, Arthur Brodeur contradicts this view and comes to the aid of the ladies. Brodeur believes that *Grettis saga* preserves the original conception of the female as the more dangerous adversary and finds Grettir's battle with the giant in the Sandhaugar episode to be an anti-climax.[15]

The main conflict among Common Origin Theory followers has, however, always been over the nature and shape of the 'old legend,' and this issue has been hotly debated ever since Guðbrandur Vigfússon announced his discovery of *Grettis saga* as a genetically related *Beowulf* analogue. Vigfússon never speculated much about the nature or the form of the 'old legend' that he had postulated, and quite possibly, he expected that it would eventually be found somewhere. After a few decades of fruitless searching, Common Origin Theory critics had to come to terms with the fact that if they wanted the legend, they would have to invent it themselves. One of the earliest such 'reconstructions' was offered by Chambers in 1929. Chambers culled his ingredients from *Samsons saga fagra*, in addition to *Beowulf* and *Grettis saga* and produced from these three sources the following summary of the 'old legend,' which he characterized as the 'residuum which is left when we have eliminated from each version what is peculiar to itself':

A creature with supernatural powers ravages a place and carries off human beings. In *Beowulf* the victims are the retainers from the King's Hall: in the *Sandhaugar* episode, the goodman and his servant: in the *Samsons saga* the Princess Valintina. In the first two cases the victims are taken by force from the hall, in the third case the Princess is enticed further and further into the forest. The ravager himself wanders abroad, but he has a mother who lives in a cave. (In the *Sandhaugar* episode the sexes have been reversed: but we have seen that this is probably a corruption.) This cave is situated behind a waterfall. This is expressed quite clearly in the *Grettis saga* and *Samsons saga*, for in Scandinavian lands vast waterfalls are familiar things, and the word *foss* is there to hand. In the Old English we have mention of the 'mountain torrent descending,' the 'mingled water rising up' (apparently the spray), and the 'water below the level of the ground': all pointing to a waterfall, although the position of the cave relative to the waterfall is not defined.

A champion arrives from a far distance, he has come purposely to the rescue. This must be an original feature of the story: for in the *Grettis saga* it persists, although quite inappropriate. Grettir, since his struggle with Glam, has been haunted by 'Glam's eyes,' and he fears the dark above all things: yet he is represented as seeking deliberately to encounter these dwellers in darkness. In *Beowulf* and the *Sandhaugar* episode the champion awaits the attack of the ravisher within the house, wrestles with and defeats him. In the *Samsons saga* Kvintalin does not come in at this stage, as he is reserved for another fate. In *Beowulf* and the *Sandhaugar* episode the hero is not completely successful: the enemy gets away with the loss of an arm, and, though this proves fatal, the conqueror has not the satisfaction of showing the corpse. Subsequently the hero plunges (in *Samson*, is plunged) into the water, where he grapples with a creature who is the mother of the ravisher. (In the *Grettis saga* the relations of male and female are of course reversed, as stated above.) The hero then penetrates into a cave behind the waterfall. (In *Beowulf* the account is ambiguous: at one time the monster appears to have carried the hero to the bottom, at another he seems to enter the cave and grapple with her. In the *Grettis saga* the hero enters the cave before he attacks his foe: in the *Samsons saga* the fight takes place at the bottom of the water: thus each of the two Scandinavian sagas follows one of the versions which seem to be combined in *Beowulf*.) In all versions a special point is made of the blood or entrails of the foe falling into the water. The hero finds treasure in the cave, but the story emphasises his taking things interesting rather than rich. (In *Beowulf* he takes nothing but Grendel's head and the hilt: in the *Grettis saga* emphasis is placed upon the bones: in the *Samsons saga* upon the personal trinkets of the Princess Valintina.) A watcher or watchers above (in *Beowulf* there are many) believe the hero to be dead. In all three cases the watchers above are led to believe that the hero is dead by observing the blood-stained water. The hero returns back in safety.[16]

In this first attempt at a reconstruction, Vigfússon's favourite element, the *hæftmece-heptisax* parallel, is noticeably absent, but Chambers, who later emended his summary in his book on *Beowulf*,[17] eventually found a way to include it: 'In *Beowulf*, *Grettir* and *Gull-Thorir* the sword which the hero meets below is characterized by its *haft* or *hilt*.'[18] The emended summary also has it that the gold in the monster's cave is cursed, and that the hero leaves the treasure behind for that reason.[19] Despite these improvements, Chambers's summary is quite vague. The Sandhaugar trolls and Grendel now descend from 'a creature with supernatural powers,' and there is no motivation for his attacks. By the same token, Beowulf and Grettir are made to hearken back to a champion from afar. Chambers and all subsequent reconstructors of the 'old legend' consider the monster's loss of an arm to be a key element which the original story contained. This is, as James Carney has pointed out, a double-edged piece of evidence:

Only in *Beowulf* and in the *Grettissaga* is there no logical reason why the arm should be hewn off. So far from proving independent origins rather does comparison point to the following conclusion: *the hewing off of the monster's arm in Beowulf must have been motivated in the original source by the arm being exposed when the rest of the body was hidden.* The *Beowulf* poet has here departed from the general picture, and the fact that the *Grettissaga* agrees with *Beowulf* in this innovation, like the *haeftmece/heptisax* agreement, points to borrowing rather than remote inheritance from a common Germanic original.[20]

These and other weaknesses in Chambers's reconstruction are understandable; he never attempts to use *Grettis saga* and *Beowulf* alone, and the outcome of trying to squeeze a common summary out of four texts is pretty bland prose.

Still, Chambers's reconstruction draws praise from Klaeber in his edition of the poem: Chambers has 'managed to reconstruct what may be considered the outlines of the original form of the Grendel story, in particular of the second adventure.'[21]

In 1950, Felix Genzmer offered a completely different version of the 'old legend' using the Bear's Son Tale, *Beowulf*, *Grettis saga*, and *Hrólfs saga kraka*[22] as his sources. Genzmer's reconstruction, which he calls 'The Geatish Saga of Biulf the Bear's Son' ('Die Gautische Saga von Biulf dem Bärensohn') is much more ambitious than Chambers's, as may be seen from the following summary:

Chapter 1: Beowulf ('Biulf') is born to a farmer's daughter. The father is a prince, Björn, whom a sorceress stepmother whose sexual advances the prince rejected turned into a bear. The boy is an unpromising but a very strong youth.

Chapter 2: Beowulf is taunted by Breki for his slackness and challenged to a swimming match. To everyone's surprise Beowulf outswims Breki. The king, Gauti, discovers that the boy is his grandson. The sorceress wife is killed.

Chapter 3: A giant who is a killer of men and cattle inhabits an island. Beowulf swims to this island and kills the giant.

Chapter 4: Beowulf turns the coward Wött into a hero by making him drink a wolf's blood.

Chapter 5: King Gauti builds himself a splendid hall. One Christmas night, when the king's retainers sleep, the hall is attacked by a troll. One of them is snatched away by the monster, who leaves bloody tracks behind. Next Christmas, King Gauti orders his men to keep watch, but towards midnight they all fall asleep, and again one of them is taken by the troll. On the third successive Christmas night, Beowulf offers to keep watch with twelve companions. The companions fall asleep, but Beowulf stays awake and fights the troll when it appears. They have a hand to hand struggle, the troll tries to get away but is held tight, and Beowulf's companions hack at it with their weapons but to no avail. Beowulf eventually rips the troll's arm off, and the monster escapes, leaving a trail of blood behind him.

Chapter 6: Beowulf, carrying his sword, Heptisax, follows the bloody trail to a waterfall. He lowers himself down by means of a rope. Behind the waterfall he discovers a cave where a fire is burning. By the fire he sees a huge trollwoman who is the mother of the attacker. Beowulf attacks her with his Heptisax, but the sword will not wound her, and he throws it down. He then catches sight of a giant sword, Gullinhjalti,[23] hanging on the wall in the cave, wrests himself free from the embrace of the troll-wife, seizes the sword, and decapitates her. She falls to the ground and her blood runs into the river.

Beowulf then proceeds to explore the cave, finds the wounded male troll, decapitates him as well, and then leaves the cave, taking Gullinhjalti with him. Above the cave the men who were supposed to be watching the rope see blood on the water, assume that Beowulf is dead, and leave. Only Wött remains. Beowulf returns in triumph to King Gauti's palace, presents the giant sword to him, and receives lands and honours in return.

Chapter 7: A dragon inhabits a cave full of cursed treasure. A golden cup is sto-len from the treasure and presented to Beowulf. Beowulf, again with twelve companions, sets out to fight the dragon. The retainers, except Wött, flee the scene of battle, Beowulf is killed in the fight, Wött kills the dragon. A funeral pyre is erected, and people mourn Beowulf's death.[24]

Genzmer believed this version of the 'old legend' to have been current in Scandinavia from the sixth century onward, and to have spread from there to England and Iceland where all but the troll fight and the swimming competition in the story was lost.[25] This basic assumption is probably the weakest link in Genzmer's theory. It is also unlikely that 'Heptisax' was the name of the sword in the original story. As Chambers points out in his book on *Beowulf*, the name of the sword would have to have been very important in the 'old legend' to sur-vive in its two late descendants, *Beowulf* and *Grettis saga*,[26] whereas in Genz-mer's reconstruction 'Heptisax' as a name has no special function or meaning. In respect to the Grendel story and the Sandhaugar episode, Genzmer – as opposed to Lawrence and Chambers – believed *Beowulf* to retain more original features of the story than *Grettis saga*.[27]

Twenty years after the publication of Genzmer's hypothesis, Larry D. Ben-son proposed yet another version of the 'old legend' in his article, 'The Origi-nality of *Beowulf*':

A hero hears of a strange monster who regularly attacks and carries off the inhabitants of some dwelling. The hero agrees to remain all night in that dwelling while its owner stays away. He is attacked by the monster, who tries to drag him away. He manages to detach an arm from the monster, and the monster falls into some inland body of water where he lives. The hero dives into the water, while one or more of his friends wait above. Beneath the water he finds a dwelling place, where he encounters another monster, of opposite sex from the first, who has treasure, the body or bodies of those he has slain, and a valu-able sword (perhaps magical in an even earlier version). After a fierce struggle, the hero manages to stab the monster. His friend or friends waiting above see the blood in the water and leave, concluding that he has been killed. But he emerges from the water with some token of his adventure, and those who thought he was dead rejoice. This is accounted a great deed, for it purged the land of the monsters that afflicted it.[28]

'We could quibble,' writes Benson, 'about some of the details of this recon-struction, but I think all could agree that it does account for both the episode in the Norse saga and the central fable of the Old English poem.'[29] This simply is not true. As we have already seen, Beowulf does not dive into an 'inland body of water'; the giant's cave in the Sandhaugar episode is not 'beneath the water,' it is behind it; Beowulf does not discover any 'body or bodies' of those the monster has slain in the monster's lair; *Grettis saga* says nothing about 'a valu-able sword' in the giant's cave; and finally, it would take a great deal of literary imagination to be able to call Grettir's fight with the giant in the cave 'a fierce struggle.'

The latest reconstruction effort to date comes from Anatoly Liberman in his article 'Beowulf-Grettir,' published in 1986:

The hero kills a cannibal devastating a large area. The cannibal is described as an evil spirit, so the hero assumes the role of an exorcist, a shaman, and not only rids the people of a monster but cleanses the area of a demon. This demon is proof against all swords except his own or against all weapons in general, but in his combat with the hero he is unarmed only because he does not anticipate resistance. Having no other choice, the hero crushes his opponent by main force. However, the misfortunes of the people soon begin anew, because the cannibal's mother or dam attempts to avenge her son or mate. The monster's habitat is a cave at the bottom of the sea or lake. The hero arms himself with a sword, a gift from his host or simply a sword of great renown, and descends to the bot-tom. He is attacked by the female monster but is unable to injure her, because his sword unexpectedly fails him and because she fights with her own magic sword, the only one that can bring her death; the magic is contained in the haft. The hero wrests the *hæft-mece/heptisax* from the monster and kills her with it. (But this sword can be used only once: when the hero wants to take it as a trophy, it melts, and nothing remains but the magic haft.) The hero returns to the shore where no one expects to see him alive.[30]

This fantasy is so far removed from events as they actually transpire in the Sandhaugar episode that it could never be its literary ancestor. But Liberman's attempt is neither better nor worse than those of Chambers, Genzmer, or Ben-son. All four base their reconstructions on different sources, and the outcome is four very different versions of the 'old legend.' As the reconstruction efforts of these critics show, the Common Origin Theory has given its followers a chance to be creative in the highest degree and ample opportunity to invent bits and pieces of the 'old legend' – to make it as it should have been – even if it meant that they had to emend both the poem and the saga in doing so. This cannot be an acceptable working method, and the results are not impressive. An enthusi-astic Common Origin Theory follower, Óskar Halldórsson, had to admit reluctantly as late as 1982 that the 'old legend' had, for more than a century, eluded scholars in their attempts to reconstruct it,[31] – and one might add that it will most certainly continue to do so.

In addition to feuding over the contents and structure of the 'old legend,' Common Origin Theory scholars have had to defend their theories against criticism from sceptics who, not surprisingly, consist mainly of those who favour the English Hypothesis. The Achilles heel of Guðbrandur Vigfússon's idea is obviously that the 'old legend' is nowhere to be found, and scholars who are critical of the Common Origin Theory were quick to point this out.[32] The Lawrence–Chambers approach also asks us – against all common sense – to believe that the Icelandic *Grettis saga* analogue, which is anywhere from three hundred to five hundred years later than *Beowulf*, preserves the basic outline of the Grendel story better than the Old English poem. We are furthermore told that in the comparison of these analogues some features, for instance the nature of the heroes and the monsters, are completely interchangeable, whereas others, such as landscapes, settings, and various details are preserved more or less intact by both *Beowulf* and *Grettis saga*. One would expect heroic exploits of the kind that the 'old legend' is presumed to have described to be linked to a specific, named hero, and a glance at *Beowulf* is enough to show us that heroic deeds are always linked to someone's name. If this was the case, was the hero's name forgotten, whereas the tale of his adventure survived in the Old English poem and the Icelandic saga? Not very likely.

Critics were also sceptical about the reluctance of Common Origin Theory scholars to discuss the origin of their 'old legend.' In his *Germanische Heldensage*, Hermann Schneider asked Chambers three questions that Chambers had carefully avoided dealing with in his book on *Beowulf*. Specifically, Schneider wanted to know where the 'old legend' had come from, how old it was supposed to be and how it might have come about.[33] Understandably, Chambers had little to say about these issues, except to hazard a guess that perhaps the 'old legend' went back to the sixth century.[34] Klaeber, however, in an uncharacteristic flight of fancy, provided Schneider with some answers:

On the whole, it seems safest to attribute the undeniable parallelisms to the use of the same or similar Scandinavian sources both in the Old English and the Old Norse accounts. There existed, we may assume, on the one hand a tale – made over into a local legend – of the freeing of the Danish court from a strange monster through the prowess of a mighty warrior, and another one – like the former going back to a primitive folk-tale – about a similar adventure expanded to a fight with two monsters and placed in picturesque Scandinavian surroundings. Both kinds of narrative circulated orally in the North. In the course of time they were attached to various persons (two of whom are unques-

tionably historical characters), Bǫðvarr, Grettir, Ormr, Bēowulf respectively. A compara-
tively early combination of the two sets was perhaps effected in Scandinavia, though it is
actually traceable in the Anglo-Saxon epic only. The artistic *Beowulf* version represents
the final result of this formative process.[35]

It goes without saying that this theory does not rest on anything other than Klaeber's imagination.

To show that the Common Origin Theory really does prove that a relationship exists between *Beowulf* and *Grettis saga*, one would ideally want the 'old
legend' or something resembling it to be discovered. A fruitless search of more
than a century has not turned up anything, and it must be said that there is something very strange about the fact that only the authors of *Beowulf* and *Grettis
saga* appear to have known the 'old legend.' Writers in medieval Iceland would
not have ignored a story of the calibre that Common Origin Theory critics postulate, and in addition the Common Origin Theory asks us to believe that the
author of *Grettis saga* – who supposedly knew the whole story – only used bits
and pieces of it and buried them in an unimportant chapter of his saga to boot.
This simply is not a very believable scenario.

In the absence of finding the legend, one might apply the usefulness of this
theory as a criterion of its validity. Can the poem be used to explicate the saga
or vice versa? Here the answer is no: all such attempts have in the end done
more harm than good for the study of the two works. It has contributed nothing
that could verify the validity of this approach. What is perhaps worst about the
Common Origin Theory is its total disregard for the very different literary characteristics of *Beowulf* and *Grettis saga*. The *Beowulf* poet cares little about verisimilitude, or about being consistent, or about making the supernatural look
natural. He paints with words, so to speak, and is first and foremost a creator of
mood and atmosphere. The saga author, by contrast, is for the most part consistent, and he nearly always presents his material in a realistic, matter-of-fact
fashion and with an eye for detail. As W.S. Mackie warned sixty years ago in
his article 'The Demons' Home in *Beowulf*,' 'we should be cautious before filling ... gaps, or interpreting ... obscurities, with the aid of the *Grettissaga*. Otherwise we may, as it were, be attempting to complete *Kubla Khan* with the help of
Robinson Crusoe.'[36]

In view of these shortcomings the great popularity which the Common Origin Theory enjoys in *Beowulf* studies is nothing less than amazing. And its
power is not to be underestimated, as the following example demonstrates. In a
recent bilingual edition of the poem, the editor informs his readers – as a statement of fact – that the poem and the saga 'both go back independently to a common original.'[37] He then has the audacity – presumably on the strength of the

poem's secure ties to *Grettis saga* – to translate *hæftmece* as 'the sword with a long wooden hilt.'[38] Faith of this kind in the Common Origin Theory can only be defined, to borrow one of H.L. Mencken's phrases, as an illogical belief in the existence of the improbable.

9

The Big Bang Theory

The history of twentieth century research into the supposed genetic relationship of *Beowulf* and *Grettis saga* falls into two clearly marked stages. During the first half of the century, critics applied old-fashioned philological methods and presented their results in a careful, almost defensive, manner. They generally looked to *Grettis saga* for something that could match the double fight of the Grendel story, and only the Sandhaugar episode was generally accepted as a candidate that could meet that demand. Only the most daring researchers were prepared to admit the possibility that the 'old legend' might somehow have split into two, and only critics who thought along those lines included the Glámr episode as a genetically related *Beowulf* analogue. This was the critical landscape of Beowulf–Grettir studies until the 1950s, when two articles on the subject – Arnold Taylor's 'Two Notes on *Beowulf*' and Nora K. Chadwick's 'The Monsters and Beowulf' – appeared and changed it for good. What was revolutionary about these articles, particularly Taylor's, was that the relationship between the poem and the saga was no longer regarded merely as a likely possibility; it was now accepted as a proven fact. Once this line had been crossed, there was no longer any need to restrict one's search for analogous material to whole sections of the saga that resembled some part of the Grendel story; bits and pieces of the 'old legend' might be anywhere in the saga, and for that matter, anywhere in Old Norse literature. Although Taylor never said it in so many words, the underlying assumption of this new approach was that the 'old legend' had somehow exploded and left literary debris all over the place. And as Big Bang Theory explained the origin of the universe, so this new approach explained the fate of the 'old legend' and its relationship to *Grettis saga*. Critics who have followed this new line of approach have not produced uniform results in their research, so in this chapter, as before, the phrase the 'Big Bang Theory' is used as an umbrella term.

Chadwick's contribution lay mostly in her extremely liberal interpretation of what elements in the poem and the saga might be considered analogous and in her purely speculative arguments – arguments which the old philological school would never have found acceptable. The following statement, in which Chadwick equates the encounter with Glámr, the Sandhaugar episode and the Grendel story, may be taken as an example of her methodology:

I regard it as immaterial that the adventure against the trolls of Sandhaugar is represented as taking place some years later than the encounter with Glámr, and that some of the details of the two encounters have been interchanged ... The visit of Glámr's ghost, the *draugr*, corresponds to that of Grendel; and this is followed, as in *Beowulf*, by the visit of the *draugr's* mother, while Grettir's encounter with the *jötunn* under the waterfall, clearly represents the quietus of the *draugr* Glámr and, as in *Beowulf*, the final episode.[1]

It was also Nora Chadwick who inserted the unfortunate Norse term *draugr* ('ghost') – meaning, as she uses the word, an evil supernatural being of any kind – into the Beowulf–Grettir debate. In doing this, Chadwick casually wipes out all distinctions between the various monstrous opponents of Beowulf and Grettir. Although this cannot be regarded as an acceptable methodology, her opinions on the subject of *draugar* in *Beowulf* and *Grettis saga* have clearly influenced a number of *Beowulf* scholars.[2] In a recent book on *Beowulf*, George Clark, who accepts most of Chadwick's theory and has himself applied it to unearth an extremely deeply buried *Beowulf* analogue in *Njáls saga*,[3] explains how her article of 1959, 'The Monsters and Beowulf,' was years ahead of its time and therefore failed to convince most *Beowulf* critics:

The closest parallels to *Beowulf* are neither Panzer's folktales nor Fontenrose's myths but the various recreations of a traditional story that Nora K. Chadwick treated in a learned but knotty, and often neglected, article of 1959. In these stories, the adventure seems an inheritance to which various members of a noble family of the Gautar (the 'Geatas,' or Geats of *Beowulf*) or members of 'the Hálogaland family of Ketill Hængr' succeed. The heroes carry on a feud with three great enemies who are frequently themselves related: 'The *draugr* Agnarr and his variants; the dragon Hárekr; and an evil supernatural woman,' a triad clearly paralleling Grendel, Grendel's mother and the dragon. Though all the texts exemplifying this recurring story are later than *Beowulf*, it seems unlikely that the Anglo-Saxon poem is their source. A common tradition older than *Beowulf* must lie behind the Anglo-Saxon poem and the various versions of Chadwick's story of the noble hero and the three monsters, or, as she puts it, 'The theme is an old one, of a high and ancient literary lineage.'

For a variety of reasons, Chadwick's paper has not much influenced the consensus of opinion on the origins of *Beowulf*: in 1959 her conclusions did not fit the dominant critical movements; her article makes hard reading; and in 1959 only two of the sagas she cites were readily available in English translation – even published editions of the Old Norse texts themselves were not widely available. Moreover Chadwick's case seems liable to some objections. The sagas she cites are much later than *Beowulf* (but earlier than most of the folktales cited by Panzer). The hero's feud with the triad of enemies paralleling Grendel, Grendel's mother, and the dragon frequently come as episodes in stories of lives filled with supernatural encounters – hence skeptical readers might have concluded that the combination was merely accidental, not a connected and recurring theme. Moreover, only two of the texts she cites include a treasure-guarding, tomb-dwelling dragon, and neither of those were available in English.[4]

Arnold Taylor – and those critics who accepted the Glámr episode as an analogue before him – assumed that bits of the 'old legend' had been used and reused by the saga author, and on the basis this approach, Taylor proposed Grettir's fight with the brown bear and his breaking into the gravemound of Kárr the Old as new *Beowulf* analogues.[5] As we shall see in this chapter, later critics have found it unnecessary conservatism to limit their search for analogous bits to *Grettis saga*, or even to postulate any well defined relationship between the saga and *Beowulf*. Richard Harris, in his article 'The Deaths of Grettir and Grendel: A New Parallel,' pauses to reflect on this issue, and what he says is quite typical of an attitude that has characterized the last forty years in Beowulf–Grettir studies:

For the purposes of this study, it will be assumed that *Beowulf* and *Grettis saga* do possess versions of a portion of the folk-tales representative of The Bear's Son Tale but that the two works [i.e., *Beowulf* and *Grettis saga*] are more closely related to each other than to the Bear's Son Tale itself ... speculation on the precise relationship between *Beowulf* and *Grettis saga* appears idle and unproductive. It is enough to conclude, as nearly all have, that some connection exists between the two works, most likely involving an indirect common source.[6]

In recent decades, Peter Jorgensen has emerged as the main advocate for the Big Bang Theory. In his work on *Beowulf* and *Grettis saga*, he favours Panzer's theory concerning the origin of the 'old legend,' but not, of course, Panzer's view of how the poem and the saga are related. In an article entitled 'Additional Icelandic Analogues to *Beowulf*,' Jorgensen describes how the state of affairs in Beowulf-Grettir studies looks to him as a critic who favours the Big Bang Theory:

Since the flurry of investigations a half century ago, the ensuing years have produced a remarkably small number of Icelandic sagas with analogues to *Beowulf*. Flateyjarbók yielded *Þorsteins þáttr uxafóts* and a single family of heroes was discerned in *Herrauðs saga, Þorsteins þáttr bæjarmagns, Hálfdanar saga Eysteinssonar*, and *Harðar saga ok Hólmverja*. *Njáls saga* was added in 1971, and the numerous parallel motifs in *Hálfdanar saga Brönufóstra* were presented in 1975. It is appropriate that the beginning of the second centenary of scholarship on this particular connection between Old English and Icelandic literature should bring forth another group of analogues. With over two dozen works attesting to the popularity of the Bear's Son Folktale in Icelandic, it should almost be expected that bits and pieces of the story would surface elsewhere in the extensive corpus of Icelandic literature, often in much reduced form. It is immaterial here whether the tale arrived from England, Ireland, or Norway, in written or in oral form, or in any combination of the above, for only after all the parallels have been enumerated and studied will conclusions about the story's genesis gain added importance.[7]

Concerning the relationship between *Beowulf* and *Grettis saga*, Jorgensen assumes that a poem about the Grendel legend existed in Iceland before the saga was written.[8] But he does not think that *Grettis saga* should have the seat of honour as the best genetically related Icelandic analogue to *Beowulf*. According to Jorgensen, a late *fornaldarsaga*, *Hálfdanar saga Brönufóstra*, is even closer to the Old English epic,[9] both on 'points of correspondence ... which can be pointed to as hard facts as well as those which conjure up remembrances and feelings of the Old English version.'[10] Furthermore, Jorgensen believes that once all the bits and pieces left by the 'old legend' in variously mutated forms have been rounded up and collated, the story itself may be reconstructed from them:

Much as philological reconstruction reaches a point where an inductively arrived at system is used deductively to explain previously anomalous phenomena, so too, has research on the Bear's Son Folktale developed to the stage at which variants of the story known in post twelfth-century Iceland can be established. The motifs examined above [i.e., in late sagas such as: *Gunnars saga Keldunúpsfífls, Sörla saga sterka, Gríms saga loðinkinna, Örvar-Odds saga, Hjálmþés saga ok Ölvis*, etc.] have not been used in such reconstructions, but their affiliation by similarity of type, place of occurrence and by sequence cannot be denied. Their value lies in what they can tell us about the composition of a saga, for they show us the saga writers, as far back as *Grettis saga*, consciously altering a well-known story in order to create one or more additional adventures for the hero. One is able to discern authors of different abilities and inclinations, sometimes being very adept at incorporating pre-existing material (as in numerous passages in *Grettis saga*), sometimes poorly motivating the episode (as in *Ólafs saga Tryggvasonar*,

Þórodds þáttr Snorrasonar), sometimes reversing the roles of hero and monster (as in *Gunnars saga Keldunúpsfífls, Hálfdanar saga Eysteinssonar, Egils saga einhenda*), often becoming trapped into *non sequiturs* (as in *Göngu-Hrólfs saga, Hrana saga hrings*) and finally, even copying verbatim from their archetype (as in *Ála flekks saga*).[11]

What Jorgensen actually discovers in these sagas are, as remains of the 'old legend,' indeed items 'in much reduced form.' In another article entitled, 'The Two-Troll Variant of the Bear's Son Folktale in *Hálfdanar saga Brönufóstra* and *Gríms saga loðinkinna*,' Jorgensen finds no less than twenty-three 'hard facts' pointing to the 'old legend' in the first of these sagas:

To begin with, the hero, Hálfdan (#1) literally 'half-Dane,' is the son of Hring, king of Denmark, which dimly echoes the location of the hall in Denmark, Heorot, ruled over by the son of Healfdene, 'half-Dane,' who was king of the Hringdenes. Hálfdan, too, has sailed from home with some companions as has Beowulf, but the Icelandic version then shifts directly to the tracking down of the monsters' lair, which also corresponds to that arduous journey in *Beowulf*. Hálfdan's is a day-long trip, along an *einstigi* (#2), a way where one must proceed single file, finally overcoming a section so steep (#5) that he is obliged to pull himself up by his axe-handle. Beowulf, too, must master steep rock faces and stretches of path which can only be taken single file. Just as Beowulf is outfitted with a weapon given to him by the king's follower, Unferth, so too, Hálfdan is equipped with a weapon given him by earl Óttarr (#3). In both the epic and the saga a tracking down of the cave is involved, and the saga differs only apparently when the tracks are said to be chiseled into the mountain (#4), for the use of the word *spor* for a niche in stone in Icelandic is strange, the expected form being *skor*. It is likely that the original *spor*[,] meaning footprints[,] has been preserved from an older version, but given the difficult ascent of the hero up the face of a mountain and the phonetic similarity to *skor*, it was left unchanged but reinterpreted in the saga to mean niche or handhold. The large size of the adversaries is not specifically mentioned in the Icelandic, but it, too, can be deduced from the tracks being spaced four yards apart. Upon arriving at the well-known large cave (#6) Hálfdan perceives the inevitable bright fire or light (#7).

Since *Hálfdanar saga* has omitted the first wrestling match with the male giant, it is not surprising that he finds both the male and the female sitting by the fire (#8). (But Hálfdan still challenges the monsters one after the other, taking on the male first and decapitating it in the cave.) That the monsters in the saga are cannibalistic as in *Beowulf* is shown by the fact that they had a kettle over the fire containing horse meat and human flesh (#9), and the carrying off of people to their lair has been replaced by their being brought to the cave by the use of magic (#11). The female's name, Sleggja (#10), meaning a large hammer, especially one to use on iron or stone, may possibly be connected semantically with a proposed etymology for Grendel as the 'destroyer,' from the Old

English verb *grindan* 'to grind,' and her return to the main cave carrying a man under each arm (#12) reminds one of Grendel's[12] lumbering away bearing the body of Æschere and the arm of her son.

Thereupon Hálfdan rushes in and challenges the male giant first (#13), but beheading it in a manner reminiscent of Beowulf's violent decapitation of the already-dead Grendel deep in the cave (#14). In a small way it lends support to the theory that the second 'battle' with Grendel is a remnant of the common folktale version in which the giant first loses his arm in the wrestling match in the house, is chased into the cave and defeated again. Sleggja's recognition of the hero she has never met (#15) is not unknown in folktales, but here it is noteworthy because the bear's son folktale has the two-troll variant which allows the return of the male monster to the female and presumably the chance to relate the outcome of the first battle. The result in the Old English epic is the revenge sought by Grendel's dam.

During the battle down in the cave, there is evidence that the motif of the ogre vulnerable only to a special sword has not been lost in the saga, for it is implicit that the axe used to decapitate Járnnefr was useless against the female, just as Beowulf's sword could not pierce Grendel's mother. As the armed hero is standing opposite the defenseless ogress, the text has him 'draw back' [*sic*], his axe is never mentioned again and his opponent has enough time to attack him 'until she reached a sword' (#16)! In the epic poem it is Beowulf who throws away his sword to begin a wrestling match, while in the saga it is the giantess who has been left holding the useless motif, throwing it down in order to initiate hand-to-hand combat (#17). As in *Beowulf* the struggle is hard and long, with the giantess enjoying a slight advantage (#18) until they come to the edge of a gorge (#19), the presence of which may be related to the gorge *under næssa genipu* into which the *fyrgenstrēam* plunges in the distorted and much-discussed scenery of the Old English epic. In the saga the troll's feet are pulled out from under her and she falls down into the gorge (#20), while the hero throws the monster to the ground in *Beowulf*. Divine intervention plays a major role, too, in both versions of the battle, allowing Beowulf to draw a golden-hilted sword from the equipment of the ogress and to decapitate her with it, while Hálfdan finds a sword which mysteriously appears, also adorned with gold, and uses it to behead the ogress (#21).

Slightly further on in the saga narrative (#22) the reader is informed that Hálfdan's men were *hugsjúkir*, 'sick at heart,' just as Beowulf's men were *mōdes sēoce*, 'sick at heart' at his absence, but the epic hero returns with valuable booty and the saga hero also comes back to camp with gold, silver, and jewels from the cave (#23).[13]

This long list of parallels is undeniably very impressive, but it is also quite misleading. Read in context, the very short chapter of *Hálfdanar saga Brönufóstra* that describes these events[14] does not – not even remotely – resemble the Grendel episode of *Beowulf*. The differences between the two stories are far too great: Hálfdan is looking for food when he chances upon the trolls, he climbs a glacier and then a rock to reach them, no particular type of relationship is indicated between the trolls, the ogress dies by falling into a gorge, and after the battle with the trolls Hálfdan frees a girl and her two brothers, who have been held captive by the trolls.

Other *fornaldarsǫgur* have not proved to be quite so full of fragments of the 'old legend' as *Hálfdanar saga Brönufóstra*, but among other discoveries Jorgensen has found:

- that the 'old legend' contained a swimming match,[15] which he then discovers to have 'parallels' in *Hálfdanar saga Brönufóstra*, *Örvar-Odds saga*, *Vilmundar saga viðutan*, *Finnboga saga*, *Hemings þáttr*, and *Egils saga einhenda*, in addition to *Grettis saga*, of course.
- that it also had 'the arrival of the hero at a court of a nobleman and his clash with an antagonistic liegeman there.'[16] Jorgensen also finds this motif in *Hálfdanar saga Brönufóstra*.[17]
- that the 'old legend' contained the gift of a useless weapon to the hero.[18] Jorgensen finds this attested in *Grettis saga*, *Hrólf's saga*, *Þorsteins þáttr uxafóts*, *Hálfdanar saga Eysteinssonar*, and *Gunnars saga Keldunúpsfífls*, among others.
- monsters attacking human dwellings, arms that are chopped off, the presence of water, single footpaths (*einstigi*), bright lights, cave battles, external aid, and treasure in a number of *fornaldarsǫgur*.[19]

These various fragments of the 'old legend' that Jorgensen has discovered in sundry sagas inevitably call attention to the methods that he uses to find them. Jorgensen's singular practice of identifying 'altered analogues' goes straight back to Nora Chadwick's tactics. Its main attraction is, of course, that it is extremely good for business, in the sense that it ensures that one's supply of eligible analogue materials will never run dry. But it is Jorgensen's tool box, as a critic in search of analogues, which is his most amazing characteristic. Things 'which conjure up remembrances and feelings of the Old English version' we have already seen, but Jorgensen also finds items 'which dimly echo' others,[20] 'role reversals,' 'deviant versions,' and the 'telescoping' of people and places in his quest for new analogues.[21] With a methodological arsenal of this kind, any critic who is worth his salt could, of course, prove that the telephone book is directly descended from the Bible, and armed with it, Jorgensen finds yet another parallel to *Beowulf* in *Grettis saga*:

In this vein it should be remarked that there occurs in *Grettis saga* an attack at night on the hero by twelve berserks. Only two survive, but flee the farmstead. The next morning all the men go out to trail the two and find them beneath a rock, dead from their wounds and the cold. Ordinarily, this passage could not be connected with the Bear's Son Folktale, except that it occurs in a saga which has varied the folktale on no less than six other occasions,[22] excluding Grettir's swimming adventures! It should also be noted that the attack was at Christmas, and the very next chapter of *Grettis saga* has the hero, at Christmas, kill a marauding bear, whose cave was under an overhanging rock (approachable by an *einstigi*, once again). Both the attacks by Glámr and by the ogress in the Sandhaugar episode are also said to take place at Christmas.[23]

Richard Harris, another Big Bang Theory critic, describes his discovery of the fifth analogue in *Grettis saga* and the saga author's working method in musical terms:

It is as if these five episodes of *Grettis saga* formed a set of fugue-like variations on a single theme, the theme found in the first part of *Beowulf* and, to some extent, in Panzer's variants of the Bear's Son Tale. Beginning with the relative simplicity of the visit to the *haugr* of Kárr inn gamli, they vary in complexity and intensity, the central confrontation, ending with Glámr's curse, being the most drastic single event in Grettir's career. When Þorbjörn comes for him in the fifth episode as he lies in a weakened state in his retreat, the details of the end are predictable, for we have already been told the story several times, but with Grettir as hunter instead of as quarry.[24]

Harris is also well informed about the intentions of the author of *Grettis saga*, and he even knows that this author was familiar with the materials on which the 'old legend' drew. 'I think it may be concluded,' Harris writes, 'that the saga's author knew more of the material, in some form or other, upon which Grendel's story is based, than could be assumed without an awareness that Grettir's death does indeed offer another parallel to the narrative in *Beowulf*.'[25] In short, both Jorgensen and Harris read *Grettis saga* as a multiple repetition of the Grendel story, the saga author sometimes directly repeating it, but more often presenting it in variously disguised forms.

As we shall see in the next chapter, it is perfectly true that *Grettis saga* contains a variety of literary patterns, including repetitions and recombinations of motifs. But so far no one has discovered anything quite so spectacular as the fivefold exegesis that Jorgensen and Harris propose. Harris's thesis presupposes that the author of *Grettis saga* was somehow obsessed by the Grendel story, and that it meant something very special to him. Why else would he want to use it and reuse it five or six times in his saga, adding new details and new characters to it at every turn? Did his audience also know the 'old legend,' and did they appreciate this peculiar handling of it, or has it – as one suspects – taken seven hundred years to fully understand what the saga author was up to? And if the 'old legend' was such an important piece of literature, why was it preserved in its entirety – or something close to it – in only one Old English poem and a single Icelandic saga? It also remains unexplained why the author of *Grettis saga* buried the fullest version of his favourite story – i.e., the Sandhaugar episode – in a late and relatively unimportant chapter of his saga. If the Sandhaugar episode appeared early in *Grettis saga* and described something really important in Grettir's life, it would not be so far-fetched to look for echoes of it later in the saga, but this is not the case, and Harris's thesis is therefore very improbable.

In chapter 37 of the book of Ezekiel, the Lord sets the prophet down in a valley full of dry bones and asks him: 'Son of man, can these bones live?' The same question may be asked of Big Bang Theory critics: do these fragments that they keep unearthing constitute the remains of something that was once a full-fledged story? The dry bones of the Old Testament are of course Israel, and the answer is yes, they can live; however, with the fragments of the scattered legend that the Big Bang Theory postulates, the answer has to be no. The main problem is, as we have seen in this chapter, the basic assumption of a proven relationship between *Beowulf* and *Grettis saga*, on which the whole Big Bang Theory argument rests. This relationship has never been satisfactorily demonstrated. It has also never been shown why the 'old legend' – over and above other stories that were current in Northern Europe during the Middle Ages – should have left the profound influence on Old Norse literature that Jorgensen and others have wanted to maintain. If the story was so important, we would expect to have more complete versions of it in Icelandic instead of late and scattered fragments. And finally, it must be said that the 'anything goes' methodology of most Big Bang Theory critics is simply not acceptable.

As we have seen in this and in the previous three chapters, none of the four theories that have been proposed to link the saga and the poem really succeeds in doing so. All four are badly flawed, and these flaws are serious enough to undermine their credibility completely. All the wishful thinking that scholars have poured into trying to establish a link between *Beowulf* and *Grettis saga* throughout the past century has, regrettably, been work in vain.

PART III
THE GENETICALLY RELATED *BEOWULF* ANALOGUES IN
GRETTIS SAGA IN VIEW OF ICELANDIC SOURCES

10

A Saga Author Shops Around:
The Eclectic Composition of
the Glámr and Sandhaugar Episodes

It is, of course, no good to reject the various theories that attempt to explain the origin of the supposed genetically related *Beowulf* analogues in *Grettis saga* if no alternative explanation can be offered instead. In this chapter I shall, accordingly, try to do so. I shall, however, concentrate exclusively on the Glámr and the Sandhaugar episodes, because it is on their 'proven' existence as genetically related *Beowulf* analogues that other episodes of the saga that have been thought to be related to the Old English poem must rest.

It has been shown that the author of *Grettis saga* was very well versed in Icelandic histories and sagas that had been written prior to his own, and that he frequently refers to them or borrows from them in the course of putting together his own story. According to Guðni Jónsson, who edited the saga in the *Íslenzk fornrit* series, the author of the saga knew and used the following texts:

1 / *The Book of Settlements* (*Landnáma*)
2 / *The Saga of the People of Laxárdalur* (*Laxdœla saga*)
3 / *The Saga of the Confederates* (*Bandamanna saga*)
4 / *The Saga of Bjorn, Champion of the Hítardalers* (*Bjarnar saga Hít-dœlakappa*).
5 / *The Saga of the Sworn Brothers* (*Fóstbrœðra saga*)
6 / *The Saga of the Battle on the Heath* (*Heiðarvíga saga*)
7 / *The Saga of the People of Eyri* (*Eyrbyggja saga*)
8 / *The Saga of Christianity* (*Kristni saga*)
9 / *The Book of the Icelanders* (*Íslendingabók*)
10 / *Egil's Saga* (*Egils saga*)
11 / *Njal's Saga* (*Njáls saga*)
12 / *The Saga of the People of Vatnsdalur* (*Vatnsdœla saga*)
13 / *Kormak's Saga* (*Kormáks saga*)
14 / *The Story of Arrow Odd* (*Örvar-Odds saga*)[1]

We may rightfully suspect that the author of *Grettis saga* knew and used even more texts, but what can be deduced from this long list of books? It tells us two things: in the first place, we are looking at a very 'literary-minded' author, and secondly, if all these texts have left their mark on *Grettis saga*, we may assume that he liked to decorate his saga with bits and pieces from books that he had read, or books that he had heard read, or stories that he knew in an oral form, perhaps to impress his readers, but more likely because he thought that they blended nicely with his own product. The first assumption is also backed by the number of literary patterns that we find in *Grettis saga* in the form of doublets and triplets and, strangely enough, repetitions and recombinations of motifs. Characters in the saga often come in identical pairs or play the same role: for example, the half-trolls Þórir and Hallmundr, the obnoxious pair Bjǫrn and Þorbjǫrn ferðalangr, and Grettir's rope watchers, the farmer Auðunn, and the priest Steinn. The berserks, Þórir þǫmb, Qgmundr illi, and Snækollr are all more or less cast in the same mould, and so are the would-be assassins of Grettir, Þórir rauðskeggr and Grímr skógarmaðr. Grettir twice swims to obtain fire, once in Norway and once in Iceland; like Glámr, Þorbjǫrg the sorceress lays a curse on Grettir; and twice someone is sent to kill Grettir. Finally, the saga frequently repeats certain phrases and parts of sentences.[2]

The Glámr Episode

As one of the few things that scholars investigating *Grettis saga* have been able to agree on is that there is a link between the Glámr and the Sandhaugar episodes; one of them must be primary, and the other a recipient. But which is which? Once this question is posed, the critical consensus ends. C.S. Smith, who was the first scholar to address the issue, was not in any doubt as he compared the Sandhaugar and the Glámr episodes: 'how much more graphic, more masterly in all its parts, is the story of the wrestling with Glam. Unquestionably that is the original, and the other a copy.'[3] R.C. Boer, in an article entitled 'Zur Grettissaga' published in 1898, concurred with Smith. Furthermore, he argued that in the composition of the Sandhaugar episode the saga author had merely combined a number of elements from Grettir's fights with Glámr and Kárr the Old. From the Glámr episode Boer believed that he had taken:

• The mysterious disappearance of people.
• Drops of blood by the doorstep.
• Most of the details of Grettir's fight with the troll-woman.

From the Kárr episode the saga author had repeated:

- Details concerning Grettir's cave fight, such as the rope, and the flight of the watchman.[4]

The counter-argument to these ideas came from Friedrich Panzer. In his book on *Beowulf* Panzer completely rejected Boer's theory, and maintained that both in the Glámr and the Sandhaugar episodes the author of *Grettis saga* had borrowed a ghost story featuring a living dead ghost called Þórólfr bægifótr, from *Eyrbyggja saga*.[5] Panzer furthermore argued that the Sandhaugar story was primary, and that as a character, Glámr was fashioned merely by combining features from the description of the troll-woman at Sandhaugar and the abovementioned Þórólfr bægifótr from *Eyrbyggja saga*.[6]

A third theory concerning the origin of Glámr was offered by Heinz Dehmer, who suggested that his relationship to Þórólfr bægifótr did not involve a literary borrowing by the saga author. According to Dehmer, many Icelandic ghost stories in the sagas shared a certain number of elements, and similarities in the description of Þórólfr bægifótr and Glámr might simply be the result of a common tradition rather than a conscious borrowing.[7] In a later article Dehmer listed what he believed to be the common characteristics of the Icelandic tradition of describing battles within a haunted house:

- The hero wraps himself in a cloak.
- He has a tug of war with the ghost over the cloak.
- A wrestling match between them follows.
- The demon is much stronger than the hero.
- A second fight in the demon's lair is never a part of this formula.[8]

Dehmer maintained that the Sandhaugar episode was not a ghost story, and was therefore not really related to the Glámr story. It featured neither a cloak nor a tug of war, and although the troll-woman is much stronger than Grettir – as is the case with fight descriptions in genuine ghost stories – he does not kill her in the traditional and decisive ghost story manner, i.e., by cutting her head off and placing it against her buttocks, which is the way in which Glámr is put to permanent rest.[9]

The most convincing analysis of the Glámr episode was, however, submitted by another German scholar, Wolf von Unwerth, in a book bearing the long and esoteric title, *Untersuchungen über Totenkult und Ódinnverehrung bei Nordgermanen und Lappen – mit Excursen zur altnordischen Literaturgeschichte* (*Studies in the Worship of the Dead and the Veneration of Odin among the North Germanic Peoples and the Lapps – with a Digression into the History of Old Norse Literature*), which he published in 1911. The Glámr episode had always been thought to go back to an oral folktale, but von Unwerth argued that both the ghost himself and his story had distinctive literary traits. It was, according to von Unwerth, a collection of literary motifs commonly found in the Icelandic saga ghost stories that he had been investigating. Such motifs included:

- a ghost who makes an entire region desolate,
- drives a few people mad,
- breaks people's bones, and
- rides roof-tops,
- kills animals,
- and after he has been 'killed,' is finally disposed of by putting his head against his buttocks.[10]

In *Eyrbyggja saga* (chapter 34), we are told that Þórólfr bægifótr drove many people away from the farm that he haunted, and killed others who stayed behind. *Laxdæla saga* (chapter 17 and subsequent chapters) tells of the evil ghost Hrappr, who also killed people. *Svarfdæla saga* (chapter 32) has the ghost Klaufi, who hurts people and animals, and Þorsteins þáttr bæjarmagns (chapters 12–13) features the ghost Agði, who has murderous intentions. *Eyrbyggja saga* (chapter 34) also tells us that Þórólfr bægifótr drove some people to madness. In *Heiðarvíga saga* (chapter 9) the ghost of Víga-Styrr drives a girl to madness and death. Ghosts who fight with humans – Hrappr (chapter 24) and Hallbjǫrn (chapter 38) – appear in *Laxdæla saga*. A description of a wrestling match between a human and a ghost inside a house, and of the damage done to it in the process, is found in *Hrómundar saga Gripssonar*,[11] (chapter 4), and in *Grettis saga*'s account of the hero's fight with the farmer Auðunn, we see the same type of wrestling match that causes great damage as we see in the Glámr episode a few pages later.[12] Fight descriptions quite similar to Grettir's struggle against Glámr occur in *Flóamanna saga* (chapter 13) and in *Hávarðar saga Ísfirðings* (chapter 2). Ghosts ride roof-tops in *Eyrbyggja saga* (chapter 34) and *Flóamanna saga* (chapter 13). The ghost kills animals (birds that touch down on Þórólfr bægifótr's gravemound) in *Eyrbyggja saga* (chapter 34). In disposing permanently of a ghost, one needs to cut off its head and place it somewhere a good distance away from where it belongs, preferably by the feet of the ghost or against its buttocks. This method is followed in *Áns saga bogsveigis* (chapter 5) to prevent a dead man from adopting a career as a ghost, and of course in the Glámr episode of *Grettis saga*.[13] As a further precaution, the body of the ghost may be burnt to cinders and the ashes securely buried, as we find in chapter 32 of *Svarfdæla saga* and in the final disposal of Glámr. It is, of course, impossible to prove that the Glámr episode consists to a large extent of a string of motifs borrowed from older sagas, but as we know that the author of *Grettis saga* was familiar with many of them, it undeniably strengthens von Unwerth's theory.[14]

Von Unwerth also demonstrated that the Glámr episode has an unmistakable connection with a little-known and highly problematic saga called *Hávarðar saga Ísfirðings*.[15] As Theodore M. Andersson has put it, *Hávarðar saga Ísfirðings* 'enjoys a particular disrepute among scholars because of evidence that it is a late reconstruction of an earlier saga and because it contains demonstrable historical errors and unprepossessing stanzas.'[16] In the form that we now have it, this saga was according to its editors in the *Íslenzk fornrit* series, originally composed sometime during the first half of the thirteenth century – some decades earlier than *Grettis saga* – and based on old legends from the Westfjords. The editors of this saga, Björn K. Þórólfsson and Guðni Jónsson, think that an older version of *Hávarðar saga Ísfirðings* had been lost by the time that the later version was composed and find it most likely that the author had either read the older version or heard it read. At one point he had known the story, but by the time that he recomposed *Hávarðar saga Ísfirðings*, he had become rusty concerning various details, such as the names of people and places.[17] Sigurður Nordal, however, does not rule out the possibility that the later redactor still had access to and used the original saga which would mean that the older version was not lost until some time after the later one had come to be written.[18] The earliest extant copies of the saga as we now have it are paper manuscripts that go back to the seventeenth century. These in turn appear to derive from a single manuscript, now lost, which is thought to have been written about 1450.[19]

In *Hávarðar saga Ísfirðings*, the hero, Óláfr, fights with a ghost named Þormóðr, who visits his widow's bed every night and who is about to frighten everyone off the farm. Von Unwerth demonstrated that a comparison of this fight with Grettir's fight against Glámr shows such an unmistakable resemblance both in the events described and in terms of language that one of the two sagas must have borrowed the episode from the other.[20] In English translation, the examples from these two sagas that von Unwerth compared are as follows:

Hávarðar saga Ísfirðings (Chapter 2)	*Grettis saga* (Chapter 35)
Óláfr was lying on a gable-end bed near the door ...	[Grettir] lay down on a bench opposite the farmer's bed closet ...
A light was burning in the hall ...	A light was burning in the hall ...
Óláfr lay down in his shirt and pants ...	Grettir did not want to take his clothes off ...

he covered himself with a cloak	he covered himself with a shaggy fur cloak ...
Þormóðr entered the hall and wagged his bald head backwards and forwards ...	Grettir saw that the thrall stretched his head inside ...
He saw that an extra bed was occupied ...	Glámr saw that some sort of heap was lying on the bench ...
he approached and pulled hard at the cloak ...	[Glámr] moved further inside the hall and pulled hard at the cloak ...
they divided the cloak between them ...	they tore the cloak apart between them ...
Þormóðr sensed that he was up against a strong man ...	[Glámr] wondered who could have pulled so hard against him ...
Þormóðr leapt under his arms ...	Glámr leapt under his arms ...
they fought hard ...	They fought very hard ...
they broke most things that were in their way ...	they smashed everything that was in their way ...
Þormóðr attacked fiercely, and in the end they fought their way outside ...	Glámr now seemed more powerful and clutched Grettir in his grip as they moved into the vestibule ...[21]

In *Hávarðar saga Ísfirðings*, however, the end of the fight has none of the high drama of the Glámr episode. Once the fight has moved out of the hall, the ghost stumbles over a piece of wood and falls on his back. The saga then merely relates that Óláfr disposed of Þormóðr in a fitting manner.

Von Unwerth thought that his comparison showed that of the two sagas, *Hávarðar saga Ísfirðings* contained the original story, and that the author of *Grettis saga* had borrowed its ghost fight and incorporated it into his description of Grettir's fight with Glámr.[22] On this issue I am convinced that von Unwerth is right, as it is very difficult to imagine that *Hávarðar saga Ísfirðings* could have borrowed this scene from *Grettis saga*. In the first place, the fight scene in *Hávarðar saga Ísfirðings* is very straightforward, almost crude in its simplicity, and it shows all the signs of going back to a local ghost story. The *Grettis saga* version is, by contrast, a more polished and more 'literary' narrative and it is considerably longer. Secondly, certain details have been embellished; the simple 'cloak' in *Hávarðar saga Ísfirðings* has, for example, become 'a shaggy fur cloak' in *Grettis saga*. And there are other ways as well in which the author of *Grettis saga* magnifies and intensifies events that take place during the fight. In *Hávarðar saga Ísfirðings* the ghost and Óláfr 'fight hard'; in *Grettis saga* they fight 'very hard.' In *Hávarðar saga Ísfirðings* they first 'divide the cloak between them' and then 'break most things that are in their way;' in *Grettis saga* Grettir and Glámr 'tear the cloak apart' and then 'smash everything that is in their way.' If the author of *Hávarðar saga Ísfirðings* had borrowed this section from *Grettis saga*, he would have had to simplify it considerably and leave out the climax of the fight, including Glámr's famous curse, his decapitation, and his burial. This is unlikely, for why would an author want to borrow a description of something from another book only to leave out the best part? This would not make too much sense.

Although it has been an established fact for decades in Old Norse studies that some kind of relationship existed between this scene from *Hávarðar saga Ísfirðings* and the Glámr episode of *Grettis saga*,[23] for some strange reason this knowledge has never entered the debate over the assumed presence of genetically related *Beowulf* analogues in *Grettis saga*. Chambers, who carefully recorded all publications that he considered relevant to these and other subjects of concern to the poem in the bibliography of his life-long and cumulative study, was obviously not aware of von Unwerth's book,[24] nor do other *Beowulf* scholars appear to have taken note of it. Had they done so, they might well have had some second thoughts about the Glámr episode being a genetically related *Beowulf* analogue. If von Unwerth is right, and we have reasonable evidence to assume that the author of *Grettis saga* borrowed his description of the hero's fight with Glámr inside the farmhouse from *Hávarðar saga Ísfirðings*, this factor alone makes it unlikely that the Glámr episode is a genetically related *Beowulf* analogue. Furthermore, we only need to add a few more sagas to the list of works that are known to have influenced *Grettis saga* and deduce that the author borrowed bits and pieces from them to have much of the Glámr episode as *Grettis saga* relates it:

- the various elements that relate Glámr's career as a ghost before he tangles with Grettir could to a large extent have come from *Eyrbyggja saga* (riding rooftops, driving people crazy or killing them, and making a region desolate).
- the parts of the fight scene and its immediate aftermath that do not come from *Hávarðar saga Ísfirðings* could have been borrowed from *Flóamanna saga* (the description of the fight after Glámr falls out of the door), and from *Svarfœla saga* (the final disposal of the ghost by burning its body and disposing securely of the ashes).

If the author of *Grettis saga* did in fact work along these lines – as indeed seems entirely possible – it goes without saying that the Glámr episode can under no circumstances be a genetically related *Beowulf* analogue, no matter how closely scholars think that it matches the Grendel story.

The Sandhaugar Episode

Any critic who believes that both the Glámr and the Sandhaugar episodes go back to the same 'old legend' has a good deal of explaining to do concerning the odd manner in which the author of *Grettis saga* relates these stories. In the first place, it would be interesting to know why he only uses half of the story in the Glámr episode, which is unquestionably the more important of the two, and then decides to give a fuller version of the Grendel story in a late and relatively obscure chapter of his saga. Secondly, it would appear that the saga author has been struck with complete amnesia over what has happened so far in his own story, when he sends Grettir to do battle at Sandhaugar. Ever since Glámr's curse, the governing theme of the saga has been Grettir's fear of the dark and of the creatures that inhabit it, and the last thing that a reader would expect is to see him voluntarily go out of his way to seek a battle with supernatural creatures. The third curious thing about the Sandhaugar episode is its picaresque nature. It is literally an adventure which is – except for Grettir's presence in it – completely independent of the rest of the saga. When the adventure is over Grettir moves on, and every single character that we met in the Sandhaugar chapters vanishes for good from the saga.

The author of *Grettis saga* wanted to write a long story about his hero.[25] We know this from the fact that after Grettir's death in chapter 82 of the saga, he adds to the story a longish appendix (eleven chapters) that describes the revenge taken for Grettir, but he does not stop even when Grettir's half-brother, Þorsteinn drómundr, has carried out his duty in Constantinople. After killing Þorbjǫrn ǫngull there, a brief fabliau-like story relating Þorsteinn's rescue from prison and his affair with a married lady is thrown in as a finale to the saga. This last part is so loosely connected to the main body of *Grettis saga* that it is commonly known by its own title: *Spesar þáttur*. If we consider the Sandhaugar episode in light of these above-mentioned points, it is very difficult to avoid the impression that it was conceived as a 'filler' by a saga author who was running low on things to do for his hero. Within the saga as a whole, one of the main characteristics of the Sandhaugar episode is that it kills time in Grettir's life. He arrives at the farm at Christmas and stays there for the remainder of the winter, and yet the only adventure that the saga author can assign to him during all this time is his early fight with the two trolls. The rest of the hero's stay at the farm – a period of four or five months – is completely uneventful and is summed up by the saga in one sentence: 'Grettir stayed at Sandhaugar during the winter in disguise.'[26]

My guess is that the troll adventure which the author of *Grettis saga* gives to his hero at Sandhaugar has its origin in a troll fight story that he knew as a legend associated with the part of the country where this farm is situated, and that he decided to use it in an amended form as a part of his own story.[27] Why else would the first fight have two different endings, and why else would the saga author have to tell us that the local population knew a version that had the troll-woman turn into a stone at sunrise? The original ending, however, was of no use to our author because it gave the real victory to the appearance of daylight rather than his hero, and he therefore changed it.

It is a curious coincidence – if, indeed, it is a coincidence – that in the Sandhaugar episode there is not a single feature which is not to be found either earlier in the saga itself or in other sagas, some of which we know the author of *Grettis saga* to have been familiar with, and others that he might have known in an oral or a written form. As to the broad structure of the first fight, I agree with R.C. Boer that it is most likely that the author of *Grettis saga* refashioned the Glámr episode into Grettir's fight with the troll woman,[28] or – as might be equally plausible – he retold an already existing regional troll fight story, inserted Grettir into it, and gave it a new ending. In the process of doing this, however, the saga author embellished his story with numerous features that he probably borrowed from other works:[29]

- A raid by a supernatural being (a dragon) on a human habitation occurs, for instance, in *Hrólfs saga kraka* (chapter 35), and a princess is abducted (by an enormous vulture) at Christmas in *Egils saga einhenda ok Ásmundar berserkjabana* (chapter 2).[30]
- The troll-woman in the Sandhaugar episode is most likely inherited from the original troll fight story. A troll-woman armed with a long knife and a trencher appears to someone in a dream in *Haralds saga harðráða* (chapter 80), and – also in a dream – in *Laxdæla saga** (chapter 48).
- The indoor fight scene is, as in the Glámr episode, borrowed from *Hávarðar saga Ísfirðings*.
- In *Örvar-Odds saga** (chapter 19) we meet a troll-woman who lives in a waterfall.
- Wrestling matches against trolls on the edge of a chasm are known from *Sörla saga sterka* (chapter 3), and *Hálfdanar saga Brönufóstra* (chapter 4).
- A hip throw by the hero occurs as a decisive move in his wrestling match with the troll in *Hálfdanar saga Brönufóstra* (chapter 6), and in *Gríms saga loðinkinna* (chapter 1).
- The arm that Grettir cuts off the troll-woman may be compared to several incidents earlier in the saga where people lose their heads, arms, or hands: Qnundr tréfótr (Grettir's great grandfather) cuts off Vígbjóðr's arm (chapter 4); Grettir cuts off the arm of Hjarrandi, and both hands off Gunnarr (brothers

of Bjǫrn, who taunted Grettir in the bear episode and was later killed by him), as they try to avenge Bjǫrn (chapter 24); Grettir cuts the hand and the head off Þorbjǫrn ferðalangr (chapter 37); and the berserk Snækollr and the would-be assassin Þórir rauðskeggr lose their heads to Grettir's sword (chapters 40 and 56). If the saga author was not simply recycling some of these incidents in the Sandhaugar episode, he might have looked to various *fornaldarsǫgur* and *þættir* in which trolls lose their hands or arms, for example: *Egils saga einhenda ok Ásmundar berserkjabana* (chapter 10); *Þorsteins þáttr uxafóts* (two trolls, male and female, in chapter 10); *Hjálmþés saga ok Ölvis* (chapter 12); *Jökuls þáttr Búasonar* (chapter 2); and *Ketils saga hœngs* (chapter 2).[31]

As for Grettir's cave adventure, certain features, such as the rope, the cowardly watchman, and the presence of treasure show striking similarity with his break-in into the gravemound and subsequent fight with Kárr the Old earlier in the saga. Boer noted this resemblance before the turn of the century,[32] and some critics, at least – including Guðni Jónsson, who, like Boer, edited *Grettis saga* – have concurred with him that these episodes must be related.[33] In the second fight, as in the first one, it is the familiarity of the various motifs that characterizes the narrative:

- Panzer points out that the name of Steinn, the watchman, and the use of a rope to reach the abode of the monster are familiar elements in different versions of the Bear's Son story, and thinks that the author of *Grettis saga* was familiar with that story and used it in the second part of the Sandhaugar episode.[34] Chambers, who on the whole rejects Panzer's theory, is inclined to agree with him on this point.[35]
- In *Þorsteins saga Víkingssonar* one of hero's opponents is described as jumping overboard from ship in terms similar to those used to depict Grettir's dive into the chasm: i.e., 'you could see the soles of his feet.'[36]
- In *fornaldarsǫgur*, it is quite commonplace to find giants living in large caves in which fires are kept burning. This occurs, for example, in *Hjálmþés saga ok Ölvis* (chapter 9), in *Örvar-Odds saga* (chapter 6), in *Hálfdanar saga Brönufóstra* (chapter 4), and in *Gríms saga loðinkinna* (chapter 1).
- A weapon with a wooden handle (*atgeirr*) fails its owner in *Njáls saga* (chapter 30).[37]
- A sword hangs on the wall in the cave of a giant in *Hjálmþés saga ok Ölvis* (chapter 9).
- Gore on the water appears in *Samsons saga fagra* (chapter 7), and in *Þorsteins saga Víkingssonar* (chapter 23).

- A watchman or watchmen who leave the rope that they are supposed to guard is a standard motif in different variants of the Bear's Son folktales.[38]
- The hero discovers human bones or finds living prisoners in the troll cave in, for example, *Hálfdanar saga Brönufóstra* (chapter 4),[39] and in *Bósa saga ok Herrauðs* (chapter 8).[40]
- It is a common expectation that the hero will find treasure in the caves of trolls, regardless of whether his encounter with them is of a friendly or a hostile nature. The following four sagas are only a small sample of the host of troll stories that follow this pattern: *Hálfdanar saga Brönufóstra* (chapter 5), *Sörla saga sterka* (chapter 4), *Jökuls þáttr Búasonar* (chapter 2), and *Hjálmþés saga ok Ölvis* (chapter 9).

If these commonplace motifs were removed from the story of Grettir's cave adventure there would not be much left of it, and the Sandhaugar episode as a whole, could never be noted for its originality.

A problem such as the one of trying to decide whether there is a literary relationship between two works must in the final analysis come down to the question of probability; there simply cannot be any other criterion upon which to base one's conclusions. Assuming influence from contemporary Icelandic sources on *Grettis saga*, particularly when they are as glaringly obvious as in the Glámr and the Sandhaugar episodes, is certainly an easier solution than accepting the existence of an 'old legend' that would have had to survive centuries of oral transmission, not to mention migration from country to country, intact. It is also simpler than tackling the thorny problem of attempting to explain how *Beowulf*, directly or indirectly, could have influenced the saga. In this case, the simplest explanation must be the most likely one.

11

Conclusion

Three centuries ago the great manuscript collector and antiquarian, Árni Magnússon, observed that there were only two kinds of scholars in the world: those who devoted themselves to helping spread errors in their field, and those who trailed after the first lot and cleaned up their mistakes. This scheme of things ensured, according to Magnússon, that both groups had something to keep themselves busy.[1] This was probably a sound assessment of the state of affairs in Old Norse scholarship in Magnússon's time, and I do not think that *Beowulf* studies have reached such a level of perfection in our day that his theory no longer applies. Of course experimentation and new ideas are necessary in the field, but so are counter-arguments and debate. Unfortunately, however, this way of looking at scholarly work seems to have become somewhat unfashionable in *Beowulf* studies in recent decades. 'Negative criticism,' i.e., the refutation of theories of other scholars, is at the moment not considered a very constructive form of research. Scholarly flights of fancy, where common sense and logic are tossed aside, have – at least as far the subject of this book is concerned – become dangerously acceptable. But if scholarly imagination is not checked by logic and common sense, and if certain theories are allowed to become such sacred cows that they are beyond criticism, then *Beowulf* studies, as a subject, will soon be at an intellectual level closer to comic books and science fiction than to other academic disciplines.

Although I have, in the previous ten chapters, argued against a generally accepted opinion concerning the supposed genetic relationship between *Beowulf* and *Grettis saga*, I am perfectly aware of the fact that it is impossible to determine with any absolute certainty whether or not the two works are indeed related. In the final analysis, the question of a relationship between the poem and the saga boils down to three possible answers:

1/*Grettis saga* is closer to the 'old legend' than *Beowulf.* Hence we are allowed
to use the saga to reconstruct the Old English poem, as Chambers, Lawrence,
and others have done.

2/*Grettis saga* is no closer to the 'old legend' than *Beowulf.* The saga only
relates and reworks bits and pieces of the original story. As a result, it cannot
be used to clarify any unsolved problems in *Beowulf.*

3/*Beowulf* and *Grettis saga* are not related in any way, although parts of each
work may – on the surface at least – appear to be similar. This possibility
obviously rules out the presence of an 'old legend' or a common ancestor for
both the saga and the poem.

In this situation, it can only be the weight of the evidence that determines which
of these possibilities appears to be the most likely one, and with that in mind,
the third one should not be ruled out quite so casually as we saw C.S. Smith and
Larry Benson do in the introduction to this book. It is perhaps well to remember
that 'there is nothing more deceptive than an obvious fact,' as Arthur Conan
Doyle has Sherlock Holmes observe in 'The Boscomb Valley Mystery.'[2]

So far, the evidence that we have examined has not suggested any form of
contact between *Beowulf* and *Grettis saga,* but one area, the question of a
mutual *genre,* remains unexplored. In the past, the debate over this has always
focused on the Grendel story, on the one hand, and on one of the five supposed
analogues in *Grettis saga,* the Sandhaugar episode, on the other, and in the following discussion I shall do the same.

What kind of story was the 'old legend' that Vigfússon thought that he had
discovered over a century ago? Vigfússon never seems to have given much
thought to this question, but others soon did. The trio of Klaeber, Lawrence, and
Chambers – in addition to Panzer, of course – were all agreed that originally the
Grendel story had to have been a folktale or a *Märchen.*[3] And there was no
doubt that the Sandhaugar episode was also a folktale; after all, the saga all but
said so. The tacit assumption upon which this conclusion had to rest was that it
was possible to peel the Old English poem like an onion, until one came upon
some kind of a reognizable folktale-like 'kernel' from which the poem as we
now have it had presumably later developed. This explanation of the poem's
growth and development from its humble origins was, however, always a bit
dubious, and Klaeber clearly had reservations, which he voiced quietly in the
introduction to his first edition of *Beowulf:*[4]

There is no evidence to show that 'a Bēowulf legend' had gradually grown up out of
popular stories that had been brought over to England by the migrating Angles. If such

were the case, it would be inexplicable why the exclusive interest in Scandinavian legends remained virtually unimpaired, and why in particular such a minute attention to the fortunes of Northern dynasties continued to be manifested in the epic.[5]

In his book on *Beowulf*, WW. Lawrence felt compelled to take issue with the unorthodox opinion that his friend and colleague was spreading: 'The answer seems clear. Interest in Scandinavian legend remained unimpaired, just as it did in Germanic legend generally. How keen this interest was, all the remains of pagan verse in Anglo-Saxon illustrate – *Widsith, Deor, Waldhere*, the Northumbrian lyrics.'[6] This is not a very satisfactory reply to Klaeber's doubts. In the first place it is rather dubious to equate, as Lawrence does, the common Germanic literary heritage with a remote and relatively provincial Scandinavian past; and secondly, none of Lawrence's examples show any signs of having a folktale origin.

The debate between Klaeber and Lawrence on the folktale origin of *Beowulf* went no further than this, insofar as I know. Perhaps they did not think that the subject matter was important enough to have a full-scale scholarly debate. Lawrence, at least, did not think very highly of folktales as a literary *genre*. In his book on *Beowulf* he characterized the folktale kernel from which he believed the poem had grown as 'a tale told among simple people with childlike imaginations.'[7] As for the competing viewpoints that were offered by the two scholars there is little doubt as to which of the two won the day. Lawrence's ideas – or Panzer's, to be exact – are repeated by *Beowulf* scholars from time to time,[8] whereas Klaeber's objections are all but forgotten.

Recent work by *Beowulf* scholars on the question of the possible folktale origin of the poem has been heavily influenced by the ideas of the Russian folklorist Vladimir Propp. Some years ago, Daniel R. Barnes investigated the poem closely from a Proppian viewpoint, with the debate between Klaeber and Lawrence in mind. He concluded that the tale that may be extracted from *Beowulf* by applying Propp's system offers 'additional support' for the folktale origin theory, but 'is not of itself sufficient "proof" that *Beowulf* is essentially a folktale.'[9] Barnes's methods and conclusion have, however, come under criticism. Bruce A. Rosenberg replied to his article shortly after its publication and dryly observed that 'the poem that has come down to us on Cotton Vitellius A XV is not a folktale,' and proceeded to take Barnes to task for the questionable methodology that he felt that his colleague had used:

we should be suspicious when we are told that 'I have applied Propp's theory to *Beowulf* by testing the poem against the structural model presented in *Morphology of the Folktale*.' And we should proceed with extreme caution when the author asserts that one of his premises is 'that examination of the poem in terms of a synthetic structural theory which attempts to describe the principles common to *all* folktales – *independent of content similarities* – offers, if not a less hypothetical means than the comparative method, at least a radically new approach to the question of the "folktale element" in *Beowulf*' ... [Barnes] admits that *Beowulf* bears 'obvious traces' of literary artistry, yet he examines the poem as though it were a folktale. Literary history is ignored, and I believe to the detriment of the author's argument.[10]

Icelandic scholars have, with the exception of Óskar Halldórsson and Vésteinn Ólason, always considered the Sandhaugar episode to be a genuinely indigenous folktale. Björn M. Ólsen thought that the saga author had merely embellished – for instance by adding the two stanzas – an already existing folktale and then attached it to Grettir's name.[11] Other critics, such as Jónas Kristjánsson and *Grettis saga*'s editor, Guðni Jónsson, have, for the most part, expressed the same opinion.[12]

If we close the circle and come back to the starting point of this debate, I think that the evidence – when considered in its entirety – confirms Klaeber's scepticism. There neither is, nor has there ever been, any reasonable evidence to suggest that the Old English poem originated as a folktale, and it is my belief that if the Grendel story had never been thought of as an analogue genetically related to the Sandhaugar episode, it would never have occurred to anybody to suggest the singular development theory that Lawrence postulated for *Beowulf*. Of course, the classification of the Sandhaugar episode and the Grendel story as different *genres* does not in itself rule out their kinship, as the 'old legend' could have taken on different shapes in different countries. But it would undeniably have strengthened the possible ties between these two stories – as Panzer, Chambers, and Lawrence indeed believed – if they could be shown to belong to the same type.

In conclusion, I want to emphasize that I do not rule out the possibility that the Sandhaugar episode and the Grendel story have a common Indo-European ancestor somewhere in the dark and distant past,[13] but if they do, that ancestor is beyond recovery. I do not think, however, that this is very likely. If we take the texts of *Grettis saga* and *Beowulf* and compare them without any wishful thinking or *a priori* notions of one being analogous and genetically related to the other, one can only conclude that any likeness that we find in the two works is accidental, because as we have seen in the previous chapters, the trail always goes cold if we try to go beyond the surface of the two texts, and – for all the scholarly ink that has been spilled on the matter – it is impossible to come up with a reasonably convincing theory to explain how the two texts are supposed to be linked. These are my two main reasons for believing that the two are not related. 'The arm of coincidence is ... long'[14] as Chambers once remarked, and ironically, the author of *Grettis saga* has his hero voice the same thought: 'many things look alike.'[15] As far as *Grettis saga* and *Beowulf* are concerned, I find myself in complete agreement with Kemp Malone's view when he observes that 'the Icelandic sagas are masterpieces of literary art but they have little in common with *Beowulf*.'[16]

Notes

Introduction

1 For a brief summary of the relevant passages see Klaeber 1950, ix–xi and xiv–xvii. Full translations of the two most widely recognized genetically related analogues from *Grettis saga* are provided, e.g., in Garmonsway, et al., 1968, 302–16, and Chambers 1959, 163–82.

2 Smith 1881, 65.

3 Benson 1970, 26. It may be added that in the years that have passed since Benson wrote his article, complete faith in a link between *Grettis saga* and *Beowulf* has been reiterated by every publication that has concerned itself with the poem and the saga. The latest such study, Andersson 1997, informs its readers, for example, that 'Among the Norse analogues only *Grettis saga* seems convincing to most students,' (125) and goes on to add that 'there is not much doubt of some connection between *Beowulf* and *Grettis saga*' (131).

4 Shippey 1978, 59.

5 Powell 1901, 395–6. Chambers 1959, 481, also notes this analogue and finds striking resemblance to *Beowulf* in the rescue of the grisly arm by the demon in female disguise.

6 Von Unwerth 1911, 167–73. Von Unwerth believes that in the first part of the Sandhaugar episode the author of *Grettis saga* borrows from his own description of Grettir's fight with Glámr, which in turn is a story made up of various literary motifs from other Icelandic texts.

1: Determining Analogous and Genetically Related Material

1 Because the word 'analogue' can both denote a general similarity between two texts and imply that the texts in question are genetically related, I want to make it very clear at the outset of my discussion that I am concerned solely with the latter use of

the word. In the chapters that follow, I am interested in *Beowulf* and *Grettis saga* analogues only as evidence that either links or fails to link the two works.

2 Guðni Jónsson, ed., *Grettis saga, Íslenzk fornrit*, 7, 1936, chaps. 64–6. All references to the saga in this book are to this edition. For an English translation see, e.g., Chambers 1959, 175–82, or Garmonsway 1968, 312–16.

3 Vigfusson 1878, vol. 1, xlix.

4 Vigfusson 1878, vol. 1, xlix, n. 1.

5 *Mece* in Old English denotes a certain type of sword, but it is not clear to what precisely the prefix *hæft-* is supposed to refer. *Grettis saga*, chap. 66, explains *heptisax* as a weapon with a wooden handle that could be used both for stabbing and cutting. Both words are discussed in detail in chap. 4.

6 Vigfusson and Powell 1883, vol. 2, 502.

7 See, e.g., Gering 1880, 85.

8 Smith 1881, 66: *Beowulf*, lines 1539–40: 'brægd þa beadwe heard, þa he gebolgen wæs, / feorhgeniðlan, þæt heo on flet gebeah.' *Grettis saga*, 212: 'bregðr hann flagðkonunni til sveiflu.'

9 Klaeber 1950, xv n. 1.

10 Halldórsson 1982, 20.

11 Malone 1958, 307.

12 Garnett 1880, 492.

13 Finnur Jónsson, 1923, 745n. 1, questions the relationship between the Sandhaugar episode and *Beowulf* that Chambers postulates in the first edition of his book on the poem (see Chambers 1959, 50) on the grounds that he assumes a common source but fails to show how the two texts are related ('han antager en fælles kilde, men ingen ligefrem sammenhæng'). Chambers eventually attempted to provide such a context; see Chambers 1959, 451–78. According to Anatoly Liberman (1986, 385), Steblin-Kamenskij, in his 1976 Russian edition of *Grettis saga* 'ascribes all the convergencies between the poem and the saga to the inevitable loci communes and peculiarities of oral transmission.'

14 Chambers 1959, 49–50.

15 Klaeber 1950, xviii.

16 Stedman 1913, 13–14.

17 *Grettis saga*, chaps. 32–5. For an English translation see, e.g., Chambers 1959, 163–75, or Garmonsway 1968, 302–12.

18 Not all critics are convinced that the text (lines 433–40b and 798–805b) actually indicates that Grendel had magical powers that made him immune to weapons. Laborde 1923, 203–4, thinks that the monster's skin was so tough that Beowulf's companions could not injure him. Boer 1900, xlii n. 1, and von Unwerth 1911, 171–2, stress the loss and the strange recovery of the horses that belong to Þórhallr on the occasion when he meets and employs Glámr as a shepherd (chap. 32) as an example of Glámr's use of magic before he utters his famous curse on Grettir.

19 Vigfusson and Powell 1883, vol. 2, 502.

20 Vigfusson and Powell 1883, vol. 2, 502.

21 Chadwick 1959, 190. The idea of linking Glámr and the troll-woman at Sandhaugar was originally proposed by Carney 1955, 95.

22 Gering 1880, 86n. 2.

23 See Boer 1898, 60; Bugge 1887, 57n. 1; Lawrence 1928, 187; Jónsson 1936, xlix (and the fact that he excludes Glámr in his discussion of the Sandhaugar episode, li–lv); and Turville-Petre 1974–7, 349.

24 See Chambers 1959, 48, and 1929, 87.

25 Smith 1881, 66–7.

26 Stedman 1913, 9. This observation is clearly based on a misunderstanding of the Icelandic text. In *Grettis saga*, chap. 32, 111, Glámr is described as 'ósǫngvinn ok trúlauss,' which must refer to his refusal to sing religious hymns, and therefore to his anti-Christian attitude. See Lie 1939, 134, for a further discussion of the meaning of *ósǫngvinn*.

27 Stedman 1913, 8–13.

28 Mossé 1933, xxxiii.

29 Smith 1881, 67, held Grendel and Glámr to be of widely different nature, whereas Stedman and many later critics thought that certain details in their description pointed to a common origin.

30 Klaeber 1950, xvii.

31 *Grettis saga*, chap. 18. Neither this episode nor the two that follow are included in the standard handbooks on *Beowulf*, such as Chambers 1959, and Garmonsway 1968. Those who wish to view the full text in English should consult a translation of the saga, e.g., Fox and Pálsson, 1974.

32 Jónsson 1936, 57. It is more likely, however, that the real function of Grettir's companion is that of a one-member dramatic audience, and it is worth noting that a page later the author seems to assume that he is there to pull Grettir out of the gravemound ('varð hann þá að handstyrkja sig upp festina').

33 Klaeber 1950, xvi n. 1.

34 Taylor 1952, 13–14.

35 McConchie 1982, 482–3.

36 Jónsson 1936, chap. 21.

37 Klaeber 1950, xiv n. 3.

38 Lawrence 1928, 187.

39 Taylor 1952, 15–17.

40 Arent 1969, 190–1. Some years later Arthur A. Wachsler, who seems to have been unaware of the work of Taylor and Arent, repeated some of these points and added others; see Wachsler 1985, 381–90.

41 Halldórsson 1982, 14.

42 Harris 1973, 31 and 52.

43 See, e.g., Jorgensen 1978, 55 and 1979, 86.
44 Jónsson 1936, chaps 70–82.
45 Harris 1973, 34.
46 Harris 1973, 52.
47 Harris 1973, 37–41.
48 Harris 1973, 50.
49 Liberman 1986.
50 Liberman 1986, 388.
51 Jorgensen 1986, 203.
52 Mitchell 1991, 59.
53 Halldórsson 1982, 34.

2: The Making of Heroes and Monsters

1 Vigfusson and Powell 1879, 404, and 1883, 502.
2 Gering 1880, 87, wonders aloud how earlier scholars like Grímur Thorkelin, N.F.S. Grundtvig, Eiríkur Magnússon, and W. Morris – all of whom knew both *Beowulf* and *Grettis saga* – could have failed to see the connection between them.
3 Jónsson 1936, lv.
4 See, e.g., Powell 1901, 396.
5 See the discussion of the Sandhaugar episode and Grettir's fight with the bear in chap. 1.
6 See, e.g., Stedman 1913, 26 and 17, and Benson 1970, 28.
7 Vigfusson and Powell 1883, 502 and n. 2 on the same page.
8 See Panzer 1910, 32–9 and 44–66, on how this feature is expressed in various tales, and 268–9 and 322–4 on his attempt to apply the idea to Beowulf and Grettir. Panzer's theory is discussed in chap. 7.
9 Jónsson 1936, 42.
10 The first section definitely relates Beowulf's exploits as a boy, but no chronology is given for the second, which may or may not refer to the same event.
11 See, e.g., Chambers 1959, 65 and Klaeber 1950, 207 (note on line 2183).
12 Arguments to this effect are summed up by Wrenn 1953, 218 (note on lines 2183–9), and Kuhn 1984, 245n. 11.
13 Seven days according to Unferð (line 517a).
14 Even Fred C. Robinson's well-known article, 'Elements of the Marvellous in the Characterization of Beowulf,' in which the author finds ways of rationalizing Beowulf's dive into Grendel's mere, his swimming contest with Breca, and his return by water from Frisia, does not alter this fact. I prefer the more traditional reading of the above-mentioned episodes of the poem, not just because it suits my argument, but because I find it futile to try to rationalize the main hero of a poem which

is neither consistent nor rational, and which asks us to believe that this same hero fought and defeated a number of supernatural enemies. In short, I prefer the mystery in a mysterious poem like *Beowulf*, and taking it away feels like being told that the parting of the Red Sea took place because of strange and unusual weather conditions.

15 See, e.g., chaps. 38, 58, and 75. Grettir's most famous water adventure, his swim from the island of Drangey to the shore of the mainland of Iceland, has been repeated several times during this century by lesser mortals.

16 Benson 1970, 28.

17 Guðni Jónsson believes Hallmundr to be a half-troll as well; see his introduction to *Grettis saga*, l. The exact nature of Hallmundr is left undefined in the saga.

18 Vigfusson 1878, xlix, and Vigfusson and Powell 1883, 502.

19 See, e.g., Chadwick, 1959, 178–91; Chadwick's use of the term *draugr* for all kinds of supernatural beings is now widely accepted.

20 See Lehmann 1901, 191–2. Early theories on the origin of the Grendels are summed up, e.g., by Kögel 1892, 274–6, and Wardale 1965, 92–3.

21 'The Haunted Mere in Beowulf.' Lawrence developed his ideas on the subject further in a later study entitled *Beowulf and Epic Tradition*.

22 Lines 1359b and 2128b. Lawrence interpreted the Old English term *fyrgenstream*, 'mountain stream,' to mean a waterfall.

23 Lawrence 1912, 241–5, and 1928, 162.

24 Lawrence 1912, 240.

25 See, e.g., Chambers 1959, 461–4; Liestöl 1930, 371–2; Fontenrose 1959, 527n. 12 and Kennedy 1940, xxi.

26 For a further discussion of this point see, e.g., von Sydow 1923, 31.

27 This has presented a dilemma to critics who look for rational explanations of everything in the poem. Klaeber 1950, 181 (note on lines 1282 ff.), for instance, offers the far-fetched but amusing theory that the reference to her weakness is 'evidently to be explained as an endeavor to discredit the unbiblical notion of a woman's superiority.'

28 See Lawrence 1928, 181–2, and Goldsmith 1970, 104.

29 See Wrenn 1953, 209.

30 See Lawrence 1928, 163–4.

31 For further reference see Klaeber 1950, xxviii–xxix, and Chambers 1959, 309–10. 'Grendel' also surfaces in English place names, often attached to water, but apart from that they throw no light on the meaning of the word according to Chambers. On the place name 'Grendill' in Iceland, see Einarsson, 1956, 79–82. He believes that the name is modern, probably given by a recent surveyor.

32 *Mære mearcstapa*. It has also been suggested, first by Edv. Lehmann 1901, 189, and later by Kiessling 1968, 191, that *mære* (with a long 'æ') – normally taken to be an adjective – might be a noun, *mære* (with a short vowel), meaning an incubus or a night monster (Old Norse *mara*).

33 See Jónsson 1936, 123–4n. 2; Janzén 1947, 51; Magnússon 1989, 252; and Jónsson 1954, 209 and 311.

34 See Boer 1898, 57–8, and 1900, xlii.

35 See von Unwerth 1911, 171–2. Von Unwerth also points to the presence of a giant named Glámr in *Bárðar saga*, chaps. 13–14.

36 See Boer 1900, xlii n. 1, and von Unwerth 1911, 171–2.

37 Carney 1955, 94–5.

38 It has been argued (see, e.g., Hume 1975, 473) that there is a causal relationship between Glámr's becoming a ghost and the fact that his death is caused by some kind of a monstrous creature. There is nothing in the text of *Grettis saga* which confirms (or denies) this view.

39 Gordon 1927, 83. Gordon, it may be added, sees little ingenuity in Glámr's behaviour as a ghost and suspects that his habit of riding the house-top 'may have been suggested originally by the cattle of Iceland getting on the turf roof to nibble the grass.'

40 See von Unwerth 1911, 167–9, and Jónsson 1936, xvii–xxxi.

41 Pálsson 1980, 98–9.

42 Pálsson 1980, 98: 'sýnast þeir með svo stórum líkömum, að höfuð ber herbergjum hærra.'

43 It appears both in *Eyrbyggja* and *Laxdæla saga*.

44 Carney 1955, 96.

45 Kiessling 1968, 200.

46 See, e.g., Halvorsen 1974, 656.

47 Christmas is very often the time when such attacks occur, but here there is nothing in the text to indicate that these particular raids are inspired by animosity towards Christianity, like the account of Grendel's ongoing strife against God.

48 There is no single word in English for this vessel. *Trog* is a cross between a tray and a trough.

49 See, e.g., Jónsson 1936, 30n. 1, and Shetelig 1937, 378.

50 See Klaeber 1950, xv n. 2.

51 See, e.g., Motz 1982, 72–3.

52 Garmonsway et al. 1968, 316.

53 Jorgensen 1973, 56. The compounds *ástvinr* and *málvinr*, which occur in the kennings for lovers that Jorgensen found ('*ástvinr meyja*' and '*ekkju málvinr*'), indicate more than just a friendship. It is difficult to see how they can be used as evidence of the semantic range of the uncompounded form *vinr* in Old Norse.

54 See, e.g., Malone 1958, 307.

55 Like the Sandhaugar episode, chap. 18 of the saga is somewhat inconsistent. The story of the high-handed practices of Kárr and his son does not accord well with the description of Þorfinnr's character, and his reaction to Grettir's robbing Kárr's gravemound makes little sense.

56 McConchie 1982, 482–3.

57 It is a fire burning on a promontory on the island that first attracts Grettir's attention, and he immediately interprets what he sees as a sign of a buried treasure. After having broken into the gravemound, Grettir pays no attention to the presence of Kárr; he merely assembles his booty and is about to leave when Kárr attacks him (cf. Jónsson 1936, 57–8). McConchie's statement (p. 484) that 'Grettir's interest in the gravemound is not given a precise motivation' is only true in the sense that the saga author does not spell it out any clearer than this.

58 Wachsler 1985, 382–3.

59 Taylor 1952, 17.

60 It is very uncertain what *þyle* really means and what Unferð's role in Heorot is. See, e.g., Rosier 1962, 1–8, and Eliason 1963, 267–84.

61 For further discussion see Hughes 1977 and Rosenberg 1975.

62 Wachsler 1985, 386.

63 Chadwick 1959, 193.

64 Chadwick 1959, 192.

65 Chadwick 1959, 193.

66 It is not clear what meaning Chadwick wants to assign to this form.

67 Arent 1969, 184–5.

68 Janzén 1947, 155. ('*Belsheim* menar mansnamnet vara samma namn som den i Normandie starkt utbredda *Grente*. Han förmodar namnet ha uppstått på "et sted i Vesten, og mindst et par generationer førend det første gang viser sig paa Isl.," och att det möjligen är ett främmande namn av oviss innebörd.')

69 Liberman 1986, 389–90.

70 For discussion along these lines see, e.g., Arent 1969, 184–5, and Chadwick 1959, 193.

71 Harris 1973, 40.

72 Harris 1973, 36.

73 Anatoly Liberman's objections to Harris's methods were noted in chap. 1.

74 Cf., e.g., item 6 regarding Grettir's death and items 6 and 7 from *Beowulf*.

75 Harris 1973, 43–4.

76 For a thorough investigation of the different roles that Grettir is made to play in the saga itself and in later tradition see Hastrup 1990, 154–83.

3: The Hero's Fight against the Monsters

1 Jónsson 1936, lv.

2 See Klaeber 1950, 155 (note on lines 736b–8).

3 German scholars have normally been more discriminating on this point than their English and American colleagues. In German these two kinds of fights are usually

called *Zerrkampf* (tug-fight) and *Ringkampf* (wrestling match). Old Norse has no term for the first type but knows the second as *glíma*.

4   In this passage the difficulty concerns the interpretation of line 749b: 'ond wið earm gesæt,' which Klaeber (1950, 155) and many other editors and translators read to mean that Beowulf sat up supporting himself on his arm. Wrenn, on the other hand, believes that the arm in question is Grendel's and that Beowulf 'sat right up violently ... so as to drive back Grendel's arm.' For further discussion of this line see Wrenn 1953, 198 (note on lines 745–9).

5   It was Heinz Dehmer who first called attention to this peculiarity of fighting with the demon's arm rather than with the demon himself. He traced the motif to Irish sources. For further discussion, see Dehmer 1928.

6   See, e.g., Whitbread 1949, Rosier 1963, and Carens 1976.

7   It should be noted that some critics believe that the best first battle analogue in *Grettis saga* is Grettir's fight with Glámr. Consequently, they see the battle against the troll-woman as an analogue to Beowulf's fight against Grendel's mother. See, e.g., Gordon 1927, 83, and Chadwick 1959, 190.

8   According to Grettir, she perished when she fell into the ravine, but the local inhabitants of Bárðardalur claim that troll-woman was caught by the light of dawn as they wrestled. She died when he cut her arm off and a stone in her likeness still stands there at the edge of the cliff. See *Grettis saga*, chap. 65.

9   See, e.g., Lawrence 1912, 234n. 1, and Puhvel 1979, 120–1.

10   See Puhvel 1979, 115.

11   See, e.g., lines 750–3a, 765b–6 and 805b–7a. Klaeber 1950, lii, complains that the fight is 'too short and easy' for Beowulf.

12   See Jónsson 1936, 212.

13   Benson 1970, 28.

14   Jónsson 1936, 120–1, 212, and 215.

15   Jónsson 1936, 120–1.

16   Chambers 1929, 87.

17   Jónsson 1936, xlix.

18   See, e.g., Dehmer 1928, 207.

19   Earle 1884, 137.

20   See, e.g., Boer 1923, 107–12, Leach 1921, 299, and Goldsmith 1970, 100.

21   See Dehmer 1927, 40–1.

22   Dehmer 1927, 41.

23   Jorgensen 1979, 84.

24   Jónsson 1936, 121.

25   Puhvel 1979, 119.

26   See chapter 9, 'The Big Bang Theory.'

27   Goldsmith 1970, 100.

28 The Devil was commonly held to have flaming eyes during the Middle Ages. See, e.g., Russell 1984, 68: 'his eyes are saucerlike and glow or shoot fire.'

29 For further discussion of these points see Taylor 1952, 15–17, Arent 1969, 190–1, and Wachsler 1985, 381–90.

30 I follow Fred C. Robinson's reading of line 1545a: *ofsæt þa þone selegyst*. For a further discussion of the meaning of the Old English verb *ofsittan*, see Robinson 1994, 1–7.

31 It is a matter of punctuation of line 1555 whether this happens through divine intervention. See Klaeber 1950, 187 (note on lines 1555 ff.).

32 It is not entirely clear whether Beowulf does this with Hrunting or the giant sword (see, e.g., Eliason 1963, 279), nor does the poem tell us why Grendel is decapitated. Klaeber 1950, xviii, finds it hard to accept that the hero would be wasting his time killing dead monsters, and proposes that in the original form of the story 'the male demon had been merely wounded; when the hero had made his way to the dwelling place of the monsters, he put the wounded enemy to death (and afterwards killed the mother).'

33 Cf. Jónsson 1936, 216: 'It is not said how much money he got from the cave, but people assume that it was a fair amount.' (Translation mine.)

34 Parks 1993, 12 and 13.

35 Chambers 1929, 85.

36 Klaeber 1950, 186 (note on lines 1506 ff.). Klaeber here accepts Lawrence's idea that *Samsons saga fagra* is yet another version of the 'old legend.' On this theory see Lawrence 1929, 172–81.

37 See McConchie 1982, 483.

38 Adapted from Stitt 1992, 155. For further discussion see his chapter 'The Gravemound Battle Tradition,' 129–69.

39 Arent 1969, 195.

40 See, e.g., Stedman 1913, 13–17.

41 Chadwick 1959, 190.

42 *Beowulf*, see, e.g., lines 194–5 and 409b–32.

43 Wardale 1965, 94.

44 Jónsson 1936, 209–10: 'Þorsteinn hvíti hét maðr, er bjó at Sandhaugum ... Þar þótti mǫnnum reimt mjǫk sakar trollagangs.'

45 Jónsson 1936, 215, explains *heptisax* as a weapon with a wooden handle that could be used both for stabbing and cutting. This now famous word, the nature of the weapon in question, and the relationship of both to Old English *hæftmece*, will be discussed in detail in the next chapter.

46 See, e.g., Brodeur 1959, 95; Chambers 1929, 91, and Lawrence 1928, 182.

47 Lawrence 1912, 234n. 1.

48 Brandl 1901–9, 994: 'Grettir erlegt ihn [i.e., the giant] mit einem Schwerthieb in die Brüst, ungefähr wie Beowulf die Grendelin.'

49 In prose word order: *ek lét heptisax hǫggva harðeggjar af skepti. See Jorgensen 1973, 54–61, and 1979, 88.
50 Liberman 1986, 391n. 3.
51 Stitt 1992, 205.
52 The motif of the gore-stained water also occurs in two Icelandic texts recorded later than *Grettis saga: Samsons saga fagra* and *Þorsteins saga Víkingssonar.*
53 Chambers 1959, 63. In the folktale, now identified as AT301, the hero goes into the lower world to rescue stolen maidens. The maidens are pulled up by the hero's companions, who in turn steal them and betray the hero by leaving him behind. He usually makes his way to the upper world through some sort of magic, finds the maidens, and punishes the treacherous companions.
54 Benson 1970, 32.
55 See Danielli 1945.

4: A Sword by Any Other Name

1 See chap. 1.
2 Chickering 1977, 133, lines 1455b–6a. Klaeber 1950, 350, simply glosses *hæftmece* as a 'hilted sword.' For the definition that *Grettis saga* gives of *heptisax*, see chap. 1, n. 4.
3 Davidson 1962, 140.
4 See Falk 1914, 10.
5 See Boer 1898, 60 and 1900, lxiii. In his 'Beowulf och Bjarke,' C.W. von Sydow also voices similar scepticism. A case for transmission through an oral tradition is made by Chambers 1959, 474, and more recently by Stitt 1992, 95–6.
6 Schneider 1934, 26–7.
7 Von Sydow 1923, 29–30.
8 Turville-Petre 1974–7, 352.
9 Taken from Chambers 1959, 180. The text in Jónsson 1936, 215, reads: 'En er Grettir kom at honum, hljóp jǫtuninn upp ok greip flein einn ok hjó til þess, er kominn var, því at bæði mátti hǫggva ok leggja með því; tréskapt var í; þat kǫlluðu menn þá heptisax, er þann veg var gǫrt.'
10 Earle 1892, 159.
11 See, e.g., Dehmer 1927, 58; von Sydow 1923, 30 and Puhvel 1979, 118.
12 See Jorgensen 1973 and Halldórsson 1982, 26.
13 Translation mine. For the original text, see Jónsson 1936:
     Þá hét konungr á berserki sína til framgǫngu; þeir váru kallaðir úlfheðnar, en á þá bitu engi járn; (5)
     Þorgeirr var fyrir búi þeira brœðra í Reykjarfirði ok reri jafnan til fiska, því at þá váru firðirnir fullir af fiskum. (26)

Skip þat, er kaupmenn hǫfðu gǫrt, var mjǫk breiðvaxit; þat kǫlluðu menn Trékylli, ok þar er víkin við kennd. (32–3)
Þorsteinn hafði látit gera kirkju á bœ sínum. Hann lét brú gera heiman frá bœnum; hon var gǫr með hagleik miklum. En útan í brúnni undir ásunum, þeim er upp heldu brúnni, var gǫrt með hringum ok dynbjǫllur, svá at heyrði yfir til Skarfsstaða, hálfa viku sjávar, ef gengit var um brúna; svá hristusk hringarnir. Hafði Þorsteinn mikinn starfa fyrir þessarri smíð, því at hann var járngǫrðarmaðr mikill. Grettir var atgangsmikill at drepa járnit, en nennti misjafnt ... (173)

14 See Jónsson 1936, xxxi–xxxvii.

15 Jorgensen 1973, 55: '... the scrambled syntax of the second stanza contains a number of details which are also found in the fight with Grendel's dam in *Beowulf*, but not in the corresponding prose version of *Grettis saga*. It is known that writers of the thirteenth century used in their prose redactions pre-classical or Old Norse verses which they no longer completely understood, and if this can be shown to be the case in *Grettis saga*, then the existence in Iceland of a poem older than the saga treating the Grendel legend must be assumed.'

16 Jorgensen 1973, 56–7.

17 Turville-Petre, 1974–7, 352.

18 In the preamble to Jorgensen's argument two other points also merit attention. It is an overstatement to maintain that *hæftmece* and *heptisax* occur 'at precisely the same point' in the relevant episodes of *Beowulf* and *Grettis saga*. The sword Hrunting is called a *hæftmece* before and not during Beowulf's battle with Grendel's mother, and the sword also has various other appellations. The issue of whether *hæftmece* and *heptisax* can be considered as cognate words will be dealt with later in this chapter.

19 Shetelig and Falk 1937, 385–6. See also Falk 1914, 68.

20 In addition to *hæftmece*, *beado-leoma*, *hilde-bil(l)*, and *wæg-sweord* are also applied to Hrunting, and these terms occur only in *Beowulf*. The same is true of the giant sword that Beowulf discovers during his battle with Grendel's mother, the *hilde-gicel* – also called *ealdsweord* and *wigbil(l)* – whose blade melts.

21 Cf., e.g., Chambers 1959, 469: 'This casual use of the word *hæft-mēce* would not have attracted attention or called for any remark, were it not for its counterpart the *hepti-sax* in the *Grettis saga*.'

22 Brady 1979, 93.

23 Beowulf's own sword is said to be 'the best of blades' (*irena cyst*) in line 673a, and lines 1023a and 2154a describe Hroðgar's gift as famous, precious, and richly adorned.

24 For a summary of early suggestions concerning the etymology of Hrunting, see Liberman 1986, 390.

25 Malone 1944 and 1946.

26 Eliason 1963, 278n. 40 and 284.

27 Shetelig and Falk 1937, 386.
28 Klaeber 1950, 360.
29 Klaeber 1950, 429.
30 Brady 1979, 101.
31 Klaeber 1950, 301.
32 Brady 1979, 101.
33 Lehmann 1967, 230.
34 See Davidson 1962, 129, and Lehmann 1967, 227–8.
35 Chambers 1959, 473–4.
36 See, e.g., Klaeber 1950, 185 (note on line 1457): 'It appears that in the original story much was made of a sword with a wonderful "haft" (or "hilt"), which later, as a result of the fight, was detached from the blade ... It was a part of such a marvelous sword, we imagine, to bring about the hero's victory. This feature is obliterated in the *Grettis saga*; in the *Beowulf*, the term *hæftmēce* has been transferred to an entirely different sword'; and also Jorgensen 1979, 89: 'It is very likely that the nonce epithet itself, i.e., *hæftmēce*, was a transferal by the *Beowulf* poet from the sword in the cave to the hero's weapon ...'
37 See Puhvel 1979, 117.
38 The traditional interpretation of *fetelhilt* has been questioned by H.R. Ellis Davidson, who points to stories about swords that are secured in some way that makes it impossible for anyone except the hero to draw them. 'It is thus possible that this unique term *fetelhilt* is not a descriptive one but one arising out of a traditional element in the story, though its significance is no longer apparent in the poem as we have it.' Davidson 1962, 142.
39 See Klaeber 1950, 189, and Wrenn 1953, 212.
40 Davidson 1962, 139.
41 Davidson 1962, 141.
42 Evison 1963, 138–9.
43 Taylor 1952, 16.
44 He referred to *hæftmece* and *heptisax* rather mysteriously as 'one word,' as we saw in chap. 1.
45 See, e.g., Jorgensen 1973, 56–7.
46 See, e.g., Chambers 1929, 94, and Puhvel 1979, 116.
47 See, e.g., Halldórsson 1982, 23: 'Augljósasta bendingin um skyldleika Bjkv. og Grettlu er hið samkynja vopnsheiti sem kemur fram í báðum verkum ... En þótt orðin samsvari hvort öðru hafa vopnin hvorki sama snið né hlutverk.'
48 Evison 1963, 138.
49 Liberman 1986, 380 and 383.
50 Mastrelli 1985–6, 405–20.
51 See Schück 1909, 18–19n. 1.

52 Arent 1969, 195. Arent's criticism rests on her belief that both words refer to a weapon which may 'merely belong to the paraphernalia of trolls and giants.'

5: Hell and High Water

1 See von Sydow 1923, 31–2.
2 See Klaeber 1950, xiv n. 3.
3 See, e.g., Arent 1969, 191, and Jorgensen 1975. It should be noted, however, that Arent believes that the scenery of the bear analogue in the saga recalls the dragon's lair rather than the surroundings of the mere.
4 Smith 1881, 65: 'In both cases we find the hero engaged in strife with two superhuman beings of different sexes, inhabiting a cave 'neath a force.'
5 Lawrence 1912, 218–19.
6 Lawrence 1912, 235–7. Lawrence later expanded his ideas on this subject in *Beowulf and Epic Tradition*, where he maintains, for instance, that the muddled picture which the author of *Beowulf* gives of a waterfall might have come about because he had never seen the real thing. See Lawrence 1928, 184–6.
7 Klaeber must have had some doubts, however, because the reference to Lawrence which follows the gloss begins with a question mark.
8 Chambers 1959, 464.
9 See, e.g., Schlauch 1956, 42–3; Chadwick 1959, 186; Jorgensen 1973, 54; Harris 1973, 41; Chickering 1977, 334; and Jack 1994, 117.
10 Mackie 1938, 457. For further a discussion of *fyrgenstream* as an epithet for 'ocean' in Anglo-Saxon literature, see also Sarrazin 1910, 5.
11 Lawrence 1939, 479.
12 Malone 1932, 192.
13 Malone 1958, 298. Malone's article is presented as a criticism of Klaeber's handling of the mere scene in his edition of *Beowulf*. However, Klaeber's notes and glosses in this section of the poem are simply an echo of Lawrence's theories concerning the landscape of the mere and its connection with *Grettis saga*.
14 This is not entirely without exception. Andersson 1997, 131, notes the findings of Mackie and Malone in their argument against Lawrence's waterfall theory, but he dismisses their impact on the question of a genetic relationship between the poem and the saga: 'Despite this curious debate over landscape features, there is not much doubt of some connection between *Beowulf* and *Grettis saga*.'
15 See, e.g., Lawrence 1912, 240: 'It is clear that the Anglo-Saxon *Beowulf*, in anything like the form in which we have it at present, could not have given a hint for the description of Grettir's adventure at the waterfall. The situation is obscure in Anglo-Saxon; it is crystal-clear in Scandinavian. The fact that the *Grettissaga* explains so well the obscurities of the Anglo-Saxon version prevents us from concluding that the

main outlines of the Scandinavian account represent a late rationalization or alteration of the original situation'; and Lawrence 1928, 182–3: 'The saga is clear where
the epic is confused; it preserves the original form of the story so much better that it
may even be used to explain obscure incidents and description in the Anglo-Saxon.
As an illustration, let us see how the tale of Grettir serves to show the original conception of the demon lair ...'

16 Neither Mackie nor Malone questioned this assumption in their objections to
Lawrence's theory. For later reiterations of the clarity and realism of the waterfall
scenery in the saga see, e.g., Arent 1969, 196; Halldórsson 1982, 32; and Liberman
1986, 374.

17 Lawrence 1912, 239: 'It is very significant, then, that the idea of a cave under a
waterfall, in a precipitous country, adhered so strongly to the story that the natural
scenery was disregarded in order to retain it.' The possibility that the saga author had
an actual waterfall in mind should, however, not be altogether discarded. In his edition of the saga Guðni Jónsson suggests the possibility that another waterfall
(Goðafoss) in a nearby river (Skjálfandafljót) may have been what he had in mind.
See Jónsson 1936, 213n. 1. Halldór Laxness, in a humorous article on Icelandic out-
laws, reports that in the 1940s the inhabitants of Bárðardalur believed the saga
description to be accurate; the waterfall had simply changed since Grettir's time.
Laxness 1949, 87–8.

18 Jónsson 1936, 214: 'en er þeir kómu til forsins, sá þeir skúta upp undir bergit; þat var
meitilberg svá mikit, at hvergi mátti upp komask, ok nær tíu faðma ofan at vatninu.'
The key word here is *skúta*, which in this context can either be a noun (acc. sing. or
pl.) meaning 'cave(s),' or a verb meaning 'to overhang.'

19 Panzer 1910, 315, takes the ten fathoms as the distance from the top of the cliff to the
cave below the fall; Boer 1900, 238n. 8, as the distance from the cave to the surface
of the pool; and Lawrence, 1912, 234n. 2, rounds up the remaining possibility by
taking them as the distance from the top of the cliff to the pool beneath. Lawrence, in
the last-mentioned article, does not seem to have realized that *skúta* was a problem,
as he only addresses the issue of the 'ten fathoms' in a footnote and concludes –
quite erroneously – that it is 'not important' for the purpose of his argument.

20 See Chambers 1959, 179. His translation of the passage reads: 'But when they came
to the waterfall they saw that the sides of the gorge hung over: it was a sheer cliff so
great that one could in nowise come up, and it was nearly ten fathoms from the top to
the water below.' Chambers further explains his vision of the waterfall landscape in
n. 2 for this page: 'The translators all take *skúta* as acc. of *skúti*, which is quite possible: but they are surely wrong when they proceed to identify the *skúti* with the *hellir*
[i.e., 'cave'] behind the waterfall. For this cave behind the waterfall is introduced in
the *saga* as something which Grettir discovers *after* he has dived beneath the fall, the
fall in front naturally hiding it till then.' It may be added that Heinz Dehmer reads

this passage to mean exactly the opposite; i.e., that Grettir sees that there is cave behind the waterfall: 'Nach Weihnachten holt Grettir Stein ab, um mit ihm nachzusehen, ob seine Ansicht richtig sei. Sie kommen an den Wasserfall und sehen eine von überhängenden Felsen gebildete Höhle, die sich weiter unter den Felsen hinzieht.' Dehmer 1927, 57.

21 See Jónsson 1936, 216–17. Stanza 60: 'fast lá framan at brjósti / flugstraumr í sal Naumu,' 'the flowing current beat against my breast in the hall of the ogress.' Stanza 61: 'Ljótr kom mér í móti / mellu vinr ór helli,' 'the ugly giant came out of his cave to meet me.'

22 Lawrence 1912, 225.

23 Lawrence 1912, 222–3.

24 Lawrence 1912, 241.

25 Lawrence 1912, 226–7.

26 See Hulbert 1929, 193–4. Mackie later argued along similar lines: 'The poet of *Beowulf* ... cares little about verisimilitude, and does not greatly trouble to be consistent; his purpose is not to make the supernatural appear natural, but to invest his narrative with an eerie atmosphere of strangeness and horror.' Mackie 1938, 456.

27 See, e.g., Goldsmith 1970, 113–14, and Niles 1983, 16.

28 Mackie 1938, 458.

29 Malone 1958, 301–2.

30 Malone 1958, 306.

31 Malone 1958, 298–9.

32 Both texts describe downward-flowing water, a grey rock, frosty woods, dark mists, and an abyss.

33 For a short summary of different theories on this subject see, e.g., Jack 1994, 110. Wright 1993, 106–74 contains a detailed and thorough discussion of St. Paul's vision and its relationship to *Beowulf.*

34 The main weakness in Malone's theory is, as Margaret Goldsmith has pointed out, that 'the place [i.e. the cave of Grendel's dam] is not in the least like hell when Beowulf arrives there.' Goldsmith 1970, 116.

35 Wright 1993, 132.

36 Chickering 1977, 334.

37 Klaeber 1950, 186 (note on lines 1506 ff.).

38 Malone 1958, 303.

39 See, e.g., Benson 1970, 28, and Turville-Petre 1974–7, 351.

40 Rosier 1963, 12. A similar argument is also presented by Dragland 1977, 614: 'If Heorot contains the symbolic darkness of Grendel, the mere-cave has something of the hall about it, described as it is as a kind of underground Germanic dwelling.'

41 Turville-Petre 1974–7, 351.

42 Klaeber explains the phrase *fyrleoht geseah* as: 'The light in the "hall" (which

enables Béowulf to see his adversary).' Klaeber 1950, 186. The suggestion that *fyr-leoht* should be translated as 'fiery light' was originally proposed by W.S. Mackie. See Mackie 1938, 461.

43 See Klaeber 1950, 188, and Mackie 1938, 461.
44 See Lawrence 1939, 478n. 2 and Chambers 1959, 466–7.
45 Mackie 1938, 461.
46 Puhvel 1979, 115.

6: The English Hypothesis

1 Vigfusson 1878, vol. 1, xlix n. 1.
2 Vigfusson and Powell 1883, vol. 2, 502.
3 Bugge 1887, 58: 'Ich vermute, dass die hier besprochene isländische sage [i.e., *Grettis saga*] aus einer nordenglischen stammt. Diese nordenglische sage ruhte, wie ich annehme, auf einem alten liede, das mit demjenigen, aus welchem der dichter des epos geschöpt hat, identisch oder nahe verwant war.' Without noticing that he was contradicting himself, Bugge completely changed his mind a few pages later and then argued that the sagas that he had been discussing did not go back to *Beowulf*, but were derived from a Danish or an English folktale that had nothing to do with the epic (see Bugge 1887, 66–7). It was, however, only Bugge's original suggestion that caught the attention of other scholars, and, as Liberman points out: 'his authority stood so high that his tentative hypothesis immediately became dogma.' Liberman 1986, 355–6.
4 Liberman 1986, 355.
5 See, e.g., Schück 1909, 20–2.
6 Liberman, in his article, mentions Bernhard ten Brink, Karl Müllenhoff, and Thomas Arnold as early supporters of Bugge. See Liberman 1986, 356.
7 See Boer 1898, 65, and his remarks in the preface to his edition of the saga: 'der interpolator hat die geschichte mit einer Beowulf-überlieferung, welche er in einer englischen fassung kennen gelernt hatte, zusammengeworfen ... Zwei strophen dichtete er hinzu; das wort *heptisax* ... verrät die englische quelle der erzählung.' Boer 1900, xliii.
8 See Olrik 1903, 248.
9 See Heusler 1911–13, 246.
10 See von Sydow 1923, 29–30, and Schneider 1934, 27.
11 Harris 1973, 28. Many prominent scholars have argued for an Irish influence on *Beowulf*, e.g., Heinz Dehmer, Max Deutschbein, Carl W. von Sydow, Gerard Murphy, James Carney, and Martin Puhvel.
12 Puhvel 1979, 137–8.
13 Friedrich Panzer's ideas are discussed in the next chapter.

14 Carl von Sydow wrote in Swedish, and not much has been done to introduce his ideas concerning the relationship between *Beowulf* and *Grettis saga* to English-speaking readers. It should therefore be noted that the latest effort to do so, *Beowulf and the Bear's Son*, by J. Michael Stitt, ascribes the notion of a common Irish source to von Sydow but omits to mention that he later changed his mind. See Stitt 1992, 95. The relevant passage in von Sydow's article, 'Beowulf och Bjarke' reads as follows: 'Beträffande förhållandet mellan Gr [i.e., the Grendel episode] och Grettis-sagas trollepisod, har jag tidigare ansett dem båda härstamma frän en gemensam irisk källa, men det har länge förvånat mig och gjort mig tveksam, att man i Grettis-saga ej, såsom i Ormsþáttr, finner något irisk drag som ej också finns i Gr under det att Gr har många sådana som ej finns i Grettissaga. Då jag nu blivit övertygad om att Beowulf-sången indirekt är källan för Grettissaga, beror detta dels på nyssmämnda faktum, dels på de båda motiven hæftmece-heptisax och runinskriften.' Von Sydow 1923, 45.

15 See von Sydow 1923, 28–9. This argument has recently been contradicted by Stitt: 'Von Sydow argued that oral tradition is incapable of preserving a specific term in a foreign language over a span of several centuries. But while the compound noun *hepti-sax* is unique each root [i.e., *hæft-* and *hepti-*] is a common word. Oral transmission is not impossible.' Stitt 1992, 95.

16 See von Sydow 1923, 30.

17 Von Sydow 1923, 31: 'En muntlig prosatradition kan ej samtidigt innehålla två sinsemellan stridande uppgifter av detta slag, utan det ena byts fullständigt ut mot det andra, om den har någorlunda god tid att utkristalliseras.' In his book *Beowulf and the Bear's Son*, J. Michael Stitt criticizes this passage in von Sydow's article with the following cryptic remark: 'Von Sydow's argument would be more convincing if the two descriptive passages [i.e., in *Beowulf* and *Grettis saga*] had detailed similarities, but the similarity here barely extends beyond the motif of a water(fall)-dwelling hag.' Stitt 1992, 95–6.

18 Liberman 1986, 383.

19 Malone 1958, 307.

20 Stedman 1913, 23, and Brandl 1901–9, 995–6.

21 Von Sydow 1923, 29–30, and Schneider 1934, 27.

22 See Einarsson 1938, 290. See also Einarsson 1933, 175.

23 Schück 1909, 21: 'Att den på angelsaksiskt språk affattade dikten om Beowulf skulle hafva varit känd på Island omkring år 1300, kan svårligen antagas, och äfven om så varit, torde språket hafva varit obegripligt. Beowulfdikten kan således icke hafva varit den omedelbara källan till de islandska sagorna.' The question as to whether speakers of Old English and Old Norse could have communicated is an issue that is still debated among medievalists. See, e.g., Fjalldal 1993, 601–9.

24 Chambers 1929, 88n. 2.

25 Chambers 1959, 50.
26 Lawrence 1912, 240.
27 Lawrence 1928, 182.
28 Chambers 1959, 53. See also pages 461–72.
29 Turville-Petre 1974–7, 347.
30 Stitt 1992, 96.
31 Chambers 1929, 91.
32 Harris 1973, 30–1.

7: Panzer's 'Bear's Son' Theory

 1 In modern folklore studies this story is now known as AT 301, or 'The Three Stolen Princesses.'
 2 Panzer 1910, 319: 'Es ist durch diese Ausführungen, glaube ich, der Nachweis erbracht, daß die Erzählung der Saga von Grettirs Abentauer in Sandhaugar in letzter Linie auf dem Bährensohnmärchen beruht. Damit aber rückt ihr Verhältnis zur Beo-wulfsage in ein ganz neues Licht. Denn damit ist offenbar die Möglichkeit gegeben, daß beide Überlieferungen durchaus selbständig nebeneinander stünden, indem beide unabhängig voneinander aus der gemeinsamen Märchenquelle sich ableiteten.'
 3 See Laistner 1889, 15–34.
 4 For a more detailed summary and a comparison of the different versions of the story see, e.g., Pizarro 1976–7, 265–9.
 5 Panzer 1910, 257.
 6 Panzer 1910, 263.
 7 Panzer 1910, 264.
 8 Panzer 1910, 268–72.
 9 Panzer 1910, 274–6.
10 Panzer 1910, 278.
11 Panzer 1910, 280.
12 Panzer 1910, 284–90.
13 Panzer 1910, 305–13.
14 Panzer 1910, 316.
15 Panzer 1910, 317.
16 Panzer 1910, 317.
17 Panzer 1910, 318.
18 Panzer 1910, 318–19.
19 Panzer 1910, 319.
20 Panzer 1910, 322–4.
21 Panzer 1910, 326–7.
22 Panzer 1910, 327–32.

23 Panzer 1910, 319–20.

24 Panzer 1910, 319.

25 Panzer 1910, 402: 'Daneben finden sich jedoch in der Grettis saga ... eine Reihe von Zügen, die auffällig mit dem Beowulf zusammentreffen und, da sie beidenmal auch formale Elemente einschließen, tatsächlich literarische Einwirkung voraussetzen. Diese Beeinflussung aber wäre auf zwei Wegen zu denken: es könnte (mittelbar) die skandinavische Vorlage des Beowulf oder aber eine mit dem Beowulf stofflich und teilweise formal identische englische Dichtung die isländische Überlieferung beeinflußt haben: beides wäre nach den allgemeinen Kultur- und den besonderen literarischen Verhältnissen an sich gleich denkbar.'

26 Chambers 1959, 478.

27 See, e.g., Chambers 1959, 380, where he refers to Panzer's elements of the different versions of the folktale as 'an artificial, theoretical composite.'

28 Chambers 1959, 62–3.

29 Chambers 1959, 380.

30 Chambers 1959, 68n. 1.

31 Chambers 1959, 380–1. For criticism of Panzer's theory in this vein see also Mogk 1919, 115.

32 Von Sydow 1923, 28: 'löftesbrott – knappast förräderi! – vilket ytterligare framhäver Grettes styrka.'

33 Von Sydow 1923, 28: 'Även om Grettissagas trollepisod kunde föras tillbaka till en med Beowulfsången gemensam källa, kan den alltså icke ge något stöd åt teorien att denna källa skulle ha tillkommit under påverkan av björnsonsagan.'

34 Mossé 1933, xl n. 2: 'C'est peut-être aller un peu loin que de voir comme le fait Panzer, (l. c., p. 319) un souvenir de ce motif [i.e., the stolen princesses] dans les rapports de Grettir avec Steinvor, la femme du bondi, assaillie par les monstres.'

35 Lawrence 1928, 171. Like Chambers, however, Lawrence has some concerns about Panzer's working method: 'What is of importance is to show that, in spite of all divergences, a common pattern is really visible. Panzer's method is to construct this common pattern, and to illustrate it, incident by incident, from his collections. This is obviously somewhat dangerous, and may lead to false conclusions. By taking many different colors and lines from many different pictures one can put together almost any kind of picture that one pleases. That this would be an unjust criticism of Panzer's book is evident when the tales themselves are read.' Lawrence 1928, 172–3.

36 Sedgefield 1935, xxviii.

37 Wardale 1965. Wardale explains differences between the Bear's Son Tale and Beowulf and Grettis saga by arguing that 'it is possible that the North-West of Europe had evolved a special form of the tale for itself.' Wardale 1965, 98.

38 See, e.g., Jones 1972, 10–11.

39 See, e.g., Pizarro 1976–7, 263: 'Friedrich Panzer's theory about the folktale of the

Bear's Son as a source of *Beowulf* and of various Icelandic sagas has met much scepticism and neglect in recent years. Klaus von See recently declared Panzer's views to be "heute zu den Akten gelegt." This dismissal of a painstaking study seems to me premature. It has often been caused by an excessively vague idea of the Bear Son's tale and of the episodes that it involves.'

40 See Harris 1973, 30.
41 See, e.g., Jorgensen 1975, 35–6.
42 See Propp 1968, 23–4, and Aarne and Thompson 1961, 7.
43 For further reading see, e.g., Rosenberg 1991, 41–6, where Panzer's methods and conclusions are critically summarized.
44 Von Sydow 1923, 25–6. See also Puhvel 1979, 86–90.
45 Klaeber 1950, xiv.
46 Boer 1912, 167.
47 See von Sydow 1923, 34, and Chambers 1959, 369.
48 See Schneider 1934, 20.
49 See Stitt 1992, 123. Women are abducted in *Egils saga einhenda*, and treacherous abandonment occurs in *Flóres saga konungs*.
50 Stitt 1992, 36.
51 Take, e.g., *Egils saga*.
52 Andersson 1997, 133.

8: The Common Origin Theory

1 See, e.g., Ólason 1993, 147: 'Augljós eru kynni Grettluhöfundar af fornaldarsögum, og væntanlega hefur hann þekkt meira af slíku efni, skráðu eða óskráðu, en varðveist hefur því að bæði í lýsingu á viðureign Grettis og Gláms og í frásögn af viðureign hans við ófreskjur í Bárðardal norður eru mikil líkindi við Bjólfskviðu. Hlýtur höfundur Grettis sögu eða fyrri sagnamenn íslenskir að hafa þekkt sagnir eða kvæði sem hafa verið skyldari Bjólfskviðu en nokkrar varðveittar fornaldarsögur.'
2 Lawrence 1928, 182–3.
3 Chambers 1959, 51–2.
4 See, e.g., Chambers 1929, 88–90.
5 See Chambers 1959, 476–7. *Samsons saga fagra* was originally proposed as an analogue by W.W. Lawrence; see Lawrence 1929, 172–81. Summaries of these stories may be found in Garmonsway 1968, 322–4, 324–7, and 328–331.
6 Lawrence 1912, 241–2. See also Chambers 1959, 51: 'it is certain that these stories – like all the subject matter of the Old English epic – did not originate in England, but were brought across the North Sea from the old home. And that old home was in the closest connection, so far as the passage to and fro of story went, with Scandinavian lands. Nothing could be intrinsically more probable than that a story current in

ancient Angel and carried thence to England, should also have been current in Scandinavia, and thence have been carried to Iceland.'

7 Schück 1909, 21.
8 Earle 1884, 139.
9 Klaeber 1950, xiv.
10 H.M. and N.K. Chadwick 1932, 437.
11 Mogk 1919, 116.
12 Smith 1881, 66.
13 See Chambers 1929, 87.
14 Chambers 1959, 49–50.
15 Brodeur 1959, 101.
16 Chambers 1929, 97–8.
17 See Chambers 1959, 476–7.
18 Chambers 1959, 477.
19 Chambers 1959, 477.
20 Carney 1955, 100, n. 1 from previous page.
21 Klaeber 1950, xx n. 1a.
22 English translations of the relevant parts of this saga are given in Garmonsway 1968.
23 Genzmer borrows this name of the sword from Chambers. See Chambers 1959, 473–5.
24 Genzmer 1950, 20–3.
25 See Genzmer 1950, 24 and 61–2.
26 See Chambers 1959, 472–3.
27 See Genzmer 1950, 30–3.
28 Benson 1970, 27.
29 Benson 1970, 28.
30 Liberman 1986, 380.
31 Halldórsson 1982, 17: 'Við rannsóknir þeirrar þjóðsögu sem hér er til athugunar hefur í heila öld verið beitt sögubundinni aðferð. Samt verður að telja að enn hafi ekki tekist að finna eina ákveðna frumsögu né teikna ættartré hennar.'
32 See, e.g., Deutschbein 1909, 110: 'Aber vergebens hat man sich in der altnordischen Literatur nach unabhängigen Spuren von Grendelkämpfen umgesehen ... An selbständigen Zeugnissen für die Existenz einer Beowulf-Grendelsage im skandinavischen Norden fehlt es bis jetzt.'
33 Schneider 1934, 28: 'Nur spricht er [i.e., Chambers] sich leider mit keinem Wort aus, wo, wann und in welcher Form sie [i.e., the original story] entstanden sein mag.' Concerning the age of the 'old legend' Ritchie Girvan maintains that 'a common source ... cannot lie very far back,' but he offers no evidence to back up this claim. See Girvan 1935, 58.
34 Chambers 1959, 474.

35 Klaeber 1950, xx.
36 Mackie 1938, 456.
37 Chickering 1977, 254.
38 Chickering 1977, 132–3.

9: The Big Bang Theory

1 Chadwick 1959, 190.
2 See, e.g., Niles 1983, 10–11, Dragland 1977, 606–7, and Clark 1973 and 1990, 30–3.
3 See Clark 1973.
4 Clark 1990, 30–1.
5 See also Arent 1969, 189–90: 'the fact that many of the motifs are reused in the
    ghost-slaying in Kár's barrow, in the Halogaland bear episode, and at Thórhalls-
    stadir, suggests an interchangeability and availability of a common stock of closely
    associated motifs.'
6 Harris 1973, 30–1.
7 Jorgensen 1986, 201–2.
8 See Jorgensen 1973, 55.
9 Jorgensen 1975, 40.
10 Jorgensen 1975, 37 and 40: 'the saga's description of the trek to the cave and the bat-
     tle with the female monster are closer to the Old English epic version than is the
     famous *Grettis saga* or any other single Norse saga.'
11 Jorgensen 1986, 208.
12 Here Jorgensen must mean Grendel's mother.
13 Jorgensen 1975, 37–40.
14 See Jónsson and Vilhjálmsson 1944, vol. 3, 330–3.
15 Jorgensen 1978, 56–7: 'The swimming contests discussed above show that
     Beowulf's swimming exploits brought up by Unferth at Hrothgar's court have
     numerous analogues in Scandinavia. Even though the saga versions show some inde-
     pendence they bear testimony to the great popularity which the tale enjoyed in north-
     ern Europe. By comparing those motifs which are found in what seems to be the
     most conservative version, *Hálfdanar saga*, with those which keep recurring in the
     other sagas, one can arrive at a probable Old Norse archetype for the swimming
     match. By cross-checking with the Old English epic, one can more reasonably say
     which motifs were present in the older Scandinavian version and common to the
     source of *Beowulf* ... Both the Old English and Old Norse variants support a Ger-
     manic original which already had an immediately following acquatic battle
     attached.'
16 Jorgensen 1978, 56.
17 Jorgensen 1978, 52.

18 Jorgensen 1979, 89: 'In the case of the English epic, *Beowulf*, it is clear that the king's gift of the useless weapon was of Scandinavian provenance and similar to the saga versions discussed above, but instead of making King Hröthgār the donor, the *Beowulf* poet protected Hröthgār's reputation by having the tainted present given by Unferth.'

19 See Jorgensen 1986.

20 Jorgensen 1975, 38.

21 Jorgensen 1986, 203–4.

22 I am, unfortunately, not aware of what Jorgensen considers to be the sixth genetically related analogue in *Grettis saga*.

23 Jorgensen 1986, 205.

24 Harris 1973, 52.

25 Harris 1973: 52.

10: A Saga Author Shops Around

1 See Jónsson 1936, xvii–xxix.

2 For examples of such repetitions, see Halldórsson 1982, 14.

3 Smith 1881, 66.

4 See Boer 1898, 62.

5 Boer had earlier noted similarities in the descriptions of Glámr and Þórólfr bægifótr in his article. See Boer 1898, 55.

6 See Panzer 1910, 334–5.

7 See Dehmer 1927, 28–9.

8 See Dehmer 1928, 205.

9 See Dehmer 1928, 205–6.

10 See von Unwerth 1911, 168.

11 See Stitt 1992, 141. Here the battle takes place inside the ghost's gravemound.

12 See Jónsson 1936, 96.

13 See von Unwerth 1911, 44–54.

14 In the above paragraph the chapter numbers refer to Guðni Jónsson's 1953 edition of *Íslendinga sögur*, vols. 1–12, and in the case of the three *fornaldarsǫgur* that I mention, *Þorsteins þáttr bæjarmagns*, *Hrómundar saga Gripssonar*, and *Áns saga bogsveigis*, to the edition of Guðni Jónsson and Bjarni Vilhjálmsson 1943–4, Fornaldarsögur Norðurlanda, vols. 1–3.

15 Translated into English by William Morris and Eiríkur Magnússon in 1891, and again by Alan Boucher in 1986.

16 Andersson 1967, 196.

17 See Þórólfsson and Jónsson 1943, lxxxix: 'að líkindum samin eftir gömlum vest-firzkum arfsögnum á fyrri hluta 13. aldar. Að vísu verður nú ekkert með vissu sagt um aldur hennar, nema að hún hefir verið eldri en Sturlubók Landnámu, sem er líklega samin á síðustu æviárum Sturlu lögmanns.' See also Þórólfsson 1923, lviii.

18 See Nordal 1968, 157 and 160: 'Samanburður við Sturlubók sýnir svo mikil frávik þess, sem hlýtur að hafa staðið í eldri sögunni, að menn hafa einna helzt hallast að því, að ekki væri um nein rittengsl að ræða milli þessara tveggja gerða. Mjög er þó varasamt að gera ráð fyrir slíku.'

19 See Þórólfsson 1923, lviii, Þórólfsson and Jónsson 1943, xc, and Nordal 1968, 159–60.

20 Von Unwerth 1911, 170: 'Die Schilderungen der beiden Kämpfe decken sich also nahezu vollständig. Die einzelnen Abweichungen sind nicht so bedeutsam, dass man um ihretwillen die beiden Erzählungen als unabhängig voneinander ansehen könnte. Literarische Abhängigheit auf der einen oder der andern Seite muss angenommen werden.'

21 Von Unwerth 1911, 169–70. Translation mine. Von Unwerth obviously followed those saga editions that were available at the time, but for the sake of convenience, I have taken the liberty of 'updating' the examples that he presented by using the text of the *Íslenzk fornrit* series. According to those editions, the original text of these passages is as follows:

Hávarðarsaga Ísfirðings, ÍF 6, 298–9	*Grettis saga, ÍF* 7, 119–20
Óláfr lá í stafnrekkju útar við dyrr ...	[Grettir] lagðisk niðr í setit gegnt lokrekkju bónda ...
Ljós brann í skálanum ...	Ljós brann í skálanum ...
Óláfr lagðisk niðr í skyrtu ok brókum ...	vildi Grettir eigi fara af klæðum ...
hann kastaði á sik feldi einum ...	hann hafði rǫggvarfeld yfir sér ...
gekk Þormóðr inn í skálann ok lét róa tinglit ...	sá Grettir, at þrællinn rétti inn hǫfuðit ...
Hann sá at rekkja var skipuð, er ekki var vani á ...	Glámr sá, at hrúga nǫkkur lá í setinu ...
snýr hann þangat ok þrífr í feldinn ...	ok rézk nú innar eptir skálanum ok þreif í feldinn stundar fast ...
þeir skipta feldinum með sér ...	kippðu nú í sundr feldinum í millum sín ...
Ok er Þormóðr finnr, at afl er í þeim, er fyrir er ...	[Glámr] undraðisk mjǫk, hverr svá fast mundi togask við hann ...
Þormóðr hljóp undir hendr honum ...	hljóp Grettir undir hendr honum ...
tókst þar inn harðasti atgangr ...	Áttu þeir þá allharða sókn ...
flest gekk ok upp, þat sem fyrir varð ...	allt brotnaði, þat sem fyrir varð ...
Þormóðr sótti þá í ákafa, ok þar kømr at lyktum, at þeir horfa út ...	Glámr fœrðisk í aukana ok kneppði hann at sér, er þeir kómu í anddyrit ...

22 Von Unwerth 1911, 171: 'aus dieser [i.e., *Hávarðar saga Ísfirðings*] hat sie der Verfasser der Grett. in seine grosse Gespenstergeschichte aufgenommen.'

23 See, e.g., Andersson 1967, 193.

24 There is no mention of it in Chambers's entries in his bibliography for the year 1911. See Chambers 1959, 576.

25 The term 'author' is a loaded word in saga studies, and I want to emphasize that in using it as I do – i.e., for convenience – I am not trying to imply anything about the actual composition of *Grettis saga*.

26 Translation mine. The original reads: 'Grettir var síðan á Sandhaugum um vetrinn ok dulðisk þó fyrir alþýðu manna.' Jónsson 1936, 218.

27 In his article 'Objects and Oral Tradition in Medieval Iceland,' Richard Perkins describes a number of interesting cases of a similar kind that are to be found within the context of the saga tradition. See Perkins 1989, 239–66.

28 See Boer 1898, 62.

29 Sagas with which the author of *Grettis saga* is known to have been familiar are marked with an asterisk.

30 The chapter numbers given throughout the following discussion refer to Guðni Jónsson's 1953 edition of *Íslendinga sögur*, vols. 1–12; for *fornaldarsǫgur* to the edition of Guðni Jónsson and Bjarni Vilhjálmsson 1943–4, *Fornaldarsǫgur Norðurlanda*, vols. 1–3; for *konungasǫgur* to the edition of Páll Eggert Ólason 1946–8, *Heimskringla Snorra Sturlusonar – Konungasögur*, vols. 1–3; and for *riddarasǫgur* to the edition of Bjarni Vilhjálmsson 1982, *Riddarasögur*, vols. 1–6.

31 Heinz Dehmer, who investigated the Sandhaugar episode as a potential ghost story, concluded that the loss of an arm by the troll-woman had no counterpart in the stories that he examined as possible parallels. See Dehmer 1927, 54.

32 See Boer 1898, 62–3. Boer thought that the first fight in the Sandhaugar episode was merely a variant of the Glámr story, whereas the second fight showed a direct contact – in some form – with *Beowulf*. For a full discussion of his position, see Boer 1923, 107–8.

33 See Jónsson 1936, xlix, and 58n. 4.

34 See Panzer 1910, 317.

35 Chambers 1959, 66 and 380: 'in Zealand, one of the faithless companions is called *Stenhuggeren* (the Stone-hewer), in Schleswig *Steenklöwer*, in Hanover *Steinspieler*, whilst in Iceland he has the same name *Stein*. which he has in the *Grettis Saga*.'

36 Translation mine. The original (see Jónsson and Vilhjálmsson 1944, 239) reads: 'Þá leiddust Faxa höggin, ok stökk hann fyrir borð ok í kaf, svá at í iljar honum var at sjá.' Grettir's dive into the waterfall is described with these words: 'síðan hljóp hann [i.e., Grettir] af bjarginu ok niðr í forsinn. Sá prestr í iljar honum ...' Jónsson 1936, 215.

37 W.P. Lehmann, who first called attention to this chapter of *Njáls saga*, is quite mistaken when he claims that 'Gunnarr cuts [this wooden weapon] with his sword.'

Lehmann 1967, 227. In reality Gunnarr's opponent, Hallgrímr, intends to stab him, but his weapon gets stuck in a piece of wood. Gunnarr hits him on the hand with his sword; the *atgeirr* comes loose, and Gunnarr kills Hallgrímr with his own weapon.

38 See Panzer 1910, 317: 'der Priester *Steinn,* der nachher das Seil hält, ist eben eigentlich der Wandergenosse des Märchenhelden ...'

39 In *Hálfdanar saga Brönufóstra* the hero notices that the trolls are cooking human flesh and horse meat together in a cauldron. He also discovers living prisoners.

40 In *Bósa saga ok Herrauðs* the hero's opponents are not trolls, but a witch and a vulture in her service.

11: Conclusion

1 Quoted from Helgason 1958, 113: 'Svo gengur það til í heiminum, að sumir hjálpa erroribus á gang, og aðrir leitast síðan við að útryðja aptur þeim sömu erroribus. Hafa svo hverirtveggju nokkuð að iðja.'

2 Doyle 1928, 79.

3 See, e.g., Klaeber 1950, xiv; Lawrence 1928, 171; and Chambers 1959, 47.

4 See also Klaeber 1950, xiv n. 1: 'it may be remarked in general that the folk-tale element is not necessarily to be considered the germ pure and simple of the Beowulfian legend. Priority may be claimed for the heroic "historical" features.'

5 Klaeber 1922, cxviii.

6 Lawrence 1928, 259.

7 Lawrence 1928, 165.

8 See, e.g., Niles 1983, 6: 'The basic plot of the poem may be the heroic equivalent of an internationally known wondertale.' Or Liberman 1986, 363: 'Once a motif got into the artistic web of the *Beowulf* poet, it was turned around and around.' See also a Proppian reconstruction of the 'old legend' in Halldórsson 1982, 18–22.

9 Barnes 1970, 432.

10 Rosenberg 1975, 205 and 207.

11 See Ólsen 1937–9, 292–3.

12 See Jónsson 1936, 213n. 1; and Kristjánsson 1978, 292–3.

13 J. Michael Stitt, for instance, has argued along this line. See Stitt 1992, 207–8.

14 Chambers 1959, 484.

15 Translation mine. See Jónsson 1936, 46: 'mart er öðru líkt.'

16 Malone 1958, 308.

Bibliography

Icelandic names are listed under the patronymic.

Aarne, Antti, and Stith Thompson. 1961. *The Types of the Folktale: A Classification and Bibliography*. FF Communications No. 184. Helsinki: Suomalainen Tiedeakatemia.

Andersson, Theodore M. 1967. *The Icelandic Family Saga: An Analytic Reading*. Cambridge, Mass.: Harvard University Press.

– 1997. 'Sources and Analogues.' In Robert E. Bjork and John D. Niles (eds.), *A Beowulf Handbook*. Lincoln: University of Nebraska Press. 125–48.

Arent, A. Margaret. 1969. 'The Heroic Pattern: Old Germanic Helmets, *Beowulf* and *Grettis saga*.' In Edgar C. Polomé (ed.), *Old Norse Literature and Mythology: A Symposium*. Austin: University of Texas Press. 130–99.

Barnes, Daniel R. 1970. 'Folktale Morphology and the Study of *Beowulf*.' *Speculum* 45: 416–34.

Benson, Larry D. 1970. 'The Originality of *Beowulf*.' In Morton W. Bloomfield (ed.), *The Interpretation of Narrative: Theory and Practice*. Harvard English Studies, 1. Cambridge, Mass.: Harvard University Press. 1–43.

Boer, R.C. 1898. 'Zur Grettissaga.' *Zeitschrift für deutsche Philologie*, 30: 1–71.

– (Ed.). 1900. *Grettis saga Ásmundarsonar*. Altnordische Saga-Bibliothek, Heft 8. Halle: Max Niemeyer.

– 1912. *Die Altenglische Heldendichtung*. Erster Band: *Beowulf*. Germanische Handbibliothek, 11. Halle: Verlag der Buchhandlung des Waisenhauses.

– 1923. 'Review of Chambers 1921.' *English Studies*, 5: 105–18.

Boucher, Alan. Trans. 1986. *The Saga of Havard the Halt together with the Saga of Hen-Thorir*. Iceland Review Saga Series. Reykjavík: Iceland Review.

Brady, Caroline. 1979. '"Weapons" in *Beowulf*: An Analysis of the Nominal Compounds and an Evaluation of the Poet's Use of Them.' *Anglo-Saxon England*, 8: 79–141.

Brandl, Alois. 1901–9. 'Englische Literatur.' In Hermann Paul (ed.), *Grundriss der germanischen Philologie*. 2nd ed. Vol. 2, pt. 1. Strassburg: Karl J. Trübner, 1901–9. 941–1134.

Brodeur, Arthur G. 1959. *The Art of Beowulf*. Berkeley, Los Angeles: University of California Press.

Brooke, Stopford A. 1905. *The History of Early English Literature: Being the History of English Poetry from its Beginnings to the Accession of King Ælfred*. New York: Macmillan.

Bugge, Sophus. 1887. 'Studien über das Beowulfepos.' *Beiträge zur Geschichte der deutschen Sprache und Literatur*, 12: 1–112.

Carens, Marilyn M. 1976. 'Handscóh and Grendel: The Motif of the Hand in Béowulf.' In Donna G. Fricke and Douglas C. Fricke (eds.), *Aeolian Harps: Essays in Literature in Honor of Maurice Browning Cramer*. Ohio, Bowling Green: Bowling Green University Press. 41–55.

Carney, James. 1955. *Studies in Irish History and Literature*. Dublin: Dublin Institute for Advanced Studies.

Chadwick, H. Munro. 1912. *The Heroic Age*. Cambridge: Cambridge University Press.

Chadwick, H. Munro, and N. Kershaw Chadwick. 1932. *The Growth of Literature*. Vol. 2, *The Ancient Literatures of Europe*. Cambridge: Cambridge University Press.

Chadwick, Nora K. 1959. 'The Monsters and Beowulf.' In Peter Clemoes (ed.), *The Anglo-Saxons, Studies in Some Aspects of Their History and Culture Presented to Bruce Dickens*. London: Bowes & Bowes. 171–203.

Chambers, R.W. 1921. *Beowulf: An Introduction to the Study of the Poem with a Discussion of the Stories of Offa and Finn*. Cambridge: Cambridge University Press.

– 1929. 'Beowulf's Fight with Grendel, and its Scandinavian Parallels.' *English Studies* 11: 81–100.

– 1959. *Beowulf: An Introduction to the Study of the Poem*. 3rd ed. with a supplement by C.L. Wrenn. Cambridge: Cambridge University Press.

Chickering, Howell D., Jr. 1977. *Beowulf: A Dual-Language Edition*. New York: Doubleday.

Clark, George. 1973. '*Beowulf* and *Njálssaga*.' In Peter Foote, Hermann Pálsson, and Desmond Slay (eds.), *Proceedings of the First International Saga Conference, University of Edinburgh, 1971*. London: Viking Society for Northern Research. 66–87.

– 1990. *Beowulf*. Boston: Twayne Publishers.

Collins, Rowland R. 1983. 'Blickling Homily XVI and the Dating of *Beowulf*.' In Wolf-Dietrich Bald and Horst Weinstock (eds.), *Medieval Studies Conference Aachen 1983*. Bamberger Beiträge zur Englischen Sprachwissenschaft, Heraugegeben von Prof. Dr. Wolfgang Viereck, Band 15. Frankfurt am Main: Verlag Peter Lang. 61–9.

Danielli, Mary. 1945. 'Initiation Ceremonial from Norse Literature.' *Folk-Lore*, 56: 229–45.

Davidson, H.R. Ellis. 1962. *The Sword in Anglo-Saxon England: Its Archaeology and Literature*. Oxford: Clarendon Press.

Dehmer, Heinz. 1927. *Primitives Erzählungsgut in den Íslendinga-Sögur*. Von deutscher Poeterey. Forschungen und Darstellungen aus dem Gesamtgebiete der deutschen Philologie 2. Leipzig: Verlagsbuchhandlung von J.J. Weber.

– 1928. 'Die Grendelkämpfe Beowulfs im Lichte moderner Märchenforschung.' *Germanisch-Romanische Monatsschrift*, 16: 202–18.

Deutschbein, Max. 1909. 'Die sagenhistorischen und literarischen Grundlagen des Beowulfepos.' *Germanisch-Romanische Monatsschrift*, 1: 103–19.

Doyle, Arthur Conan. 1928. *Sherlock Holmes: The Complete Short Stories*. London: John Murray.

Dragland, S.L. 1977. 'Monster-Man in *Beowulf*.' *Neophilologus*, 61: 606–18.

Earle, John. 1884. *Anglo-Saxon Literature*. London: Society for Promoting Christian Knowledge.

– (Trans.). 1892. *The Deeds of Beowulf: An English Epic of the Eighth Century Done into Modern Prose*. Oxford: Clarendon Press.

Einarsson, Stefán. 1933. *Saga Eiríks Magnússonar*. Reykjavík: Ísafoldarprentsmiðja.

– 1938. 'Review of Guðni Jónsson's edition of *Grettis saga*.' *JEGP*, 37: 289–91.

– 1956. 'Bjólfur and Grendill in Iceland.' *Modern Language Notes*, 71: 79–82.

– 1961. *Íslensk bókmenntasaga 874–1960*. Reykjavík: Snæbjörn Jónsson.

Eliason, Norman E. 1963. 'The Þyle and Scop in *Beowulf*.' *Speculum*, 38: 267–84.

Evison, Vera I. 1963. 'Review of Davidson's *The Sword in Anglo-Saxon England*' *Medium Ævum*, 32: 136–40.

Falk, Hjalmar. 1914. *Altnordische Waffenkunde*. Videnskapselskapets Skrifter. II. Hist.-Filos. Klasse. 1914. No. 6. Kristiania: In Kommission bei Jacob Dybwad.

Fjalldal, Magnús. 1993. 'How Valid Is the Anglo-Scandinavian Language Passage in *Gunnlaugs Saga* as Historical Evidence?' *Neophilologus*, 77: 601–9.

Fontenrose, Joseph. 1959. *Python: A Study of Delphic Myth and Its Origins*. Berkeley: University of California Press.

Fox, Denton, and Hermann Pálsson. (Trans.). 1974. *Grettir's Saga*. Toronto: University of Toronto Press.

Frank, R. 1986. '"Mere" and "Sund": Two Sea-Changes in *Beowulf*' In P.R. Brown, G.R. Crampton and F.C. Robinson (eds.), *Modes of Interpretation in Old English Literature: Essays in Honour of Stanley B. Greenfield*. Toronto: University of Toronto Press. 153–72.

Fry, Donald K. 1969. *Beowulf and the Fight at Finnsburh: A Bibliography*. Charlottesville: The University Press of Virginia.

Garmonsway, G.N, Jacqueline Simpson, and Hilda Ellis Davidson. 1968. *Beowulf and Its Analogues*. London: J.M. Dent & Sons.

Garnett, James.1880. 'Review of *Anglia*, volume 3, 1879–1880.' *American Journal of Philology*, 1 (1880): 491–7.

Genzmer, Felix. 1950. 'Die skandinavischen Quellen des Beowulfs.' *Arkiv för nordisk filologi*, 65: 17–62.

Gering, Hugo. 1880. 'Der *Beówulf* und die islaendische *Grettissaga*.' *Anglia*, 3: 74–87.

Girvan, Ritchie. 1935. *Beowulf and the Seventh Century*. London: Methuen.

Goldsmith, Margaret E. 1970. *The Mode and Meaning of 'Beowulf.'* London: Athlone Press.

Gordon, E.V. 1927. *An Introduction to Old Norse*. Oxford: Clarendon Press.

Halldórsson, Óskar. 1982. 'Tröllasaga Bárðdæla og Grettluhöfundur.' *Skírnir*, 156: 5–36.

Halvorsen, Eyvind Fjeld. 1974. 'Troll.' In Finn Hødnebø (ed.), *Kulturhistorisk Leksikon for nordisk middelalter*, vol. 18. Oslo: Gyldendal Norsk Forlag. 655–7.

Halvorsen, Eyvind Fjeld, and Anna Birgitta Rooth. 1962. 'Jotner.' In Finn Hødnebø (ed.), *Kulturhistorisk Leksikon for nordisk middelalter*. Vol. 7. Oslo: Gyldendal Norsk Forlag. 693–700.

Harris, Richard L. 1973. 'The Deaths of Grettir and Grendel: A New Parallel.' *Scripta Islandica*, 24: 25–53.

Hasenfratz, Robert J. 1993. *Beowulf Scholarship: An Annotated Bibliography, 1979–1990*. New York: Garland Publishing.

Hastrup, Kirsten. 1990. *Island of Anthropology: Studies in Past and Present Iceland*. The Viking Collection: Studies in Northern Civilization. Vol. 5. Odense: Odense University Press.

Hatto, A.T. 1957. 'Snake-words and Boar-helms in *Beowulf*.' *English Studies*, 38: 145–60.

Helgason, Jón. 1958. *Handritaspjall*. Reykjavík: Mál og menning.

Heusler, Andreas. 1911–13. 'Beowulf.' In Johannes Hoops (ed.), *Reallexikon der germanischen Altertumskunde*. 245–8.

– 1924. 'Review of "Beowulf och Bjarke" by C.W. von Sydow.' *Anzeiger für deutsches Altertum und deutsche Litteratur*, 43: 52–4.

Hübener, Gustav. 1927–8. 'Beowulf und nordische Dämonenaustreibung.' *English Studies*, 62: 293–327.

Hughes, Geoffrey. 1977. 'Beowulf, Unferth and Hrunting: An Interpretation.' *English Studies*, 58: 385–95.

Hulbert, James R. 1929. 'A Note on the Psychology of the *Beowulf* Poet.' In Kemp Malone and Martin B. Ruud (eds.), *Studies in English Philology: A Miscellany in Honor of Frederick Klaeber*. Minneapolis: University of Minnesota Press. 189–95.

Hume, Kathryn. 1975. 'The Thematic Design of Grettis Saga.' *JEGP*, 73: 469–86.

– 1980. 'From Saga to Romance: The Use of Monsters in Old Norse Literature.' *Studies in Philology*, 77: 1–25.

Irving, Edward B. 1968. *A Reading of Beowulf*. New Haven: Yale University Press.

Jack, George (ed.). 1994. *Beowulf: A Student Edition*. Oxford: Clarendon Press.

Janzén, Assar. 1947. *Nordisk Kultur VII Personnamn*. Stockholm: Albert Bonniers Forlag.

Jones, Gwyn. 1972. *Kings, Beasts, and Heroes*. London: Oxford University Press.

Jónsson, Finnur.1923. *Den oldnorske og oldislandske Litteraturs Historie*. Vol. 2. 2nd ed. Copenhagen: G.E.C. Gads Forlag.

Jónsson, Guðni (ed.). 1936. *Grettis saga Ásmundarsonar*. *Íslenzk fornrit*, 7. Reykjavík: Hið íslenzka fornritafélag.

– (Ed.). 1953. *Íslendinga sögur*. 12 vols. Reykjavík: Íslendingasagnaútgáfan.

– (Ed.). 1954. *Edda Snorra Sturlusonar, Nafnaþulur og Skáldskapartal*. Reykjavík: Íslendingasagnaútgáfan.

Jónsson, Guðni, and Bjarni Vilhjálmsson (eds). 1943–4. *Fornaldarsögur Norðurlanda*. 3 vols. Reykjavík: Bókaútgáfan Forni.

Jorgensen, Peter A. 1973. 'Grendel, Grettir, and Two Skaldic Stanzas.' *Scripta Islandica*, 24: 54–61.

– 1975. 'The Two-Troll Variant of the Bear's Son Folktale in *Hálfdanar saga Brönufóstra* and *Gríms saga loðinkinna*.' *Arv*, 31: 35–43.

– 1978. 'Beowulf's Swimming Contest with Breca: Old Norse Parallels.' *Folklore*, 89: 52–9.

– 1979. 'The Gift of the Useless Weapon in *Beowulf* and the Icelandic Sagas.' *Arkiv för nordisk filologi*, 94: 82–90.

– 1986. 'Additional Icelandic Analogues to *Beowulf*.' In Rudolf Simek et al. (eds.), *Sagnaskemmtun: Studies in Honour of Hermann Pálsson on His 65th birthday, 26th May, 1986*. Vienna: Hermann Böhlaus. 201–8.

Kennedy, Charles W. (trans.). 1940. *Beowulf: The Oldest English Epic*. New York: Oxford University Press.

Kiessling, Nicolas K. 1968. 'Grendel: A New Aspect.' *Modern Philology*, 65: 191–201.

Klaeber, Fr. (ed.). 1922. *Beowulf and the Fight at Finnsburg*. 1st ed. Boston: D.C. Heath.

– 1950. *Beowulf and the Fight at Finnsburg*. 3rd ed. Boston: D.C. Heath.

Kögel, R. 1892. 'Beowulf.' *Zeitschrift für deutsches Altertum*, 37: 268–76.

Kristjánsson, Jónas. 1978. 'Bókmenntasaga.' In Sigurður Líndal (ed.), *Saga Íslands*. Vol. 3. Reykjavík: Hið íslenzka bókmenntafélag, Sögufélagið. 261–350.

Kuhn, Sherman M. 1984. '*Beowulf* and the Life of Beowulf: A Study in Epic Structure.' In his *Studies in the Language and Poetics of Anglo-Saxon*. Ann Arbor: Karoma Publishers. 243–64.

Laborde, E.D. 1923. 'Grendel's Glove and His Immunity from Weapons.' *The Modern Language Review*, 18 : 202–4.

Laistner, Ludwig. 1889. *Die Rätsel der Sphinx. Grundzüge einer Mythengeschichte*. Vol. 2. Berlin: W. Hertz.

Lawrence, William Witherle. 1912. 'The Haunted Mere in *Beowulf*.' *PMLA*, 27: 208–45.

– 1928. *Beowulf and Epic Tradition*. Cambridge, Mass.: Harvard University Press.

– 1929. '*Beowulf* and the *Saga of Samson the Fair*.' In Kemp Malone and Martin B.

Ruud (eds.), *Studies in English Philology: A Miscellany in Honor of Frederick Klaeber.* Minneapolis: University of Minnesota Press. 172–81.

– 1939. 'Grendel's Lair.' *JEGP,* 38: 477–80.

Laxness, Halldór Kiljan. 1949. 'Lítil samantekt um útilegumenn.' *Tímarit Máls og menningar,* 2: 86–130.

Leach, Henry, G. 1921. *Angevin Britain and Scandinavia.* Harvard Studies in Comparative Literature. Vol. 6. Cambridge, Mass.: Harvard University Press.

Lehmann, Edv. 1901. 'Fandens oldemor.' *Dania,* 8: 179–94.

Lehmann, W.P. 1967. 'Atertanum Fah.' In Walter W. Arndt et al. (eds.), *Studies in Historical Linguistics in Honor of George Sherman Lane.* University of North Carolina Studies in Germanic Languages and Literatures, no. 58. Chapel Hill: University of North Carolina Press. 221–31.

Liberman, Anatoly. 1986. 'Beowulf-Grettir.' In Bela Brogyanyi and Thomas Krömmelbein (eds.), *Germanic Dialects: Linguistic and Philological Investigations.* Amsterdam and Philadelphia: John Benjamins Publishing Company. 353–401.

Lie, Hallvard. 1939. 'Noen metodologiske overveielser i anl. av et bind av *Íslenzk Fornrit.*' *Maal og Minne.* 97–138.

Liestöl, Knut. 1930. 'Beowulf and Epic Tradition.' *The American-Scandinavian Review,* 6: 370–3.

Mackie, W.S. 1938. 'The Demons' Home in *Beowulf.*' *JEGP,* 37: 455–61.

Magnússon, Ásgeir Blöndal. 1989. *Íslensk orðsifjabók.* Reykjavík: Orðabók Háskólans.

Malone, Kemp. 1932. 'Review of *Beowulf: An Introduction to the Study of the Poem with a Discussion of the Stories of Offa and Finn* by R.W. Chambers.' *English Studies,* 14: 190–3.

– 1944. 'On the Etymology of *runt*' *Language,* 20: 87–8.

– 1946. 'Hrungnir.' *Arkiv för nordisk filologi,* 284–5. Reprinted in Stefán Einarsson and Norman E. Eliason (eds.), *Studies in Heroic Legend and in Current Speech,* Copenhagen: Rosenkilde and Bagger, 1959. 202–3.

– 1958. 'Grendel and His Abode.' In A.G. Hatcher and K.L. Selig (eds.), *Studia Philologica et Litteraria in Honorem L. Spitzer.* Bern: Francke Verlag. 297–308.

Malone, Kemp, and Martin B. Ruud. 1929. *Studies in English Philology: A Miscellany in Honor of Frederick Klaeber.* Minneapolis: University of Minnesota Press.

Mastrelli, Carlo Alberto. 1985–6. 'Motivi indraici nel *Beowulf* e nella *Grettis Saga* (ags. *hæftmēce* e a.isl. *heptisax*).' *AIUON, filologia germanica,* 28–9: 405–20.

McConchie, R.W. 1982. 'Grettir Ásmundarson's Fight with Kárr the Old: A Neglected *Beowulf* Analogue.' *English Studies,* 63: 481–6.

Mitchell, Stephen A. 1991. *Heroic Sagas and Ballads.* Ithica: Cornell University Press.

Mogk, Eugen. 1919. 'Altgermanische Spukgeschichten. Zugleich ein Beitrag zur Erklärung der Grendelepisode in *Beowulf.*' *Neue Jahrbücher für das klassische Altertum, Geschichte und deutsche Literatur und für Pädagogik,* 22: 103–17.

Morris, William, and Eiríkur Magnússon (trans.). 1891. *The Story of Howard the Halt. The Story of the Banded Men. The Story of Hen Thorir. Done into English out of the Icelandic. The Saga Library.* Vol. 1. London: B. Quaritch.

Mossé, Fernand (ed.). 1933. *La Saga de Grettir.* Paris: Éditions Montaigne, Aubier.

Motz, Lotte. 1982. 'Giants in Folklore and Mythology: A New Approach.' *Folklore*, 93: 70–84.

Murphy, Gerard (ed.). 1953. *Duanaire Finn. The Book of the Lays of Fionn.* Part 3. Irish Texts Society, 43. Dublin: The Educational Company of Ireland.

Niles, John D. 1983. *Beowulf: The Poem and Its Tradition.* Cambridge, Mass. Harvard University Press.

Nordal, Sigurður. 1968. *Um íslenzkar fornsögur.* Trans. Árni Björnsson. Reykjavík: Mál og menning.

Ólason, Páll Eggert (ed.). 1946–8. *Heimskringla Snorra Sturlusonar: Konungasögur.* Vols. 1–3. Reykjavík: Menntamálaráð og Þjóðvinafélag.

Ólason, Vésteinn, et al. (eds.). 1993. *Íslensk bókmenntasaga, 2.* Reykjavík: Mál og menning.

Olrik, Axel. 1903. *Danmarks Heldedigtning: En Oldtidsstudie.* Copenhagen: Universitetsboghandler G.E.C. Gad.

Ólsen, Björn M. 1937–9. *Um Íslendingasögur: kaflar úr háskólafyrirlestrum.* In *Safn til sögu Íslands og íslenzkra bókmennta að fornu og nýju.* Vol. 6. Reykjavík: Hið íslenzka bókmenntafélag.

Orchard, Andy. 1995. *Pride and Prodigies: Studies in the Monsters of the Beowulf Manuscript.* Cambridge: D.S. Brewer.

Pálsson, Hermann. 1980. 'Glámsýni í Grettlu.' In Jónas Kristjánsson (ed.). *Gripla*, 4. Reykjavík: Stofnun Árna Magnússonar. 95–101.

Panzer, Friedrich. 1910. *Studien zur germanischen Sagengeschichte.* Vol. 1. *Beowulf.* Munich: C.H. Beck'sche Verlagsbuchhandlung.

Parks, Ward. 1993. 'Prey Tell: How Heroes Perceive Monsters in *Beowulf*.' *JEGP*, 92: 1–16.

Perkins, Richard. 1989. 'Objects and Oral Tradition in Medieval Iceland.' In Rory McTurk and Andrew Wawn (eds.), *Úr Dölum til Dala: Guðbrandur Vigfússon Centenary Essays.* Leeds Texts and Monographs. New Series 11. Leeds: Leeds Studies in English. 239–66.

Pizarro, Joaquín M. 1976–7. 'Transformations of the Bear's Son Tale in the Sagas of the Hrafnistumenn.' *Arv*, 32–3: 263–81.

Powell, F. York. 1900. 'Review of Boer's Edition of *Grettis saga*.' *Folklore*, 11: 406–14.

– 1901. 'Béowulf and Watanabe-No-Tsuna.' In *An English Miscellany Presented to Dr. Furnivall in Honour of his Seventy-Fifth Birthday.* Oxford: Clarendon Press. 395–6.

Propp, Vladimir. 1968. *Morphology of the Folktale.* Trans. Laurence Scott. Ed. Louis A. Wagner. Austin: University of Texas Press.

168   Bibliography

Puhvel, Martin. 1979. *Beowulf and Celtic Tradition*. Waterloo, Ontario: Wilfrid Laurier University Press.

Ranisch, W. 1902. 'Review of Boer's edition of *Grettis saga*.' *Anzeiger für deutsches Altertum und deutsche Litteratur*, 28: 216–35.

Robinson, Fred C. 1974. 'Elements of the Marvellous in the Characterization of Beowulf.' In Robert B. Burlin and Edward B. Irving (eds.), *Old English Studies in Honour of John C. Pope*. Toronto: University of Toronto Press. 119–37.

– 1994. 'Did Grendel's Mother Sit on Beowulf?' In Malcolm Godden, Douglas Gray, and Terry Hoad (eds.) *From Anglo-Saxon to Early Middle English: Studies Presented to E.G. Stanley*. Oxford: Clarendon Press. 1–7.

Rooth, Erik G.T. 1917. 'Der name Grendel in der Beowulfsage.' *Beiblatt zur Anglia*, 28: 335–40.

Rosenberg, Bruce A. 1975. 'Folktale Morphology and the Structure of *Beowulf*: A Counterproposal.' *Journal of the Folklore Institute* [Indiana University], 11: 199–209.

– 1991. *Folklore and Literature: Rival Siblings*. Knoxville: University of Tennessee Press.

Rosier, James L. 1962. 'Design for Treachery: The Unferth Intrigue.' *PMLA*, 77: 1–8.

– 1963. 'The Uses of Association: Hands and Feasts in *Beowulf*.' *PMLA*, 78: 8–14.

Russell, Jeffrey B. 1984. *Lucifer: The Devil in the Middle Ages*. Ithaca: Cornell University Press.

Sarrazin, Gregor. 1910. 'Neue Beowulf-Studien, 7. *Fyrgenstrēam*.' *Englische Studien*, 42: 1–37.

Schlauch, Margaret. 1934. *Romance in Iceland*. Princeton: Princton University Press.

– 1956. *English Medieval Literature and Its Social Foundation*. Warsaw: Państwowe Wydawnictwo Naukowe.

Schneider, Hermann. 1934. *Germanische Heldensage*. Vol. 2, pt. 2. In *Grundriss der germanischen Philologie*, 10/3. Ed. begun by Hermann Paul. Berlin and Leipzig: Walter de Gruyter.

– 1952. *Edda, Skalden, Saga: Festschrift zum 70. Geburtstag von Felix Genzmer*. Heidelberg: Carl Winter Universitätsverlag.

Schück, Henrik. 1909. *Studier i Beowulfsagan*. In *Uppsala Universitets Årsskrift*, 1909, Program M.M. Uppsala: Almqvist & Wiksells Boktryckeri.

Sedgefield, Walter J. (ed.). 1935. *Beowulf*. 3rd edition. Manchester: Manchester University Press.

Shetelig, Haakon, and Hjalmar Falk. 1937. *Scandinavian Archaeology*. Trans. E.V. Gordon. Oxford: Clarendon Press.

Shippey, T.A. 1978. *Beowulf*. London: Edward Arnold.

Short, Douglas D. 1980. *Beowulf Scholarship: An Annotated Bibliography*. New York: Garland Publishing.

Sigfússon, Björn. 1960. 'Grettis saga Ásmundarsonar.' In Finn Hødnebø (ed.), *Kultur-historisk Leksikon for nordisk middelalter*, vol. 5. Oslo: Gyldendal Norsk Forlag. 461–2.

Smith, C.S. 1881. 'Beówulf Gretti.' *The New Englander*, 4: 49–67.

Stedman, Douglas. 1913. 'Some Points of Resemblance Between *Beowulf* and the *Grettla* (or *Grettis Saga*).' *Saga Book of the Viking Society*, 8 (Part 1): 6–28.

Stitt, J. Michael. 1992. *Beowulf and the Bear's Son: Epic, Saga, and Fairytale in Northern Germanic Tradition*. New York: Garland Publishing.

Sveinsson, Einar Ól. (ed.). 1934. *Laxdœla saga. Íslenzk fornrit*, 5. Reykjavík: Hið íslenzka fornritafélag.

Sveinsson, Einar Ól., and Matthías Þórðarson (eds.). 1935. *Eyrbyggja saga, Grænlendingasögur. Íslenzk fornrit*, 4. Reykjavík: Hið íslenzka fornritafélag.

Sydow, Carl W. von. 1923. 'Beowulf och Bjarke.' *Studier i nordisk filologi* 14:3. In *Skrifter utgivna av svenska litteratursällskapet i Finland*, 170. 1–46.

Taylor, A.R. 1952. 'Two Notes on *Beowulf*.' *Leeds Studies in English and Kindred Languages*, 7 and 8: 5–17.

Turville-Petre, Joan. 1974–7. '*Beowulf* and *Grettis saga*: An Excursion.' *Saga Book of the Viking Society*, 19: 347–57.

Unwerth, Wolf von. 1911. *Untersuchungen über Totenkult und Ódinnverehrung bei Nordgermanen und Lappen mit Excursen zur altnordischen Literaturgeschichte*. Germanistische Abhandlungen, 37. Heft. Breslau: Verlag von M. & H. Marcus.

Vigfusson, Gudbrand (ed.). 1878. *Sturlunga Saga Including the Islendinga Saga of Lawman Sturla Thordsson and Other Works*. Vol. 1. Oxford: Clarendon Press.

Vigfusson, Gudbrand, and F. York Powell (eds.). 1879. *An Icelandic Prose Reader with Notes, Grammar and Glossary*. Oxford: Clarendon Press.

– 1883. *Corpus Poeticum Boreale: The Poetry of the Old Northern Tongue*. Vol. 2. Oxford: Clarendon Press.

Vilhjálmsson, Bjarni (ed.). 1982. *Riddarasögur*. 6 vols. Reykjavík: Íslendingasagnaútgáfan, Haukadalsútgáfan.

Wachsler, Arthur, A. 1985. 'Grettir's Fight with a Bear: Another Neglected Analogue of *Beowulf* in the *Grettis Sage Asmundarsonar*.' *English Studies*, 66: 381–90.

Wardale, E.E. 1965. *Chapters on Old English Literature*. New York: Russell & Russell.

Whitbread, L. 1949. 'The Hand of Æschere: A Note on *Beowulf* 1343.' *Review of English Studies*, 25: 339–42.

Whitman, F.H. 1977. 'Corrosive Blood in *Beowulf*.' *Neophilologus*, 61: 276.

– 1977. 'The Kingly Nature of Beowulf.' *Neophilologus*, 61: 277–86.

Wilson, David. 1971. *The Anglo-Saxons*. Harmondsworth, Middlesex: Penguin.

Wrenn, C.L. (ed.). 1953. *Beowulf: With the Finnesburg Fragment*. London: George G. Harrap.

Wright, Charles D. 1993. *The Irish Tradition in Old English Literature*. Cambridge Studies in Anglo-Saxon England, no. 6. Cambridge: Cambridge University Press.

Þórólfsson, Björn K. (ed.) 1923. *Hávarðar saga Ísfirðings*. Copenhagen: J. Jørgensen.

Þórólfsson, Björn K., and Guðni Jónsson (eds.) 1943. *Vestfirðinga sǫgur. Íslenzk fornrit*, 6. Reykjavík: Hið íslenzka fornritafélag.

Index

— CASE FILE —

COMPENDIUM

Bing An Ben

1

— CASE FILE —
COMPENDIUM
Bing An Ben

1

WRITTEN BY
ROU BAO BU CHI ROU

COVER ILLUSTRATION BY
BOKI

INTERIOR ILLUSTRATIONS BY
DanKe

TRANSLATED BY
BEN BINGHAM

Seven Seas

Seven Seas Entertainment

CASE FILE COMPENDIUM: BING AN BEN VOL. 1

Published originally under the title of 《病案本》 (Bing An Ben)
Author © 肉包不吃肉 (Rou Bao Bu Chi Rou)
US English edition rights under license granted by 北京晋江原创网络科技有限公司
(Beijing Jinjiang Original Network Technology Co., Ltd.)
US English edition copyright © 2024 Seven Seas Entertainment, LLC.
Arranged through JS Agency Co., Ltd
All rights reserved

Cover Illustration: Boki
Interior Illustrations: DanKe

Seven Seas press and purchase enquiries can be sent to press@gomanga.com.
Information regarding the distribution and purchase of digital editions is available
from Digital Manager CK Russell at digital@gomanga.com.

Seven Seas and the Seven Seas logo are trademarks of
Seven Seas Entertainment. All rights reserved.

Follow Seven Seas Entertainment online at
sevenseasentertainment.com.

TRANSLATION: Ben Bingham
ADAPTATION: Kayce Teo
COVER DESIGN: M. A. Lewife
INTERIOR DESIGN & LAYOUT: Clay Gardner
COPY EDITOR: Jade Gardner
PROOFREADER: Stephanie Cohen, Hnä
EDITOR: Laurel Ashgrove
PREPRESS TECHNICIAN: Melanie Ujimori, Jules Valera
MANAGING EDITOR: Alyssa Scavetta
EDITOR-IN-CHIEF: Julie Davis
PUBLISHER: Lianne Sentar
VICE PRESIDENT: Adam Arnold
PRESIDENT: Jason DeAngelis

ISBN: 978-1-68579-772-0
Printed in Canada
First Printing: February 2024
10 9 8 7 6 5 4 3 2 1

TABLE OF CONTENTS

OPENING SHOT

C *LICK.* The darkness illuminated. The TV screen flickered, and an image began to appear.

The faculty dorm was located in the building crammed into the furthermost corner of this centuries-old university campus. Placed out of the way, it was where the school mostly sent their young and sprightly teachers. The exterior was gorgeous—all red brick and white steps, with delicate ivy vines encircling the old Western-style building. No passersby would be able to resist taking a lingering gaze, but only those lucky enough to become a teacher and enter it would realize that, under its beautiful facade, this building had undergone many rounds of repairs. The interior walls were mottled and layered, like an aged face caked with countless layers of makeup. The dorm was so old that it didn't even have digital televisions; the ones here were cable TVs that could only be described as antiques.

"The Yangtze Plain is experiencing several torrential rainstorms in succession..."

A young man walked past the corridor as the sound of the TV program filtered through the cracked glass window of the receptionist's office. Usually, the old lady on shift would stop him and shout, "Hey, little student, dontcha know? This is a faculty residence for teachers. You're a student, you can't keep coming here."

But today, the receptionist didn't scold him. Perhaps it was because she was staring off into space, or that her eyesight was failing in her later years, but she didn't notice him pass by in the dark night.

He walked directly up to the third floor and knocked on a familiar iron door.

It opened with a creak; the woman inside poked her head out. "It's you?"

"Xie-laoshi," the young man said softly.

It was quite late, and he was an unexpected guest. But the woman was his teacher, as well as the person closest to him in the entire school. After a moment of surprise, she welcomed him inside.

She brewed a cup of tea and added some sliced ginger. It was raining outside, and she could feel that the youth was soaked and cold; hot ginger tea could drive out the chill.

Xie-laoshi placed the steaming cup down on the tea table before her student, who was standing uncomfortably in front of the sofa. "When did you get back?"

"Just today."

"Please sit down," Xie-laoshi said.

Only then did he sit, his hands curled over his knees. He was stiff and reserved, and didn't touch the tea.

"Why didn't you let me know that you were coming back? Are there even buses this late?"

"...Mm."

"How did things go with your family?"

The youth was quiet for a while, then lowered his head to pick at the rip in his jeans. "My mom still wants me to drop out..."

Xie-laoshi fell silent.

He was already a university student; if he chose to drop out, the school didn't have much say in the matter. Even so, she had spoken with his mother and promised to lower the tuition fees due to their financial difficulty in hopes that his mother would allow her son to finish his studies at the university he had worked so hard to get into.

But his mother had shrilly refused.

"What studies?! Studying Chinese? Who doesn't know how to speak Chinese? You're all just pulling a scam!"

Xie-laoshi had patiently and gently tried to explain, "Your son is very bright. Look, he's already in his second year. Wouldn't it be a huge waste to give up halfway? Plus, once he graduates, it'll be easier for him to find a job. He told me he wants to be a teacher. With his grades, he'd have no trouble getting employed as one. This is your son's dream, and teaching is a stable job..."

"He could never become a teacher! It's not like you haven't seen his face!"

The mother's words were like a dull blade cleaving right down the middle of an invisible current.

Xie-laoshi was furious, but she didn't know how to respond.

"I want him to come back to work right now! Our family is broke! He needs to stop wasting time! With that...that face... What can he do even if he studies! What school would want this kind of teacher?!"

So what was his face like?

She peered at her student, his face dimly illuminated by the weak incandescent lamp in her room.

Xie-laoshi had already grown used to his features, but everyone who saw him for the first time would gasp. Due to some unknown disease, half of his face—from forehead to neck—was covered in purple blotches, as if concealing rotting flesh.

It was a horrifying sight, undisguised in its abnormality.

"Freak!"

"Stay away from him, it might be contagious."

"Hey! Half-and-half!"

Having grown up with this face of his, mockery and ridicule followed him like a shadow.

Because he had a disease, and moreover because he didn't have the sense to cover up his ailment, his ugliness, he was shunned wherever he went. No matter how hard he studied, no matter how gently he interacted with others, he was like an evil dragon flying through a clear sky: conspicuous and frightening. He could never receive any equal treatment.

People like Xie-laoshi, who could see that the unblemished half of his face was very lovable and gentle, were a rarity.

He would always gently and numbly bear everyone's mockery. Sometimes, he too would laugh along, as if he had actually done something wrong.

But what exactly had he done wrong?

Xie-laoshi noticed it all. When studying, he'd always be the most focused; he'd dutifully do his part and silently take on the most work in group projects. When people bullied him, he would just endure it without getting angered or saying much.

"It's fine, Laoshi, I'm already very happy that you'd chat with me. Back in my village, everyone would cross the street as soon as they saw me coming. There's never been anyone like you, who would listen to me so attentively. The other students are very nice too. At least no one's thrown bricks at me."

His words were calm, but his head was forever bowed, his shoulders hunched. Years of humiliation had caused his spine to bend, deforming from the pressure.

Later, she said to him, "If you'd like, you can always come to me for private tutoring after the evening self-study session. If there's anything you don't understand or you need my help with, just let me know."

He smiled in deep embarrassment, the blush of shame appearing on the unblemished half of his face.

In the two years she'd known him, she'd grown used to opening her dorm door after he had knocked to see him standing there with his stooped posture. He would be carrying the papers, prose, and even poetry that he wrote, having come to ask her for pointers.

These days, many people liked to curse, but very few liked to write poetry.

But he persisted, even as other students mocked him, calling him an ugly freak who wrote ugly things: *So rancid, even more rancid than your rotten grape face.*

He would smile a little and just keep writing.

Now, he didn't even have the right to do that anymore.

As these thoughts filled Xie-laoshi's mind, she felt a pang of sorrow and gazed with pity at the boy in front of her.

"Laoshi, this time, I came to say goodbye," he said. "I'll be leaving tomorrow."

"You're going back home?"

"...Mm, more or less."

He paused. "Laoshi, if my disease weren't on my face, if it were somewhere people couldn't see, people would be a little nicer to me. How nice would that be."

The rims of Xie-laoshi's eyes reddened. She'd already done everything she could, but she wasn't his kin; she didn't have the final say, nor could she save him. His family situation was worsening by the day, and his mother regretted letting her child leave home to study, especially since she had a healthy second son who was still in junior high school. If they called the sick child back home, they could let the healthy one take his place.

Xie-laoshi didn't blame his mother; having to weigh the pros and cons of the family situation, she was being quite fair.

"The...the essay that you left with me, the one you wanted me to look over, I'm not done editing it yet—" Xie-laoshi hastily changed the subject, feeling that soon she wouldn't be able to hold back her tears anymore.

"But I read through the first parts very carefully. Why don't you start the academic withdrawal process a little later? Wait until I've edited the entire thing..."

"No." He shook his head with a smile. "I must go when morning comes."

She felt so remorseful; why had she always thought that there was still time?

Why hadn't she stayed up all night to edit his essay?

And why had she gone out to shop and chat and attend those long and meaningless meetings?

Her student's dreams were about to shatter, and his heart about to give out. As his teacher, she couldn't even offer up a bouquet of flowers to bid his dream farewell.

"I'm sorry..."

"It's fine," he said. "But I wrote one last poem. Can I give it to you?"

She readily nodded.

He took a piece of paper out of his backpack and handed it to her. The paper was thin, almost weightless.

She read every word. It was an adoring love poem, searingly passionate yet tentative and careful. She'd read the works of many masters who spoke of romance, from the "when will the moonlight in our bed dry the tears on our faces"[1] of the past, to the "my eyes are more beautiful because they have you in them"[2] of the present. Yet at this moment, it seemed like none of them could compare to this sheet of paper that her student had presented to her.

He didn't put anything out in the open, as if doing so would spoil the meter of the poem.

This young man was a poet. He knew that if the love between two people from different social statuses lost its poetry, all that would be left was embarrassment.

"It's a memento for you."

Tenderness was written all over his face—both on the grotesque and ordinary halves.

"I'm sorry, Laoshi. I can't afford to buy you any gifts."

"There's nothing better than this." She turned around, suppressing her sobs. "You...you should eat something. I'll find you some snacks to go with the tea."

In a bid to keep her emotions in check, Xie-laoshi rummaged through her cabinets. She picked up a tin of butter cookies and placed it on the table.

He thanked her politely. Under Xie-laoshi's gaze, he finally touched the teacup tentatively, only to pull back instantly. Softly, he said, "It's so hot."

Xie-laoshi touched the cup. "Huh? It's lukewarm."

Nonetheless, she added some cold water to the cup. Her student chewed on his favorite cookies and slowly began to drink. By the time he finished the cookies and the tea, the night was still young.

"Laoshi, can I stay here for a little while longer to read?" he asked.

---

1   From the poem "Moonlit Night" by Du Fu, a Tang dynasty poet.
2   From the poem "Your Eyes Are So Beautiful" by Yu Kwang-chung (1928–2017).

"Of course."

He smiled again, slightly sheepish. "I'm inconveniencing you so much, even when I'm about to leave."

"It's fine, you can stay for as long as you'd like... Right, give me your address—I'll send you a copy of all the good books I see. Given how clever you are, even if you only study on your own, you won't do too poorly." Xie-laoshi could only offer some words of comfort. "If you need any help with anything, you can contact me on WeChat."[3]

He looked at her. "Thank you." He paused. "If only everyone were like you, then perhaps..."

He lowered his head and didn't continue.

Her dorm had no shortage of books. With his undisguised disease, his grotesque appearance made him the center of attention every time he went to the library. Thus, she invited him to the faculty dorm and lent him her own books to read.

In that same spirit, he spent the whole night reading inside the faculty dorm, as if he wanted to bring all the words back to his hometown using this night.

He rarely acted so selfishly. In the past, he would never stay too late, worried that he'd disrupt his teacher's routine. But today was an exception.

Xie-laoshi didn't blame him for this final willful streak. She stayed up with him, but into the latter half of the night, she grew tired. Without realizing it, she drifted off to sleep at her desk.

In her hazy unconsciousness, she heard her student suddenly say, "Xie-laoshi."

She blearily made a noise of assent.

"There's one more thing. I want to apologize to you. Those thefts in our class that you got criticized for... When those students kept

---

3   Chinese messaging app.

losing their belongings and couldn't find them no matter what... Actually, I was the one who took their things."

Shocked, she stirred from her slumber, but her body was too tired, too heavy to get up.

"But I didn't keep any of those things. I didn't take any of their money," he said sorrowfully. "When they mocked me, I really hated them... I threw all their bags into a pile of straw and burned it all. They suspected me, but you chose to vouch for me without question. But in truth, I was the culprit. I didn't have the courage to admit it. Only in one person's eyes have I ever been a normal person, or even a good person—that's you. Laoshi, I'm very vain, aren't I?" He paused. "I wouldn't know what to do if you were disappointed in me. You're the only person who has ever acknowledged me."

His voice trailed off.

But his gaze was clear, almost transparent, as if a weight had been taken off his shoulders.

"This is the one thing I regret the most... Xie-laoshi, I'm truly sorry. My disease seems to have metastasized from my face to my heart. If there is a next life, I really want to be a normal person... I don't want to be so sick that I don't even have the right to be loved. Xie-laoshi..."

Wind rushed in through the window, making the papers on the table flutter, like soul-summoning flags.

Then silence returned.

The tea on the table cooled.

When Xie-laoshi woke up the next morning, she found that she'd slept the night away at her desk. Her room was neat and tidy. Her student was always polite, but this time, he hadn't said goodbye to his teacher before packing up his things and leaving.

Unable to suppress a twinge of melancholy, she rose sleepily and went to the living room. When she looked down at the tea table, her eyes flew open, as if a basin of ice water had just been poured over her head.

The tea she'd made for the youth had frozen over, but how? The room was clearly 27 or so degrees Celsius!

Her dark eyes wide, she looked around the room only to be plunged into even deeper shock. Last night, she'd clearly seen her student eat the butter cookies, yet not a single one was missing from the tin. The tea which had frozen into ice was untouched, and finally...

That veiled love poem, the contents of which she still sheltered in her heart, the paper farewell he'd gifted her...

It had disappeared.

Or, perhaps it was more accurate to say that the paper had never existed in the first place.

She was almost shaking. Suddenly, her phone alerted with a *ding*, causing her to jump in fright. She grabbed it immediately, only to find that it was a spam message. She let out a breath of relief, but then, as if struck by a thought, as if waking from a dream, she quickly dialed the student's number.

Beep. Beep. Beep.

Her heart pounded with every beat of the mechanical tone.

"Hello?"

The call had gone through.

On the other end of the line was the familiar voice of a middle-aged woman. It sounded coarse, but right now, it was also nasal with tears. Xie-laoshi exchanged a few words with the young man's mother.

Her heart sank into a pitch-black hole, careening downward.

After a pause, she heard a flurry of accusations—"It was you people! You again!! I haven't had time to come for you, yet you actually called us first!"

Xie-laoshi couldn't remember what she had said at the beginning anymore; her mind had blanked out. All she could hear was the miserable shouting at the other end, like a bludgeoning wake-up call. "He's dead! Dead!"

Blood froze in her veins.

Dead?

"It's all your fault!! He got into an argument with me and ran out. There was a torrential storm outside, and the police said a section of an electric cable was exposed..."

Xie-laoshi's ears were ringing.

Amid the intense castigation and mournful sobbing, she could barely make out a few words, ghostly and ghoulish, like an other-worldly farewell.

The woman on the other end of the line gave an ear-splitting shriek.

"Why bother calling? Why bother?! Yesterday was his seventh day!!"[4]

---

4   It is a traditional Chinese belief that the spirits of the deceased will return home for a visit on the seventh day after their death.

2

I WAS STILL A STUDENT BACK THEN

"*YESTERDAY WAS HIS seventh day!!*"

The tapping of the keyboard stopped. He Yu stood up from the desk in the faculty dorm room. The apartment wasn't even sixty square meters. Next door, in the living room, a tedious variety show about poetry was playing on an old-fashioned TV. The program was accompanied by the static humming of the faulty signal.

The sofa was still that sofa in the story. The snacks for the tea, the tin of biscuits—they were all still there. But the time on the clock read 8:09, and the streetlights were on outside. It was the middle of summer, and the air was very humid. Moths circled beneath the lights, mosquitoes buzzed low to the ground, and rain had yet to fall.

He Yu left the little study in the faculty dorm. When he opened the door, light spilled in at an angle through the filthy windowpanes, making the entire space seem rather surreal, more so than the story he had just finished writing.

A young woman lay on the sofa. The air conditioning was set to a very low temperature, and she was sleeping under a coral fleece blanket. Before her were several crumpled tissues that had been used to wipe away tears and snot.

"Wake up," said He Yu.

"Ngh..."

"Get up."

"Not so loud... I barely even fell asleep..." The young woman groaned wearily, smacking her lips. "Gonna nap for a bit longer..."

He Yu was about to say something else, but the variety show on the TV started introducing an old movie.

"There's a *Brokeback Mountain* in every person's heart..."

He gave up trying to wake her up and took the remote to change the channel.

He Yu really disliked homosexuality.

"Welcome, everybody, to our medical wellness program today..."

He changed the channel again. He Yu also disliked doctors and hospitals.

"Once, Zhuangzi dreamt he was a butterfly, a butterfly fluttering about..."[5]

This time, he left the program on. Given his tastes, he could accept this as background noise.

He Yu put down the remote and glanced over at the snoring woman still lying on her back. He turned and walked into the kitchen. He opened the greasy refrigerator, and the light from the appliance illuminated his face.

After he surveyed the refrigerator's contents several times, he took out two eggs and a chunk of ham, as well as a bowl of yesterday's leftovers. Then, he raised his voice to ask the woman sleeping in the living room, "Xie Xue, do you have green onions here? I can't find any."

The woman didn't move.

"I'll make you Yangzhou fried rice."

---

5   From a story about Zhuangzi (Zhuang Zhou) in which he had a dream about becoming a butterfly and then wondered whether he was a man dreaming he was a butterfly or a butterfly dreaming he was a man.

There was no response from the living room. He Yu glanced back again to see that the young woman had gotten off the sofa and was leaning against the kitchen doorway.

"...Then you'll need two eggs, plus a big piece of luncheon meat," the woman said, then hesitated. "Do you know how?"

He Yu rolled up his sleeves and looked back at her with a suave smile. "Sit outside and wait. It'll be ready soon."

The woman named Xie Xue tottered away to wander around the other rooms. Seeing that the computer in the study was switched on, she sat down to skim over the opened Word document. "He Yu! Did you use me as your muse?"

The range hood was too loud. "What?" He Yu asked.

"I said! Did you! Use me! As your muse?!" Xie Xue brought his laptop out. "For the Xie-laoshi in this ghost story!"

"Oh." He fell silent for a while before cracking an egg with a smile. "Yep. You're exactly the person I imagined. Art imitates reality, Xie-laoshi."

"But you wrote that you were secretly in love with me?"

"...Art is not the same as reality, Xie-laoshi."

But that last part was a lie.

He really was secretly in love with her.

He Yu and Xie Xue had known each other for more than ten years. Xie Xue was five years older than him. This was her first year as a lecturer teaching screenwriting and directing in the School of Fine Arts at Huzhou University. He Yu was one of the students in her class.

When Xie Xue first saw the roster for the incoming screenwriting and directing majors, she had sent a shocked message to He Yu. "Fuck, what a coincidence! One of the boys in the two classes I'm teaching has the same exact name as you!"

At the time, He Yu had been on a plane. He was sitting in a window seat and looking out at the flickering lamplight of the airport tarmac with his cheek propped up on one hand. His phone dinged, and a familiar profile picture popped up. He looked at the message from the girl he had been in love with for ten years and was just about to reply when the request for all passengers to switch their devices to airplane mode sounded over the intercom.

He Yu tilted his head and thought for a minute. He didn't reply to her message before turning off his phone.

How could there be so many coincidences in this world?

Idiot.

He had fought for this opportunity himself, of course. It was completely unlike the story He Yu had written.

As for He Yu himself, not only was he not penniless, he wasn't ugly either. He was blessed with a very handsome face, and as the son of a pharmaceutical tycoon, he had been born with a silver spoon in his mouth and attended high school overseas. But less than thirty minutes after finding out that Xie Xue had become a lecturer at Huzhou University upon graduating, He Yu applied for the institution's School of Fine Arts.

Several months later, the semester began.

However, the newly appointed Xie-laoshi was too young; she didn't understand how treacherous workplaces could get.

Jiang Liping, the morality advisor[6] in charge of the screenwriting/directing classes one, two, and three, was an infamous eccentric. Supposedly, she had no relevant education or training and had gotten this fluff position in the school simply by sleeping with the board of directors. Jiang-laoshi was ostentatiously beautiful and

---

6   University role overseeing the ideological and political education of students according to the national party line.

didn't feel a bit of shame about using sex to get what she wanted. She spent every day blatantly flirting with the board members in broad daylight and was overtly hostile toward any female student or teacher with decent looks.

When Xie Xue rushed into the classroom for her first lecture with her laptop in her arms, she saw Jiang Liping there in a floor-length red dress, hogging her lectern to discuss important items with the new students.

"I'm sorry, Jiang-laoshi, the first class is starting..." Xie Xue tried to remind her.

But the other woman merely waved her hand. "Just wait a minute, the morning study period was too short. I still have two items to go over."

Who knew if she was picking on her on purpose, but Jiang Liping stretched out the last two points for fifteen, almost sixteen, minutes before she finally finished. "All right, that's all I had to cover. I won't disrupt your class anymore." She then turned to Xie Xue. "Uhh...I'm sorry, I didn't catch your name earlier. Anyway, stay focused, don't be nervous."

Professor Jiang strutted away, her towering scarlet heels clicking against the ground. Her vintage Hong Kong-style dress fluttered in proud crimson waves in her wake, leaving the dejected Xie Xue to shuffle up to the lectern, laptop still in her arms.

She was so fucking screwed.

Maybe things would have been all right if Jiang Liping hadn't said anything. But now that she had, Xie Xue had to gulp nervously.

Most students in prestigious schools were exceptionally talented and not easily won over. They didn't trust younger teachers as much as they did older ones in the first place. Now, Jiang Liping's parting words were nothing short of a vicious kick to Xie Xue's knees.

This group of prodigies immediately understood that, oh, their instructor was still a teacher-in-training—one whose name their advisor didn't even know.

What an outrage! No matter how much fiery motivation burned in Xie Xue's heart, it couldn't fend off the disparaging comments that this class was spitting at her. It only took ten minutes for the new faculty member Xie-laoshi to devolve from a confident woman to a stuttering mess. She began to feel dizzy and faint.

So caught up was she in her emotions that she didn't even notice the tall young man who was leaning back in his seat in the last row of the classroom, watching her while spinning his pen idly.

"Hello, everyone. I'm your screenwriting and directing teacher. My name is Xie Xue. Um..."

The students weren't buying it. "Laoshi, how old are you?"

"Jiejie, why don't you order milk tea with us too?"

"Ooh, Laoshi, you look even younger than me..."

The situation was spinning out of control. Xie Xue had no choice but to feign sternness like a paper tiger. "Silence! I'm not messing around with you. Don't waste your precious youth during your university years. You must study hard and gain knowledge. I'll have you know, I'm a very strict and uncompromising person, and the percentage of students I fail is far higher than my colleagues. So all of you need to be on your toes; don't you dare brush off my words."

He Yu couldn't contain his mirth. He looked down as the corner of his mouth curved carelessly upward.

She was just a fucking dumbass.

The students in the classroom fell silent, staring at her as if she were an animal in a zoo. One student even sighed and picked up his backpack to leave.

"Hey! You there! You—"

"Laoshi, I won't fail no matter how much you threaten me. I have a date with my girlfriend, so I'll be leaving now."

"Fascinating. So Huzhou University actually hires teachers-in-training who threaten to fail us if we don't attend class? We got into this university after enormous effort—we're not here to become lab rats for the teachers to experiment with, are we? How come you're the one teaching us while Professor Shen teaches next door? I'm going to write a letter of complaint to the dean later. Excuse me for not staying."

Xie Xue was in a terrible predicament.

Although she forced herself to calmly ask for the students' names and took points off on her tablet, this sequence of events had dealt her such a heavy blow that she wasn't able to recover for a long while. Her carefully prepared lesson had become a half-forgotten mess. She blathered pointlessly for an age before finally reaching what she had previously thought would be a very interesting interactive activity. However, not a single person was willing to come onstage and participate.

Just as she was on the verge of tears, thinking of running away in defeat, a male voice suddenly came from the last row of the classroom.

"Laoshi, I'll do it."

Xie Xue was so miserable that she didn't even realize how familiar that pleasant voice was. She immediately sought out the source of the sound, looking for her savior through eyes filled with grateful tears.

When she saw the boy she hadn't seen in three years, Xie Xue was so surprised that she gaped at him without regard for her image. "H-He Yu?!"

The boy sat at his desk. His eyes were bright and clear, the corners of his mouth were upturned, and his lips were strikingly thin.

He looked a little haughty, a little mischievous—much like the moment when a young Lau Kin Ming in *Infernal Affairs II* raised his head and gazed toward a drunk Mary, with some of the smugness of a young man who had discovered his prey and sated his desire.

He arched a brow. "Long time no see, Xie-laoshi."

Long story short, that's what happened.

After returning to the dorm, Xie Xue couldn't hold back anymore and began to sob in an almost cathartic manner. He Yu had a crush on her, but he wasn't particularly tactful and didn't know how to comfort her properly. He actually said, "Go ahead and cry it out, then. I'll go write in your study for a while. Once you feel better, I'll come out and have dinner with you."

"He Yu, do you know how to cheer people up at all?!"

"Do I have to finish the homework you assigned or not?"

"...Just go."

But when He Yu came out after finishing the story, Xie Xue had already cried herself to sleep.

She didn't wake when he called for her, but he wasn't in a rush.

Xie Xue's favorite activity was eating, with sleeping a close second. As long as you made her something yummy, she'd definitely crawl out of bed right away. Even as a university instructor, this trait wouldn't change.

Fifteen minutes later, she was staring down at the food He Yu held before her.

"...What's this?"

Looking down at the pathetically mushy "fried lumps of rice with egg and ham" in his hands, He Yu felt a little embarrassed. He told his teacher extremely loftily, "Can't you tell? It's Yangzhou fried rice."

"You call *this* Yangzhou fried rice?"

"...Fine, don't eat it then. I can order delivery." The student picked up his phone with a deadpan expression and looked up the highest-rated restaurant. He was filling in the delivery address when the doorbell rang.

He Yu raised his almond eyes. "Who is it? A colleague here to see you?"

"Probably not, I haven't gotten to know them yet." Xie Xue put down her chopsticks and looked up at the clock. "Who would come at this hour..."

As she spoke, she shuffled over to the doorway in her slippers.

A few seconds later, Xie Xue's excited voice came from the doorway. "Ge! Why are you here? You're not working overtime today?"

The sound of the word "Ge" crashed down like thunder. He Yu's original scoundrel aura and his careless lazy mood were instantly shattered. Countless dark memories flashed through his mind like a knee-jerk reaction.

Springing to his feet, he grabbed that appallingly disgraceful fried rice from the table and strode quickly toward the trash can in the kitchen.

But it was too late. Xie Xue had pulled her big brother into the room.

"Ge, I haven't even told you yet. He Yu's back from overseas, and he's one of my students. He's sitting inside right now. You two haven't seen each other in a long time either, right? Hey, He Yu!" Xie Xue's call stopped him midstride. "Where are you going with that plate?"

He Yu froze stock-still in silence.

Never mind.

Since he'd come back, he'd inevitably have to face him again.

He Yu stood with his back to them, wiping his genuine emotions from his face before slowly turning around, looking gentle and refined, elegant and poised.

Facing the elder brother of the Xie family who was a full thirteen years older than him, he actually seemed to match the man in his presence. He gazed toward the head of the Xie family, at the man who somewhat resembled Xie Xue. Then, he reached up to pinch his own nape, his eyes lingering momentarily on the man's features. "Long time no see, Doctor Xie. You look..."

He Yu paused, assessing him.

This man hadn't changed a bit. His features were indifferent and grim, while the planes of his face were sharp and hard, outlining a strong, combative face. His eyes were pretty—a pair of peach-blossoms similar to Xie Xue's. Though they would appear alluring on anyone else, his eyes were a testament to what it meant to have your features align with your personality. On this extraordinary man, they could freeze even thousands of leagues of peach-blossom pools into dark ice. Despite the similarities to Xie Xue's lovely eyes, his pupils were ice-cold. With his rigidly poised physique, he exuded an aura of absolute detachment.

Very tyrannical, very dictatorial. He resembled the big boss of an autocratic feudal clan—all he needed was an atmospheric black fur coat to contrast against his pale face and two of those silver cloak clasp chains worn by military warlords to complete the look.

In the end, He Yu smiled warmly, but there was no mirth in his eyes.

"You look the same as before. You haven't aged a bit."

3

I DISLIKED HIM FROM THE START

THIS WAS XIE XUE's older brother, Xie Qingcheng.

Xie Qingcheng had once treated He Yu's illness as his family's personal physician.

He Yu looked like a normal person on the outside. The impression he gave others was always gentle and kindhearted, and he excelled in conduct, learning, and career. However, the He family had a closely kept secret: this enviable golden child had suffered from a rare mental disorder since birth.

It was an orphan disease, with only four recorded cases having occurred throughout history. The circumstances of each patient were similar: They had congenital deficiencies in the endocrine and nervous systems. When disrupted, their personality would drastically change. Usually, they were numb to pain, but when their condition flared up, they would lose touch with reality, become bloodthirsty, and gain intense destructive tendencies toward themselves or others, resulting in a standard antisocial personality. Physical symptoms included a high fever and confusion, with each flare-up being more severe than the last.

In clinical practice, this disorder was nicknamed "psychological Ebola." It gradually caused the patient's mind to collapse, consequently paralyzing and numbing their body. In the end, they would suffer the deaths of first their mind, then their body. Like a metastasizing cancer, the symptoms would worsen step by step, breaking down a fully functioning member of society into one who'd have difficulties with the most basic of social tasks until eventually becoming a complete lunatic.

In this manner, Patients 1–3 had all been tormented to death before succumbing to that final stage.

He Yu was Patient 4.

His parents brought him to many famous doctors, both local and international, but it was no use. The doctors all believed that the only way to delay the progress of the disorder was to hire a medical caretaker to stay by He Yu's side and carry out long-term supervisory care in order to lower the frequency of flare-ups.

Ultimately, with various considerations in mind, the He family found Xie Qingcheng, who was only twenty-one at the time.

That year, He Yu was eight years old.

But now, He Yu was already nineteen, and Xie Qingcheng was thirty-two.

Xie Qingcheng looked even more unflappable than before; one could even call him indifferent and cold. He was not easily affected by anything, so He Yu's sudden return had not shaken him. He only spent a few seconds looking over the young man he hadn't seen in more than three years from head to toe, ignoring He Yu's polite greetings.

With his age and social standing, he had neither the interest nor the need to play along with a boy who wasn't even twenty years old. He only asked, "Why are you here?"

"I..."

"It's already so late. This is the female faculty dorm."

He Yu smiled. Though he wanted to curse, "Why the fuck are *you* here then?!" he nevertheless responded politely, "I hadn't seen

Xie-laoshi in a very long time. We were talking for so long I forgot the time. Sincerest apologies, Doctor Xie."

"You don't need to call me Doctor Xie anymore. I'm no longer a doctor."

"My bad. Old habits," He Yu responded lightly.

"...Aiya." Seeing the atmosphere between them grow tense from the sidelines, Xie Xue rushed to mediate. "Um, Dage, don't look so stern and serious... He Yu, sit down, don't be nervous. We haven't seen each other in so long."

As she spoke, she distanced herself from He Yu, acting quite courteously. She was always like this: When she was alone with He Yu, she was very casual and behaved as though they were quite close. However, as soon as anyone else was present, especially when it was Xie Qingcheng, she would maintain a polite boundary between herself and He Yu.

He Yu figured that Xie Qingcheng had used fear from a very young age to inspire this behavior. This older brother who acted so much like a family head from a feudal society was the epitome of straight man cancer[7] and egregious chauvinism.

Such a man would be ever-vigilant about threats to the safety of · their female dependents. When Xie Xue was young, Xie Qingcheng didn't even let her wear dresses with hems above the knee. One time, her school organized a talent show for families and classmates, in which Xie Xue had breakdanced. As Xie Qingcheng watched from beneath the stage, his expression had gone black. When the young Xie Xue stepped off the stage, he interrogated her about why she would participate in such an improper dance performance with a grim look on his face, then forcefully draped his suit jacket over her shoulders.

---

7   Derogatory slang term for sexist, paternalistic men, similar to the concept of toxic masculinity.

Though it was only eight or nine at night, Xie Qingcheng probably thought it was extremely improper for a single man and an unmarried woman—like He Yu and his sister—to be alone together at such a late hour.

Just as expected, as soon as Xie Qingcheng walked into the room, he pulled up a chair and sat down. The head of the household crossed his long legs, loosened his cuff links, and looked impassively at He Yu.

"Tell me, how exactly did you just happen to get accepted to Xie Xue's university, and into her exact field of study at that?"

His forceful attitude from his occupation had seeped into his personal life. At that moment, He Yu felt like he was a patient at the hospital stuck with a moody doctor who asked, "Tell me where it hurts," in a flat, indifferent tone.

When He Yu thought of it like this, he found it sort of funny.

Xie Qingcheng saw that He Yu didn't respond for a while, and the corners of his mouth seemed to carry a slight smile. Xie Qingcheng's gaze iced over. "You can't explain?"

He Yu was wrong. He wasn't a doctor examining a patient— Xie Qingcheng's tone sounded exactly like a policeman interrogating a criminal.

He Yu sighed and replied, "It's not like that."

"Then enlighten me."

"I couldn't get used to being abroad, and I like screenwriting and directing. You're asking me why it's such a coincidence, but how can I explain it?" He Yu smiled as he spoke, patience dripping from every word. "It's not like I'm a fortune teller."

"You like screenwriting and directing?"

"Yes."

Xie Qingcheng didn't press further, because his eyes were drawn to the "fried lumps of rice with egg and ham" that He Yu was holding.

Xie Qingcheng furrowed his brow. "...What is that?"

He Yu wanted to throw the plate at Xie Qingcheng's face—a face that looked as if others owed him a fortune—then follow up with "What's it to you?"

But because Xie Xue was present, he smiled at her brother politely and replied, "Yangzhou fried rice."

Xie Qingcheng looked at it closely for a few more seconds. With a cold expression on his fatherly face, he said, "Take off the apron. I'll make another one."

He Yu stared at him, dumbfounded.

"How did you survive abroad for all these years?"

"...By ordering delivery."

Xie Qingcheng's gaze sharpened, a hint of condemnation flashing in his eyes.

Under his penetrating glare, He Yu was transported back to the first time they met. On the villa's freshly mowed lawn, Xie Qingcheng had looked down at the eight-year-old He Yu with a gaze so sharp it could practically dissect his heart.

That day was He Yu's birthday. A crowd of children were playing at the He family's enormous villa. They had tired themselves out and were chatting on the white pebbles of the lakeshore about their ambitions.

"When I grow up, I wanna be a celebrity!"

"I'm gonna be a scientist."

"I'm gonna be an astronaut!"

There was a chubby kid who didn't know what he wanted to be, but he didn't want to show it either. As he looked around, he happened to catch sight of the housekeeper ushering a young doctor through the front yard.

The grass was lush and vibrant, and the sky was a clear and pristine blue. The young doctor was carrying a bouquet of flowers for his boss. The splendidly blooming summer hydrangeas were wrapped in pale silver tissue paper, arranged with silvery willow catkins and bright double roses. As a unique touch, the bouquet was covered in a layer of decorative tulle.

Xie Qingcheng held the flowers in one hand and casually stuck his other hand in his pocket. He was wearing a clean, close-fitting white lab coat with two ballpoint pens clipped to his breast pocket. Since he wasn't working at the moment, the front of the coat was unbuttoned, revealing a lead-gray shirt beneath, as well as a pair of long, shapely legs clad in loosely tailored pants.

The chubby kid gaped at him. After a while, he pointed at Xie Qingcheng with his short, stubby, sausage-like fingers and declared, "I'm gonna be... I'm gonna be a doctor!"

There was a sudden gust of wind, and since the florist really hadn't paid enough fucking attention when they wrapped the flowers, the wind managed to blow away the tulle covering Xie Qingcheng's bouquet. The white fabric immediately floated into the sky over the lawn, only to fall when the wind died back down again.

All the children craned their necks to look at that piece of white tulle. It finally fell precisely in front of He Yu, the only one who wasn't interested at all.

Although He Yu didn't like the doctors, pharmaceutical representatives, and researchers who often appeared in his home, he was habitually courteous. Therefore, he lowered his head, picked up that square of soft tulle, and brought it over.

"Doctor, you dropped this."

He looked up at those indifferent eyes.

It was the height of summer, but inexplicably, they still made He Yu, who was learning Tang dynasty poetry at the time, think

of a particular phrase: "Snowfall whispers onto the neighboring bamboo grove."[8]

Xie Qingcheng looked down and took the tulle. The movement made his lab coat flutter lightly in the breeze, like the cast-off feathers of a crane that had transformed into a demonic spirit. "Thank you."

At that moment, He Yu suddenly caught a whiff of a faint medicinal smell coming from his cuffs.

Research had shown that the feelings between people were largely dictated by the scents on each other's bodies. That was to say, if someone gave off a scent that you liked, then it would be easier for you to fall in love at first sight. On the other hand, if their smell made you annoyed or afraid, then you probably wouldn't have a very promising future together.

He Yu didn't like Xie Qingcheng's scent.

It was ice-cold and unyielding—like the countless bitter pills he'd swallowed ever since he was a child, like the alcohol and iodine solution they would wipe on his arm before injections; like pale, white, ice-cold hospital rooms, devoid of human company and suffused with the odor of disinfectant.

He was almost instinctively terrified of this kind of smell. Subconsciously, he frowned.

But the housekeeper grabbed his shoulder and smiled as he introduced him to that doctor big brother who made him feel unwell all over. "Doctor Xie, this is our boss's young master."

Just when he was about to look away, Xie Qingcheng paused and fixed his dark eyes on He Yu. "...So, it's you."

The look in his eyes irrationally reminded He Yu of a surgical knife. It was abnormally incisive, giving He Yu the strange feeling that he was going to cut open his heart and put it under a microscope.

---

8   From the poem "New Year's Eve in Guilin" by Rong Yu.

"Nice to meet you," the young doctor said. "I'll probably be the one treating your illness in the future."

He Yu was afraid of doctors. He deeply disliked even gentle female doctors, to say nothing of this terrifying apparition emanating stern iciness from head to toe. The eight-year-old boy immediately felt unwell. He forced a smile, then turned around and left.

His mother, Lü Zhishu, happened to see this scene from the balcony. When she finished work that night, she called her son into the study. There was a cup of hot cocoa at just the right temperature on the tea table covered in emerald-green velvet. She pushed the cocoa over to He Yu.

"That Doctor Xie, you met him today?"

"I did." He Yu's family upbringing was strict. He was always very prim and proper to his mother, and a distance was maintained between them.

Lü Zhishu was considerably disappointed in this abnormal son. At that point in time, she had already birthed a second child. Although the younger boy wasn't as clever as the elder, he was at the very least cute, sweet, and healthy, so she focused all her attention on him. When she talked to He Yu, she had nearly no patience. "His name is Xie Qingcheng. He'll be your personal physician from now on, and he'll come to our house every week to examine you. You must cooperate with him, and if you ever feel unwell, you can call him over at any time."

"Mm."

The composure of the eight-year-old boy in front of her always made Lü Zhishu feel a little scared, a feeling she tried to dispel with a sigh and a bit of teasing. "He Yu, we've signed a slave contract with Doctor Xie. If he can't cure your condition, he'll end up as a long-term laborer for us. He'll never get paid or be able to take any days off. He won't even be able to find a wife and get married. Do you know what this means?"

"Not really."

"It means, if you don't cooperate, you'll lower the efficacy of his treatment, keep him from regaining his freedom, and leave him unable to eventually find a wife. Then, you'll have to take responsibility for him and support him for life."

Even though he was mature for his age, He Yu was still only eight—young and gullible—and was thus horrified. He looked up at once. "Can I cancel his contract?"

"No." On her flights the past few days, Lü Zhishu had obsessively watched Republican-era dramas about torturous love and family infighting. With a fleeting thought, she added something even more cutting. "Also, he might want you to take responsibility by becoming his wife. Look at how pretty you are—you'd make a decent foster bride."[9]

Back then, He Yu had no interest whatsoever in love, nor did he have any desire to learn more, so he didn't even know marriage was restricted to heterosexual couples in this region. At Lü Zhishu's words, his psychological trauma deepened; there was even a period when Xie Qingcheng's silhouette would appear in his nightmares.

"No, I don't like you... I don't want to marry you...!"

These nightmares weren't dispelled until six months later, when He Jiwei heard the story and roundly cursed out his own wife. "What the hell did you tell our son?"

Then he cursed out He Yu. "How'd you fall for this kind of joke? Where has your usual intelligence gone? You're a man, Xie Qingcheng is also a man—what do you mean you need to marry him and be responsible for him? Do you have rocks for brains?"

---

9   A girl adopted into a family with the intention of having one of their sons marry her in the future.

He Yu felt very dispirited.

Over the course of the past half a year, at the thought of how he'd end up as that ice-cold doctor's foster bride if he didn't cooperate and let Doctor Xie cure him of his psychological condition, all he could do was constantly pretend to be stupid and foolish in front of the doctor. He hoped to leave a very negative impression on this man, so that even if matters got to that point in the future, Doctor Xie would definitely never develop any untoward interest in himself.

However, he didn't expect that after playing the fool in front of Xie Qingcheng for six months straight, his dad would tell him, "Your mom was teasing you."

If not for He Yu's strong self-restraint, he might have already blurted out a "Fuck you!" Unfortunately, he was monitored too closely. Forget about curse words—at age eight, even the word "bastard" had yet to enter his childhood vocabulary.

But, in any case, through those six months of diligent effort, persevering hard to embarrass himself before Xie Qingcheng, He Yu had more or less managed an extraordinary feat: no matter how hard he strove, in the following six or seven years...

No, it was longer than that. Even after he parted ways with Xie Qingcheng at age fourteen, even today, to Xie Qingcheng, He Yu was still a massive, three-dimensional, living and breathing dumbfuck with a capital D.

And in this moment, the hideous bowl of fried rice in his hands was the strongest evidence of the fact that, in Xie Qingcheng's eyes, after four whole years, he was still the ultimate dumbfuck who couldn't even make fried rice properly.

He put down the offending dish and handed the apron to the head of the Xie family, the elder brother who was dressed immaculately in a pressed suit and leather shoes. He Yu appeared calm and collected, but he was a little dejected. *That was a miscalculation,* he thought to himself. He shouldn't have personally done the cooking to begin with. Wasn't this just giving Xie Qingcheng free entertainment?

4

WHEN WE MET AGAIN,
I NEEDED TO LOOK
DOWN AT HIM

HE SIZZLING SOUND of frying rice filled the narrow
kitchen. He Yu and Xie Xue sat at the somewhat greasy
little dining table. Xie Xue was in a better mood, a relaxed
smile on her face as she waited for her elder brother to finish cooking. He Yu also smiled perfunctorily, but on the inside, he was
rolling his eyes.

The kitchen door covered in posters slid open. The familiar aroma
of cooked rice wafted out first. Then Xie Qingcheng walked out
and took off his apron. As usual, he was wearing a shirt tucked into
tailored dress pants. Despite his cold personality, he was still a good
elder brother. Because his parents had died young, he had become the
head of the household by default, looking after his younger sibling
since childhood. As a result, his culinary skills were quite excellent.

Seeing her brother with his rolled-up sleeves bring a tray over and
put it down on the simple little table, Xie Xue cried out in surprise
and quickly jumped up to help him arrange the food and set the
table.

"It smells amazing. Ge, you're the best, you're the best! I love you
so, so, so much! Let's eat! I'm starving!"

Xie Qingcheng's expression was solemn. "Girls shouldn't blather
on like this. It's inappropriate. Go and wash your hands first."

Then he turned to He Yu and said, "You too."

It had been ages since He Yu had eaten this kind of fried rice.

The rice Xie Qingcheng made was fluffy and golden, each and every grain distinct—when He Yu was little, he would stand by the stove and watch Xie Qingcheng make his little sister's favorite dish. He knew good fried rice needed to be made from leftover rice that was neither too moist nor too dry. Before the rice went into the pan, Xie Qingcheng would first mix it with beaten eggs in a large bowl until every grain of rice was evenly coated in golden yellow.

Once the oil in the pan was hot, he would swiftly add in two more fresh eggs, scramble them, and immediately scoop them up. Then he would add lard and pour the egg-coated rice into the frying pan and stir-fry on high heat.

But this wasn't exactly authentic Yangzhou fried rice. To suit Xie Xue's tastes, Xie Qingcheng modified the recipe and never added peas, but this didn't make it any less delicious.

All three plates of golden, piping-hot fried rice glistened under the lights, with small pieces of diced ham, tender shrimp, and delicate green onions sprinkled throughout. They looked and smelled extremely appetizing.

As He Yu ate, he schemed in secret.

He hardly tasted the food as it passed through his mouth. Xie Xue talked and laughed at the table, but because Xie Qingcheng was present, she directed most of her cheerful chatter toward her brother. The two siblings conversed comfortably, but because He Yu hadn't interacted with the two of them in so long, he struggled to get a word in edgewise, becoming a nonexistent backdrop.

Said backdrop wasn't happy at all. He needed to find an excuse to send Xie Qingcheng away.

"Do you want some more?"

While lost in thought, he'd already silently finished the fragrant fried rice. He Yu snapped out of it and politely responded to Xie Qingcheng, who was looking at him, "I'm good."

"Ge, I want more! Give me some more!"

Xie Qingcheng left with Xie Xue's plate. Xie Xue bit down on her chopsticks and said to He Yu, "My brother's fried rice is way better than yours. It's so delicious—why don't you have another bowl?"

He Yu faked a smile. "One person who can break the scales is enough. I won't cause further trouble."

"Hey! What's your problem?! You don't like me, huh?"

"You're the one who complained that mine wasn't as good as his!"

As the two of them squabbled, Xie Qingcheng's voice sounded from the kitchen. "Xie Xue, what's this bucket of water doing here?"

"Oh." Xie Xue immediately stopped quarreling with He Yu. As if she hadn't just been giggling with him, she sat up straight and said solemnly, "The school said the water's going to be shut off tomorrow. I filled a bucket with water just in case, but the kitchen is too small and it gets in the way if I put it anywhere else, so I can only put it on top of the chest."

"If you put it up so high, what if it falls when you open the kitchen door without paying attention?"

"Aiya, Ge, you don't need to pay it any mind," the dumbass replied. "It'll be fine."

Xie Xue spoke off-handedly, but He Yu was listening intently. He was someone who liked to pull a girl's pigtails if he had a crush on her. As he listened to their conversation, his pretty, pure almond eyes glanced toward the kitchen as a terrible idea suddenly occurred to him.

The three of them finished eating dinner. Xie Qingcheng didn't like to clean up, so He Yu, with his image of being a gentle, reliable, and exceptional boy, naturally took on the task of washing the dishes and pans.

"Do you need help?" Xie Xue asked.

"I'll let you know in a bit if I do," He Yu said with an insincere smile. He turned to walk into the kitchen and closed the door.

The moment the door shut, his smile disappeared.

He Yu carefully examined the angles in the room. He first moved the bucket of water a bit farther outward on the chest of drawers, to a position where it would fall when the kitchen door was opened. Then he very calmly took out the hair dryer that Xie Xue kept in the second drawer. Without batting an eyelid, he put it into the sink and turned the faucet on.

Xie Xue had saved up half a month's salary to buy this high-end hair dryer. With a loud splash, Young Master He—whom she'd never suspect—thus drenched it into an impressive-looking but useless piece of scrap.

Excellent.

He Yu wiped the water off the hair dryer and placed it back into the drawer.

The preparations were complete.

He glanced coolly through the ajar door at the girl chatting with Xie Qingcheng, then turned around and rolled up the sleeves of his white shirt. He calmly turned on the faucet again, dispensed some detergent, and began to wash the dishes.

He simply looked like the epitome of a good person! A shining example of an upstanding young man!

However, those who had done too many bad things were likely to encounter retribution.

He Yu was on the cusp of seeing his carefully devised and meticulously planned efforts come to fruition. He shook the water off his hands and was getting ready for the female lead to run into the disaster of the "coincidence" that he'd orchestrated when he suddenly heard footsteps outside the kitchen. He Yu immediately turned his head, only to see the shadow of a tall, straight-backed man through the frosted glass.

He Yu's almond eyes widened, but before he could prevent anything, he heard Xie Qingcheng say, "He Yu, I'm coming in to wash my hands."

"Wait—"

The word was halfway out of his mouth before he heard a massive noise. The bucket of water that He Yu had intentionally readjusted on the chest of drawers rocked in a circle. Then, with an almighty crash, that full bucket of water—the bucket that should have landed on Xie Xue according to He Yu's original plans—tipped over, its contents cascading right over Xie Qingcheng's handsome face!

Fuck!

Not a single fucking drop was wasted!

Both men were at a complete loss for words.

Water splashed everywhere, rendering the entire room a mess. The bucket, which had achieved its goal with smashing success, dropped to the ground and rolled around beside Xie Qingcheng, who was drenched from head to toe. In the end, it leisurely rolled out of the living room, like an old man taking a walk, and came to a perfectly satisfied stop before Xie Xue, who had hastily run over at the commotion.

Xie Xue had witnessed the entire series of events from outside the kitchen. Now, she was trembling in fear.

She was done for...

She was fucking done for!

Xie Xue watched as her completely soaked big brother slowly turned toward her. His skin was quite fair to begin with, but after being drenched so thoroughly out of the blue, his complexion seemed even paler while his eyes and brows looked even darker. Water dripped from the wet wisps of hair plastered to his forehead, streaming past his eyebrows to his eyes, wide open in disbelief. He narrowed them subconsciously before returning to his senses.

"XIE XUE!!"

Xie Xue flinched, shrinking in terror.

Xie Qingcheng flipped his dripping bangs back and raged, "I already told you not to put the bucket on the drawers!!"

"I'm sorry—I'm sorry!" Quivering, Xie Xue scurried into the room and grabbed a mop and paper towels. She handed the paper towels to her brother as she rummaged through the drawers for her hair dryer. "Ge, I didn't expect it to fall either... It was clearly fine earlier... Dry your hair first, don't catch a cold."

Behind her, He Yu guiltily blinked his warm almond eyes.

Xie Xue pulled Xie Qingcheng into the living room, completely oblivious as she took out the hair dryer that He Yu had ruined with water. She plugged it in and pressed the button to switch it on.

Nothing happened.

"Eh?"

She pressed the button again.

Still nothing.

Speechless, she could only keep on pressing the button to no avail.

"...Ge." As Xie Xue looked at her brother's extremely dark expression, she felt like her death was practically imminent. In a shaky voice, she said, "Th-the hair dryer seems to be broken..."

Xie Qingcheng shot her a glance through icy peach-blossom eyes. "This is the four-thousand-yuan hair dryer you told me about?"

Xie Xue nearly fell to her knees. How could she be so unlucky?!

Xie Qingcheng hadn't understood why she needed to buy a hair dryer that was more expensive than a regular television in the first place. He'd cursed her out roundly for it, but she kept reiterating how great this hair dryer was, how good it was for the hair. Most importantly, it was very high-quality and would last at least twenty years.

"I swear that I'll use this hair dryer for twenty years!" Xie Xue had proclaimed. "Otherwise, you can chop my head off as idiot tax!"

Her words from back then echoed in her ears. Under Xie Qingcheng's chilling gaze, Xie Xue felt her nape prickle with cold. She involuntarily took a few steps back and reached up to cover her neck.

Just as she was at a loss for what to do, Xie Xue glimpsed He Yu wiping his hands and walking out from the kitchen, as if he had done nothing wrong. Suddenly struck by an idea, she ran hastily over to He Yu as though she had seen a life-saving deity and wept.

"He Yu! Can I ask you for a favor?" she cried. "My hair dryer broke! Who knew I'd be so unlucky?! Do you have spare clothes in your dorm? You have a hair dryer, right? Can you take my brother over there to change? Laoshi thanks you!"

She was acting so courteously in front of her brother again. After a moment's silence, He Yu smiled and decided to play along. "Xie-laoshi, you're really being too formal."

He looked toward Xie Qingcheng.

Xie Qingcheng was sitting with his back against the couch, water still dripping from his chiseled jaw. His casual gray shirt had been completely soaked through. The fabric stuck to his skin and faintly exposed the outline of his chest and his slim waist. His thin lips were slightly pursed as he stared darkly at Xie Xue, as if he were getting ready to choose righteousness over family and obliterate this failure of a sister on behalf of the world.

He Yu looked at him and felt the onset of a slight headache.

According to his original plans, the person who was supposed to end up soaked and helpless was Xie Xue. She should have been the one following him back to his dorm to blow-dry her hair.

How did it become Xie Qingcheng instead?

He Yu was straight, and he also disliked doctors. His Elderliness Xie Qingcheng was completely unwelcome in his room.

But he had no other choice; there was no turning back now. He'd already gotten Xie Qingcheng into such a state, and Xie Xue had already asked him for help.

He could only sigh softly and walk over to Xie Qingcheng. To the gloomy-faced doctor sitting on the sofa, He Yu said, "You're already-soaked, so you should stop glaring, Doctor Xie. Why don't you come with me to get changed? My dorm's only ten minutes away from here. Let's go."

The male dorms at the School of Fine Arts in Huzhou University were four-person rooms. It was still dinnertime when He Yu and Xie Qingcheng arrived. All his roommates had gone out to eat, so no one was inside the dorm.

"Wear these." He Yu took out a clean shirt and a pair of pants from his closet and handed them to Xie Qingcheng.

"A sports T-shirt?" Xie Qingcheng scoffed.

"What's wrong with it?"

What was wrong with it? Well, men only wore such clothing when they were in school; Xie Qingcheng hadn't put on something like this in decades. He couldn't even remember how he looked in shirts like this anymore, not to mention they didn't suit him at all now.

"Give me a dress shirt."

"Tsk, sorry about that, Doctor Xie. You don't get to choose." He Yu's smile was so light and perfunctory it was like gauze. Since Xie Xue wasn't here, he could drop all pretense. His pitch-black eyes were devoid of the slightest hint of sincerity, and his tone was less than courteous when he said, "Ah, I really only have one shirt that's in your size. My dress shirts are too big for you."

Xie Qingcheng looked up, his gaze piercing through his wet bangs and landing on He Yu's face. The mockery lurking at the corners of He Yu's mouth seemed much more obvious now that he'd done away with his feigned politeness. He arched a brow as he met Xie Qingcheng's eyes. "Don't want to wear it? Then you'll have to walk out naked."

Xie Qingcheng silently snatched the clothes out of He Yu's hand. His expression was stiff as he trudged to the washroom.

While waiting for Xie Qingcheng to change, He Yu was struck by déjà vu...

He said to the man behind the frosted door, "By the way, Doctor Xie, I remembered something all of a sudden. Remember that time when I went to your university dorm—"

"I don't remember. Get lost."

He Yu laughed. He hadn't even completed his sentence before Xie Qingcheng cut him off with his denial—how was this any different from admitting outright that he hadn't forgotten that old grudge?

Clearly, both he and Xie Qingcheng recalled that incident from before.

Grievances didn't stem from nothing; even something as minor as this article of clothing was long-awaited retaliation against Xie Qingcheng.

He Yu found himself feeling a little pleased at this thought. Perhaps this was how it felt to turn the tables many years later.

"Then hurry up." Without Xie Xue, He Yu could barely keep his true colors from shining through brightly in front of Xie Qingcheng. He leaned against the bathroom door with his arms crossed and smiled. He knocked on the pane of frosted glass. The roguish note in his voice was apparent as he said, "We still need to go back and see your sister after you're done."

A few minutes later, Xie Qingcheng flung the door open. It slammed into He Yu, nearly knocking him over. Caught off guard, He Yu let out a muffled groan and bent over, clutching his nose.

Xie Qingcheng looked at him indifferently. "Why were you standing so close?"

He Yu was in so much pain that he let his mask slip. "Xie Qingcheng, why are you so unreasonable? You're the one who slammed the door into me!"

When his stubbornness got the better of him, he still used Xie Qingcheng's full name in private.

Xie Qingcheng hesitated. "Go get some ice for it."

"Where am I supposed to find ice?" He Yu let go of his reddened nose bridge and kneaded it. He managed to suppress his anger but couldn't resist talking back. "You look a lot like ice to me. Might as well hold your hand to my nose instead."

Xie Qingcheng imagined the scene for a moment. With a chilly expression, he tersely replied, "Too gay. I'm homophobic." Xie Qingcheng shoved He Yu away. He circled around him to enter the dorm and began searching.

He Yu was at a loss for words. "What? That's not what I meant. If you're homophobic, then I'm even more homophobic…"

"Where's the hair dryer?" Xie Qingcheng didn't let him continue. He also couldn't be bothered to listen to his explanation.

"…On the chair."

Xie Qingcheng plugged the hair dryer in and began blow-drying his hair. He Yu, who was still somewhat upset, stood on the balcony. From a distance, he stared at Xie Qingcheng. He simply couldn't understand how a person like this could be Xie Xue's biological brother.

Xie Xue worshipped her elder brother and saw him as a savior of sorts, but He Yu didn't understand what it was about Xie Qingcheng that made him so worthy of her devotion. He was just an old man.

But as he stared, He Yu's mind began to wander.

Xie Qingcheng was the young He Yu's childhood nightmare. He Yu had always feared him, yet he still had to see him because Xie Qingcheng was his doctor. In front of him, He Yu had embarrassed himself and lost all his composure. Xie Qingcheng had witnessed all the times he had gone mad. Once, He Yu was struggling wildly against his medical restraints, screaming at him like a crazed, trapped beast. Xie Qingcheng had leveled a cool gaze at him and walked toward him under the glare of surgical lights. He Yu had caught a whiff of the icy-cold scent of disinfectant on Xie Qingcheng before a needle pierced his skin...

At that time, he thought that Xie Qingcheng was so tall. And so cold.

Xie Qingcheng was strong and irrefutable, hovering over him like a dark cloud—a bogeyman he could never escape in his lifetime.

Who would have thought that, after a few years apart, He Yu was now the one who had to look down at Xie Qingcheng.

He Yu lowered his gaze to look at Xie Qingcheng.

What had happened?

Xie Qingcheng didn't seem as scary anymore.

Perhaps people's childhood impressions were enduring, even if they were inaccurate. For example, if one looked back at TV shows that seemed endlessly long when they were a child, they'd realize that the shows might have had but twenty-something episodes; or the sheepdog that they had once feared, that seemed bigger and sturdier than a horse, in fact only came up to an adult's knee in old photographs.

Perhaps this was the sort of psychological discrepancy He Yu felt toward Xie Qingcheng. He Yu's gaze lingered on Xie Qingcheng— long enough for him to notice.

Xie Qingcheng shot He Yu a cold look. "What are you looking at?"

He Yu was quiet for a moment. "Just seeing whether or not my clothes suit you."

Xie Qingcheng didn't reply.

"They really are too big," said He Yu. "Xie Qingcheng, I remember you used to be very tall."

"I don't feel the need to show off my height and build," Xie Qingcheng said coolly.

He turned around and continued to dry his hair. However, just before he faced away, his expression seemed a bit dark.

In that instant, He Yu realized that his childhood bogeyman was merely an ordinary person—a slightly slender man, at that. He Yu's white T-shirt hung loose on Xie Qingcheng, the dip at the collar exposing pale skin, like a gulf at the base of a snowy mountain stream, cast in shadow by the garment.

Weird—why had he been so afraid of Xie Qingcheng back then?

He Yu was still caught up in his musings when Xie Qingcheng finished drying his hair. Straight men didn't bother much with their appearance; he only casually ran a hand through his locks in front of the mirror before putting down the hair dryer and turning back to He Yu. "I'll get going. I'll return your shirt tomorrow."

"No need. I'm not accustomed to wearing clothes that other people have worn. Just toss it after you change—it was getting old anyway."

Xie Qingcheng didn't press. He pushed aside the still-damp ends of his hair once more and said, "All right, then I'll be on my way."

"You're not going back with me to Xie Xue's?"

"No," said Xie Qingcheng. "I have other plans tonight."

"Writing papers?"

Xie Qingcheng wasn't in the habit of hiding his personal affairs, or maybe he just didn't care. He glanced over at He Yu as he was putting his watch back on his wrist and said, "A matchmaking date."

He Yu, who was only making small talk and not paying much attention, didn't react to these words right away. He even felt secretly happy that Xie Qingcheng finally had the good sense to leave. Several seconds later, however, his words finally registered in his brain, as if the distance from his ears to their destination was a reflex arc long enough to loop the earth.

He Yu's head whipped around in shock, his almond eyes flying wide open.

Wasn't Xie Qingcheng married?

Why was he going on matchmaking dates?

Why hadn't Xie Xue mentioned this to him before?

Countless questions surged through his head. He Yu blinked as he grasped at the central thread of this jumble of thoughts.

He practically gaped at Xie Qingcheng's apathetic face, half of which was submerged in shadow. After a moment's hesitation, he asked, "You...got divorced?"

5

HE GOT DIVORCED

IT DIDN'T SEEM LIKE Xie Qingcheng planned to explain further. He merely asked, "Xie Xue never told you?"

"She didn't."

"Maybe she thought it was my personal business."

He Yu fell quiet for a moment. "You and Li Ruoqiu weren't right for each other?"

Li Ruoqiu was Xie Qingcheng's ex-wife.

He Yu had a very deep impression of this woman—he thought there was something wrong with her. How could someone walk into marriage, often touted as the grave of love, with a man as paternalistic and cold as Xie Qingcheng?

In He Yu's memory, Xie Qingcheng seemed devoid of desires. It was like he ought to be always sitting at his office desk in a neat and proper white lab coat, against the backdrop of some over-flowing bookshelves, giving off the ice-cold and sobering scent of disinfectant.

He Yu found it hard to believe that Xie Qingcheng would love anyone. He found it even harder to believe that anyone would love Xie Qingcheng.

But Doctor Xie really had gotten married.

He Yu still remembered Xie Qingcheng's wedding day—he had gone at his mother's behest to bring gift money to the newlyweds.

He hadn't even bothered to change out of his school uniform. After the driver dropped him off at the hotel, he walked in casually wearing his white athletic shoes, his backpack slung over his shoulders, hands shoved into the pockets of his school-issued gym shorts.

Xie Qingcheng was welcoming the guests.

The team of wedding professionals had put makeup on him. He stood in the center of the crowd, his back as straight as a ruler, his bearing dignified, with pitch-black brows and eyes that resembled fallen stars. The master of ceremonies was saying something to him— it was too loud, and Xie Qingcheng was tall and couldn't hear clearly, so he tilted his head and leaned down to let the emcee speak directly into his ear. In contrast to those around him, Xie Qingcheng's face seemed shockingly pale, like thin porcelain under a spotlight, so fragile it would shatter at the slightest touch. His lips were slightly pale too, as though the blood in his veins had been frozen under a layer of ice.

Skin clear and pristine, lips like red plum blossoms frosted with snow.

Though He Yu didn't like men, he was someone who appreciated beauty.

At that moment, He Yu imagined that the proposal between Li Ruoqiu—who was very pretty, to be honest—and Xie Qingcheng might have gone like this:

Xie Qingcheng would be dressed in pure white, his usual ballpoint and fountain pens clipped to his breast pocket, with his hands in his pants pockets, standing like an untouchable alpine flower. Then, in an unrepentantly insufferable tone, he would say to the young lady, "I'm going to marry you. You can go ahead and thank me on your knees."

He Yu was a master at pretending, so of course he wouldn't voice his genuine thoughts. With his messenger bag slung over his shoulder, He Yu walked up to the handsome groom and beautiful bride. Smiling, he said, "Doctor Xie, Saozi."

"This is..." began Li Ruoqiu.

"A friend's son," Xie Qingcheng said by way of introduction.

He had an agreement with the He family; he wouldn't tell outsiders that He Yu was his patient.

"So pretty—what a good-looking kid," Li Ruoqiu complimented.

He Yu gave her a polite, gentlemanly bow, with a faint smile in his dark black eyes. "Nonsense. Saozi is the real beauty."

The teenager retrieved a thick sealed red envelope from his canvas bag. He said, gentle and refined, "Wishing you and Doctor Xie an everlasting and blissful marriage."

Everlasting and blissful his ass.

Back then, he already had an inkling that no one would be able to put up with a man like Xie Qingcheng, but he hadn't expected that this marriage would really be so short-lived. Could he have magically manifested this?

He Yu resisted the building schadenfreude and asked evenly, "Why'd you get divorced all of a sudden?"

Xie Qingcheng said nothing.

"I remember she really liked you back then. When the two of you visited my house after you got married, she only had eyes for you."

Xie Qingcheng broke his silence. "He Yu, this is indeed my personal business."

He Yu arched a brow slightly.

He assessed Xie Qingcheng's arrogant expression. Now that he was facing Xie Qingcheng again, He Yu suddenly felt that many things had changed over the course of the years he had spent abroad.

But He Yu wasn't actually interested in what had changed about Xie Qingcheng, so in the end, he just smiled. "Then never mind. Hope you have a successful matchmaking date."

Xie Qingcheng shot him a cool glance and, without bothering to thank him, turned to leave.

The dorm door closed behind him.

Because He Yu had brought up his ex-wife, Xie Qingcheng found himself involuntarily reminded of his marriage with Li Ruoqiu, a union that could be described as a complete failure.

Xie Qingcheng was well aware of the reason why Xie Xue hadn't mentioned the divorce to He Yu: it was immensely embarrassing. While it was true that Li Ruoqiu had once loved him, it was also true that her love didn't last.

She cheated on him.

This was something that Xie Qingcheng could never accept. He didn't know what love was, but he did know familial duty. With respect to certain issues, his way of thinking was extremely conservative.

But Li Ruoqiu was different.

She believed that the most important thing in a marriage was love, not duty. Thus, their marriage eventually fell apart. Even though she was the one who had fallen in love with a married man, she still cried and lashed out at Xie Qingcheng afterward. She told him he only had eyes for his work, that marrying him was no different from marrying a frigid copy of his work schedule.

In all honesty, this wasn't an unreasonable criticism. Xie Qingcheng knew he wasn't a sentimental man.

Throughout their relationship, Xie Qingcheng had never felt any sort of love for her. She had pursued him for many years, and as they got to know each other, he also began to feel that she was a suitable partner. In due course, they got married.

After they tied the knot, he didn't shirk a single duty or responsibility expected of him as a husband.

But that wasn't the type of marriage she wanted.

Xie Qingcheng was very responsible, but he wasn't romantic, and his personality was rather indifferent. He could remain rational and calm even in bed, never succumbing to or indulging in any desires. It was as if he were completing a task or fulfilling a duty that one was obligated to do after marriage, but he did so without much passion.

Thus, her heart gradually cooled.

She cheated on him, then told him, "Xie Qingcheng, you're a heartless person. Even to this day, you still don't understand. What I want is love, not just a marriage."

But what was love?

Xie Qingcheng only felt the onset of a splitting headache. Who knew how much effort it took for him to refrain from slamming the table in rage. He gazed at her for a very long time. In the end, he spoke numbly, his voice as calm as still water. "Does that man love you? He has a wife and daughter. How sincere do you think he is about you?"

She looked up, her eyes burning with something that Xie Qingcheng couldn't understand at all.

"...I don't care if he has a wife and a kid," Li Ruoqiu said. "I just know that at the very least, he's passionate when he holds me. I can hear his heart beat faster, unlike you, Xie Qingcheng. You're perfectly prim and proper, you never mess around with other women, you let me manage the money and the household—but your heart when you're with me is like a dead man's ECG. We've been married for so many years, but it's only ever been a flat line.

"Life is short—just a few decades. He was once bound by an unhappy marriage, just like me. Now, I've come to a realization:

I don't need status, money, or even reputation. Other people can call me loose or a slut if they feel like it, but I only want to be with him."

Xie Qingcheng closed his eyes, the cigarette in his hand about to burn his fingers. "Li Ruoqiu, have you gone insane? There's no such thing as love. Love is just a reaction caused by the dopamine in your body—it's your hormones acting up. But responsibility does exist, and so does family. You're crazy about him, but is he willing to get divorced and live with you?"

After a moment of silence, the flame in Li Ruoqiu's eyes blazed even more wildly. Finally, she said with tearful resolve, "I just don't want to have regrets. Xie Qingcheng, love does exist. It might defy norms and be shunned by society, or maybe it's so lowly that it's buried in mud and unspeakable filth, but it does exist. It has nothing to do with hormones or dopamine. I'm sorry—there's no way I can continue living with you like this, because now I know what love is. I love him, even if it's wrong."

Despite the many years that had passed since the divorce, Xie Qingcheng still found the conversation absurd every time he thought of it.

If "love" was what made someone walk into the fray, despite knowing very well that it was wrong—if "love" made them stand by their mistakes, despite knowing full well that they were stepping into a bottomless abyss, to the point that they could disregard anything, from infamy, scorn, principles, morals, to life itself—then, to him, this seemed less like a type of affection and more like some kind of disease.

He couldn't empathize at all.

Although Xie Qingcheng's personality was staunch, when all was said and done, he was still a straight man who had internalized traditional chauvinistic ideals. When his wife cheated on him and ran off with a married man, that betrayal pained him deeply.

After his divorce, Xie Qingcheng carried on. He went to work, wrote his manuscripts, and taught his students as usual; he didn't seem upset at all. Yet it was plainly obvious to everyone around him that he was rapidly losing weight, his cheeks were becoming slightly sunken, and his voice rasped when he spoke.

Concerned that the university would go viral on Weibo[10] if Xie Qingcheng kicked the bucket, the dean advised him solicitously, "Professor Xie, if you're feeling unwell, just take some time off and go rest at home. You mustn't push yourself too hard."

To the dean's surprise, Xie Qingcheng tossed a flash drive at him. In it was a compressed folder of PowerPoint presentations—the most recent materials for his course. Given how complex and dense the contents were, the dean realized that even at the height of his intellectual and physical prowess, he would have had difficulties putting them together so quickly.

"Do you still want me to go home?" Xie Qingcheng leaned back against his office chair, interlocking his slender fingers. He was so slight he resembled tissue paper and so thin his silhouette seemed like dark smoke. Yet when he looked up, his gaze was still unexpectedly clear—one could even call it coldly sharp.

"I do want to rest," Xie Qingcheng continued, "but please make sure that there's someone other than me who can prepare the first lecture of this course to this standard."

Naturally, there was no one else who could step up to the plate.

The dean could also tell from Xie Qingcheng's blazing gaze that his worry that the university would go viral on Weibo was

---

10 *Popular microblogging platform in China.*

unfounded for the time being. Those were not the eyes of someone who was about to shrivel up and die.

But hardly anyone knew that in order to keep working properly, in order to bury those shattered emotions at the bottom of his heart, Xie Qingcheng would sit in his bedroom and smoke when he was at home. Even when he started coughing uncontrollably, he refused to stop. It was as if he wanted to dye his lungs black, as if he wanted to turn the entire house into a nicotine paradise.

His neighbor Auntie Li simply couldn't bear to see him in this state.

In the beginning, the Xie family had been quite well off, as both his parents were high-ranking members of the police force. Later, however, they committed a major error when handling a case and were both demoted to the lowest rank. At that time, his mother also fell ill. In order to pay for her treatment, they sold their large house and moved into an apartment in a small alley in the old city district of Huzhou. They pinched pennies to survive but came to know many enthusiastic neighbors along the way.

Xie Qingcheng hadn't even come of age when his parents passed away, yet he had to take on the responsibility of being the head of the household. All the neighbors pitied the Xie children and made sure to look after them, and Auntie Li was especially attentive to Xie Qingcheng.

Auntie Li was a little younger than Xie Qingcheng's mother. She liked kids, but she never married and had no children of her own. She treated the Xie siblings as though they were her own precious babies, especially after their parents died. This untethered woman and the two orphaned children grew deeply attached to each other.

After Xie Qingcheng's divorce, Auntie Li wept for a long, long time. Then, like an old mother going bald from stress, she mustered up the energy to introduce girls to him.

In order to avoid hurting Auntie Li's feelings, Xie Qingcheng attended every meeting she set up, but really, he was just going through the motions. Besides, from the perspective of those girls, he wasn't a great catch either.

Xie Qingcheng's circumstances were considered excellent the first time he got married. He was handsome and tall, a doctor in his twenties at a provincial-level hospital. He was in the prime of his life, with boundless future prospects. His only tangible shortcoming was that he hadn't been born into a wealthy family and didn't have much money.

But now, he was a divorcé, and his salary as a professor wasn't as high as when he had been a doctor. He wasn't that young anymore either, so naturally, his flaws became all the more conspicuous, like a set of unusually protruding ribs. Not only was he a divorced man pushing forty without a nice house or car, but he also had an unmarried younger sister he needed to look after, dragging him down like a child from a previous marriage.

No matter how handsome he was, he wasn't a celebrity, so he couldn't cash in on it to make a living.

How could a girl's parents not mind?

Turning up for matchmaking meetings and dating weren't the same. It was said that compatibility was determined by first impressions, but in reality, one's overall circumstances were the deciding factor. Thus, the conversations often went like this:

"Your job is pretty good, right? Do you have time to take care of a family?"

"I don't. Because I'm a medical school professor, the course materials need to be very detailed and accurate. The students also have many questions, so I often work overtime."

"Oh... Well, your salary isn't bad, right?"

"I'll probably need to teach for another three years or so before I get a raise. But I'm not sure if I'll still be at the university at that time."

"Ah, I see... Do you have any other family?"

"...I have a younger sister."

"Is she married?"

"Not yet."

Silence.

The interrogation was usually sharp and direct, dissecting one's circumstances like a surgical knife, and Xie Qingcheng's answers would completely erase the woman's initially hopeful smile.

Auntie Li became terribly anxious when she found out about this. "Hey, you have to talk yourself up on a matchmaking date! It's all an established convention. Everyone else is bragging, but you get there and downplay yourself from the get-go. People will think you're even lousier than you say you are. Who would know if you embellished a bit?"

Xie Qingcheng originally wanted to say, "I don't want to remarry," but when he met Auntie Li's worried and sorrowful eyes, the words that came out of his mouth turned into, "I've grown used to it. Sorry."

Auntie Li looked at him with wide eyes. After a while, she sounded slightly choked up as she said, "Child, you're so wonderful. How could Buddha possibly not bless you... I burn incense and pray every day, asking the heavens to find a fated marriage for my precious one. Then even if I died right now, it would be worth it..."

"Auntie Li, please don't talk nonsense."

"I'm an old bag of bones, why should I be afraid? But you're different—you're still young. If you don't live well in the future, how could I face your dad and Muying in the underworld..."

Auntie Li cast her net wide, looking for all types of girls, in hopes that she could find a suitable marriage partner for him. Xie Qingcheng didn't like this one bit. He was a proud, arrogant, and unyielding man; he was unwilling to lie and disliked being scrutinized. As a result, his state of mind had done a one-eighty compared to when he had gone on a matchmaking date with Li Ruoqiu. Now, he was certain he would never share the rest of his life with anyone else.

But with his patriarchal personality, how could he bear to let his friends and family cry and hurt because of him? He had to see them live happily under his protection and care.

Thus, in order to make Auntie Li a little happier, he still agreed to go on those matchmaking dates that were akin to job interviews, even though the result was always a foregone conclusion.

His matchmaking date today was with a much younger woman named Bai Jing, who worked at a luxury sales counter in Huzhou's most fashionable mall. A relative of hers was apparently a professor at a famous medical school.

In this coastal city overflowing with wealth, there were plenty of rich people with millions in assets. Bai Jing spent her days amid the excessive extravagance of the luxury goods counter, listening to the obnoxious bragging of the men and women who frequented the store. This inevitably gave her the misconception that she was also very posh and glamorous. With her nose in the air, she judged people by the logos on their clothes—those boys wearing Adidas and Nike were immediately labeled as penniless wretches in her mind. At any rate, they'd have to throw on some Prada at *least* to be good enough to talk to her.

When Xie Qingcheng arrived at the café, Bai Jing was talking to her bestie on the phone. "Aiya, totally. You have no idea—I run into those kinds of dumbasses every single day at work. Today, there was a mother and son, I dunno what the son was wearing—it was probably from Taobao. If I weren't such a professional, I would've rolled my eyes *so* hard. Ah, wearing Taobao to shop at our counter, dontcha think that's hilarious?"

Holding a teaspoon with her diamond-adorned pinky outstretched, she stirred her little cup of coffee. Bai Jing listened to her friend's reply and covered her mouth as she laughed.

"What can you buy with that? They definitely won't be able to afford it. The both of them would probably need half a year's salary to pay for a single pair of slippers from our counter. And let me tell you something, babe—do you know what that boy asked when he came up to me? He said, 'Do you sell baseball caps here? My mom likes working out and it's her birthday today. I want to buy her a baseball cap.'"

Bai Jing laughed so hard she shook.

"I straight up told him, 'I'm so sorry, the brands we carry here have never made baseball caps. Sir, are you unfamiliar with our brands?' Ha ha ha ha, if only you could've seen his face! It was incredible... Aiya, hold on, I think my date is here. I'll talk to you later then. Let's try out Bulgari for afternoon tea later, babe. Love you! Mwah!"

Unfortunately, the café was noisy so even though Xie Qingcheng was looking for Bai Jing, he didn't hear her obnoxious bragging.

Bai Jing caught sight of Xie Qingcheng peering around and noticed that he fit the description given by the matchmaker. "Very tall, very handsome, peach-blossom eyes, but with a cold demeanor." She waved to him at once. "Hi! Are you Xie Qingcheng, Professor Xie?"

Xie Qingcheng walked over. "Mm. Hello."

Bai Jing gave him a once-over before finally locking her gaze on his simple T-shirt. Suddenly, a smile spread across her face as her voice coyly went up an octave. "Hello, hello, I'm Bai Jing."

6

And He Still Had to Go on Matchmaking Dates

B EFORE XIE QINGCHENG arrived for their date, he had heard that this young woman cared a lot about a man's income. But contrary to his expectations, her enthusiasm didn't ebb after he told her his salary wasn't high at all.

"Professor Xie, you're such an intellectual, truly so modest," Bai Jing beamed. "Aiya, it's not easy to find such straightforward men these days, you know."

Xie Qingcheng was at a loss for words.

"Professor Xie, you seem to have great taste," continued Bai Jing. "You're someone who appreciates the finer things in life, right?"

Xie Qingcheng frowned, "No, I—"

"I could tell the moment I saw the way you're dressed."

Xie Qingcheng was even more dumbfounded.

He had no idea what Bai Jing meant until she finally blurted it out, unable to hold herself back any longer, "Professor Xie, the T-shirt you're wearing is a genuine article from our counter. There were only five or six pieces in stock in all of Huzhou, so they were extremely hard to get. Even if you buy its price in accessories, you still wouldn't be able to purchase it.[11] You're so low-key."

---

11   A common practice for luxury goods in China requires consumers to spend a certain amount of money at the store before they can purchase a desirable item. Often, the amount they need to spend is equal to (or sometimes even more than) the price of the item.

Only then did Xie Qingcheng finally understand that the strange trajectory this date had taken was a result of the change of clothes He Yu had offhandedly given him.

He pondered the girl's words for a moment and then remembered what He Yu had said so casually.

No need. I'm not accustomed to wearing clothes that other people have worn. Just toss it after you change—it was getting old anyway.

The depravities of capitalism.

"Professor Xie, you're not being sincere with me on this date," Bai Jing smiled. "The price of this shirt of yours is nearly a year's salary for many people, and it's very hard to purchase it domestically without connections, yet you only invited me out for coffee?"

"You've misunderstood," replied Xie Qingcheng. "I borrowed this shirt from a friend."

"Borrowed?" Bai Jing's eyes immediately widened.

After this point, the conversation took a rather unremarkable turn. As soon as the formerly delighted salesgirl learned the truth, the matchmaking date returned to reality.

Bai Jing's interest in Xie Qingcheng waned noticeably. After she coerced him into taking some selfies together, she pointed her camera at the dessert and clicked away before turning it on herself and doing the same. She was occasionally interrupted by messages from her customers, to which she replied with voice messages without the slightest hesitation or embarrassment.

"Mrs. Zhang, please don't worry. Of course I've kept that limited-edition bag for you. Aiya, you don't need to send me any more thank you gifts, it's not worth the trouble."

"Executive Wang, the dress you ordered has arrived. When would it be convenient for you to come to the shop? Yes, it's already been altered to your size—plus size, but the front collar needs to be taken in two centimeters. Don't worry, I've noted it all down here."

The meal was exceptionally awkward. Xie Qingcheng footed the bill and lowered his head to glance at Bai Jing. This young woman was about the same age as his students. He never harbored any genuine matchmaking intentions and only wanted to fulfill Auntie Li's wishes, so he didn't take any of Bai Jing's words or actions to heart. Plus, he had old-fashioned ideas about chivalry, so he said, "I'll call a taxi for you."

"All righty, all righty," Bai Jing said, without a trace of politeness. "Thanks a bunch, Professor Xie."

They were on Huzhou's busiest street, and it was the evening rush hour. The two of them waited for a long time, but all the taxis that passed by were already occupied.

Xie Qingcheng sighed. "If you don't mind, I can walk with you for a bit. It'll be easier to call a car if we turn the corner up ahead."

"That's fine," Bai Jing replied, "but I have to start a livestream at eight o'clock. I've already scheduled it, and my fans will be upset if I bail at the last minute. Do you mind?"

Xie Qingcheng didn't use streaming apps, but he'd heard a bit about them from Xie Xue. Hearing Bai Jing's words, he asked without thinking, "You're a streamer as well?"

"Yup, I work very hard. I'll become a top streamer soon enough, heh."

Xie Qingcheng nodded. "It's always good to have a dream. Let's go then, I don't mind."

"Oh, thank you, Gege. You might not be very rich, but you're still pretty handsome." Bai Jing caught up to him with a smile. "One more thing—if you're in the frame a little, that's okay, yeah? Everyone likes to see good-looking guys."

"...Do as you like."

Ten minutes later, Xie Qingcheng very much regretted his words.

He was truly out of the loop and had no idea that young people would watch streams like *this* nowadays. Bai Jing took a pink selfie stick out of her bag and started waving it around in random directions. The words that came out of her mouth somehow seemed like meaningless lines spoken by an actor; even after she had rambled on at length, he still didn't know what she was trying to say.

"This is Huzhou's busiest street, full of beautiful guys and gals. Hey, everyone... See the bag that person's carrying over there? That's a high-quality fake, I can tell with just one look. If you wanna learn how to tell whether something's authentic or not, remember to follow me.

"Oh yeah, next to me here's a nice piece of eye candy I met today. He has a great personality, is an extremely educated professor, and has a salary in the millions. Do you all see that sold-out T-shirt he's wearing? Ah, yes—that's right, he's the one who took me out to dinner, and now he's walking me home. Thanks for your blessings, everyone! Thank you!"

Xie Qingcheng suspected his ears might have stopped working. Just when he was about to turn around and refute her, Bai Jing had already muted the mic with a nimble tap of the screen.

"Sorry, Gege, it's not easy to make a living. Could you please not expose me?"

Xie Qingcheng had no words. He simply couldn't understand why some people liked to put up a front online, showing off manufactured happiness and using inflated materialism to attract viewers.

But, whatever—he didn't want to argue any further with a silly girl either.

This matchmaking date would have just ended like this, with Xie Qingcheng silently enduring this ordeal—if they hadn't run into someone, that is.

That someone appeared unexpectedly at a three-way intersection.

Xie Qingcheng and Bai Jing had already walked for more than ten minutes and stopped at a less-crowded section of the block to wait for a taxi. Bai Jing was in the middle of animatedly introducing the new high-end products of the season to her fans on the stream.

Halfway through her spiel, the perceptive Bai Jing suddenly noticed a blurry shadow close in behind her through her front camera. That shadow was swaying back and forth in hesitation.

She didn't pay it any mind at first, but shortly thereafter, the shadow began to approach her quickly. By the time she realized it, the face of a dirty old homeless man was already reflected on her screen, rushing directly at her.

Startled, Bai Jing glanced behind her and let out a scream.

It was an unkempt old man emanating an unbearable odor. His clothes were so tattered with holes of varying sizes that they'd never be wearable again once they were taken off. A lame yellow dog dashed over on his heels and began to bark wildly at Bai Jing.

"Daughter! Daughter! I've finally found you, Daughter!"

"Eek! What's your problem?! Who's your daughter?! Go away!"

"No, no no no—but you're my daughter? Daughter, don't you recognize your dad? Come here, let Dad take a look at you, Dad hasn't seen you in so long..." The old man didn't seem to be in the right state of mind. Weeping and overcome with emotion, he tried to hug Bai Jing.

Bai Jing's pretty face turned pale with shock. She took several steps back, her stream still running as she shrieked hysterically. "Are you insane?! Who are you?! Get the hell away!"

"Daughter, how can you not recognize me?" Tears streamed down the old man's face. He scrambled forward, his blackened and shriveled fingers extending like coals unwilling to die in the fading embers. He tried to wrap his trembling arms around the girl before him. "I...missed you... Papa missed you..."

The man spoke with a thick rural accent from the central plains. Obviously, he wasn't the father of Bai Jing, who was a Huzhou native. Xie Qingcheng immediately figured out what was going on and pulled Bai Jing behind him. "It's okay—stay behind me," he reassured her.

"He's so scary!" Bai Jing wailed in fright. "How can this kind of person be out wandering the streets? Doesn't the city care? AHHHH!"

She let out another hysterical scream as she jumped up and down. As it turned out, the yellow dog that had followed the old man over was circling and sniffing at her feet.

"Help! I-It wants to bite me! What's wrong with this dog?! Where's its leash?!"

Bai Jing took off running as she screeched. Panicked, she wanted to use the phone in her hand to call the police. To her, a homeless old man was already alarming enough, but an ugly street dog like this was even more terrifying. They both deserved to get locked up! Especially since they scared her and interrupted her livestream... Hey, wait a minute—her livestream!

Bai Jing suddenly realized that she had been streaming the entire time. She hurriedly raised her phone to take a look. A few seconds later, her pupils shrank violently in complete disbelief. Her ordinary and unremarkable livestreams usually only had twenty or thirty viewers, but this time, because of this unexpected surprise, her audience had grown to more than three hundred viewers in just a few minutes!

The viewer count was still increasing rapidly, and the scrolling comment section filled instantly with remarks in real time:

"Shit, what happened—a nightmare in Huzhou?"

"Looks like a run-in with a crazy homeless man. Streamer! Are you all right? Turn the camera, we want to see what's happening!"

"So thrilling! This is right next to my house!"

"That homeless old man's not a pervert, is he? He actually tried to hug the streamer! Streamer, look! If it's serious, you need to call the police immediately!"

Amid those comments rising like helium balloons, a rocket suddenly flew up and exploded on the screen—somebody had sent her a 500 RMB tip.

Bai Jing flinched. The shock of this explosion brought her back to her senses. She suddenly realized what she should do. Hastily running her fingers through her hair, she adjusted the camera angle, then rushed out from behind Xie Qingcheng before he could react.

"Be careful!" yelled Xie Qingcheng.

He never could have imagined that the girl who had been so terrified a second ago would now be standing with her pretty face upturned, heedless of danger, next to the homeless old man. She'd even made sure to adjust her pricey little purse beforehand so that it was hanging off her back, out of the old man's reach.

"Let's get this straight," Bai Jing cried. "Your accent is from out of town, so how could you possibly be my dad? Stinky old man, you're a pervert who wanted to use this chance to take advantage of me! Do you think I couldn't tell? Have some sense of dignity, okay?!"

Shocked, the old man retreated.

The situation was turned on its head. Xie Qingcheng realized that the old man's intentions might not have been malicious at all.

Upon closer examination, the grief in the man's expression was too profound to be feigned.

Xie Qingcheng couldn't help but frown. "Miss Bai, can you turn off the livestream? This old gentleman doesn't look like he's in a very good state. He might have mistaken you for someone else. Why don't you call city management first? Let's take care of this."

But why would Bai Jing listen to him? The viewer count in her stream was rising steadily; she didn't even find the old man stinky anymore. She brought her powdered face even closer to him.

"Hey, come take a look—everyone, come take a look." Bai Jing had the homeless man look at her phone screen. She positioned the selfie stick so that the front-facing camera had them both in frame. "Old pervert, look at me, then look at yourself. You think *I'm* your daughter? Take a good look—look at your shabby clothes, your messy hair and filthy face. Can you still say that you weren't trying to be a lecher?"

The homeless old man was stumped for a moment. His eyes then followed the direction of her pointed finger, and he squinted as he looked up along the selfie stick.

After getting a good look at the two of them on the phone screen, the old man was taken aback at first. Then, as if suddenly realizing how utterly pathetic he appeared, he tried to make a hasty escape.

Once he began to run, Bai Jing got even more excited.

Apparently, all that was needed to make a clean-freak streamer overcome her phobia to film herself pressed up against an unkempt old man was a surge in her follower count.

"Look, everyone! This is a perfect example of covert harassment! He must be faking his psychological issues—watch me expose his true colors!" Bai Jing chased after the old man to get him into the frame. "Hey! Get over here!" she shouted. "Didn't you just call me your daughter? Huzhou is such a big city with good public security, yet you still dare to scam people here?! Have you gotten a whiff of yourself? You reek! Get over here!"

The old man's head seemed to have cleared a bit, but not entirely. His gaze was half-muddled, half-lucid.

Watching from the sidelines, Xie Qingcheng was certain this old man wasn't trying to take advantage of her. The man's mental state seemed very poor. If Xie Qingcheng had to describe him, he would say that this old man was like a scrawny dog who had wandered across half of China before finally drifting into the misty rains of Jiangnan.[12] The concept of searching had been carved into his bones—with just one glance, one could tell he had lost something and had been looking for it all this time.

But Bai Jing didn't care about any of that. Although she had been a streamer for over half a year, her performance was mediocre, and she hadn't been able to attract many viewers. She was furiously envious of her hardworking peers, who were able to make a living through livestreaming.

Not long ago, when she had failed to garner attention despite trying everything she could think of, she had gone to the pages of a few well-known influencers in a rage to flood their comment sections with hateful remarks.

One day, she cursed one out, "Why are you putting on a show like this?! Acting like you have some perfect life, as if everything doesn't just run on money?! The rural lifestyle you're showing isn't real at all!"

The next day, she targeted another. "Here's a man using the money that a woman earned with her blood, sweat, and tears to buy a luxurious villa. Everyone's said it already—every tube of lipstick

---

12 The geographical area south of the Yangtze River known for its wet climate. In this setting, Huzhou is part of the Jiangnan region.

you buy was made from the skeletons in his closet! When are the women still buying his things going to wake up?!"

And the day after, she focused her wrath on yet another influencer. "I can't believe you call yourself an independent, self-made modern woman. You're just selling your trauma all day long. Isn't livestreaming your job? You're tired, but you're still earning money. You get cussed out, but you're still earning money. Everyone gives you so much money, what do you have to complain about?"

No one knew about the vicious expression that would appear on her face when she was tapping furiously away on her phone under her covers. On the subways whizzing through tunnels, in the bustling skyscrapers, amid the whirl of designer clothes and expensive perfume, bathed in the golden dazzle of luxury, everyone called her Cindy, never Bai Jing. In her towering high heels, she toiled at her job, bowing deferentially to her honored guests.

Bending at the waist, she always gave her all to maintain her composure as she crouched down to buckle Mrs. Chen or Mrs. Li's shoes with slender, pale, jade-like hands, and then walked them out through the spacious golden foyer with a respectful bow. No one knew how many times she had stared after those graceful figures and thought, *One day, I'll have the proudest salesgirls welcome me with a bow too.*

She wanted money and fame so badly her eyes reddened with hunger. Thus, she forgot her fears and lost her germaphobic tendencies. She also failed to see the old homeless man's trembling lips and the hot tears welling up in his blurry eyes.

"Is your daughter from Huzhou? Your *daughter*?" she scoffed, her words dripping with disdain. "Who knows if a stinky old man like you was ever married. All you do is make up reasons to act crazy and harass women! What are you hiding for? Weren't you acting all grabby with me just now? Let everyone see your face! Come on!"

"No... No..."

Terrified, the old man shrank his head back and stooped over. The cries coming out of his mouth sounded like the wails of an infant, mixed with vague mumbling.

"I'm sorry... I...I got the wrong person..."

"You're sorry? What use is that?! Get over here! Look at the camera! Take a look at what you're wearing! If you wanna come out and scam people, you could at least make yourself look presentable first!"

In the comments filling the screen, audience members who didn't understand the full situation were cheering on the "courageous female streamer who was fighting back against street harassment from a crazed homeless man." Tips began to flow and balloons began to rise, and Bai Jing's heart felt like it was swelling up right alongside them.

The harried old man feebly shrunk away, plummeting from the excitement of reuniting with his daughter only to realize that he was mistaken. The throes of his delusion gave way to helplessness as he came to his senses and tried to flee the escalating situation. Under the watchful camera lens, he was like an old dog with nowhere to run. Dazed by the relentless pursuit of this so-called justice, he held his head and cowered, just like the stray dog that accompanied him.

"Please stop filming, I beg you... I got the wrong person... Stop filming... Young Miss, please stop filming..."

The old man's entire body was trembling, his legs shaking like sifting chaff underneath his tattered pants. He covered his face, wanting to shield it from the camera, only to realize that he also wanted to cover his ratty clothes. In the end, he didn't know what he should hide. It felt as though every bit of flesh on his body, every article of clothing, was not fit to be seen, an embarrassment not to be shown to others. A flood of tears rushed down the creases of his wizened face. He shrank to the ground, practically kneeling as he begged for Bai Jing's mercy.

"Please, Miss, spare me..."

"I—" Undeterred, Bai Jing was about to say something when her selfie stick was suddenly snatched away.

Without the slightest courtesy, Xie Qingcheng removed her phone and tossed her selfie stick to the side.

"Hey! You! What are you doing?!"

"What are *you* doing? I've already told you—this old man seems to be mentally unwell, and I asked you not to trigger him. Can't you hear, or are you too daft to understand?"

Xie Qingcheng cut off the stream.

A series of brilliant colors like a carousel lantern flashed through Bai Jing's face. She stomped her high heels and raged at Xie Qingcheng. "How's this any of your business? Give me back my phone! I have a right to stream! Don't you know that I need to earn money? I want to be an influencer!"

"Whatever you want has nothing to do with me." Xie Qingcheng's expression was frosty. His paternalistic tendencies surfaced once more as he scolded her without blinking an eye. "However, Miss Bai, do you have any shame? Can't you see what state he's in? To get views, you'll keep on going even though you know it's wrong; you choose unscrupulous methods even when you know the consequences. Despite knowing full well the pain your actions will bring to others, you have no qualms about exploiting it for attention because you're not the one getting hurt. Have you no conscience?!"

"What are you saying?! Stop trying to discipline me, are you my dad? You're just someone who had a matchmaking date with me today! It's none of your business!" Bai Jing's temper flared as she rushed up to Xie Qingcheng to snatch her phone back.

But Xie Qingcheng's temper was fiercer than hers. He pinned Bai Jing in place and stared down at her, his eyes cutting into her like razor blades.

"To you, a person's dignity and life are worth less than the viewers you can attract in a single livestream. You really are a fucking freak of nature."

"You have the guts to call me names?" Bai Jing cried. "You wretched beggar!"

Enraged, she pounced forward and tried to slap Xie Qingcheng.

But Xie Qingcheng grabbed her by the wrist. With a sudden burst of force, he twisted her arm, making her shriek in pain.

"If you keep making a fuss," said Xie Qingcheng icily, "not only will I have the guts to call you names, but I'll also have the guts to beat you up."

"L-let go! If you don't let go, I'll call the police! I'll scream for help!"

Although there weren't many people on this street, they had caused a rather loud disturbance; some passersby had already stopped to observe from afar. But Xie Qingcheng couldn't care less—to him, the gazes of others were nothing more than empty air to begin with. However, he was caught off guard by a sudden shout from a sharp-eyed older woman from the crowd.

"Oh my god! What's wrong with that old man?"

Xie Qingcheng looked down at him immediately. The old man's mental state was fragile in the first place. But after mistaking Bai Jing for his daughter, and then being filmed and chased by her, his heart couldn't handle the emotional distress anymore. His lips turned pale, and the blood drained from his face. He clutched at his chest and doubled over, curling like a shrimp before suddenly collapsing to the ground with a thud.

7

HE ASKED ME ABOUT
MY DRIVING SKILLS

AS A FORMER DOCTOR, Xie Qingcheng acted without
hesitation. He flung Bai Jing away and bent down to check
the old man's condition.

In clinical medicine, an acute myocardial infarction—or a severe
heart attack—was a cardiovascular emergency with an extremely
high mortality rate. A sudden onset of intense emotion was one of
the major triggers for the condition in elderly people.

Bai Jing, who hadn't realized what was going on, was still busy
cursing at him.

Xie Qingcheng rolled up his sleeves to begin administering first
aid. He turned back and snapped at her, "Don't just stand there and
stare! The patient is having a severe heart attack! Call an ambulance!
Hurry up!"

"What does a severe heart attack have to do with... A severe heart
attack?!"

Bai Jing was dumbstruck.

Her glittery gold eyeliner only emphasized the shock and fear
in her eyes. The color in the girl's face drained instantly. She stood
frozen, like a dazed goose, not knowing whether to advance or
retreat.

"Don't you know the emergency services number?!" Xie
Qingcheng snapped.

Bai Jing might have known it at one point, but with the situation devolving so quickly, she drew nothing but a blank. "Wh-what is it?"

"120!"

"Ohhh...!" Bai Jing didn't expect that things would turn out like this, with a precious human life in danger. She hastily picked up the phone that Xie Qingcheng had tossed back to her and dialed the emergency number.

"Hello? 110? Ah, no, no! Don't hang up! I misspoke! I don't want to call the police, I was calling your number! I—there's an old man here who's had a severe fainting attack... Ah, no, what was it, severe heart failure..."

"Severe heart attack!"

"Ah! Yes! A heart attack, heart attack!"

After stammering her way through the call, Bai Jing let out a breath and managed to collect herself a bit. However, she was still too afraid to get close to Xie Qingcheng and the old homeless man.

Xie Qingcheng wiped away the secretions from the old man's mouth and nose and carefully laid him down flat so that he wouldn't choke. His forehead was already dripping with sweat when he looked up at Bai Jing and said, "Come help."

"No way!" Bai Jing immediately retorted. "It's so disgusting! Who knows if he has AIDS or some other contagious disease! And my clothes are very expensive; they'll be ruined if I get them dirty."

Xie Qingcheng was furious. "AIDS isn't transmitted like that! What's more important: your clothes or someone's life?! Come here and help!"

"Absolutely not. Is this emotional blackmail? Do you know how long I had to work to buy an outfit like this, how long I had to wait?

Besides, he must have some underlying condition that's just acting up, so it wasn't my fault. I..."

With a cry, the old man spat out another mouthful of white foam. Bai Jing's throat tightened at the sight, and she nearly retched. She retreated, taking one step after another backward. "Don't force me... I can't."

Luckily, an older woman ran out from the circle of observers at this moment. "Little girl, do you have a conscience?" she yelled at Bai Jing. "You'll grow old one day too! You're dressed in such flashy, glamorous clothes, and yet your heart is so rotten?!"

"I..." Bai Jing started.

The older woman rolled her eyes, ignoring her, then turned to Xie Qingcheng, "Tell me what to do. I'll help."

This was a classic example of herd mentality. When a crowd quietly watches from afar, no one is willing to take the initiative to step forward and help. But once a single person breaks from that crowd to lend a hand, others emerge like spring shoots after rain.

Soon, those who had been observing from a distance and afraid of getting involved started to inch closer. People appeared, offering to look around for a pharmacy to buy emergency medicine and waving fans to cool them down, and Bai Jing found herself forcibly pushed to the side.

However, no matter how enthusiastic the crowd, they couldn't resolve the urgent matter at hand. They could only anxiously wait as the minutes ticked by.

Alas, things didn't go so smoothly—right at this juncture, Bai Jing's phone rang. It was a call from the hospital.

"There's been a very unfortunate situation—a surface collapse broke a water main. The main highway to your current location is flooded, and there's no way for an ambulance to get through. There's another path through local streets, but we can't get in at all—there's too much traffic, and it's also the wrong way up a one-way street, so we had to turn around."

Bai Jing reported the situation to Xie Qingcheng, who was still administering first aid to the old man. "How much longer?" Xie Qingcheng asked sharply.

This time, Bai Jing was cowed. She hurriedly conveyed his question. "H-how much longer will it take?"

"We have to take another route. It'll be at least thirty minutes."

Xie Qingcheng looked at the old man's situation. Thirty minutes would be the difference between life and death.

How were they so unlucky that something went awry now? And for a broken water main to flood a whole major highway!

He was still at a loss as to what to do when two glaring headlights suddenly flashed from the intersection. A black Rolls-Royce Cullinan adorned with a little winged hood ornament cruised silently under the glow of the streetlamps. The car glided right over to the corner of the one-way street where the incident was unfolding, its rectangular tail lights calmly illuminating their surroundings.

Bai Jing's instinct to stream about all things luxurious—even at this critical juncture when someone's life was on the line—was difficult to temper. She barely repressed her urge to raise her phone and aim it at the Cullinan, for fear that if she were a second too late, it would drive off and disappear.

But she never could have anticipated that this Cullinan would actually slowly make its way over to them and come to a stop.

Bai Jing's eyes widened at the incredulous events unfolding.

Her pupils only contracted even further as she watched the rear window of the luxury car of her dreams silently roll down. A young woman poked her head out and shouted to Xie Qingcheng, who was in the middle of administering emergency treatment to the old man beside her.

"Ge!"

Bai Jing was flabbergasted.

"He Yu invited me out for barbecue, so we were just passing by," said Xie Xue. "I saw someone in the distance and thought it looked just like you, so I had him come take a look. It really is you... Ah! Oh my god! What's wrong with the person next to you? Did something happen?!"

Xie Qingcheng looked up at his sister. He Yu was sitting in the recesses of the genuine leather seat, hidden in the darkness on the other side of the vehicle. Those looking in could only make out his calm and elegant profile. His silhouette was especially handsome and refined, but upon closer examination, one could almost sense a bestial and depraved aura emanating from the young man.

Xie Qingcheng didn't want to inconvenience He Yu, but he didn't have many options. "We ran into an ill person. He was emotionally triggered and had a severe heart attack. I gave him some basic treatment, but he needs to go to the emergency room."

Xie Xue was stunned. "Where's the ambulance?"

"We called, but the road conditions are poor. It'll take thirty more minutes before they arrive."

Upon hearing this, Xie Xue immediately opened the car door and jumped out, rushing to the old man's side. She didn't show the slightest disdain toward him, but she had no medical training whatsoever and could only stand by helplessly. She shouted anxiously at the car, "He Yu! He Yu, come out and help!"

The depraved gentleman stepped out of the car, took one look at the old man's purpling lips, and immediately said, "We'll go in my car."

Xie Xue, the fool, asked, "What will you do if other drivers don't make way for you? I mean, it's still rush hour."

"I'd like to see 'em try," He Yu sneered.

He turned to the driver and asked, "Lao-Zhao, can you drive smoothly?"

"I can drive smoothly, but I'm used to being careful, so I might not be fast..."

Besides, Young Master He, even if you told me to crash the car, I wouldn't dare!

"Then get out." He Yu rolled up his sleeves. With one long-legged step, he got into the driver's seat. He pulled down the handbrake without even glancing at it, chewing his gum as he said, "Get in. We'll be at the municipal hospital in ten minutes."

"Do you have a license?" Xie Qingcheng asked.

"Nope," replied He Yu expressionlessly. "Are you coming or not?"

"He does!" Xie Xue was truly fed up with the two of them, especially He Yu. Even at a time like this, he was still sparring with her brother. "He just finished converting his overseas license to a domestic one! Ge, don't listen to his nonsense!"

Under Xie Qingcheng's guidance, they carefully lifted the old man into the Cullinan. After everyone got into the car, He Yu fastened his seat belt. He was about to floor the gas pedal and bring the vehicle to a death-defying speed when that lame little dog darted up and started to bark incessantly at the people on the other side of the slowly closing car doors.

Xie Xue was softhearted. When she saw the tiny, pitiful dog limping behind its master to the car, she couldn't help but say, "Poor thing..."

He Yu glanced at her, then the passenger-side door opened again. "Bring it inside."

Xie Xue immediately jumped down to pick up the dirty little yellow dog by its armpits and carried it into the car.

The pitiful animal whimpered. As if sensing that it hadn't been abandoned, it turned to look at the old man lying in the backseat, then raised its fluffy snout, its black bean nose sniffing gratefully at Xie Xue's cheek. Then it stuck its head over to the driver's seat, giving the young man a careful lick on the cheek with its damp tongue.

He Yu ignored the dog's affections. With the press of a button, his rearview mirror returned to his customized position as he gripped the steering wheel with long, slender hands. "Call emergency services back and explain our situation. Let's go."

Thankfully, because the old man had received professional first aid immediately and had been promptly taken to the hospital, he was finally no longer in critical condition after half a night's rescue efforts.

Outside the emergency care unit's patient ward, Xie Qingcheng signed a stack of forms and opened an app on his phone to pay the bill only to find that he didn't quite have enough money. Just as he was wondering what he should say to the worker at the service window, a hand reached out from behind him and passed a credit card through the slot.

Xie Qingcheng turned to see He Yu's face.

"Why are you here?"

"It's fine," He Yu said. "No need to thank me."

Because the old man was homeless, they couldn't find or contact any of his family members. He also didn't have his ID card on him, so certain administrative procedures were very inconvenient. If it weren't for the fact that Xie Qingcheng had once worked at this municipal hospital and knew the director of the emergency care unit's night shift, this might have caused a bigger issue. Now, even though the old man was no longer in danger, many administrative orders of business needed to be retroactively completed. The hospital even contacted the municipal department in charge of the homeless population for assistance.

As for the enthusiastic group of Good Samaritans, He Yu and the others also couldn't leave for the time being. After paying the bill, He Yu and Xie Qingcheng went out to the gardens behind the hospital for some fresh air, and He Yu struck up a conversation.

"That Bai woman, she was your matchmaking date?" He Yu asked.

"Mm. Where is she?"

"Resting with Xie Xue in the underground parking lot. Since it was so late, both of them had grown a little sleepy. Xie Xue was worried, so she had me come up to see how you were doing." He Yu then asked, "How come you were on a matchmaking date with a girl like that?"

Xie Qingcheng's expression was flat. "It was just dinner."

"Then you should have just rejected the matchmaker outright. The way I see it, you weren't taking it seriously either. Plus, isn't she about the same age as Xie Xue? You're already middle-aged. It's not very appropriate."

Since Xie Qingcheng was less tense now, He Yu's words irritated him. Thirty-two years old was middle-aged? What a nutcase. If it weren't for the fact that He Yu had helped him out today, he definitely would have said, *Little devil, it's none of your fucking business.* But he had just used He Yu as a driver and then as an ATM, so he had no right to curse him out too viciously. Xie Qingcheng shot him a glance through bloodshot eyes, stiffly enduring the word "middle-aged," and coldly replied, "You're right, Young Master He. I truly don't want to waste my breath on little kids below the age of thirty anymore."

Both of them fell silent.

The little kid and the middle-aged man verbally sparred each other tit for tat, but neither of them could get the upper hand. Thus, Xie Qingcheng decided to simply turn away.

The wisteria-covered walkway behind the municipal hospital was very long. With his hands in his pockets, Xie Qingcheng walked silently ahead, his expression flat. Ten years ago, he'd often pass through this way, though back then, the garden hadn't been fully completed yet. There were even unauthorized stall-keepers at the two ends of the pathway selling Tianjin-style jianbing,[13] porridge, noodles, and rice balls before the city management officers arrived to put an end to the illegal activity. Now, the garden presented a scenic picture with every step.

Later, Xie Qingcheng resigned from his post at the municipal hospital, and in the years that followed, he never walked through this wisteria path again.

This literal walk down memory lane reminded him of the past. After a lengthy silence, Xie Qingcheng abruptly spoke up. "Hey, little devil?"

"Hm?"

"Do all of you youngsters these days want to become internet celebrities?"

"I'm not interested. But they earn a lot of money, so it's true that there are many who do. Is that Bai Jing an internet celebrity?"

"...How did you know?"

He Yu grinned. "I could tell." Then he asked, "Did that old gentleman's sudden illness have to do with her?"

The night wind blew past, rustling through the vines.

---

13 Thin pancakes wrapped around fried dough sticks (youtiao) with a sweet and savory sauce (tianmianjiang).

"He mistook her for his daughter, so Bai Jing chased after him while she was livestreaming," replied Xie Qingcheng. "He was hiding from the camera the whole time, begging her to stop filming, but she refused to listen; she could only see how many people had entered her livestream and how many people wanted to follow her account." After a pause, he asked, "What is the point of it all?"

He Yu sighed. "Xie Qingcheng, the things you find meaningless are tickets to a whole new life for certain people. You find the way they chase fame and profit bizarre, but in the same vein, they can't understand your way of thinking either. Humans are all the same species, but we're also the ones with the greatest barriers to empathy; we're often incapable of mutual trust, much less mutual understanding. Sometimes, when two people look at each other, it's as if they're looking at organisms from an entirely different genus."

At this point, He Yu's phone suddenly rang. It was his driver; as it turned out, He Yu had terrorized the streets with his wild driving. The traffic police on patrol had flown into a rage and chased them all the way to the hospital.

"Young Master He, why don't we ask the doctor to explain things to them..." the driver suggested. "There were extenuating circumstances..."

"It's nothing," replied He Yu. "Just let them deduct the points and pay the fines; there's no point in wasting time on this."

He hung up.

"Is your spare cash burning a hole in your wallet?" asked Xie Qingcheng.

"To me, time is money. I don't like to waste time on unnecessary things, like needless explanations to government employees. Who knows, they might even ask a reporter to write some moving story about it."

He Yu's almond eyes lowered, his pitch-black pupils appearing so apathetic they seemed to hold a hint of subtle perversity, even as the corners of his mouth curved up in a smile. "I may as well chat a little longer with you. In any case, you can do the same things they do, right? For example, checking my driver's license."

Xie Qingcheng didn't respond.

As the man's expression grew uglier, the teasing mockery at the corners of He Yu's mouth slowly diffused into his eyes. With his hands in his pockets, he cast his glance ahead—not at Xie Qingcheng's face anymore, but rather at a random spot before him. Then, he leaned forward slightly, tilting his face toward Xie Qingcheng's neck. He lowered his head, his thin lips stopping just short of Xie Qingcheng's carotid artery.

Maintaining his position, he gazed into the distance and spoke quietly into the man's ear. "Ge, how was my driving?"

Xie Qingcheng answered with silence, his expression growing even cloudier.

Why was He Yu still holding a grudge against him for asking about his driver's license?! Just how petty was this person exactly?

Xie Qingcheng scoffed a little, and with a chilly look, he responded, "Practice some more when you get the chance. If you stop being so hot-headed, young man, you can become a driver after you graduate."

He didn't want to waste any more breath on He Yu after that, so he brushed away the dangling vines in front of him with a frigid expression and walked on ahead.

But He Yu wasn't finished with him yet, or maybe he'd gotten into the swing of mocking him. He continued his sarcastic questioning, like a dog with a bone. "Executive Xie, if I worked as your driver, what kind of car would you have me chauffeur you in? How much would I get paid per month?"

Xie Qingcheng didn't look back as he answered, "A Hongguang Mini,[14] and then I'll give you a drug prescription. Take it if you want, get lost if you don't."

With his hands in his pockets, He Yu stared at his back. He kicked at something with his sneakers, his expression perverse as he cursed softly. "A prescription? You sure are something else, Xie Qingcheng. I'll really need to pay you back for that one."

---

14   A tiny electric car model.

8

HE EVEN ORDERED ME AROUND LIKE A SERVANT

HALF AN HOUR LATER, an employee from the Department of Homeless Services of the Bureau of Civil Affairs showed up. He thanked the medical staff and everyone who had come with Xie Qingcheng as he explained the situation.

"This old man is called Zhuang Zhiqiang. He really is a stubborn old nail house."[15]

Xie Xue and Bai Jing—who'd insisted on hitching a ride—had also come up from the underground parking garage. They sat on the sofa in the doctor's office to listen to the details.

"Mr. Zhuang Zhiqiang...his situation is rather unique. Homeless Services has been struggling to resolve this problem." The employee wrung his hands and took a sip of the tea that the nurses had brewed in disposable paper cups. He smacked his lips and sighed. "He came to Huzhou about three years ago and said that he was looking for his daughter. But we checked the registry—he's just an old man who lives all by himself. He doesn't have any family. He used to reside in a yaodong[16] in Shanzhou, a place so poor even birds don't want to live there. He didn't have any neighbors whatsoever, and he had to walk over a mile just to get water. We even sent people down to inquire

---

15   钉子户, "nail house," is a term for people who refuse to vacate their residences even under pressure from property developers.
16   A type of rural dwelling carved out of a hillside.

with the other villagers, and they all said that the old man was very antisocial and that they didn't know anything about him at all."

"But that's not an excuse for you to shirk your responsibilities!" Bai Jing blurted out stridently. "Shouldn't you lock up people who pose a danger to society? He disrupts the municipal environment and might even attack others!"

"Miss, you must understand," the employee said with an awkward expression. "We can't lock up the homeless, they are citizens as well. We can only arrange housing for them or send them to a hospital for medical care…"

Bai Jing's tone was vicious. "I don't care. Nutcases should all be forcibly institutionalized. Shouldn't all these abnormal things be quarantined?"

Before this exchange, He Yu hadn't yet formed an opinion on this woman. He was someone who didn't have a particularly strong moral compass—in other words, he had a rather high tolerance for all sorts of people. To him, what Xie Qingcheng had told him about her wasn't even worthy of comment—everyone had their own way of living, their own choices.

But Bai Jing's rant about "nutcases" really was tap-dancing right on Young Master He's nerves.

The corners of He Yu's mouth suddenly curved into a slightly mocking smile, but he lowered his head and kept quiet.

The employee from the Department of Homeless Services wiped away his sweat. "Young lady, please calm down a little. Since Mr. Zhuang Zhiqiang's condition does seem likely to worsen to the point where he might lose his ability to function in society, we'll take him to our affiliate psychiatric hospital for treatment and supervision once his situation here improves…"

"Which psychiatric hospital?" Xie Qingcheng suddenly asked.

"Given the current situation, it'll probably be Cheng Kang. Even though it's not the best in terms of facilities and management, the accommodations we have reserved with Wanping have already been filled up. There's nothing we can do."

Hearing this, Bai Jing was finally satisfied. "That's more like it..." she muttered.

Just as they were talking, the emergency doctor arrived.

He informed them about Zhuang Zhiqiang's condition: Because he had been treated in time, he was no longer in mortal danger. One visitor was allowed if they wanted to go check on him. "A girl would be best," the doctor explained. "The patient is still in a state of confusion. He keeps trying to look for his daughter."

Xie Xue stood up. "I'll go." She followed the doctor out of the room.

He Yu had been sprawled over the reception room sofa with his elbow propped up on its back, listening to the conversation with his head lowered and an indifferent expression on his face. However, now that Xie Xue was leaving, he swung his long legs down and prepared to get up as well.

"Hold it," said Xie Qingcheng, his guarded wariness obvious.

"What's wrong?"

"Why are you following my sister around all the time?"

The schoolboy sat back down on the sofa, falling silent for a moment. Though it seemed like they were having a sophisticated and courteous conversation, his almond eyes were, in fact, full of derision and ridicule. "Then, what if I follow *you* around all the time instead, Doctor Xie?"

To this, Xie Qingcheng had no reply.

With a steady warmth in his voice, He Yu said, "Both you and your matchmaking date are here. Isn't it inconvenient for me to be around? I'll give you some room. I don't want to be in your way."

Bai Jing immediately snatched the bait and yelled, "There's no chance we'll get together!"

He Yu laughed softly without looking at Bai Jing. Tilting his head, he added quietly at a volume only Xie Qingcheng could hear, "Doctor Xie, don't you think your charisma is fading with old age? You can't even get that little girl."

Xie Qingcheng said nothing.

Wicked thing.

Could it be that his ancestral tomb had been renovated into an outhouse? How'd they produce such a depraved beast?

Xie Qingcheng's expression was cold as his lips moved just enough to reply, "Hurry up and get lost."

He Yu smiled. He stood up suddenly, and his arm shot over Xie Qingcheng's shoulder. Xie Qingcheng started, bewildered as to what this depraved gentleman, who was flouting normal etiquette, was doing. Even though they were several centimeters apart, he could pick up the scent of He Yu's adolescent hormones, as well as feel the heat emitting from the boy's chest as he loomed over him.

The domineering aura unique to young males made Xie Qingcheng, a fellow man, extremely uneasy. As a rather traditional man, he immediately felt a sense of irritation at his "male territory" being invaded.

Xie Qingcheng was just about to shove He Yu away when this invasive and imposing schoolboy straightened back up. In his hand was a large bag of coffee he had picked up from the counter behind him—the drinks He Yu had just ordered.

"Ge, I was just getting the drinks," he said.

He Yu's derisive smile widened at the sight of the man's dark expression. He took out the cups of coffee from the paper bag and passed them to the employee from Homeless Services, the doctors, and the nurses. He also asked someone to bring one to Xie Xue and even handed a cup to Bai Jing.

But then, he clicked his tongue and looked at Xie Qingcheng. "Would you look at that. I'm so sorry, I forgot to get one for you."

After a brief pause, He Yu held out his cup of iced coffee to Xie Qingcheng. "Why don't you drink mine?"

But this clearly wasn't a sincere offer. He had already inserted the straw into the cup and was holding it right up to Xie Qingcheng's lips, as if it were the most natural thing to do.

He was certain Xie Qingcheng would refuse.

But to his surprise, it sparked Xie Qingcheng's temper instead. Xie Qingcheng subverted all of He Yu's expectations as he sat right there on the sofa with the air of a man getting waited upon by a little brat. With a sly lift of his gaze, he stared into He Yu's eyes, parted his pale lips and slowly closed them around the straw that had been shoved in front of his face.

Without breaking eye contact, he sucked deeply on the straw without a hint of courtesy.

Xie Qingcheng's throat bobbed as he swallowed the drink. It was as though he were egging He Yu into a fight.

Then he let go of the straw, his wet lips glossy, his eyes sharp. "You can put it over there. I'll take it as a gesture of filial piety."

He Yu was speechless.

When he saw Xie Qingcheng dip his head and close his lips around the straw, he felt a maddening heat in his chest, probably from sheer anger. He thought that this person really deserved to be tormented thoroughly, more than words could describe. He had wanted to see Xie Qingcheng stuck in an awkward dilemma or snap back in embarrassed rage.

But in the face of He Yu's challenge, Xie Qingcheng had answered him with an air of composure, radiating arrogance.

For a second, He Yu had the urge to toss the coffee all over that fatherly ice cube of a face, to see how miserable he would look with his face dripping wet and his clothes soaked through.

But in the end, he only smiled and set the iced coffee lightly down onto the tea table. Ducking his head for a moment, he spoke quietly to Xie Qingcheng. "All right, since you wanted it, be sure not to waste a drop. Drink it all, drain the cup, and let me know if it's not enough. I'll get you another."

"How could I possibly impose? You've acted as my driver and handed over your checkbook tonight, and now you're even offering to become my delivery boy." Xie Qingcheng laughed coldly and picked up the coffee, his long, slender fingers sliding through the droplets of condensation collecting on the cup. "You're dismissed."

After Xie Qingcheng finished speaking, he swirled the cup at He Yu.

He Yu walked away, a dark expression on his face.

After witnessing this verbal pissing contest, it was clear to everyone present that the two of them weren't exactly on the best terms. It was somewhat awkward, but Xie Qingcheng acted as if everything were fine.

He got up, and under the circle of watchful eyes, tossed the coffee into the trash. Only schoolboys ordered coffee so late. How was he to get any sleep that night if he messed around like this at his age?

Xie Qingcheng sat back down, his expression calm as he looked toward the Homeless Services staff. "Sorry about making such a scene. My client's son doesn't know any better."

"I-it's fine." The worker laughed awkwardly.

"So where were we... Oh, that's right... So, you're certain that Zhuang Zhiqiang doesn't have a daughter?"

The employee snapped out of it. "That's right, he doesn't. Mr. Zhuang Zhiqiang doesn't have any relatives at all. We help homeless individuals get in touch with their family or other community members, but there was no one we could contact for this old man."

Xie Qingcheng fell silent.

From his experience, he felt that Zhuang Zhiqiang's reaction didn't seem like a meaningless or random dissociative episode. The matter of his "daughter" had to be a weight on his mind.

"Daughter..." The old man lay on the hospital bed with an oxygen cannula, still muddled and rambling under his breath about the person who might have been a figment of his imagination. "My wonderful daughter... Your old man watched you grow up right before his eyes, watched you go to school with your little backpack on your shoulders, watched you pass the college entrance exam and move to the big city..."

He stopped for a moment, a cloudy tear seeping out from the wrinkled folds of his eyelids. The old man's sleep-talking was tainted in pain and choked with sobs. "Why couldn't you...ever come back to see your old man...?"

Xie Xue was softhearted, and her tears flowed freely as she listened at his side. After getting the nurse's permission, she reached out for Zhuang Zhiqiang's hand and said from his bedside, "Uncle, don't cry anymore. I...I'm here. I'll stay here with you. Please get better soon..."

As he was still ill, she couldn't spend too much time with the patient. After she comforted the old, confused man for a while, the doctor told her it was about time to leave.

After disinfecting herself, Xie Xue walked out of the emergency room. She reached into her bag for tissues to wipe her tears, only to discover that they'd already been used up.

A pretty hand passed her a man's handkerchief.

Xie Xue looked up. Her slightly swollen and red eyes were met with the sight of He Yu's gently smiling face.

With Xie Qingcheng, He Yu had behaved like a degenerate beast, but with Xie Xue, he was rather like a well-behaved show dog. The handkerchief he passed over was a square of snowy white silk of a very delicate and exquisite make, without a single crease marring its surface.

"Here you go."

"Th-thank you."

"It's nothing."

He'd already known that Xie Xue would react like this.

Xie Xue's parents died soon after she was born, and her grandparents had already passed away long before that. Ever since she was little, she'd been very envious of others who could shout "Daddy," "Mommy," "Grandpa," or "Grandma." In her case, it was only during the annual Qingming festival[17] that she could quietly say those words as she stood beneath Xie Qingcheng's black umbrella with a bouquet of dainty white chrysanthemums in her hands, facing those ice-cold, rain-soaked gravestones.

Thus, the one thing she couldn't bear was seeing people of her parents' or grandparents' age without children to keep them company.

"Doctor?" Wiping her tears, she spoke to the emergency physician again. "Can you please let me know when he's moved to the psychiatric hospital? I'll go with him."

He Yu frowned slightly. "What would you go to that kind of place for?"

---

17 A holiday for honoring departed ancestors.

"It's no trouble. It just so happens that the university wants me to go to several prisons and psychiatric hospitals to discuss whether we can bring students to visit. They said it's to give the screenwriting and directing students some hands-on experience in civic engagement, but I haven't had the chance to discuss it with them yet." Xie Xue blew her nose. "It's not like I'll be going out of my way."

Since she'd put it that way, He Yu couldn't really say anything else. He could only walk over to the side and pick up that little yellow stray.

He Yu put his hands under its chubby front legs and lifted it up to his face. Its yellow-and-white-striped legs kicked a few times in midair, and its black bean nose met his almond eyes as it fell into somewhat of a daze.

He Yu said gently, "I'll get a dog permit so that you can stay at my place for the time being. Once your owner's better, I'll send you back to him."

Trembling and shivering, the little dog let out a whimper.

It is said that animals have a sixth sense, allowing them to detect danger and madness hidden behind a person's smile. So, despite the kindness of He Yu's words, the little dog was frightened but attempted to get on He Yu's good side anyway. It nervously stuck out the tip of its soft tongue and gave He Yu a lick.

He Yu laughed and reached out to stroke the dog's head, letting the dog lick the tips of his fingers. Eyes dark, he said, "Good boy. You're much more sensible than *him*."

9

BUT NEVER MIND HIM, I DECIDED TO TELL HER MY FEELINGS

AFTER FINALLY RESOLVING this unexpected mishap, the group was both tired and hungry, so He Yu asked if they wanted to get a late-night snack. The first person to raise their hand and agree enthusiastically with this suggestion was the one who had absolutely nothing to do with them: Bai Jing.

"Okay, okay! How does congee sound? There's a restaurant over by the Bund[18] that serves the best shark fin sea urchin congee. Why don't we go there?"

He Yu turned to look at Xie Xue.

Xie Xue dabbed at her tears and shot Bai Jing a disgruntled look. "I wanna eat barbecue. I wanna eat on Laji Street."[19]

"Then let's go eat on Laji Street."

Bai Jing said, "Ah...isn't that too... All right then..."

With Xie Xue present, He Yu was a bit more courteous to Xie Qingcheng, asking him, "What about you?"

"I'll pass. I'm taking this dog to get its shots, and then a pre-adoption health assessment. If you want to keep it, I'll bring it to you later." He shot a glance at the little yellow dog sitting obediently by his feet as he spoke.

---

18 A Shanghai waterfront district.
19 垃圾街, "garbage street," a street in Hangzhou with many food stalls.

Surprisingly, the dog took a liking to Xie Qingcheng, happily circling around him and wagging its fluffy yellow tail. "Woof!"

Half an hour later, the other three found themselves at the night markets of Huzhou.

"Laoban, can I get fifty skewers of chicken cartilage, fifty skewers of lamb, ten skewers of roasted rice-cakes, ten skewers of roasted mushrooms, a dozen baked oysters, and five bottles of beer?" Xie Xue started ordering as soon as she stepped into the barbecue shop, as though she knew the place inside and out.

"Isn't this sort of place kinda dirty...? I'd never eat here." Bai Jing extended two fingers to flip through the greasy menu, as if she'd wanted to touch it with nothing more than the tips of her fingernails.

Irritated, Xie Xue rolled her eyes. "Weren't you the one who forced your way into the car and insisted on coming along?"

"Aiya, little sis, why are you so angry? I'm hungry too." Bai Jing set her venerated buttocks onto the seat closest to He Yu without the slightest courtesy or hesitation as she spoke. "I'd just like to ask that you go a little easy on the grease. It's so late, I'm afraid of getting fat."

Xie Xue glared at her and viciously slammed a hand on the table, raising her voice as she shouted, "Laoban, get me another ten fucking fried rabbit heads!"

Bai Jing exclaimed, "You—!"

He Yu said mildly, "Get twenty instead. I want some too."

Bai Jing could only respond with silence.

Grilling skewers is a skill that's easy to pick up but difficult to master. The same chicken cartilage would not taste the same—as though some key element were missing—if the cook were helming the grill. However, all it took was a jerk of the boss's arm and a jolt of the bamboo skewers to have the excess fat and grease from the juicy cartilage that had been grilled to a golden yellow drip onto the charcoal, creating a miraculous chemical reaction.

The aroma of searing fat and a shower of brilliant sparks flew out in unison as the boss worked. Enveloped in dark smoke, he was like a reclusive grandmaster; with a slight flare of his nostrils and the merest whiff of the air, he could discern the subtle delicious elements within the smoke that indicated it was time to remove the skewers from the grill.

Then, he plated the food and set the dishes on the table, serving the food while it was still hot. The preparations were done flawlessly, down to the degree of heat used for each and every one of the skewers, as if the platter of comfort food were the personal creation of a master chef from the world of fine dining. A little less time, and they would be undercooked, but a little more, and they would be too tough; these were crunchy and scorched to perfection, each crackling bite of fragrant juiciness melting like snowflakes in one's mouth.

Xie Xue could be considered a regular at this restaurant and had ordered a full table's worth of barbecue skewers. The little table covered in a thin plastic tablecloth almost buckled under the weight of the food. However, while she was working on inhaling the smorgasbord of delicacies, Bai Jing stayed in character, doing her best to perform a quintessential Sichuan opera technique: swapping faces.[20]

"It seems that Young Master He isn't a native of Huzhou like me?" Bai Jing batted her lash extensions, and her lips, coated with shimmery lipstick, curved into a wide grin. "Your accent doesn't sound like it."

He Yu asked with a smile, "Miss Bai, are you checking my household registration?"

---

20 Bianlian (变脸) refers to the performance art of swapping masks faster than the eye can see. The same term is used figuratively for being two-faced/having an instant change in demeanor.

"Aiya, not at all, not at all." Bai Jing hastily waved her hands, awkwardly smoothing down her hair. "Um, I did my grad degree with the School of Business Management at Yanshi University of Economics. Your Mandarin sounds pretty standard, so I wondered if you were a northerner."[21]

"You must have been quite a talented student." He Yu smiled with a refined air as he selected a rabbit head—one with its eyes still wide open in unresolved rabbity grievances—from the barbecue tray.

Unsure if she could take his comment at face value, Bai Jing kept rambling, "Right, so my main reason for working at the sales counter is to gain experience so that I can be promoted to manager in the future. I can gain a lot of knowledge and experience being on the front lines, and I've served plenty of celebrities and CEOs. A few days back, I even met an actor, the one from that TV show that's been airing on primetime—"

With a crunch, He Yu's gleaming white teeth chomped the rabbit skull into pieces.

Bai Jing choked on her words. She felt as though He Yu had swooped in and bitten through her windpipe, leaving the shattered remains of her unfinished speech within. She suddenly felt a slight ache in her neck.

He Yu gave a slight smile. It was only at this moment that Bai Jing discovered he had sharp canines. They weren't obvious—their tips only peeked out from beneath his thin lips when he gave a crooked grin—so she hadn't noticed earlier. He Yu ate the rabbit brains slowly, with perfect composure. "Miss Bai should eat as we chat. Seeing as you've come with us, we can't have you go hungry. Do you not like rabbit heads?"

---

21   Standard Mandarin is based on dialects spoken in northern China, especially Beijing.

Bai Jing waved her hands hastily, "M-my appetite is usually really small, and I get full with just a couple of sips of Coke, I don't need..."

"Is that so?" He Yu tossed the shattered rabbit bones onto his plate and smiled. "That's really such a shame."

At the end of their meal, even though Bai Jing had restrained herself a little, she still couldn't resist temptation and tried to add He Yu on WeChat. Seeing this, Xie Xue finally snapped. This woman was her older brother's matchmaking date—what was she adding He Yu's WeChat for?! She was so disrespectful!

Seething with anger, she said, "So sorry, but he can't give you his WeChat."

"Why's that? Are you his girlfriend?"

"I-I'm not!" Xie Xue said furiously. She made up some nonsense. "But He Yu does have a girlfriend, a real beauty with an especially vicious personality who gets jealous easily. She's way older than him and manages him strictly. She slaps him when he disobeys and makes me monitor his behavior when we go out. Isn't that right, He Yu?!"

He Yu's reply was dry. "What you're talking about is a special agent from the NBIS."[22]

Fuck!

Xie Xue stomped on his foot under the table in anger.

He Yu said, "I don't have a girlfriend like that. I also don't like super jealous beauties with vicious personalities."

Fucking hell!

Xie Xue stepped down even harder until her own foot began to hurt. She looked down and—great, she had been stomping on the table's leg.

He Yu smiled, retracting his long legs from where they had been resting against the table's leg frame without batting an eye as

---

22   *The military intelligence agency of the Republic of China.*

he picked up the grilled skewers covered in Sichuan peppercorn powder and set them on Xie Xue's plate. Then he turned to Bai Jing, who was brimming with excitement, and said, "However, Miss, I do already have someone that I like, so I don't add girls on WeChat so casually. Please forgive me."

Bai Jing couldn't hide her disappointment. "We can't even be ordinary friends?"

This time, even He Yu's half-hearted smile had vanished. In an instant, that amiable, youthful quality seemed to disappear completely as he calmly glanced at the girl.

"Thank you, but I don't think we come from the same world."

With this simple sentence, he had essentially and imperceptibly eliminated Bai Jing's chances of getting out of this embarrassing situation unscathed. For a moment, the atmosphere became incredibly strained.

He Yu pulled out a napkin and wiped the oil from the skewers off his fingers one by one. Then, he tossed the napkin, squinted indifferently at the flabbergasted woman sitting beside him, and calmly said, "I'm going to go wash my hands."

Not everyone in this world was a socially incompetent fool incapable of understanding human speech. Bai Jing had received the message loud and clear that this handsome rich guy regarded her with nothing but cold disdain. As for that Xie woman, it was quite evident that after what had happened earlier, she had no desire to waste any more words with her either. Unable to bear the awkwardness any longer, Bai Jing finally gave a weak excuse and left the table in defeat.

After a while, He Yu returned to find Bai Jing's seat vacated. He raised an eyebrow but didn't even bother to ask after her as he sat down next to Xie Xue as though nothing had happened.

Xie Xue rolled her eyes and cursed Bai Jing a few more times. Only then did she begin gnawing on a couple of chicken cartilage skewers, turning to ask He Yu, "You said just now that there's someone you like? Are you serious? Who is it?"

"I was just teasing you."

Xie Xue patted her chest in relief and took another tiny sip of beer. "Oh, well, you really scared me to death there..."

He Yu's hands stilled momentarily as he gazed at this girl's open and candid profile.

"Whatcha looking at me for?"

"Are you scared of me having a crush?"

"Of course."

"Why?"

"Because I'm still single. Once you're in a relationship, I won't be able to come and hang with you so often, right?"

...What kind of dumbfuck excuse was that?

"What're you laughing at?" asked Xie Xue.

He Yu reached up, gently thumbing away some black pepper that had gotten onto the corner of her mouth without her noticing. His expression cleared, then he acted as though nothing had happened. "How do you manage to get a mess on your mouth even when eating barbecue?"

Actually, he'd been wanting to tell her how he felt for a very long time and had planned to do so ever since he came back from overseas. But when He Yu considered it carefully, he felt that a declaration of love should be a solemn and serious event. He shouldn't be blurting out all those feelings he'd kept hidden for so many years in the middle of a noisy street on a hot-blooded, hot-headed impulse.

So, he changed the subject. "You shouldn't let your brother go on matchmaking dates with those kinds of young women in the future.

He's not young anymore, and his personality is so stiff that even aunties his age can't stand him, never mind those girls. The generation gap between her and your brother is just too wide."

"What are you bad-mouthing my brother for? It's not like he's ever treated you badly!"

He Yu said, "I'm speaking the truth."

"As if!"

He Yu rolled his eyes, completely baffled by Xie Xue's reverence for her brother. "Really, just take off your rose-colored glasses and take a closer look. Your brother's already an old divorcé. It's enough just to find a decent person with a good personality. Someone so young really wouldn't suit him."

"Save your breath. My brother is so handsome and great, why should he settle?"

"He's handsome, but he looks down on and side-eyes everyone all day long. It's not like they owe him anything." At this point, it was as if Xie Qingcheng's indifferent face appeared in front of He Yu. He remembered the way he had opened his mouth slightly, leaned forward, and caught the straw between his teeth.

His attitude was just like that of a CEO accepting his assistant's services in a matter-of-fact manner when he didn't even have the money to pay medical fees. How could he be so calm and unruffled, so contentious and mocking?

He Yu was angered just thinking about it. He wondered what should be shoved in "Executive Xie's" face instead to sweep away every shred of his composure, to make his expression go dazed, for his features to be subsumed by wretchedness and humiliation.

But would that face of Xie Qingcheng's really reveal such weakness?

He Yu had never seen it before. After pondering for a moment, he realized he couldn't even imagine it.

"What are you thinking about?"

"Your brother," He Yu said absentmindedly.

"Ah?"

"I'm thinking about whether there's ever been a time when your brother was helpless, lost control, and found himself bested by someone else."

"Oh, well. You can give up on that thought because I don't remember ever seeing him like that. My dage is super awesome; he's so coolheaded and tough. Nowadays, he's always wearing a suit and carrying a book, but when he was your age, he was the best fighter on our block. Once, when a gang of hoodlums bullied me, he grabbed a steel pipe and took out a dozen of them all by himself, dragging them to the police station. After that, those little punks practically threw themselves down at his feet like a carpet for him to walk on, bowing down and calling him 'Ge.' Well, all except for one person... But that's another matter, so it doesn't count."

Seeing her eyes sparkling, He Yu was only more irritated. He laughed. "How come you're still the same as when you were little? The moment he's mentioned, your face lights up with adoration. It always feels like your brother is your savior."

"But he is! You have no idea how difficult it was for him to be my mom *and* my dad *and* my brother all rolled into one *and* raise me all by himself..."

"Well, you were also a good kid and saved him a lot of trouble."

"...Ah, I'm no good. He's ten times more capable than me." Xie Xue shook her head as she ate a skewer. "I'm nothing compared to him."

As the two of them talked in the restaurant's hubbub, he watched her self-deprecating demeanor. Finding her somewhat laughable, He Yu's expression slowly softened. He thought, surely, he couldn't be the only person who would like such a nice girl.

He really couldn't wait any longer.

That night, He Yu didn't return to his dorm. It was far too late, and he didn't want to disturb his roommates. So after taking Xie Xue back to the faculty dorm, he had his driver drop him off at a hotel he often visited. He took a shower and lay down amid the fluffy goose-down pillows.

"I'm back, are you..."

His fingers flew over his phone screen, but his thoughts hit a snag halfway through the message.

In the end, He Yu sighed and deleted the words in the text box. He stared at the profile picture of a sleepwalking bear for a while, then sent the simplest message.

"Good night."

He heard a ding just as he was about to turn off his phone. Thinking it was Xie Xue's reply, He Yu immediately picked his phone back up.

But the message was from that "savior." It was a bank transfer notice.

"Earlier at the hospital, I hit my e-banking limit. I've sorted it out now, so here's the money for the bill."

He Yu had always hated it when Xie Qingcheng acted this way. Plus, the fact that the message wasn't the reply from Xie Xue he was hoping for made his reply all the more frigid.

"I was just saving someone's life. Why should you pay me back?"

Xie Qingcheng also hated when He Yu acted like this, but he was too lazy to argue, so he just said, *"Then consider it a service fee."*

"What?"

"A service fee for driving me. Even if I found another driver on the spot, I wouldn't be able to find a driver as strong and youthful, as skilled at revving engines as you."

He Yu was speechless.

How impressive.

How many people in this world truly dared to use Young Master He as a driver and then pay him a service fee?

Also, why did it sound just like a prostitution fee?!

He Yu's expression grew dark. He was just about to reply when he accidentally exited out of the conversation and noticed his chat window with Xie Xue.

He thought again of Xie Xue's sparkling eyes when she spoke of Xie Qingcheng, and those words she had said, "You really have no idea how difficult it was for him to raise me all by himself..."

He was quiet for a moment.

Forget it. He was her brother, after all.

Thus, He Yu replied, *"You're welcome, Xie-ge. Call me anytime if you need me again in the future. I'll make sure you have a comfortable ride, satisfaction guaranteed."*

"Show me your car insurance claims report from when you were abroad first, then we'll talk."

He Yu's expression darkened once more. He shouldn't have been courteous in the first place!

His phone dinged again.

This time, it wasn't Xie Qingcheng but Xie Xue.

"Good night! Thank you for today."

She had walked out of the bathroom in her Huzhou University faculty dorm, yawning while toweling dry her dripping hair. She saw the "good night" He Yu had sent her the moment she picked up her phone. She couldn't help but smile as she replied to his message.

Then, she sat down at her desk and opened her notebook. Though hardly anyone journaled their daily life in a physical book these days, there were always a few eccentrics who held onto this nostalgic hobby of yesteryear, lingering in the past with the accompaniment of bitter ink, a sharp pen, and rice-yellow paper.

Xie Xue turned up the brightness of the lamp on her desk and began to write her bedtime diary entry.

"Today, my brother went on another matchmaking date, but I don't like the girl, I think..."

She poured out more than five hundred words. Perhaps because she had touched upon Xie Qingcheng's love life, she couldn't help but think about how she had always been single up until now.

Xie Xue sighed as she looked out at the night sky beyond her window, lit by the flickering glow of streetlamps.

She was different from her brother. He was someone who had lost faith in love and marriage. He was too clearheaded in life, and his peach-blossom eyes regarded each person he caught sight of with the same degree of slight impatience.

But she had someone she liked.

An indistinct figure appeared before her eyes. Ever since her youth, he had often been in her presence, so close yet so far.

She knew full well that they were worlds apart, that the gap between their social circles and classes was an impassable void—not to mention the fact that he was even younger than her...

But now, they were both at Huzhou University, and she could tell that there was no shortage of girls who were interested in him. They came one after another, turning to him more eagerly than waves of windblown wheat before the fall harvest.

If she didn't hurry and tell him her feelings, she would soon lose her chance. If they slipped past each other just like this, then maybe she would regret it in the future, and she would end up like her brother—bickering over the trivialities of life with someone she didn't really have feelings for, speaking an insincere vow and walking into the grave of matrimony. Then, one day, she too might find herself popping back to life like a reanimated corpse, alone again and doomed to go on matchmaking dates so as not to upset her elders.

There were times when she really couldn't bear to see her brother like this. She felt that Xie Qingcheng was living mostly for other people. Regardless of whatever he said about not caring about the opinions of others, he was actually the one who cared about his friends and family the most.

Xie Qingcheng lived an utterly stressful life.

It wasn't like she hadn't tried to talk to him, but every time she got the words halfway out of her mouth, her big brother would shoot her a glare and tell her to study properly and focus on her own future, or he'd scold her about sticking her nose into the business of adults, saying, *What do you know, a little girl like you?*

In fact, the one who understood emotions the least was Xie Qingcheng himself. Despite having lived through nearly half his life, he'd only had that one extreme failure of a marriage.

"I want to try expressing my feelings to the one I like. Ever since I was young, Gege always told me to be brave, and I think this is the same. Whether I succeed or not, I'll have tried my best. And when I think back on it in the future, I'll have no regrets."

After writing down her last sentence, Xie Xue closed the notebook.

What she didn't know was that in a hotel suite a few miles away, He Yu was having similar thoughts...

10

ON THE DAY I WAS GOING TO TELL HER, SOMETHING WENT WRONG

A FEW DAYS LATER, He Yu made a reservation at a rooftop restaurant and asked Xie Xue to meet him on a weekend evening. He was planning to formally express his feelings to her there.

Xie Xue was confused when she picked up his call, but once she heard that there would be food, she was immediately overjoyed. "All right! I'll be there! I'll definitely be there!"

"Then let's do six o'clock on the 20th. See you there."

"Eh? The evening of the 20th?"

"What is it?"

Xie Xue felt a bit distressed. "I might be a little late if it's then. The Emergency Department at Huzhou First Hospital just called me and said that Homeless Services would be taking Uncle Zhuang to Cheng Kang Psychiatric Hospital that evening. I also reached out to Cheng Kang, since I wanted to discuss bringing students over to visit with their director..."

He Yu sighed. "Then I'll pick a different time."

"But it's so hard to get reservations at that restaurant. The last time I called, they told me I would need to do it at least three months in advance."

He Yu smiled. "Don't worry, we can go anytime you want. My family is one of the restaurant's investors."

Xie Xue was speechless.

Capitalism. What a disgusting thing. It robbed all the satisfaction of a hard-won prize.

"Don't. It's so much trouble for the restaurant managers, and I don't like doing things that way," said Xie Xue, "Let's just go with the 20th. I'll try to finish up as quickly as possible. If anything changes, I'll tell you on WeChat beforehand."

He Yu pressed a hand against his forehead, smiling even more widely. "Okay, it's all up to you."

Xie Xue happily ended the call.

There was going to be good food to eat!

The 20th arrived in the blink of an eye.

Because Xie Xue was discussing business on behalf of the school, she wore a classic Huzhou University faculty uniform suit to accompany Zhuang Zhiqiang to Cheng Kang Psychiatric Hospital with the employee from Homeless Services.

Unlike Wanping 600, Cheng Kang was a privately run and very old psychiatric hospital. As soon as they stepped out of the car, they were assaulted by a horrible stench. A staff worker was in the middle of directing a cleaning cart to drag off a load of bedsheets that had been soiled with patients' feces and urine with a look of aversion on their face. Off to the side, two people in charge of refueling a car were arguing, their faces turning red as they debated whether or not some gas had gone missing.

Uncle Zhuang was a bit afraid, and he shrank back, tugging on Xie Xue's hand. "Daughter, this…"

"Don't worry, Uncle. You'll only be here for a short while. They'll take you somewhere else later, okay?"

Only then did Uncle Zhuang slowly follow Xie Xue into the building.

The decor in the psychiatric hospital's reception area could be considered comforting. Though the facilities were all aging, at least the air inside the room was clean and fresh, and the color scheme was soothing.

"Xiao-Zhang from Homeless Services? You're here to arrange Mr. Zhuang Zhiqiang's temporary guardianship service, correct?"

"Yes."

"The boss mentioned you'd be coming. This way, please."

Zhuang Zhiqiang's condition was classified as a relatively minor case, so he was placed on the first floor. Accompanied by an employee, Xie Xue toured the room and surrounding areas, which relaxed her slightly. A young staff member began to speak with Uncle Zhuang, her expression all smiles. Mistaking the staff for his daughter, he began to ramble on again.

"Well then, we'll be leaving him in your care." The Homeless Services employee returned to the office with the director of long-term hospitalizations and signed a stack of forms.

But Xie Xue's appointment wasn't with the receptionists. She needed to talk to Director Liang, who was upstairs. The receptionist couldn't step away from her post to guide her, so she gave Xie Xue directions to the third-floor shift office where she could find him.

The third floor of the Cheng Kang Psychiatric Hospital was the ward set aside for acute cases. As soon as Xie Xue stepped out of the elevator, she felt a chill—the entire atmosphere on this floor was completely different from downstairs.

It felt like a prison, with its barred windows and reinforced doors lining the entire corridor. Shrieks and sobs filled the air, making the whole area seem as frightening as a scene out of a horror movie.

The incandescent bulbs flooded the corridor in bright light around the clock, rendering it an abnormal, deathly white.

"I'm dying! I'm dying, ha ha ha ha ha ha—"

"*You're* sick! *You're* the sick ones!"

"I'm not human, I'm a ghost, no, I'm not a ghost, I'm human! ...Who exactly am I? Am I a human or a ghost...?"

Each patient's room was sealed with a heavy steel door, and each steel door had a copy-paper-sized tempered glass window through which it was possible to peer inside.

Trembling with fear, Xie Xue ventured a bit further down the corridor. In the end, she couldn't contain her curiosity and stopped at the doorway of a relatively quiet patient's room, lifting herself onto her toes to peek in the window.

A woman was sitting inside, laughing foolishly to herself. The entire room was fully furnished with soft objects that ensured the patient could not harm or kill herself. There were no tables or chairs. Even the bed was a special type that didn't have corners, and it came equipped with pitch-black restraints that trailed down to the floor.

That madwoman was sitting there and caressing the restraints, clinging to them intimately and shoving them into her ample bosom, giggling stupidly. "Who told you to cheat with that bitch? Look, now... I've already chopped you into strips... Other than me, who else would be willing to touch and hold you? Husband..."

Xie Xue moved on to the next room, but it was empty. Perhaps the patient had been taken away for treatment.

The window of the room after that showed the silhouette of a hunchbacked man, sitting facing a corner and smearing something on the wall. He appeared extremely calm and peaceful, but as Xie Xue stared, she realized that what he was smearing was his own excrement!

Continuing to the next room, she saw the patient was a young boy. Perhaps because he had mutilated himself too badly, he had been completely bound to a specialized bed—who knew for how long. He was laughing and sobbing hysterically with his face up-turned. "Fuck you! What right do you have to tie me down? I want to die!! Why can't I want to die?! If you don't let me die, once I get out, I'll kill you all...! Once I get out, I'll kill every last one of you!! Let me out! Set me free!!"

The more Xie Xue watched, the more terrified she became; the more terrified she became, the more she stared, stupefied.

Eventually, her eyes moved along the glass window, to the next—

"AH!!!" Xie Xue screamed.

A face pressed against the glass window caught her off guard. Horribly frightened, Xie Xue retreated to the opposite side of the corridor, leaning against a door on the other side and panting harshly.

The man at the window was cross-eyed, and he stared at her with terrifyingly huge, bloodshot eyes. Seeing her frightened expression, he started laughing loudly with delight from inside the room. His nose, red and swollen from rosacea, was pressed tightly to the glass, rubbing sebaceous streaks all over the window.

Xie Xue's heart pounded. She had just struggled to collect herself when she suddenly felt something ice-cold on her ankle.

She looked down and screamed even louder than before.

"AAHHHHHHH!!!"

It was a hand!

In addition to the eye-level windowpane, there was also a flap for delivering meals at the bottom of the steel door. Taking advantage of this, a tiny pale hand had reached out from the opening and was grabbing tightly onto her ankle, which was pressed against the door.

Xie Xue nearly had a breakdown. She jumped up immediately, crying and screaming while stomping her feet. The little hand retreated, but the patient went back to the center of the room, standing where he could be seen through the windowpane. It was a young boy with albinism. His entire body looked as if he'd been bleached—even his pupils were nearly translucent. He stared calmly at her, baring his gleaming white teeth in a grin.

"Jiejie... Heh heh heh..."

Cheng Kang had poor soundproofing. All the patients along the corridor had taken notice of the ruckus. They squeezed up to their respective windows and stared at Xie Xue while filling the corridor with a cacophony of strange noises. The patients shouted among themselves, and a number of them stuck their hands out through the opening flaps, swaying them back and forth and grasping the air blindly like floating seaweed.

"There's a woman here to see us!"

"Who is it? A doctor?"

"A doctor, my ass! A visitor!"

"It's a female ghost!"

"Grab her legs!"

They couldn't reach Xie Xue, of course, but they laughed with extreme and unbridled abandon. For a moment, Xie Xue practically felt like she'd walked into a forest filled with owl spirits, surrounded by ghoulish cries.

Xie Xue couldn't bear it anymore. She prepared to flee back to where she had come from. No matter how long the receptionist took, she'd wait until they were done before coming back up with them!

But right at that very moment, someone tapped her on the shoulder.

"HELP AAAAAAAAHHHHH!!!" Bad things came in threes; Xie Xue's mental defenses broke down completely.

"Shh."

Xie Xue's face was soaked in cold sweat. She turned in the direction of the shushing sound in horror only to see an exceptionally attractive countenance.

It was a beautiful woman.

That woman wore an old-fashioned, vintage-looking red dress with a pair of red heels. She was a little along in years, about fifty or so, but one could still see the stunning beauty she must have possessed when she was younger. Even though they'd begun to shrivel away like a drying apple, one could still imagine the beguiling allure her features once had.

A name tag hung over her chest: "Liang Jicheng."

Xie Xue let out a sudden sigh of relief like a leaking ball on the verge of collapse. "D-Director Liang..."

Liang Jicheng smiled, but for some reason, her face was a little stiff, as if she couldn't move her muscles fully and could only manage that superficial expression.

She told Xie Xue quietly, "You must not scream here. The more you scream, the more it thrills the patients, and the more they'll try to scare you. Come, let's go to my office."

At five-thirty, He Yu suddenly received a message from Xie Xue. *"I probably won't be late."*

He replied to her. *"Did the talks go smoothly on your end?"*

"Quite smoothly. They agreed to let me bring a group of students here to visit, but they have more requirements than I expected, so I'm still hashing out the details."

After a while, she texted, *"Oh, right. The Director Liang in charge of showing me around today is beautiful! A real stunner, and super poised. It's really too bad that you didn't come along."*

He Yu didn't want to bother himself with her anymore. He tossed his phone aside and got ready to wait for her at the restaurant.

It was still early when he arrived. The manager reverentially led him to the table at the rooftop observatory he'd booked in advance. Even though there were private rooms, He Yu had chosen an open balcony seat so that they could look down at Huzhou's scenery. Plus, the night wind was very calming, and the rosy sunset was beautiful and majestic. He felt that Xie Xue would like this better.

At 6:05 p.m., Xie Xue still hadn't arrived.

He Yu sent her a message asking where she was and whether she was caught in traffic. Right after that, he heard a nearby server say, "Ladies and gentlemen, please be careful on these steps."

He looked up to see a large group of people had arrived. It looked like some business conference or a gathering for the higher-ups of a company.

He Yu found it a little noisy. Just as he was thinking about whether he should get a different seat, however, the sight of an indifferent-looking man among the crowd startled him. "Xie Qingcheng?"

As luck would have it, the medical school that Xie Qingcheng worked at had an important event at this venue, which was chosen months in advance. Now that the event was over, it was dinnertime for the attendees.

When arranging a date at such an upscale spot, He Yu never could have imagined that he would be so unfortunate as to still end up bumping into Xie Qingcheng.

How could he possibly express his feelings to Xie Xue with this feudalistic patriarch at the scene?! God knows, Xie Qingcheng might throw him off the top floor into the river below!

Xie Qingcheng had noticed He Yu as well. He said a few words to his colleague and walked over to greet He Yu. "Waiting for someone?"

"...Yes."

One of Xie Qingcheng's nosy coworkers approached. Upon seeing He Yu, they said, "Ooh, what a handsome young man. Professor Xie, is this your relative?"

"A client's son."

"Oh... Young man, are you on a date with your girlfriend?" In this world, there were always irritating social butterflies who pried without the slightest respect for boundaries.

He Yu had a good sense of self-restraint. He smiled, saying, "I'm waiting for Professor Xie's little sister."

The colleague grew even more excited, turning to bat their lashes in Xie Qingcheng's direction. "Your brother-in-law is so handsome."

At the sight of Xie Qingcheng's expression, He Yu knew that if he dared tell Xie Xue how he felt today, Xie Qingcheng would flip a table and start a fight with him on the spot.

...What if he gave up? He could tell her some other day and just have dinner with Xie Xue this time round.

His mind set, he voluntarily took the first step to smile and say, "You've misunderstood, we're just friends."

Xie Qingcheng was still frowning. "Why did you make plans with her?"

"I haven't had the chance to treat her properly since I came back from overseas."

Just as Xie Qingcheng was about to say something else, his colleagues at their table started calling for them to get seated. With his colleague pulling him away, he had no other choice but to leave. He shot He Yu a look of warning before returning to his own table.

When 6:15 p.m. rolled around, the food had already begun to arrive at the medical school professors' table. Xie Xue, however, had yet to make her appearance.

Not only that, but she also hadn't even replied to the messages that He Yu sent her ten minutes ago. He Yu sent another text, but there was still no response.

Feeling something was off, He Yu decided to call Xie Xue directly on WeChat.

She didn't answer.

He then tried calling her cell number.

At first, the dial tone beeped, but after a long time, there was still no response.

He called her again...

Something was definitely wrong.

"Hello, the user you are calling has their device switched off. Please call back later."

Xie Xue's phone had suddenly been switched off.

This time, He Yu was certain that something had happened. He immediately stood up and made to walk straight out of the rooftop restaurant. At the sight of Young Master He moving so quickly and with such a dark expression, the manager was terrified out of his wits. With panic in his voice, he asked, "Young Master He, was there a problem with the service?"

"No." He Yu pressed the elevator buttons, his expression growing increasingly severe. "Have the lobby call a car for me, immediately."

"Oh! Yes, straight away."

He Yu's temper was beginning to flare; why the fuck was this building so tall? He even had to switch elevators to get all the way down!

With a loud ding, the offending elevator finally reached his floor. The gunmetal-gray doors opened, and He Yu strode in. Just as the doors were about to close, a hand shot between them and pushed them open again.

He Yu looked up viciously to see which tactless bastard was wasting his time. What he saw was a beautifully slender hand wearing a wristwatch. His eyes traced their way up the length of that arm, only to meet Xie Qingcheng's gravely stern face.

"What happened?"

Forty minutes later, after running too many red lights to count and breaking numerous traffic regulations, the restaurant's luxurious shuttle bus came to a stop outside Cheng Kang Psychiatric Hospital.

He Yu and Xie Qingcheng entered the building together.

By this time, the sky had already turned dark. The lights were on in the lobby and the first floor. Several patients with mild conditions were doing rehabilitation exercises under the nurses' supervision.

Upon seeing He Yu and Xie Qingcheng's harried expressions as they pushed open the door, the nurse at the reception desk stared briefly in surprise before addressing them. "Who are you looking for?"

"A young female teacher from Huzhou University came to see Director Liang to discuss a project this afternoon," said Xie Qingcheng. "I'm her older brother. Where is she?"

"In that case, she should be on the third floor." The nurse looked Xie Qingcheng up and down and suddenly smiled, her face reddening. "You're worried about your little sister, handsome? You don't need to be so nervous," she teased in a saccharine voice. "We're a licensed hospital here. Nothing can go wrong. They probably just got carried away while chatting. Plus, our Director Liang is in his fifties and has a wife and kid. There's no way he would—"

"What did you say?!" He Yu suddenly cut her off. "You said Director Liang has a wife and a kid?"

"Y-yes."

He Yu's face blanched. Originally, he only had an unfounded suspicion that something was wrong, but now He Yu was completely certain.

He still had the last message that Xie Xue sent to him. She had said, *"The Director Liang in charge of showing me around today is beautiful! A real stunner, and super poised."*

But Director Liang wasn't a woman!

He Yu immediately sprinted up the stairs.

At that very moment, within Cheng Kang Psychiatric Hospital's shift office, drifting snippets of a children's nursery rhyme echoed throughout the space. "Drop, drop, drop the hanky, set it lightly behind your friend's back, no one let her know..."

"Liang Jicheng" absentmindedly hummed this song as she hacked at something on the ground again and again with the surgical scalpel in her hand.

The fan above her head whirred with a droning hum. It threw the stark lines of shadow and light into a chaotic mess, but the object in front of her was still illuminated.

It was a body, still fresh.

Blood had already dyed the Huzhou University faculty uniform bright red... The Huzhou University faculty uniform...

And in it was Xie Xue.

"Liang Jicheng" finally managed to hack off Xie Xue's entire hand. Holding it up, she examined the hand for a while before apathetically tossing it aside. The disembodied body part fell to the ground next to where Xie Xue's ice-cold corpse lay...

11

HE BECAME A HOSTAGE

THE MAIN DOOR of the office was locked securely from the inside. Because it was designed specifically to be both burglar- and blast-proof, it didn't even budge when Xie Qingcheng and He Yu threw themselves at it. Sensing that something was wrong, the receptionist hastily rushed upstairs with the key in hand.

"There're sounds coming from inside," He Yu said.

Xie Qingcheng slammed his hand against the door. For as long as He Yu had known Xie Qingcheng, he had never seen such a terrifying expression on his face. He seemed to have gone berserk.

"Xie Xue! Xie Xue!! Are you there?!" Xie Qingcheng yelled. "Whoever's inside, say something if you can hear me!! Xie Xue!!"

No one responded.

There was only the gentle sound of that woman's voice, drifting eerily in the air. "Drop, drop, drop the hanky..."

"Th-the key... The key!!" The receptionist rushed over and handed him the key.

Xie Qingcheng took it from her. His hands were trembling so violently that it took him two tries to line it up with the keyhole. After a few turns, the lock clicked, and he threw the door open with a bang. The heavy stench of blood assaulted them as Xie Xue's grisly, mutilated body immediately came into view before Xie Qingcheng's eyes!

Xie Qingcheng fell apart at once, his vision going dark as though he'd been struck over the head, like the sky had fallen and smashed down onto his body. His tall figure tipped forward; if he hadn't grabbed the doorframe in time, he might have ended up falling to his knees.

The fan was still wobbling in its orbit, circulating the sickening stench through the air.

Xie Qingcheng didn't usually get dizzy at the sight of blood, but at this moment, it was as if he were about to drown in the vivid shades of crimson. At the sight of Xie Xue, it felt as though Xie Qingcheng's soul had wrenched itself out of his body, lest he break down completely. He began to lose his sense of awareness, hearing, sight, touch... The world had been reduced to a haze.

Someone seemed to be screaming behind him, perhaps the receptionist who had accompanied them upstairs, he wasn't sure. He couldn't hear anything clearly anymore.

Yet, his sense of smell alone had become horrifyingly acute.

The sickly stench of blood overpowered everything else as it surged into his sensory and internal organs, purifying and disintegrating his lungs.

He stumbled into the room. Mortality and danger meant little to him—even if the murderer inside were to rush up and kill him right now, he wouldn't care.

That was his little sister!!

He could hear someone mumbling, though he didn't know who it was. "Xie Xue... Xie Xue..."

That voice trembled alarmingly, but it also sounded like the quavering cry escaping from his own shattered, hoarse throat.

"Xie Xue!!"

"Don't go over there!!" Someone seized his hand and grabbed him around the waist, forcefully pulling him back. "Don't go over there!! Xie Qingcheng!!"

He didn't even blink or try to throw that person off; all he cared about was moving forward, which he did so with astonishing strength. He had already gone numb. There were only so many people he cared about in this world...

In that moment, it was as though an earth-shattering deluge had suddenly poured down over everything before his eyes. The scent of the rain was putrid, and he stood there like a withered husk in the downpour. That had been the first time he ever witnessed death...

His parents had died in a pool of blood, their mangled bodies smashed to bits. Half of his mother's body had practically been crushed to a pulp, and one of her severed hands had fallen far into the distance. He staggered to that severed hand, right until it was at the tips of his toes.

He looked at it with vacant eyes...

"Xie Qingcheng! It's not Xie Xue! Wake up! Take a good look!!"

It was as though these words had shattered the curse of a terrifying demonic mirror. They slammed into his chest, and the sudden jolt dragged his sense of reason back from the overwhelming fear that had consumed him.

He slowly turned his head, his peach-blossom eyes focusing on the face of the person who had spoken those words to him.

It was...

He Yu.

It was He Yu who had spoken those words.

It was fake.

It wasn't real.

Xie Xue wasn't dead...

All of a sudden, Xie Qingcheng snapped out of it, abruptly turning around to stare...

The faculty uniform that had belonged to Xie Xue was the most glaringly eye-catching item on the dead body. But upon closer examination, he realized that the height and build of that mutilated corpse didn't resemble Xie Xue at all. Xie Xue's uniform had been forcibly wrapped around it—the buttons couldn't even be fastened over the chest. It was the corpse of a man.

Xie Qingcheng's legs gave out; it felt as though his escaped soul had been relentlessly shoved back into his body in an instant, the force so brutal he could hardly bear it.

He closed his eyes, taking a moment to gather his wits. Only then did he manage to swim through the inundation of shock and terror from a moment ago and climb ashore. However, he was already soaked through, his body and forehead covered in cold sweat.

Normal people would not have been able to identify a corpse that had been mutilated to this degree in such a short amount of time. The smell of blood alone would have been sufficient to make one lose their sense of awareness and muddle the mind.

But He Yu had a rare mental illness called "psychological Ebola." He was psychological Ebola's Case #4, who had the highest tolerance for blood.

He wasn't afraid of blood; in fact, during flare-ups, he actually became bloodthirsty. That was why he could tell that the deceased wasn't Xie Xue in such a short amount of time.

He asked "Liang Jicheng" in a cold voice, "Where's the girl?"

"Liang Jicheng" raised her head.

She was exactly the same as Xie Xue had described in her final message to He Yu—an exceptionally attractive woman who had prevailed remarkably untouched over the cruel march of time, far more beautiful and alluring than most women her age.

Upon seeing "Liang Jicheng's" face clearly, the receptionist behind Xie Qingcheng and He Yu, who was so frightened she'd fallen to the floor and wet her pants, let out a twisted scream that could have been better described as an anguished wail.

"It's her!! It's her!!"

Right then, the security guards rushed over. They had intended to ask what was going on, but the scene that greeted them frightened them out of their minds. Only a few people had the wits to shout hoarsely.

"Jiang Lanpei!!"

"How did she get out?!"

Jiang Lanpei was considered an "elder" at Cheng Kang Psychiatric Hospital. There was an unspoken custom in these institutions, as well as the morgues of normal hospitals, to refer to the patients without anyone to bring them home or corpses that were left unclaimed for too long as "elders."

Jiang Lanpei had been here for nearly twenty years. Nobody had ever come to visit her.

Due to the switch from paper to digital records, even the files containing the information about how she had come to the hospital had been lost.

The people at Cheng Kang Psychiatric Hospital only knew that she was a madwoman who shouldn't be provoked because her condition wasn't obvious. While other patients looked messy and unkempt, and spoke unclearly, she styled herself every day to look bright and beautiful and was able to respond to others without missing a beat.

However, everyone in the hospital knew that, despite the logical consistency of her words, this was just an act. To put it bluntly, it was deranged nonsense that sounded very much like normal speech.

"Don't interact with her too much and leave right after you've finished attending to her. This madwoman is a skilled manipulator."

This rule had remained unchanged since the former boss, Liang Zhongkang, had established it. Even when he died and the hospital was taken over by his younger brother, Liang Jicheng, and other associates, it remained the same.

The man lying on the ground was the real Liang Jicheng.

Jiang Lanpei regarded the growing crowd outside the door with a menacingly cold expression. "Do not call the police."

"Hurry up and call—"

"Don't you dare!" Jiang Lanpei raised the scalpel with a sweeping motion and pointed it at everyone before her, her eyes flashing with a gleam of madness.

"I've been here for almost twenty years, and I've had enough! I want to leave now! I want to go home! My children are still waiting for me!"

"Wh-what children are you talking about, Jiang Lanpei?!" The captain of the security guards, bravely leaned forward and shouted nervously at Jiang Lanpei, "You don't have children! You're alone! We've cared for you for twenty years—"

"Bullshit! You guys cared for me for twenty years? How could that be considered care? Let me go! I want to leave, right now! Get out of the way! All of you, get out of the way! Otherwise... Otherwise, you'll never find the other girl!"

Upon hearing this, He Yu and Xie Qingcheng's expressions darkened.

"Where is she?!" Xie Qingcheng demanded sharply.

"Do you think I'm stupid?! Why would I tell you?! If I tell you, they'll just take me away!"

Xie Qingcheng's complexion paled as he suddenly thought of something. He stepped forward.

Jiang Lanpei retreated a few steps, pointing the sharp scalpel that was still dripping blood at Xie Qingcheng's chest. "What are you doing? I told you not to come any closer!"

"You took her to use as a hostage, right?"

Jiang Lanpei said nothing.

Xie Qingcheng lifted his hand and, as he stared into her eyes, suddenly grabbed the bloody blade. Jiang Lanpei shrieked and tried to pull the scalpel out from his grip. Xie Qingcheng's palm was immediately cut open and blood dripped down in rivulets.

"What are you doing?! You want to throw away her life? You—"

Xie Qingcheng pulled the blade toward himself and pressed it against his chest.

The entire room was shocked.

Without blinking, Xie Qingcheng said, "Take me."

Jiang Lanpei froze.

Slowly releasing the blade, Xie Qingcheng spoke with deliberate emphasis. "I'll take her place. Tell them her location right now and have them bring her out in front of me! I'll wait right here. If a single strand of her hair is out of place, I don't care if you're insane or just pretending to be, I'll fucking kill you!"

Jiang Lanpei considered his offer for a moment, but her muddled mind couldn't come to a decision.

Xie Qingcheng's gaze was much too terrifying. Even a crazed corpse-dismembering murderer like her found it difficult to so much as breathe as she returned his stare. Thus, she gave up on thinking and yanked him closer, pressing the blade to Xie Qingcheng's carotid artery.

"Xie Qingcheng!" He Yu cried.

"That little girl is in my room, B3009."

"We've checked it already! Don't believe her lie!" one of the security guards shouted. "Jiang Lanpei! There's no one in your room!!"

Jiang Lanpei scoffed. "Move the bed aside—there's a loose floorboard underneath. Pry it open. It's a very small secret chamber. You'd best go together. Other than that little girl, there's another surprise waiting for you as well."

The security guards looked at each other in dismay before making to leave.

"Wait a minute!" Jiang Lanpei suddenly exclaimed. After a pause, she continued, "All of you, take out your phones and throw them onto the ground."

They had no choice but to comply, and so they followed her orders. Because there were no telephones installed in any of the other rooms on this floor, and the stairwell was fully within view, the three phoneless security guards were now allowed to go to the nearby room B3009 to look for Xie Xue. The others remained where they were.

Shortly thereafter, the security guards who had left rushed back.

Who knew what the three of them saw inside the secret chamber, but sure enough, their faces were as gray and pallid as unevenly mixed wet concrete. They had used a bedsheet as a makeshift stretcher to carry the unconscious Xie Xue over.

The moment Xie Qingcheng saw Xie Xue, his heart couldn't take it anymore.

On the one hand, he could finally breathe a sigh of relief. Xie Xue truly was fine and had likely only been drugged unconscious.

On the other hand, he was overcome with devastation because Xie Xue's clothes had been taken off. With fall still approaching, it was sweltering hot outside, so Xie Xue had worn the bare minimum amount of clothing. With her school uniform removed, she was clad in nothing but her thin, lacy white underclothes.

Xie Qingcheng looked away after a single glimpse, his body trembling in rage. He reached up—

"What are you doing?" Jiang Lanpei shouted. "Don't move!"

"That's my fucking sister!" Xie Qingcheng took off his shirt and tossed it to He Yu even as Jiang Lanpei's trembling blade was still viciously pressed against him.

He commanded He Yu with bloodshot eyes, "Drape it over her!"

He Yu didn't need him to say so—he'd already taken the shirt and put it on Xie Xue, covering her up. Her entire body leaned limply into his arms when he picked her up. He turned to ask Xie Qingcheng, "What about you?"

"What do you think?!" Xie Qingcheng snapped. "What else can I do? Whenever I meet you, it's always bad luck. Why didn't you dig through the Cinderella one back then—you should've just mistaken the poison for candy and died right there!"

He Yu immediately narrowed his eyes.

He knew what Xie Qingcheng meant with these reproachful words.

He knew, but Jiang Lanpei didn't.

"All of you, follow me to the roof," said Jiang Lanpei. "Once we're on the roof, I'll let him go."

When a murderer who was trying to escape took a hostage, they would usually say something like, "Get me a car, and don't call the police. I'll let them go once I drive away." This Jiang Lanpei really was a lunatic who looked normal on the surface. Not only did she not head downstairs, she wanted to go to the roof instead.

Could there be a helicopter waiting?

But since she had given this order, the others present could only comply.

"Go! All of you, go first! Walk in front!" Jiang Lanpei snapped. "To the top of the building! Hurry up!"

She rushed them along, one after another. It was only after everyone had gone out that she carefully went up to the roof herself, Xie Qingcheng in tow.

Cheng Kang Psychiatric Hospital was located in a remote area, rather far away from the city. The lighting on the roof was sparse, and the strong night wind blew so hard that it dried the cold sweat on their bodies and caused gooseflesh to rise in its wake.

Jiang Lanpei ordered everyone to sit down some distance away from her. She retreated to the side of the water tower with the scalpel still pressed to Xie Qingcheng's neck.

"What is your goal?" asked Xie Qingcheng.

"I said, my goal is to escape!"

"That's not your goal."

"What do you know?" said Jiang Lanpei. "The people in the sky will come and take me away..." The blade pressed firmly against Xie Qingcheng's skin; blood had already begun to trickle out.

She stood up on her tiptoes and whispered in Xie Qingcheng's ear, "When the time comes, you'll all die."

After determining that Xie Xue was safe, Xie Qingcheng had calmed down completely. His mind was perfectly clear—to him, his own life truly didn't matter that much.

"If that's the case, then why don't you kill me right now?" he asked Jiang Lanpei, his voice cold. "According to you, we're all going to die anyway."

"*You!*"

"Are you too afraid to do it?"

Jiang Lanpei didn't respond.

"What are you waiting for, people to come down from the sky?" Xie Qingcheng continued. "What people are there in the sky? The smog is so dense we can't even see the stars."

"Just you wait," Jiang Lanpei said darkly. "You'll see."

At this point, she had probably also felt that her strength was waning even as she spoke. After all, she was a woman in her fifties, and she had to stand on her tiptoes and tense her whole body to reach Xie Qingcheng's neck; she could not constantly coerce Xie Qingcheng into obeying her while simultaneously keeping a watchful eye on the others for an extended period of time. Realizing this, she glanced out of the corner of her eye around the water tower and caught sight of a length of hemp rope that had been left behind during construction. Hooking a foot around the rope to bring it closer, she continued to press the blade against Xie Qingcheng's throat.

Rope in hand, she began to tie him up. Using plenty of knots, she bound him firmly to the water tower.

"You seem quite experienced," Xie Qingcheng scoffed. "Is this the only thing you practiced for the past twenty years in the loony bin?"

He seemed to have struck a sore spot. She sharply backhanded him across the face and spat, "Shut your mouth!"

After tying him up tightly, she backed away a few steps and finally let out a sigh of relief.

Hatred flashed through her eyes. "All of you men are beastly bastards."

Behind them, the security guards couldn't help but whisper among each other. Those who hadn't gone to save Xie Xue asked the three who did, "Was there really a secret chamber in Jiang Lanpei's room?"

The three security guards were clearly disturbed in comparison to the others. Two of them couldn't collect themselves at all as they fixed their terrified eyes on Jiang Lanpei.

Only one could barely eke out an answer. "There was."

"What was inside?"

What was inside? Collectively, the three security guards began to tremble.

Jiang Lanpei had overheard this question. Before the guards could speak, she slowly turned her head, the sharp blade still gripped in her hand.

She smiled. "What was it?"

The hatred in her smile began to blaze, the scent of smoke and flame seemingly materializing in an instant. "What's inside? Ha ha... ha ha ha ha... Love! A very, very intimate sort of love! Isn't that right?" Jiang Lanpei's face contorted—she truly was a madwoman.

The only security guard who could still speak, a man slightly older than the others, clutched his head with his hands. His own daughter on his mind, the guard explained, "Liang Jicheng was raping her."

The other guards stared at him in shock.

"For more than ten years... He did it every night, no matter what condition she was in... And every night, Liang Jicheng left a photo, so that when you enter the room, it's on every wall, everywhere..."

"That's not all," Jiang Lanpei smiled slightly. "Did you see the skeleton in the corner?"

No one responded.

"That was a tasty little morsel that Liang Jicheng brought," Jiang Lanpei continued, as though sharing a secret with friends, but in a voice that was loud and hoarse, like a crow cawing and wailing. "He was afraid he would leave crumbs and that the scent would attract cats if he ate outside![23] So, he brought his food here, to the secret chamber in the mental hospital he and his brother shared. They nibbled away at their tasty little morsel...but that little girl couldn't stand the defilement and killed herself by hitting her head against the wall!

The more she spoke, the more horrified the listeners' expressions became.

Only He Yu's face remained calm.

Xie Qingcheng's, on the other hand, grew increasingly hateful and furious.

"The morsel killed herself in the end, but she couldn't be thrown in the trash can, could she? So, they kept her in the secret chamber, immersed in sulfuric acid. It didn't take long for the flesh to disappear, and there wasn't much left of the bone either...but they still left some for me to look at, to scare me. To keep me from trying to seek death because I would end up the same way if I did." As Jiang Lanpei recounted these memories, her mind crumbled into delirium and her speech became disjointed, but the madness in her expression never faded.

"I pretended to be scared and catered to their whims every day... Later, he died...and there was only his brother left... Pfft! That brother was even more disgusting—a perverted deviant through and through..."

"Why didn't you tell us?! Why didn't you ask us to call the cops?!"

The young nurse couldn't bear it anymore, and her eyes brimmed with tears. "If you reported it, we could have helped you!"

"Who would have believed me?! I'm a madwoman! A madwoman!! They told you not to talk to me! They told you to stay as far away from me as possible! Every single day, you fed me medicine!

---

23   "To eat outside" is a euphemism for cheating in a relationship.

Medicine! You didn't care! Did anyone ever listen to me? Did anyone ever believe me?!" Jiang Lanpei raged. "I'm a lunatic! To all of you, I'm just a dangerous beast! You don't have to take me seriously, you don't have to care for me sincerely—what would I dare to tell you? If I told you, Liang Jicheng would just turn around and kill me!"

B3009 was like a rusting forge, filled with almost twenty years of lust and depravity.

Because of her illness, normal people wouldn't be able to see past their preconceived notions. Between an insane woman and the asylum's director, who would believe her? Gradually, the secret chamber beneath the woman's bed became a spider's lair untouched by sunlight, a web where the flesh of women turned to rot.

"All of you disgust me. I hate all of you!!" At this point, the light in Jiang Lanpei's eyes grew even more terrifying. Her voice gradually softened as she clutched at her head. "No one can help me... I've long since...long since forgotten who I am, forgotten where I came from... I can only... I can only return to the sky."

She suddenly looked up at the others and announced, "All of you must come with me."

Just as she finished speaking, she realized that one of the security guards was looking at her with an odd anxiety. She was stunned for but a moment before she reacted, turning swiftly.

At that very moment, she suddenly felt a gust of wind behind her. Though she just barely managed to dodge, she was immediately and ferociously kicked down by her opponent's long legs and pinned to the rough cement floor of the roof. She stared in disbelief at the man standing before the cloudy nightscape, the man with a bare upper body, wiry shoulders, and a sharp expression.

"The knots, how...how could you..."

"I forgot to mention," Xie Qingcheng said icily. "My parents were both police officers. I've been playing around with knots like these since fucking childhood."

THE MURDERER TURNED
INTO A BLAZE OF FIRE

PINNED TO THE GROUND, Jiang Lanpei panted for breath, her eyes bloodshot, an insane smile forming at the corner of her mouth. "Ha ha ha ha... Police... What use are the police? The police are all trash! In all these years, has a single police officer ever found me trapped in this godforsaken place? No! They're all useless!"

Her befuddled mind latched onto the triggering keyword and began to spiral. The wind blew messy hair into her mouth as she spat curses with a ferocious gaze.

"Now what? You're going to kill me, aren't you? Officer? You're going to kill me to cover up your negligence, aren't you?" A beautifully indifferent smile appeared on her face as she spoke. Though she was restrained, her eyes were nevertheless filled with mockery.

"I knew it! All you men are like this! Trash! The only thing you know how to do is take out your frustrations over your own uselessness on women! You're completely incompetent when it comes to anything else! I've been treated like livestock for twenty years... Do you know what I used to keep track of the days? I used the photos that that bastard posted on the wall! I looked at those disgusting things every day. In the first photo, I was only twenty-nine! Twenty-nine!!

"I turned fifty this year...huh? Or maybe fifty-two? Fifty-one? Or perhaps I haven't hit fifty yet?" Shaking off her confusion, her red lips curved into an arsenic-laced, bewitching smile. "Forget it, that's not important... The important thing is that I'm out. Do you know how I got out?

"I spent so many years as a lunatic and a slut, coaxing and pandering to him. He looked down on me, yet he still wanted to fuck me, to strut around and show off before me, to recover some of his pathetic male ego... Ha ha ha ha... I indulged him until he was giddy with glee. Bit by bit, that man lowered his guard. Once, when he took off his pants, he actually left the key to my room behind in the secret chamber."

She acted like she was letting them in on a secret, but she couldn't help but laugh loudly in delight. "But I didn't take it. That night, I handed him the key and asked him what it was. His face blanched the moment he saw it, but after seeing how stupid I was, he relaxed. He determined that I was far too ill...that I couldn't even recognize a key, ha!" Her gaze sharpened dramatically alongside her voice. "Who could possibly live like this for twenty years and not go crazy?!

"So he used that key to tease me, like he thought I was a stupid dog that had the key to my escape but didn't know what it was! He had no idea that I saw all the delight in his eyes, that I was so disgusted I wanted to hurl! But I could fake it—who said lunatics don't know how to fake it? I faked it so well that I completely deceived him. Later, he became even more relaxed, even more heedless. So long as he left the key behind, I would sneak out... I've touched every single brick in this loony bin! But I didn't leave! I wanted all these men to go to hell!

"I finished putting everything in place at last, just yesterday... I took advantage of the fact that he had once again left the key behind and took it. When night fell, I went out and quietly stole a scalpel."

She was still gripping the surgical knife tightly in her hand. The blood on its shiny silver blade had already dried up and congealed into an ugly brown. Xie Qingcheng knew that if he were to loosen his grip, however slightly, the woman would once again leap up and plunge the blade into his chest.

The animalistic aggression in her face was far too strong. She regarded the entire world with loathing. Twenty years had transformed her from an artlessly simple patient into a bloodthirsty, trapped beast with wicked teeth.

"I hid the knife under the bed, and when he came to rub his greasy mouth all over me once more, I humored him as I stretched my hand under the mattress. And then..."

Liang Jicheng's blood and miserable screams from when she had murdered him in vengeance seemed to sparkle in her eyes as she began to cackle. "Warm blood... Tell me, how can such a coldhearted person have such warm blood? It shouldn't be like that!

"Afterward, I dragged him into the office... I wanted to dismember him, but I heard something outside and, through the crack in the door, I saw a strange girl looking for something. Of course, I couldn't let her ruin my plans! I'd waited for so many years! So, I hid the body in the closet, clipped on his name tag, and walked out...to speak with your sister..."

Her face contorted, as if she were narrating a story to Xie Qingcheng, but also as if she were talking to herself. "The girl was very pretty, and even looked a bit like that *tasty little morsel* that had been brought back. You know, the one who killed herself by hitting her head against the wall? If I had to guess... Heh, she was the reincarnation of that little morsel... And even if she wasn't, that was fine as well. To be honest, I don't really remember what that girl looked like, but she was about the same age, so I thought it must be fate. So, I lied to her and got her to follow me into the office, then drugged her drink with a sedative when she wasn't paying attention... Of course, I knew which one was the sedative! The most laughable thing about you normal people is that you look down on lunatics. I know that special sedative all too well. Whenever I was disobedient, that Liang bastard would force a whole cup of it down my throat!

"After she passed out, I dragged her to the secret chamber. I thought that after I finished taking my revenge, when her loved ones came to look for her, they'd definitely...definitely turn this place upside down! Unlike me... Unlike me...me..." Her eyes dimmed, her expression unexpectedly lonely.

Xie Qingcheng stared at her with a sharp gaze. "So, you hoped that after everything was over, someone would find the secret chamber when looking for her?"

The woman's smile was stiff and distorted. She didn't answer his question. "None of that matters anymore."

"After I locked your sister in the secret chamber, I dragged Liang Jicheng out of the closet. I wanted to end it all in that place, in the very spot where I first met him! Just me and him, like the first time we met...and no one else! I'd cried out to heaven and earth, but no one ever responded, so I wanted to personally cut him apart, piece by piece."

She paused. Her gaze gained a hint of bone-deep hatred as she stared at Xie Qingcheng. "But you people came. You interrupted me and wouldn't let me carry out my final revenge against him there! You interrupted me... You're a police officer, aren't you? You're a police officer! You policemen are all supporters of evil, so just kill me. Kill me, and sooner or later, I'll come and take your life too!"

Loathing, determination, malevolence, and insane laughter all practically erupted from her face, turning into long fangs and stabbing through the man before her.

But Xie Qingcheng only stared at her, speaking with deliberate emphasis. "I'm not a police officer, nor do I plan on killing you."

The woman trembled. This was beyond her expectations. Her eyes bulged as she bared her teeth and said, "Then what do you want?"

"He wants to help you call the police." He Yu handed Xie Xue off to a young female nurse to look after and walked to Xie Qingcheng's side. In the darkness of night, it was difficult to see his expression clearly. "He wants you to tell the authorities everything."

"I won't!" Jiang Lanpei began to shout hysterically. "I won't! Nobody will believe me!! I won't go! Liars... You're all liars!"

As He Yu slowly approached her, Xie Qingcheng turned his head and sternly asked, "What are you coming over here for?!"

"Xie Qingcheng, you don't understand her," said He Yu. "You've talked with her for so long, but other than cursing you out, has she listened to anything you've said?"

The young man walked over to them, pulled Xie Qingcheng away, and helped Jiang Lanpei to her feet. With a burst of astonishing strength, Jiang Lanpei immediately pointed the knife at He Yu as if she were about to stab him.

His gaze unwavering, He Yu said, "Jiang Lanpei, I'm also a lunatic."

Jiang Lanpei's hand froze.

Their faces were less than a hand's width apart.

The youth's almond eyes reflected the madwoman's gaze.

His voice was very soft. Aside from Xie Qingcheng, who was the nearest, no one else could hear him. He slowly lifted his hand and, gazing into Jiang Lanpei's eyes, steadily grasped the ice-cold blade with utmost calm.

If Jiang Lanpei were to regain her awareness and lash out with the knife at this moment, he would certainly get injured. But He Yu seemed far too detached—his whole body was tense, but his face did not reveal a single hint of emotion. It was as though he were speaking to a completely ordinary woman, a mother, a normal person.

"That's right, I'm also a lunatic."

Silently, the blade passed into his hand.

It was only when Jiang Lanpei lost the knife that she suddenly became aware of the danger she was in. She glared at He Yu, her face deathly pale. "You..."

But he had no intention of hurting her.

He slowly smoothed the messy strands of hair at the woman's temple back and tucked them behind her ear. Peering into her eyes, he said, "My illness is unique. Look at my eyes—I'm a madman. Can't you tell that we're kin?"

Though Jiang Lanpei's expression remained guarded, she carefully stared into He Yu's eyes. She even started sniffing him.

He Yu remained calm and expressionless as he let her use the most primitive, animalistic means to confirm his identity. Perhaps every type of person had their own ways of determining safety; perhaps lunatics had a stronger animal instinct and sixth sense than ordinary people.

At last, Jiang Lanpei said in a low voice, "You are."

"I am."

"Who hurt you?"

"I was born this way," He Yu replied. "I don't even have a target for revenge."

Jiang Lanpei said nothing.

"However, even though I'm a madman, they'll believe everything I say."

"Why?"

He Yu smiled. The clouds parted, and under the pale moonlight, his eyes seemed as though they were gilded with a bright layer of frosty silver, his exposed canines appearing coldly sinister and sharp.

He leaned in close, as though sharing a wonderful secret on how to defeat some illness with a fellow patient, and whispered into her ear in a low and gentle voice, "Because, just like you, I know how to fake it. You fake being a fool. I fake being a normal person."

He Yu smiled slightly, his eyes like overflowing pools of ice-cold frost as he continued, "I've faked it for nineteen years already, but very few people have discovered that I'm sick. We all need some means of camouflage, don't we?"

Confusion flickered across Jiang Lanpei's face, but she quickly cleared her head once more.

"No... I've already killed someone. My disguise has been exposed."

"You can't trust them, but maybe you can trust me. First, let me tell you a secret."

Jiang Lanpei's eyes widened as she listened.

He Yu raised a finger and pressed it lightly to his lips. "Very soon, the police will arrive."

Jiang Lanpei's pupils suddenly contracted. "What do you mean? They called the police?! They still called the police! They deceived—"

"I called them." He Yu's expression was very calm.

"Why would you... We're the same... Why would you stand on their side... You should...you should..." The woman began to mutter incoherently.

"I'm standing on your side," He Yu said. "But don't you want Liang Jicheng's reputation to be completely ruined after his death?

After twenty years, you'll allow him to die pointlessly like this—as a victim, perhaps even to be memorialized as an outstanding entrepreneur, with flowers spread over his gravestone and the oblivious relatives of his patients all lamenting his death? Meanwhile, you'll be known as a murderer, with your reputation tarnished, the newspapers splashing your ugliest photo across their front pages, and everyone saying you're a beast who bit the hand that fed you. No one will know the suffering you've endured, and after your death, you'll still be beneath him, with everyone vilifying you. Think about it—is that worth it for you?"

Jiang Lanpei remained silent.

"If you tell the police everything, you might not find yourself at a dead end," He Yu continued. "Liang Jicheng's posthumous reputation would be finished, and you could have him die twice over—once in person, once in name." He Yu tilted his head, speaking quietly into her ear in an enticing tone. "It would be such a good deal. Why don't you do that?"

For a split second, Jiang Lanpei seemed to have been moved by what he had said. At that very moment, however, the sound of sirens came like a distant tide from all directions, rushing toward the psychiatric hospital that loomed in the night.

"Out of the car!"

"Everyone, get out of the car!!"

Jiang Lanpei's gaze shifted as she struggled to stand. Seeing this, the security guards all looked like they wanted to stop her, but He Yu very gently helped the woman to her feet.

"I'll go with you to take a look," said He Yu. "Take a good look. Before you, there might still be light on the path out of here."

Jiang Lanpei seemed to have been enticed. Shivering, she walked forward to the rooftop railing. She abruptly grabbed onto the ice-cold, rusty metal handrail and craned her neck to peer down.

In her hazy field of view, everything was lit up by the red and blue flashing lights of police cars. At first sight, it was indeed a scene that she had never witnessed in all her years in this prison.

It was as if all the injustice, humiliation, and suffering she had endured could be illuminated, and that secret chamber, hidden in the dark for twenty years, could also see the light of a bright and sunlit day.

As she continued to look, she became overwhelmed with emotion, and tears slipped from her eyes.

She turned around slowly. In the night wind, her red dress—the dress Liang Jicheng had bought for her under the pretense of caring for an abandoned patient to satisfy his own perverse desires, the dress he had given to her but then kept lasciviously stripping off her—billowed noisily in the wind.

"...So bright," she murmured in a soft voice. "It's like the breaking of dawn. Thank you. But..."

The last few syllables that fell from her bright red lips overlapped with the sounds of the police loudspeakers from below.

"All civilians, please remain calm! All civilians, please remain calm! Do not take the elevator! Try to seek out a nearby source of water! Soak a cloth with water and cover your mouth and nose! Stay low! The firefighters have already arrived! If you can, please use any nearby conspicuous object to help mark your location! We will immediately begin the rescue!!"

The light in Jiang Lanpei's eyes dimmed. "It's already too late. Twenty years is more than enough time for me to grow to despise everyone. The moment you charged into that office, my plan reached its final step." She paused. "Young man, I can't turn back anymore."

As if corroborating her words, the boom of a massive explosion suddenly echoed through the air.

The hospital staff trapped on the rooftop rushed to the building's edge in panic—near the linen room of the psychiatric hospital, a set of tightly closed doors and windows had finally exploded violently from the blazing flames inside.

Backlit by the flames, Jiang Lanpei slowly said, "Cheng Kang Hospital has many unspeakable secrets. Liang Jicheng created several secret rooms in the hospital, storing gasoline and ignition systems inside... He didn't dare speak about it in front of anyone and only dared show it off in front of a fool like me. He said that all he had to do was press that hidden button in his office and everything would start to burn in less than ten minutes...

"He had a guilty conscience, and he allowed the smoke alarms and surveillance system in this damned place to break down ages ago. He even called people to discuss these matters while he was doing those things in my bed. He let me hear everything. These past few years, I got to know Cheng Kang better than anyone.

"...Originally, I wasn't planning on going this far, but you just had to show up when I was hacking up his corpse... I don't want to end up in police custody, so I had already pressed the button when you went to the secret chamber to fetch that girl."

"You!" Xie Qingcheng exclaimed in anger.

"That's right. The reason I brought you all up here was to stall for time. Once the fire spreads, no one's getting out. We'll all die together, and it won't hurt so much after death... You want me to turn back now?" Jiang Lanpei let out a wretched laugh and added, "It's too late. Too late... Too late for me, and too late for all of you as well..."

Amid the lashing of the wind, the hoarse voice of a stranger yelled out, "It's not too late!!"

Jiang Lanpei whipped around to find that a specially trained firefighter had climbed up using a rope ladder slung over a wall still unaffected by the flames.

The firefighter was a bearlike man wearing protective gear. He probably hadn't heard what they had been talking about with any clarity and only heard this trapped woman saying, "It's too late, it's too late" the moment he got onto the roof.

Wasn't this doubting his professional capabilities?

The little firefighter bear couldn't take it and loudly yelled, "It's not too late! I was very fast! Everyone, come over here! Get down now! The fire's gonna reach the north side soon!! Hurry up, hurry up!! Women and children go first!!"

"Me!! Me first!!"

The nurse was scared silly. To her, the firefighter looked like a god descended from the heavens. She ran over, sobbing, as a few more firefighters climbed up the rope ladder and took everyone away before the fire got out of control and spread closer.

Xie Xue and the other female employees were the first group to be brought down. A firefighter shouted at Jiang Lanpei, "Jie!! Come here!! Why are you standing so far over there?! We'll take you down! We'll protect you, don't be scared!! We'll take you home! Hurry!!"

Jiang Lanpei's entire body twitched, as if she'd been struck with electricity. She stood beneath that high water tower, the wind blowing through her long, blood-colored dress.

But where was home?

And who was she?

If she were saved, where could she go? She'd been insane for so long, she'd long since forgotten the world outside. Her world was a dark and secluded room filled with thousands of photographs, a heart full of hatred, and boundless misery.

She was going to hell with all of it in tow.

She was just waiting for the fire to burn its way to the top, waiting for the flames to spread and to take all the darkness up into the sky, transforming it into the first glimpse of dawn after a long night.

"Jie! Come here!"

The expanding gases shattered the windows, and the flames, no longer silent below them, surged out like a fiery dragon spitting furious black smoke as it howled, and illuminated the night sky with their glow.

Jiang Lanpei took a shaky step forward.

And then, she stopped.

She turned her face to look up at the water tower behind her. That backup water tower was rarely used, and there wasn't much water inside—no, that wasn't water.

The corner of her mouth curved up in a grim smile.

That was the gasoline she'd obtained from countless trips to the storage site after stealing the key from an oblivious Liang Jicheng and sneaking out. And, in the lapels of her dress, lay the final item that would allow her to go up into the sky.

"He Yu, get over here!!" Struck with a sudden realization, Xie Qingcheng grabbed He Yu by the arm and hurtled in the opposite direction.

At that very same moment, Jiang Lanpei smiled and pulled a metal lighter out from her dress, flicking it alight and tossing it toward the water tower where gasoline was dripping ceaselessly.

Fire swirled upward with a loud roar, engulfing Jiang Lanpei's entire body in an instant.

Xie Qingcheng tackled He Yu to the ground as waves of roiling heat surged behind them. The firefighters were struck dumb, staring as the woman spread her arms and looked up—as if anticipating holy redemption, as if wanting to fly into the sky—before she was swallowed by the raging flames.

Xie Qingcheng and He Yu turned around, speechless.

Sparks flew in all directions. The raging, pungent inferno viciously spat out terrifying black smoke. A pillar of malevolently twisting dark gases took shape, its thick fumes combining with Jiang Lanpei's miserable howl and festering life. That fire danced madly, splitting through the skies and shattering the earth. The furious flames and smoke rose into the inky sky that had been forcibly torn apart by the blaze, smashing through the vault of the heavens, surging away in a spectacular, all-consuming wave.

"It's been twenty years. I don't trust anyone anymore."

"There's no way for me to turn back."

"The people in the sky will come to take me away. I want to go up into the sky."

I'll never turn back.

13

WE SURVIVED THE CALAMITY

XIE QINGCHENG was the last person to descend the rope ladder with the firefighters.

By the time he made it to the ground, the blazing flames had already begun to approach them. The dense, roiling smoke made it difficult to keep their eyes open. After their perilous escape, the rescue workers ran over immediately to examine his injuries.

Xie Qingcheng caught sight of Xie Xue in the crowd, surrounded by several doctors and nurses. He rushed over. "How is she?"

"And you are..."

"I'm her brother."

"Oh, don't worry. She's fine now. Her vitals are stable, so she should wake up once the drugs in her system wear off."

At last, Xie Qingcheng let out a sigh of relief.

The paramedics took in this tall, bare-chested man. It wasn't the time or place for lustful distractions, but the mere sight of this handsome man seemed to invigorate them, so they couldn't help but steal a few more glances as they worked.

However, Xie Qingcheng wasn't aware of his effect on the paramedics. The allure of his well-proportioned shoulders and back and his long, slender waist tapering into his silver-buckled belt was lost on the stoic man who paid little attention to his own appearance or the gaze of others. The stares of the enamored paramedics went unnoticed as he looked up from his sister to watch as Cheng Kang Psychiatric Hospital continued to burn.

A myriad of emotions welled up in Xie Qingcheng's heart as he watched the raging fire engulf the rooftop. Patients who had yet to be rescued shrieked in terror from their windows, banging against the casements that were securely bolted shut with metal bars.

"Help!!"

"Save us! Fire! The fire's almost here!!"

"I don't want to die yet... I'm begging you, please save me!!"

The bars that had originally been installed to prevent patients from jumping out of the windows and running away had now become their greatest obstacle to a timely rescue. Unable to utilize their usual tactic of a rope ladder, the rescuers' only option now was to risk their lives by rushing into the building and unlocking each of the rooms to save their occupants.

The ghoulishly desperate shrieking transformed Cheng Kang Psychiatric Hospital into an earthly purgatory under Jiang Lanpei's curse. In the ward closest to the linen room, an old man wailed continuously, calling out for his mother and father. The old man had dementia and would often have spells of madness, prompting his children to shun him and send him here.

Perhaps he was vaguely aware that they would rejoice at his death.

His parents, who were long gone, were the only ones who truly loved him. Thus, with death approaching, he sobbed and bawled like a child, screaming continuously for his mom and dad...

The firefighters attempted to break the windows using brute force, but it was too late—the old man's room was too close to the origin of the fire. As the crowd looked on, he was swallowed by the towering flames, with one hand still trying to reach beyond the metal bars, frozen in place...

No one knew if, in his final moments, he was ultimately an old man abandoned on account of his illness or a child longing for his parents.

Lips trembling, a firefighter turned their head to the crowd and bellowed, "Where are the keys? When all of you escaped, did anyone take the keys?"

"N-no... Who could possibly remember..."

"They're hanging in the director's office on the third floor!"

Another deafening explosion sounded as window glass and wooden debris flew outward.

One of the workers who had just been rescued stood up and said, "Comrades, don't go in there anymore!! It's much too dangerous!!"

"That's right... It's too late... It's impossible to rescue them..."

There was even someone who said in a hushed voice, "Those are all severely ill patients... The higher up you go, the worse the patients' symptoms. Even if you were to get them out, it wouldn't be worth it..."

Order broke down as chaos reigned.

Suddenly, Xie Qingcheng noticed a lone figure standing amid the bedlam. That individual looked up at the burning building for a short spell before turning to head away from the locus of everyone's attention, deeper into the thick undergrowth and winding around toward the northern entrance.

Xie Qingcheng was astounded.

He Yu?!

"Excuse me, let me borrow a mask."

Xie Qingcheng took a moment to gauge the state of the fire as he grabbed two protective masks and ran after He Yu.

"Hey! Comrade!" The paramedic abruptly came back to her senses. Fucking hell, even if he was hot, he couldn't be this impulsive! "What are you doing?!" she shouted after him. "Don't go back into the fire!!!"

Ignoring her shouts, Xie Qingcheng stared at He Yu's back as he chased after him like a cheetah.

He never could have imagined that He Yu would go back into the fire—what was he planning to do?

Unexpectedly, He Yu did not head over to the northern entrance where the firefighters were gathered. Instead, he grabbed one of the rope ladders that had yet to be removed and climbed directly up to the rooftop from which they had just escaped. Xie Qingcheng followed suit. As they climbed, flames licked at the rope under them, burning the fiber into ash. With the rope gone, there was no hope of anyone coming after them.

He Yu flipped over the roof's railing and shot a glance over at the area below the water tower. Only one thing remained there: a still-burning, charred black body, curled up in a fetal position.

Jiang Lanpei's corpse.

Throwing the door open with a loud *bang*, he quickly assessed the intensely burning fire before running toward the director's office.

Xie Qingcheng thought He Yu really was a madman—but, of course, he had always been one.

Catching up, he grabbed He Yu's arm, yanking him back outside of the door and rebuking him severely, "What are you doing?! Do you want to die? Come with me to the northern entrance, now!! The fire on this side hasn't gotten so bad yet. We can still make it."

Puzzled, He Yu stared at Xie Qingcheng's face. "What are you doing up here?"

Xie Qingcheng couldn't be bothered to waste words with him. With sharp eyes, he yelled, "Fucking come down with me!"

"I can't. This time, it's different. This time, I want to save them."

"You—"

"They're my kin. Only I can save them. Only I can help get all of them out in time. You heard what those people said down there. That old man was burned alive, just like that, before their very eyes. There are still more people who are about to die, yet they just said, 'forget about them.'"

He Yu's eyes almost terrified him.

Softly, He Yu said, "The mentally ill are not worth saving, and in these circumstances, they should all be abandoned. They deserve to die."

He stared into Xie Qingcheng's eyes. The corners of his mouth slowly curved into a grim, bone-chilling smile. "Is that what you think as well, Doctor Xie?"

"They only say that because there really isn't enough time... Be reasonable! You can't possibly open the doors one by one." Xie Qingcheng's voice had gone hoarse. "There's simply no time left."

He Yu did not speak any further. He threw Xie Qingcheng's hand off with great strength and turned to run toward the office.

Fortunately, the office was separated from the area where the fire raged most fiercely by a large section of lavatories. Back in the day, the construction workers had skimped on the job by only using ceramic tiles without bothering to set any wooden frames. Consequently, the fire spread slowly here.

After finding a large panel full of jangling keys in the office, He Yu headed for the section of sickrooms that remained untouched by the fire on the third floor.

"Help..."

"Save us!!"

"I don't want to die yet... I don't want to die yet!!!"

"Waaah, has the devil's fire burned its way here? It's the devil's fire!!"

The lights in the corridor had long been extinguished. Though sounds of sobbing filled both sides of the hall, there were even more rooms from which such noises would never be heard again...

The keys were labeled with room numbers. He Yu grabbed the one for the nearest room and began unlocking the door.

By the time Xie Qingcheng managed to catch up to He Yu again, he had already opened the first door. A woman with disheveled hair ran out, shouting hysterically. A chill went through Xie Qingcheng's heart—she was completely out of control.

Even normal people would lose their sense of reason under these circumstances, so it went without saying for these patients.

With a shrill scream, the woman darted mindlessly toward the fire like a headless chicken. Xie Qingcheng was about to stop her when he saw He Yu reach out and drag her back. "Don't go that way!" He Yu said.

"She won't listen to you—" Xie Qingcheng began.

"Fire! There's a fireeeeee!!" the woman wailed.

A flash turned Xie Qingcheng's attention away from the chaos to see He Yu holding the blade that he had taken from the office. He clutched it in one hand and slashed his palm.

Blood immediately began to ooze from the wound. Xie Qingcheng didn't understand why at first, but like a computer displaying old data, he unconsciously remembered something that sent a chill down his spine.

The next second, his eyes widened as he saw He Yu remove one of the rings of keys from the panel and smear it with his own blood. He spoke to the insane woman in a light but commanding voice, "Take this ring of keys and go open the doors. With every opened door, give the person inside some of the other keys and order them to open even more doors. Go quickly. The faster you go, the more patients we can save. Go on."

Something terrifying had happened. The moment that woman, who had only just been in a state of hysteria, smelled the scent of He Yu's blood, her eyes suddenly became extremely calm, as though she had been injected with a tranquilizer.

It was as if He Yu's blood had triggered some reflex in her brain through her sense of smell, allowing him to control her.

The woman took the ring of keys and immediately ran off toward the other metal doors.

The scene lasted but a few moments yet sent a chill down Xie Qingcheng's entire body, right down to his fingertips.

Case #4, He Yu. The comorbid ability that he had manifested after reaching adulthood was...

Blood toxin! Among all the abilities linked to psychological Ebola compiled by computational modeling, this was the one whose existence had always been regarded as the most dubious.

Given the lack of clinical data on the disease, the medical community's only option was to refer to the previous three cases and design a series of computational models to simulate a patient's future condition. Thus, it could be determined that, in addition to the baseline characteristics, every patient that suffered from this type of mental illness had their own unique comorbid abilities.

Simply put, the disease would continue to evolve inside the body. Given that each person possessed different genes, the evolutionary pathways would also vary by person. This differentiation typically occurred as the patient grew older, stabilizing and becoming fully apparent with the onset of adulthood.

The comorbid ability that Case #1 developed was acute hyperosmia, or an enhanced sense of smell.

The illness altered her olfactory nerve, causing her nose to become unusually sensitive. Generally speaking, the olfactory epithelium of dogs is four times as sensitive as that of humans. After her disease mutated, Case #1's sense of smell became more than eight times as acute as the average human; even the slightest odor in the air was sufficient to irritate her olfactory nerve and cause her such torture that she became increasingly mentally aberrant.

Cases #2 and #3 had also exhibited their unique comorbid abilities before their deaths.

As for Case #4, He Yu had not shown any signs of disease differentiation while under Xie Qingcheng's care.

Xie Qingcheng had originally thought that perhaps disease differentiation in psychological Ebola did not occur in all cases, that perhaps He Yu was an exception. He never would have expected that of all the abilities predicted by computational modeling, He Yu would have the most terrifying comorbid ability of them all—blood toxin.

This so-called blood toxin meant that, under certain conditions, He Yu's blood had the hypnotic power of persuasion, specifically over those afflicted with mental illness. Like serotonin, it could immediately stabilize a patient's mood, and, like a drug, it could stimulate the reward system in the patient's brain, causing them to develop the misconception that by following his orders, they could receive more. Thus, in this way, the patient would fall under the control of He Yu's words, as if becoming intoxicated.

The conclusions reached by researchers back then had been mere conjecture. When the computational models had predicted the blood toxin disease variant, there were even some researchers who had refused to believe the results.

But now, the patients under He Yu's influence opened the doors, one after another.

Their speed was astonishing. With every opened door and rescued patient, another fell under He Yu's spell to rescue others themselves. With the efficiency of a unit of well-trained soldiers, the blood-intoxicated and crazed patients distributed all the keys and unlocked every door.

He Yu wove between them with a stern expression, like a spiritual leader surveying his congregation. He strode to the very end of the corridor to the northern entrance—the last remaining path to safety. The firefighters' voices were already echoing through the corridor; they would soon reach the third floor.

By that point, however, the flames at the end of the corridor had already closed in, rushing toward them like a roaring dragon of fire accompanied by billows of choking smoke, as though trying to slay them in this ominous corridor with suffocating poison gas and all-encompassing heat.

There was no water here, nor was there any way to moisten fabric to cover their faces; they could only go faster.

Standing before the fire door, He Yu turned his head slightly as he issued an order to the patients. "Get as low to the ground as possible and come this way. Go downstairs and find the firefighters. Quickly."

The patients surged forward into the corridor with such robotic obedience and coordination that even mind-controlled zombies in a sci-fi movie couldn't compare.

By the time the last patient had run downstairs, the inferno was dangerously close. The smoke grew thicker and thicker, leaving only a thin layer of breathable air close to the ground. He Yu watched as Xie Qingcheng approached him with a deeply unpleasant expression. Without a word, he merely stepped to the side to allow Xie Qingcheng into the corridor as well.

The fire door closed behind them with a heavy thud, cutting off the fiery dragon's approach for the time being.

In the dark corridor, ice-cold almond eyes met shocked peach-blossom eyes. "Xie Qingcheng. Do not tell a soul."

Xie Qingcheng's face turned terribly ashen, but he could not think of how to respond. Instead, he passed a gas mask to He Yu, saying, "Take that. Let's go."

The flames raged against the fire door as He Yu and Xie Qingcheng rushed downstairs, following the rescued patients.

"Ge!! Ge!!"

Xie Qingcheng and He Yu were the last two people to run out under the firefighting crew's support. Two cries from a voice nearly cracking with emotion welcomed them, and Xie Qingcheng took off his mask when he saw the now-awake Xie Xue charging at him with a face full of tears. She ran so fast that the shoes the firefighters had found for her fell off her feet.

"Ge, aaaaaaah... Dage!! Dage!! Are you trying to scare me to death? Huh, are you?! I thought even you were abandoning me too!! Even you!! Ge, waaaah..."

She threw herself into Xie Qingcheng's arms and held him so tightly she nearly snapped his waist in half. The sounds of explosions and screams of those they couldn't save continued around them.... She was so scared, it was as though all the blood had been sucked out of her body, leaving nothing behind but a thin painted skin[24] in the human realm. It was only when she was tightly embracing her brother's tall figure, choking on sobs as she breathed in Xie Qingcheng's scent, that her heartbeat finally recovered and warm blood flushed through her veins once more.

Tears streamed down her face, splotching it like the patterns on a cat's fur. She opened her mouth and wailed with absolutely no

---

24   In legends, a magical skin worn by monsters to take on the appearance of a beautiful maiden. More generally, it can refer to a deceivingly lovely superficial layer that hides what's within.

concern for her image, tripping over her words as she yelled, "You can't abandon me like Mom and Dad!! You just can't, Dage!! I was so scared... I was really so scared... Hug me, hug me!!"

"Everything's all right, okay? Everything's all right."

Xie Qingcheng very rarely accepted such intense displays of emotions. Although his love for his family was strong, it was also reserved, and often only expressed in the form of scolding.

But at this moment, he also found it a bit difficult to maintain his usual demeanor. He held his sister as she shivered beneath a long coat and leaned down to kiss her messy bird's nest of hair. The rims of his eyes were tainted red as he spoke soothingly, "Everything's all right, Xie Xue."

Xie Xue wailed in Xie Qingcheng's arms for a long while before spotting He Yu. Despite just managing to calm down a bit, she broke down once again and threw herself, sobbing, into He Yu's arms—or rather, to be more precise, she dragged He Yu over and hugged both him and her brother at the same time. As a result, He Yu was forcibly squeezed against Xie Qingcheng as well.

An awkward expression surfaced on He Yu's handsomely refined face. He had never been so close to another man before; and considering the fact that the man in question was Xie Qingcheng, he felt extremely unsettled. One look at Xie Qingcheng's expression told him the feeling was mutual.

But out of consideration for Xie Xue, neither of them moved. They allowed her to squeeze the three of them together into an unyielding hug, carving out a little reunion for them amid the chaos.

"Help! Help me!! Comrades! There's someone here! I'm over here!!"

A man with salt-and-pepper hair was screaming in panicked fear beside the door of the elevator in Cheng Kang Psychiatric Hospital. He was one of Cheng Kang's oldest directors, a friend of Liang Jicheng, who had recently broken his leg while playing polo with Liang Jicheng, confining him to a wheelchair for the time being. If it weren't for the fact that there had been some matters that he needed to take care of at the office today, he wouldn't have been there in the first place.

The man trembled in the wheelchair, urine trickling down the legs of his trousers from his already-soaked crotch. It was his first time experiencing just how terrifying it was to be in a condition where he couldn't look after himself. The blazing fire was pressing toward him at that very moment, and although he probably knew that he couldn't take the elevator, that it was likely already broken, he still couldn't stop himself from frantically pressing the button.

"Quick! Quick... Someone come save me... I have money... Who's gonna come and save me... I have a lot of money!"

The muscles in his cheeks twitched violently, spasming from anxiety.

Suddenly, as if the heavens had heard his pleas, someone wearing a gas mask who looked like a firefighter ran out of the pitch-black escape corridor and saw him sprawled in the wheelchair.

It was as though the man had seen a god appear before him. "Comrade!! Save me!! Quick, save me!!!"

His nostrils trembled in agitation, and fine beads of sweat hung from the pale flesh of his nose. His pupils dilated in excitement, reflecting the figure of the person walking up to him with firefighting equipment in hand.

A moment later, he froze, and his pupils abruptly shrank.

A sinister sneer flashed from behind the goggles of the person in the firefighting uniform. Then, they took the lid off the equipment in their hands... It wasn't a fire extinguisher! It was...gasoline!!!

"You, you're—!"

"This shithole Cheng Kang is beyond saving. I'm the 'janitor' they sent over to clean this place up." The muffled sound of a man's voice came from under the mask. "You can take your time spending that money of yours on the other side."

"NO!!!"

The newcomer simultaneously tossed the gasoline and lighter into the man's panicking and grotesquely contorted face.

A massive boom ripped through the air, and that face seemed to resemble the warped visage in Edvard Munch's *The Scream* as it was completely swallowed up by the flames...

14

WE TALKED ABOUT
SECRETS AND THE PAST

AFTER HE YU AND XIE QINGCHENG finally managed to calm Xie Xue down and get her to sit on a stool to rest obediently with the other survivors, they received a stern tongue-lashing from the head of the firefighting squad.

Thoroughly reprimanded, the two of them walked off to the side. Out of the corner of his eye, He Yu shot a glance at Xie Qingcheng, who was lighting a cigarette that he'd gotten from a police officer, of all people. Unable to fathom the reasons for Xie Qingcheng's actions earlier, He Yu asked, "Xie Qingcheng, why did you run into the fire with me?"

"The area you entered hadn't become too dangerous yet." Xie Qingcheng took a drag from the cigarette, then slowly let it out. Only then did he fully relax.

The embers glowed and dimmed between his fingers, the ashes drifting down like a whisper of snow.

"Tell me about your condition." Xie Qingcheng flicked the ash away and gazed straight ahead. "When did it start?"

He was asking about the blood toxin.

"Shortly after you left," He Yu replied after a brief pause. "When I went to a private psychiatric hospital for another checkup, I ran into a mentally ill patient and found out by accident. When I used my blood as bait, they would listen to me. You knew about this condition?"

"I did." Xie Qingcheng coughed softly and took another drag as he tried to describe it as indifferently as possible. "Blood toxin is a mutant variant of psychological Ebola." He hesitated. "You haven't told anyone else about this, have you?"

He Yu smiled, his eyes a bit dark. "You're the only one who knows."

Xie Qingcheng let the information sink in before replying.

"If I wanted to silence all the witnesses someday, all I would need to do is kill you."

Xie Qingcheng rolled his eyes at He Yu. "I'd like to see you try."

The police officer's cigarette didn't suit Xie Qingcheng's tastes; it was too effeminate and contained a menthol-flavored capsule. Such was his distaste for it that Xie Qingcheng choked several times while he smoked, so he stubbed it out in irritation.

"Don't tell anyone else about this. Not even your doctors."

"I'm not that stupid, Xie Qingcheng," He Yu said mildly. He really was one hell of a rich young master; despite having gone through so much, he was still the most immaculately dressed one in the crowd, looking unbearably handsome and refined. Some of the rescued people nearby were even sneaking looks at him.

"Psychological Ebola is already an exceedingly rare disorder. Now, with this ability that allows me to force mentally ill patients to obey me, I can forget about living a peaceful life. But remember this, Xie Qingcheng..."

He Yu suddenly drew closer to Xie Qingcheng, slowly assessing him through apathetic almond eyes. "Those eyes of yours are the only pair to have personally witnessed it all."

He was very close, his lashes on the verge of brushing against Xie Qingcheng's own. That low and unhurried voice whispered into Xie Qingcheng's ear; amid the chaos, the words that He Yu wanted only this one person to hear sounded like a murmur, but also like a threat.

"This mouth of yours is the only mouth that can reveal the truth."

His soft gaze fell on Xie Qingcheng's thin, pale lips, as if caressing them as it sought out something unknown. But the menace hidden within the depths of his eyes was anything but light.

As He Yu stood before Xie Qingcheng, staring into his face, he reached out to adjust the collar on the shirt the older man was now wearing courtesy of the firefighters. The way in which He Yu straightened out Xie Qingcheng's clothes might have seemed courteous to onlookers, but only the two men themselves knew how much force He Yu used as he smoothed out Xie Qingcheng's shirt and silently pulled his collar taut, the warning and coercion communicated in his actions.

He Yu finished straightening out Xie Qingcheng's clothes and smiled in an extraordinarily gentle and refined manner. "Therefore, about this secret...you'd better hold it safely in your mouth. Hold it in there nice and tight. Don't let it fall out."

"You're threatening me?" Xie Qingcheng retorted icily.

"I wouldn't dare. This is just a reminder." He Yu's hands slid down from Xie Qingcheng's collar as he sighed. "I just want to live a normal life."

Xie Qingcheng really couldn't be bothered to waste his breath on this nutcase.

Why did He Yu bother going to such lengths? If Xie Qingcheng had really planned on telling others about He Yu's symptoms, he wouldn't have reminded him not to reveal it to anyone else to begin with.

But He Yu didn't think that way. He didn't trust Xie Qingcheng that much. He only felt that Xie Qingcheng's mouth had become a threat that he badly wanted to silence. It would be best for something to be savagely shoved inside, reducing him to garbled incoherency like a bound hostage, unable to spill his secret.

Xie Qingcheng looked at him. "You say you only want to live a normal life. In that case, why did you take the risk of entering the fire and using your blood toxin to save those patients when time was not on your side?"

"Because what you want and what you are are never the same," He Yu said. "I want to be a normal person, but I've always been a madman. However, first of all, there was never a danger of time as the flames had not yet reached that side of the building. Secondly, do you remember what I said to you? That humans will never be able to understand nor empathize with each other? Just like two completely different species. I feel that, compared to all of you, those people are more like my kin. The only way I differ from them is that I wear a better disguise."

He Yu continued impassively, "If even I thought that their lives were insignificant and expendable, then who else would treat them as living, breathing humans?"

All humans—in any society, community, righteous coalition, or nefarious alliance—craved to be with their own kind, regardless of the type of person they were.

Because absolute solitude would drive one insane.

He Yu was an overly solitary person. No one could understand what ailed him; they could only listen to his words and see the suffering he revealed on the surface. All three of the patients who had been afflicted with the same disease as him, his true kin, were already dead. Thus, he could only hope to enter similar communities and try to find a shaky, floating bridge that could link him to the rest of the world.

Yet, He Yu was dangerous because he could bewitch those who were his kin. His blood was a reward to the mentally ill, and his words were commands that they could never disobey. He could even use his ability to commit crimes if he desired, so it was no wonder that he didn't want others to know of this.

So it was no wonder that he wished to seal the lips of the only other person in the world to know his true power.

"Is kinship really so important to you?" Xie Qingcheng asked. "To the point that you would even put your own life at risk?"

"Doctor, you wouldn't understand us," replied He Yu coldly. "One cannot see the dark night while standing in the light."

Xie Qingcheng sighed. Discussing this topic was proving fruitless. "Final question," he said. "Since you have blood toxin, why didn't you use it earlier with Jiang Lanpei?"

"Because it's unstable," He Yu replied. "There's a possibility that my blood would make the patients go even more insane. Under those circumstances, I couldn't afford to take that risk, unlike you..."

He Yu's words came to a sudden halt, before shifting gears and starting again. "You're really something else. You'd already fallen into that person's hands but still had to mention Cinderella. You took such a big gamble—weren't you afraid that I wouldn't catch on?"

"I took that gamble because I consider you to be quite clever," Xie Qingcheng said lightly. "Besides, wasn't Cinderella the very thing you wanted to bring up that time when I went to your dorm to change?"

He Yu fell silent for a while before finally dropping his head with a sneer. Feeling the tension ease, Xie Qingcheng pressed his hand against his forehead. At this juncture, the two finally felt some degree of the relaxation and ease that came with surviving a calamity, and their minds drifted to the past.

Yes, both of them still remembered that event that happened when He Yu was about eight or nine years old. Therefore, it had unexpectedly become their secret code for calling the police in the nick of time.

Back then, Xie Qingcheng felt that, aside from the basic regimen of medical treatment, He Yu also needed to get outside more, get some sun and fresh air, and relieve his boredom. Many doctors believed that treatment for the mentally ill should prioritize medication, but Xie Qingcheng took a different approach. He believed that a patient's mental illness was a product of their environment and that one shouldn't isolate and cut a mentally ill patient off from society. Therefore, mental illness was not a battle to be won with medication but with rehabilitating patients to rebuild the bridges linking them to their family and society as a whole.

And so, he gave his recommendation to Lü Zhishu.

Lü Zhishu, who was in the middle of attending to a flurry of business calls, looked up at Xie Qingcheng and gave him an embarrassed laugh. "I don't have the time, Doctor Xie. Why don't you take him?"

Xie Qingcheng forced down his anger. "He's your son."

Having grown accustomed to talking business, Lü Zhishu didn't even bother to look up as she countered, "I'll give you a raise."

Xie Qingcheng was at a loss for words.

Lü Zhishu then took her phone and left in a whirl of arrogant, idle chatter. It was as though she was a businessperson first and a mother second; from start to end, the chubby and wealthy matron remained smiling as she addressed "Executive Zhang, Executive Li" over the phone, her line of sight never once landing on Xie Qingcheng.

Never mind He Yu, who stood behind him.

Xie Qingcheng turned around and looked down only to see that He Yu didn't appear to be troubled much at all by his mother's actions. He seemed to be accustomed to this kind of mother-son relationship. Sitting on the sofa, he didn't even bother looking up as he peeled a large, golden-yellow navel orange for himself.

That orange was bigger than his hands, and He Yu lost his grip halfway through. It fell to the floor and rolled under the tea table. He hopped off the sofa and went to pick it up only to see a glistening Christmas apple appear before his eyes.

"You're going to eat something that's fallen on the floor?" Xie Qingcheng let out a sigh, unsure as to why his heart had grown soft. He passed He Yu the Christmas apple and picked up the dusty orange. "I'll take you to the amusement park tomorrow," he said.

Thus, Xie Qingcheng brought his little sister and He Yu to the amusement park the next day. Xie Xue had a sweet disposition, smiled often, and was good at looking after the younger boy. As a result, He Yu's entire condition seemed to improve significantly.

But on their way back, it suddenly started to pour.

By the time they finally managed to catch a taxi, the three of them had already become ridiculously soaked. However, the He family's villa was quite a distance away in the outskirts of the city, so Xie Qingcheng brought the two children to his medical school dormitory first.

Xie Qingcheng's university housing was the same as He Yu's present dorm, a four-person room. His roommates were all busy working on their projects in the lab, so he and the two drowned rats had the place to themselves.

"Gege! Your cactus is blooming!" As soon as she walked in, Xie Xue pounced over to Xie Qingcheng's desk like she owned the place, smiling brilliantly and poking at the ball cactus that was crowned with a circle of small, goose-yellow flowers inside its egg-shaped pot. "Whoa...so pretty."

This was clearly not her first time visiting her brother's dorm.

Xie Qingcheng poured hot ginger tea for the children and firmly shoved the cups into their hands. "Drink it while it's hot."

Xie Xue liked spicy foods and began sipping away as soon as she got the ginger tea in her hands, quickly finishing off the drink. But He Yu was not so eager. The young master couldn't stand strong flavors, so he sat with his head down and cradled his cup, hardly able to force himself to take even a single sip.

Xie Qingcheng went to the bathroom to wash his hands. Just as He Yu was trying to figure out what to do with this cupful of pungent spiciness, Xie Xue let out a satisfied sigh beside him. "It's so good."

He Yu turned, flabbergasted, and assessed her with a calm expression.

Sensing his gaze, Xie Xue turned and giggled at him with her eyes fixed on his cup. "If you don't like it..."

"No, I like it very much," He Yu said, his voice bland.

"No way! Look, you've only had a tiny bit of it after all this time!"

He Yu smiled. "It's because I like it that I can't bear to drink it."

"...Oh." Apparently convinced, Xie Xue nodded regretfully as she moved to look away.

It was only then that He Yu passed her the mug he'd long since been ready to give away. "Here."

"Ah? B-but I thought you liked it?"

"If you want it, I'll give it to you."

The fucking idiot's eyes widened as she gratefully accepted the hot ginger tea.

He Yu made sure to calmly remind her, "Drink it quickly. We can't let your big brother find out I gave mine to you. Otherwise, he'll scold you again."

"Yes, yes." Xie Xue, who was so pure she'd help her kidnapper count her ransom, gratefully chugged the hot tea in one gurgling gulp. She nearly choked on it and broke into a flurry of coughs.

Smiling, He Yu patted her on the back.

"I love ginger tea." Having regained her energy, Xie Xue cupped her hands around the still-steaming mug and told He Yu quietly, her eyes suffused with a gentle brightness, "Back when I was little and it snowed outside, we lived in the little alley and didn't have anything to help us keep warm, so my brother would make this for me..."

It was clearly a difficult memory filled with heartache, but when she spoke, her eyes shined as though she were recalling some incomparably fun event from the past.

When Xie Qingcheng returned, he looked at the two children sitting next to each other on the edge of his dorm bed. "Are you two done drinking?"

The children glanced at each other and exchanged a secret look. While He Yu was very calm, Xie Xue was a little flustered and nodded quickly. It could be that she'd drunk too much, so she couldn't help but open her mouth a little to quietly let out a small burp as she was nodding.

Xie Qingcheng turned to fetch a change of clothes from his closet. The little girl's kickboxing lessons were located close to the medical school, so Xie Qingcheng always had a few sets of dry clothes on hand for when she'd inevitably show up soaked with sweat after class. They came in handy this time around as well.

While poking around in the closet, soft fairy-tale princess names passed through the elder brother's thin lips. "Do you want Belle or Cinderella?"

The little girl was delighted. "I want Belle!"

Xie Qingcheng passed her a light-yellow princess dress. Xie Xue cheered with glee, grabbing the clothing before scampering into the bathroom to change.

He Yu remained standing by the edge of the bed, dripping wet as Xie Qingcheng continued digging around in his closet for a bit. In the end, he sighed, collected himself, and did something extremely inhumane.

"Why don't you wear this, then?"

He Yu took the proffered clothes and unfolded them to take a look. Calmly, he said, "Doctor Xie, you've made a mistake."

"I have not."

He Yu froze for a moment, then slowly looked up, his eyes narrowing as a chilly undisguised darkness gradually stole over his features.

"You've given me a dress."

More importantly, it was a baby blue Cinderella princess dress.

It was unclear whether Xie Qingcheng had done this on purpose, but faced with He Yu's suppressed fury, a slight smile spread over Xie Qingcheng's lips. However, it was hard to tell if he was mocking He Yu or being sincere, even when there was a smile on that frosty, cold face of his.

"You don't get to choose. This is all I have in your size."

"I think I can wear one of your dress shirts," He Yu said.

Xie Qingcheng crossed his arms and leaned back against the ladder of the bunk bed as he looked down at him loftily. "Little devil, my dress shirts are too big for you."

He Yu was silent.

"Don't want it? Then you'll have to walk out naked."

He Yu still said nothing.

Outside, the rain continued to fall, its pitter-pattering becoming the background music for that bygone conversation...

The firefighters gradually contained the fire at Cheng Kang Psychiatric Hospital. They continued their efforts while the police officers busied themselves with the investigation. Xie Qingcheng and He Yu exchanged a glance, seeing reflections of the past in each other's eyes.

"Back then, you even told me that I wasn't losing out on anything, that there was even a piece of candy in the pockets of that princess dress," said He Yu. "You suggested that I check the pockets and consider it a form of psychological reparation. But I said what you gave me was poison and that I wouldn't eat it at all. Looking back on it now, you really were evil."

"...I don't remember anymore," Xie Qingcheng replied. He turned to leave.

"You're full of crap." He Yu reached up to block his way, setting his hand on the large tree behind Xie Qingcheng. He narrowed his eyes. "You don't remember? If you don't remember, then why did you mention Cinderella's candy when you had me rifle through your pockets for your phone as Jiang Lanpei held you hostage?"

Xie Qingcheng didn't back down at all. With a cold expression, he answered, "A coincidence."

He Yu's anger flared. He felt like Xie Qingcheng had gotten off far too easily when he had taken him back to his dorm and given him a T-shirt to wear. Now, it seemed like even if he'd had to use the one-hour delivery option, he should've bought him a wedding dress instead—the sexy kind complete with a lace garter belt. He should've gotten him stockings too, and if he refused, then he could've handcuffed him, tossed him onto the bed, and forced it onto him! Anything less than that wouldn't be enough to humiliate Xie Qingcheng; after all, he had no shame!

"You don't remember, huh?" He Yu lowered his head, warning Xie Qingcheng, "Then you'd better be careful not to get yourself so wet in the future..." He Yu's gaze slid over Xie Qingcheng's eyes as he added softly, "Otherwise, the next thing I give you to wear might not be an old T-shirt."

Xie Qingcheng lifted his hand and patted He Yu on the face. "Don't worry, little devil. You won't get that chance. Even if I'm soaked through, I can still walk out naked."

"Naked?" A police officer walked over. Upon seeing that it was the two lunatics who had run into the fire earlier, he immediately said, "You can't go in there naked again! That's so dangerous! No, wait, I mean, even if you're not naked, you can't go in there..."

He Yu smiled warmly, his eyes gentle. "Yeah, I was just telling him. That's so dangerous, right, Xie-ge?"

"Why are you scolding him? Didn't your ge run into the fire because you rushed in first?" The little police officer stared at them. "Ah, forget it. Have your wounds been treated? If so, then please come back to the station with us. We have much to sort out tonight."

Due to the grave severity of the case and the amount of people involved, the police had a long night ahead of interviewing and recording the testimonies of each person in writing. As there were far too many people to handle at once, the witnesses were divided into groups to be taken back to the station in police cars. Several break rooms at the station were also set up as makeshift bedrooms so that those who had yet to be questioned about the chaos could spend the night.

Xie Xue arrived shortly after Xie Qingcheng and the others. Since she was a woman, she was assigned to a room with a female nurse while He Yu and Xie Qingcheng were given the room next door.

Xie Xue had already calmed down quite a bit before she went to take a nap. Due to the fact that she'd been unconscious the whole time and didn't see much blood, she wasn't too shaken up and was instead comforting that panic-stricken nurse.

"It's all right now. You'll certainly have good fortune after surviving such a catastrophe. Let's get some rest now, and the officers will come and get us when it's our turn."

"I can't fall asleep, waaah..." the nurse whimpered.

"I can sing a song to help you sleep. Drop, drop, drop the hanky..."

"Aaahhh. Don't sing that hellish song!!"

Oblivious to why the nurse had such a reaction, Xie Xue said, "I don't know why this song appeared in my head. I feel like when I was passed out, someone kept singing it next to me... Anyway, I'll switch to another song. In the blue, blue sky and the Milky Way, there's a little white ship..." Xie Xue began to softly chant another children's song.

The nurse was visibly unsettled.

Dismayed and confused by the nurse's reaction, Xie Xue apologized. "I'm a little out of it. I'm sorry, I'm sorry. Okay, let me tell you a joke instead."

Meanwhile, Xie Qingcheng and He Yu arrived at their break room.

"You two can sleep here. The conditions aren't very good, but you'll have to make do. Come find us any time if you need anything. Someone will come for you when it's your turn," the little police officer explained in a hurry before he turned on his heel and left. There were still plenty more witnesses to sort out.

Together, Xie Qingcheng and He Yu pushed open the doors only to freeze upon seeing the layout.

This really was a break room that had been rearranged at the last minute...

There was only a single fucking sofa bed inside.

How were they supposed to sleep?!

15

WE SLEPT ON THE SAME SOFA BED

THE TWO OF THEM STOOD in the narrow break room. The space had just been cleared out, leaving behind little more than an old sofa bed and a chair to place their clothes. The furnishings were reminiscent of a "massage parlor" that authorities needed to investigate. It was unnerving.

Both men looked around the room in dismayed silence.

He Yu tossed down his phone carelessly, turned to Xie Qingcheng, and said, "Why don't you go ahead and sleep? You're getting old."

Xie Qingcheng's face darkened. "Am I already at the stage where I need others to give up their seats and beds to me?"

He Yu had been weary for some time by now, so he didn't feel like wasting his energy arguing with Xie Qingcheng. "Whatever. This sofa bed isn't that small, and I'm a quiet sleeper. Do you mind?"

This could be taken as the young man making a graceful concession.

He Yu had never slept with anyone else before; in his memories, a bed was just a place to rest. But Xie Qingcheng wasn't the same. To a man who'd once been married, sharing a bed with someone else would always feel a bit strange.

Xie Qingcheng furrowed his brow slightly. "I'm not tired. I'll just sit."

But his face was pale, and even if he'd been forcing himself to bear with the exhaustion this whole time, his features nevertheless revealed a hint of fatigue.

"I'm not gonna eat you, so what're you so afraid of?" He Yu shot back. "Scared I'll go crazy in the middle of the night and kill you?"

"...What nonsense are you spouting?" Xie Qingcheng retorted.

This mentally ill young man was surprisingly sensitive.

However, Xie Qingcheng really was bone-tired. Even a wild beast would have run out of strength after such a rough day. Without the energy to squabble with He Yu any longer, he gave in with a sigh and said, "Fine, let's sleep."

He lay down on the sofa bed, resting on his side and facing the wall. After a while, he felt the other side of the bed dip slightly, then heard He Yu settle down a short distance behind him.

Xie Qingcheng still felt a bit uneasy. He abhorred having someone else sleep on the other side of his bed, especially someone like He Yu, who was young and had a high body temperature. Even if they weren't especially close to each other, Xie Qingcheng was still fully aware of his heat and scent in this narrow little room. Once silence settled over them, he could even hear the faint sound of He Yu's breathing.

Furthermore, Xie Qingcheng's instinct as a patriarch and protector kept him alert and unable to truly relax. When he was very young, it was Xie Xue who had slept by his side; later, it was Li Ruoqiu. The only ones he had been able to allow into his territory—barely so, at that—were the women who were dependent on him.

But the aura of an eighteen- or nineteen-year-old boy wasn't the same. Those male hormones put Xie Qingcheng on edge. The sense of encroachment He Yu gave him was too strong and foreign to him.

So, he closed his eyes and furrowed his brow, shifting a bit closer to the edge of the bed.

Just a bit closer.

Just...

"If you keep moving that way, you'll be sleeping on the ground," a cool voice suddenly said from behind him.

He Yu hoisted himself to a sitting position without warning. Before Xie Qingcheng could react, He Yu was already leaning over him, half of his body hovering over his, close enough to touch. The boy's unique scent crashed over Xie Qingcheng in a forceful and impetuous wave.

Xie Qingcheng opened his peach-blossom eyes. "What are you doing?"

He Yu misunderstood Xie Qingcheng's motivations, believing he was moving away out of disgust for his illness. And so, feeling a bit malicious, he leaned even lower, pressing his lips to the side of Xie Qingcheng's neck and letting the tips of his teeth brush against the older man's skin as he spoke quietly. "My illness is acting up. I want to kill you to shut you up. Are you going to run?"

Like hell was his illness acting up!

He Yu didn't act like this at all when it did. Xie Qingcheng could see right through him and knew it was little more than an adult tantrum, so he said in a very cold and hard tone of voice, "Get off me first."

"I'm getting my phone." Not only did He Yu refuse to get off, he leaned down even lower.

Regardless of whether he was really reaching for his phone or not, Xie Qingcheng couldn't take this intrusion into his personal space. He Yu was far too close to him, and for a moment, his every breath was filled with the heat emanating from the other man's body.

Xie Qingcheng turned his face away to endure it, but before long the discomfort became too much to handle. He sat up abruptly and grabbed He Yu's wrists. His back arched like a cheetah's, and his shoulder blades spread like a butterfly's wings as he forcefully flipped over and pinned He Yu under him.

"Why are you throwing yourself at me?" He Yu asked in bemusement. "Aren't you scared of me?"

"Why would I be scared of you? I'm teaching you how to behave."

He Yu simply stared in response for a while before sighing softly. "Ge, you're hurting me, you know?" It had occurred to He Yu that Xie Qingcheng's aversion had only stemmed from the fact that he was a man, not his mental illness, and so, he stopped resisting Xie Qingcheng's tight grip on his wrists.

In the stillness, Xie Qingcheng could see himself reflected in the younger man's unnervingly apathetic gaze as he spoke in an equally apathetic voice. "Okay, okay. I'll behave." He Yu said. "Could I please trouble you to hand me my phone?"

Xie Qingcheng didn't take well to being coerced at all, but he found it much less intolerable when he was the one looking down at the other young man. He didn't like feeling invaded and suppressed by any other member of his own sex, but the closeness didn't bother him so much when he was in control.

With He Yu sufficiently subdued, Xie Qingcheng got up to search the area off to the side of the sofa bed and, sure enough, found He Yu's phone. He'd probably carelessly left it there earlier.

He handed the phone to him.

"Thank you." He Yu took it and tilted his head back as he swiped the screen. He remarked casually, "Doctor Xie, we may both be men, but we're secure in our sexuality, wouldn't you agree? So, why are you so nervous? Never shared a bed with a man before?"

"I'm used to being alone," Xie Qingcheng replied, his expression and voice bitterly cold.

He Yu laughed. He was still looking at his phone, and the luminescent glow of the screen made his long eyelashes appear to be covered with a layer of frost. They trembled faintly with each breath he took. In a mocking tone, He Yu asked, "Then, did you and Saozi sleep in separate beds?"

Despite the apathetic front, Xie Qingcheng knew that He Yu was feeling a kind of empathetic pain after seeing those mentally ill patients today, souring his disposition. However, no matter how bad of a mood He Yu was in, Xie Qingcheng had no duty or obligation to become the dumping ground for his anger.

Besides, he was hardly in a better frame of mind himself.

Xie Qingcheng glared at He Yu. "I'm going to sleep, so stop disturbing me," he berated the younger man before turning over to lie back down. Unfortunately, Xie Qingcheng found it difficult to sleep. He Yu, on the other hand, hadn't planned on sleeping at all; he was just lying down to get comfortable. He stared at Xie Qingcheng in silence for a while, wondering how this person could be so paternalistic and give him a tongue-lashing as though he were scolding his own son.

The notion that, given the opportunity, he really ought to get a wedding dress and force Xie Qingcheng into it appealed to He Yu more than ever. If Xie Qingcheng wore it, then he could forget about lifting his head in front of He Yu again for the rest of his life.

With this thought and plenty of time to kill, He Yu opened an online shopping site on his phone and typed "wedding dress" into the search bar.

The styles that popped up were all perfectly normal, each one extremely beautiful and dignified; however, he felt that none of them could achieve the best effect for what he had in mind.

After pondering for a spell, He Yu glanced up at Xie Qingcheng's back. Then, he looked back down and added another keyword.

"Humiliation."

This time, the search results were a gold mine.

Black silk garters, white silk garters, lacy silk garters, bondage kink, sheer skirts... Everything you could think of—a complete collection in a countless variety of styles—was right at his fingertips. As He Yu swiped through page after page, his eyebrows inched higher and higher.

It was quite interesting; the human imagination truly was boundless when it came to seeking pleasure.

Every time he found an interesting item, he would hold his phone up to Xie Qingcheng's back, fantasizing about how Xie Qingcheng would look if he were to one day succumb to He Yu's control and get tied up and stuffed into this kind of attire. As he envisioned Xie Qingcheng's humiliation at his hands, He Yu's weariness faded away without a trace.

When he was young, he had been rather afraid of Xie Qingcheng, but it was simply the nature of boys that the more loftily and oppressively a mountain towered over them when they were young, the more they'd want to conquer it when they grew up. Only once they stood upon those snow-capped peaks and stood even higher than the summit would the young man feel that they had truly matured, that they had finally taken hold of the prize they had long been seeking.

That was why He Yu felt that butting heads with Xie Qingcheng was something that could bring him the most exquisite pleasure.

Perhaps it was because he had become too enthralled by his scrolling, but with a slip of the finger, He Yu ended up accidentally tapping on a livestream link—incredibly, he had forgotten to put his phone to silent mode.

In this cramped little break room with an area of less than ten square meters, the girlishly coy voice of a livestreamer rang out. "This sexy wedding dress really is incredibly gorgeous. If you wear this on your wedding night, your husband will definitely lose control..."

He Yu quickly turned off the sound and froze, his eyes on Xie Qingcheng's back.

It was dead silent in the room.

He Yu hoped dearly that Xie Qingcheng had already fallen asleep.

But his hopes were not answered. Xie Qingcheng turned over and looked at him with an exceedingly frigid gaze that was exactly the same as the past; like a sharp blade, as if he wanted to cut He Yu's heart open.

"What are you doing?"

There was no point in hiding it. Smiling slightly, he politely replied, "Browsing shopping websites."

"You're buying a wedding dress?"

"What, I'm not even allowed to look?"

Incredibly annoyed at the mere sight of him, Xie Qingcheng sneered as he asked, "Why are you looking at wedding dresses? Who's gonna wear it?"

He Yu's eyes shifted around, as though searching his mind for just the right answer. *I wonder if he would just kill me immediately if I told him "you are"?*

A murder in the police station was a terrible idea—the civil servants would be terribly inconvenienced.

So, suppressing his mischievous inclinations, He Yu simply said, "I believe this has nothing to do with you."

"Turn off your phone," Xie Qingcheng ordered with an ice-cold expression. "Stop looking at this trivial nonsense. You're so young and haven't even started dating yet, so what's the point of looking at such things?"

He Yu surprisingly found himself feeling a little upset at Xie Qingcheng's incredibly frosty tone and his disgust-flecked eyes.

What right did he have to interfere so much in his business?

What was their relationship, anyway?

He Yu's urge to provoke him welled up again.

He took a moment to stare at those peach-blossom eyes in silence before letting a mocking, meaningful smile slowly spread across his lips. "There's no need for you to worry about me, Xie-ge. I'll be dating very soon."

He paused briefly, then continued, "When the time comes, I'll ask you for guidance. You're older than I am and have a lot of experience, seeing as you've gotten married and even divorced already. With all that experience, you're sure to know how to treat girls well too. So, Professor Xie, when I come to ask you for advice, please remember to give me lots of tips."

He Yu's eyes flashed as the roguishness and malice in his smile intensified.

"But I'm curious about one thing. You and Li-sao were married for so long, so why didn't she have any kids?"

Xie Qingcheng's expression clouded over. He didn't reply.

This schoolboy, who pretended to be cultured and refined, and practiced great self-restraint in front of everyone but Xie Qingcheng, was, in this moment, a malicious beast that had returned to his cave and stripped off his human mask.

He Yu cast his almond eyes lazily downward, and, with a hint of ridicule in his voice, asked, "Was it because you couldn't get it up?"

Silence filled the room for but a few seconds before Xie Qingcheng grabbed the brat by his collar and threw him heavily onto the ground, followed by his pillow and blanket, burying He Yu in bedding.

Although He Yu wanted to provoke him, he hadn't expected he'd elicit such a huge reaction. Xie Qingcheng seethed. Sure, he wasn't keen on sex—quite indifferent to it, actually—but that little brat was spouting nothing but nonsense!

"He Yu." Xie Qingcheng stared at him, his gaze and voice peppered with shards of ice. "Just how fucking immature are you?"

He got up, adjusted his clothes, and left the break room, the loud slamming of the door betraying his anger.

Xie Qingcheng stepped out onto the station's portico, lit a cigarette, and took a deep drag.

He despised the mere mention of Li Ruoqiu's name, but He Yu always knew just how to twist a knife into his weak point for maximum pain.

Xie Qingcheng leaned against a pillar and took another long drag. His clothes and hair were in disarray, a far cry from his usual meticulous and stern appearance. As dark clouds closed in again, the distance between his eyebrows narrowed above his bloodshot eyes. He bit the cigarette filter with rough, chapped lips, as he stared vacantly into the night, a picture of decadent beauty despite his disheveled state.

The police officers who passed by couldn't help but steal glances at him. After a while, a young male officer dashed over and handed him a cold can of beer. "Comrade, one of those days, huh? I get it. What happened tonight was—eh? Xie-ge? Why're you here?"

Suddenly recognizing the voice, Xie Qingcheng snapped out of his brooding and looked over at the police officer.

"...Chen Man?"

Chen Man was Xie Qingcheng's acquaintance through his older brother, who had also been a police officer and a mentee of

Xie Qingcheng's father, no less. Unfortunately, Chen Man's brother had died in the line of duty.

Chen Man followed in his brother's footsteps by attending university to become a police officer and was now slowly rising through the ranks. Xie Qingcheng had even bumped into him on several occasions at the local police station before now.

Chen Man's name was actually Chen Yan, but because he always did things a little too quickly, his family gave him the nickname "Chen Man"[25] in hopes that he would slow down a bit. Over time, everyone came to prefer calling him Chen Man, and the name stuck.

"Xie-ge, how did you get pulled into this case?"

"It's a long story." Xie Qingcheng sighed with the cigarette still in his mouth and opened his beer. He bowed slightly in Chen Man's direction as a gesture of thanks, then went back to leaning glumly against the pillar and gazing into the darkness.

Chen Man stood silently with him for a while, but realizing that he had no intention of elaborating, decided to change the subject. "Xie-ge, aren't you cold? Why don't I give you my jacket…"

"It's fine, I'm not cold. How could I be on such a hot day?"

"According to the calendar, it's already fall…"

Xie Qingcheng was already quite vexed, and this kid blabbering on about nothing of consequence wasn't doing his mood any favors. "You can go," he said without looking back at Chen Man. "I don't really have anything to talk about. Thanks for the beer, though."

"You're sure you're okay?"

"I'm fine."

It was only then that Chen Man reluctantly walked away, glancing back every couple of steps.

---

25   *"Man" (慢) means "slow."*

"Wait," Xie Qingcheng suddenly called after him. "Come back."

Chen Man rushed back over without hesitation.

To his surprise, Xie Qingcheng grabbed him by his police uniform. Given their familiarity, Xie Qingcheng wasn't too concerned about politeness as he reached into Chen Man's pocket and fished out a pack of cigarettes.

Although Chen Man didn't smoke, most of the other officers did, so it was convenient to have a pack of cigarettes in his pocket while working with different units.

Cigarettes successfully acquired, Xie Qingcheng straightened out Chen Man's uniform and patted him on the shoulder. "*Now* you can go."

"...Oh. Don't smoke too much, Ge. You've been smoking way too much these days."

Chen Man's concern fell on deaf ears as Xie Qingcheng simply leaned back against the pillar to finish his cigarette, taking no notice as the police officer took his leave.

His reprieve would not last long, however, as the sound of footsteps came from behind him once again.

"Don't you have work to do tonight?" Xie Qingcheng growled without a hint of patience.

"What work do *I* have to do?"

It was not Chen Man's voice. Xie Qingcheng turned his head to confirm that his latest disturbance was He Yu. Seeing that it was indeed him, Xie Qingcheng's expression became even more ruthlessly cold, and he looked away again without a word.

He Yu quietly stood next to him for a while before reluctantly breaking the silence. "Doctor Xie, I'm sorry. About you and Saozi, I'm very sorry..."

This was the final straw for Xie Qingcheng. He Yu was truly far too tactless and had pushed him past his limit. Xie Qingcheng was dispassionate by nature on the surface, but that only meant that he was constantly holding back.

This apology felt no different than mere mockery, which only served to enrage him even more. He could deal with He Yu's impudence, but his anger flared the moment he heard He Yu apologize in this pretentiously fake manner. He Yu's lack of sincerity was just like his parents, people who treated personal and business relationships the same, who just went through the motions for the sake of harmony. It was as if his very apology were modeled on *The Capitalist Manifesto*.

That apology cracked his stoic mask, and his pent-up irritation rushed into his heart, propelling his arm to throw the beer Chen Man had given him in He Yu's face.

"What are you apologizing for?" The beer dripped from He Yu's hair and slid down his face, the liquid bone-chillingly cold. But Xie Qingcheng's tone was even colder. "There wasn't a shred of sincerity in your apology. That pretense of yours may serve you in front of others, but it's useless on me. Don't you realize I know all your tricks?"

He Yu didn't utter a word. This was the first time someone had ever dared to throw a drink in his face. He was still processing it when Xie Qingcheng continued his verbal attack.

"Also, stop saying 'Saozi.' We've already divorced, and even if we hadn't, I'm not your biological brother, so she wouldn't be your Saozi. Just the sight of you irritates me right now, so don't let me see you again tonight!"

He Yu considered Xie Qingcheng's words for a short while, then said, with deliberate emphasis, "Then what do you want me to do? Take back what I said?"

He Yu was truly unhinged. Droplets of beer rolled down between his dark brows as a smile slowly formed on his lips, a smile so gentle it was terrifying. "Or... Perhaps I should get down on my knees and say sorry? In order to show my sincerity, that is."

"You don't need to do anything." Xie Qingcheng stiffly crushed the empty beer can in his hand as he spoke. He stared into He Yu's eyes as he tossed the can into the rubbish bin.

"He Yu, just remember: even though I'm a failure when it comes to my love life, you're in no position to mock me. With the deceitful and sick way you treat others, no one is ever going to sincerely like you either. Didn't you say just now that you're going to tell someone your feelings soon? Just try it and see."

He Yu simply stared back.

"I don't care who it is that you like—if she can stay with you for more than a month, I'll take your fucking surname."

16

BUT WE ARGUED UNTIL WE PARTED WAYS AGAIN

H E YU AND XIE QINGCHENG ignored each other throughout the rest of the investigation process.

When they were released, Xie Qingcheng took the liberty of hailing a taxi for himself and Xie Xue. Xie Xue wanted to wait for He Yu so that they could leave together, but Xie Qingcheng refused outright and shoved her down by the back of her head, stuffing her into the car without a word of explanation.

He Yu simply leaned back quietly against a pillar with his hands clasped behind his back as he watched the scene. He didn't make a sound, nor did he try to force the matter. He looked like a dog that knew it had been abandoned but couldn't chase after its master; this made Xie Xue feel extremely uncomfortable.

"He Yu... Ge, why don't we wait for him..."

"Get in."

"But..."

"Get in!"

"...Then, He Yu? Let me know when you get home, okay?" Xie Xue said weakly.

"Are you done?" Xie Qingcheng snapped. "We're leaving."

Xie Xue wanted to say more, but He Yu quietly shook his head, signaling for her to stop talking.

Once Xie Xue had reluctantly settled down into the car, he merely waved at her, then watched as their car drove away.

Xie Xue sunk into her seat and couldn't help but let out a sigh. "Ge, what's up with you two *this* time?"

Xie Qingcheng didn't feel like responding. He opened the pack of cigarettes he'd pilfered from Chen Man and was just about to light one when he remembered that Xie Xue was behind him in the back seat and stopped. He held the cigarette between his teeth as he rested his elbow against the open window and gazed with a dazed expression at the city nightscape flashing by on the other side of the glass instead.

"Did He Yu mess up and say something wrong and make you angry...?" Xie Xue ventured quietly.

Xie Qingcheng answered her question with stony silence.

"Ge, don't blame him too much. He's a bit volatile at times, but he's still a good person at heart. I heard that this time, if it weren't for him, you two wouldn't have realized I was missing in time and rushed over and things might have been a lot worse. He—"

"He what?" Xie Qingcheng snapped. He held the cigarette between his fingers and continued in a condemning tone. "I told you to stay away from him, so why're you hanging out with him all the time?"

Xie Xue felt a bit wronged too. "But he's a good person, he treats me nicely, and he's respectful to you..."

Xie Qingcheng was so disgusted he couldn't even speak.

Respectful.

Like *hell*, he was respectful!

It was and had always been just him putting on an act in front of others. But even so, he couldn't tell Xie Xue about He Yu's disease. Xie Xue only ever saw He Yu's usual virtuously elegant and gentlemanly disguise. Even if he were to speak of the indignities he had suffered at He Yu's hands, even his own sister wouldn't be able to believe him. He could only bite his tongue and bear it.

"Ge..."

"Shut up!"

Xie Xue froze.

This was what always happened with family. The moment after surviving a calamity, everyone would think, *We'll never fight again for the rest of our lives! We'll live happily together and talk to each other properly by communicating gently.*

But the heightened tender affections brought upon by the shock of traumatic events were no more than a buff,[26] and once they wore off, the disciplinarian would go back to disciplining while the person receiving the discipline would go back to being disciplined. Everyone would return to their familiar roles, and exchanges would be just as foul-mouthed as ever.

It really fucking was just a temporary panacea.

Xie Xue felt mistreated, but there was nothing she could do. Who made him her elder brother?

Ah, whatever, whatever—if she didn't coddle him, then who would? She would just have to indulge that parental temper of his.

At this thought, she crossed her arms and somewhat exasperatedly pursed her lips. She didn't know why her brother kept telling her to keep her distance from such a talented, refined, and morally virtuous boy like He Yu; it had reached the point where it seemed as if her brother actually had some major objection to him, but what could it be? It was truly baffling...

After a while, Xie Xue spoke up again. "Oh, by the way..."

---

26 Slang used in gaming to describe temporary positive status effects on characters.

Xie Qingcheng didn't bother acknowledging her, but Xie Xue knew that her brother's silence meant: *"If you have something to say, spit it the fuck out."*

Thus, she cautiously said, "Earlier when I was resting, he...called... and asked what happened, I..."

Xie Qingcheng didn't ask who "he" was, as though both siblings had tacitly agreed to refer to *"him"* as such.

"What did you say to him?" Xie Qingcheng asked.

"What else could I say? I just said everything was fine. I didn't talk to him very much."

Xie Xue paused for a moment. "Ge, are you feeling better now?"

"Do you think he would make me feel better?"

Out of options, Xie Xue could only nudge closer and stick her head out from the backseat. She pawed at the edge of the passenger seat like a kitten, as though trying to catch her brother's attention with sheer cuteness. "Then look at me, look at how I'm perfectly fine—doesn't it make you feel better?"

"...In the future, don't go to such dangerous places by yourself," said Xie Qingcheng. His tone had finally softened slightly.

"All right, I'll be careful..." Xie Xue hastily replied as the car sped off in a swirl of dust.

The next day, news about the Cheng Kang Psychiatric Hospital was plastered on the front pages of the newspapers.

The article drew on the statements that all the people who had been forced onto the rooftop had given to the police. It described in detail how this case of murder and arson, prompted by the flare-up of Jiang Lanpei's illness, was actually the story of a woman who lived a life worse than death during her nearly twenty years of imprisonment. But unfortunately, Liang Jicheng was already dead, Liang Zhongkang had passed away before his younger brother, and the other higher-ups who might have known about the details of the case were deceased as well—several of them having died in this very inferno.

It was as though the fire of vengeance lit by Jiang Lanpei had taken on a life of its own and swallowed up everyone who had ever been involved in this crime.

Just as He Yu predicted, the papers chose Jiang Lanpei's ugliest photo to print onto their pages. Even so, she still looked very stunning in it—the now-dead woman gazed directly out of the newsprint, her expression showing a hint of resolve, yet one could also see a trace of bewilderment...

Beneath her photo, the reporter wrote: "There is a possibility that Jiang Lanpei is not her real name as such information was processed before digital recordkeeping began. The police are currently conducting genetic testing on Ms. Jiang's remains, but due to the length of time that has elapsed, results may be inconclusive. If members of the general public have any leads, please contact the relevant department at the number below."

Inside his villa, He Yu folded the newspaper shut.

Recently, the topic of psychiatric hospitals and the mentally ill had become the object of public scrutiny. From greasy uncles to naive little girls, everyone discussed it with an air of unflappable logic, as though they were all experts in sociology or medicine.

In most people's eyes, they had become accustomed to labeling the mentally ill as "them," with their natural antithesis being "us." It was impossible for "them" to become "us," no matter how pitiful they were.

But how did mental illnesses arise then?

He Yu remembered something Xie Qingcheng had once said to him.

"The vast majority of mental illnesses are normal people's responses to abnormal circumstances. Obsessive-compulsive disorder, major depressive disorder, bipolar disorder... In these patients' daily lives, there is certain to be one or more abnormal situations that place them under great pressure. For example, bullying at school or cyberbullying, sexual violence against women, or social inequality—these kinds of abnormal situations, that is, the main culprits dealing the greatest damage to their psyches, very ironically, nearly all originate from their families, from their workplace, from society—they originate from 'us.'

"I think that mentally ill people shouldn't be locked away unless there is no other alternative. Rather, they should be allowed to roam freely in the world just like any normal person. This is how they can heal their state of mind and become one of us again. Cages should be reserved for criminals, not for patients who have already suffered so much."

He Yu didn't like Xie Qingcheng, but he agreed with him on this point.

The reason why he allowed Xie Qingcheng to stay by his side for so long was precisely due to this perspective. It made He Yu feel that, at the very least, Xie Qingcheng regarded him as a living, breathing human being.

Thus, after what happened yesterday, upon realizing that he had gone too far and offended Xie Qingcheng, he had felt that he should at least apologize to him.

But who could have known that Xie Qingcheng's familiarity with his disguise would actually lead him to believe that even his apologies were false and end up splashing beer all over his face?

Merely thinking of it filled He Yu with sorrow. He closed his eyes, determined to shake the humiliating feeling of the icy droplets of liquid streaming down his face that still lingered.

Forget it... Don't think about it anymore.

At least Xie Qingcheng had only sworn at him and thrown a drink in his face—others would treat a mentally ill person like him like an animal. If his family had put him in a loony bin like Cheng Kang, his illness might've long since gotten much worse.

Jiang Lanpei had stayed there for twenty years. Did her illness ultimately improve or worsen? Perhaps she wouldn't have ended up taking this path in the first place if she'd never been admitted.

Lao-Zhao knocked on the door of He Yu's room. Upon receiving permission, he entered with the little yellow dog trailing behind him, cautiously wagging its tail. "Young Master He, your instructions have all been carried out." He proceeded to give He Yu a status update on several matters. "I've already given Homeless Services a heads up and explained your intentions to Executive He. Arrangements have been made for Zhuang Zhiqiang to stay at our rehabilitation center for the time being. He won't be sent to Wanping."

"Good. Thanks for all your hard work," said He Yu.

Zhuang Zhiqiang was also pretty damn fortunate—his room was on a lower floor, and he had been quickly rescued by the firefighters. If nothing else, they'd been brought together through fateful coincidence. So, He Yu had no intention of abandoning him after what they had gone through.

Besides, Xie Xue would definitely worry about him.

All the people who had been involved in the massive fire at Cheng Kang received about a week of vacation to recover both mentally and physically. With this experience behind them, they now had to look to the future. Seeing as they had escaped the fires of purgatory, they really ought to live their lives happily and peacefully from now on, including He Yu.

He Yu let his mind drift back to that night, out on the portico.

Didn't Xie Qingcheng say no one would be willing to be with him? Didn't Xie Qingcheng say that if anyone could stay with him for more than a month, he would take his surname?

Very well. He would just *have* to get together with Xie Xue then.

He wanted to be with the person closest to Xie Qingcheng, to steal his younger sister away from his side—and when the time came, Xie Qingcheng would have to live up to his word and change his name to He Qingcheng. He Yu could only imagine how that man would feel when that happened.

The thought delighted him.

That insufferably arrogant and frigidly stern face...would it reveal an expression that he'd never seen before?

After a week of rest, He Yu returned to the university campus with renewed motivation.

He was ready to make a fool of Xie Qingcheng and confess his feelings to Xie Qingcheng's most beloved little sister.

The outdoor lamps on the villa's balcony were just bright enough to attract a few hovering insects searching for light. Droplets of moisture clung to the glass of the lamp like a sheen of cold sweat, and an armchair that had its back facing the grand doors of the balcony was enveloped in its dim glow.

Someone was sitting in the armchair.

The subordinate who pushed open the door to enter could only see a sliver of the person's hidden silhouette, their elbow lying slanted against the armrest.

"Is that so? There was an instance of patients successfully escaping in an extremely short period of time?"

"Yes, Duan-laoban."

"Fascinating..." Duan-laoban let out a soft chuckle from the chair. "The power of teamwork? Cheng Kang is a psychiatric hospital, not a nursery for teaching little children manners and conduct. This really is quite unusual."

Cold sweat beaded on the subordinate's forehead. "Duan-laoban, Cheng Kang's surveillance was decrepit to begin with, and no equipment survived the fire. We want to extract footage from the incident, but it's really..."

"I didn't hope to extract useful footage from that squandering Liang Jicheng's death in the first place."

Duan-laoban paused.

"Has there been news from the police department?"

"There has, actually. A few patients said that a fellow patient gave them the keys and told them to help each other open the doors, but that was the extent of their information."

Duan-laoban scoffed quietly. "Even if you gave them keys and told them to open doors, would they listen?"

Silence answered him.

"There was a blazing inferno," Duan-laoban continued. "It was a critical moment between life and death."

The subordinate shivered. "Duan-laoban, do you mean to say..."

The man in the armchair didn't speak again. The dim light illuminated the scrap of paper he'd carelessly tossed before him.

Two words written on top, circled, and punctuated with a question mark. *Blood toxin?*

17

HE AND I WERE
TRAPPED TOGETHER

S URVIVING THE INCIDENT at the Cheng Kang Psychiatric
Hospital made Xie Xue into a legendary teacher at the school.
When she returned to the lectern, not a single student
arrived late or left early without a legitimate excuse. The classroom
was jam-packed every lecture, with students from other classes attending the lesson if they weren't busy—even the dreamboat from
the fourth-year drama class stumbled in to take a good look at her.
All the students wanted to see this lucky duck who had supposedly
escaped the clutches of a deranged and violent murderer.

Even more outlandishly, there were those who believed that if
you printed out Xie Xue's photo and hung it on your dormitory
door, the entire dorm would be sure to pass their classes.

But Xie Xue was oblivious to all of this. She believed with great
confidence that the reason behind the current unprecedented surge
in popularity of her screenwriting and directing classes must be
because her teaching methods were extremely interesting.

"Aiya, I really must be a genius educator who teaches in the best
of ways," Xie Xue said gleefully to He Yu, who had come to deliver
the class's homework to her. "Oh yeah, He Yu, are you feeling better? The school wants to give you an award—granted, the way you
rashly charged into the fire shouldn't be imitated, but the university
president said that your selfless act of courage is commendable..."

He Yu smiled. "I'm much better. That award is mostly for my parents, anyway."

He Jiwei and Lü Zhishu had found out about what happened, but they made no special efforts to return home upon hearing that their son wasn't severely hurt. It was a surprising decision for Lü Zhishu in particular—she always dealt with her clients with a smile, cracking one joke after another. Those who weren't familiar with her would get the impression that she was very charming and placed great value on family and life.

But people more familiar with her like Xie Xue and Xie Qingcheng knew all too well that her humor and kindness were a facade. As far as she was concerned, her business away from home was naturally far more important than her eldest son who had merely experienced a somewhat distressing ordeal. She simply called the school's administration and told the board of directors to pressure the school into consoling He Yu properly.

Therefore, He Yu didn't care one bit about these frivolous awards.

Xie Xue didn't know what to say. She felt pity for He Yu, but not wanting to pry into He Yu's family matters, she hurriedly switched to a more lighthearted topic. "Uh, umm, so, the school's hosting a campus exploration event on Friday. You've been through so much recently, so this is a perfect opportunity to unwind and have fun with your classmates. Why don't you join?"

"I can't. I have something I need to do on Friday."

"I see..." Xie Xue's face fell. "That's too bad. I was going to ask you to keep me company."

He Yu's aloof expression perked up a bit as he looked at her, asking, "You're going?"

"I have to." Xie Xue took out a giant, furry fox head from behind her desk and, after digging around some more, fished out a snowy white tail as well. "Look at this."

"What is this?"

"A costume for a nine-tailed fox mascot. The school organized it so that every department needs to select one teacher to wear a costume and welcome guests. My luck is so rotten, not only did I get volunteered as tribute, but I even drew the most boring activity venue."

"Isn't it always that those who are dumb at least have good luck? So how come you not only have a low IQ but shitty luck too?"

Xie Xue's face crumpled. She didn't even feel like dealing with He Yu's snide remarks.

He Yu sighed and then asked, "Where are you being banished to?"

"The newly revamped Neverland Island in the central lake. You know, that damned place might be called Neverland, but seriously? Even though the students strung up some lanterns and projected an image of the night sky over that useless place, it's pretty much the same as it has always been. Plus, it's so far away... Ah, the whole thing was supposed to be canceled this year, but the dean thinks of this event as a tradition, so we still kept it in the end..."

She dejectedly tossed the fox head and tail away and sprawled out limply in her chair.

He Yu picked up the furry, snow-white tail she'd tossed onto the desk and looked at it thoughtfully for a moment. He didn't say anything, but an idea popped into his head.

Friday arrived in the blink of an eye.

The buttery aroma of warm sponge cake wafted through the bakery classroom. He Yu carefully put the finishing touches on the freshly made cake, covered it with a pure-white sheet of wax paper, and packed it into a box. Then, he diligently tidied up the bakery classroom that one of the teachers had allowed him to use and walked out.

The campus exploration event was boisterously underway.

He "I don't have time to hang out" Yu took a leisurely stroll around the campus with one hand carrying Xie Xue's favorite whipped cream mango mousse cake and the other tucked into his pocket.

He checked out a world travel-themed maze and won a small stuffed toy dog—a white Samoyed that looked like a smiling angel with round, dark-chocolatey eyes that gazed up at him as he hugged it in the crook of his arm.

"Look!"

A group of schoolgirls were standing nearby with their little fists pressed to their mouths. Fragments of their conversation floated over to He Yu's ears from time to time.

"It's He Yu-xuezhang! The xuezhang who rescued his teacher from the fire! He's even hotter in person than in his pictures!"

"What xuezhang, you silly girl. He's a xuedi!! He's in the 1001 screenwriting and directing class!"

"Huh? But he's so tall...he looks like he's gotta be almost 180 centimeters. Wait, no. He has to be like 190..."

"I have a friend in his class who said that He Yu's family is super wealthy—and he's gorgeous and has perfect grades to boot."

"Isn't that just like Wei Dongheng-xuezhang?"

"Forget it, Wei Dongheng doesn't behave like a man at all. He's so full of himself and prettier than a flower, yet you still wanna call him 'xuezhang'? You might as well call him 'xuejie' instead. He's such a show-off, flaunting his family's wealth, and clearly spoiled rotten. Last week, the prettiest girl in the Class 5 drama course confessed to him, and do you know what he said?"

"What?"

"You? Why don't you look in the mirror—want me to send you a set of skincare products?"

The first girl couldn't muster a reply to this.

"But He Yu's not like that. He has such an easygoing personality and is so well mannered, he won't even raise his voice at people. Heck, he even risked his life to save Xie-laoshi! Where can you even find such a nice boy?"

Hearing them talk about him like this, He Yu gave them a little smile. The schoolgirls quietly squealed "he heard us!" and then immediately scattered into the distance in embarrassment.

In his usual gentle and refined manner, He Yu held back a second smile as he watched them go, his gaze darkening. *Xie Qingcheng should really get a load of this.*

How could anyone not like him?

He didn't actually have any interest in these schoolgirls. But that person...

That person was the only one he wanted.

The phone in his pocket buzzed, breaking him out of his thoughts. He Yu checked the message.

"He-laoban, you really want me to chop down the rope bridge?"

It had come from a second-year outdoor recreation club member.

Neverland Island lay in the middle of Huzhou University's garden lake; the center of the island had a campsite set up by the university's outdoor recreation club. This message was from the senior who usually managed it.

He Yu replied, *"The rope bridge has gone a long time without repairs. It'd be dangerous to keep it up. Besides, chopping it down would also make it easier for the dean to replace it."*

The second-year texted back, *"But the dean just had workers do a maintenance check at the beginning of the term. Our club is responsible for managing Neverland Island, so if it broke in such a short period of time, our outdoor recreation club would have to pay for it. Even though it's just a small floating bridge, it would cost at least 3,000 RMB to fix..."*

In response to this message, He Yu solved the problem with a few taps on his screen. He imagined the sudden clinking-coins sound effect that his fellow senior's phone was making at this very moment accompanying the message: *"5,000 RMB has been sent to your Alipay account."*

Executive He's message followed right on its heels. *"Please make sure to chop it down thoroughly."* The communication methods of the bourgeoisie were so simple and decisive.

The penniless club member was speechless.

According to the directions on the campus exploration event map, the nine-tailed fox would wait for students at the dock, then accompany those who wanted to take the duck-shaped boats to Neverland Island.

He Yu walked toward the lakeshore covered in withered leaves and dead branches. As expected, he saw Xie Xue wearing the white nine-tailed fox mascot costume and waiting for the students who would come for the boat rides.

The white fox sat quietly in the boat, seemingly unaware that one of its nine tails had fallen onto the water's surface, setting off ripple after ripple from the swaying vessel.

He walked closer to the fox, the fallen leaves crunching softly beneath his feet. The zoned-out nine-tailed fox mascot didn't hear him approaching until he was standing by the shore.

"Xie Xue."

The nine-tailed fox was stunned for a moment before it turned its head to look at him in surprise.

He Yu smiled. "Bet you didn't think I'd come."

He glanced around at their surroundings. "They really sent you far away from everyone. I doubt anyone else would bother coming out here, so if I didn't come, you'd be left sitting around here all day."

The nine-tailed fox looked at him in silence, as if it didn't quite agree with what he said.

"Who else do you think would come visit you? Your brother?"

After a pause, He Yu said gently, "Your brother is nearing menopause, and yet he keeps getting forced into matchmaking dates out of his age cohort. He spends all his days so pissed off by those little girls that he needs to drink Women's Soothing Tonic to calm down; he probably doesn't have the time or energy to care about you."

The nine-tailed fox didn't react.

He Yu stepped gracefully onto the boat. "Come on, I'll go with you. To Neverland Island."

A lake on a university campus couldn't be all that big, so even though the island was in the central lake, it took less than two minutes for the two of them to reach that lump of dirt called Neverland.

The island looked as pathetic and deserted as expected. There were a few strings of lanterns hung up just for show and some tent-building materials strewn around the campsite covered in a thick layer of accumulated dust. There were too many mosquitoes out right now, so even though it had already been a month since school started, the outdoor recreation club had yet to organize a single event.

He Yu said, "I'll be your customer. So, where do I get the stamp?"

The nine-tailed fox silently moved its head, gesturing toward a certain direction.

He Yu looked at the full-body fox costume, and his amusement reared its head once more. "It's so hot today, don't you feel stuffy wearing that? Why don't I help you take it off?"

At the sight of him reaching out, the nine-tailed fox took a quick step back, holding its paws up in front of it.

"...You don't want to?"

It nodded.

"Ah, okay, keep wearing it then. Don't come crying to me if it gets too hot."

The nine-tailed fox lowered its snowy paws indifferently and crossed its arms.

He Yu gazed at it. "To be honest, it's pretty cute. If you look like this, Gege will give you full marks on your performance review later."

Once again, silence hung between them.

"Go ahead and lead the way, then," He Yu said.

The stamp was located in the middle of Neverland Island and atop a small, simple desk. The nine-tailed fox silently leaned against a tree and turned its head to gaze off into the distance.

He Yu turned to look at it after getting his stamp. While he found the whole thing amusing, he also felt that the costume's head must be too heavy for Xie Xue. Not to mention, given his predisposition to bullying people, the more Xie Xue didn't want him to remove the headwear, the more he wanted to get it off.

And so, seeing that the nine-tailed fox had turned in a different direction, he found himself seized by a sudden whim. Setting his things on the ground, he walked over silently, and once he was close enough, he grabbed the head abruptly and, with a big smile on his face, pulled up.

"Xie Xue—"

What? How could it be?!

The face covered in disheveled hair that appeared from beneath the headpiece didn't belong to Xie Xue at all! It was a clearly furious Xie Qingcheng!

Both men were at a loss for words.

Professor Xie's mouth opened and shut several times in succession. After pressing his lips tightly together for a while, he pushed his messy fringe out of his eyes and gave a glare that pierced He Yu like a dagger. The tips of his white teeth were just barely visible under his thin lips as he gritted his teeth.

He broke the silence with a terrifyingly chilly voice, "Are you fucking insane?!"

Executive He's expression darkened the moment he saw Xie Qingcheng. "No, but why did you crawl your way into this stupid mascot getup without telling me?"

Xie Qingcheng tossed the headpiece into He Yu's arms and pulled himself out of the costume with a frown. It was truly a rare occasion; the elite Professor Xie was always immaculate, so He Yu could never have imagined that he'd ever be able to see something as wretched as Xie Qingcheng laboriously climbing out of the suit with disheveled hair.

"Why would I tell you? You said so much nonsense the entire way here, when would I even have had the chance? If you're done getting your stamp, then scram."

He Yu stared at him in dissatisfaction. "Where's Xie Xue?"

"She found it too hot and asked me to take her place. Now, who's the one busy with matchmaking dates and needs to drink Women's Soothing Tonic again?"

He Yu didn't reply.

Meeting Xie Qingcheng's incisive, scalpel-like gaze, He Yu recalled what he had said earlier and smiled. "Please don't take it to heart. Those were just idle remarks."

This was the first time they'd met since parting ways at the police station. After the initial horror of the situation faded, the atmosphere became a bit awkward, especially for Xie Qingcheng. Shortly after throwing beer in He Yu's face, he felt that his actions had been entirely unnecessary. He was accustomed to keeping a cool head, but that day, the pressure of his emotions had gotten the better of him. So, when He Yu happened to hit a sore spot, he lost his temper and started a fight with the younger man. Under normal circumstances, he wouldn't have stooped so low as to squabble with a boy thirteen years his junior.

Now, as He Yu apologized to him again, Xie Qingcheng paused while running his hands through his messy hair. His tone eased slightly as he broke the tense atmosphere and responded, "...Forget it. Weren't you busy today?"

"...Yeah. How did you know?"

"Xie Xue said she asked you because she planned on having you take her place, but you said you were busy today and had no time, so she felt awkward asking."

He Yu fell silent for a long while. Instead of responding to Xie Qingcheng, he set the mascot head and the Samoyed plushie to the side. He stood with his hand to his forehead as he processed the situation. Then, he turned around and walked back toward the dock, the bag with the mango mousse cake in hand.

"...I should have checked the almanac today before coming out."

However, when He Yu returned to the Neverland Island dock with a sliver of hope in his heart, all he saw were the bobbing duck-shaped boats that had already been moored on the opposite bank.

The boats swayed back and forth, their golden beaks distorted into mocking smiles by the warped light reflecting off of the waves.

It was only then that He Yu remembered that he'd personally asked his xuezhang to cut off all means of transport after he landed on the island so that he could trap Xie Xue here alone and tell her his feelings.

Was this what it meant to shoot oneself in the foot?

He Yu's eyebrows twitched slightly.

"What's wrong?"

The sound of footsteps approached him from behind; he didn't need to turn back to know that the only other featherless biped on this island was Xie Qingcheng. He Yu had originally planned for a single man and a single lady to stay on this island—a perfect scenario for romance. But now, not only were two single men trapped on this island, but the other was the one man whom he detested the most.

The more he thought about it, the more vicious he felt. It was to the point where he kind of wanted to handcuff Xie Qingcheng's hands behind his back, tie him to a tree, and torment him half to death for an entire night in this lonely wilderness until Xie Qingcheng's complexion turned pale and his body was covered in bits of grass, until he passed out, until he died. There was nobody else coming anyway, and if he couldn't declare his love to Xie Xue, then it was just as well if he could personally destroy this man. In any case, he shouldn't waste this no man's land that he had built so carefully.

Who asked him to ruin his plans, anyway?

Having removed the mascot costume, Xie Qingcheng's figure appeared tall and slender as his aura abruptly changed. When he caught up to He Yu and walked beside him, it was as though He Yu could smell that elusively cold scent of medicine and disinfectant that he couldn't stand all over again.

He Yu composed himself and tamped down on the unrealistic urge to commit a crime as he turned around once more.

"I don't know why the boats are all on the other side."

"...Maybe they're being operated from the control room?" Xie Qingcheng stuck his hands in his pockets as he expressionlessly mulled things over for a while. "It's okay; there's still a rope bridge. Follow me."

Five minutes later, Xie Qingcheng stared at the now-mostly sub-merged rope bridge in silence with disbelief written all over his face.

"It seems the rope bridge has also broken."

"Ah, how unlucky. Someone must have pulled a prank." Although He Yu feigned calm on the outside, on the inside he was considerably dispirited. *Would you look at that! If it isn't the consequences of my own actions. After a while, you'll also find that there's no phone signal either.*

He had originally planned on staying on this island with Xie Xue until around midnight. To that end, he'd even managed to get his hands on a set of signal jammers that were used for the university entrance examinations to prevent cheating. Actually, it could be said that they were even more effective than the ones used in the examination because he'd reprogrammed the devices himself.

He Yu was rather capable in this respect. He would often distract himself when bored by focusing all his attention on studying how to break into computer systems and signal interference. Given his opponents' firewalls, breaking into computer programs was a race against time. It was quite effective at diverting his attention from his pain and keeping his illness under control. After so many years of practice, he had inadvertently become a formidable first-rate hacker.

Of course, he wouldn't tell his senior that the signal jammer was of his own making. He only had him activate the device on the other side of the shore, thus ensuring that Xie Xue would get no response no matter what. If anyone tried to come to Neverland Island, his xuezhang would also tell them that this activity was too boring and had already been shut down.

He Yu had originally thought that this was a perfectly seamless plan.

For the sake of it, he'd even made sure to stress the details to his accomplice. *"Remember to wait on the opposite shore until midnight before sending the boats back over."*

"Understood, He-laoban."

"You must ignore us no matter how much we call for help during this time. I want to put on a convincing act in front of her, otherwise she'll get suspicious very easily."

"No problem, He-laoban."

At present, as He-laoban gazed at Xie Qingcheng's slender and poised silhouette, he felt a slight headache coming on.

What do you mean, no problem? He Yu inwardly scolded himself. *This problem is turning out to be a bit too big...*

"Wait a minute, there's someone on the other side." Xie Qingcheng had walked halfway around the lump of dirt that was Neverland Island and discovered the senior club member standing watch on the other shore. "I'll call for him."

"It's useless for you to do it." He Yu sighed, mustering his final wisp of hope. "It's better if I do it."

Xie Qingcheng asked, "Why is that?"

"I'm just being filial. I respect the elderly and cherish youth—is that a good enough reason for you?"

He Yu felt like he was truly at the end of his rope and didn't want to bother wasting his breath with Xie Qingcheng anymore. He began waving on his own toward his wingman across the water, but to no avail.

Fifteen minutes later, the dry-mouthed Young Master He leaned back against the tree trunk.

Xie Qingcheng mocked mildly, "Now that you're done being filial, do you still have any energy left?"

Young adult men who had just come of age had the biggest of egos; to them, the most unbearable thing was to hear others say that they were impotent. However, He Yu genuinely had no explanation to offer, and so he simply turned to his other side, unwilling to even look at Xie Qingcheng. He picked a knee-length stalk of foxtail grass and slapped in frustration at the mosquitoes buzzing around him.

The more he stood there and thought, the more irritated He Yu became. He tossed the stalk of grass away with a flick and turned to walk into the forest.

"Where are you going?" Xie Qingcheng asked.

"I'm going to get a drink of water from the campsite." The boy's voice had already gone hoarse from yelling.

After walking some distance away, He Yu took out a different, un-blocked phone and sent his accomplice a message with a nauseated expression. "*Something's gone wrong. Please help us get off the island.*"

The senior club member replied in an instant, and he didn't even forget to suck up to this member of the bourgeoisie. "*Very impressive, Executive He! Your acting's so good! Even this message is fake, right?*"

Another few seconds passed, and another message arrived.

"*Executive He, I remember that you told me before not to let you two out no matter what you said. I'll take care of everything, so don't you worry. I'll only come pick you up after midnight. If other people try to get close to Neverland Island, I'll chase them off. So, don't worry and enjoy your private time together.*"

He Yu couldn't come up with a suitable reply.

What was he supposed to enjoy on this deserted island?

Enjoy Xie Qingcheng?

If murder weren't illegal, he could certainly chain Xie Qingcheng up, toss him into a heap of straw, and enjoy himself all night long, but what was he supposed to enjoy now?

18

I REMEMBERED THE DAY HE LEFT HIS JOB

GIVEN THAT HE LIVED in a lawful society, He Yu obviously couldn't toss Xie Qingcheng into the underbrush to torture him for the sake of vengeance. But in any case, there was no way for them to leave, so the two of them ended up accepting their fate and returned to the camping grounds with nothing to do but stare at each other and make idle conversation.

Perhaps this is what actually happened with Adam and Eve—they weren't really in love, they simply had no other options than each other. After all, they could hardly spend all their time talking to the snake in the tree.

"Little devil," Xie Qingcheng spoke up.

Aside from Xie Qingcheng, no one else ever called He Yu "little devil."

Furthermore, whenever he called him this, it usually meant that Xie Qingcheng intended to have a proper conversation with him.

He Yu turned. "Mm?"

"Has the injury on your hand healed?"

"It has." He Yu smiled. "Doctor Xie, why are you worrying about my hand? That day at the police station, you seemed like you were half-tempted to stab me again."

"You know that I genuinely don't want to hear others talk about the past."

"Then did you know that I was genuinely trying to apologize to you that day?"

Xie Qingcheng looked up without a word.

He Yu's smile remained, but his eyes were cold and indifferent when returning Xie Qingcheng's gaze. "It's just how I am, Xie Qingcheng. I wasn't being insincere that day, nor was I, as you said, speaking like a member of the bourgeoisie giving a PR statement. Ever since I was little, it was always you guys who demanded that I control my emotions. Could it be that it's been too long since you left your job that you've forgotten what you once told me yourself?"

A few beats of silence passed, and Xie Qingcheng said, "It's true that it's been a long time since I left my job."

"It's been four years."

"And in that time, I still haven't had the chance to ask you properly," said Xie Qingcheng. "How are you doing?"

"Much better." He Yu smiled once more. "There's no need for you to worry. Regardless of how I see you as a person, I've always considered your medical philosophy to be sound and kept the instructions you gave me in mind."

Xie Qingcheng took in the youth's indifferent expression and said, "That's great. Your illness demands that you save yourself. No matter what doctor you have, the most important thing is your own mindset."

He Yu fell silent for a spell, then lowered his head and smiled. "Just listen to yourself—these words of yours, why do they sound so familiar? Ah," he paused as his eyes glazed over with a chilly sheen. "I remember now. You said those words to me once before, Doctor Xie. It was the day when you left..."

The day when Xie Qingcheng had quit being his doctor.

The previous day, after He Yu and Xie Xue had finished doing some reading at the library, it began to rain. He Yu walked Xie Xue home under his umbrella.

"Thanks for walking me all this way."

"It's nothing."

"Do you wanna come in for a bit? Though my house is kinda small..."

"Won't I be intruding?"

"Of course not. I was just worried you'd feel uncomfortable." Xie Xue smiled as she pulled He Yu's hand and led him toward the alleyway where her house was located.

Xie Qingcheng wasn't home, but Li Ruoqiu was.

The woman was sitting at her desk and in the middle of messaging someone on her phone with an irrepressible smile on her face. She didn't even look up when her little sister-in-law stepped into the house, as she said, "Xie Xue, you're back."

He Yu rarely interacted with Li Ruoqiu. As he entered the house, he very politely said, "Li-sao, sorry for the disturbance."

Li Ruoqiu started in surprise at the sound of his voice and lifted her head. "...Ah, a VIP, a VIP. Quick, take a seat."

She got up in a hurry to make him some tea.

He Yu smiled. "Saozi, there's no need to trouble yourself. I was just walking Xie Xue home, so I'll be leaving soon."

"What are you saying? Take a seat, I'll go fetch you guys some snacks."

She turned and left.

Xie Xue leaned over and said, "Saozi's a pretty good person, and super enthusiastic. But if you refuse her, she'll get angry."

Li Ruoqiu was a very strong-willed woman indeed; He Yu could tell based on the handful of fleeting encounters he'd had with her.

Not to mention, what kind of ordinary woman would want to marry a cold and patriarchal man like Xie Qingcheng?

So, he obediently took a seat. The old houses in Huzhou's alleyways were very cramped. This one in particular was a studio that had been partitioned with curtains. The junior-high-school boy had already reached puberty and hit his growth spurt and all the changes that came with it.

This was the first time he had entered Xie Qingcheng's personal territory. His gaze flickered across the furnishings of the room and paused for a moment on that double bed half-hidden behind gauze curtains. A strange sort of feeling arose in his heart.

It was difficult for him to imagine what Xie Qingcheng and Li Ruoqiu would do there.

He Yu very politely averted his gaze.

"Here's the tea, now. And I've brought some snacks too. I don't know if you're used to eating this sort of thing, though." Li Ruoqiu handled the household tasks with a smile. She brought over a pot of hot tea and little pastries; there was even a platter of cut fruit on the tray. "Give it a try. I baked the pastries myself."

"Saozi, you've really gone to a lot of trouble."

Li Ruoqiu covered her mouth with a hand and laughed. Her clever eyes sized up He Yu and Xie Xue in turn.

Although these two children had a significant age gap, adolescent boys grew very quickly. Plus, He Yu wasn't wearing his school uniform today—instead, he was dressed in fall clothes: a high-collared black shirt, jeans, and a baseball cap. He was also already nearing 180 centimeters, so he didn't look much like a junior high schooler at all. When he sat next to Xie Xue, who was a few years older than him, their heights and appearances were, in fact, quite well matched.

A brief silence fell over the room.

After a few minutes, unable to help herself, Li Ruoqiu let out a "pfft" of laughter and waved a hand. "Okay, you two chat, you two chat. I'll go visit Auntie Li for a while."

"Ah," Xie Xue said. "Saozi..."

But Li Ruoqiu had already waltzed out of the room.

Even an idiot would know what she was thinking, what with the eyebrow-waggling smile she had graced them with before leaving. Xie Xue immediately felt a bit awkward, and her little face visibly flushed red.

"Um, He Yu, I'm sorry. My sister-in-law really likes to watch idol dramas, and the more she watches, the more likely she is to overthink things."

"It's all right." He Yu looked down and drank a mouthful of warm tea. Li Ruoqiu's misunderstanding made him quite happy, so he smiled and said, "I don't mind."

He liked Xie Xue a lot, so Li Ruoqiu hadn't misunderstood much at all.

"Oh, right. Your brother's not working tomorrow, but he's coming to my house to take care of some business. Do you want to come with him? After he's done, I'll take you out to barbecue."

Hearing that there would be food, Xie Xue happily agreed.

However, when He Yu got home that evening, he saw the lights were on in the living room. Lü Zhishu was sitting inside reading the newspaper when he walked in—a surprising sight.

Lü Zhishu and He Jiwei were rarely home. The He family had two permanent villas: one in Huzhou and the other in Yanzhou, which was the primary residence. He Yu had only ever lived in Yanzhou when he was very young. When he was five, he had been taken to live in Huzhou. But it was different for his younger brother, who was expected to study and was used to raising hell with his rich playboy friends in the area. He had a heart attack whenever he saw that elder brother of his who excelled in all areas, so he pretty much only stayed in the primary residence.

So it came to be that the brothers lived on opposite sides of the Yangtze River, and when their parents were free, they were naturally more willing to stay with the precious, innocent, and cute younger brother. Unless there was pertinent business to take care of, they very rarely came to stay with He Yu.

"Why are you back?" He Yu ventured hesitantly.

"I just had some business," Lü Zhishu said as she put down the newspaper. "Sit down, I have something to tell you."

Instead, the young teenager took off his backpack and shoes and walked into the room to stand in front of his mother, making her look up at him.

He Yu looked down. "Go ahead."

Lü Zhishu poured a glass of red wine for herself, took a sip, and then said, "Tomorrow will be the last day Doctor Xie comes to treat you. After that, he will no longer be our family's personal physician."

He Yu froze in shock. He had not expected this.

After a long time, he heard himself say in a seemingly calm tone, "Why so sudden?"

"Mm. I didn't tell you beforehand because I was afraid you'd make a fuss if you knew."

"Why?"

Lü Zhishu didn't answer his question directly. Instead, she said, "We are already in the process of wrapping everything up and settling the medical bill. Once he comes to report to me tomorrow, he will also say his goodbyes to you. As for after that..."—she took another sip of wine before landing the final blow—"you should stop interacting with their family."

He Yu fell quiet.

"Do you understand my intentions? We aren't members of the same class. Lao-Zhao told me you were visiting Doctor Xie's home in Moyu Alley with his sister when I had him pick you up this afternoon." Lü Zhishu sighed. "To tell the truth, you've made me quite disappointed. Mencius's mother moved thrice, carefully selecting neighborhoods in which to live.[27] All parents hope their sons can be surrounded by appropriate companions."

She assessed the boy's figure, already tall and broad. Then, she shifted her gaze up to land on He Yu's face, which was already distinctly handsome.

"Especially female companions."

Silence hung over the living room for a long time before He Yu finally asked, "Are these Doctor Xie's intentions?"

"Resigning is his intention. Having you keep your distance from their family is mine." Lü Zhishu spoke honestly as she smiled and closed the gap between herself and He Yu. She looked up as she lifted her hand to smooth back his fringe.

"But I think Doctor Xie understands my intentions as well. He wouldn't want to maintain superfluous connections after his work is finished either. He's a very rational person; it's one of the reasons why your father and I appreciate and trust him so much."

When He Yu didn't respond, Lü Zhishu added, "If you don't believe me, you can ask him yourself tomorrow."

The next day, Xie Qingcheng came.

---

27 Mencius, or Mengzi, is a famous Confucian philosopher held to be second in importance only to Confucius himself in the Confucian ideology. According to legend, his mother, seeking to find the best place to raise her son, first moved near a graveyard, where the young Mencius began to mimic the rituals of the mourners. Then, she moved near a market, where he began to mimic the merchants selling their wares. Finally, she moved near a school, where Mencius began to imitate the etiquette and study habits of the scholars.

After signing and handing over the papers, he gave He Yu one last medical checkup. When it was completed, he said softly to the boy lying on the medical recliner, "Your mother should have already told you."

He Yu didn't say anything.

"Starting from tomorrow, I will no longer be serving your family. If you feel unwell in the future, don't distract yourself by self-harming like you did in the past. In addition, no matter which doctor comes to treat you in the future, remember that the most important thing is your own mindset."

As expected, when the young doctor said these words, he didn't bring any of his personal emotions into it.

Lü Zhishu was right. To Xie Qingcheng, the boundary between He Yu and himself had always been perfectly clear. Their families were from completely different worlds; He Yu was the young master of the He family, the son of He Jiwei, and Xie Qingcheng was simply a doctor their family had hired.

It wouldn't be beneficial for He Yu either, to always rely on a doctor to manage his mental plights.

Xie Qingcheng was very calm because he understood this better than anyone else.

He provided his patients with care, support, and powerful mental encouragement, but there was no sentimentality in his farewells. He always handled doctor-patient relations in this crisp and clean manner. So, in the end, he only said, "All right, little devil. I wish you a speedy recovery."

The boy who had just reached puberty suppressed the anger in his heart and stared at him. "You don't have anything else you want to say to me?"

He waited for a while, but Xie Qingcheng didn't respond.

He Yu said, "All right. If you don't, then I do."

Xie Qingcheng still said nothing.

"Xie Qingcheng, I've gone through many doctors these past years. They had me take medicine, gave me shots, and looked at me with an expression that said I was a singular, unique patient. You were the only one who was different. It's true that I really don't like you, but I've taken in every word you said because you were the only one who treated me like someone who could and should integrate into society. You told me that taking medicine and getting shots weren't the most important things, that it was most crucial for me to make connections with others and build up a strong sense of self—that's the only way I can keep holding on and move forward."

He Yu paused briefly. "Doctor Xie, we're not very close, but I still... I..."

At this point, He Yu found himself unable to continue for a long time. He stared fixedly at Xie Qingcheng's face through his almond eyes. "I thought you saw me as a normal person with feelings, not just as a patient."

"I do see you as a normal person with feelings," replied Xie Qingcheng.

"And yet you'd leave so suddenly, just like this?" The teen's anger radiated from his mature body in a frightening aura of tangible pressure as he struggled to contain his emotions. "Are relationships between two normal people like this?"

Xie Qingcheng took a moment to choose his words. "He Yu. I know that you might find this sudden, and I certainly should have let you know earlier, but your parents and I have already discussed this matter. I cannot go against their wishes, especially not your father's. Not only can he be considered an old friend of mine, but he's also my employer. Therefore, so long as I do not betray my own principles, I must respect his wishes first…"

"Then what about my wishes?"

Xie Qingcheng said, "I'm just a doctor."

"I'm your employer too." He Yu stared at him. "Why didn't you ask what I wanted?"

Xie Qingcheng sighed. "Control yourself, young man. I don't mean to disrespect you, but you're still a student. My salary isn't something that you'd be able to afford."

He Yu didn't know what he was thinking. At this point in his life, he was already very calm and unflustered, and could navigate adult interactions without losing his composure. But when he thought about how Xie Qingcheng and Xie Xue were going to leave, he suddenly felt extremely helpless and blurted out, "I have a lot of allowance, I can—"

"Save it to buy cakes."

He Yu stared at him silently.

"I'm not a slice of cake that you can buy just because your father won't get it for you," Xie Qingcheng reasoned. "I came to treat you largely as a favor to him. It's impossible for me to go against his wishes, do you understand?"

"Why does he want you to leave?"

"He didn't want me to leave," Xie Qingcheng said. "It was my own choice. Didn't you ask me just now if such a separation, this end to our relationship, is normal between people?" Xie Qingcheng gazed into He Yu's eyes as he continued, "It is. Although I see you as a normal person with feelings, the relationship we've established between us is that of a doctor and his patient. Relationships between people must always come to an end; even your parents, the people closest to you, cannot accompany you for life."

Xie Qingcheng paused, letting his words sink in. "Now, our doctor-patient relationship is at an end, so I must leave. This is a very normal conclusion to relationships between normal people."

He Yu didn't reply.

"Your father and I agreed at the beginning that the duration of this relationship would be seven years." Xie Qingcheng looked into He Yu's eyes again. "It's not suitable for someone to continue staying with you at this stage of your illness. Sooner or later, you'll have to depend on yourself to walk out of the shadows in your heart. Do you understand?"

"So, you think the same way as my mother—that after today, there shouldn't be any other contact between you and me, between Xie Xue and me?"

"If you need our help, you can contact us at any time," said Xie Qingcheng. After a pause, he added, "As for the rest of the time, it's really not necessary."

He Yu held his tongue.

"Also, your mother told me that you went out with Xie Xue alone," Xie Qingcheng said. "As her guardian, I do feel that this is rather inappropriate."

He assessed the teen and said in a calm and sensible voice, "I know that the two of you have a large age gap, that what you feel for her is only a sense of dependence and that you have no other intentions. But it's inevitable that certain ugly rumors will crop up in time, and that wouldn't be good for either of you."

He Yu didn't correct his excessively archaic and naive thinking. He only said, "So, you approve of my mother's methods."

"I do."

He Yu stared at him for a very long time. Then, he sat back down and sunk into his chair. He propped his chin in his hand as he smiled slightly. That smile seemed like clouds obscuring the sun, thoroughly and completely covering the millimeter of genuine emotion that he only ever revealed with so much difficulty.

He Yu said, "Doctor, you're really...so calm. It makes it seem like you're even more heartless than me even though you're not ill. Very well. Since it's already come to this, you may go. I will keep note of what you said. I will save myself, very calmly, and live on, very calmly. In addition, I wish you every success and a smooth-sailing career moving forward. However,"—He Yu changed the topic—"Although Xie Xue is your sister, she has the right to make her own decisions. So, no matter what you say, I will still go looking for her."

Xie Qingcheng frowned, and his stare grew sharp as a knife. "She's a girl, and you're already fourteen. You should have some sense of appropriate distance. Why do you insist on sticking to her?"

"Because she's not like you."

A beam of light cut decisively across the ground, leaving one of them in the light and the other in the darkness, like two broken fragments splintered down the middle.

"She is the only bridge I have to the outside world."

Xie Qingcheng paused for a moment before replying, "Then you should find another bridge."

The time had come. He had other matters to attend to and couldn't keep talking to He Yu, so he left.

For the remainder of the day, from dusk until the dead of night, He Yu sat in the chair without moving a muscle.

He Yu thought, Xie Qingcheng was such a cunning person. Xie Qingcheng always spoke reasonably. He was the one who had told He Yu that he hoped for him to treat himself as a normal person; he was the one who had told him that people could walk out from the shadows in their hearts all on their own. He was even the one who caused He Yu to develop the delusion that no matter how close He Yu got to Xie Xue, Xie Qingcheng, as her older brother, would still be able to accept him.

But on that day, Xie Qingcheng's actions made him realize that he had gotten too far ahead of himself.

When it came to social relationships, the one between an employer and employee was the simplest and clearest of them all. Regardless of whether it had been maintained for ten or twenty years, they could settle all the accounts without the slightest emotional entanglement when the relationship ended, leaving no loose ends.

Similarly, a personal physician could leave after being paid for his services because he had no reason to stay. In comparison to the other doctors He Yu had seen in the past, Xie Qingcheng wasn't actually all that special. In fact, he was even more cruel than the ones who saw He Yu as a different species, because he'd lied to him for the longest and benefited the most from his blood and pain. It was Xie Qingcheng who made He Yu mistakenly believe that the relationships he'd built could last; it was he who made him mistakenly believe his affection for Xie Xue was something that her parental guardian could accept.

But he had been wrong on all accounts.

Now, on this isolated island, He Yu gazed at Xie Qingcheng's face as he thought about this part of his past.

So many years had passed since then. Xie Qingcheng was still that elder brother of the Xie family, and nothing had really changed in the end. He was still unwilling to let Xie Xue be alone with him, still standing guard before his sister in a tyrannical, dictator-like and protective position—even the words he used to admonish He Yu were completely identical.

Xie Qingcheng might very well be a great doctor with medical philosophies deserving of praise, a righteous way of thinking, and a strong sense of responsibility toward his patients, but unfortunately, he had no heart.

"Are you still thinking about what happened in the past?" Xie Qingcheng's voice pulled He Yu back to the present.

Snapping out of his musings, He Yu said, "You mentioned it, so it came to mind. Now that I think about it, you probably don't actually remember the way I used to speak in the past." He Yu smiled at last. "In the end, the relationship between the two of us is merely a doctor-patient relationship that has already ended, isn't that right?"

Before Xie Qingcheng could reply, a streak of light suddenly flared overhead. A loud bang sounded as a firework blossomed in the night sky. It was the brilliant fireworks that served as the campus exploration's finale every year. Countless flowers burst in midair with a barrage of explosions.

"Right," said Xie Qingcheng.

Amid this brilliant resplendence, the muffled boom of thunder suddenly rang out—a rain shower had begun. Ultimately, the tender blaze born from the fireworks couldn't stand up to the lightning's fierce, ice-cold chill, and quickly surrendered in defeat. In the distance, students giggled as they darted into lecture halls or dorms to avoid the rain as droplets the size of soybeans pitter-pattered down onto the bustling world below.

Beneath the darkening sky, He Yu maintained that small smile on his face as he said, "Then let's hide from the rain together, Doctor Xie. If I use your clearheaded style of reasoning to analyze this, aside from our doctor-patient relationship, you're also my teacher's older brother now. If you end up soaked in the rain, it'll be hard for me to explain myself to her."

He paused briefly, and a mocking lilt entered his voice once more. "For two people who have already ceased their doctor-patient relationship, hiding from the rain together should count as normal behavior that doesn't violate any boundaries of propriety, right?"

Xie Qingcheng knew that He Yu still held a grudge against him, but he didn't have the patience or magnanimity to coax He Yu any longer. His tone was cold as he responded, "Right."

He Yu smiled. "There's a cave up ahead. After you."

While He Yu and Xie Qingcheng were looking for a place to hide from the rain on the island, He Yu's senior was still cautiously taking care of things on his end. He continued to guard the dock entrance and prevent any other participants in the campus-wide event from approaching.

The club member pondered a bit. Everyone probably already had their share of fun, and it was unlikely that anyone had absolutely nothing better to do than come all the way to Neverland Island for a stamp, so he allowed himself to relax a bit.

"Aiya, this rain is really too heavy." He sat ruefully on the duck boat, gazing stupidly toward the island in the hopes of catching a glimpse of something, but the island was too far away. Earlier, he could only vaguely make out He Yu and someone with a rather tall and slender figure. This beautiful lady looked like she was pushing 180 centimeters—maybe she was wearing high heels? He was near-sighted and couldn't see them too clearly, so he couldn't say for sure.

But it sure seemed Young Master He had unique tastes to like tall girls, especially one this tall.

Ah...the lives of the bourgeoisie truly were something to be envied.

A feeling of temptation rose in his heart as the thought crossed his mind; he really wanted to know how the two people on the island were getting along under the downpour right now. The two of them hadn't brought an umbrella, and the only shelter on Neverland Island was a cave; it was a blind spot in the school's campus surveillance system and students rarely went there, though the club member had heard that some couples liked to go to the cave in the middle of the night for an outdoor tryst. He reckoned that He Yu, with his looks and family background, and after putting so much effort into pursuing that 180-centimeter beauty, must have succeeded in his mission by now.

Should he send that member of the bourgeoisie a text and remind him to use protection?

At this thought, he pulled out his phone.

Going all the way on the night of a declaration of love—that would only be fitting for someone living life in the fast lane, wouldn't it?

So he composed his message. He planned to send it to He Yu's unblocked phone in order to curry some more favor with that member of the bourgeoisie.

"He-laoban, there's a first aid kit inside the cave on the island. It has boxes of condoms in the second compartment. If you need them, you can check inside the kit, and remember to send me a red packet[28] afterward..."

---

28 A function for sending money via WeChat.

19

WE FINALLY STOPPED ARGUING

THE SENIOR CLUB MEMBER had just finished writing out and sending his message when someone's voice suddenly came from behind him.

"Little student."

Lost in his dirty thoughts, the sleazy club member was easily startled and nearly fell sideways right into the water.

The speaker was very nimble and immediately steadied the boat. He smiled and asked, "Little student, did I scare you?"

"Ah, no, not at all."

The club member looked up to see a man with scraggly facial hair who was at least thirty or forty years old. He looked ridiculously unkempt in his white tank top and flip-flops, but there was a bright gleam in his eyes. Who knew what business he had here.

Flip-Flops smiled as he asked him, "Are you using that boat?"

"Ah, the boat?" The club member thought fast, blurting out, "The boat's broken."

"It's broken?"

"Yep, there's a leak at the bottom. It's unusable and can only be docked in the shallow area."

Flip-Flops hummed thoughtfully. "What a coincidence. The rope bridge leading to this island also seems to have broken."

"Sure has." The club member spoke with righteous conviction. "I chopped"—he coughed—"Someone must've chopped it down. Who are you?"

Flip-Flops grinned, baring his teeth. "I'm the school's electrical maintenance worker. As a matter of fact, I got a notice to come to the island to take a look. See, I've even brought my toolbox."

The senior club member felt guilty as soon as he heard that the man was a worker for the school. He cleared his throat a few times, glancing left and right before inching closer and saying, "Dage, I'll be honest with you. There's a nouveau riche student declaring his love on the island today. He's paid to have the whole place to himself. Think about it, wouldn't getting in their way be a dick move? Of course it would."

Flip-Flops understood immediately. His eyes shone as he likewise responded very foolishly. "Ah, reserving the island to declare one's love? So romantic. You youngsters sure know how to have fun."

"That's not it." The club member slapped his thigh and raised his other hand to make a money gesture by rubbing his index and middle fingers with his thumb. "The main thing is, he's rich."

Flip-Flops beamed. He was surprisingly understanding. "All right then. When will this boat of yours be usable?"

"Probably after midnight. I'm mostly worried that the little couple won't be able to hold themselves back after he tells her how he feels. You know, tasting the forbidden fruit for the first time and being unable to stop. It's possible that it won't be until a bit later, even." He began to gossip as well when he saw how amiable this uncle was.

Men. When they got together and talked about these types of things, there would inevitably be a depraved glint in their eyes.

The club member lewdly implored the older man, "Uncle, why don't you come back tomorrow morning? They'll definitely be gone by then. One of them is a xueba, there's no way he would skip class."

A gregarious laugh burst up from Flip-Flops' belly. "Fucking hell, not even a beautiful lady can keep a xueba from going to class."

"Well, of course. Otherwise, how can they be a xueba?"

The uncle chatted with the club member for a little longer before leaving with his toolbox. After arriving at a deserted location, he came to a stop, lit a cigarette, and dug a cell phone out of his toolbox. It was the oldest model of brick phone, a product that had almost gone extinct from the market. "Hello. Captain Zheng, maybe push the deadline back a few more hours. I won't be able to get onto the island tonight. Uh, problem? There's no problem. It's just that two students have reserved the island for a bit of romance. Mhm, yes, yes, I know, I'll go early tomorrow morning."

He flicked away some cigarette ash and sighed in exasperation. "Honestly, isn't this spy of ours a little *too* cautious? Won't even send texts. Every time there's intelligence to be reported, it needs to be fucking written in the student guestbook. And what's with that excuse of 'this won't invite suspicion'... Ahh...screw it, I'm going back to the station. You know, I came here to pick up the intelligence report only to end up being force-fed PDA by bratty children instead. This police officer job of mine sure ain't easy..."

Flip-Flops left in a whirl of disgruntled mumbling.

The cave on Neverland Island wasn't particularly large, and it was very dark inside. If not for the pouring rain, Xie Qingcheng felt that no one would ever bother to come in here. However, it was only when he crouched down like a cat and entered the cave that he realized he was wrong.

By the dim light of his phone, he could see some outdoor recreational gear strewn about the inside of the man-made cave: hurricane lamps, waterproof canvas, oxford cloth folding chairs, Wolf-Eyes flashlights, and even a little camping stove.

"A secret utopia."

"What?" Xie Qingcheng turned around.

He Yu shone his phone flashlight over one of the cave walls. "That's what this says."

Only then did Xie Qingcheng discover the masterpieces written on the damp walls of the cave, left behind from the ancient past for successive generations of intrepid explorers—they were all the graffitied scribblings of students who had discovered this secret place by mistake.

The biggest words were the ones that said, "Secret Utopia."

Xie Qingcheng wasn't interested in these scribbles. After glancing at it briefly, he sat down at the entrance of the cave to watch the rain fall.

But He Yu was a student of writing and directing and was more than willing to read all the words that appeared before him with care.

"Buddha saved the people by bringing them to the shores of enlightenment, yet why does he not ferry me out from the sea of academia?"

"Zhou-xiansheng is the love of my life, but how can it be that when we met, he had already become the husband of another? I long for him, yet I cannot have him, and I become mad, so unspeakably mad, as the only thing that remains for me is endless waiting."

He Yu lifted his phone, casting light on the walls as he read the words out loud, and shook his head. "So poetic, so wretched."

Then he illuminated the other side.

Now, that side was something else—filled with all kinds of content. He read, "May advanced mathematics get the hell out of the curriculum soon."

"Graduating soon, I hope I can become a famous director. Jiayou."

"In sheltering here for rain, we..." He Yu's voice trailed off, and he stopped reading.

This only piqued Xie Qingcheng's curiosity. "We what?"

"...Nothing."

Xie Qingcheng didn't believe him, so he turned to look and was immediately left speechless.

"In sheltering here for rain, we fell in love. Thanks be to the heavens for bestowing us with this fateful opportunity."

These two illicit lovers had even left their names underneath, encircled in a massive heart.

Given this situation, awkwardness was inevitable. No wonder He Yu didn't finish reading it. Xie Qingcheng spoke apathetically, "It's only been a few years since we last saw each other, yet now you've developed dyslexia. No choice but to read everything out loud."

"Don't you think it's quite interesting? Who knows where these people are now—they might have entirely forgotten about what they've written here." He Yu reached up and stroked a line of mottled handwriting. "Maybe some of them have already turned to dust, yet these words still remain."

Xie Qingcheng said coldly, "Then why don't you leave your own written masterpiece for later generations to admire?"

He'd only meant to mock He Yu and was a bit surprised when He Yu picked up a thin shard of stone from the ground, chose a blank spot on the wall, and said thoughtfully, "You're right. What do you think I should write?"

He Yu even shot a glance at Xie Qingcheng. There was a hint of irrepressible disdain in his eyes. *That's right... Here, we take shelter from the rain and join in love, thanking the heavens for bestowing us with this fateful opportunity—how many quintessential classic love stories started like this? The White Snake smiling as she asked to borrow an umbrella from Xu Hanlin in the boat,[29] while Benigni laid down an entire red carpet for Nicoletta in the rain so that she could descend the steps.*

If this were Xie Xue, perhaps he would find this night much more pleasant. Perhaps they could have followed the example set by their predecessors and carved the words "so did we" beneath the handwriting of their xuezhang and xuejie who had gotten together because of the rain.

Too bad the person trapped on the island with him right now was Xie Qingcheng.

It was exceedingly boring for two straight men to be stuck together, especially when they weren't on particularly good terms with each other.

Xie Qingcheng sensed his grumpy gaze and adopted an even crabbier expression in response. "What are you looking at me for?"

"I'm sorry, but there's no one else I can look at." He Yu tossed the rock into the air a couple of times, then carelessly scratched out a few words. "May my dreams come true."

Powdered stone fell with a whisper as he worked.

When he finished writing, He Yu tossed the rock away and turned around. "Doctor, why don't you also have a go at a little immaturity?"

Xie Qingcheng's eyes lit up slightly, but in the end, he shifted his gaze back to the downpour outside. In the mist-like, hazy warm

---

29 The character Xu Xian from the classic Chinese love story Legend of the White Snake. As Xu Xian was a scholar, Hanlin may be a reference to the Hanlin Academy or a misspelling of his courtesy name, Hanwen.

light, his silhouette was as thin as a sheet of fine calligraphy paper[30] that could be dispersed by a mere gust of wind.

"No need. My wish is a fantasy."

"Oh?" He Yu said offhandedly, "Then why don't you tell me what kind of daydream it is. *Can* I ask? I hope I'm not offending you."

For some time, the only sound was the howling of the wind and the shower of rain outside. Just when He Yu thought that he didn't want to bother with talking to him anymore, Xie Qingcheng spoke in a calm voice as he gazed at the rivulets of rainwater streaming over the rocks beyond the cave. "I didn't want to be a doctor."

"Nor are you one, right now anyway."

"I never wanted to study medicine when I was young."

At this point, He Yu was a bit perplexed. He raised his almond eyes to examine the older man. "Then what did you want to study?"

Xie Qingcheng got up and walked deeper into the cave. He stared at the "May my dreams come true" that He Yu had carved, then said, "It's been too long, I can't remember anymore."

This was a lie spoken without the slightest bit of sincerity, entirely perfunctory to the point that he didn't even bother to hide the frustrated disappointment in his eyes. He Yu almost suspected that he was using this as an opportunity to insult his intelligence.

Xie Qingcheng turned away, as though he didn't want to address this subject any further. He returned to the center of the cave and asked He Yu, "Is there anything to eat?"

It was indeed dinnertime by now. The only food He Yu had brought onto the island was the mango mousse cake he had originally made for Xie Xue.

But now, it looked like it would need to be sacrificed for the sake of their rations.

---

30   浣花纸, *a type of special pink paper invented by Xue Tao, a Tang dynasty poet.*

He Yu didn't have much interest in Xie Qingcheng anyway, so if Xie Qingcheng didn't want to talk about his former life plans, then he likewise had no interest in asking him.

He took out the cake and passed a piece to Xie Qingcheng. Xie Qingcheng must have been starving, as he wolfed the dessert down immediately without even sparing it a glance.

"Do you have any napkins?" Xie Qingcheng was a stickler for cleanliness, so after he finished eating, he even asked Secretary He for napkins.

Secretary He looked around and spotted a first aid kit on the canvas table. Thinking that this type of kit might have napkins and such inside, he went over and rummaged through it. The light was too dim, so he searched by touch and, when he found a package that seemed to be roughly the right size to be napkins, he tossed it to Xie Qingcheng.

Xie Qingcheng caught the package and was just about to open it when he suddenly realized the texture wasn't quite right—why was it a paper box instead of the usual plastic wrapping?

He examined the box, then sighed. "What?"

Without a word, Xie Qingcheng tossed the Durex box back to He Yu.

"Do you have eyes or not?"

He Yu looked at it, paused for a few seconds, then quietly put the box back into the first aid kit.

Fucking fantastic.

And it was even the textured kind with a delay lubricant.

Granted, both of them were rather thick-skinned in this area. Generally speaking, it was difficult to faze He Yu, and this was just a mistake, so it wasn't anything to make a fuss over.

As for Xie Qingcheng, he was calm and steady by nature and rarely let his emotions get the best of him. Besides, he was already a man who had gotten married and divorced. Though he wasn't particularly interested in these kinds of things, seeing adult products could hardly offend his delicate sensibilities.

Xie Qingcheng merely furrowed his brows. "Why are all you students these days so depraved?"

"This isn't so bad," He Yu said mildly. "You haven't even seen the worst of it yet."

As he spoke, he noticed a notebook lying next to the medical kit.

Utopia Guestbook

These notebooks usually served as anonymous confessionals, with writers adding on to previous comments over time. Even if previous writers might never see the ensuing comments, those who came later could carry on the discussion and add their own juicy tales. Reading these tomes from cover to cover was also quite interesting, especially considering that these books usually ended up containing exciting stories of romance or friendship.

He Yu was suddenly struck with an idea. He picked up the notebook and asked Xie Qingcheng, "Would Doctor Xie like to see? This notebook should have a lot of content that'd help you better understand the ways of modern youth."

With nothing else to do, the two of them began to read it together.

As expected, the notebook was chock-full of all kinds of different handwriting. The contributors wrote mainly about declarations of love, the beginnings of friendship, secret confessions, and the like.

They were leafing their way through when He Yu let out a sudden hum of surprise.

"Xie Qingcheng, someone's mentioned you here."

20

ONLY FOR HIM TO
CATCH ME IN THE ACT

A T FIRST, Xie Qingcheng wasn't paying much attention to the book, but when he heard what He Yu said, he looked over the page again. He discovered that there was a box in the very corner of the copy-paper-sized page labeled with the words "Group Chat for Gays," in which his own name appeared with great frequency.

Xie Qingcheng had an ominous feeling about this.

Sure enough, as the two of them read through this section, it turned out to be written by a whole group of little bottoms who were deep in a heated discussion about the "ideal tops" from the surrounding colleges and universities. In short, there were too many bottoms, not enough tops, and all of them were looking to get laid.

The first mention of Xie Qingcheng's name was written in ballpoint pen. The handwriting was faded and somewhat aged. The writer wrote, "There's a new professor at the neighboring medical school named Xie Qingcheng. He's extremely hot and has a very cold and alpha-like aura. I really want him to fuck me."

In the comments below, people began to mock him for being such a slut.

But shortly thereafter, a new comment entered the fray. That's when the atmosphere began to turn a little absurd. "Holy fuck! The older students upstairs should really stop laughing. If you ever get to read this guestbook again, you guys need to head over to the medical school and see him for yourself. He really is so fucking handsome he'd make all you bottoms wet. His legs are soooo long and he's got broad shoulders and a narrow waist; he's so tall and his whole body is as straight as a javelin pole. It nearly fucking kills me whenever he wears a suit and tie. After meeting him, I had wet dreams about him for three nights in a row..."

The comments that followed were even more outrageously uninhibited.

"I want Gege to take care of me sooo bad."

"I hear that Professor Xie's divorced. Maybe he's like us."

"My god, are you for real? If he's like us, then I'd be willing to stay single my whole life if he rails me just once."

After reading this section, He Yu fell silent for a long time. He really couldn't bear it anymore.

He'd be an idiot if he gave up his chance to mock Xie Qingcheng for this. The jokes had practically written themselves!

And so, He Yu grinned. "Doctor Xie, who could have thought you're the ideal top for all the bottoms. Seeing as they all want you to fuck them, why don't you take one for the team and choose a concubine?"

Xie Qingcheng's face twisted into an extremely ugly expression as he tried to flip the page.

He Yu pressed down on the paper, stopping him. "I haven't finished reading."

"I'm turning the page."

"Wait a while longer."

"I'm turning it."

He Yu insisted with a mocking smile, "Just a little while."

Feeling humiliated, Xie Qingcheng forcibly turned the page.

He Yu's laughter was particularly cruel as he continued reading, searching for any more mentions of Xie Qingcheng later in the book.

However, he'd only flipped through a few pages when his laughter died.

Because He Yu saw his own name.

It was written in the same style as the "Group Chat for Gays" from previous pages. Evidently, Xie Qingcheng had noticed as well, and the two of them began to read together once more.

"Why were all the earlier pages filled with bottoms chatting with each other? Anyway, this is the tops' chat. Anyone have any recommendations for pretty boys at school?"

After a bunch of random names, He Yu's name appeared.

"Oh, He Yu. It seems like he's nice to everyone, but really? He's extremely snooty and so standoffish. Not to mention, he looks way too delicate and refined. He may be tall, but his skin is as pale as a girl's. Though, I've seen him play basketball before, and he's pretty strong. I'm sure it'd feel great to fuck him."

"OP, have you gone mad? That's the young master of the He family."

"It's exactly that kind of status that makes him more fuckable!! He really turns me on."

"Don't you guys know that not only is He Yu good at playing basketball, but he's also really good at beating people up? Yeah, he's nice on the eyes, but haven't you guys seen that swimmer's body of his when he takes off his clothes at the school's swimming pool? He'd kill you with a single blow."

"But I still want him..."

Xie Qingcheng turned to the ashen-faced He Yu when he was done reading. "Amazing. In the future, you should bring a self-defense flashlight when you go out at night. Worst-case scenario, you can give me a call if you're really too scared. Seeing as we're old acquaintances, I can even walk you home."

"Turn the page," said He Yu.

"I haven't seen enough yet."

He Yu fell silent.

A depressed gloom settled over He Yu for a long while. In the end, it seemed that he no longer felt like wasting his energy arguing with Xie Qingcheng; he simply tore those two pages out of the notebook and set them on fire with a lighter.

After reducing the pages to ashes, he even went so far as to pull out a tissue to wipe the fingers that had touched them clean, his face devoid of emotion while he worked.

Xie Qingcheng simply continued perusing the notebook silently as the stoic-faced He Yu stood nearby.

For a long time, the only sounds in the cave were the echoes of the rain splashing down outside.

Summer rainstorms didn't last long, however, so by the time their cell phones read eight o'clock, this boundless thunderstorm had already weakened into a lightly pattering rain shower. Xie Qingcheng lifted a pale and slender hand to close the notebook, but just before the book was completely shut, something a bit strange at the corner of a page caught his eye.

Xie Qingcheng's hands froze. He made the hurricane lamp brighter and locked his gaze on that spot, his expression attentive yet grave...

A few seconds later, He Yu heard Xie Qingcheng's voice float over, his tone so chilly it sounded a little peculiar.

"He Yu, come take a look at this."

It was a line of writing squeezed into a very unremarkable corner of the notebook.

"WZL will be murdered soon."

These words were written with a fountain pen in a crooked scrawl; it looked as though someone wrote it with their left hand. However, what made this message so intriguing was that the person had signed her name at the end.

It was a name that no one could've expected to see here—

"Jiang. Lan. Pei."

Thunder boomed outside, but within the cave, they could have heard a pin drop.

"Wasn't Jiang Lanpei locked up in a psychiatric hospital for twenty years?" He Yu finally broke the silence in a quiet voice.

Xie Qingcheng frowned in contemplation. "Though she did get a key in the end and had plenty of opportunities to come and go as she pleased..."

"But she was probably limited to the grounds of Cheng Kang Psychiatric Hospital." He Yu continued Xie Qingcheng's train of thought. "Do you think she could have left and returned without a single soul noticing? And run off to this cave on Neverland Island at Huzhou University and leave a message like this in such an unremarkable tree hollow book?"

Of course, it was impossible.

"Plus, this writing looks very new, like it was only left within the past few days." Xie Qingcheng examined those red words written in the book under the searchlight's illumination. "And who's this WZL..."

The two of them pondered over this old worn-out notebook for a very long time.

He Yu suddenly said, "I just remembered a rumor I overheard a few days ago on campus!"

"What was it?"

"Some students feel that although Jiang Lanpei is terrifying, she's also quite a tragic figure—the type that spawns legends. Plus, when she died, she was wearing the kind of red dress that's associated with vengeful spirits. Those students made up a saying that if you have a grudge against someone, you can picture how that person will die and write it down on a piece of paper. Then, you write down Jiang Lanpei's name using a red pen, and her ghost will kill your enemy for you."

He Yu paused and added, "But your enemy must be a man; it won't work if they're female."

"Why is that?"

"Because the newspapers published a story about what Jiang Lanpei went through, so the students who made up this rumor thought that Jiang Lanpei's resentment would only target men."

He Yu took another look at the writing in the notebook.

"Say, do you think someone might have come to this island recently and remembered the rumor about Jiang Lanpei's murderous ghost when they were flipping through this book and reading the messages people left before? Maybe that person happened to loathe this WZL guy just like the author of the previous message, so they were struck with the idea of changing this simple rant into a proper curse?"

Shaking his head, Xie Qingcheng pulled out his phone and casually took a photo for documentation. Then, he said, "I'll bring this book to the public security bureau later. I keep feeling that there's a certain link between Jiang Lanpei and your Huzhou University."

The light in He Yu's eyes flickered as he said softly, "I agree."

"Oh?"

"The school uniform."

Xie Qingcheng sighed, and his eyes hardened. "So, we're on the same page. I suppose the Department of Public Security's thinking along the same lines too—I've seen plainclothes officers at your school the past few days. Some of them are even veteran officers who used to work with my parents. They seem to be investigating something."

The day Jiang Lanpei murdered Liang Jicheng, there was a seemingly unremarkable detail that was extremely odd: why did Jiang Lanpei go through the trouble of taking off Xie Xue's Huzhou University uniform and putting it on Liang Jicheng's dead body before dismembering and mutilating the corpse?

"Mentally ill people rarely act without reason, especially when it's something this highly purposeful and unusual," said Xie Qingcheng. "The way I see it, the investigation of Jiang Lanpei's case will implicate certain people at your school sooner or later."

He Yu raised a hand and smiled. "I definitely won't be included among those people."

Xie Qingcheng made no reply.

"I might not even have been born yet when she got locked up."

Exasperated, Xie Qingcheng said, "This isn't something either of us should worry about. I'll hand the book over to the police after we get out of here—let's leave it to them to figure it out."

He Yu hummed in response. Since they were talking about Cheng Kang Psychiatric Hospital, he suddenly had a thought. "Oh yeah."

"What?"

"I've been wondering recently, how we would be doing now if Xie Xue had actually been murdered when we rushed over there that day?"

Xie Qingcheng fixed his black pupils on He Yu indifferently. "Why can't you think about something good for once?"

"I wish her more good than anyone else."

In his annoyance, Xie Qingcheng didn't catch the meaning behind He Yu's words. He only irritably tossed out a careless reply. "Me too."

"But if something really happened to her—"

"Then I'd go on living just as I am now, just so long as I'm not dead myself."

It wasn't as though Xie Qingcheng hadn't experienced something similar before.

That one time when the devastating incident had occurred, there wasn't even a chance for him to turn back or get a shot at redemption.

In the middle of a downpour, he'd seen the ice-cold bodies of his parents sprawled across the ground. Behind him was the yellow- and white-striped police tape that cordoned off the area. The belated wail of piercing sirens filled his ears. The front end of a truck was engulfed in violent flames. In the light of the towering fire, he could see that only half of his mother's body was intact. Her wide eyes stared vacantly at him. A hand, severed by the truck's wheel, lay near the toe of his shoe.

Back then, he'd thought that there was no way for him to continue living.

But nineteen years had already passed since then.

He Yu didn't know what Xie Qingcheng was thinking about. But when he heard the older man's response, he fell silent for a while. He gazed at Xie Qingcheng with an unreadable expression in his eyes, and then gave him a very light, icy smile. "As expected of you, Xie Qingcheng. You live every moment of your life with such a cool head that you would only ever lose control for a minute at a time."

"People can't live their whole lives in grief," said Xie Qingcheng. "When tragedy strikes, even if it's impossible for you to accept it immediately, you'll still be able to slowly digest what happened in the end. Rather than wallowing in your pain and refusing to move on, it's better to not waste this time and instead pull yourself together to do the things that need to be done, in order to prevent more tragedies from happening."

"Ah," He Yu said softly. "A stone-cold pragmatist indeed."

Mood heavy, he didn't want to remain in this cave with Xie Qingcheng any longer. Since the rain had let up some, he walked outside alone.

He Yu spent some time calming himself down until the stroke of midnight, when he saw some signs of activity on the opposite shore. It turned out that his conscientious, money-seeking club member had wrapped up his responsibilities and was paddling the duck boat to return to Neverland Island right on time.

He became quite animated the moment he saw He Yu, standing up and waving frantically from the swaying boat. "How was it? I'm very punctual, aren't I? Was He-laoban's declaration of love successful?"

He peered impatiently behind He Yu as he spoke.

"Huh? Where's the lovely lady?"

What declaration of love?

The only person on the island was a stone-cold pragmatist; to whom was he supposed to declare love?

He Yu responded to the dumbfuck on the boat with a smile. "I don't believe xuezhang should be nosy about that."

"Look at you, you're *shy*. Ha ha ha, I get it, I get it." He winked at He Yu with a suggestive expression, then pulled up the Alipay QR code on his phone.

"The rest of the payment."

He Yu rolled his eyes and took out his phone. It still had no signal. He unlocked it with an icy expression. "Please turn off the signal jammer first."

The senior club member did as he was told, then asked with great excitement, "Did you see the message I sent you? On the other phone."

"What message?"

He Yu fished out his other phone and looked at it.

"He-laoban, there's a first aid kit inside the cave on the island. It has boxes of condoms in the second compartment. If you need them, you can check inside the kit, and remember to send me a red packet afterward..."

His accomplice silently edged over with a nosy expression on his face.

"It's even the kind with the special delay lubricant, guaranteed to wear your lady out."

He Yu smiled slightly. "Don't put these kinds of things in the first aid kit anymore. It's terribly immoral, don't you think, Xuezhang?"

He finally picked up on the bourgeoisie member's poor mood. After a brief moment of shock, he suddenly realized that this was because *He Yu didn't get any!*

The senior club member couldn't help but feel immense admiration for that unknown 180-centimeter beauty.

Originally, he'd thought that the reason the beautiful woman didn't come to the shore with He Yu was because she had been left so weak after receiving his affections for the first time that she couldn't rise.[31]

But now, it seemed that the towering beauty was, in fact, a cold mistress who was unswayed by wealth and riches!

Young Master He was so tragic. How did he end up falling for someone so high-maintenance? Tsk, tsk. A waste of money... Such a waste of money...

The club member shut up. Even after receiving the last installment of his payment, he behaved professionally and called a friend to get a kayak out from the storehouse. The two of them departed first, leaving the duck boat on the shore for He Yu to use.

---

31 Referencing "The Song of Everlasting Sorrow" by Tang dynasty poet Bai Juyi, a description of Yang-guifei, the beloved consort of Emperor Xuanzong.

He Yu finished dealing with the scene of the crime and was about to go to the cave and call Xie Qingcheng over. But the moment he turned around, he froze.

That man was already standing in the moonlit forest with his hands in his pockets, leaning against a cedar tree as he gazed at He Yu with a blank expression. Who knew how long he'd been there, silently listening under the shadows of the trees?

He Yu was silent.

Xie Qingcheng lit a cigarette and, like a cop conducting an interrogation, said, "I'll give you one chance to explain."

He slowly exhaled a faint ring of gray smoke and locked eyes with He Yu. "Go ahead."

21

IN TURN, I CAUGHT
HER IN THE ACT

AT THAT VERY MOMENT, Huzhou University's indoor gymnasium was bustling with an unusual amount of noise and excitement thanks to the students who had set up several rows of temporary vending booths inside of its walls.

This was one of the places that campus exploration event attendees usually visited the least, but due to the rain outside, it was impossible for the outdoor events to continue. Thus, a crowd of participating students had gathered here.

"Oh, look. There's a love letter mailbox here."

"It was here? Yes! I finally found it! I've been looking forever."

A group of grinning female students crowded around a capsule-shaped mailbox, falling over each other to write the names of the recipients of their love letters and stuff them into the box.

It was a mailbox specifically prepared for shy and socially anxious folks to avoid the awkwardness of personally delivering a love letter. It was set up every year during the campus exploration event and was wildly popular with the students.

Xie Xue sat in a corner, drinking warm milk as she finished writing her letter and sealed it in a pure white envelope. She looked the envelope over before carefully writing down, one delicate stroke after another, the name of the boy with whom she was secretly in love.

A satisfied smile spread over her face as she got up and walked over to the capsule mailbox. However, just as she was about to deposit her love letter, a droplet of blood suddenly fell from above, dotting the envelope's surface.

Xie Xue gasped in surprise.

"Ah, Xiao-jiejie, your nose is bleeding..." An observant bystander quickly took out a pack of tissues from her bag and offered it to Xie Xue. "Here, wipe your nose before more drips."

Xie Xue hastily tilted her head up as she covered her nose with the tissue. "Th-thank you."

How could she be so unlucky as to suddenly get a nosebleed?

It had been a long time since this happened. Now that she thought about it, the last time it happened, she was still a little kid.

"Your letter... Why don't I get you another one..."

"Ah, it's fine, it's fine, it's fine! I wrote it for no reason! Just for fun! It's not important! Not important at all!" Fearing that someone would see the name on the envelope and laugh at her, Xie Xue hurriedly nudged her way through the crowd. She stuffed the blood-stained letter into the mailbox slot in a flurry, then turned tail and ran off without another glance, still clutching at her nose.

It was only then that the student standing by the mailbox realized, "Eh? I think that was Xie-laoshi..."

After running some distance away, Xie Xue thought she ought to give her brother a call and ask what it meant when someone suddenly got a nosebleed.

However, when she dialed his number, all she got was, "Hello, the user you are calling has their device switched off. Please call again later."

Xie Xue was taken aback. Ahh...could it be that her brother had already returned to his dorm and gone to bed?

Xie Xue could never have possibly imagined that her big brother wasn't asleep at all, that because he had taken her place as the nine-tailed fox, he was trapped by He Yu on an island for a good few hours.

And despite his careful planning, He Yu had been caught red-handed by her big brother in the end.

The two gentlemen stood by the water's edge, both with their hands shoved into their pockets as they faced each other with icy stares.

Xie Qingcheng was waiting patiently for He Yu's explanation.

"...The moon's reflection in the water is a beautiful sight to behold." He Yu turned his face up to the sky and spoke at last, unhurried, "The moon is very beautiful tonight.[32] Do you understand what I mean?"

"Speak normally."

"I *also* think you're very good-looking, and I want to date you."

"Have some sense of fucking shame." Xie Qingcheng flicked off the ash from the cigarette he was holding. "I'm not joking."

Slowly, He Yu's smile faded. He finally removed his frivolous mask, likely because he knew Xie Qingcheng could see right through it, and his expression darkened. "Seeing as you already heard me, what else is there for me to explain?"

He met Xie Qingcheng's sharply cold eyes once again, and with a pause and a sigh he laid things out in simple terms.

"Very well. I have someone that I like. I was originally planning on telling her tonight, but she didn't come. Do you finally get it now?"

32 *This phrase is commonly used as a veiled declaration of love.*

Xie Qingcheng had a vague hunch that something wasn't quite right, but he couldn't quite pinpoint what exactly it was at the moment.

He was distracted by the very fact that He Yu had a girl he liked. "Someone at your school?"

"Yes."

"Who?"

He Yu smiled. "That is none of your business."

Xie Qingcheng straightened out his legs, then slowly walked over to He Yu. Though he was shorter than He Yu, the higher ground he was standing on allowed him to look down at the younger man from above. His peach-blossom eyes looked as though they were lightly frosted by the moonlight.

"He Yu, do you know what kind of illness you have?"

He Yu said indifferently, "Psychological Ebola."

"Then what are you doing trying to date someone before you've fully recovered and gotten your symptoms under control?"

He Yu did not react.

It was almost as though he had long anticipated such a reaction from Xie Qingcheng.

After a moment of silence, He Yu looked back at him and said softly, "Weren't you the one who once said that I ought to form connections with others and build a bridge to society? You encouraged me to interact with other people, to make friends and find affection, to seek love. Not to mention, weren't you the one who said I hadn't even gotten into a relationship, that I'd forever be just a little devil?"

"I said that out of anger." Xie Qingcheng's eyes were as sharp as a blade, "You're so smart, you should be able to tell the difference between truth and provocation."

"Thank you for thinking so highly of me," He Yu said. "But I'm also only nineteen years old. I'm not as perceptive as you think I am."

Xie Qingcheng's expression hardened. "You'd better be more careful, He Yu. Do you know just how many people become depressed after a breakup? Even ordinary people can lose their minds over love, suffering terribly and hovering between life and death. What you need is a steady and calm state of mind. Once all your lab results have returned to normal, you can date whoever you want, and it'll have nothing to do with me. I won't even bother to ask."

He Yu suddenly thought of Xie Xue's dimpled smile.

It was kind of funny that Xie Qingcheng had no idea that the person He Yu liked was Xie Xue. He had no idea, yet he was already reacting like this. If he had known that the person that he had originally planned on trapping on this island was his beloved little sister, Xie Qingcheng probably would've already slapped him viciously across the face.

"Have you ever been able to exercise complete control over your emotions these past few years?" Xie Qingcheng asked. "If not, then what right do you have to pursue someone romantically?"

He Yu met Xie Qingcheng's gaze with his dark eyes. "The fact that I made such a decision in the first place means that I believe I can control myself."

"You really are far too conceited."

"Conceited?" He Yu repeated with a chuckle. Then, he asked softly, "Doctor Xie, have I ever hurt anyone in these nineteen years?"

Xie Qingcheng did not answer.

"I just like someone, that's all." He Yu paused. "But I don't get such a right, do I?"

"You have no idea just how this illness will manifest in the future," Xie Qingcheng warned. "Not to mention, you're a patient with the blood toxin variant, you—"

"Professor Xie." He Yu calmly interrupted the older man's speech. "You are no longer my personal physician. I know that you are lonely in your middle age, and that's causing you sleepless nights. So it's perfectly normal that you like to poke your nose into the affairs of young people. But, frankly speaking, I think this matter of mine has very little to do with you."

Provoked by He Yu's tone, Xie Qingcheng's temper also flared. "Do you think I *want* to poke my nose into your business? I'm only doing this out of respect for your father. Not to mention, I treated your illness for seven years. It's hardly unreasonable to feel concern for a dog that you've looked after for seven years, much less a person."

He Yu lowered his head with a smirk as he ran the tip of his tongue over his teeth. "Ah, what a pity it is that I'm not your dog."

Xie Qingcheng could only stare in response.

"It's late. I don't want to continue standing here feeding the mosquitoes. Are you getting onto the boat or not?" He Yu loosened the iron chain that secured the boat into place and said to Xie Qingcheng in a slightly mocking tone, "Your back must hurt after sitting for so long. Do you need me to assist you in any way?"

In the end, the two of them parted on bad terms once again.

After returning to his dormitory, Xie Qingcheng took a shower and thought over the recent events. Even though it was a bit late, he gave He Jiwei a call.

"Oh, Doctor Xie! Long time no talk, long time no talk." He Jiwei was surprisingly rather polite when speaking to Xie Qingcheng, "What a coincidence; I was just thinking about giving you a call."

"There's a matter that Executive He would call *me* for?" Xie Qingcheng felt a little taken aback.

"That's right. I wanted to ask you about the incident at Cheng Kang Psychiatric Hospital."

That made sense.

He Jiwei sighed heavily. "These past few days, I've managed to get the gist of what happened. That boy, He Yu, really worries me far too much. I heard that you were with him through the whole thing."

"I was."

"The officers at the police station told me that you were looking after him all day that day. I really must thank you."

It seemed that He Yu had not told He Jiwei the whole story.

Xie Qingcheng disliked being thanked for no good reason, and so he gave He Jiwei a rough account of what happened during the Cheng Kang incident—omitting, of course, any mention of the blood toxin. He Jiwei fell silent for a short while after he was done giving his report. "So, that's what happened. That little brat. Ah..."

After a moment of deliberation, Xie Qingcheng said, "Executive He, you treated me kindly in the past, so even though I'm no longer employed with the He family, I still take note of his condition when I see him. So, if you don't mind, I'd like to ask how He Yu has been doing over the past few years?"

"Thanks to you, he's doing much better. Didn't you say back then that he needed to become independent once he reached that stage? I was rather worried at first, but who could have expected that he actually had that level of self-control? He gets shots occasionally or takes medicine when he feels unwell, but he hasn't had any other issues."

"Then, would you say he's dependent on medication?"

"That..." He Jiwei hesitated slightly before forcing out a laugh. "You know very well that his mother and I are both very busy with our work. To be honest, it's impossible for us to pay much attention to how much medicine he takes... According to the housekeeper, it's not too bad; he doesn't medicate all that much. Why? Has he been acting strangely?"

"No." Xie Qingcheng hesitated for a moment. Despite his concerns, he wasn't intending to divulge He Yu's dating plans to He Jiwei. "It's nothing, really. I was just asking, that's all."

He Jiwei said, "You can return at any time, if you'd like. You're the best fit for someone like He Yu. There's no one else like you."

"Executive He, you flatter me, surely," Xie Qingcheng said. "I've left the healthcare system for so long, even my medical license has expired."

"Well, you were only a student when you came to us... Ah, forget it... Since you're unwilling, then I won't press the issue any further. However, Doctor Xie, seeing as you and He Yu now live quite close to each other, could I please trouble you to help look after him from time to time? He may seem mature, but he's still quite young. He often acts on his emotions and does some rash things on impulse. His mother and I can't watch over him, so there are times when we really are quite worried about the boy."

He Jiwei then added, "But please, don't force yourself if you don't have the time..."

"No, it's fine. After all, he was my patient for a very long time," Xie Qingcheng said. "Not to mention, he's Executive He's son. These are all things that I ought to do."

The two of them chatted idly for a while longer before hanging up.

Xie Qingcheng leaned back against his chair and reached up to massage his temples. To him, He Yu was a unique patient who was enmeshed in a very complicated network of personal relationships.

But after all was said and done, He Yu had grown up and become independent—he might not even listen to what He Jiwei said anymore. There were certain things that were truly beyond his control.

Xie Qingcheng could only observe for now.

With an aching head, Xie Qingcheng blow-dried his hair and changed into clean clothes. Even if He Yu truly wasn't ready for dating, there was no guarantee the poor unlucky girl would even say yes if he were to ask her out.

Xie Qingcheng should just wait and see.

With this in mind, he picked up the notebook he'd brought home from Secret Utopia and pushed open the door to go downstairs. There, he called a taxi and headed off to the local police department.

At the conclusion of the campus exploration event, the handful of students in charge of clearing the scene were moving the activity fixtures, one of which was the massive love letter mailbox.

"The love letter capsule is way too heavy this year…"

"Just how many love letters are there?"

"Is everyone so shy and unwilling to say their feelings outright? Ahh…"

"Hey! Don't step on my foot… Aiyo!!"

In a flurry of limbs, the two students handling the mailbox stumbled to the ground together with the box. Its cheap plastic flap cracked open upon impact, and the letters within spilled out with a whoosh all over the synthetic rubber surface of the track. With a gust of the night wind, the flyaway letters scattered in all directions, as though they had grown legs.

One of the students went pale with alarm. "Oh no!"

These love letters from those young men and women hadn't even been delivered into the hands of their recipients yet—how could they lose them? The students scrambled up and hastily dusted themselves off before running after the flyaway envelopes.

But there were too many letters that had been scattered away by the wind for the two of them to even hope to pick up all by themselves. They were reduced to raising their voices and yelling desperately for passersby to lend a hand. All the students were also very enthusiastic, and they cornered and chased down the letters, grabbing them in handfuls from all around.

He Yu just so happened to pass by as this scene played out.

As expected of a warm, kind, and gentle rich young master and perfect role model in front of others such as him, He Yu didn't hesitate to help his xuezhang and xuejie pick up all those runaway love letters.

"Thank you, thank you so much!"

The xuejie was so busy she didn't even look up as she bowed repeatedly.

The girl beside her pinched her and whispered, "It's He Yu!"

"Ah!" The xuejie yelped and looked up. Sure enough, it was He Yu. With her heartbeat accelerating like a rocket, she stuttered out, "Hi, hi, Xuedi..."

He Yu smiled and passed her the letters before continuing to help pick up some more.

There was a letter stuck in the bushes beside the basketball court. He Yu walked over and picked up that pristine white envelope. He flicked off the dust only to suddenly freeze.

There were bloodstains on that letter.

Beneath the stains, a row of exceedingly, beautifully written words were still visible.

"To Wei Dongheng."

Wei Dongheng was the class idol in Class 1 of the senior cohort in the drama department of the School of Fine Arts. He was also someone He Yu had known for a very long time.

Among the wealthy business social circles in Huzhou, theirs were the two names that were mentioned the most frequently when the subject of different influential families' young masters came up. The reason for this was none other than the fact that Young Master He and Young Master Wei were very similar in many respects—even their birthdays were on the same day, though they were born in different years. However, the results of their upbringings were completely different: in this social circle, Young Master He was famously well educated and refined while Young Master Wei was known for his licentious behavior and debauchery.

The Wei family was an aristocratic military family. However, one of their ancestral tombs might've been unfortunately renovated into a nightclub or the like. As a result, people probably desecrated their clan by popping-and-locking on the grave every single night, so perhaps that was how such a refined family had managed to pop out a degenerate like Wei Dongheng.

Ever since childhood, Wei Dongheng had spent his days street-racing, skipping classes, and revving engines with disreputable thugs; he stirred up endless trouble for the Wei family. If not for their family's influence, they might've long since been cooked up into a pot of shit stew. In this social circle, the number of times parents cried in humiliated rage, "Look at He Yu! Then look at yourself! What good are you?!" was exactly equal to the frequency with which their teary children retorted, "Look at Wei Dongheng! Then look at your me! What's wrong with how I am?!"

The entire Huzhou University knew that Wei Dongheng was unbelievably wild. When the school provided the drama students with audition opportunities, Wei Dongheng didn't attend a single tryout. The reason why he was a drama major was because it was the one major in the Department of Fine Arts that had the lowest passing grade requirement; in short, he was only there to coast by and collect a degree.

Which visually impaired girl would write him *a love letter?* He Yu thought, somewhat incredulously.

He was getting ready to return the envelope when he paused, suddenly struck by a feeling that something wasn't quite right.

He glanced at the envelope once more...

To Wei Dongheng... To Wei Dongheng...

Then, he froze.

The handwriting.

He could never mistake it.

He felt like he'd been struck by an invisible, staggering blow.

This was Xie Xue's handwriting!

"Oh my, what's going on? Did the letters fall out?" A group of male students who had just finished their game of basketball emerged from the court while wiping away their sweat. One of them glanced over casually and saw the letter in He Yu's hands.

A smile immediately broke out over the student's face as he turned and said, "Young Master He, you've gotten another great harvest this year!"

Another student stepped off the basketball court. He was about He Yu's height and had an honest and respectable face, but his hair was bleached and dyed a flashy silver, and he had five piercings in his ears. He wore a carefree expression of uninhibited degeneracy.

It was Wei Dongheng, the man himself.

Wei Dongheng and He Yu's eyes met.

Wei Dongheng nodded first. "Young Master He."

He Yu returned the gesture, but the words "To Wei Dongheng" kept swinging back and forth before his eyes, every line and stroke carrying those familiar flourishes.

Usually, Wei Dongheng had no interest in these idiotic love letters, but since this particular one was in He Yu's hands, he couldn't suppress the urge to at least take a second glance. That's when he spotted the bloodstain on the envelope.

Wei Dongheng furrowed his brow. "A threatening letter?"

He Yu seemed exceptionally nonchalant—even the movements of his lips were very slight. "Looks like it. Want me to toss it for you?"

"I have no interest in love letters. They all go in the trash can. I'm sure that Young Master He understands. But this is the first time I've gotten a threatening letter! I'll have to go back and read it properly." Wei Dongheng smiled at He Yu and plucked the letter from his hands. "Thanks."

Out of habit, He Yu replied blandly, "No problem."

After Wei Dongheng left, a very long time passed before He Yu managed to slowly clear his mind.

He still didn't dare believe that what he saw was really Xie Xue's confession letter to Wei Dongheng. Out of the corner of his eye, he noticed that the two girls in charge of the capsule mailbox were gazing over at him and Wei Dongheng in excitement just now. He made his way back toward them.

"Excuse me, about that bloodstained letter..."

"Oh, that girl with all the luck, Xie-laoshi, wrote it."

"Yeah, it was her. Maybe it was because it gets so dry in the fall, but her nose started bleeding while she was writing. I was the one who passed her a tissue."

"...Okay." After a moment, He Yu said quietly, "Thank you."

He Yu returned to his bedroom that evening, and after washing up, he lay in bed and endured a sleepless night thinking about Xie Xue and Wei Dongheng.

Xie Xue had also known Wei Dongheng all this time.

When they were young, the Wei family's Young Master would come over to play. Xie Xue would be there too, and she and He Yu would always team up to target Wei Dongheng. Back then, He Yu thought that Xie Xue disliked this arrogant boy who thought himself higher than the heavens.

But at the time, none of them asked themselves: why would anyone go out of their way to bother someone if they genuinely didn't care about them?

Xie Xue and Wei Dongheng attended the same high school.

When Xie Xue was a second-year student, Wei Dongheng was in his first year.

When Xie Xue was a third-year student, Wei Dongheng was yet again in his first year.

Later, when Xie Xue graduated, Wei Dongheng was still in his first year.

This joker actually used the fact that he had been held back twice to become a legend in their circles and even passed it off as an impressive feat as he held the position of the first-year idol for three years in a row.

He was a perennial rulebreaker—when Xie Xue was hall monitor at school, Wei Dongheng had walked right past her with complete indifference to eat barbecue off-campus for lunch. She furiously warned him against it only for him to ignore her. Even the clique of hoodlums who followed him around started to ridicule her.

"Wei-ge, is this our little saozi? She really keeps you on a short leash. She said she's gonna take points off you if you dare to go out! Oh, I'm so scared, ha ha ha ha!"

"Saozi, not only are you super short, but you're also flat as a board."

"Wei-ge! This little girl's really writing down in her notebook that you broke the rules! Why aren't you trying to keep her happy?"

The gangsters whistled and jeered. Xie Xue, who was wearing the school's red hall monitor armband, became so angry her eyes began to fill with tears. She dashed over to Wei Dongheng's swaggering figure as he walked away with his backpack slung over one shoulder, stood on her tiptoes, and yelled furiously, "Wei Dongheng! You're trash! You're the most irritating person in the universe!!"

But despite that, why did she come to Huzhou University's School of Fine Arts to be a teacher after graduating?

She was the top of her class and had gotten exceptionally good grades, so she clearly could have tried to get a job at Yanzhou's Academy of Drama, where the pay was better and the program was much more prestigious. But back then, she had told He Yu over WeChat that she lacked confidence in herself. That's why she decided to accept an offer at the somewhat less-challenging Huzhou University.

He Yu had his doubts at the time.

Xie Xue had always been a very brave person. Other than Xie Qingcheng, He Yu had never seen anyone more courageous than her. So why would someone like her lack the confidence to even apply for a job?

It was only now that He Yu finally understood that what Xie Xue had actually been chasing after was Wei Dongheng, who was attending Huzhou University.

And He Yu had been completely oblivious, rejecting offers from top overseas universities to come after her.

...How laughable.

He Yu lay on his bed the entire night, quiet and numb as he continued mulling over the situation until the sky began to brighten with the coming dawn.

"He Yu, we've got morning classes. Are you getting up? Let's go have breakfast," his roommate urged him from beyond the curtain.

He Yu agreed and sat up.

But a brief moment later, his chest suddenly contracted with a sharp pain which rapidly spread throughout the rest of his body.

He propped his slightly cold forehead up with a hand and took a pill from the bedside table. "I'm not feeling very well," he said in a low voice. "You guys go ahead."

He Yu felt unwell, but Xie Qingcheng's night wasn't much better.

By the time he made it to the police department, he was already feeling a little off.

Xie Qingcheng wasn't sure if he'd caught a chill on the island or what, but he kept feeling dizzy and hearing a faint ringing in his ears.

He handed the notebook with the suspicious message off to a police officer on duty and explained the circumstances of its discovery before turning to leave.

However, he'd only made it to the staircase before he suddenly collapsed.

"Xie-ge?!"

Xie Qingcheng turned his head with difficulty and saw that it was Chen Man, who was in the middle of helping his coworker transport some files.

"Xie-ge!" As Chen Man sprinted over, Xie Qingcheng was overcome by a bout of intense dizziness; it was only after Chen Man grabbed him around his waist that he was able to steady himself.

Chen Man looked him over anxiously. "What's wrong?"

"I don't know. I suddenly felt a little dizzy..."

"Your face looks awfully red too. Let me take a look... Aiya, why do you feel so hot?" Chen Man hastily propped him upright and turned to shout at his coworker, "Um, Xiao-Zhou, take over for me for a bit, okay? I'm taking someone to the infirmary!"

I TORMENTED HIM
UNTIL HE GOT A FEVER

THE STATION'S INFIRMARY didn't have much diagnostic equipment—it mostly contained supplies for treating external injuries—so Chen Man ended up bringing Xie Qingcheng to the hospital.

Chen Man rushed back and forth, registering at overnight urgent care, picking up medicine, and waiting for the blood test results, while Xie Qingcheng reclined in the hospital's ice-cold metal chair and rested with his eyes closed.

After a while, Chen Man returned from the service window with a freshly printed examination report in hand. Written on this report was a line of text that made Chen Man wonder whether he'd gone blind: an allergic reaction to mango.

"Comrade, shouldn't you know what you're allergic to at your age?" The overnight urgent care doctor pushed up their glasses as they scolded Xie Qingcheng. "You really were too careless—just look at your test results. How terrifying."

Brandishing their pen imperiously as they spoke, the doctor prescribed a slew of medicines in an indecipherable script.

"We usually give patients with such serious allergic reactions antihistamine injections, but given the severity of his current state, he would need to receive them over the course of three days. If he's too busy to take time off from work, there's a new type of IV saline solution that will alleviate the symptoms overnight. Think it over and decide which option you'd prefer."

Xie Qingcheng disliked antihistamine injections. He detested the thought of having to go to the hospital three days in a row even more.

"I'll have the IV," he said, and Xie Qingcheng and Chen Man were led into the infusion room.

Xie Qingcheng had a delicate constitution and tended to feel dizzy and nauseated if the IV drip delivered the medicine too rapidly, so he slowed down the infusion himself after the nurse left.

Chen Man busied himself with swiftly taking care of the administrative procedures, and then sat down next to Xie Qingcheng, who was resting with his eyes closed.

Chen Man stared at his profile for a while, then said quietly, "Ge, don't you always avoid eating mango?"

Feeling unbelievably unfortunate, Xie Qingcheng said, "I was so unlucky I went fucking blind, okay?"

Chen Man was already used to being cursed out for no good reason. His older brother had been Xie Qingcheng's father's mentee, so he had known Xie Qingcheng since childhood and was familiar with this dage's personality. When this dage lost face, you'd better pretend not to see it—if you dared point it out, you'd definitely end up just like him right now, thoroughly chewed out.

Chen Man sighed. "Sit tight. I'll go pour some hot water for you."

He returned in a heartbeat and held a paper cup out to Xie Qingcheng. "Ge, you should drink some."

Only then did Xie Qingcheng open his eyes to receive the cup of piping-hot water with his slightly cool fingertips and drink a few sips.

"So, who tricked you into eating mango?" Chen Man took in his sickly appearance and mumbled, "What a fucking asshole."

After finishing the water, Xie Qingcheng's voice seemed to have finally warmed back up to a certain degree. "It was payback..."

That's what it was, wasn't it? he thought.

Nothing good ever happened whenever he ran into He Yu.

Of course, Xie Qingcheng knew that he had a mango allergy, and a severe one at that. His skin wouldn't just burn up and flush red, he would also come down with a high fever. He had known since he was seven or eight years old that he needed to avoid this fruit as if it were a biological weapon; even his little sister, who craved mango so much she would literally drool when she saw it, had to accommodate him. In fact, in the interest of his health and safety, she never brought any mango-flavored foods into their home.

It had been so long that he'd forgotten what mango tasted like. When He Yu brought out the cake on Neverland Island, it was already too dark for him to see what type it was, so he had eaten the mango mousse cake thinking it was peach-flavored.

Xie Qingcheng sighed. "I'm going to sleep for a bit. Are you in a rush to get back?"

"Oh," Chen Man said hastily. "No, I'm not in a rush. I'll keep you company."

Xie Qingcheng truly was too tired and miserable. He lowered his lashes, leaned back against the chair, and fell asleep.

The air-conditioning was rather cold in the IV ward, and patients receiving IV treatment were susceptible to the cold to begin with. Chen Man saw a slight frown appear on Xie Qingcheng's sleeping face, as though he was displeased with the temperature. In response, Chen Man got up and removed his own navy-blue uniform jacket and draped it over Xie Qingcheng.

Sensing the warmth, Xie Qingcheng's brow slowly smoothed out.

Chen Man fixed his eyes on Xie Qingcheng's handsome, chiseled features and felt that the time wasn't passing too slowly at all...

Sometime later, an emergency room nurse came over. "Time for a new bag?" she inquired.

The nurse was doing her rounds while taking over for the next shift, but as soon as she walked over and saw that the patient receiving the IV transfusion was Xie Qingcheng, she became instantly dumbfounded.

She was an old colleague of Xie Qingcheng's at Huzhou First Hospital, but their relationship wasn't the greatest. Her expression darkened slightly as her gaze darted back and forth between Xie Qingcheng and Chen Man before landing on the police uniform draped over Xie Qingcheng's shoulders for several seconds.

An oblivious Chen Man replied with utmost politeness, "Yes, thank you."

The nurse laughed humorlessly and dragged out her words in a singsong manner as she said, "No problem. May I ask who this person is to you?"

"...My..." Chen Man's cheeks subconsciously flushed. "My friend."

"Oh, your *friend*." The nurse smiled. "Officer, you're going to a lot of trouble, bringing your friend here in the middle of the night and keeping watch over him so closely."

Chen Man didn't know how to respond. He found her words a bit odd, but he didn't take them to heart.

The nurse sashayed away after she was done changing the IV bag. As she left the room, she took out her phone to tap some messages into the group chat that she had with her colleagues.

It had been late at night when Xie Qingcheng was first hooked up to the IV, so by the time the three IV bags were in his system and he woke up, it was already morning.

He had an allergic constitution—his reactions were intense, and his recovery slow, so he still felt rather unwell even after the IV needle had been removed. Realizing this, Chen Man said to him, "Ge, keep my jacket for now. Don't catch a cold."

Xie Qingcheng hummed weakly in agreement and walked out of the treatment room with Chen Man's uniform jacket on.

The hospital lobby was already brimming with people when they checked out—Huzhou First Hospital was the busiest hospital in the area, after all. Chen Man took the medical report to fetch the oral prescription while Xie Qingcheng waited in a less crowded area.

Xie Qingcheng leaned against the wall with his eyes closed and head hanging down. After a while, he heard footsteps approaching.

Someone stopped before him.

Thinking it was Chen Man, Xie Qingcheng opened his eyes. "All done?" he asked without looking at the newcomer and simply straightened up. "Thanks for today. Now, let's go."

"...Xie Qingcheng."

Xie Qingcheng's head shot up at the sound of that voice.

A handsome face with well-defined features appeared before his eyes. It was the culprit who had reduced him to such a sorry state: He Yu.

He Yu stared at him. "Why are *you* here?"

Xie Qingcheng's expression soured in an instant.

The fact that they'd just had a falling-out on the island the night before aside, it seemed that, ever since Xie Qingcheng and He Yu reunited, they would get into an altercation every time they met. He Yu had grown up into a full-fledged adult in the time that they had been apart, so he didn't find Xie Qingcheng as scary as he did when he was a child, nor did he feel the same powerful reverence toward him anymore. What's more, He Yu had found many ways to vex this man and make him feel ill at ease—and found it deeply satisfying to boot.

Xie Qingcheng emphatically refused to let a young man laugh at him. His features grew sharp and cold while he stood up perfectly straight, as if he were not ill at all. "It's nothing. I had some business to take care of." He sized up He Yu. "And why are *you* at the hospital?"

As he spoke, his gaze slid downward to land on the bag of medicine that He Yu was holding.

He Yu moved the bag behind him without batting an eye and replied mildly, "My roommate is sick. I'm getting him some medicine since it's more convenient for me to drive."

The two of them stared at each other in silence, hiding their true selves.

After a while, He Yu said, "The jacket you're wearing…"

It was only then that Xie Qingcheng realized that Chen Man's uniform was still draped over his shoulders; layered on top of his snowy white dress shirt, the police jacket really was quite conspicuous. No wonder He Yu had been able to spot him immediately in the bustling crowd.

"It's my friend's."

"You're waiting for him?"

Xie Qingcheng nodded perfunctorily.

He Yu was still in a terrible mood. Xie Xue's love letter had given him such a great shock that he could no longer suppress the symptoms of his illness with his usual medicine, so he had come to the hospital to pick up a new prescription. To be honest, he'd wanted to ignore Xie Qingcheng when he spotted him earlier, but upon remembering that Xie Qingcheng was Xie Xue's elder brother, he thought that he should at least check in on him since they'd run into each other at a hospital.

But right now, he didn't want to talk much more with Xie Qingcheng either, much less meet his friend.

"I'll be leaving first then," said He Yu. "I still have other things to do."

And so, he left just like that.

Xie Qingcheng frowned slightly as he watched He Yu make his way through the bustling crowd. He knew that when He Yu's illness worsened, some of the medication he used could only be prescribed at provincial-level hospitals. Could it be...

"Xie-ge." At that moment, Chen Man returned, interrupting Xie Qingcheng's thoughts. "I got your medicine. I'll take you back now."

He noticed Xie Qingcheng's gaze and followed it, but He Yu had already disappeared.

Chen Man asked, "What's wrong?"

"...Nothing," Xie Qingcheng replied.

What else could he say?

That he'd met the culprit responsible for this whole mess?

Of course not. So, Xie Qingcheng simply said, "Let's go."

"Oh, okay. Ge, be careful on the steps."

They arrived half an hour later at the single faculty dormitory of Huzhou University's Medical Science Department in Chen Man's car. Chen Man hung his uniform jacket on a clothes rack beside the door and went into the kitchen to prepare the medicine. He handed it to Xie Qingcheng and watched as he slowly drank it down.

"Ge?" Chen Man thought for a moment and then said, "Did you run into an acquaintance at the hospital just now?"

Xie Qingcheng didn't reply.

"By the way, a nurse came by last night to change the IV bag, but she was acting kind of weird."

This time around, Xie Qingcheng acknowledged him. "Did that nurse have a long face, a mole below her lips, and look to be around thirty or forty years of age?"

"Yes."

"That's Nurse Zhou. She used to work under an older doctor," Xie Qingcheng said. "It's fine. She and I just don't get along very well."

After taking his medicine, Xie Qingcheng started to feel tired again. He lay down on the sofa with his arm over his eyes and annoyed himself with thoughts of Nurse Zhou and He Yu.

Regardless if it was his former coworker at Huzhou First Hospital or He Yu, they both irritated him to no end. When he was vexed, he liked to smoke. He didn't even get to touch his lighter at all last night as he was stuck in the IV room. Now, he lifted his arm from his eyes and said to Chen Man, "Hand me a cigarette."

Chen Man paled in shock. "You can't smoke! Your test results! Look at them, they—"

"Look at what? Who's the doctor here, me or you? Hand me a cigarette."

"I don't have any. I won't give it to you!"

"You don't or you won't?"

"I won't! I-I don't!" Chen Man stammered.

Xie Qingcheng yanked Chen Man forward by the lapels, swiftly rifled through his pockets, and fished out a pack of Liqun brand cigarettes from Chen Man's police uniform. He rolled his eyes as he tore the pack open and drew out a cigarette. He then held it between his teeth and looked at Chen Man expectantly.

Chen Man was silent.

Xie Qingcheng said, "Light."

Chen Man sighed deeply, truly at the end of his rope. "Xie-ge, it's really bad for you to continue like this. If Aunt and Uncle knew..."

Chen Man hadn't intended to bring up Xie Qingcheng's parents. When he saw how ugly Xie Qingcheng's expression had become, he didn't dare to speak another word. Instead, he quietly mumbled, "Sorry."

He handed Xie Qingcheng the lighter with utmost reluctance and looked on helplessly as Xie Qingcheng proceeded to slowly poison himself right before his eyes.

Xie Qingcheng took a few puffs from the cigarette, his pale, slender hand dangling from the edge of the sofa as he lay back to stare at the ceiling with an empty expression.

"You've been busy rushing around all night," he said to Chen Man. "I've also gotten in the way of your work. Thank you. You can go back now, I'll be fine."

"How could this be called getting in the way?"

But Xie Qingcheng couldn't make Chen Man bustle about anymore. "Go back and rest," he insisted.

Reluctantly, Chen Man thought things over and said, "Ge, I'm worried for you. I feel like your allergic reaction to the mango must have been planned out by some malicious bastard. If anyone tries to harass you, tell me. I'm a police officer now, and I can take care of him real—"

"What can you do?" Xie Qingcheng finally shifted his gaze and looked at the young man whose face still held a touch of childish innocence. He raised his hand and pulled down hard on his police hat until it covered his eyes. "You talk about doing this and doing that, but you're still a rookie, so what can you even do? I'm telling you to go back and do your civil policeman duties properly. Don't show off when there's nothing happening. Your brother is already gone, and you're the only son left in the family, so don't make your parents worry so much."

"Got it..." Chen Man mumbled and then lowered his head in silence.

Xie Qingcheng leaned back against the soft cushion once more, exhausted and rather listless. "Go home."

Chen Man had no choice but to comply.

Chen Man was a good kid, but he was just too brash and impatient in everything that he did. Xie Qingcheng knew he became a police officer because his brother had died in an anti-gang operation and he wanted to get revenge. But the silly child was foolish and never capable enough, so he ended up getting assigned to a local police station instead of the criminal investigation team to which his brother had belonged. Xie Qingcheng could tell that this was a fact that Chen Man had never truly gotten over in his heart.

But Xie Qingcheng thought it was for the best.

Chen Man's brother had stuck too closely to Xie Qingcheng's own parents, getting swept deeper and deeper, one step after another, into intrigue and danger. Because of this, Xie Qingcheng had always felt a sense of remorse toward Chen Man's family.

It was best for Chen Man to be a base-level civil police officer and spend his days catching thieves, doing things like finding lost dogs for grandpas and such. It'd be even better if he stayed at this level for the rest of his career.

Pushing these thoughts aside, Xie Qingcheng fell into a dizzy sleep that lasted until the next morning when he was awoken by his phone's ringtone.

"Hello?"

"Hey, Ge...eh?" It was Xie Xue, calling him as she was getting ready in her dorm. "What happened to your voice?"

"It's nothing. I wasn't paying attention when I was eating and ate some mango."

"What?! You're allergic and you still—"

"I already said I wasn't paying attention. Why are you calling me?"

"Oh, it's nothing," said Xie Xue. "I was just letting you know that there's a fall trip after class today. We're going to Nanshi."

Xie Qingcheng coughed a few times. His body felt so hot it was as though he were on fire. "Then go. Stay safe on the way and don't go to any remote places with anyone by yourself. I told you, you got lucky at Cheng Kang Hospital. If–"

"Okay, already! I got it. Don't worry! Ge, you take care of yourself too."

Worried that she was disrupting Xie Qingcheng's rest, the siblings only exchanged a few more words before Xie Xue hung up. She deliberated for a while after ending the call, then sent a voice message to He Yu.

Xie Qingcheng fell asleep again.

He was someone who excelled at taking care of other people, but wasn't particularly good at doing the same for himself. Other than taking two pills after Chen Man brought him back, he had done nothing but smoke a handful of cigarettes—he still hadn't even eaten. But he felt ill and wasn't in the mood to cook, so it was only natural that he just fell right back to sleep without doing anything else.

This time, he slept for who knew how long. While drifting in and out of slumber, Xie Qingcheng heard the faint click of the lock. His consciousness was like a kite floating in the air as he dreamt, but the sound of the lock was the string that pulled him back to reality.

He didn't open his eyes, but he knew that someone had come.

In his daze, he thought it was Xie Xue. She was the only one who had the key to his dorm.

Didn't she have to go on the fall trip? It was frowned upon for new teachers to miss events like these at universities. Why did she come here?

Despite his concerns, Xie Qingcheng nevertheless turned over in an attempt to avoid being disturbed by his sister. He instinctually wanted to curl up under the covers, but unfortunately, there were no covers to grab and he realized he'd been lying on the couch ever since he got home. He hadn't even undone the buttons of his cuffs.

Just as he furrowed his brow in irritation, a sudden warmth descended over him.

The person who entered his house had walked over, stared at him for a while, and placed a thin summer blanket over his body.

Xie Qingcheng wanted to open his eyes, but he really was exhausted. There was only the blurry image of a tall young man reflected between the fluttering of his lashes before his heavy eyelids fell shut once more.

It was already dusk by the time he woke up again. Someone had diligently mopped the floor of his dorm and opened the windows to let in fresh air. A slightly damp breeze blew in through the curtains and set the snowy-white gauze fluttering under the glow of the setting sun.

Xie Qingcheng narrowed his eyes slightly. He stuck an arm out from under the summer blanket that had been warmed by his body heat and covered his eyes with the back of his hand.

There was the sound of another man talking within the room, as if on the phone. "Mm...okay. Then I'll come in a few days. Don't worry about it. You aren't asking for a lot of time. I also want to gain some experience unrelated to my major, so it's no trouble at all."

"Rest assured, Feng-jie. I've already asked for time off. I know it's difficult for you. There won't be any surprises."

I TORMENTED HIM UNTIL HE GOT A FEVER

"Mm, yes. Then I'll let you go now."

The sickly Xie Qingcheng finally realized that this was He Yu's voice.

Xie Qingcheng bolted up and turned in the direction of the voice.

He Yu had just finished his call and came out of the kitchen carrying a wooden tray in his hands. He walked to Xie Qingcheng's side and set the tray down on the tea table. On the tray was a large Mino ware ceramic bowl. It was filled to the brim with chicken porridge that had simmered for a very long time until it turned an appetizing milky white. The porridge had taken on the chicken stock's flavors, with each grain soaking up the rich and milky soup enveloping it. Snowy-white pieces of chicken floated within the porridge, and fragrant and crispy white sesame seeds had been sprinkled on top.

"Oh, you're awake? Since you're awake, you should eat this while it's hot. I made it following a recipe I found online."

He Yu paused for a few moments, then said, "I saw the lab results and the medical prescription on your desk."

Xie Qingcheng didn't respond.

"You went to the emergency room last night for an IV, didn't you?"

With a hand pressed to his forehead, Xie Qingcheng spent some time gathering himself before adjusting his position on the sofa.

After ensuring that his voice wouldn't sound as pathetic as he felt, he finally said, "Why did you come here?"

He Yu didn't seem to be in the greatest shape either. He was calm—so calm that there was a sense of darkness lurking within.

Even though Xie Qingcheng was sick, he could still faintly sense He Yu's strangeness. He traced his gaze along He Yu's arm and discovered that there were bandages wrapped around his wrist. He looked higher and found that the almond eyes that had been kept lowered this whole time seemed to be slightly red. Xie Qingcheng thought once again of the medicine He Yu got at the hospital.

But before he could ask He Yu about it, the younger man had bent down and reached over Xie Qingcheng's shoulder to push a hand into the sofa behind him. He Yu looked down at the man and said, "Xie Qingcheng, if you are having such a severe allergic reaction to mango, why did you tell me nothing was wrong at the hospital?"

"Xie Xue told you?"

"Yes. She asked me to come visit you, saying that you didn't feel well and that your voice was all hoarse when you spoke to her."

Xie Qingcheng made no reply.

The boy watched him intently. "I was the one who gave it to you. I was the one who caused you to end up like this. Why did you hide it from me? Why didn't you come find me? Why didn't you tell me the truth at the hospital?"

"There was no need." Xie Qingcheng said in a very calm and cold tone. "You didn't mean it. You didn't know that I'm allergic to mangoes. Besides, I was already being taken care of."

But these words didn't satisfy He Yu; on the contrary, they triggered the appearance of something slightly dangerous in his eyes as he stared at Xie Qingcheng. "I don't think I'm so evil that I'd stand back and ignore someone I hurt like this."

Xie Qingcheng said nothing.

"So, what exactly do all of you see me as?"

All of you? Xie Qingcheng furrowed his brow silently. Aside from him, who else was there at the hospital? But given He Yu's deteriorating mood, Xie Qingcheng held his tongue and didn't ask.

He Yu stilled before him. He, too, might have felt that he'd gone a bit overboard. He slowly straightened back up and said, "Never mind."

He poured Xie Qingcheng a cup of water, then tidied up his examination results. He sighed at the sight of the terrifying data printed at the top detailing the allergic reaction.

"If there's nothing else you need, I'll be going now."

Out of instinct born from serving as He Yu's doctor for seven years, Xie Qingcheng stopped him. "He Yu."

"What is it?"

Xie Qingcheng frowned slightly. "Did something happen to you?"

"...No."

"Then what's with the bandages on your wrist? And the medicine you went to the hospital for?"

He Yu draped his uniform jacket over his shoulders and replied without a backward glance, "I already told you about the medicine. It was for a friend. My wrist is bandaged because your stovetop was too messy, and I burned myself while cleaning up."

He straightened his arm, and that bandage disappeared beneath the wide sleeves of his uniform jacket. He Yu stood motionless for a moment, as though trying to decide what to say. He turned his head slightly to address Xie Qingcheng again. "I still have the evening self-study session to get to, so I'll be leaving now. Remember to give Xie Xue a call and tell her I came over."

Xie Qingcheng nodded, but he still felt that there was something vaguely off about He Yu as he watched him getting ready to leave. After some thought, he asked, "Even Xie Xue went on the fall trip, so why didn't you?"

He Yu paused for a moment while tying his shoes. From Xie Qingcheng's line of sight, he couldn't see the younger man's entire face clearly, only part of his sharp and elegant jawline that was half-hidden in the shadows.

"It's too boring. Most of the people going on the trip are acting majors. I have nothing in common with them, so I didn't want to participate."

He Yu knotted his shoelaces with a yank, pushed open the door, and left before Xie Qingcheng could ask any more questions.

THE MURDER CASE WE WERE EMBROILED IN HAD YET TO CONCLUDE

XIE QINGCHENG RECOVERED completely from his illness a few days later and was eating with Xie Xue in Huzhou University's dining hall. Upon seeing the chicken porridge in his bowl, he suddenly realized that it had been quite a few days since he last saw He Yu. He also hadn't come across any of He Yu's posts when browsing his WeChat Moments either.

He frowned slightly as he recalled He Yu's strange behavior on the day that he had come to check on him in his dormitory. Xie Qingcheng was an extremely rational person, but he wasn't completely heartless. Not to mention, he had promised He Jiwei that he would help him keep an eye on He Yu. So it was a matter of course that he'd have some concern for the boy.

And so, once Xie Xue carried over her meal tray and sat down at the table across from him, he asked her how He Yu had been doing recently.

Who would have thought that, in response to her brother's inquiry, Xie Xue would suddenly widen her eyes and say, "Huh? You don't know? He requested a leave of absence and went to Hangshi to film a drama. Didn't he tell you?"

Xie Qingcheng's hand that was holding his chopsticks froze. "Isn't he majoring in screenwriting and directing?"

"Ah, it's only for a little while. He's helping to step in for another actor and playing a minor supporting role. They took a shine to him when he was buying breakfast by the school's front gate, and he's somewhat interested in it as well. Frankly speaking, with his looks, it's kinda hard to say which side of the camera he'll be working on in the future. He's also a highly motivated person, so he definitely wouldn't waste an opportunity to gather some experience."

"But why so suddenly?"

"Well, it's because the actor originally slated for the fifth male lead role got into an accident. That kid was a drama major, but he crashed into a taxi while biking around the campus gates before he even arrived on set. He got a huge gash on his face and had to get a bunch of stitches. The production team needed to get someone to fill in for his role fast and ended up finding He Yu..."

As Xie Xue explained the situation, Xie Qingcheng vaguely recalled the phone call that He Yu had that day in his home; it seemed as though that was what that conversation was about.

Xie Xue rambled on. "But there's one thing that I find a bit strange. I've seen the script for this drama before. It's a super crappy little web drama. With his tastes, I would've thought he'd definitely look down on such a show, but he suddenly agreed, just like that. Even if it won't take much time—something like ten days or so—I still have no idea what he's thinking... He seemed to be in a pretty bad mood when he was asking me for time off too. He was so closed off when I talked to him."

Upon hearing this, Xie Qingcheng's expression turned grave.

He thought back to the bandage that had been perfunctorily wrapped around He Yu's wrist that day and the bag of medicine from the hospital...

"Has anything bad happened to He Yu recently?"

"Of course not!" For some reason, Xie Xue's mood seemed to have improved by leaps and bounds ever since the fall trip; she appeared to almost give off an aura of a sumptuous peach blossom in full bloom. She chewed on her ice cream spoon thoughtfully, and it was only after a while that she began to waver and say hesitantly, "I don't really know either... But I don't *think* anything's happened..."

Xie Qingcheng watched Xie Xue pensively, noticing her shining eyes and strikingly good mood. He could sense that she'd been exceptionally happy the past few days since returning to campus. Her head was constantly bowed as she tapped away at her phone and responded to message after message. Who knew to whom she was talking?

It was the same with her WeChat Moments. In the past, her posts were all along the lines of "a new xx restaurant opened on xx street, anyone wanna go check it out with me?" But recently, the posts had suddenly and inexplicably become much more artistic and refined. They were things like excerpts from youth literature that Xie Qingcheng couldn't understand no matter how hard he squinted or strange photographs, such as a stretch of lake water or two leaves from a tree. Late last night, she even posted a picture of a shadow cast upon a wall with the words, "He he, li'l white floof." It was difficult to tell just whose shadow it was with the fuzzy lighting; perhaps it was her own.

Xie Qingcheng had even commented on it, asking her, "Who's this li'l white floof?"

A long time later, Xie Xue finally replied, "A cute little puppy."

Xie Qingcheng said, "Stop posting such pointless things in your Moments. Hurry up and go to bed."

Xie Xue responded with an emoji of a face with its tongue sticking out. A while later, Xie Qingcheng discovered that she had also changed her profile picture to a swan that was facing away from the camera.

Recalling these details, Xie Qingcheng asked, "Then what about you? Has anything good happened to you recently?"

Xie Xue's cheeks flushed red. She turned her face away and continued biting on her spoon, carefully tucking the secret incident that happened during the fall trip into the bottom of her heart. "Oh, n-nothing."

Xie Qingcheng folded his arms as he silently observed her body language and the details of her embarrassed expression. His gaze slowly became keenly perceptive.

"Oh right, Ge?" Xie Xue, who felt a bit bashful under Xie Qingcheng's fixed stare, tried to change the subject. "I brought some specialty pastries from the fall trip back for you and He Yu. Are you busy this weekend?"

"No, why?"

"I... Uh, there's a conference at school so I can't take the day off, but pastries go bad so quickly. So, if you have time, could you make a trip down to Hangshi and check on He Yu for me? That way, you can bring him the pastries too."

Xie Qingcheng frowned slightly. He felt as if Xie Xue was keeping something from him, but he did not question her any further.

"All right," he agreed. He was rather worried about He Yu's condition to begin with, so it was a convenient excuse for him to visit the production team and check on He Yu's mental state.

At dusk that very day, the ruins of Cheng Kang Psychiatric Hospital stood empty, bordered by white and yellow police tape. When the wind blew, the police tape trembled as dust rose over the field of scorched earth beyond. Recently, a lot of people had made their way to this place from the city; some were here to mourn the victims' deaths, while others were only here for the novelty and to join in on the excitement.

Among the thronging crowd was an inconspicuous man wearing horn-rimmed glasses. Having squeezed his way through the group of people, he stared in terror and hesitation at the charred grounds of Cheng Kang Psychiatric Hospital with his slightly protruding eyeballs.

"...Yeah, they're all dead. Not a single higher-up is still alive."

"Could it really be Jiang Lanpei's vengeful spirit coming for their lives?"

"That woman was wearing a red dress when she died. I hear these kinds of ghosts are the most powerful, so it's no wonder that the fire seemed like it was going for Liang Jicheng's accomplices on purpose."

"Aiya, you're gonna scare me to death!"

As the chatter increased around him, the man in glasses began to tremble harder. On such a hot day, his entire body was covered in sweat and his back was almost completely soaked through.

He swallowed his saliva and turned back—he needed to go home.

His parents had already been living separately for a long time. He lived with his father, who was also part of the "organization." But among his parents' shared assets, there was a safe in the old residence where he lived when he was still a child. Inside the safe was a stack of dusty old papers with moth-eaten corners.

Those were Jiang Lanpei's real files.

His father had once told him that if something were to ever happen to him, he should hand over those papers to the police and then turn himself in. It would be fine even if he went to jail, because at least he'd get to stay alive.

He was a coward—following his father's lead, he'd only dipped his toes into the organization. He was too scared to say anything and even threw up in a terrified daze the day the police came to his home to investigate. But now that he'd returned to his senses... Now he knew that this issue absolutely wasn't so simple; the list of the dead posted in the newspaper told him as much.

He didn't want to die. He didn't want to be killed. He was terrified and urgently hoped to retrieve the items from the safe and run to the police department.

In the past, he had been afraid of police sirens. He'd jolt upright in fear and tremble like a mouse whenever he heard police cars in his nightmares. But now, he finally realized in hindsight that only the police could save him.

He broke into a sprint the moment he entered the little group of villas. The houses were set in a community that could have been considered posh twenty years ago. He was petrified, terrified that "those people" would catch up to him, terrified that Jiang Lanpei's ghost would catch up to him.

Crimson tongues of raging flame, crimson waves of a ghostly dress.

"Ah... AHH!"

The more he thought about it, the more terrified he became. He couldn't help but start screaming as he ran. He came close to pissing himself, and his glasses nearly slipped off the greasy bridge of his nose.

He forced his way into the garden of the old villa and immediately charged through the doors.

He was afraid—so afraid that he didn't question why the door of this old home that had lain deserted for more than a decade would be unlocked, nor did he wonder why the main doors would only be half-closed...

The man in glasses was so disoriented, his head was like a pot of porridge. He panted heavily as he hurtled down the stairs to the basement. The rotting floorboards seemed like a lineup of corpse after corpse of the dead patients at Cheng Kang Psychiatric Hospital, heaving low and heavy sighs beneath his feet. His mind was on the verge of breaking completely, and his lips trembled uncontrollably.

Help me...

Help me...

With a bang, he smashed through the basement door and charged hastily toward the safe.

He remembered the passcode. It was his mother's birthday. Even though his father was a filthy lecher—the reason his strong-willed mother always looked down on him when she was younger and why they later divorced—the password was never changed.

Now that he thought about it, his mother also liked curling her hair and wearing red dresses when she was younger. Hong Kong fashion was popular back then, and many pretty women liked to dress up the way Hong Kong celebrities did in the papers—the most popular trend was those billowing red dresses.

Fingers trembling, the man in glasses turned the dial, once, and once again...

The door of the safe clicked open.

He reached in.

A few seconds later, he suddenly spasmed, almost convulsing, as if he'd been electrocuted.

It was gone!

That stack of papers—they were gone!!

Impossible... How could this be?

Amid the crushing disappointment and heightened sense of horror, he suddenly felt something warm land on his forehead with a soft plop.

All the bones in his body seemed to be on the verge of turning tail and fleeing, but trapped within his flesh, they could only remain inside him in despair.

Once again, there was that same sound and sensation.

Yet another drop of something warm fell. This time, it landed on his lips.

It smelled metallic.

The man's eyes suddenly bulged out. He hyperventilated, and his features contorted as he slowly looked up.

He saw a woman.

A woman who'd died on the staircase, with a gun still in her hand. She had been shot through the head, and her blood was pooling out all over the ground. The blast had destroyed her eyes, but her face was still barely recognizable, her eye sockets staring fixedly in his direction.

The woman looked as though she'd committed suicide, but the man in glasses knew for certain that she hadn't.

Because that was his...

"Mom..." The man in glasses cried out involuntarily, whether in extreme horror or sorrow, one couldn't tell. "Mom!! MOM!!!! AH!! AHHHHH!!"

His mother *didn't live here*... His mother had already left more than ten years ago without ever coming back...

Did she know about these files too? Did she also want to take these files to protect her son?

The man in glasses broke down and immediately crumpled to the floor. His face was a mess of tears, snot, sweat, and blood. Beastlike howls emitted from his mouth, but not even he knew what he was wailing for.

Then, he heard footsteps coming from behind him. It was the sound of high heels tapping against the floor.

Click, click, click.

The heels were bespoke counter-surveillance shoe covers with the latest, most innovative technology. The man in glasses didn't even have the chance to turn his head when he felt something hard pressed against the back of his neck.

A female voice giggled softly from behind him in a singsong tone. "Drop, drop, drop the hanky, set it lightly behind your friend's back, no one let him know..."

The woman held a yellowed file before his eyes.

Warm breath brushed against the man's temple as the newcomer asked gently, "Were you looking for this?"

"You..." The man in glasses didn't dare to turn around; his teeth clattered as he trembled.

"So was your mama."

The man was too terrified to speak.

"Your old man was a cowardly hamster, so disloyal to the boss that he even hid something like this at home." The woman sighed into his ear, elegant as an orchid. "He *really* shouldn't have... Did he think the boss wouldn't know?"

"W-who are...you..."

The woman smiled. "What kind of answers can a disloyal man seek?"

He made no reply.

"Save your questions for Hell."

Those were the last words the man in glasses ever heard.

A few seconds later, an ear-piercing gunshot stirred up the dust of the basement.

The woman steered clear of the filthy mess of blackened blood on the floor and cleaned up the scene with an air of indifference. Then, she looked down, leafed through Jiang Lanpei's files herself, and walked out of the old and abandoned building without a backward glance...

24

HE CAME INTO MY HOTEL ROOM

"LAST NIGHT, the residents of Golden Magnolia Garden reported hearing two gunshots. When the police arrived at the scene, they found the bodies of a man and a woman in an abandoned residence. The victims were a 52-year-old woman and a 26-year-old man. The two were mother and son—the wife and son, respectively, of Cheng Kang Psychiatric Hospital's administrative director, Liang Jicheng. The police discovered suicide notes written by the deceased within the residence. As both were involved in the Cheng Kang case, their cause of death is suspected to be suicide to evade punishment..."

On a weekend evening, Xie Qingcheng was sitting on the high-speed rail when he received a push notification for a news article on his phone.

He frowned slightly and opened it.

The article wasn't long; as these things usually went, the more serious the matter, the fewer the words.

Liang Jicheng's wife and son...

He recalled how the young nurse who greeted them at Cheng Kang Psychiatric Hospital that day had indeed said that Liang Jicheng had a wife and child—those were the very words that made He Yu realize that the "Liang Jicheng" Xie Xue had met was an impostor.

Did those two really die by suicide?

Something about this case unnerved Xie Qingcheng, but, ultimately, he wasn't a police officer, and the details were too scant. The article didn't even include a picture. Even if he wanted to, there were no clues for him to ponder over in the first place, so he turned off the display of his phone screen and let out a soft sigh. The flames from the rooftop of Cheng Kang Psychiatric Hospital that day seemed to flicker before his eyes.

Jiang Lanpei had cackled hysterically and said that no one had ever come to see her over the course of twenty years; no one had ever even thought of her.

She wanted to become a vengeful ghost and turn all of Cheng Kang into Hell.

Was this some kind of otherworldly karmic retribution?

"Good evening, this is the G12 regular service train. We will arrive at Hangshi Station in ten minutes. Please gather your belongings and prepare to disembark the train. Thank you for riding with us today. The next station is Hangshi Station."

The sound of the high-speed train's announcement pulled Xie Qingcheng out of his thoughts.

He politely excused himself to the young girl sitting beside him. Her face turned red as she made room for him to pass. Holding the gift box, he walked down the aisle and waited to exit the train. He pushed the matter of Liang Jicheng's wife and son out of his mind; after all, the case of Cheng Kang was a thing of the past.

The production He Yu had joined was a small-budget web series.

The screenwriter was a newbie, the director was a newbie, and the actors were newbies... Since there was little to no investment, the entire cast and crew were all new while the props were all old.

However, there were good things about being newbies too. As everyone was equally inexperienced, their faces had yet to be stained by the grease of smoke-filled celebrity banquets, and the soles of their shoes had yet to be tainted by the mud of powdered fame. Most of their hearts still resided in their chests, wrapped only in a thin layer of flesh, and could be easily worn on their sleeves; while it was difficult to say just how much sincerity they possessed, they weren't completely fake, at the very least. According to Xie Xue, the overall atmosphere was quite amiable.

By the time Xie Qingcheng's taxi arrived at the filming location, the cast and crew were shooting the final scene before dinner break.

Xie Xue had already given the crew a heads up prior to Xie Qingcheng's arrival, so once he got there, he was ushered to the seat next to the director's playback monitor to watch the filming while he waited.

He Yu was in the middle of the shoot.

To be honest, Xie Qingcheng didn't know what kind of production He Yu had joined before he came. After observing for a while, he realized it was a melodramatic and extremely clichéd campus love story.

In the drama, He Yu played a bourgeois male cannon fodder character who'd silently crushed on the female lead for years; the character actually fit his real personality quite well. In this particular scene, the capitalist was to declare his love to the female lead, be rejected, and then leave on his own.

This scene had to be filmed in a rainstorm, and since it was a drama with such paltry investment that even the director's great-aunts and grandmothers had been dragged into playing the extras, the crew would no doubt look to save money on artificial rainfall if they could. So, when the stingy producer happened to get a rainstorm gifted by the heavens, he started to frantically pull actors in and torture them with repeated takes.

As a result, He Yu had to repeat this emotional, explosive scene in the heavy downpour, over and over.

Acting wasn't his major, and it was also his first time doing it. But He Yu managed to control his emotions very well when filming this scene. It didn't seem like he was acting at all. Instead, it felt like he was rather freely expressing his own emotions.

Xie Qingcheng was quite surprised, and he wasn't the only one who felt this way. Everyone standing before the monitors under the makeshift tent was shocked as well.

"Wow, is this stud really not an acting major…?" a staff member rolled the script into a little megaphone and said in an extremely soft whisper.

By the time they finished shooting this scene, the sky was already completely dark.

The embarrassingly poor production team had erected a make-shift tent by the side specifically for the actors to rest and change in. He Yu dipped into this tent after he finished filming his scene. For a long while, there was no discernible movement from within.

Xie Qingcheng sent him a message, and about ten minutes later, a young assistant pushed aside the hanging screen and came out. The assistant, who was carrying a large black umbrella with a carbon fiber handle, ran over to the tent where Xie Qingcheng was waiting and invited him to the one that He Yu was in.

He Yu's tent was very small and contained only a white plastic outdoor table and a couple of chairs. When Xie Qingcheng entered, He Yu was sitting in one of the chairs toweling his hair dry. Hearing movement, he lifted his head and glanced at Xie Qingcheng.

This glance of his was not quite what Xie Qingcheng had expected.

He had thought that He Yu's condition would be exceedingly poor. He Yu's unbridled emotional performance just now had somewhat affected even the staff members who were watching in the tent and caused them to shed a few tears, but the actor himself was unexpectedly apathetic. He Yu lounged in the tent, listening to music with his Bluetooth earbuds stuffed into his ears and his slender, fine-boned left hand nonchalantly tapping a beat against the table.

On the contrary, his mental state seemed even more normal than when they had run into each other at the hospital.

"Xie Xue told me that you were coming." He Yu removed one of his earbuds and tossed it carelessly onto the table. He even gave Xie Qingcheng a smile. "Are your allergies better?"

Xie Qingcheng relaxed slightly. "If they weren't, I'd be dead." He glanced at He Yu's phone screen. "What're you looking at?"

"The news," He Yu said. "The aftermath of Cheng Kang Psychiatric Hospital. Liang Jicheng's wife and son died last night. The reporter said the authorities suspect suicide. You saw it too, right?"

Xie Qingcheng nodded.

He Yu smiled. "Even a man like this had a wife and son... Even *he* had someone who liked him before."

Xie Qingcheng didn't notice the darkness in He Yu's words. He pushed the gift box Xie Xue had him bring into He Yu's arms. "From Xie Xue."

Carrying the heavy box, He Yu stilled for a moment before he said, "Thanks."

Xie Qingcheng accepted his thanks with a clear conscience. After standing in the tent for a while, he asked, "Enough about Liang Jicheng, let's talk about you. Why did you suddenly want to act?"

"I want to try some more things and the opportunity happened to fall into my lap. Plus, I like this character."

Xie Qingcheng nodded. He pulled a chair over, sat down, and put a cigarette in his mouth.

But before the lighter could touch the cigarette, he heard He Yu say, "Could you not smoke?"

Xie Qingcheng was silent.

He Yu often watched his parents' guests puff out clouds of smoke when he was young, so he had developed an aversion to smoking that was difficult to put into words.

Xie Qingcheng slid the cigarette back into its box, but he still subconsciously bit down on his lip out of habit.

He Yu watched him. "You didn't smoke in the past."

"...Mm."

"When did you start?"

Xie Qingcheng pursed his lips and seemed to be deep in thought. Finally, he looked up and replied with a slight shrug, "I don't remember."

The man paused, as though reluctant to continue with this topic. He looked at the boy sitting across the simple plastic table. "Your acting is rather commendable. I thought you really got into character."

He Yu pressed the tip of his tongue to the back of his teeth, then smiled slightly. He smiled often, regardless of whether his mood was good or bad, gloomy or sunny. In his case, a smile was not an indicator of his state of mind. Rather, it had been forged into the mask that he was accustomed to wearing when he interacted with people—an extremely alluring hallucinogen he employed at will to prevent others from discovering his true self.

"No, I'm not that stupid. It's a script written by someone else. Who would take it seriously?"

"Then how did you act it out?"

"It's just like lying. Haven't I been faking it all these years?" He Yu stared at Xie Qingcheng. His voice was so soft that the other man could just barely hear it. "I have an illness, but I pretend to be a normal person."

He Yu leaned back and fiddled languidly with the earbud on the table, spinning it as if it were a top.

"I thought that perhaps something had happened to you and this was all just an outlet to vent your feelings about it," said Xie Qingcheng.

He Yu raised his head and gazed at Xie Qingcheng. "Is my acting that good?"

"It's not bad. How's the burn on your wrist?"

He Yu subconsciously touched his wrist before quickly letting go.

He calmly, casually, almost carelessly revealed it to Xie Qingcheng.

"It's fine. But I can't have too many scars showing on screen. They took care of it, sorta."

The makeup artists had drawn some delicate tattoos onto his arm, many of them in Sanskrit. The solemnity of the Buddhist texts blurred and entwined with the brashness of the tattoos in a way that suited the character's introverted, gloomy personality quite well.

"Does it look good?" He Yu asked.

"It looks terrible. It looks even worse paired with your school uniform."

"He doesn't have tattoos in high school, so when we change costumes in a bit, they'll have to redo the makeup and find a way to cover the scars," He Yu explained. "Are you going to stay and watch? The shoot will probably go on till pretty late."

"I'm not watching. I've seen you in a school uniform for almost a decade. My eyes have had more than enough."

But although he said he wouldn't watch, Xie Qingcheng still asked, "What are you shooting tonight?"

"An exam scene." He Yu said with a hint of a mocking smile, "There's not much to see. Why don't you help me bring these things over to the hotel? I'll give you my room card." He Yu paused for a moment, then asked, "Are you staying at the same hotel as the cast and crew tonight? Don't worry about it if you're not. I'll just bring them back myself after I'm done filming."

Xie Qingcheng checked the message with the plans that Xie Xue had sent him earlier.

"I'm in 8062."

"That's right next door to me."

Xie Qingcheng accepted He Yu's request. Since he had confirmed that He Yu's illness wasn't acting up, he took the room card He Yu passed to him and stood up to head to the hotel and rest. After all, he still needed to catch an early train tomorrow to make it back for his class.

When Xie Qingcheng swiped the key card and entered He Yu's room, he didn't notice anything unusual.

The room was what one would expect from a male college student: there were a few unwashed articles of clothing tossed onto the bed, a basketball in the corner, a couple pairs of athletic shoes, and some books lying on the table.

Xie Qingcheng placed the box of pastries beside He Yu's desk, then returned to his own room next door to take a shower. Dressed in the hotel's loose-fitting white bathrobe, he was in the middle of towel-drying his hair while walking over to the writing desk when his phone began to ring.

It was Chen Man.

"Xie-ge, I came to visit you at your dorm; why aren't you home today?"

"I'm in Hangshi."

Surprised, Chen Man said, "You've only just recovered. What're you in Hangshi for?"

"Checking on a patient."

"What patient? Didn't you stop being a doctor a long time ago?"

Xie Qingcheng lit a cigarette, glad he could finally smoke now. "A little devil around your age," he said, then paused. "A little younger than you, actually."

For some reason, Chen Man was silent for several seconds on the other end of the line.

Then, very abruptly, he asked, "Male or female? Ge, how come you went out of your way to visit them?"

Xie Qingcheng breathed in a lungful of smoke. He found Chen Man's behavior baffling, but still he responded, "Male. His father and I know each other, and I used to treat his illness. Otherwise, I really couldn't be bothered. Why are you so curious?"

Inexplicably, Chen Man's tone relaxed once more. With a laugh, he said, "I'm just asking for no reason."

"So, why did you come looking for me at my school?"

"Oh, I wanted to give you some of the crab roe sauce my mom made. It's really good mixed with noodles."

"You can leave it with Xie Xue."

Alarmed, Chen Man said, "No way! She has such a huge appetite, there's no chance there'd be any left over for you. Forget it, I'll just wait till you get back."

"Very well."

"Ge, you sound pretty tired. I'll stop bothering you so you can have a good rest..."

Xie Qingcheng said indolently, "Mm."

He didn't bother with pleasantries with Chen Man either and ended the call.

Chen Man wasn't this clingy in the past, but after his brother passed, he was depressed for a long time. Xie Qingcheng often went to see him during this period of mourning. Later, after Chen Man recovered, he would come over to Xie Qingcheng's house from time to time. It was only when Xie Qingcheng started to find him annoying that he finally stopped somewhat.

But Chen Man was right. After spending an entire day rushing about, he really was a bit tired. And so, dressed in a bathrobe, he lay down in bed and closed his eyes to take a short rest.

That short rest turned into a long nap. When he woke up, the digital clock on the table read 11:10 p.m.

He Yu should have already been back for a while, but Xie Qingcheng must've been sleeping too heavily to hear him return.

There was no other option—he was leaving first thing in the morning and He Yu began filming early as well, so it was difficult to say whether they would be able to run into each other again. After a moment of contemplation, Xie Qingcheng picked up the thin key card from the table and headed over to He Yu's room next door; in any case, he should make sure to return the key.

Xie Qingcheng knocked on the door several times, but there were no signs of movement inside He Yu's room. Recalling that He Yu had spent the evening repeatedly filming scenes in the torrential downpour, Xie Qingcheng supposed that the boy had fallen asleep from exhaustion. He lowered his hand and crouched down, intending to slide the key card under the door and then send He Yu a message to tell him so that he'd see it when he woke up in the morning.

But before he slid the key card under the door, Xie Qingcheng suddenly realized...

The lights were on in He Yu's room.

It wasn't very bright—only one of the floor lamps was on—but he could still see very clearly through the gap at the bottom of the door and confirm that the lights in the room were indeed on inside the room.

Xie Qingcheng inexplicably started in surprise. He straightened up and, sensing something amiss, instinctively knocked a little louder, "He Yu, are you in there? I've come to return your room key."

There was no response.

Xie Qingcheng took out his phone and dialed He Yu's number. A moment later, he heard He Yu's ringtone through the door.

Xie Qingcheng couldn't shake his anxiety about He Yu's condition. He knocked a few more times on the door, then raised his voice and called out at the tightly closed grayish-brown door, "He Yu, if you don't respond, I'm going to open the door and come in."

There was no response.

"Can you hear me?"

Still no response.

Xie Qingcheng pressed the rather worn-out key card to the sensor of the lock and, with a light beeping sound, the door opened.

The thick curtains were drawn, and a heavy smell of alcohol permeated the room.

Xie Qingcheng was immediately overcome with an ominous feeling.

He swept his eyes over the room and spotted the boy, curled into a ball in the corner.

The worst of his fears had come true. Xie Qingcheng was so angry he didn't even know where to begin. "...You!"

Like a little dragon in a cage, the boy shifted slightly but did not respond any further.

Xie Qingcheng finally saw through He Yu's disguise. His intuition had been correct: He Yu had indeed not come all this way for this role and to waste time with this production team for no good reason. He came here to find an outlet, a vent for his troubled mind.

In fact, He Yu's illness had begun to flare up ever since he found out that Xie Xue liked Wei Dongheng. However, it hadn't yet reached its peak and could still be controlled.

Upon realizing that he was unwell, He Yu had immediately gone to the hospital to get a new prescription before joining the production team in an effort to distract himself. But although he could pretend to be calm and collected when he was in front of others during the day, he could not control himself when he was alone at night. He ended up self-medicating by randomly taking all the various medicines he had brought to prevent his illness from worsening. And when that didn't work, he turned to drinking alcohol. Thus, when Xie Qingcheng entered the room, he was greeted by the sight of wine bottles—as well as pillboxes—strewn all over the floor.

He Yu was popping pills indiscriminately.

Xie Qingcheng had expressly informed He Jiwei of the importance of strictly controlling He Yu's drug usage before he left his job. If these medicines were to lose their effectiveness, the only option left when He Yu's illness worsened would be to physically restrain him at a hospital.

He didn't even mention the word "treatment."

Because he would end up in the exact same situation as the patients at Cheng Kang Psychiatric Hospital—forcibly subdued, tied down with restraints, subjected to electroconvulsive therapy, imprisoned—none of it would lead to recovery; it would only make him deteriorate into a vicious beast and force him into manacles and a muzzle so that he couldn't harm others.

He Yu would become a madman through and through.

No doctor could bear seeing a patient ruin themselves like this. Xie Qingcheng walked over to He Yu and said with a voice tinged with anger, "...He Yu."

No response.

"He Yu."

Still nothing.

"HE YU!"

The boy finally moved, and his beautiful almond eyes shifted beneath long, thick lashes. His gaze slowly inched over to the halo of light cast by the floor lamp where Xie Qingcheng stood in a bathrobe. "It's you," he muttered.

Before Xie Qingcheng could respond, He Yu leaned his head back against the bedside cabinet and said softly, "Tsk, seriously... What did you come in here for?"

Xie Qingcheng ignored him.

"I'm just exhausted from work and drank a little wine. It's nothing, okay? You can go."

The alcohol allowed him to control his violent bloodlust, but it also caused his mind to become befuddled; the normally intelligent He Yu suddenly found himself unable to spin up any good lies. In fact, he was so tired that he no longer wanted to continue making up stories at all. "Go, stop poking your nose into my business."

What he received in return was a hand wrapping painfully around his wrist as he was forcefully yanked up off the floor. Before he could come back to his senses, he was tossed onto the armchair. Looking around hazily, He Yu could only see Xie Qingcheng's familiar and severe face.

A pair of peach-blossom eyes.

As though he'd been stabbed, He Yu immediately turned his face away to stare fixedly at the completely innocent and uninvolved decorative painting hanging in the corner: Van Gogh's *Starry Night*.

He Yu's voice sounded very congested when he spoke, despite his best efforts. "Xie Qingcheng, I said that I'm fine, so what are you still doing here? Are you gonna monitor my drinking too?"

Xie Qingcheng said, "Do you think I want to monitor you? Just look at yourself right now—what kind of behavior is this?"

He Yu didn't bother responding to him and covered his eyes with his hand instead.

It was at this very moment that Xie Qingcheng was able to finally get a good look at his wrist under the dusky glow of the dim floor lamp.

The tattoo that had been drawn on top of it, as well as the concealer the makeup artist used, had already been washed away, revealing a deep and recent gash on He Yu's naked wrist.

Xie Qingcheng's heart sank immediately.

"You're fucking cutting yourself again!"

"Is that any of your business?! It's not like I'm cutting *your* wrist!"

Xie Qingcheng truly didn't want to make it his business.

But considering psychological Ebola, considering what He Jiwei had said to him before, Xie Qingcheng nevertheless said through gritted teeth, "Fine. I won't argue with you. I won't argue with you, okay?"

He walked over to He Yu's desk, on top of which there lay a box—a box of pills.

Xie Qingcheng returned from the desk with a big cup of hot water. He took out the two pills that he'd selected, the type with calming properties, and passed them to He Yu, who was still sitting on the ground in a fetal position. "Hurry up and take them," Xie Qingcheng ordered.

He Yu turned his face slightly to the side.

"Are you going to take them yourself, or do you want me to force them down your throat?"

He Yu stayed silent.

"Take them. Once you're done, I'll keep out of your fucking business."

He Yu seriously didn't want to seem pathetic in front of Xie Qingcheng, especially since he was a bit dazed from drinking so much. He looked up wanly and took the pills and water from Xie Qingcheng's hand and swallowed them with a gulp of water from the cup he was holding.

"I've taken them. *Now* can you get out?"

But Xie Qingcheng was not the type of gentleman who kept his word no matter what, so he grabbed He Yu by the wrist. "Sit down."

He Yu yanked his hand back with an icy expression.

"I said, sit *down*," Xie Qingcheng firmly ordered.

"Didn't you say you'd leave me alone after I took the pills?!" He Yu leaned back against the wall with his face upturned, his Adam's apple bobbing.

Xie Qingcheng didn't respond to him.

He Yu closed his eyes. "...Just let me calm down like this by myself, okay?" His long eyelashes fluttered, and the jut of his throat bobbed up and down. "Just stop bothering me."

It seemed as though he was truly depressed. A dying fish would still flop around when they had the will to live, but at this moment, He Yu seemed to have completely resigned himself to fate, just waiting for his final breath of air to slip out of his lungs.

Xie Qingcheng grabbed He Yu's wrist and looked down at him through peach-blossom eyes. Sternly, he asked, "What happened to you?"

He Yu gave no answer.

Xie Qingcheng said, "You have a mental illness; there's nothing to be ashamed of. The fault lies with the disorder and not with you. It's been seven years, He Yu—I thought that by now, you wouldn't hide your troubles and refuse to seek help anymore, yet you degrade yourself like this."

He Yu remained silent. He simply sat there, brows furrowed, face upturned, and wrist still firmly in Xie Qingcheng's grip. His heart struggled against the effects of the alcohol and medication, pounding so fast that it was practically skipping beats.

Xie Qingcheng could feel this increasingly erratic pulse through his hands around He Yu's wrists. Like countless times in the past, Xie Qingcheng's intuition and knowledge of He Yu pierced directly through his facade to see all the thoughts and symptoms he tried so hard to hide.

Sensing that he couldn't continue like this, He Yu instinctively began to struggle and tried to yank his wrist out of Xie Qingcheng's grasp. The two of them began to tussle, but as the effects of He Yu's drunkenness overwhelmed him, he leaned back against the wall and gazed upward while panting.

"Xie Qingcheng, you're refusing to let go?"

The boy tilted his face away. By the time he turned back, the rims of his eyes were blood-red with a mix of intoxication and hatred. He sneered, "You're right, I *am* unhappy. I *am* upset. I *can't* control myself. Everything is just as you said. You predicted it all. Are you satisfied now? You wanted to have a good laugh. Are you laughing now?"

With a dark expression, Xie Qingcheng calmly replied, "You really think you're that entertaining? I'm looking out for you on your dad's behalf. I'm worried you'll get into trouble."

"You're worried I'll get into trouble?" He Yu said, his voice tinged with mockery and his eyes bloodshot. "Our doctor-patient relationship is over, so why are you doing this, huh? Has he paid you to look after me? You're letting my dad screw you over!"

He Yu withdrew his hand with a vicious jerk. This time, he managed to extricate himself from the slightly stunned Xie Qingcheng's grip.

Xie Qingcheng didn't know what "screw you over" meant in the modern youth lexicon. Momentarily infuriated in his misunderstanding, he scolded He Yu sharply, "What the hell are you saying?! Screwing? He's your *dad*! What kind of imagination do you have?!"

"You're so obedient to my dad, you do everything out of consideration for his reputation. If that's the case, go look for him—come back after he pays you. After all, *I* sure can't afford your service." He Yu was deeply drunk and extremely depressed. He sneered and stared at Xie Qingcheng. "If you insist on babysitting me, then I can only screw you over. 'Screwing over' means not paying, Doctor Xie—you cool with that?"

Xie Qingcheng looked into He Yu's eyes without speaking.

They were wet, empty, and filled with ridicule for them both. Despite being hidden by such thick lashes and the dimness of their surroundings, those eyes could still show such conflicting emotions. He Yu tilted his head back and turned his face to the side. Xie Qingcheng thought he saw tears brimming at the corners of his eyes, but it might have been a trick of the light.

He Yu leaned back haphazardly and glared at Xie Qingcheng as he asked, "It's not worth it, is it? Xie Qingcheng? You won't do it, right? So what's the point in poking your nose into other people's business...? Cutting my wrists won't kill me, so why can't you just let me let loose a little without feeling guilty? I've already tried my hardest—I didn't kill anyone or set fire to anything, so why can't I just fucking cut myself? Does my depression get in your way? Do you all want to fucking hound me to death?! Haven't you had enough?!"

He Yu's mind grew increasingly muddled. His sense of awareness was visibly slipping away. Usually, he didn't have much to say to Xie Qingcheng—it was only when he got drunk that he became irritable and talkative.

Xie Qingcheng looked down at him, and just like this, listened to him for a long, long time before he suddenly reached up and covered He Yu's eyes.

The unexpected action stunned He Yu for just a moment, but then he forcefully grabbed Xie Qingcheng by the wrist.

His voice was almost whisper-soft as he said, "Xie Qingcheng?" The lips visible beneath the palm that covered his eyes parted. "What are you trying to do?"

25

I KISSED HIM

"XIE QINGCHENG... What are you trying to do?"

Logically, as a doctor and an elder, the appropriate response would be for him to offer comfort to the other party. But Xie Qingcheng didn't do that.

He bent down, allowing He Yu's larger hand to grip him tightly by the arm.

"He Yu, honestly, I don't have a lot of patience for you," Xie Qingcheng said. "When you recklessly take drugs and hurt yourself like this, it takes all my willpower just to talk to you properly. So, know what's good for you and stop looking at me with such distaste. Close your eyes and calm down. Stop thinking about such trivial nonsense."

He Yu had no way to respond.

Xie Qingcheng was pressing down on him with a lot of strength. The words he said weren't comforting at all, but it somehow felt like there was a great force that traveled through his hand and bore into He Yu's heart.

He Yu gradually stopped struggling, but his head was still considerably woozy. So he sat there, just like that, and quietly allowed Xie Qingcheng to continue covering his eyes.

After a while, He Yu blinked, his eyelashes brushing against Xie Qingcheng's palm.

Sensing that he'd calmed down somewhat, Xie Qingcheng was about to relax when something caught his eye—in addition to his wrist injury, He Yu also had a small bruise on his cheek.

Xie Qingcheng was utterly speechless. "What happened to your face? You hurt yourself on your face even though you have to appear in front of the camera?"

"I fell on a rocky incline when I was rehearsing."

"You think I'd believe that?"

"If you don't believe me, then forget it. Get out," He Yu said, eager for Xie Qingcheng to leave. The irritation was making his mind fall apart once again.

The young man's thin lips, still exposed under Xie Qingcheng's palm, opened and closed as he tried his hardest to maintain his lucidity.

"Get out already."

Seeing him like this, Xie Qingcheng grew furious. "Let me make something clear, He Yu. Even if you think that I don't understand and can't empathize with you, an illness ought to be treated. This is nothing to be ashamed of. If you feel uncomfortable anywhere, you can ask someone to help you alleviate the pain. If your heart feels heavy, then you should take your medicine on time. If your medicine is too bitter, you can say something or eat a piece of candy. Nobody would blame you for asking for a spoonful of sugar to help the medicine go down. You don't need to tough it out like this, and you definitely shouldn't hurt yourself."

He Yu remained silent.

"You're only nineteen, He Yu. To put it bluntly, you're still three years from being able to legally marry—you're still just a child. You can cry when it hurts, you can ask for sweets. There's not a single doctor or nurse who would make fun of a patient for being afraid of pain and suffering. We even made it through the great catastrophe of Cheng Kang Psychiatric Hospital—you should be happy that you managed to escape with your life. What could've possibly made you so upset?"

He Yu silently leaned against the wall as his chest heaved slowly.

Xie Qingcheng quietly watched as He Yu's breathing slowly relaxed and grew gentler. He was still covering the upper half of He Yu's face, so he couldn't see the expression in those almond eyes, but he could feel that He Yu had stopped struggling so much.

Xie Qingcheng hesitated briefly, then raised his other hand and brushed it through the sweat-soaked hair scattered and stuck across the young man's forehead.

He Yu shrank back slightly.

From the center of Xie Qingcheng's palm, there came a distinct sensation.

Xie Qingcheng started in surprise—he could feel wetness on the palm of his hand.

He couldn't be certain—and didn't dare to make certain of it—because he'd rarely ever seen He Yu cry. At most, the rims of his eyes would redden. For a moment, he dared not remove his hand, going so far as to wonder, *Is my sense of touch failing me?*

But he didn't know that this spiel of his had caused the dazed and drunken He Yu to fall into the indiscernible abyss between dreams and reality.

He Yu thought of Xie Xue.

Xie Xue had once told him something similar before. Back when he was young, she had tilted her head and asked the boy who looked so polite yet never paid anyone any mind, "Didi, are you upset?"

He Yu made no response.

"I heard that my brother knows your dad. He's working for your dad, so we'll see each other a lot in the future."

The little girl grabbed his hand as she spoke. "Let me tell you something. If you're unhappy, you can ask my brother for chocolate—unless you have cavities and can't have sweets, of course. But otherwise, he won't make fun of you or refuse you. I ask him for chocolate like this all the time! See? I got one just this morning!"

As she spoke, she dug around a bit in the pocket of her floral-print dress before fishing out a piece of milk chocolate, just as promised. Her mouth split open into a grin as she stuffed the soft, sweet chocolate into He Yu's ice-cold palm.

"You can have it—even though you have a big house, you don't have my brother's chocolate."

He Yu was at a loss for words.

"My name's Xie Xue. You're He Yu, right? Once you eat this chocolate, you'll be my friend."

He was completely dumbfounded.

"You have to be happy in the future, okay? If you're upset, come play with me. I'm great at cheering people up. I can stay with you the whole day..."

Children truly were the easiest people to please. To them, a whole day was already enough. It was a vast stretch of time, nearly equal to what adults meant when they spoke of a lifetime. So, children would speak of a whole day so seriously, while adults would speak of a lifetime like it was nothing at all.

In his drunken stupor, it seemed to He Yu that it was still that afternoon from ten years ago.

He and Xie Xue still had an endlessly long day before them.

He Yu sighed. After a while, he suddenly tightened his grip. Holding Xie Qingcheng's well-defined wrist, he forcefully dragged the hand Xie Qingcheng was using to cover his eyes down, bit by bit.

The warm lamplight shone into the young man's dim and hazy eyes. In that moment, perhaps because they had yet to adjust to the transition from dark to light, He Yu's eyes seemed a bit unfocused.

Suddenly, he couldn't discern who the person in front of him was. He stayed frozen in place for some time.

As for Xie Qingcheng, he could clearly see his own reflection in those almond eyes at such a close distance.

"Those words..." He Yu finally whispered. He stared at Xie Qingcheng, but his vision was still somewhat blurred and out of focus. "You've said them to me before."

Xie Qingcheng furrowed his brows, faintly sensing that something was wrong as the young man's warm, intoxicated breath invaded his every pore.

But he had no way of knowing that He Yu was recalling the first time he met Xie Xue, nor did he realize that He Yu's mind was already so muddled that he could no longer recognize him. Xie Qingcheng only found his words inexplicable and strange.

"Now, tell me: if I'm devastated, how long can you stay with me this time?"

Xie Qingcheng didn't respond.

"How long?" He Yu asked again, louder this time.

Xie Qingcheng returned to his senses. "What nonsense are you talking about—"

"I'm asking you a question."

Xie Qingcheng fell silent again.

"Answer me," He Yu insisted.

By this point, He Yu's tone had already become a bit hostile and overly forceful. It was the first time he'd ever had such a wolfish gleam in his eyes, like a male beast watching a female beast that was determined to leave him. He'd never revealed such a gaze to Xie Qingcheng before.

Xie Qingcheng instinctively felt a chill run down the back of his neck—that look was enough to make even a tough guy like him feel uneasy.

"You're drunk. He Yu, you should get up first."

The alcohol had really begun to kick in, causing He Yu's mind to grow increasingly chaotic. He grunted in response but didn't let go, staring into Xie Qingcheng's eyes as his gaze gradually hazed over. "You're lying. You think I'm a fool too."

Xie Qingcheng didn't know what to say.

Under such a stare, Xie Qingcheng tensed up even more, the most primitive genetic code deep within his flesh beginning to sound the alarm after sensing danger.

It was impossible to get through to He Yu anymore.

The younger man was already halfway into a flare-up. He was like a remote island, entirely sealed off. He only said what he wanted to say and rejected anyone who tried to pry into his inner self.

At this moment, Xie Qingcheng also realized that they weren't at the He family residence, with its restraints and specialized tranquilizers. He had no tools to help him handle He Yu.

In truth, he shouldn't have been alone with He Yu at all when he was in this state.

He Yu had already taken his medicine, and given its potency, it would put him to sleep soon. Whatever it was that they needed to talk about, it would be better to save it for the next morning when he was a bit more lucid.

"Forget it," Xie Qingcheng said as he rose to his feet. "You should rest up tonight first—"

Unfortunately, this realization had ultimately dawned on him a little too late, as He Yu grabbed his hand so tightly he couldn't even budge.

He Yu had been staring at his eyes—the part of him that most resembled his sister—the entire time. They were the exact same peach-blossom eyes, only differing in terms of their character. Xie Xue's eyes were very warm, constantly emanating her curiosity and passion for life. On the other hand, Xie Qingcheng's were downright frigid—out of all the eye shapes in the world, this kind was the most emotive, but his aura made his gaze sharp and incisive.

Under ordinary circumstances, there was no way He Yu could ever mix them up. But right now, in his downcast mood and drunken stupor, under the dim lights of the hotel, what he drowsily and blurrily saw were the eyes of the person he wanted to bed.

He Yu looked and looked, until finally, he could no longer tell the two of them apart at all.

"Fine. You insist on leaving, is that it?"

"What are you doing?"

The young man ignored his question. "I'm asking you. You insist on leaving, is that right?"

Xie Qingcheng tore himself out of He Yu's grip. "Just what exactly are you trying to do?"

He Yu dropped his head and sneered. His normally upright and refined features could not hide his deviant and sinister nature that lurked just underneath once he lost control.

A shiver ran down Xie Qingcheng's spine as he took in the faint smile curling the corners of the younger man's lips.

He jerked to his feet, intent on leaving, but he had only taken a single step when He Yu seized his wrist again with a slap of skin on skin.

Before Xie Qingcheng could react, He Yu yanked him close with the powerful strength of a young man. With one hand gripping Xie Qingcheng's wrist and the other hand wrapped around his waist, He Yu rose and forcefully pressed him onto the long tea table nearby!

The back of Xie Qingcheng's head knocked audibly against the hard surface. He let out a muffled groan and the world spun before his eyes. "He Yu!"

He couldn't be blamed for failing to react to such a brutal and sudden attack. It was as if an evil dragon lying dormant in its lair put up with a noisy intruder until it lost its last shred of patience, spreading its enormous, terrifyingly rugged wings and ferociously swiping at the walls of the cave, fiercely shoving the offering that had encroached upon its territory onto a bed of rock. The intruder would stand no chance as its powerful claws brought a shower of debris down while tearing through that unfortunate soul's neck with its teeth.

In truth, given Xie Qingcheng's strength, he could have broken free at this point. Unfortunately, Xie Qingcheng was too straight-laced and he hesitated, thinking the violent bloodlust that was a symptom of He Yu's illness was about to manifest itself. His imagination didn't extend to any other possibilities, so he missed his final opportunity to escape.

As the two of them stumbled and collided with each other, their feet caught on the floor lamp's power strip. The lamp fell onto the thick carpet with a muffled thump, plunging the room into darkness. Meanwhile, when Xie Qingcheng and He Yu tripped, He Yu knocked over Xie Qingcheng and ended up pinning him down hard onto the middle of the table.

His breathing was rough and ragged, reeking of alcohol.

Only their silhouettes could be seen in the faint glow of the city's streetlights beyond the window. He Yu's gaze carefully traced over these outlines to land on that pair of unbearably familiar peach-blossom eyes.

Between the alcohol and the dim light, He Yu's mind and vision blurred. As he lowered his head to look down into those eyes that were only centimeters away, the rift in his heart began to expand violently outward.

All the dissatisfaction, pain, emptiness, and unrequited love that he had suppressed for so long broke through the surface and shattered those accumulated layers of sedimentary rock transforming into heartache, manifesting in the trembling of his eyelashes, becoming the unyielding force of the hand with which he grabbed Xie Qingcheng's wrist, accumulating into the hot teardrop that fell down in his sorrow.

He Yu didn't know where that tear fell.

But Xie Qingcheng stopped struggling as he felt something warm drip onto his chest.

"He Yu, you..."

Before Xie Qingcheng could finish his sentence, the young man hovering over him with his head lowered and his throat choked with sobs suddenly cupped the back of his head with his hands. Then, with his eyes closed, he leaned closer and caught Xie Qingcheng's slightly cool mouth with warm, wet lips.

Xie Qingcheng felt as though he had been struck by lightning. His eyes abruptly flew open as time ground to a stop, and his mind went blank.

He couldn't make sense of anything amid this chaos; it didn't even occur to him to push He Yu away. He Yu was kissing him, his every breath burning with fervor. The force behind this kiss was something intense and searing, urgent yet distraught. He had never felt anything like it.

And it wasn't as though Xie Qingcheng had never kissed anyone before. He and Li Ruoqiu had slept together, of course, but neither he nor Li Ruoqiu had any passion for the deed—it had always felt as though they were simply going through the motions.

But now he was pinned under a strapping young man who had caught him off guard and kissed him. As He Yu's lips pressed against his own, Xie Qingcheng was assailed by the feverish scent of adolescence. Unlike a mature adult, the young man lacked technique, but his kiss was terrifyingly hot. As their lips came together and intertwined, Xie Qingcheng began to struggle on instinct, but He Yu held him firmly in place.

"Mmph!"

The desire of young people was too raw to be restrained, as though they would suffer helplessly all the way until their death if you didn't help them find relief. However, if you didn't get away in time, the heat from their body would radiate unchecked until it melted you to your core.

Every nerve in Xie Qingcheng's head seemed to snap in an instant.

He felt as though he had simply gone crazy—was this real, or was it a nightmare? It wasn't until another one of He Yu's tears fell, dripping onto his cheek to roll down the side of his face into the hair at his temples, that Xie Qingcheng jolted awake from this shockingly immoral position and abruptly began to resist. But unfortunately, He Yu had taken him for Xie Xue; there was no way he would let Xie Qingcheng go so easily. He Yu forcefully wrapped a hand around his pulsating neck, pulling away slightly in the process, and then leaned down to draw him into yet another kiss.

Xie Qingcheng's strength was formidable, but his shock hindered both his mind and body. He hadn't even had the time to react when He Yu grabbed him around the waist and pulled him to the bed.

"He Yu... HE YU! Use your fucking eyes... *Fuck...*" Xie Qingcheng was far too masculine to stand being subjected to something like this. He was still wearing that bathrobe he had carelessly left his room in, and when He Yu grabbed the side of his waist, the heat that he felt from the younger man's palm through the thin layer of fabric was impossible to ignore.

Xie Qingcheng's scalp had practically gone numb. He began to resist He Yu's advances, but although he was a full-grown man standing no less than 180 centimeters, He Yu was both younger and taller than him. And while the brat had a pretty face with his red lips and white teeth, he was in excellent shape. His abs were clearly defined when he took off his shirt, and his strength was truly, frighteningly explosive.

Xie Qingcheng had cleared his head, but between that strength and the fact that He Yu had the upper hand, breaking free wouldn't be so easy. Not to mention, this was also He Yu's first fucking kiss!

What was it like for a nineteen-year-old virgin, who had never been with anyone before and suppressed his desires for so many years, to kiss someone for the first time?

It was practically the same as an animal getting its first taste of meat after a yearlong famine.

He Yu was drunk and sick, his awareness muddled, but he could still feel pleasure and arousal. He yanked violently on Xie Qingcheng's hair to keep him from escaping, and the rims of Xie Qingcheng's eyes turned red—perhaps out of pain, but more likely out of anger and frustration.

The boy who had gotten a taste of carnal desire refused to let him go. He Yu sensed that Xie Qingcheng's furious struggles were indeed difficult to deal with, so he eased his hand out of the man's hair to clamp down tightly on his nape instead.

Xie Qingcheng lifted his foot in a savage kick, but He Yu simply used the force of this motion to pin down the man who'd rather die than get onto the bed.

"You—!"

Xie Qingcheng felt as though the entire world was spinning as he fell heavily onto the soft, springy mattress. He Yu's searing weight pressed down on top of him a moment later.

Xie Qingcheng's chest tensed in overwhelming shock and his pupils contracted...

Beside him on the bed was a handful of unwashed, sweat-drenched high school uniforms that He Yu had worn for the drama. There were even some half-read textbooks next to the pillow. The bed, with its consummate schoolboy vibe, made Xie Qingcheng feel as though he was being defiled by a high schooler.

He Yu truly could no longer identify the person before him. Driven by his desire, he silently tightened his grip on Xie Qingcheng's neck and stared at him, waiting for his captive's strength to fade away as he lay beneath him.

About a dozen seconds later, Xie Qingcheng's face was red from lack of oxygen. There was a brief moment when He Yu's gaze seemed extremely terrifying, as if he wanted to gouge Xie Qingcheng's peach-blossom eyes right out of his head.

But once that moment passed, he suddenly became extremely helpless and despairing again. Startled, he slowly loosened his grip on Xie Qingcheng's neck...

Air rushed back into Xie Qingcheng's lungs as he took huge, gasping breaths and started coughing violently.

"...I'm sorry..." He Yu seemed to have sobered a bit, though his eyes remained confused. Even though he was speaking to him, he was really trying to tell "her," "I'm sorry... I didn't want...I didn't want to hurt you... I just..."

Unsure of what to say, he lowered his head and slowly closed his eyes. The tip of his elegant nose rubbed against the side of Xie Qingcheng's neck, and he dropped light kisses repeatedly on the bruises dotting the older man's throat.

Scalding lips murmured against his carotid, "I didn't want to hurt you..."

Xie Qingcheng shook with anger. The blood vessels in his head were on the verge of bursting.

After kissing his neck, He Yu stared at him again, before passionately forcing a kiss on Xie Qingcheng once more. He eagerly sucked on Xie Qingcheng's bottom lip and buried his fingers into the older man's messy black hair as he was made to endure the plundering kiss...

He Yu even went so far as to try prying open Xie Qingcheng's teeth to stick his tongue in!

Unable to bear the assault any longer, Xie Qingcheng viciously bit He Yu's lip. The smell of blood filled the air. Seizing his opportunity, Xie Qingcheng turned his face away to avoid the young man's scorching breath and began to yell at him.

"Are you fucking insane?! Let go...! You've drunk so much that your mind is confused! Get the hell up!"

Xie Qingcheng pushed at He Yu's chest with his hand, but the young man only clasped his own hand over it. He even went as far as to interlace their fingers.

Xie Qingcheng's scalp prickled as goosebumps broke over his entire body and he had to fight the impulse to violently throw He Yu off himself.

It was at this time that He Yu shed his third tear.

It fell just near his eyes.

He Yu's finger followed the teardrop, tracing the outline of Xie Qingcheng's peach-blossom eyes.

Before Xie Qingcheng could scold him again, he heard He Yu sigh softly. He Yu's gaze was unfocused as he looked at Xie Qingcheng's face and curved a finger to touch the man's cheek. "Xie..."

His voice softened and he paused, only allowing Xie Qingcheng to hear "Xie," but not the following "Xue."

Xie Qingcheng didn't know how to respond.

He Yu leaned over and trapped Xie Qingcheng beneath him with his broad shoulders. He turned his head and murmured softly into the side of Xie Qingcheng's neck, "I like you... I really like you..."

26

AFTER I SOBERED UP

WITH HIS HEAD BOWED, the young man lifted up slightly, his breath tickling that tiny space just above Xie Qingcheng's lips. His loose fringe hung over his brow, a curtain over his confused yet scalding gaze.

He clasped Xie Qingcheng's hand tightly, but Xie Qingcheng was so stunned by He Yu's sudden confession that he was nearly catatonic.

He had only been furious and bewildered before, but this shock sent a bolt of paralyzing electricity throughout his body.

He was so confounded that he even forgot to resist...

Who liked whom?

He Yu liked *him*?

How could this be...

They were both men, and He Yu had never shown any inclination toward homosexuality; not to mention, Xie Qingcheng was thirteen years older than him...

As he lay on He Yu's hotel bed, his bathrobe in disarray and his body drenched in sweat, Xie Qingcheng slowly lifted his gaze to look into the eyes of the boy leaning over him in the darkness. But he had no idea that when this boy looked at him, he saw only that girl who resembled him.

"I love you so much... Listen to me: don't get together with him..."

It was only after this sentence that Xie Qingcheng finally snapped out of his astonishment. "...Fucking hell!" he cursed through gritted teeth.

He Yu had drunk too much and mistaken him for the wrong fucking person!

Xie Qingcheng tore his eyes away from He Yu's face as the puzzling mysteries from before came together like pearls on a string: He Yu joining the drama production, the sudden flare-up of his illness, what he said on Neverland Island about declaring his love to a girl, the drunken words he muttered over and over again...all the pieces fell into place.

Xie Qingcheng understood everything.

He Yu had expressed his feelings and then was rejected by that poor unfortunate girl...

Xie Qingcheng pressed his fingers to his brow. All the furious tussling in their wrestling match of dominance had coated Xie Qingcheng's forehead in sweat. He pushed his messy, drenched bangs out of his face in irritation as his chest heaved with each breath.

His neck still ached from where He Yu had grabbed it, but it didn't hurt as much as his head. The night's incident had been an unbelievably hideous, hellish mess, but he couldn't help but be glad for the sake of that faceless girl he had yet to meet.

At least this disaster hadn't befallen her.

Then, there was the matter of He Yu.

For starters, patients with psychological Ebola needed to stay calm; they could maintain rationality and self-control by keeping their mood fluctuations to a minimum. Romance could really disturb one's mood, so it was better to avoid it where possible.

But He Yu seemed to have developed "Xie Qingcheng PTSD"—he was willing to listen to literally any advice so long as it didn't come from Xie Qingcheng.

So much for following the doctor's orders.

It was no surprise, then, that He Yu had fallen into his current state.

That said, it was fortunate that he had only unraveled this much, because he could still be saved.

Xie Qingcheng was still pinned beneath the young man's tall, broad, and feverishly hot body. But after sorting out his thoughts, he once again pressed his hand to He Yu's chest with a grim expression. "You... Get the fuck off me. Get *off*!!"

The intensity in He Yu's eyes had already faded. The medicine's tranquilizing properties were finally taking visible effect. He was still staring at Xie Qingcheng, but his grip slowly began to weaken and, as his breathing gradually steadied, signs of his madness ebbed away.

There was even an instant when a flash of sobriety flickered in his eyes before quickly dissipating once again.

Xie Qingcheng seized the opportunity to throw He Yu off his body. Tightening his hold on his bathrobe, he got up from the bed. His wrist was still throbbing in pain.

He Yu finally quieted down, though it might have been more accurate to say that the medication had finally subdued his savagery. He didn't struggle after being viciously pushed away, only opened his eyes in a vacant stare. After a long while, he whispered, "Did you know? I can't find the bridge anymore..."

"What?"

"I can't find it... I can't get out of here... I...I can't get out of here, no matter what I do..."

These quiet murmurs weren't spoken to Xie Qingcheng or any-one else. He Yu's expression was empty. He seemed lost, as he spoke like a madman raving in the darkness.

He Yu slowly closed his eyes, his lashes quivering.

Xie Qingcheng had no idea what bridge He Yu was talking about. The events of tonight had nearly driven him mad. He forced down his anger and discomfort, threw He Yu onto the bed with a strained expression, and tossed the blanket over him. Then, he went to the bathroom to brush his teeth and rinse his mouth.

Xie Qingcheng was somewhat apathetic toward sex and disliked having unnecessary physical contact with others, much less getting kissed by someone of the same sex, so he was unbearably disgusted. With tap water gushing out of the faucet, he thoroughly rinsed out his mouth and splashed a handful of water onto his face. Leaning against the vanity, he finally managed to compose himself as he looked up into the mirror at his own face, which was still dripping wet.

The relationships between young people were simply a train wreck waiting to happen; the slightest bump in the tracks and everything would promptly fly off the rails. If not for the fact that this incident had happened to him personally, he could hardly be bothered to deal with this mess at all.

Seriously, what the hell? What the *fucking* hell?

All things considered, He Jiwei really ought to be paying him—it'd be inexcusable if he didn't. Later, he ought to seek He Jiwei out for compensation.

Xie Qingcheng's expression was grim as he pressed a hand to his aching temple, turned off the faucet, walked out to the sofa by the bed, and sat down in a daze.

The medicine had already knocked He Yu out by the time Xie Qingcheng stepped out of the bathroom. The docile-looking boy hugging a blanket on the bed was nearly indistinguishable from his usual model student self and completely different from the beast that had been clinging to him earlier.

Xie Qingcheng's mood soured as he looked at He Yu. He twisted open a bottle of the hotel's complimentary spring water and was about to take a sip to quell his anger, but a sudden flash of pain jolted through him the moment his mouth touched the bottle. Gasping, he lifted a hand to his lips, only to discover that they had been bitten bloody by He Yu. In all his thirty-two years, no one had ever dared to ravage his lips like this. Xie Qingcheng's expression darkened completely.

He slammed down the bottle of water, lit a cigarette, and began to smoke right there in the room—He Yu's preferences be damned. It was only after he had forced the little bastard sleeping on the bed to breathe an excess amount of secondhand smoke that he finally stubbed out the cigarette.

...Forget it. Just forget it! Xie Qingcheng thought, incandescently furious. *Seeing as he's already fucking kissed me, then so be it. What else is there to be done?*

As a man, he had nothing to lose; aside from feeling somewhat disgusted, there wasn't really an issue. Not to mention that, ultimately, this was nothing more than a misunderstanding.

Xie Qingcheng was too rational a person to waste much grief on a silly misunderstanding.

Objectively, the most important thing right now was He Yu's current condition.

He had finally personally experienced one of He Yu's flare-ups in their present stage. It was true that He Yu had been unhinged, yet this was still merely a partial flare-up as he had retained some semblance of control over his actions.

The question was, what would happen when He Yu fell completely ill and had a full-blown episode? How horrible would that be?

Perhaps his prognosis wasn't nearly as optimistic as it appeared on the surface.

Xie Qingcheng closed his eyes. He had long predicted that He Yu's condition would fluctuate a certain degree if he were to fall in love. That day on the island when he had tried to warn He Yu against pursuing his feelings, it hadn't only been out of consideration for that girl but for He Yu himself as well. However, his words fell on deaf ears.

He Yu had told him, "Doctor Xie, have I ever hurt anyone in these nineteen years? I just like someone, that's all. But I don't get such a right, do I?"

At the time, Xie Qingcheng had looked into He Yu's eyes and suddenly found himself unable to say anything.

He had watched He Yu grow up and knew his illness was too severe. He Yu had wandered between the twin abysses of his mental and physical states for nearly twenty years now, but he had yet to find a way out. The minds of patients with psychological Ebola were plagued with an intense viciousness; when their mental illness flared up, they could even become extremely violent and bloodthirsty.

Yet, He Yu chose to direct that viciousness at himself.

Whether it was howling in anguish or smashing his head against the walls, he always retreated to his evil dragon's lair whenever he felt things getting out of hand. Rather than risk harming the innocent, he would endure the torment in isolated darkness.

So, that mystery girl, was she the light at the end of the tunnel that He Yu was chasing?

Thinking of the tears He Yu had shed tonight, and recalling how the boy had sobbed out how much he loved her, Xie Qingcheng couldn't help but turn back once more and look at the young man slumbering on the bed.

Was this why He Yu had left school, why he couldn't take it anymore, why the disease lying dormant in his heart had been triggered?

Xie Qingcheng subconsciously reached up and touched the spot on his lips where He Yu had kissed him. He Yu may have been a loathsome beast, but Xie Qingcheng couldn't help thinking that he was a pitiful beast as well.

However, Xie Qingcheng had suffered too much of a shock to think about things too deeply. He still believed that the "Xie" He Yu had uttered in his half-muddled daze was referring to himself, and it never crossed his mind that He Yu could possibly have been thinking of Xie Xue at all.

And why would it? Even though He Yu and Xie Xue were of the same generation, they were still five years apart in age. To Xie Qingcheng, this age gap signified that they were unlikely to develop romantic feelings for each other, so he never once suspected that He Yu had inappropriate feelings for Xie Xue.

Not to mention, how old was He Yu again? Nineteen—still a teenager. In olden times, he wouldn't yet have had his coming-of-age crowning ceremony. He would have still been considered a minor.

Truth be told, to the stiff and traditional Xie Qingcheng, nineteen was still far too early to be dating. Nineteen-year-old boys barely had any hair on their chest and would still be in school, yet he was thinking of romance? He didn't even know who he was yet, so how long could this relationship last? And if he happened to knock her up, could he take the girl to the Bureau of Civil Affairs and make an honest woman out of her? Could he be self-sufficient enough to raise a family of three while caring for two sets of aging parents? Without financial support from his parents, could he earn enough money to raise the child and make sure his wife wouldn't have to worry about making ends meet while she was pregnant?

Nonsense, he couldn't do any of that at all.

So, he was still a boy, not a man.

Xie Qingcheng would never equate this sort of person with his future brother-in-law, so it was only natural that the thought wouldn't have even crossed his mind.

The sleeping student on the bed furrowed his elegant brows as though upset by something in his dream. Xie Qingcheng didn't want to look at him any longer, and he wanted to look at that hopelessly messy bed even less.

He got up and walked out the door.

It was already early the next morning by the time He Yu woke up. He opened his eyes in a daze, ran a hand through the messy hair scattered over his brow, and pressed against his slightly cool forehead.

His memories of the night before were like shattered fragments of porcelain: it was difficult to avoid being cut by their jagged edges when piecing them back together.

He Yu endured the spasming pain inside his skull as a rough outline of events from the night before formed in his mind. But the second he remembered the misdirected kiss, his entire body froze as he realized...

It seemed...he had...kissed Xie Qingcheng...

He Yu's immediate reaction was to hope that he was having a nightmare, but the broken skin on his bitten lip was still a little bloody. When he licked it, it stung with an utterly sobering kind of pain that made it patently clear that everything that had happened last night was indeed real.

As an all-encompassing model student since childhood, He Yu had honed the extremely high resilience and lightning-fast reaction time common to all star xueba. However, nothing could have prepared him for something like this.

His face was pale as he sat on the bed in a daze.

As his mind struggled to make sense of his memories, he heard the beeping sound of a key card being swiped. He Yu looked on helplessly as his door was abruptly pulled open and the victim of his inadvertent sexual harassment from the night before walked in with a calm and collected expression.

Xie Qingcheng had stayed up the entire night. He had spent several hours lost in thought after returning to his room, which gave him ample time to compose himself. He had just finished getting ready for the day before He Yu woke up. Upon walking into the room, he immediately saw that this little lunatic, with a crown of messy hair atop his head, was already awake and staring back at him through wide almond eyes.

Incredibly, He Yu appeared to be innocently baffled. This expression, in addition to his pretty and delicate xueba face, made it seem as though *he* was the actual victim in this scenario.

That beast.

Xie Qingcheng immediately picked up He Yu's T-shirt from the sofa and flung it into the beastly xueba's face, obscuring that irritating gaze.

"Get up," he ordered with an audible chill in his voice.

The beastly xueba pulled the shirt from his face and said with great difficulty, "Xie Qingcheng, last night, we... You and I... Did I..."

Terrifyingly, Xie Qingcheng replied, "Yes."

He Yu's expression crumbled.

"But there's no need for us to discuss such a stupid matter any further," Xie Qingcheng added.

He Yu started once again in surprise. He never could have imagined that Xie Qingcheng's attitude would be so cold and callous the moment he opened his mouth. If not for the fact that he was certain there was nothing wrong with his memory, he would have doubted the truth of what had happened the night before—that he hadn't kissed the wrong person in a moment of befuddlement, but rather, Xie Qingcheng had had a premeditated plan to take advantage of the moment and sexually assault him instead.

The cold and callous Xie Qingcheng leaned against the TV stand and crossed his arms. He looked at He Yu with a gravely apathetic expression and said, "Get dressed. We need to talk."

Last night, they had experienced such an embarrassing instance of physical contact together. Even if it was a misunderstanding, it was still sufficient to make He Yu feel guilty.

Seeing as he was the one who had initiated the kiss, He Yu found himself grasping for words. Under ordinary circumstances, he absolutely would've rebelled against Xie Qingcheng, but today, he was still struggling to wrap his mind around what had transpired. So, all he could do was follow Xie Qingcheng's words to the letter.

"Did you tell that girl you like her?"

"...No."

"You're still trying to lie to me? Did you forget what you said to me last night?"

He Yu could vaguely recall some of it, but he wasn't quite sober yet. After a while, he finally said, "I mistook you for the wrong person. I didn't say anything to her, I found out she likes someone else... Forget it. Why am I telling you all this? If you're gonna laugh, then go ahead and laugh."

He looked up. "I know that you're ecstatic. Everything happened just as you said it would: no one likes me, and I can't control myself. Aren't you glad? All your predictions came true."

Xie Qingcheng stared at him. "I'm glad that you didn't go completely mad."

He paused as he looked at He Yu's guarded expression. It seemed as though He Yu expected him to say, "Dear patient, after a night of reflection, I've come up with two treatment options. Please look them over and decide whether you would like to be chemically or physically castrated. Feel free to choose either one."

Xie Qingcheng sighed. Truth be told, he had no desire to belabor the issue. It was childish and a waste of time, so he simply said, "Forget it, He Yu. About this matter, about last night—just forget about it."

He Yu looked at him. Xueba were all accustomed to speaking up and proving themselves at every opportunity; the particularly beastly xueba sitting on the bed was no exception. And so, He Yu asked, "However?"

"However," Professor Xie swept his severe gaze over He Yu's face, displeased by his speaking up. "I thought things over and what happened last night leads me to believe that your current condition is extremely poor. To be honest, when I previously spoke with your father over the phone, he did ask me to regularly check in on you. Your indiscriminate abuse of drugs when your illness flares up and your attempts to hide the truth from everyone are extremely inappropriate. Therefore..."

He Yu's "father"—Executive Xie—began to lecture him.

However, he only managed to hear the opening of his "father's" speech. He Yu hadn't quite recovered yet, and his head was a bit dizzy as his thoughts wandered about absent-mindedly. Every word

Xie Qingcheng spoke went in one ear and out the other. What could Xie Qingcheng possibly be talking about if not how he would never ever forgive him?

But on second thought, he never asked Xie Qingcheng to come and look after him in the first place. It was Xie Qingcheng who had barged into his room and approached him. They were both straight men who hadn't the slightest interest in the same sex, so it was just a matter of bad luck on both their parts. He didn't owe Xie Qingcheng anything.

Thankfully, He Yu hadn't said Xie Xue's name aloud yesterday. Otherwise, it'd be even harder to clean up this mess...

"...That's basically the gist of it."

At some point, his "father" had already finished his lecture and summed up his main points.

"Did you hear me?"

He Yu lifted his head and met Xie Qingcheng's frosty gaze.

Parched from speaking so long, Xie Qingcheng picked up the bottle of spring water he had left untouched the night before, unscrewed the lid, and took a drink. "If you agree, then we'll consider this matter resolved," he said with cool indifference.

In reality, He Yu hadn't managed to absorb a single thing Xie Qingcheng had just said. His hungover, dully aching head only registered that final "we'll consider this matter resolved." However, as someone accustomed to being an outstanding student, he nevertheless nodded his head instinctively.

Xie Qingcheng looked down at him with disdain. "Good. In that case, come find me at the medical school once you've wrapped your scenes and returned to campus."

Only then did He Yu snap out of his daze. Realizing that he had seemingly agreed to some kind of demand while he was spacing out just now, he finally woke up completely and asked in a hoarse voice, "Wait. Sorry, what did you say?"

Xie Qingcheng's expression immediately darkened. "Do you have any other terms you would like to discuss with me?" he asked stiffly.

What terms?

He hadn't caught a word of what Xie Qingcheng had said—not even whatever Xie Qingcheng had been roughly paraphrasing as he moved his lips just a moment ago...

Dammit, what the hell did he promise Xie Qingcheng?

Meanwhile, Xie Qingcheng felt that he was being rather lenient with He Yu. He didn't even berate He Yu for the damn mess that happened last night.

Of course, the main reason for that was because he truly didn't want to bring up that scalp-prickling kiss again.

When it came to He Yu's current medical condition, it was one thing if he didn't see it, but since he had, he couldn't just stand by and do nothing. Even if it weren't for He Jiwei, even if he were just a regular patient acting this way in front of him, Xie Qingcheng wouldn't be able to remain an idle spectator.

He couldn't treat He Yu like he had in the past, as his personal doctor, but he could at least help restrain He Yu's emotions a little and give him a few pointers.

And it didn't hurt that over the course of this process, he could have He Yu do some grunt work for him. He Yu's ability to do manual labor was quite useful when he was being obedient. He was clever and quick-witted, sturdy and strong. If Xie Qingcheng could make use of him like he did in the past, it would count as a way of evening the score after he got licked by a dog.

He would be able to kill two birds with one stone.

Noticing that He Yu had zoned out, he impatiently repeated his proposal in simple terms. "After you wrap up filming, come to the medical school and train yourself under my supervision. During that time, I'll have you do some work for me as a form of distraction. Don't spend all your time wallowing and overthinking. Since you have someone you like, you should promptly adjust your mental state and learn to control your emotions as quickly as possible. It's for your own good."

After a moment of silence, He Yu said, "She has someone she likes right now, and it's not me."

Xie Qingcheng sighed. "The girl you like is young, right?"

"...Yes."

"The future is unpredictable. Not to mention, even if she doesn't fall for you in the future, you might start liking a different girl. If you can control your symptoms when the time comes, then that would be good too."

He Yu took a moment to think, then asked, "Why aren't you asking who it is that I like?"

"What does that have to do with me?"

He Yu bowed his head and a hint of mockery flickered in his lowered eyes. "True."

He thought back to their conversation at the police station.

At the time, Xie Qingcheng said there was absolutely no one who could possibly fall for someone like He Yu, that he would fail as a matter of course.

He had felt as though he'd been viciously slapped across the face. Back then, he thought that if he could get together with Xie Xue, he would insist on seeing Xie Qingcheng lose control. He wanted to see Xie Qingcheng break down. But now, everything was reversed.

It was Xie Qingcheng who got to see him in this unspeakably pathetic state instead.

If he were to retreat at this point, then he really would have lost all his pride before Xie Qingcheng...

He Yu closed his eyes for a moment, then smiled. "Be honest. In the end, did you come just to watch me make a fool of myself?"

"You can think that if you like."

He Yu didn't know what to say.

Upon meeting that man's apathetic yet slightly challenging gaze, the darkness in He Yu's heart deepened.

He truly disliked seeing this type of expression on Xie Qingcheng. He'd seen it countless times as he grew up, and each time, he could vividly sense Xie Qingcheng's apathy, as well as his irritating aura of strength.

He Yu brooded for quite some time before he finally looked up at Xie Qingcheng and asked, "You want me to distract myself by working for you? What exactly do you want me to do?"

"I haven't decided yet," Xie Qingcheng answered, utterly blasé. "But you've worked for me before and you know the type of person I am. To give you a taste of hardship, I'm not someone who will let you off so easily."

"...Are you doing this to punish me, Professor?"

Xie Qingcheng paused, then arched his brow slightly. "Are you afraid?"

Having lost his pride already, He Yu didn't want to lose his dignity as well. "Professor, you must be joking, I'm not afraid of anything."

Hearing his answer, Xie Qingcheng lowered his head and took out a cigarette. He held it between his teeth and mumbled, "Hopefully you mean it. Don't start crying and say you want to give up after just three days. The lighter's by the head of the bed—pass it to me."

He Yu ignored him and got off the bed. He headed toward the bathroom to brush his teeth and gargle. Even though any lingering aftertaste of the kiss from yesterday was already long gone, He Yu was still deeply disgusted. At the thought of how he'd gotten the wrong person yesterday and actually kissed a *man* with such passionate fervor, his entire body felt uncomfortable and he was determined to clean himself properly.

Before he entered the bathroom, he turned back to glance at the person who'd been the recipient of his passionate advances yesterday once more. This time, his head was crystal clear—an exemplary gentleman, as though the person who had pinned Xie Qingcheng down and kissed him like he was in heat was someone else entirely. "Forcing me to inhale secondhand smoke cannot be considered a part of my training; it is no different than a drawn-out murder. If you want to smoke, please do it outside."

With that, He Yu closed the bathroom door and went to wash up.

Facing the bathroom mirror, He Yu pensively touched the lips that Xie Qingcheng had bitten to the point of bleeding last night...

He bent down to wash his face and grabbed the faucet.

Tendons protruded slightly from the back of his hand as he forcefully twisted the tap tight; the flow of water ceased in an instant. He straightened up and gazed at the person in the mirror.

What training? Didn't Xie Qingcheng just want to keep laughing at his expense, tormenting him and exploiting him?

This time, he'd really miscalculated when he messed with that old pervert Xie Qingcheng.

27

HE WENT TO SEE CHEN MAN

THE FRIGID, STRAIGHT-AS-AN-ARROW, and masculine Xie Qingcheng never could have imagined that there would come a day when a boy would curse him out as an old pervert in his head.

Nor could he have dreamed that said boy had climbed on top of him the previous night like a little pervert himself and forcibly kissed him with such hot-blooded urgency that he nearly shoved his tongue into his mouth.

It seemed that some schoolboys these days took the wholly unreasonable path of weaponizing their good looks, excellent grades, and the fact that they would have still been considered minors centuries ago in order to act with such impunity.

He Yu was one such wholly unreasonable xueba who was using acting in a drama as a means of softening the heartache from his unrequited crush. But he was a last-minute replacement for a rather insubstantial role, and the series was short. As a result, filming wrapped up quickly and he returned to school.

Before heading back, he sent a message to Xie Qingcheng, then left the hotel with his suitcase in tow.

The day He Yu returned to school, Chen Man invited Xie Qingcheng to visit the cemetery with him bright and early in the morning.

The little police officer had just solved his first case all by himself and felt that this occasion was worth commemorating, so he wanted to have a chat with his big brother.

"It was an interprovincial case." Chen Man was carrying a fruit basket and paper money as he walked through the cemetery over to his brother's gravestone. His movements were hurried, and he nearly tripped over a bush.

"An interprovincial bicycle gang thievery case," said Xie Qingcheng.

Chen Man's face turned red. "B-bicycles are vehicles too. They're still assets of the people..."

Xie Qingcheng paid him no attention. He took the fruit basket, set it before the grave as an offering, and lit the paper money on fire. The heat from the flames created a halo of distortion in the air. Xie Qingcheng looked at the photograph of the striking, young police officer on the gravestone and the row of characters traced over with gold dust.

In remembrance of Chen Lisheng.

Chen Lisheng's life had been cut short in his early twenties. Xie Qingcheng's impression of him had already grown fuzzy—he only remembered that, unlike Chen Man, Chen Lisheng had been a serious and steady young man. When he brought Chen Man, who was still very young at the time, to visit the Xie family's home, every other phrase out of the elder brother's mouth seemed to be "thank you" or "sorry for the trouble."

Even the last message he sent to his colleagues before he was murdered was, *"Something's come up today. I'll probably be late. Sorry for the trouble."*

Xie Qingcheng looked at the pitch-black headstone and said, "Your little brother has also become a police officer capable of handling cases all by himself now."

Chen Man hurriedly added, "I'll be even more awesome in the future! I want to be transferred to the Criminal Investigation Department."

Xie Qingcheng shook his head. "Your IQ is too low."

Chen Man couldn't muster a response to this.

"Unfortunately for you, your brother got all the intelligence."

Chen Man knew that Xie Qingcheng didn't want him to climb up the ladder. The higher he climbed, the stronger the headwinds—one misstep and he would be blown down and fall to a grisly death. So, in his own way of caring, Xie Qingcheng always discouraged him like this.

Chen Man didn't get angry. Instead, he muttered a few more words under his breath to his older brother, lit a cigarette, and set it down in front of his brother's offering stand.

He closed his eyes and spoke with his palms pressed together, "Ge, one day I'll solve that unfinished case of yours."

Silence fell between them. Xie Qingcheng knew that Chen Man was referring to the case of his parents' murders.

The case was a frustrating one. Anyone with a discerning eye could tell that it was no ordinary car accident that had killed Xie Qingcheng's parents. Likewise, everyone at the police department had their suspicions. But even so, what could be done? Xie Qingcheng's mom and dad didn't die in the course of an investigation, so they couldn't be posthumously honored as fallen heroes.

Additionally, the person who had orchestrated the crash left no indication of foul play. To complicate matters further, there were too many suspects who might have held a grudge against his parents as they had both once been high-ranking members of the force and were involved in countless major criminal cases. Crime syndicates and drug-trafficking organizations alike could've been involved.

In the end, all the evidence indicated an accident involving a large, out-of-control vehicle was to blame, and the police could only wrap up the case accordingly. It was absolutely impossible to open an investigation on a cold case like this.

Xie Qingcheng had done his utmost to seek answers regarding his parents' death himself, but he'd given up eventually. It was still a struggle for someone who was so coolheaded to gaze toward the path to the future, even when their tears had yet to dry and their heart had already died.

Xie Qingcheng finished arranging the incense. Seeing as Chen Man still needed a little more time, he went ahead and began to wander around.

His parents' graves weren't in this cemetery. A plot in this place was very expensive; the price of some graves that included a mausoleum could easily get you a house in a second-tier city with change to spare. The annual maintenance fee alone was also shockingly high. Only the wealthy and influential could afford to be laid to rest here.

As Xie Qingcheng strolled through the graves, he found himself standing before a statue.

Tomb effigies were a type of funereal practice modeled after the European style in which a life-sized figure of the deceased was typically carved out of marble and placed over the tombstone. This particular statue standing in the quiet cemetery was one of a doctor wearing a white coat. He had thick-rimmed glasses and sat on a chair looking at the book in his hands.

Beneath the statue was the inscription:

Qin Ciyan (1957–2017)
In the end, the only thing he couldn't cure was human nature.

Xie Qingcheng knew Qin Ciyan.

The two of them used to be colleagues.

Qin Ciyan was a famous alumnus of Huzhou Medical School and an awe-inspiring figure in the field of neurosurgery. He graduated several decades ago, went to the United States to pursue additional training, and returned upon the completion of his studies. He was once a professor at his alma mater, where he led a research team. Half a lifetime of efforts culminated in him accomplishing more than most could in an entire lifetime; there was no doubt that he'd already attained success and recognition, and absolutely could have enjoyed a leisurely life sitting with a warm cup of tea below the glow of a lamp in his later years, but Mr. Qin chose to remain on the front lines.

It was impossible for a surgeon to give up the scalpel for the pen.

So, when Professor Qin retired from Yanzhou at age sixty, he returned to his hometown and rejoined the workforce at Huzhou First People's Hospital. It was there that he and Xie Qingcheng became colleagues.

However, one evening four years ago, when sixty-year-old Qin Ciyan was in his office packing his bag and preparing to go home to celebrate his wife's birthday, a young man with scraggly facial hair holding a fruit basket and a silk banner suddenly appeared in the doorway. The man said he was the family member of a patient and that he'd come all the way to the hospital just to thank Director Qin personally for the gift of life he'd bestowed upon his mother.

Qin Ciyan had many such patients. Seeing as the man was covered in sweat and his complexion was pale, Doctor Qin deduced that he must have spent a long time on the road and invited the man into his office for a cup of tea.

But no one could have anticipated that, just as the old doctor bent his head to pour water to steep the tea, this timid-looking young man would silently rise to his feet and pull out a sharp knife from the bottom of the fruit basket, its steel blade gleaming in the cold light. In the time it took Qin Ciyan to finish preparing the tea and turn back with a smile, the man's expression had completely changed. His eyes bulged out hideously, and, with a loud yell, he committed a brutal murder.

This was the Yi Beihai medical murder case that shocked the nation four years ago.

According to the surveillance footage that the police collected afterward, the criminal Yi Beihai had pinned the elderly doctor, Qin Ciyan, against the wall and stabbed him in the chest and abdomen thirteen times. Fresh blood sprayed all over the relatively small office. From the handwritten patient files on the desk to the silk banner the murderer had brought as a cover, everything was painted a hair-raising crimson.

When those who heard the commotion came running into the office, Yi Beihai was already covered in so much blood that it was difficult to discern whether he was human or demon. Before everyone and their shocked cries, he lifted the body of the old man who'd dedicated his entire life to the medical profession into the air and hurled him out the window.

Thrown from such a height, the mangled corpse completely smashed to a pulp as it hit the ground with a great thud.

Seeing his work, Yi Beihai retracted his head from the window and stood gleefully in the pool of blood as he held the dripping, glinting knife. He tilted a smile toward the skies and shouted, "Payback! For cheating others of their money! I'll kill you! I'll kill you!"

But what caused this bloody, deep-seated hatred?

What exactly led the young family member of a patient to do such an inhumane thing to an old doctor graying at the temples?

The findings that the police reported after their investigation infuriated all levels of society, and public opinion boiled over like hot oil.

It was revealed that Yi Beihai's mother was a brain cancer patient with a glioma. The tumor was malignant, and its location within the brain was precarious. Despite having visited a number of hospitals, there wasn't a single doctor who was willing to operate on her.

The single mother was afraid that seeing a doctor would be a waste of money, so she didn't want to treat it, preferring to wait for death instead. However, her son, who was already past thirty, still expected to be waited on hand and foot and lazed around all day without looking for a job. Fearing that no one would look after her incompetent son once she kicked the bucket, she didn't dare die yet.

Her condition continued to deteriorate as she waffled on what to do. In the end, she heard that the Department of Neurology at Huzhou First Hospital was very famous and that the doctors there had a strong sense of medical ethics. On top of having the best surgical skills, some Buddha-hearted members of staff even went so far as to help find ways to raise money for impoverished patients or reduce the medical fees out of pity.

With her heart full of hope, the mother carried a burlap sack packed with local seafood specialties from her hometown and got on the green train[33] that took her to this unfamiliar metropolis.

But after she arrived, she was left utterly disoriented by the city, with its thousands of layered buildings and tens of thousands of terraced streets. It took this woman, who didn't even know how to make electronic payments, an eternity to find the hospital. Though she eventually managed to find her way, she didn't know how to

---

33 Trains dating back to the 1950s with forest green livery and yellow trim. They are much slower than modern trains, with few, if any, amenities. Although these trains are being phased out, they are still the only train service serving some remote areas.

register for an appointment. With her timid nature, she ended up standing in the bustling hospital lobby for an entire day.

At the end of the workday, a doctor finally noticed this woman emanating a pungent, fishy odor.

The doctor inquired as to the purpose of her visit and asked for her information. He even gave her his phone number and told the woman that he'd help her think of a solution.

Following this meeting, the woman's thick stack of medical files was handed over to the Department of Neurosurgery at Huzhou First Hospital. No one knew what was discussed behind closed doors, but in the end, the mother did indeed receive the discount she had hoped for and her surgery was scheduled. With her heart filled with gratitude, she began to wait for the dawn of her new life.

Meanwhile, her gambling addict of a son remained in their faraway hometown without accompanying his mother for even a single day.

The surgery fee was reduced, but in an opulent place like Huzhou, where the ground was paved with pearls, and gold was hardly better than iron, the living expenses were still immense for this mother. She lived frugally in a tiny hotel room stuffed with eight beds and smelled of damp mold. For food, she would split a single Gaozhuang steamed bun into three meals and drink hot water from a charity booth.[34]

At the end of the month, the woman's battered old cell phone rang. The caller was her son, and the contents of the call were wholly predictable—he wanted money.

"I'm in Huzhou for treatment and have to spend money on a lot of different things. I really don't have anything left over this month..."

---

34 *Marketplace stalls reserved for vendors who are elderly, or disabled, or come from low-income backgrounds.*

"What?!" The young man on the other end of the line immediately erupted in fury, his shout nearly puncturing the sickly old woman's eardrums. "No money?! Then what am I gonna do this month? Who's gonna take care of me? I don't care! You have to come up with something! I don't even have any fucking food to eat!"

The woman stooped down and clutched the scratched-up cell phone between her hands. She stammered as though she had done something wrong. "I really don't have any more money. When I first got here, I didn't know my way around and had to spend money on some bus rides. But now that I remember the way, I can walk. My medical fees have also been reduced... I'll save up some more so that next month I'll definitely have money... Don't worry..."

"Who told you to get treated in Huzhou?" the man continued shouting furiously. "I already told you! That place is only good for scamming rich idiots with too much money on their hands! What are you doing joining in on the action? Isn't there more than enough for you to see in our county? You eat and drink to your heart's content all day long. What serious illness could you possibly have?! What a waste of money!"

As the woman listened, large teardrops rolled down from the spidering creases at the corners of her eyes and fell onto the greasy concrete floor of the tiny hotel.

Meanwhile, her son raged on. "Why are you so eager to pay those doctors, huh? Don't you know that they're only after your money? Every day, they make a fortune off people's lives, hoping that dumbasses like you will fall ill so that you'll line up to give them money! How else would they be able to keep their hospitals open? And now that you've gone and let them rob you blind, you can't even take care of your own child!" he spat contemptuously.

After cursing her out, Yi Beihai slammed down the phone, unwilling to continue wasting words on the woman. He angrily threw on his clothes, dug out the last fifty yuan he had from under his bed, and headed for the illegal gambling den by the entrance of the village.

For a moment, in her overwhelming grief, the woman no longer wanted to seek treatment. Ultimately, it was the doctors at the hospital who consoled her and reached out to Yi Beihai.

In the end, Yi Beihai impatiently agreed that so long as they didn't try to take his money, she could get the surgery if she wanted to. He didn't want to waste time and energy rushing over to Huzhou either, so he verified the operational risks over the phone and left behind a voice recording stating that, when the time came, his mother could just sign the medical consent forms herself.

The process went somewhat against standards, but in spite of objections from within the hospital itself and out of respect for Qin Ciyan's prestige, the entire procedure was nevertheless carried out as planned. Hospitalization, rehabilitation, preoperative briefing... Everything was methodically arranged and systematically executed.

The day of the operation finally arrived, and the doctors once again reviewed the risks of the surgical procedure with that solitary woman, informing her that the location of the tumor was extremely dangerous. If she did not go through with the procedure, she would likely only be able to live for another three months, but the operation also came with grave risk—in the event that the surgery failed, she could die on the operating table.

"Then...then, I'd like to make another phone call, if that's okay?" the woman lying on the hospital bed asked somewhat timidly.

The cell phone was passed over, and the woman dialed a number with shaking hands, hoping to speak a few more words with her son before she stepped into the gate between life and death.

But after waiting through the endless trill of the ringing on the other end, the only response she received was the same ice-cold automated voice of the pre-recorded answering machine she'd heard the day before.

Yi Beihai was a gambling addict. He lost all sense of reason the moment he placed his first bet; there was no way he would find the time to answer calls from his elderly mother.

In the end, the woman slowly set down the phone, her eyes wet. Sniffling, she smiled. "Thank you, Doctor. Um..."

"What is it?"

The woman hesitated slightly, visibly conflicted as though too ashamed to ask.

The young doctor responsible for conducting the preoperative procedures said gently, "Auntie, you can say whatever you want. It'll be all right."

The woman's voice trembled slightly as she asked, "Will it hurt?"

"Mm?"

"The surgery, will it hurt?" the woman asked, feeling her face grow warm as a light flush of shame struggled to surface from beneath the waxy yellow pallor of her skin.

"Oh." Realization dawned on the young doctor, and he soothed her with a smile. "It won't hurt, Auntie. We'll be using anesthesia— it's a medicine that will make you fall asleep for a short while. It won't hurt at all. When you wake up, it'll all be over."

Hearing the young doctor's gentle assurance, something akin to yearning spilled into the woman's eyes.

So, it won't hurt at all...

As she was being wheeled into the operating room, she looked up at the pristine white ceiling of the hospital corridor, and at the doctors and nurses around her, scrubbed up and ready to do their best. In her mind, she was still thinking of those final words she had heard as her shrunken lips curved into a faint, slightly humble smile.

The surgeon in charge of the operation was Qin Ciyan. Qin Ciyan was getting on in years, and he had already performed three major surgical procedures that day, so he was not in his best condition. However, he was the only one who could be trusted to perform such a difficult operation.

The minutes and seconds ticked by as sweat gradually soaked through the elderly doctor's protective green scrubs.

"Forceps."

"Gauze."

"Hand me two more pieces of gauze."

Calm and steady.

His muscles were tense, and his eyes did not blink once during the most crucial moments.

The first to realize that something was off was the assistant surgeon. When he took the surgical tray from Qin Ciyan, he noticed that the doctor's body was swaying slightly.

Doctors are doctors, but sometimes, doctors are patients as well.

The moment the assistant surgeon glanced nervously at Qin Ciyan, Qin Ciyan also realized that he couldn't continue any further. He slowly and carefully completed the step that he was in the middle of. Then, in a composed voice that wouldn't alarm the others, he said, "My vision is blurred, and I'm experiencing some dizziness."

As he spoke, he backed up a few steps. He was about to say something else when his world went black and he collapsed...

This was the first time such a thing had happened to Qin Ciyan. He had high cholesterol and suffered from severe internal jugular vein thrombosis. Due to his condition, he often experienced nausea and headaches, but it had never become so severe as to induce dizziness or fainting.

Although such accidents rarely happened in a hospital, it wasn't unheard of. During residency, doctors were taught how to finish an operation smoothly with the remaining doctors should an unexpected situation arise. But the location of the woman's tumor was too risky. Even though the other doctors tried their best, the operation still ended in failure.

The mother was gone.

All of a sudden, the son became very filial; he couldn't afford to be unfilial, since he had eagerly waited for the measly allowance that his mother provided him every month. What's more, when she passed away, his housekeeper, cook, and servant...all disappeared. Yi Beihai felt as though he had plummeted into hell; there was no way he could accept it.

After some rumination, he eventually concluded that it was the doctors' fault.

They must have tricked his mother into having surgery and staying in the hospital because they were after the last bit of her money. Assistance? Reduced fees?

How could such a golden goose just fall from the sky? They must have thought that they hadn't squeezed enough money out of her and that this old bag of bones could be used as a free specimen in medical experiments. Those scammers must've tricked his poor mother, lost and alone in an unfamiliar place, into wrongfully dying under the knife.

The more he thought about it, the more convinced Yi Beihai became. He lay on his bed in the deep, dark night as the strange hooting of owls outside in the tiny village began to resemble laughter, swarming in his head until it became a whirlpool of hate that dragged him down into its depths.

The next day, the economically impoverished and culturally backward Yi Beihai, who owed money to anyone and everyone, scrounged up a rusty butcher knife at home, ground it on a whetstone until it shone, and wrapped it in a thick, dirty towel.

Then, he went to the small shop at the village entrance and threatened the shopkeeper into handing over all his cash before setting off for Huzhou.

A few days later, the news of the Yi Beihai medical murder incident exploded across the country like a clap of thunder, striking the heart of the public.

The news and social media platforms brimmed with shock at the incident, resentment toward the criminal, and reminiscence for Qin Ciyan. But gradually, some slippery snakes and venomous scorpions began to emerge from their nests in the middle of this chaos.

"Was Qin Ciyan really as kind and compassionate as he seemed?"

"It's true that the death of Yi Beihai's mother is quite suspicious."

"Yi Beihai deserves sympathy. He and his mother lived in such poverty, never knowing where their next meal would come from, so it's normal for such a child's mind to become twisted..."

Thanks to certain official and verified WeChat and Weibo accounts, these sensational articles and arguments began to circulate. To gain attention, many people began to doubt Qin Ciyan—from his academic papers to his moral character. Some even believed that he should have retired if he was getting on in years—after all, there was no need to selfishly cling to his position and authority only to bring harm to both others and himself.

Moreover, they began to find ways to dig up information about Qin Ciyan and his family. They questioned why his daughter married a foreigner and moved abroad—because what was so good about a foreigner? Wasn't that the same as providing for a traitor with the motherland's money?

They asked why Qin Ciyan's wife married him when she was more than ten years younger than him, concluding that it was definitely because she was after his wealth. Maybe she wasn't even his lawfully wedded wife!

"Everyone, dig a little harder; maybe we'll find out that she was actually a mistress who displaced the rightful spouse!"

The victim's personal affairs became an intoxicating drug for this audience, blocking their ability to smell the yet-undissipated blood in the hospital and allowing them to willfully sink into a revelry as they tore down the walls of privacy and abandoned their conscience.

There was also another verified Weibo user who unearthed a documentary from the depths of the Internet. It dated back more than a decade and covered Qin Ciyan's trip to the front lines of a certain disaster relief effort to treat the wounded.

That account knew how to create a commotion without being punished. They expertly clipped a part out of context that showed Qin Ciyan and his colleagues sitting in an ambulance and presented it without comment. A young doctor, who felt bad seeing how bone-weary and desperately thirsty his mentor was, handed Qin Ciyan a bottle of dextrose solution.

Some of the comments read:

"I'm not trying to disrespect Qin-laoshi's goodwill, but I have to ask—aren't supplies extremely limited in these disaster areas? There definitely aren't enough supplies to go around for the patients, but he took such a huge sip... Did he even think about the dying patients on the hospital beds?"

"Did he pay for that dextrose solution...?"

"Professionals have a lot of power. Look, he can waive an operation fee at will, so there's no way he'd pay for the dextrose solution. I know someone on staff at Huzhou First Hospital—they said the professionals are all corrupt. Surgery fees are no less than five figures, so if you see them including a discount, it just means that they'll sometimes use those patients for risky experimental procedures. Otherwise, how else would they hone their medical skills?"

But the most shocking and disappointing of all was the rationalization of Yi Beihai's actions.

When the results of the investigation were publicly announced, it was revealed that Yi Beihai was a patient with transient psychotic disorder.

According to Article 18 of the Criminal Law, "If a mental patient causes harmful consequences at a time when he is unable to recognize or control his own conduct, upon verification and confirmation through legal procedure, he shall not bear criminal responsibility..."[35]

However, evidence collected in the investigation ultimately demonstrated that Yi Beihai was mentally sound when he killed Qin Ciyan, that he hadn't lost control of himself at all. Consequently, Yi Beihai was still sentenced to death. However, many doctors and nurses felt immeasurably resentful and hurt due to how the dispute was dragged out, as well as some of the baffling opinions expressed by the general public at the time.

Even now, there were still those who remained fixated on these incidents and commented on them...

With the events of the past on his mind, Xie Qingcheng gazed at the gravestone with a blank expression for some time before walking up to it.

---

35 "Criminal Law of the People's Republic of China," Congressional-Executive Commission on China, January 15, 2013, https://www.cecc.gov/resources/legal-provisions/criminal-law-of-the-peoples-republic-of-china.

"Xie Qingcheng?"

The sound of approaching footsteps accompanied by a woman's astonished voice suddenly came from behind him. "Why...are *you* here?"

28

I ALSO SAW CHEN MAN

XIE QINGCHENG turned around. What a coincidence. Was the cemetery having a huge bargain sale today? Everyone was coming to visit the graves in droves.

The small group of people standing before him were his former colleagues from Huzhou Medical School.

To be honest, they didn't really count as colleagues although Xie Qingcheng referred to them as such. Rather, they were Qin Ciyan's students who were mostly in neurosurgery, a different department from Xie Qingcheng's.

"...Long time no see," Xie Qingcheng offered after a long pause.

Among these doctors was Nurse Zhou, the one who'd changed Xie Qingcheng's IV drip in the urgent care unit the other night. In stark contrast to Xie Qingcheng, Nurse Zhou was a forthright person with an irascible temper, making it quite difficult for them to see eye to eye, After glaring at him for a while, she couldn't help but say, "Xie Qingcheng, what's the meaning of this? What...what are you doing, coming to Qin-laoshi's grave?"

Xie Qingcheng remained silent.

"Hurry up and get out of here. Someone like you shouldn't be paying respects at Qin-laoshi's grave."

"I've no intention of paying respects," Xie Qingcheng said. "I just happened to pass by."

"You—!"

Upon hearing this person speak with *that* attitude, the other doctors standing by couldn't hold back anymore either.

"Professor Xie must be living it up at Huzhou Medical School, isn't that right?" one of them sneered.

"Must be nice, having so much free time that you can come and stroll around in a cemetery. Teachers really do have it easier than doctors."

Xie Qingcheng looked at them dispassionately. "What's wrong, everyone? Did I commit a crime or do something wrong? If you want to become the next Qin Ciyan, then be my guest. There's no need to expect everyone to follow in his footsteps."

"Xie Qingcheng!" Nurse Zhou was scandalized by his words. Her horselike face pulled even longer in her disgust. "Have you no shame?!"

"I'm unenlightened," Xie Qingcheng replied. "I have a sense of self-preservation."

"...Leave! Just hurry up and leave!"

"That's right! And don't let us see you here again!"

The young doctors couldn't control their emotions and were on the verge of strangling Xie Qingcheng to death right there in the cemetery.

The clamor grew so loud that one of the cemetery's gray-clad groundskeepers came over, hastily stopping the fight. "What are you doing? Remember to be solemn and respectful! And keep the volume down!"

As he scolded them, he pointed to a sign in the distance.

Then, he sternly added, "Acting like this will disturb those at rest. If you have any grudges or debts, go settle them outside. Once you're out of the cemetery, you can make as much noise as you want, so stop shouting when you're in here!"

Nurse Zhou rolled her eyes so hard that they nearly popped out of her head. "Who'd willingly meet with this guy once they're out of the cemetery? Just the sight of his face makes me feel like I'm choking on anger..."

"I also find the sight of fools like yourselves rather inauspicious," Xie Qingcheng retorted coolly.

"Xie Qingcheng, you—!"

"Xie-ge!" Chen Man called out as he rushed over. He had heard the ruckus while paying respects to his brother and came to help. "What's going on?"

As he was in full police regalia, the people around them naturally quieted down.

Nurse Zhou immediately narrowed her eyes in recognition.

It was that young cop again, the one who stayed by Xie Qingcheng's side all through the night that time...

"What's wrong?" Chen Man asked.

"It's nothing." Xie Qingcheng's peach-blossom eyes swept over each doctor's face in succession. Then, he turned to Chen Man and said, "Let's go."

"Oh..." Chen Man guessed that some conflict must have arisen between them, but Xie Qingcheng might not want to waste time talking about it, so he said, "Xie-ge, be careful. It just rained and the ground is quite slippery."

As the two of them made to leave, Nurse Zhou seriously couldn't bear her disgust anymore. At the thought of what had happened at Huzhou First Hospital before, and seeing Xie Qingcheng's prim and proper figure right now, a wave of violent loathing surged up in her chest.

She didn't know what she was thinking either, but seeing how close Chen Man and Xie Qingcheng were, she spat at him and said,

"Xie Qingcheng, I spoke up for you back when there were rumors going around the hospital that you were a homosexual. But now I see that Professor Xie is capable of enticing even cops into his bed. With a little police officer keeping you warm at night and at your beck and call during the day, serving and protecting you, you sure seem safe now. You'll never need to worry about getting—"

"What the fuck are you saying?!"

This time, it was Chen Man who was enraged. He didn't even wait for Nurse Zhou to finish before he was raring up for a fight.

Xie Qingcheng grabbed him. "Don't bother."

"But the way she was insulting you—"

"Let's go, Chen Man. You're still in uniform. Think of your reputation," warned Xie Qingcheng. The reminder was like a splash of water to the face, and it brought Chen Man back to his senses. Chest heaving and jaw clenched, he glared viciously at those people once more before finally leaving the cemetery with Xie Qingcheng.

Although the offending doctors were out of sight, Chen Man was still incandescently furious and kept swearing under his breath in the car on the drive back.

"How could they insult you like that...

"Xie-ge, there was nothing wrong with your decision to begin with...

"What right do they have to emotionally blackmail you like that, what right do they have to talk to you like that..."

But Xie Qingcheng was rather composed, as though he hadn't heard what they said at all, as if nothing had happened and they hadn't met anyone whatsoever.

"Ge, why aren't you angry at all?!" Chen Man exclaimed.

"Why should I be angry?"

"Th-they talked about you like that—"

"They are the last students of Qin Ciyan. And as for Nurse Zhou, she was personally hired by Qin Ciyan. It's perfectly normal for them to take issue with me."

"They even said that you and I, that we...we..."

"Are gay?"

Chen Man didn't know how to respond.

"I'm not gay, but people can say whatever they like. It doesn't affect me." As Xie Qingcheng spoke, he picked up and unlocked the phone that he hadn't looked at all morning. As they had been in the cemetery, his phone was on silent mode, so it was only now that he noticed that He Yu had sent him a text.

"I returned to school today. When will our arrangement begin?"

Xie Qingcheng frowned slightly.

He suddenly recalled the passionate kiss that had transpired in the chaos of the hotel room and couldn't help but feel slightly ill at ease. After all, the rumors at Huzhou Medical School that he was gay had all begun thanks to this brat, He Yu.

He Yu had come to the hospital to look for him one day. The kid was too damn tall; despite being just a junior high schooler, he'd already shot up to nearly 180 centimeters. He hadn't been wearing his school uniform, so he completely fooled the young, not-yet-married Nurse Zhou. She assumed that he was a twenty-something young man and ran over to ask for his number. But who knew what that goddamn degenerate He Yu was thinking. Perhaps he was trying not to hurt Nurse Zhou's feelings or perhaps he hoped to avoid awkwardness, but he actually smiled at her request and told her, "Ah, but I'm Doctor Xie's boyfriend. I'm waiting for him to get off work."

Just the thought of it ticked off Xie Qingcheng, so he sighed and locked his phone again, not in the mood to reply to He Yu.

"I'm going to nap for a while," he told Chen Man. "I have class in the afternoon."

Chen Man was still grumbling, but when he heard Xie Qingcheng's unexpected words, he shut up.

"Oh...then sleep, Ge. I'll wake you when we get there."

Xie Qingcheng said his farewell and fell asleep.

Light splintered between the tree branches and spilled through the window, streaming over Xie Qingcheng's well-defined face and the elegant line of his slender neck, illuminating his pale skin before burying itself beneath his neatly tailored shirt...

Everything about this man exuded a sense of composure, reserve, and strength.

For some reason, when Chen Man thought of the vulgarities Nurse Zhou had spewed at them back at the cemetery and her accusation that Xie Qingcheng had seduced a cop into bed, his heart skipped a beat as a subtle feeling rose alongside his fury.

His gaze swept over Xie Qingcheng's brows, eyes, and nose bridge, and eventually landed on the man's ice-cold lips. When Xie Qingcheng was awake, the words that came out of those lips were rarely cordial. Even his tone was always very stiff. But now that his eyes were closed in sleep, those lips seemed very soft...

Chen Man watched him, mesmerized by the sight before him, his warm breath becoming just the slightest bit hotter than usual.

Fall brought an end to the loud clamor of cicadas at Huzhou University, but as though irritated by the tranquility settling over the human world, the dry leaves fell in succession, crunching underfoot as students walked by, smoothly shifting the noise from the tree branches to the ground.

When He Yu returned with his luggage in tow, he had the good fortune of running into Xie Xue, who was leaning against the doorway of the little shop by the school's gate with her head tilted upward.

"...What's up with you?" He Yu asked by way of greeting.

At first, he wanted to go the other way and pretend he hadn't seen her, but then he felt that there was no need for him to avoid her. He hadn't told her how he felt, and Wei Dongheng might not even accept her affections. The two of them could at least continue to interact as friends for the time being.

Xie Xue had a tissue pressed to her nose, and her voice was nasal when she spoke. "I don't know, maybe it's the dry fall weather, but my nose is bleeding again, ugh... Oh, wait, you're back! Why didn't you tell me earlier?"

"What's the point? But you—if you're constantly getting nosebleeds, then you should go get it checked out. Take some time off and I'll go with you to the hospital."

"It's fine, it's fine. It's not that big of a deal."

"What do you mean it's not a big deal?" He Yu frowned. "When I got sick in the past, you always promised to go with me to the hospital. Can't you take this as my returning the favor?"

Xie Xue blanked for a moment. Maybe the nosebleed sapped her of her IQ. "It's been so long, I don't even remember what I said back then anymore..."

He Yu sighed, then took out a pack of tissues and gave it to her. "I'm used to it. I don't know how you managed to get into university and become a teacher with that memory of yours."

He watched as Xie Xue covered her nose with a clean piece of tissue. "Have you told your brother about your nosebleeds?"

"My brother's busy. I don't wanna bother him."

At this moment, Xie Xue spied someone walking over from a distance. That person waved to her, and Xie Xue's face suddenly flushed bright red.

Before He Yu noticed just what had flustered Xie Xue all of a sudden, she reached out and pushed him slightly with her free hand. "Uhhh, didn't you just get back? Hurry up and go unpack. Don't worry! If I get another nosebleed, I'll go to the infirmary to get it looked at. And if it's really a problem, I'll go to the hospital. I have a faculty meeting soon, so I'll be going now."

"...All right, go on then," He Yu said.

So, Xie Xue left.

He Yu found her behavior a little strange, but he didn't think much of it as he dragged his suitcase toward his dorm.

He had no intention of telling Xie Xue about his feelings now. After the recent events, especially when he had lost control and forcibly kissed Xie Qingcheng in the hotel, he realized that although he hadn't completely abandoned all sense of reason, he was indeed still a patient with a potentially dangerous condition.

He couldn't be certain whether he would always be able to maintain his present state of rationality in the future.

What if he went even crazier?

Perhaps Xie Qingcheng was right...

He should first get a hold of himself and strive to reach a stable condition that Xie Qingcheng would approve of. At that point, it wouldn't be too late for him to tell Xie Xue how he felt.

In any case, he had already waited for so many years, so it wouldn't hurt to bide his time a bit longer. Plus, He Yu figured that a scoundrel like Wei Dongheng wouldn't actually get together with Xie Xue.

When He Yu returned to his dorm, all his roommates happened to be out. He spent some time unpacking his things, and when he sat down to rest, he saw that there was an unread message on his phone.

It was from Xie Qingcheng.

After leaving him on read all day long, Xie Qingcheng finally deigned to grace him with a reply.

"6 p.m. Wait for me in front of the medical school's Laboratory #3."

He Yu needed to honor his agreement with Xie Qingcheng and begin receiving the so-called "training."

He Yu arrived outside the medical school's main laboratory right on time, but it was another thirty minutes before Xie Qingcheng finally made his appearance.

Professor Xie's neat, snow-white lab coat meant that he had probably just finished teaching a specialized course. Huzhou was warm in the early autumn, as the city remained blanketed in lingering heat and humidity, so now that his class had ended, Professor Xie unbuttoned his white coat, revealing the light gray blazer and sharply tailored trousers underneath.

With a swipe of the employee ID card hung around his neck and a *beep*, Xie Qingcheng walked out of the main building's sliding doors. His coat fluttered in a passing draft, and he reflexively tamed it with the clipboard in his hand without pausing as he descended the tall flight of stairs of the laboratory, calm and unruffled.

He Yu watched him coolly, one hand wrapped around the strap of his messenger bag and the other stuffed into his pocket.

"Your sense of time is really lacking."

"Class ran late," Xie Qingcheng said. "Have you been waiting for long? Come and eat with me first."

The food at the medical school's dining hall was excellent, far better than that of Huzhou University. Professor Xie and He Yu made their way there.

Dinnertime had already passed, so there were only a few stations cooking made-to-order dishes that were still open. A scant handful of latecomer students were scattered throughout the spacious dining hall.

Xie Qingcheng swiped his employee ID card at one of the order windows and then returned to his table with the receipt scribbled out by the dining hall auntie in his hand.

While they were waiting for their food, a pair of male students walked up beside them—surprisingly, they were holding hands. Xie Qingcheng didn't even notice at first, but later, after the two of them sat down across from each other and chatted for a while, the taller of the two leaned forward and tenderly kissed the other student on his fair-skinned cheek.

Xie Qingcheng and He Yu stared in mute horror at this gay couple.

Then, the two homophobic straight men moved in astonishing unison. Without waiting for the other to react, they both stood up and moved to the table furthest to the side.

"Why are you..." He Yu began.

"I can't stand it."

"...Aren't you a doctor?"

"My medical philosophy and personal life perspective are two separate matters." Xie Qingcheng pushed one of the beers he had grabbed from the fridge toward He Yu, then pulled open the tab of his own can with a pop. The creamy white foam bubbled to the top. He took a sip. "Why would men get together with someone of the same gender... Wouldn't it be very awkward?"

He Yu also opened his can of beer and touched it to Xie Qingcheng's. "I've gotta say, Doctor Xie, I really do approve of some of your ideas. A gay classmate even asked me out once before... He gave me a huge bouquet of roses."

"What happened then?"

"I broke his shin."

Xie Qingcheng had nothing to say to that.

The dining hall auntie stuck her head out of the order window and shouted at the top of her lungs, "Number 19 is ready! Two spicy dry pots, come and get 'em!"

Xie Qingcheng stood up and went to fetch their meals.

Of the two spicy dry pots, one was vivid red in color, filled to the brim with diced chicken stir-fried with dried chilis, facing heaven peppers, and Sichuan peppercorns. The crispy cubes of chicken were hidden within a sea of deep-fried chili peppers, studded with glistening and tender pieces of chopped green onion. Slices of garlic fried over high heat gently emitted an extremely appetizing aroma from where they lay atop the mountain of chicken and dried chilis.

This was Xie Qingcheng's order.

As for the other dish, though it was called spicy dry pot in name, it wasn't spicy at all. It was a pot of pork ribs that had been mixed with fermented bean curd and onion powder, and then fried until they were crisp on the outside and juicy on the inside. Plump slices of king oyster mushrooms scored with a crosshatch pattern curled up into themselves, while boldly sliced sections of leek diligently drew out the fragrant juices from the mushrooms and meat. Although the light in the dining hall wasn't all that bright, this hot, aromatic, and hearty dish had a mouth-wateringly soft shine to it, not to mention the smell of garlic and fermented bean curd that seemed to rush through one's nostrils straight into the belly.

Xie Qingcheng pushed the pot of fried ribs toward He Yu.

He Yu frowned at the dish.

Xie Qingcheng glanced at him. "You don't like it?"

"I don't really like fried food," He Yu said. "Plus, I'm allergic to fermented bean curd." He smiled. "Are you using this opportunity to get back at me for feeding you mango?"

"...A close acquaintance of mine—not much older than you—gets this every time he comes here. I thought all you young boys liked this kind of dish. Don't eat it if you're allergic. Go order something else."

"Which acquaintance? Do I know him?" He Yu asked nonchalantly.

"You don't know him. He's the one who was at the hospital last time, but you didn't meet him."

Just as Xie Qingcheng finished speaking and was about to hand He Yu his employee ID, his phone suddenly began to ring. He glanced at the screen and set down his chopsticks. "...Speak of the devil. Let me get this."

"Hello? Xie-ge, I'm near your school right now." Chen Man's voice came from the phone. It wasn't very clear, but He Yu could vaguely make out some of his words. "Are you done with class?"

Xie Qingcheng looked over at He Yu. "I'm with a patient. I have to talk with him a bit tonight. Why did you come?"

Chen Man paused for a few seconds. "I-I just got off work and happened to pass by. You accidentally left your notebook in the car this morning, so I wanted to give it back to you. I won't bother you if you're busy though."

He Yu was rather interested in checking out this devil. Anyone who managed to have a stable relationship with Xie Qingcheng was a curiosity, so after a moment of consideration, he said, "It's fine— seeing as he's already here, let's have dinner with him. I can't eat this anyway, and didn't you say that he likes it?"

"You don't mind?"

"Not at all."

So Xie Qingcheng invited Chen Man to join them.

He Yu went back to the window and ordered a pot of lightly seasoned seafood congee and a few more cans of beer.

Just as he finished ordering, Chen Man rushed into the dining hall carrying a paper bag with Xie Qingcheng's notebook inside.

Holding three beers in one hand and tucking his other hand into his pocket, He Yu casually walked back to their table. His gaze was fixed straight ahead and his messenger bag was slung over his shoulder.

They met in front of Xie Qingcheng's dining table and looked each other over.

Both young men were eye-catching. Chen Man had a fresh, lively appearance and exuded a sunny vibe while He Yu was exceedingly beautiful and elegant. Anyone would give pause when they saw their faces.

When their eyes met, they both froze for a moment.

He Yu felt that Chen Man looked a bit familiar, and the feeling appeared to be mutual.

But neither of them could figure out where they had met before.

Chen Man was a very amiable person. Shaking off the odd feeling, he smiled at He Yu first. Meanwhile, He Yu slipped on his refined, public-facing mask as per usual and offered Chen Man a polite smile. To make a somewhat inappropriate comparison, if you gender-swapped him and placed him in an ancient setting, Young Master He would be like the young lady of some wealthy estate, someone who wouldn't lose her sense of decorum so easily in front of an intriguing stranger.

"Hello," Chen Man said.

"Hello, Officer." He Yu returned the greeting.

Chen Man started in surprise. "You know me?"

"Professor Xie's mentioned you before," He Yu responded. *Also, I saw Xie Qingcheng wearing your uniform jacket in the hospital.*

Xie Qingcheng looked at the two of them standing there like a noble consort meeting a low-ranked concubine in some harem drama and furrowed his brow. "Why are you two just standing there? Come sit."

As a police officer, Concubine Chen had the modest nature of a public servant. He smiled as he said, "Comrade, please sit."

Accustomed to being in business settings with his parents since childhood, Noble Consort He followed the courtesies of capitalism, so he returned the smile. "After you, sir."

Suddenly being addressed as "sir" threw off the civil police officer. He scratched his head and cautiously sat down.

Likewise, the member of the bourgeoisie was surprised to suddenly be called "comrade," but took it in stride. Smile still intact, he also sat down.

Neither of them bothered with detailed introductions.

Social interaction in the present day was just like that. People often didn't give their full names when they met friends of friends—there was no need to. This was a barrier established by common convention as both parties understood that they were only sharing a meal together and wouldn't interact on a deeper level.

But this didn't prevent the two young men from making friendly conversation at all. After all, they were similar in age and had a lot of shared interests. Plus, He Yu's desire to scope out the weirdos that made up Xie Qingcheng's acquaintances kept the conversation flowing from gaming to sports stars, and sports stars to championships, all without sharing each other's names.

Toward the end of their chat, both these dashing youngsters, Chen Man and He Yu, were all smiles. The communist and the capitalist had a very friendly and amicable interaction—almost as though the Chinese Communist Party and the Chinese Nationalist Party had agreed to present a united front.

The generational gap between the two of them and Xie-dage might as well have been as wide as East Africa's Great Rift Valley. He watched from the sidelines, unable to contribute even a single word.

"...Ha ha ha ha, right? That kick was *amazing*."

"A complete shut-out—that's really quite rare."

"Did you see the game against England?"

"I was on call that day, but I watched the replay..."

The middle-aged man was getting fed up with the two youngsters' chatter. "Are you two going to eat or not?"

Chen Man reacted immediately. He realized that he was chatting a bit too pleasantly with his peer, so he hurriedly passed Xie Qingcheng a can of beer. "Ge, have a drink."

He Yu lowered his head without batting an eye and pressed a bent finger lightly to his temple, hiding the mocking smile playing at the corners of his mouth.

Of course, he had done it all on purpose.

Chen Man had accompanied Xie Qingcheng to the hospital, so their relationship must be pretty good. He Yu's interest in this police officer's personality had been piqued, so he wanted to see just what kind of person could put up with a paternal man like Xie Qingcheng.

Now, he could see that Chen Man was indeed a silly little fool with an extremely sunny disposition.

Xie Qingcheng's grumpy scolding led Chen Man to worry about neglecting the older man, so he didn't dare to chat with He Yu any further. Instead, he started to ramble idly to Xie Qingcheng.

As they neared the end of their meal, He Yu figured there wasn't much else to say. With a smile, he said, "Professor Xie, shall we talk business? I'll leave once we're done."

Xie Qingcheng didn't intend to keep him either, so he handed He Yu a list of names. "These are some students who often skip class. I'll give you a week to talk to each of them and see if their behavior changes after that."

He Yu accepted the slip of paper and looked it over. "Why are they all female students?"

"Male students are on my list."

He Yu examined his list carefully.

"The number of students on my list is the same as yours," Xie Qingcheng said. "I'll also talk with them over the course of this week. I'll take attendance at next week's lecture, and if you manage to convince fewer students to come back to class than me, you lose. If you lose, you have to do grunt work for me."

"Won't it be very difficult for me to succeed?" He Yu asked. "Since you're the teacher, won't they come if you threaten to fail them?"

"How can something easy be called training? You might as well ask me to spoon-feed you milk."

He Yu didn't want to waste any more time arguing with him. A xueba wasn't afraid of a challenge, so he haphazardly stuffed the list into his messenger bag. "I'll be going then. You'll see the results in one week."

Then, he nodded very politely at Chen Man. "Take your time eating, Officer. Maybe I'll run into you again sometime," he said with a smile.

After He Yu left, Chen Man turned to Xie Qingcheng. "Ge, is he a patient? He seems rather cheerful."

"...His issue is minor. He got rejected by his crush. His dad is worried about him and wanted me to give him some guidance."

Chen Man was stunned. "Huh? That guy got rejected? With *that* handsome face? That girl's standards are way too high..."

"What use is a handsome face?" At the mention of relationship troubles, Xie Qingcheng thought of Hangshi; when he thought of Hangshi, he thought of He Yu's indiscriminate kiss; and when he thought of that kiss, he felt rather uncomfortable. He said to Chen Man with a cold expression, "Just look at him. Does he look like the kind of guy who knows how to earn money or support a family?"

For some reason, Chen Man stilled for a moment before breaking into a smile. "Ge, I can earn money, *and* I can support a family."

Xie Qingcheng didn't take this to heart at all. He only treated it as some sort of bizarre competitive impulse between handsome youngsters. "Great, now go and find yourself a partner while you're still young."

Chen Man was dumbfounded.

"Eat your vegetables," Xie Qingcheng said blandly.

"Okay..."

29

HE BROKE THE RULES

A FEW DAYS LATER, at Huzhou Medical School, a boy was crying bitterly inside Xie Qingcheng's office.

"Waahhh, Professor Xie, I was wrong! I was really wrong! I'm heartless! I'm unworthy of being human! I betrayed your trust, betrayed the party and the country's expectations of me. I'll never skip class again, waaaah..."

Xie Qingcheng sat in front of his desk, his fountain pen skimming over the paper as he made a check mark on the list of names. "All right. You may leave," he said without even lifting his gaze.

The boy left, still sobbing.

Xie Qingcheng had plenty of ways to deal with problematic students. That clinical medicine major may have strutted in all high and mighty, but he left with tears streaming down his face. On his way out, he bowed several times to Xie Qingcheng and promised, in a voice choked with sobs, that he would turn over a new leaf and behave properly, that he would never skip class again; even if he were to do so, it wouldn't be Professor Xie's class.

Xie Qingcheng closed his notebook and steepled his fingers before himself.

All the problematic male students with questionable attitudes toward studying had already promised him that they'd straighten themselves out in the future. Unless He Yu was able to get all the female students on the list on board as well, he really would end up losing this round.

Sitting straight-backed in his office chair, Xie Qingcheng felt that victory was near, and thus began to placidly ponder how he'd go about training the defeated little xueba.

After some time considering his options, his thoughts were interrupted by the phone ringing.

"Hello?"

"Professor Xie, it's me."

The caller was a female student, a first-year forensic science major.

Like He Yu, she was also a xueba. Though she appeared on the list of people that He Yu needed to talk to, she was one of Xie Qingcheng's most disciplined students.

Xie Qingcheng had deliberately put her name on the list.

As an impassive woman who studied cadavers more than Dior and Chanel, she was specially exempted from attending class for no other reason than that this lofty ice queen could learn the course material much faster through self-study.

An academic goddess like this was usually rather unsociable. She rarely interacted with her classmates and didn't always listen to what her professors had to say, but she greatly respected Xie Qingcheng.

The first reason was because Xie Qingcheng was at the top of his profession and could engender the xueba's appreciation for those stronger than her. The second was because the school rejected her application when she first applied for independent study and only relented after Xie Qingcheng fought for her by saying that an institution should teach students according to their aptitude. Therefore, she held strong gratitude for his efforts on her behalf.

"Professor Xie, the boy named He Yu came looking for me."

"What did he say?"

"He didn't try to convince me right away to focus on studying. He said that you sent him to me so that we could have a heartfelt conversation, and then he arranged to have coffee with me tomorrow."

"You can go, but don't listen to him."

"I know. You can count on me," the female xueba said. "But Professor Xie, he's from Huzhou University next door, not our medical school. How did you meet him? Is he your relative?"

"He's the son of a close acquaintance," Xie Qingcheng said. "His father helped me out in the past, so I teach his son a lesson now and then when he runs into problems."

It happened to be the truth too. If not for He Jiwei, Xie Qingcheng might not have looked after He Yu for so long.

"Oh." The xueba didn't ask any more questions. "In that case, leave it to me. I won't let you down. I'm off to study now. Goodbye."

Xie Qingcheng ended the call and tossed his phone into his pocket before packing up his teaching materials and returning to his dorm.

Of course, Xie Qingcheng knew that He Yu wasn't someone who was easy to deal with. He looked on with the cool eye of a bystander as those distracted girls returned to class one after another, the number ticking up one by one. By Thursday, all eleven girls on the list except for the female xueba had remorsefully adjusted their behavior and come back for lectures.

The female xueba was the last holdout.

On Thursday evening, she came to ask Xie Qingcheng for help with a workbook problem. Afterward, he asked, "Has He Yu spoken to you yet?"

"He has." The neat and competent girl with her hair pulled up in a ponytail responded. "We met up twice this past week and had afternoon tea both times."

But after saying this, she hesitated briefly before adding, "But he... he didn't talk to me about skipping class or anything like that. He really did just take me out to walk around and have a heart-to-heart."

Xie Qingcheng frowned slightly.

It was already Thursday, yet He Yu still hadn't talked about the matter at hand?

There were three more days before the week was over. What exactly was He Yu planning?

While he was lost in thought, the girl xueba coughed quietly. "Professor Xie?"

"Hm?" He lifted his gaze and glanced at her distractedly with dispassionate eyes.

"I have a question I'd like to ask you."

"Go ahead." Xie Qingcheng had already picked up the fountain pen that he'd used to solve the previous problem from the table.

But he put the cap back on the pen upon hearing her question.

What she wanted to know had absolutely nothing to do with learning. "Um, is He Yu from the 1001 screenwriting and directing class at Huzhou University?"

Only a man as staunchly masculine as Xie Qingcheng would be oblivious enough to feminine fancy to fail to understand the reason behind her question. He frowned and sized up the formidable girl before him. Why was she asking him this?

He nodded stiffly. "Yes. What about it?"

"Nothing much," she answered firmly. She spread out her notebook and diverted her teacher's attention with her studies. "Professor Xie, these are the questions related to your field that I've collected over the course of this week. Please help me answer them."

Sunday came in the blink of an eye.

The female xueba sent him a message. "Professor Xie, are you free tonight? I've spent all day thinking and come to a realization about something. Can I discuss it with you?"

Thus, Xie Qingcheng arrived at the door of his office at the agreed-upon time of 6:30 p.m.

His office was at the very end of a winding hallway in Teaching Building 5. As he made his way down the long corridor, he completely failed to recognize the female student standing next to the handrail near his office.

Upon arriving at the door to his office, he began to dig for his keys to open the door without acknowledging the girl's presence. Even when she opened her mouth and called out, "Professor Xie!" his first reaction wasn't to glance at this young lady, but rather, to look around in an attempt to find that student with her straight, unstyled hair who was always in T-shirts and jeans that he'd arranged to meet.

"...Professor Xie, I'm over here."

Xie Qingcheng turned around and froze.

After a moment, he subconsciously took a step backward, hitting his head on the aluminum security door of his office with a loud *bang*. Gasping sharply in pain, he touched a hand to his head and narrowed his eyes.

"Professor! Are you okay?"

"...I'm fine."

His hitting his head was indeed fine, but the appearance of the girl before him posed a much bigger problem.

The female xueba looked nothing like her usual self.

She had let her hair down from its customary ponytail and had a stylist blow it out. Her face was carefully made up, and she wore a gauzy, pure white dress. Her slim legs looked as if they'd been carved from jade, forming pin-straight lines that ended in a pair of black satin heels. Those high heels had silver buckles and straps that looped around her delicate ankles, setting off the nude-pink of her toenails.

Xie Qingcheng had to confirm it several times before he finally concluded beyond any doubt that this wasn't an impostor but the genuine article.

His headache suddenly intensified as he began to feel a faint sense of foreboding.

The female xueba wasted no time in bluntly revealing her reason for requesting their meeting. "Professor Xie, um, I came here to tell you that I went out with He Yu again. This time, he talked to me about returning to class, but he also told me about the agreement between you two."

Xie Qingcheng was speechless.

"Professor Xie, I respect you a lot, but I don't think it's good to take advantage of someone when they're in a difficult position. It's not something a teacher should do."

Xie Qingcheng's hand, which was about to grab the key and open the door, came to a stop. "...What did He Yu say to you?"

"He told me everything. He said his declaration of love ended in failure, so you wanted him to train more and gave him some extremely difficult challenges."

Xie Qingcheng lifted his hand to run his slender fingers through his bangs. His neat coif ended up tousled and messy; several dark strands tumbled back down over his eyes.

He stared at her through his disheveled hair with his coldly incisive peach-blossom eyes. Then, with a click of his tongue, he looked away and said, "It's not as simple as you think."

After a pause, he continued, "Forget it. You may leave."

But she didn't leave. She stared at him intensely with the tenacity of a true xueba. "Laoshi, you have to put yourself in He Yu's shoes and stop making things difficult for him at this time. Also, I really think that you're the one in the wrong here. I hope you can apologize to He Yu in the future when the opportunity arises."

In the ensuing silence, a thought occurred to Xie Qingcheng: *He Yu used his blood toxin on her, didn't he?*

Xie Qingcheng's expression cooled. Beneath his messy fringe, his eyes were piercingly sharp. "I asked you to leave. Do you understand me?"

"I do. But before I leave, I wanted to be honest with you, Professor. I've already told He Yu about our private agreement."

Xie Qingcheng was at a loss for words.

"I had no choice. He was sincere to me, and I didn't want to lie to him either. The fact that you put me down on his list so that you'd win—I really couldn't keep it a secret for you any longer."

This little traitor didn't even forget to give Xie Qingcheng a courteous bow at the end of her speech.

"Please forgive me."

As the last syllable fell from her lips, the young girl turned around and strode gracefully away in her heels. There was even a little sashaying spring in her step that Xie Qingcheng had never seen in all the time he'd known her.

Xie Qingcheng felt a raging headache beginning to build, but he didn't want to argue with the female student. So, he merely gritted his teeth and growled in a low voice, "He...Yu..."

A shadow moved.

The sound of footsteps came from somewhere nearby.

And then, he appeared.

"Professor Xie, you were looking for me?"

Xie Qingcheng suddenly raised his head, his hair becoming even messier as his gaze zeroed in on the direction of that voice.

A tall boy stood with his hands in his pockets and a backpack slung over one shoulder. His expression was calm and indifferent, and beneath the smooth expanse of his exposed forehead, a pair of disdainful almond eyes looked out from under lowered lashes and a mouth curved in a nearly imperceptible smile.

He Yu had been hiding behind a large gothic pillar at the end of the corridor this whole time. Neither Xie Qingcheng nor the female xueba knew he had been watching.

When the girl had been vigorously fighting injustice on his behalf, when Xie Qingcheng had been scolded so thoroughly by this student that he couldn't get in a word edgewise, He Yu had actually been leaning there with his hands casually thrust into his pockets, listening from behind that damned gothic pillar that was large enough to require three people to encircle it.

Was he even fucking human?

With an ashen face and a glare that could kill, Xie Qingcheng said, "You—"

"Oh, you can't blame me." He Yu raised his hand and made a shushing motion. His slightly narrowed eyes took on a roguish quality undetectable to anyone but Xie Qingcheng.

He gave Xie Qingcheng a once over, then laughed coldly. "You got someone to help plot against me first, teaming up to make sure I couldn't win. If I used similar methods against you, no one could accuse me of being petty, right?"

Xie Qingcheng didn't bother dignifying his words with a response.

He had already lost. Anything he said would just result in him losing more face.

And so, Xie Qingcheng clenched his teeth and held his tongue.

After a long silence, he finally asked, "How did you trick her? Just look at her in that getup—is that how a student is supposed to look? A halter top minidress..."

"What's wrong with it?" He Yu circled closer, closing the gap between himself and Xie Qingcheng with one hand in his pocket and the other wrapped around the strap of his messenger bag. At this proximity, the only difference was that the way that He Yu lowered his lashes to look down at Xie Qingcheng became even more evident.

"Then tell me, how should a student look?"

He Yu pressed closer, like he was about to nail Xie Qingcheng through the door.

"A graphic T-shirt, jeans, high ponytail, and no makeup?

"Doctor Xie," he sighed. "Actually, I've wanted to tell you this for a while: I'm not the only one who's sick. You ought to get yourself checked out too. You're way too controlling. Don't you know about 'straight man cancer'? What year is it, and you *still* think that it's improper for a girl to wear a halter dress?"

He Yu took another step closer, bringing them nearly nose-to-nose.

Were they of opposite genders, such a distance would be dangerous in a suggestive way, but as they were both straight men, the proximity took on an aggressive and invasive quality that seeped wordlessly right into Xie Qingcheng's flesh and bones.

With He Yu looming over him, Xie Qingcheng had no choice but to lean back against the ice-cold panels of the door. The extreme discomfort of this position finally brought Xie Qingcheng to his senses. Not wanting to waste any more time with He Yu, Xie Qingcheng reached up to press a hand against his broad and sturdy chest.

"Forget it. I won't talk nonsense with you. Step aside."

Xie Qingcheng shoved He Yu back hard, then rubbed at his wrist. He lowered his arm, shot He Yu a glare, and then trudged past He Yu to leave.

"...Wait a minute, Xie Qingcheng."

After walking a few dozen meters away, He Yu turned again and leisurely called out from behind him.

Xie Qingcheng's expression was already extremely overcast, but after standing there grimly for a moment, he nevertheless turned back. "What?" he asked, face ashen.

He Yu had pulled out his list of names from his bag at some point and was now waving it at Xie Qingcheng. "You lost this round."

But he didn't leave it at that. The degenerate stuffed the list back into his bag, then took out something covered in pink wrapping paper.

He glanced up at Xie Qingcheng with an aloof expression as he slowly tugged at the ribbon around the package. "Professor, even though you're playing a training game with me, there should be consequences when you lose too," he said, voice unhurried. "Otherwise, wouldn't that be way too boring?"

Xie Qingcheng stared at him in silence.

"Tell me, as a professor, a member of the older generation, and my former personal physician, how should I punish you for breaking the rules like this? What should I do to teach you a little lesson?"

You can lose a bet to someone, but you should never lose your graceful demeanor. If you were willing to place a bet, then you had to be willing to accept your losses.

"What do you want?" Xie Qingcheng asked impassively.

"What a pity, I've not decided yet," He Yu said gently. "You can just owe me for now—when I think of something, you can repay it all at once."

"All at once?"

"Mm. I think you'll lose to me again in the future."

Xie Qingcheng was finding it a challenge to control his temper. "He Yu, don't get ahead of yourself."

"I wouldn't dare." He Yu smiled. Despite his words, he very much "dared" to look Xie Qingcheng over with open provocation in his eyes. "But, you'd do well not to cheat again in the future, Professor Xie. You're not very good at it, and it's so easy for me to find out when you're up to something."

His tone was still courteous and polite.

But as he spoke, he had already torn open the pink wrapping paper to reveal a piece of chocolate, albeit a misshapen one—it didn't look like it was bought off the shelves, but rather clumsily made by some amateur.

"Didn't you ask me just now how I got through to her? Actually, it wasn't much—I just invited her out for afternoon tea twice, and then we went to a chocolate-making class today. She doesn't have many friends at school, you know. The other students all think she's weird and antisocial, but actually she's quite easy to get along with. It's just that no one really invites her along when they're going out for fun."

As he spoke, he broke off a chunk of chocolate with a snap and took the small, brown piece of cocoa butter between twin rows of pearly-white teeth before walking past Xie Qingcheng, his messenger bag slung over his shoulder.

As they brushed past each other, the schoolboy stared straight ahead, not even sparing Xie Qingcheng a glance as he sucked the chocolate into his mouth and chewed it slowly.

"So sweet."

And with that, the xueba was on his way, leaving Xie Qingcheng with the sight of his gentlemanly figure lit by the setting sun.

At that very moment, in a villa somewhere in Huzhou, under the slanting rays of twilight, a woman's high heels clicked across the bricks of the balcony. The hem of her red dress skimmed over a man's legs.

"Executive Duan." The woman sat down next to the man, cuddling up to him with a smile as she lit him a cigarette.

"Has everything in Liang Jicheng's home been destroyed?"

"It's all been cleaned up."

Duan-laoban smiled and accepted the proffered cigarette, taking a drag. The woman swept aside her cascade of long, wavy hair and leaned in for a kiss, but Duan-laoban turned his face away and sniffed at the side of her neck instead.

"How many people did you sleep with today? I can smell them on you."

"Isn't it all for you?" the woman replied lazily. "When can we go after Huzhou University? I'm tired of sleeping with the board of directors, the greasy old geezers."

"Those board members are old geezers, but Executive Huang isn't? You seem to like him quite a lot."

The woman twirled her hair flirtatiously with her fingertips. "Executive Huang's young at heart, so he's aging like a fine wine. But..." She smiled. "I like you more, Executive Duan..."

Duan-laoban lifted a finger and pressed it to her soft lips. "If you keep misbehaving like this, I'll have to speak with your Executive Huang," he cautioned mildly. "Take a guess—if he finds out, do you think he'll be mad?"

The woman stiffened slightly, then forced a smile. "I'm just teasing you. Why are you so serious?"

Duan-laoban reached up and stroked her hair with a calm expression. "Just do what you're supposed to do. After that fiasco with Cheng Kang Psychiatric Hospital, I can tell that a number of people are getting restless and impatient. Keep playing with those hamsters. Once our hackers receive the equipment they ordered from America, we'll be able to start showing those rodents who's boss."

He lifted the woman's chin and examined her face.

In a soft, slow voice, he said, "When the time comes, the technological aspects will depend on the hackers, but when it comes to cleaning up the hamster cages at Huzhou University, that will depend on you and her."

The light from the lamps illuminated the woman's delicate and lovely face.

The face of Huzhou University's instructor, Jiang Liping.

"You can be as vicious as you like." Duan-laoban stroked her cheek with his fingers. "I know you've suffered many grievances these past few years... Once we're done, you won't have to be a mole among that horde of old hamsters any longer..."

CHARACTERS, NAMES, AND LOCATIONS

CHARACTERS

> The identity of certain characters may be a spoiler; use this guide with caution on your first read of the novel.

MAIN CHARACTERS

He Yu
贺予   SURNAME HE, GIVEN NAME YU, "TO GIFT"

A nineteen-year-old screenwriting/directing student and Case #4 of a rare disease called psychological Ebola. He Yu enrolled in Huzhou University to pursue Xie Xue, his crush and childhood friend who is a young lecturer at the same university.

Xie Qingcheng
谢清呈   SURNAME XIE, GIVEN NAME QINGCHENG, A CLOSE HOMONYM FOR "DAWN"

He Yu's former doctor and Xie Xue's elder brother, who currently works as a medical school professor. He and He Yu had a falling-out years ago and now often find themselves at odds.

SUPPORTING CHARACTERS

Xie Xue
谢雪   SURNAME XIE, GIVEN NAME XUE, "SNOW"

A young screenwriting and directing lecturer at Huzhou University with a carefree nature. She looks up to her elder brother Xie Qingcheng very much due to his active role in her upbringing following the death of their parents when she was young.

Chen Yan
陈衍   SURNAME CHEN, GIVEN NAME YAN, "PLENTIFUL"

NICKNAME: Chen Man 陈慢 / Surname Chen, given name Man, "slow".

A young police officer and close family friend of Xie Qingcheng.

Lü Zhishu
吕芝书   SURNAME LÜ, GIVEN NAME ZHISHU, "GORGEOUS," "TO WRITE"

He Yu's mother, a wealthy businesswoman who habitually prioritizes work over her eldest son.

He Jiwei
贺继威   SURNAME HE, GIVEN NAME JIWEI, "TO CONTINUE," "PRESTIGE"

He Yu's father, a wealthy businessman who is often away from home.

Li Ruoqiu
李若秋   SURNAME LI, GIVEN NAME RUOQIU, "LIKE AUTUMN"

Xie Qingcheng's ex-wife. Cheated and left the marriage because she felt he didn't truly love her.

Jiang Liping
蒋丽萍   SURNAME JIANG, GIVEN NAME LIPING, "BEAUTIFUL," "DUCKWEED"

The morality advisor in charge of He Yu's screenwriting/directing class.

Qin Ciyan

秦慈岩 SURNAME QIN, GIVEN NAME CIYAN, "COMPASSION," "STONE"

A neurosurgeon and Xie Qingcheng's former colleague who was killed by the angry son of a patient who passed away while under his care.

Zhuang Zhiqiang

庄志强 SURNAME ZHUANG, GIVEN NAME ZHIQIANG, "STRONG IN WILL"

A mentally ill homeless man convinced he has a daughter despite there being no records of her existence.

Jiang Lanpei

江兰佩 SURNAME JIANG, GIVEN NAME LANPEI, "ORCHID," "PENDANT"

A patient in Cheng Kang Psychiatric Hospital.

Liang Jicheng

梁季成 SURNAME LIANG, GIVEN NAME JICHENG, "SEASON," "ACCOMPLISHMENT"

The director of Cheng Kang Psychiatric Hospital.

Duan-laoban

段老板 SURNAME DUAN, TITLE -LAOBAN, SUFFIX FOR "BOSS"

A mysterious figure working in the shadows who knows more than he should about the incident at Cheng Kang Psychiatric Hospital.

Wei Dongheng

卫冬恒   SURNAME WEI, GIVEN NAME DONGHENG, "WINTER,"
"CONSTANT"

A senior drama student at Huzhou University and He Yu's acquaintance who was a big troublemaker in his youth.

LOCATIONS

CITIES

Huzhou
沪州

A fictional major city in the Jiangnan region of China (to the south of the Yangtze River). "Hu" is the abbreviation for Shanghai.

Yanzhou
燕州

A fictional capital city in the north of China. "Yan" is the name for an ancient city that includes modern-day Beijing.

Hangshi
杭市

Another fictional major city in the Jiangnan region, not far from Huzhou. "Hang" is the same character used in the city Hangzhou.

PLACES

Huzhou University
沪州大学

A prestigious university located in Huzhou with a School of Fine Arts, among others.

Huzhou Medical School
沪州医科大学

A prestigious medical school located in Huzhou that neighbors Huzhou University.

Neverland Island
梦幻岛

A man-made island in the middle of a lake on the Huzhou University campus.

Cheng Kang Psychiatric Hospital
成康精神病院

An old psychiatric institution on the outskirts of Huzhou.

NAME GUIDE

Diminutives, Nicknames, and Name Tags

DA-: A prefix meaning "big" or "elder," which can be added before titles for elders, like "dage" or "dajie," or before a name.

DI/DIDI: A word meaning "younger brother." It can also be used to address an unrelated (usually younger) male peer, and optionally used as a suffix.

GE/GEGE: A word meaning "older brother." It can also be used to address an unrelated male peer, and optionally used as a suffix.

JIE/JIEJIE: A word meaning "elder sister." It can also be used to address an unrelated female peer, and optionally used as a suffix.

LAO-: A prefix meaning "old." Usually added to a surname and used in informal contexts.

LAOSHI: A word meaning "teacher" that can be used to refer to any educator, often in deference. Can also be attached to someone's name as a suffix.

LAOBAN: A word meaning "boss" that can be used to refer to one's superior or the proprietor of a business. Can also be attached to someone's name as a suffix.

SAOZI/-SAO: A word meaning "elder brother's wife." It can be used to address the wife (or informally, girlfriend) of an unrelated male peer.

XIAO-: A prefix meaning "little" or "younger." Often used in an affectionate and familiar context.

XUEZHANG: Older male classmate.

XUEDI: Younger male classmate.

XUEJIE: Older female classmate.

XUEMEI: Younger female classmate.

PRONUNCIATION GUIDE

Bìng Àn Běn

Bìng as in **Bing**ham

Àn as in **on**

Běn as in hus**ban**d

Hè Yǔ

Hè as in **huh**

Y as in **you,** ǔ as in b**ee**, but with lips rounded as for **boo**

Xiè Qīngchéng

X as in **sh**eep, iè as in **yet**

Q as in **ch**arm but more aspirated, īng as in s**ing**

Ch as in **ch**arm, éng as in h**ung**

GENERAL CONSONANTS

Some Mandarin Chinese consonants sound very similar, such as z/c/s and zh/ch/sh. Audio samples will provide the best opportunity to learn the difference between them.

X: somewhere between the **sh** in **sh**eep and **s** in **s**ilk

Q: a very aspirated **ch** as in **ch**eat

C: **ts** as in pan**ts**

Z: **ds** as in su**ds**

S: **s** as in **s**ilk

CH: very close to **c**-, but with the tongue rolled up to touch the palate.

ZH: very close to **z**-, but with the tongue rolled up to touch
the palate.

SH: very close to **s**-, but with the tongue rolled up to
touch the palate. Because of this, it can give the impression of **shh**, but it's a different sound compared to the
x- consonant.

G: hard **g** as in **g**raphic

R: partway between the **r** in **r**un and the **s** in mea**s**ure. The
tongue should be rolled up to touch the palate.

GENERAL VOWELS

The pronunciation of a vowel may depend on its preceding consonant. For example, the "i" in "shi" is distinct from the "i" in "di,"
where the first is a buzzed continuation for the sh- consonant and
the latter a long e sound. Compound vowels are often—though not
always—pronounced as conjoined but separate vowels. You'll find a
few of the trickier compounds below.

IU: as in **yo**-yo

IE: **ye** as in **ye**s

UO: **war** as in **war**m

APPENDIX

GLOSSARY

GLOSSARY

EYES: Descriptions like "almond eyes" or "peach-blossom eyes" refer to eye shape. Almond eyes have a balanced shape, like that of an almond, whereas peach-blossom eyes have a rounded upper lid and are often considered particularly alluring.

FACE: *Mianzi* (面子), generally translated as "face," is an important concept in Chinese society. It is a metaphor for a person's reputation and can be extended to further descriptive metaphors. For example, "having face" refers to having a good reputation, and "losing face" refers to having one's reputation hurt. Meanwhile, "giving face" means deferring to someone else to help improve their reputation, while "not wanting face" implies that a person is acting so poorly or shamelessly that they clearly don't care about their reputation at all. "Thin face" refers to someone easily embarrassed or prone to offense at perceived slights. Conversely, "thick face" refers to someone not easily embarrassed and immune to insults.

JADE: Jade is a semi-precious mineral with a long history of ornamental and functional usage in China. The word "jade" can refer to two distinct minerals, nephrite and jadeite, which both range in color from white to gray to a wide spectrum of greens.

UNIVERSITIES AND CLASS STRUCTURE: In Chinese universities, students are assigned to a class of students in their major. Each class takes their major courses together for the duration of their university career.

WECHAT: A Chinese instant messaging, social media, and mobile payment app ubiquitous in modern Chinese society. People use its text, call, and voice message functions for both personal and business communications.

WEIBO: A popular Chinese microblogging social media platform similar to Twitter.

XUEBA: 学霸, literally "academic tyrant," is a slang term for high-achieving students. Usually complimentary.